THE College WRITER

A Guide to Thinking, Writing, and Researching

Fourth Edition

WADSWORTH
CENGAGE Learning

Australia • Brazil • Japan • Korea • Mexico • Singapore • Spain • United Kingdom • United States

Randall VanderMey
Westmont College

Verne Meyer
Dordt College

John Van Rys
Redeemer University College

Pat Sebranek

WADSWORTH
CENGAGE Learning™

**The College Writer: A Guide to
Thinking, Writing, and Researching,
Fourth Edition**
Randall VanderMey, Verne Meyer, John
Van Rys, and Pat Sebranek

Publisher: Lyn Uhl

Executive Editor: Monica Eckman

Acquisitions Editor: Margaret Leslie

Development Editor: Judy Fifer

Assistant Editor: Amy Haines

Editorial Assistant: Elizabeth Ramsey

Media Editor: Janine Tangney

Marketing Manager: Jason Sakos

Marketing Coordinator: Ryan Ahern

Marketing Communications Manager:
Stacey Purviance

Content Project Manager: Rosemary
Winfield

Art Director: Jill Ort

Print Buyer: Betsy Donaghey

Rights Acquisition Specialist, Images:
Mandy Groszko

Rights Acquisition Specialist, Text: Katie
Huha

Production Service: Sebranek, Inc.

Text Designer: Sebranek, Inc.

Cover Designer: Sebranek, Inc.

Cover Image: vanya 2010/used under
license from www.shutterstock.com;
Tischenko Irina 2010/used under
license from www.shutterstock.com

Compositor: Sebranek, Inc.

Sebranek, Inc.: Steve Augustyn,
April Barrons, Colleen Belmont,
Chris Erickson, Mariellen Hanrahan,
Rob King, Chris Krenzke, Lois Krenzke,
Mark Lalumondier, Janae Sebranek,
Lester Smith, Jean Varley

For product information and technology assistance, contact us at
Cengage Learning Customer & Sales Support, 1-800-354-9706.

For permission to use material from this text or product,
submit all requests online at **cengage.com/permissions.**
Further permissions questions can be emailed to
permissionrequest@cengage.com.

Library of Congress Control Number: 2010935800

Casebound Edition:

ISBN-13: 978-0-495-91585-0

ISBN-10: 0-495-91585-8

Paperbound Edition:

ISBN-13: 978-0-495-91583-6

ISBN-10: 0-495-91583-1

Wadsworth
20 Channel Center Street
Boston, MA 02210
USA

Cengage Learning is a leading provider of customized learning solutions
with office locations around the globe, including Singapore, the United
Kingdom, Australia, Mexico, Brazil and Japan. Locate your local office at
international.cengage.com/region.

Cengage Learning products are represented in Canada by
Nelson Education, Ltd.

For your course and learning solutions, visit **www.cengage.com.**

Purchase any of our products at your local college store or at our
preferred online store **www.cengagebrain.com.**

Credits begin on page 706, which constitutes an extension of this
copyright page.

Printed in the U.S.A.
3 4 5 6 7 14 13 12

Brief Contents

Contents

III. Research and Writing

Documentation and Format Styles

IV. Handbook

Punctuation, Mechanics, Usage, and Grammar

Thematic Table of Contents for Readings

Diversity and Equity

Education and Learning

Environment and Nature

Ethics and Ideology

Ethnicity and Identity

Family and Friends

Fashion and Lifestyle

Gender and Integrity

Humor and Humanity

Language and Literature

Memory and Tradition

Science and Health

Terror and Our Time

Work and Play

Preface

The fourth edition of *The College Writer* is a fully updated four-in-one text—with a Rhetoric, a Reader, a Researcher, and a Handbook. These four sections help college students connect their reading, writing, and thinking. The book's visual format allows students to grasp the big picture and easily locate supporting details.

What's New in the Fourth Edition?

- **Learning outcomes** at the beginning of each chapter and learning-outcome checklists at the end track student performance.
- **All-new exercises in the Handbook** give students practice with punctuation, mechanics, usage, grammar, sentences, and trouble spots for English language learners.
- **More high-interest academic models** from students and professionals help writers understand and create a scholarly tone.
- **New overviews and revamped guidelines** accentuate the reading-writing connection.
- **Updated MLA and APA documentation** aids students in finding reliable sources and creating strong research papers.
- **Increased attention to the rhetorical situation**—role, subject, purpose, form, audience, and context—gives students a tool to analyze the works of others and create their own works.
- **A new emphasis on thesis and outline creation** ensures that students will organize their thinking as they write.
- **New charts, graphs, and photos** help visual learners grasp concepts.
- **Cut-out tabs** make flipping to any of the four sections of the book easy.

What Other Features Are There?

- **At-a-glance format** presents each concept in one or two pages.
- **Writing with sources features** are integrated into the writing-process chapters.
- **A friendly, coaching tone** develops students' self-confidence as learners.
- **Cross-curricular writing instruction** is offered throughout the text.
- **Critical thinking and critical viewing** help students analyze and evaluate written and visual arguments.
- **Additional Handbook exercises** are available on the text's website, **www.thecollegewriter.com/4e.**

 A thematic table of contents supports instructors who employ themes such as community and conscience or ethics and equity.

New to This Edition

1 Critical Thinking Through Reading, Viewing, and Writing

When you write something or create an image, you are sending a message into the world. When you read something or view an image, you are receiving a message. Whatever side you find yourself on, you should think critically about all elements of the rhetorical situation—the sender, message, medium, receiver, and context.

This chapter provides strategies for deepening your understanding of each element as you read, view, and write in college. By deepening your critical thinking, you'll find that college classes become easier and much more rewarding.

Learning Outcomes

▸ Use the SQ3R reading strategy.
▸ Read actively.
▸ Respond to a text.
▸ Summarize a text.
▸ Actively view images.
▸ Interpret images.
▸ Evaluate images.
▸ Think critically through writing.

Visually Speaking ▸ In the photograph above, what examples can through reading, viewing, and writing? How d the experience of touring an art museum?

Learning Outcomes and Learning-Outcome Checklists: The goals of each chapter appear in a set of learning outcomes at the beginning of the chapter. At the end, a checklist helps students and instructors track whether the outcomes have been achieved.

Visually Speaking: Visual prompts throughout the text— and many new graphics—help students develop visual literacy.

---

26   Reading, Thinking, Viewing, and Writing

Critical-Thinking and Writing Activities

As directed by your instructor, complete the following critical-thinking and writing activities by yourself or with classmates

1. Northrop Frye has argued that "[n]obody is capable of free speech unless he [or she] knows how to use language, and such knowledge is not a gift: It has to be learned and worked at." How does Frye's claim relate to the discussions of critical reading, viewing, and writing in this chapter?

2. What thinking, reading, viewing, and writing skills are required in your field of study? Reflect on those possibilities.

3. Choose a subject you know something about. Practice thinking about that subject both inductively and deductively. Then write two paragraphs—one developed inductively and the other developed deductively.

4. Select a sample essay from the "Strategies and Models" section. Read the piece carefully and identify where and how the writer uses different thinking modes. Do the same analysis on a recent sample of your own writing, rating your analysis, synthesis, evaluation, and application.

Learning-Outcomes Checklist

_____ I use the SQ3R reading method for important reading assignments for my courses and research projects, thinking about the rhetorical situation. (See pages 4–5.)

_____ I read actively rather than passively by taking thoughtful notes, annotating texts, mapping, and outlining. (See pages 6–9.)

_____ I respond to texts in an honest, fluid, reflective, and selective way. (See page 10.)

_____ I effectively summarize texts, capturing the text's main argument and providing the main supporting details—all in my own words and in a concise form. (See page 11.)

_____ I view images actively instead of passively, thinking about the rhetorical situation. (See pages 12–13.)

_____ I interpret images, asking deeper questions about each part of the rhetorical situation. (See pages 14–15.)

_____ I judge the value of images, considering the purpose of the image and its quality. (See pages 16–17.)

_____ I think critically through writing, analyzing, synthesizing, evaluating, and applying information. (See pages 18–25.)

Exercises in the Handbook: The Handbook—which has always provided succinct rules and examples for punctuation, mechanics, usage, grammar, and sentences—now also provides engaging exercises to practice these rules. And students who need even more practice can find it online at www.thecollegewriter.com/4e.

More High-Interest Academic Models: Students are writing now more than ever, but most of their writing occurs through informal social media. By focusing on third-person essays, *The College Writer,* Fourth Edition, helps students learn to write with greater formality.

The Reading-Writing Connection: In the Reader, revamped chapter overviews focus on strategies for reading a specific type of selection—narrative, cause-effect, comparison-contrast, persuasion, and so on. Reworked guidelines at the end of the chapter help students focus on writing the same form. These guidelines also provide trait-based instruction.

288 Persuasive Writing

Reading Persuasive Writing

How should you read a paper that urges you to act on an issue? The instructions below offer helpful instructions.

Consider the rhetorical situation.

When reading an appeal to act, anticipate what the writer wants people to do, what audience he or she has in mind, and how the topic is treated.

- **Purpose:** Whether in academics, the workplace, or public life, writers call for action because they believe change is needed. Something is not right. Something needs to be improved or fixed. The writer's goal is to convince readers to care about the issue strongly enough to take a concrete step.
- **Audience:** The intended readers are people whom the writer believes need to be pressed to act. Readers may be unaware of the issue, may feel overwhelmed by it, may have an interest in not acting, or may not care enough about the issue to actually act. The writer thus educates and urges such readers.
- **Topic:** In academics, the topics addressed might be related to a specific discipline (e.g., educational mentoring campaign, expanding an arts program), a political or social issue (e.g., shelter for abused women, Special Oly humanitarian concern (e.g., help for victims of an epide

Look for convincing qualities.

When reading an appeal to act, look for the following:

- **Compelling Argument:** The writer accurately describes of its importance, and calls for a doable and effective ac fact based and reasonable, not extreme, trivial, or unqua
- **Logical Argument:** The argument is based on reliable e anecdotes, tests, experiments, analogies, and expert test and the argument avoids logical fallacies such as half-tr attacks against a person, and false analogies (see pages 2
- **Mature Voice:** The writing sounds informed and genui manipulative appeals, quarrelsome language, or demean

Reader's Checklist

_____ What is the issue, and what action is requested to add

_____ Who are the intended readers, and what capacity to a

_____ Are the writer's claims accurate, compelling, and logi

_____ Is the argument's tone informed, genuine, and respec

_____ Is the writing convincing—does it move readers to d

4 Reading, Thinking, Viewing, and Writing

Using the SQ3R Reading Strategy

Obviously, reading a novel, a textbook, and a webpage are all different activities. Nevertheless, all college reading assignments can be approached systematically, especially when your goal is to absorb and engage the text. One strategy for critical reading, especially of information-rich texts, is called **SQ3R: Survey, Question, Read, Recite, and Review.** Here is how SQ3R works.

Survey

The first step in SQ3R is to preview the material. Check for clues to each part of the rhetorical situation:

Rhetorical Situation

Sender (Creator) → Message (Subject + Purpose) → Receiver (Audience)

Medium (Form)

Context (Environment)

Read about the author. Then read the title and the opening and closing paragraphs to get a sense of the main points. Glance at all other pages, noting headings, topic sentences in paragraphs, boldface type, illustrations, charts, maps, and other cues to the content and organization.

Benefits: Surveying helps you (1) focus on the writer's message, (2) identify its organization, and (3) anticipate how the text will develop.

Question

As you survey, begin to ask questions that you hope to answer as you read.

- **Read any questions that accompany the reading.** Look at the end of the reading or in a study guide.
- **Turn headings into questions.** If a subhead says, "The Study," ask, "How was the study conducted?"
- **Imagine test questions for major points.** If the reading draws conclusions about self-control, ask, "What conclusions does the author draw about self-control?"
- **Ask the journalist's questions:** Ask *who, what, where, when, why,* and *how*? Whose attitudes are changing? What are their attitudes? Where is the change strongest? When is it occurring? Why is it happening? How?

Benefits: Asking questions keeps you actively thinking about what you are reading and helps you absorb information.

The Rhetorical Situation: Writing is no longer an academic exercise for students, but a daily communication activity. By teaching students to think about the rhetorical situation—role, subject, purpose, form, audience, and context—*The College Writer* gives students a tool that helps them read, think, view, and write.

MLA and APA Documentation: The fourth edition includes fully updated sections on MLA and APA styles. A completely revised and updated chapter on conducting research on the Internet (chapter 29) provides full coverage of how to evaluate online sources, with examples of authoritative and nonauthoritative sites, and an Evaluation Checklist that helps students avoid biased or unreliable sites.

More Online Supplementation for the Student

The College Writer E-book *The College Writer* is also available as an e-book that offers students online access to the entire text, along with video and audio explanations that enhance the text, writing tutorials, grammar exercises, additional writing models, and links to carefully selected websites.

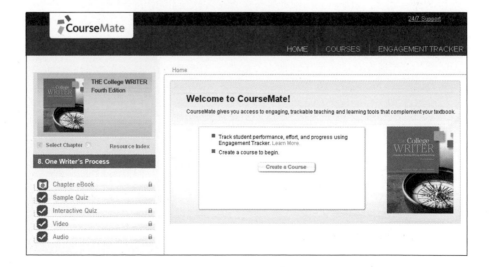

Student Voices: A Sampling of College Writing This 64-page supplement of student papers illustrates each of the modes and provides additional writing formats. This resource can be packaged with the text for only $5.00.

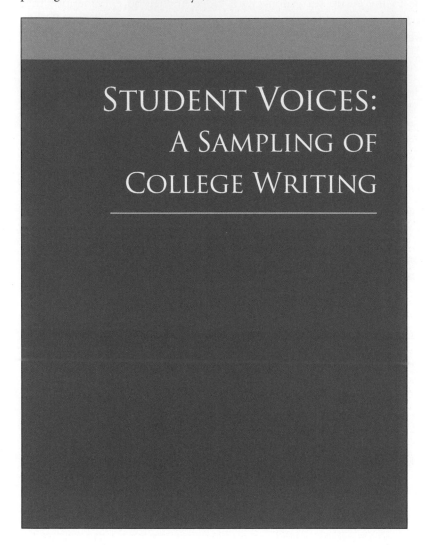

STUDENT VOICES:
A SAMPLING OF
COLLEGE WRITING

More Online Supplementation for the Student

- **The College Writer e-Book** *The College Writer* is also available as an e-book that offers students online access to the entire text, along with video and audio explanations that enhance the text, writing tutorials, grammar exercises, additional writing models, and links to carefully selected websites.

- **Student Voices: A Sampling of College Writing** This 64-page supplement of student papers illustrates each of the modes and provides additional writing formats, and can be packaged with the text for only $5.00.

- **CourseMate for *The College Writer*** English CourseMate brings course concepts to life with an integrated eBook as well as interactive learning tools, including quizzes, flashcards, videos, and more. *Make the Grade with CourseMate!*

- **Enhanced InSite for *The College Writer*** Insightful writing begins with Enhanced InSite™ for *The College Writer*, 4th Edition. From a single, easy-to-navigate site, you and your instructor can manage the flow of papers online, check for originality, and conduct peer reviews. You'll access a multimedia eBook with text-specific workbook, private tutoring options, and resources for writers that include anti-plagiarism tutorials and downloadable grammar podcasts—all designed to help you become a stronger, more effective writer. Learn more at www.cengage.com/insite.

More Online Supplementation for the Instructor

- **Online Instructor's Resource Manual** This manual is available for download or printing on the instructor website. The *Instructor's Resource Manual* includes assessment rubrics, learning objectives, an overview of the course, sample syllabi, chapter summaries, and teaching suggestions. Whether you are just starting out or have been teaching for years, the authors have designed this manual to accommodate you.

- **Instructor Website** This password-protected site, accessed through www. cengagebrain.com, provides a downloadable version of the Instructor's Resource Manual, assessment rubrics, learning objectives, and access to all materials in the student website.

- **CourseMate for *The College Writer*** Interested in a simple way to *complement* your text and course content with study and practice materials? Cengage Learning's English CourseMate brings course concepts to life with interactive learning, study, and exam preparation tools that support the printed textbook. Watch student comprehension soar as your class works with the printed textbook and the textbook-specific website. English CourseMate goes beyond the book to deliver what you need! Learn more at cengage.com/coursemate.

- **Enhanced InSite for *The College Writer*** Easily create, assign, and grade writing assignments with Enhanced InSite™ for *The College Writer,* 4th Edition. From a single, easy-to-navigate site, you and your students can manage the flow of papers online, check for originality, and conduct peer reviews. Students can access a multimedia eBook with text-specific workbook, private tutoring options, and resources for writers that include anti-plagiarism tutorials and downloadable grammar podcasts. Enhanced InSite™ provides the tools and resources you and your students need plus the training and support you want. Learn more at www.cengage.com/insite.

Acknowledgments

The authors express their gratitude to the following people, who have contributed to the development of this edition of the text or to prior editions and supplements.

Reviewers

Belinda Adams, *Navarro College;* Alena Balmforth, *Salt Lake Community College*; Cherrie Bergandi, *Chippewa Valley Technical College;* Mary Burkhart, *University of Scranton;* Hugh Burns, *Texas Woman's University;* Michael D. Cook, *Everest College—Phoenix;* Tamera Davis, *Northern Oklahoma College—Stillwater;* Mary Etter, *Davenport University;* Patrick L. Green, *Aiken Technical College;* Jennifer Haber, *St. Petersburg College;* Julie Hemker, *De Anza, UC Berkeley, University of San Francisco;* Patricia A. Herb, *North Central State College;* Elizabeth Huergo, *Montgomery College;* David Jacobsen, *Westmont College;* John L. Liffiton, *Scottsdale Community College;* Molly Luby, *Central Carolina Community College;* Kelly B. McCalla, *Central Lakes College;* Christine A. Miller, *Davenport University;* Boyd Minner, *Navarro College;* Nancy W. Noel, *Germanna Community College;* Julianne Palma, *Monroe Community College;* Francie Quaas-Berryman, *Cerritos College;* Christine A. Saxlid, *Wisconsin Indianhead Technical College;* Vicki Scheurer, *Palm Beach Community College;* Catherine Scudder Wolf, *Susssex County Community College;* Susan M. Smith, *Tompkins Cortland Community College;* Donald Stinson, *Northern Oklahoma College;* Christine Szymczak, *Erie Community College;* Carolyn Towles, *Liberty University;* John Williamson, *Thomas More College*

Instructors

Mary Adams, *Peru State College;* Jim Addison, *Western Carolina University;* Susan Aguila, *Palm Beach Community College;* Cathryn Amdahl, *Harrisburg Area Community College;* Edmund August, *McKendree College;* Richard Baker, *Adams State College;* Thomas G. Beverage, *Coastal Carolina Community College;* Patricia Blaine, *Paducah Community College;* Tammie Bob, *College of DuPage;* Candace Boeck, *San Diego State University;* Charley Boyd, *Genesee Community College;* Deborah Bradford, *Bridgewater State College;* Linda Brender, *Macomb Community College;* Colleen M. Burke, *Rasmussen College;* Vicki Byard, *Northeastern Illinois University;* Susan Callender, *Sinclair Community College;* Sandra Camillo, *Finger Lakes Community College;* Sandy Cavanah, *Hopkinsville Community College;* Annette Cedarholm, *Snead State Community College;* James William Chichetto, *Stonehill College;* Sandra Clark, *Anderson University;* Beth Conomos, *Erie Community College, SUNY;* Keith Coplin, *Colby Community College;* Sue Cornett, *St. Petersburg College;* Debra Cumberland, *Winona State University;* David Daniel, *Newbury College;* Sarah Dangelantonio, *Franklin Pierce College;* Rachelle L. Darabi, *Indiana University, Purdue University Fort Wayne;* Judy C. Davidson, *University of Texas, Pan American;* Helen Deese, *University of California, Riverside;* Darren DeFrain, *Wichita State University;* Sarah Dengler, *Franklin Pierce College;* Linda Dethloff, *Prairie State College;* Steven Dolgin, *Schoolcraft College;* Carol Jean Dudley, *Eastern Illinois University;* Chris Ellery, *Angelo State University;* Ernest J. Enchelmayer, *Louisiana State University;* Anne K. Erickson, *Atlantic Cape Community College;* Kelly A. Foth, *University of Dubuque;* Julie Foust, *Utah State University;* Lyneé Lewis Gaillet, *Georgia State University;* Gregory R. Glau, *Arizona State University;* Patricia Glynn, *Middlesex Community College;* Samuel J. Goldstein, *Daytona Beach Community College;* Kim Grewe, *Wor-Wic Community College;* Loren C. Gruber, *Missouri Valley College;* Michael Hammond, *Northeastern Illinois University;* Katona Hargrave, *Troy State University;* Dick Harrington, *Piedmont Virginia Community College;* Karla Hayashi, *University of Hawaii, Hilo;* Anne Christine Helms, *Alamance Community College;* Stan Hitron, *Middlesex Community College;* Karen Holleran, *Kaplan College;* Barbara Dondiego Holmes, *University of Charleston;* Maurice Hunt, *Baylor University;* Barbara Jacobskind, *University of Massachusetts, Dartmouth;* Linda G. Johnson, *Southeast Technical Institute;* Alex M. Joncas, *Estrella Mountain Community College;* Nina B. Keery, *Massachusetts Bay Community College;* Sandra Keneda, *Rose State College;* Margo LaGattuta, *University of Michigan, Flint;* Richard Larschan, *University of Massachusetts, Dartmouth;* Dusty Maddox, *DeVry University;* Bonnie J. Marshall, *Grand Valley State University;* Daphne Matthews, *Mississippi Delta Community College;* Claudia Milstead, *Missouri Valley College;* Kate Mohler, *Mesa Community College;* Meghan Monroe, *Central Michigan University;* Ed Moritz, *Indiana University, Purdue University Fort Wayne;* Linda Morrison, *Niagara University;* Deborah Naquin, *Northern Virginia Community College;* Julie Nichols, *Okaloosa-Walton Community College;* Robert H. Nordell, *Des Moines Area Community College;* Christine Pavesic, *University of Wisconsin, Waukesha;* Sherry Rankin, *Abilene Christian University;* Laura Robbins, *Portland Community College;* Matthew Roudané, *Georgia State University;* Robert E. Rubin, *Wright State University;* Nancy Ruff, *Southern Illinois University, Edwardsville;* Christine M. Ryan, *Middlesex Community College;* Larry W. Severeid, *College of Eastern Utah;* Donna K. Speeker, *Wallace State Community College;* Talbot Spivak, *Edison College;* Joyce Swofford, *Clayton College & State University;* Terry Thacker, *Coastline Community College;* Diane Thompson, *Northern Virginia Community College;* Monica Parrish Trent, *Montgomery College;* Dori Wagner, *Austin Community College;* Shonda Wilson, *Suffolk County Community College;* Frances J. Winter, *Massachusetts Bay Community College;* Kelly Wonder, *University of Wisconsin, Eau Claire;* Benjamin Worth, *Bluegrass Community and Technical College;* Deanna L. Yameen, *Quincy College.*

Students

Lindsi Bittner, *St. Petersburg College;* Danielle Brown, *Oakton Community College;* Marie Burns, *University of Tampa;* Will Buttner, *University of Tampa;* Debra Cotton, *St. Petersburg College;* Jessica de Olivera, *Northeastern Illinois University;* Petra Hickman, *St. Petersburg College;* Anne Hsiao, *Oakton Community College;* Cassie Hull, *St. Petersburg College;* Courtney Langford, *St. Petersburg College;* Sandy Lehrke, *Hillsborough Community College;* Michael Pistorio, *Oakton Community College;* Crystal Smuk, *Triton Junior College;* Marc Sordja, *St. Petersburg College;* Johnny Velez, *Hillsborough Community College;* Anthony Zalud, *Harper Community College;* Omar Zamora, *Northeastern Illinois University.*

Special Thanks

A special thanks goes to Sarah Dangelantonio and Sarah Dengler of *Franklin Pierce College* for their work on the *Instructor's Resource Manual.* Also, thanks to Mark Gallaher, Kelly McGuire, Julie Nash, Dee Seligman, and Janet Young.

I. Rhetoric:
A College Student's
Guide to Writing

Reading, Thinking, Viewing, and Writing

1 Critical Thinking Through Reading, Viewing, and Writing

When you write something or create an image, you are sending a message into the world. When you read something or view an image, you are receiving a message. Whatever side you find yourself on, you should think critically about all elements of the rhetorical situation—the sender, message, medium, receiver, and context.

This chapter provides strategies for deepening your understanding of each element as you read, view, and write in college. By deepening your critical thinking, you'll find that college classes become easier and much more rewarding.

Learning Outcomes

Audio

▸ Use the SQ3R reading strategy.

▸ Read actively.

▸ Respond to a text.

▸ Summarize a text.

▸ Actively view images.

▸ Interpret images.

▸ Evaluate images.

▸ Think critically through writing.

Visually Speaking ▸ In the photograph above, what examples can you find of critical-thinking through reading, viewing, and writing? How does critical thinking enhance the experience of touring an art museum?

Using the SQ3R Reading Strategy

Video

Obviously, reading a novel, a textbook, and a webpage are all different activities. Nevertheless, all college reading assignments can be approached systematically, especially when your goal is to absorb and engage the text. One strategy for critical reading, especially of information-rich texts, is called **SQ3R: Survey, Question, Read, Recite,** and **Review.** Here is how SQ3R works.

Survey

The first step in SQ3R is to preview the material. Check for clues to each part of the rhetorical situation:

Rhetorical Situation

Read about the author. Then read the title and the opening and closing paragraphs to get a sense of the main points. Glance at all other pages, noting headings, topic sentences in paragraphs, boldface type, illustrations, charts, maps, and other cues to the content and organization.

Benefits: Surveying helps you (1) focus on the writer's message, (2) identify its organization, and (3) anticipate how the text will develop.

Question

As you survey, begin to ask questions that you hope to answer as you read.

- **Read any questions that accompany the reading.** Look at the end of the reading or in a study guide.
- **Turn headings into questions.** If a subhead says, "The Study," ask, "How was the study conducted?"
- **Imagine test questions for major points.** If the reading draws conclusions about self-control, ask, "What conclusions does the author draw about self-control?"
- **Ask the journalist's questions:** Ask *who, what, where, when, why,* and *how*? Whose attitudes are changing? What are their attitudes? Where is the change strongest? When is it occurring? Why is it happening? How?

Benefits: Asking questions keeps you actively thinking about what you are reading and helps you absorb information.

Read

As you encounter facts and ideas, ask these questions: What does this mean? How do the ideas relate to each other and to what I know? What's coming next?

Keep track of your answers by taking notes, annotating the text, mapping, or outlining. (See pages 6–9 for more on these active-reading techniques.) Read difficult parts slowly; reread them if necessary. Look up unfamiliar words or ideas, and use your senses to imagine the events, people, places, or things you are reading about. Imagine talking with the writer. Express agreement, lodge complaints, ask for proof—and imagine the writer's response or look for it in the text.

Benefits: Engaging actively with the text in this way will draw you deeper into the world of the writing. You'll trigger memories and make surprising connections.

Recite

After finishing a page, section, or chapter, recite the key points aloud. Answering *Who? What? When? Where? Why?* and *How?* questions is a quick way of testing yourself on how well you understood what you read. You can also recite the key points by listing them or writing a summary (see page 11).

Benefits: Reciting tests your comprehension, drives the material deeper into your long-term memory, and helps you connect the content with what you already know.

Review

As soon as you finish reading the material, double-check the questions you posed in the "question" stage of SQ3R. Can you answer them? Glance over any notes you made as well. But don't stop there if the reading is especially important. You will remember the material much better by spacing out your reviews; spend a few minutes reviewing each text over the next few days. Consider the following helpful memory techniques:

- **Visualize the concepts in concrete ways.** *Example:* If a text discusses a study about self-control, imagine a television panel discussing the topic.
- **Draw diagrams or develop clusters.** *Example:* See the cluster on page 8.
- **Put the material in your own words.** *Example:* See the summary on page 11.
- **Teach it to someone.** *Example:* For a study about self-control, explain the main points to a friend or relative—in person, on the phone, or by e-mail.
- **Use acronyms or rhymes.** *Example:* "*i* before *e* except after *c*."

Benefits: Research shows that reviewing within 24 hours helps considerably to move information from your short-term memory to your long-term memory. You will also improve your memory if you create a network of associations with the information you want to remember, if you link the memory to two or more senses, or if you reorganize the material while still retaining the substance with accuracy.

■ Reading Actively

Truly active reading is a kind of mental dialogue with the writer. Use these strategies to read actively:

- **Pace yourself.** Read in stretches of thirty to forty-five minutes, followed by short breaks.
- **Anticipate.** When you break, think about what is coming next and why.
- **Read difficult parts aloud.** Or take turns reading aloud with a partner.
- **Take thoughtful notes.** Find a note-taking system that works for you. (See pages 432–435). This is especially true for research projects.
- **Annotate the text.** Mark up the text (if you own it) or a photocopy. Underline or highlight key points. Write a "?" beside puzzling parts. Write key words in the margin and add personal observations.

Read, annotate, and respond to a text. ■■·■

The following article first appeared in June 2, 2010, in a monthly column in the *Fast Company* newsletter. The author, Dan Heath, is also coauthor (with his brother) of the best-selling business books *Made to Stick* and *Switch*. He is currently a consultant to the Policy Programs at the Aspen Institute. Read the following article, using SQ3R and active-reading strategies.

Why Change Is So Hard: Self-Control Is Exhaustible

You hear something a lot about change: People won't change because they're too lazy. [1] Well, I'm here to stick up for the lazy people. In fact, I want to argue that what looks like laziness is actually exhaustion. The proof comes from a psychology study that is absolutely fascinating.

The Study

So picture this: Students come into a lab. It smells amazing—someone has just baked [2] chocolate-chip cookies. On a table in front of them, there are two bowls. One has the fresh-baked cookies. The other has a bunch of radishes. Some of the students are asked to eat some cookies but no radishes. Others are told to eat radishes but no cookies, and while they sit there, nibbling on rabbit food, the researchers leave the room—which is intended to tempt them and is frankly kind of sadistic. But in the study none of the radish-eaters slipped—they showed admirable self-control. And meanwhile, it probably goes without saying that the people gorging on cookies didn't experience much temptation.

Then, the two groups are asked to do a second, seemingly unrelated task—basically a [3] kind of logic puzzle where they have to trace out a complicated geometric pattern without raising their pencil. Unbeknownst to them, the puzzle can't be solved. The scientists are curious how long they'll persist at a difficult task. So the cookie-eaters try again and again, for an average of 19 minutes, before they give up. But the radish-eaters—they only last an average of 8 minutes. What gives?

The Results

The answer may surprise you: They ran out of self-control. Psychologists have discovered that self-control is an exhaustible resource. And I don't mean self-control only in the sense of turning down cookies or alcohol; I mean a broader sense of self-supervision—any time you're paying close attention to your actions, like when you're having a tough conversation or trying to stay focused on a paper you're writing. This helps to explain why, after a long hard day at the office, we're more likely to snap at our spouses or have one drink too many—we've depleted our self-control.

> *Psychologists have discovered that self-control is an exhaustible resource.*

4

And here's why this matters for change: In almost all change situations, you're substituting new, unfamiliar behaviors for old, comfortable ones, and that burns self-control. Let's say I present a new morning routine to you that specifies how you'll shower and brush your teeth. You'll understand it and you might even agree with my process. But to pull it off, you'll have to supervise yourself very carefully. Every fiber of your being will want to go back to the old way of doing things. Inevitably, you'll slip. And if I were uncharitable, I'd see you going back to the old way and I'd say, You're so lazy. Why can't you just change?

5

This brings us back to the point I promised I'd make. That what looks like laziness is often exhaustion. Change wears people out—even well-intentioned people will simply run out of fuel.

6

Reading for Better Writing

Working by yourself or with a group, answer these questions:

1. In a single sentence, state the thesis of the essay.
2. In a few sentences, tell how the findings of the study help explain why change is difficult.
3. Compare your notes and annotations with a partner. Which parts of your notes and annotations are the same? Which parts are different? How does discussing the content of the essay reinforce or otherwise alter your understanding of the essay?
4. Think about you own life. What sorts of activities require you to exert a great deal of self-control? What sort of activities do you find too tempting to resist when you have "run out" of self-control? How could this information help you avoid temptation?

Map the text. ■■■

If you are visually oriented, you may understand a text best by mapping out its important parts. One way to do so is by "clustering." Start by naming the main topic in an oval at the center of the page. Then branch out using lines and "balloons," where each balloon contains a word or phrase for one major subtopic. Branch out in further layers of balloons to show even more subpoints. If you wish, add graphics, arrows, drawings—anything that helps you visualize the relationships among ideas.

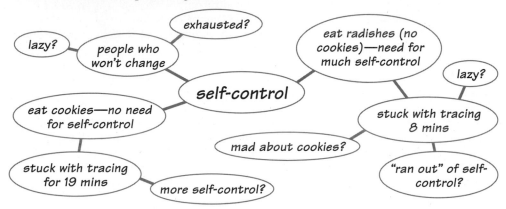

Outline the text. ■■■

Outlining is the traditional way of showing all the major parts, points, and subpoints in a text. An outline uses parallel structure to show main points and subordinate points. See pages 48–50 for more on outlines.

Sample Outline for "Why Change Is So Hard: Self-Control Is Exhaustible"

1. Introduction: Change is hard not because of laziness but because of exhaustion.
2. A study tests self-control.
   a. Some students must eat only cookies—using little self-control.
   b. Some students must eat only radishes—using much self-control.
   c. Both sets of students have to trace a pattern without lifting the pencil—an unsolvable puzzle.
      - Cookie-only students last an average of 19 minutes before quitting.
      - Radish-only students last an average of 8 minutes before quitting.
3. Results show that self-control is exhaustible.
   a. Avoiding temptation and working in a hard, focused way require self-control.
   b. Change requires self-control.
   c. Failure to change often results from exhaustion of self-control.

Evaluate the text.

Critical reading does not mean disproving the text or disapproving of it. It means thoughtfully inspecting, weighing, and evaluating the writer's ideas. To strengthen your reading skills, learn to evaluate texts using the criteria below.

1. **Judge the reading's credibility.** Where was it published? How reliable is the author? How current is the information? How accurate and complete does it seem to be? In addition, consider the author's tone of voice, attitude, and apparent biases.

   Discussion: Dan Heath, the author of "Why Change Is So Hard" is a *New York Times* best-selling author, a consultant to the Aspen Institute, and a monthly columnist for *Fast Company.* How do these credentials affect your reading of the article? How does the article itself build or break credibility?

2. **Put the reading in a larger context.** How do the text's ideas match what you know from other sources? Which details of background, history, and social context help you understand this text's perspective? How have things changed or remained the same since the text's publication? Which allusions (references to people, events, and so on) does the writer use? Why?

   Discussion: "Why Change Is So Hard" centers around a single psychological study and draws from it specific conclusions about self-control. What other studies have attempted to track self-control? Is this a new subdiscipline in psychological research, or a well established one?

3. **Evaluate the reasoning and support.** Is the reasoning clear and logical? Are the examples and other supporting details appropriate and enlightening? Are inferences (what the text implies) consistent with the tone and message? (Look especially for hidden logic and irony that undercut what is said explicitly.)

   Discussion: In "Why Change Is So Hard," Heath identifies exhaustion of self-control as the reason for the difference between the performance of the two test groups. What other explanations could there be for the difference in performance between the two groups of subjects? Is Heath's reasoning sound and convincing?

4. **Reflect on how the reading challenges you.** Which of your beliefs and values does the reading call into question? What discomfort does it create? Does your own perspective skew your evaluation?

   Discussion: What self-control issues have you faced? What might this article have to say about those who work two jobs, run single-parent households, serve extended terms in war zones, or otherwise must exert superhuman levels of self-control? What social changes could help keep people from "snapping"?

 For additional help evaluating texts, see pages 426–429. For information on detecting logical fallacies, which weaken writers' arguments, see pages 257–260.

■ Responding to a Text

In a sense, when you read a text, you enter into a dialogue with it. Your response expresses your turn in the dialogue. Such a response can take varied forms, from a journal entry to a blog to a discussion-group posting.

Follow these guidelines for response writing. ■ ▪ ■

On the surface, responding to a text seems perfectly natural—just let it happen. But it can be a bit more complicated. A written response typically is not the same as a private diary entry but is instead shared with other readers, whether your instructor or a class. You develop your response keeping in mind your instructor's requirements and the response's role in the course. Therefore, follow these guidelines:

1. **Be honest.** Although you want to remain sensitive to the context in which you will share your response, be bold enough to be honest about your reaction to the text—what it makes you think, feel, and question. To that end, a response usually allows you to express yourself directly using the pronoun "I."

2. **Be fluid.** Let the flow of your thoughts guide you in what you write. Don't stop to worry about grammar, punctuation, mechanics, and spelling. These can be quickly cleaned up before you share or submit your response.

3. **Be reflective.** Generally, the goal of a response is to offer thoughtful reflection as opposed to knee-jerk reaction. Show, then, that you are engaging the text's ideas, relating them to your own experience, looking both inward and outward. Avoid a shallow reaction that comes from skimming the text or misreading it.

4. **Be selective.** By nature, a response must limit its focus; it cannot exhaust all your reactions to the text. So zero in on one or two elements of your response, and run with those to see where they take you in your dialogue with the text.

Sample Response

Here is part of a student's response to Dan Heath's "Why Change Is So Hard" on pages 6–7. Note the informality and explanatory tone.

> Heath's report of the psychological experiment is very vivid, referring to the smell of chocolate-chip cookies and hungry students "gorging" on them. He uses the term "sadistic" to refer to making the radish-eaters sit and watch this go on. I wonder if this mild torment plays into the student's readiness to give up on the later test. If I'd been rewarded with cookies, I'd feel indebted to the testers and would stick with it longer. If I'd been punished with radishes, I might give up sooner just to spite the testers.
>
> Now that I think of it, the digestion of all that sugar and fat in the cookies, as opposed to the digestion of roughage from the radishes, might also affect concentration and performance. Maybe the sugar "high" gives students the focus to keep going?

■ Summarizing a Text

Writing a summary disciplines you by making you pull only essentials from a reading—the main points, the thread of the argument. By doing so, you create a brief record of the text's contents and exercise your ability to comprehend, analyze, and synthesize.

Use these guidelines for summary writing. ■ ˙ ■

Writing a summary requires sifting out the least important points, sorting the essential ones to show their relationships, and stating those points in your own words. Follow these guidelines:

1. **Skim first; then read closely.** First, get a sense of the whole, including the main idea and strategies for support. Then read carefully, taking notes as you do.

2. **Capture the text's argument.** Review your notes and annotations, looking for main points and clear connections. State these briefly and clearly, in your own words. Include only what is essential, excluding most examples and details. Don't say simply that the text talks about its subject; tell what it says about that subject.

3. **Test your summary.** Aim to objectively provide the heart of the text; avoid interjecting your own opinions and presence as a writer. Don't confuse an objective summary of a text with a response to it (shown on the previous page). Check your summary against the original text for accuracy and consistency.

Sample Summary

Below is a student's summary of Dan Heath's "Why Change Is So Hard," on pages 6–7. Note how the summary writer includes only main points and phrases them in her own words. She departs from the precise order of details, but records them accurately.

> In the article "Why Change Is So Hard," Dan Heath argues that people who have trouble changing are not lazy, but have simply exhausted their self-control. Heath refers to a study in which one group of students was asked to eat cookies and not radishes while another group in the same room was asked to eat radishes and not cookies. Afterward, both groups of students were asked to trace an endless geometric design without lifting their pencils. The cookie-only group traced on average 19 minutes before giving up, but the radish-only group traced on average only 8 minutes. They had already used up their self-control. Heath says that any behavioral change requires self-control, an exhaustible resource. Reverting to old behavior is what happens due not to laziness but to exhaustion.

INSIGHT: Writing formal summaries—whether as part of literature reviews or as abstracts—is an important skill, especially in the social and natural sciences. For help, go to **www.thecollegewriter.com/4e.**

■ Critical Thinking Through Viewing

Video

Images are created to communicate, just as words are. Most images in everyday life are made to communicate very quickly—magazine covers, ads, signs, movie trailers, and so forth. Other images require contemplation, such as the *Mona Lisa*. When you view an image, view actively and critically.

Actively view images. ■ ∙ ■

Survey the image. See the image as a whole so that you can absorb its overall idea. Look for the image's focal point—what your eye is drawn to. Also consider the relationship between the image's foreground and background, its left content and right content, and its various colors.

Inspect the image. Let your sight touch every part of the image, as if you were reading Braille. Hints of its meaning may lurk in the tiny details as well as in the relationship between the image's parts.

Question the image. Think in terms of each part of the rhetorical situation.

- **Sender:** Who created the image? Why did the person create it?
- **Message:** What is the subject of the image? What is the purpose?
- **Medium:** How was the image originally shown? How is it currently shown?
- **Receiver:** Who is the intended viewer? Why are you viewing the image?
- **Context:** When and where did the image first appear? When and where does it appear now? How does the image relate to its context?

Understand the purpose. Different images have different purposes. Ask yourself, "What is this image meant to do?" and then decide on an appropriate response:

- **Arouse curiosity?** Open your imagination, but stay on guard.
- **Entertain?** Look for the pleasure or the joke, but be wary of excess or of ethically questionable material in the image.
- **Inform or educate?** Search for key instruction, noting what's left out.
- **Illustrate?** Relate the image to the words or concept being illustrated: Does the image clarify or distort the meaning?
- **Persuade?** Examine how the image appeals to the viewer's needs, from safety and satisfaction to self-worth. Are the appeals manipulative, clichéd, or fallacious? Do they play on emotions to bypass reason?
- **Summarize?** Look for the essential message in the image: Does that main idea correspond with the written text?

View an image. ■■·■

The use of *minors* as *miners* is no *minor* problem.

Discussion

The illustration and caption above by Chris Krenzke effectively combine humor with instruction. Originally published in a high school writing handbook, the image's aim is to teach students about a specific word-usage problem while also entertaining them. The image is line art in the "comic" genre, using a humorous scene to convey a serious message. Here are some thoughts on how you might actively view this image:

1. **Survey.** The image tells a story of heavily burdened children working under the heavy supervision of an authoritarian male. That story moves from left to right, from breaking rocks to loading rocks to carrying rocks toward a likely distant destination, the destination pointed to by the man. The black-and-white medium accentuates the starkness.

2. **Inspect.** In terms of the illustration's details, each figure is striking. The individual children share a thinness in their bodies and a strain in their faces. The four children in the line are pictured as beasts of burden bent over by bags that dwarf them. The repetition of figures emphasizes the trudging repetition of their work, and each child in line is pressed farther toward the ground. As for the man, his back is straight and his posture tall. His enormous chin, large nose, overly long but skinny arm, and sharply pointed finger suggest a negative authority. His stubbly face and his caveman clothing add to this figure's prehistoric character.

3. **Question.** Who is the artist Chris Krenzke? When did he first create this image? In what book was it published? When? Why did Krenzke use this caveman style? Who or what do "minors," "miners," and "minor" refer to in the illustration?

4. **Relate.** The connection between the sentence and the image becomes clear when the viewer realizes that "minors" are children not of a legal age to work, "miners" refers to an occupation, and "minor" means insignificant. But the image prompts other connections: the history of horrific child-labor practices during the Industrial Revolution as well as continuing child-labor issues in today's global economy. With these allusions, Krenzke succeeds in deepening the instruction offered by his art.

Interpreting an Image

Interpreting an image follows naturally from viewing or "reading" the image. Interpreting means figuring out what the image or design is meant to do, say, or show. Interpreting requires you to think more deeply about each element of the rhetorical situation, and complications with each element.

- **Sender:** Who created the image—a photographer, a painter, a web designer? Why did the person create it? What other people might have been involved—editors, patrons?
  Complications: The sender might be unknown or a group.

- **Message:** What is the subject of the image? How is the subject portrayed? What is the main purpose of the image—to entertain, to inform, to persuade, to entice, to shock?
  Complications: The message might be mixed, implied, ironic, unwelcome, or distorted. The subject might be vague, unfamiliar, complex, or disturbing.

- **Medium:** What is the image—a painting, a cartoon panel, a photo? How might the image have been modified over time? What visual language has the sender used?
  Complications: The medium might be unusual, unfamiliar, or multiple. The visual languages might be literal, stylized, numeric, symbolic, and so on.

- **Receiver:** Whom was the image made for? Are you part of the intended audience? What is your relationship with the sender? Do you agree with the message? How comfortable are you with the medium? What is your overall response to the image?
  Complications: You might be uninterested in, unfamiliar with, or biased toward the message.

- **Context:** What was the context in which the image was first presented? What context surrounds the image now? Does the image fit its context or fight it?
  Complications: The context might be disconnected, ironic, changing, or multilayered.

INSIGHT: Like words, visuals can be clichés—trite, misleading, or worn-out expressions of concepts or ideas. For example, TV ads for weight-loss drugs commonly picture scantily clad, fit young people, deceptively linking use of the drug to beauty, youth, and sex.

Interpret an image. ■■■

Discussion

This color photograph shows a multireligious commemoration of the 229,000 victims of the Indian Ocean tsunami of December 26, 2004.

The symbolism is clearly rooted in the points of light created by the candle balloons, where light itself is a cross-cultural symbol of hope, endurance, the human spirit, and God's presence. The skyward angle of the photograph, with the clusters of candle balloons floating up and the people in the lower right of the frame, creates this sense of vertical longing and release, emphasizing perhaps humanity's longing to solve life's mysteries, including death and disaster. Although the large, just-released candle balloons are most prominent, the viewer's eyes are also drawn upward, where clusters of far-off candles become constellations of starlike lights. The mourners in the right of the frame, forming a loose circle, are all gazing skyward, like the viewer. Ordinary people in ordinary clothes, they appear to be clapping and, for some, the clapping shows their hands virtually in a posture of prayer. In this way, the image both mourns the dead and celebrates life.

Sender:	Photographer Bazuki Muhammad; authors of *The College Writer*
Message:	Thais release candle balloons during a mass prayer for victims of the Indian Ocean tsunami. The message is to remember those who died, but move forward with hope.
Medium:	Digital color photograph
Receiver:	The intended viewer was anyone reading a newspaper, magazine, or web article. The current viewer is likely a student or an instructor in a composition course.
Context:	This photograph was part of a series provided by Reuters for global newspapers. It now is part of a composition text.

■ Evaluating an Image

When you encounter an image, you must do more than understand and interpret it: You must assess its quality, truthfulness, and value. In other words, you must evaluate it. When you have done that well, you can fairly say you have thought it through. The following questions will guide your assessment.

Consider the purpose. ■ ■ ■

What purpose does the visual image best seem to serve?

- **Ornamentation:** Makes the page more pleasing to the eye
- **Illustration:** Supports points made in the accompanying text
- **Revelation:** Gives an inside look at something or presents new data
- **Explanation:** Uses imagery or graphics to clarify a complex subject
- **Instruction:** Guides the viewer through a complex process
- **Persuasion:** Influences feelings or beliefs
- **Entertainment:** Amuses the reader

Evaluate the quality. ■ ■ ■

Essentially, how good is the image?

- Is the image done with skill? A map, for example, should be accurately and attractively drawn, should use color effectively, and should be complete enough to serve its purpose.
- Does the image measure up to standards of quality? See **www.thecollegewriter. com/4e** for design tips for a variety of visuals.
- Is it backed by authority? Does the designer have a good reputation? Does the publication or institution have good credentials?
- How does the image compare to other images like it? Are clearer or more accurate images available?
- What are its shortcomings? Are there gaps in its coverage? Does it twist the evidence? Does it convey clichéd or fallacious information? (See pages 257–260 for a discussion of logical fallacies.)
- Could you think of a better way to approach the image's subject? If you were to produce the visual, what might you improve?

Determine the value. ■ ■ ■

What is the image's tangible and intangible worth? Its benefits and drawbacks?

- Is the visual worth viewing? Does it enrich the document by clarifying or otherwise enhancing its message?
- Does the visual appeal to you? Listen to authorities and peers, but also consider your own perspective.

Evaluate an image. ■ ▪ ▪

Discussion

Evaluating an image such as this WWII poster aimed at U.S. servicemen reveals its strong stereotypes of both men and women, stereotypes related to the historical period. As with all images, evaluation begins with understanding and interpreting the poster.

In the poster's center is a woman in evening dress, her hair done up, wearing jewels and a corsage. She is seated, at ease, looking at us. Perhaps she represents beauty, both sensual attractiveness and sophistication. The colors used to present her are pale and muted, except for her blue eyes and red lips.

Surrounding the woman are three men, individually dressed in the uniforms of Army, Air Force, and Navy. Drinking and smoking, the men seem to be competing for her attention.

The poster implies that all service personnel were male, which was not true even in WWII, when WACs and WAVEs served in the armed forces. It cautions that these male members of the armed forces should be wary in seemingly innocent social situations, since even a beautiful woman, whom popular stereotypes of the day characterized as "dumb," might not be what she appears. Such a woman might, in fact, be a spy—an idea perhaps inspired by the famous case of WWI spy Mata Hari. The statement that "careless talk costs lives" is a version of another common phrase from the period: "Loose lips sink ships."

Evaluating this poster involves considering its original context while assessing it from our current perspective. In the heat of WWII, this poster could be considered a fair piece of military persuasion. Today, however, what is striking are the gender stereotypes at work in both image and words. Not only are service personnel today both male and female, in every branch of the armed forces, but they fulfill the same roles, including combat positions. With respect to the men, the image implies that in social situations (which are assumed to include smoking and drinking), they are untrustworthy and apt to boast or compete in the presence of an attractive woman. With respect to women, the image both denounces and warns, implying that women, especially attractive women, are cunning and dangerous. Today, such stereotypes press us to question the quality, truthfulness, and value of the image.

Video

Critical Thinking Through Writing

In college, your writing often must show your ability to think critically about topics and issues by analyzing complex processes, synthesizing distinct concepts, weighing the value of opposing perspectives, and practicing new applications of existing principles. The following tips can help you.

Develop sound critical-thinking habits.

Like everything worthwhile, improving your critical-thinking skills takes time and practice. But cultivating the habits below will pay off in sound, thoughtful writing.

1. **Be curious.** Ask "Why?" Cultivate your ability to wonder; question what you see, hear, and read—both inside and outside the classroom.

2. **Be creative.** Don't settle for obvious answers. Look at things in a fresh way, asking "what-if" questions such as "What if Ophelia didn't die in *Hamlet*?"

3. **Be open to new ideas.** Approach thinking as you would approach a road trip— looking for the unexpected and musing over mysteries.

4. **Value others' points of view.** Look at issues from another person's perspective and weigh that against your own. Honestly examine how the core of her or his perspective compares to the core of your perspective, and how each basis for thought might lead to different conclusions.

5. **Get involved.** Read books, journals, and newspapers. Watch documentaries. Join book clubs, film clubs, or political and social-action activities.

6. **Focus.** Sharpen your concentration, looking for details that distinguish a topic and reveal key questions related to its nature, function, and impact.

7. **Be rational.** Choose logical thinking patterns like those discussed in this chapter, and then work through the steps to deepen your understanding of a topic.

8. **Make connections.** Use writing to explore how and why topics or issues are related. Use comparisons to identify and name these relationships.

9. **Tolerate ambiguity.** Respectfully analyze issues not readily resolved—and acknowledge when your position requires further research or thought.

10. **Test the evidence.** Be properly skeptical about all claims (see pages 252–253). Look for corroboration (or verification) in other sources.

11. **Develop research-based conclusions.** Focus on understanding issues, assessing their history, development, function, and impact. During the process, gather details that lead to and support a reasonable conclusion.

12. **Expect results.** Consider each paper to be a benchmark that reflects your progress in developing your thinking and writing skills. Save your papers for periodic analyses of your progress and revision of the writing.

Ask probing questions.

Every field uses questions to trigger critical thinking. For example, scientific questions generate hypotheses, sociological questions lead to studies, mathematical questions call for proofs, and literary criticism questions call for interpretations. A good question opens up a problem and guides you all the way to its solution. But not all questions are created equal. Consider the differences:

- "Rhetorical" questions aren't meant to be answered. They're asked for effect. *Example:* Who would want to be caught in an earthquake?
- Closed questions seek a limited response and can be answered with "yes," "no," or a simple fact. *Example:* Would I feel an earthquake measuring 3.0 on the Richter scale?
- Open questions invite brainstorming and discussion. *Example:* How might a major earthquake affect this urban area?
- Theoretical questions call for organization and explanation of an entire field of knowledge. *Example:* What might cause a sudden fracturing of Earth's crust along fault lines?

To improve the critical thinking in your writing, ask better questions. The strategies below will help you think freely, respond to reading, study for a test, or collect your thoughts for an essay.

Ask open questions. Closed questions sometimes choke off thinking. Use open questions to trigger a flow of ideas.

Ask "educated" questions. Compare these questions: (A) What's wrong with television? (B) Does the 16.3 percent rise in televised acts of violence during the past three years signal a rising tolerance for violence in the viewing audience? You have a better chance of expanding the "educated" question—question B—into an essay because the question is clearer and suggests debatable issues.

Keep a question journal. Divide a blank notebook page or split a computer screen. On one side, write down any questions that come to mind regarding the topic that you want to explore. On the other side, write down answers and any thoughts that flow from them.

Write Q & A drafts. To write a thoughtful first draft, write quickly, then look it over. Turn the main idea into a question and write again, answering your question. For example, if your main idea is that TV viewers watch far more violence than they did ten years ago, ask *Which viewers? Why?* and *What's the result?* Go on that way until you find a key idea to serve as the main point of your next draft.

For more help with critical-thinking skills such as making and supporting claims, recognizing logical fallacies, and dealing with opposition, see "Strategies for Argumentation and Persuasion," pages 249–264.

Practice inductive and deductive logic. ■ ■ ■

Questions invite thinking; reasoning responds to that challenge in an organized way. Will the organization of your thoughts be inductive or deductive? Inductive logic reasons from specific information toward general conclusions. Deductive logic reasons from general principles toward specific applications. Notice in the diagram below that inductive reasoning starts with specific details or observations (as shown at the base) and then moves "up" to broader ideas and eventually to a concluding generalization. In contrast, deduction starts with general principles at the top and works down, applying the principles to explain particular instances.

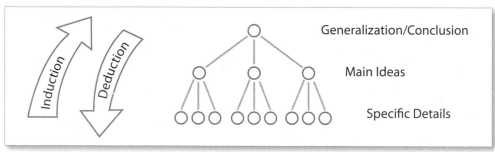

Sentences, paragraphs, and entire essays can be organized either inductively or deductively. Use induction when you want to postpone your conclusions. Use deduction for logical clarity, directness, and strength, or to apply what is already agreed on to what is still under dispute. Narrative or personal essays tend toward inductive organization, whereas analytical essays (particularly those written in the social or natural sciences) typically use both induction and deduction.

Example: Read through the paragraphs below from the student essay "If We Are What We Wear, What Are We?" by Allison Young (**www.thecollegewriter.com/4e**). The first paragraph works deductively, the second paragraph inductively. Note how each approach affects the message.

Deduction: generalization to specific details

The American excuse for owning multiples is that clothing styles change so rapidly. At the end of the '80s, trends in high fashion changed every two and a half months (During 95). Even for those of us who don't keep up with high fashion, styles change often enough that our clothing itself lasts much longer than the current trend. Perhaps this is one of the reasons the average American spent $997 on clothing in 1996 (U.S. Department of Commerce).

Induction: specific details to generalization

While Americans are spending a thousand dollars on clothing a year, people in Ethiopia make an average of only $96 a year, those in Bangladesh $280, and the average Filipino worker makes $1,052 (United Nations Statistics Division). I, on the other hand, made over $5,000 last year, and that job was only part-time. When an American college student can earn more money at her part-time job than three billion people each make for a living, it's time to question our culture and ask, as Alan During did, "How much is enough?"

■ Practicing Modes of Thinking in Your Writing

In your various writing assignments, you will need to practice specific modes of thinking. The table below maps out these modes (from elementary to complex) and the tasks each requires. The more complex modes are then fleshed out on the following pages.

When you are asked to _____, be ready to _____.

Know

define	memorize
identify	name
list	recall
match	recognize

Call to mind what you have learned

- Recall information
- List details
- Define key terms
- Identify main points

Understand

comprehend	interpret
connect	restate
explain	summarize
grasp	

Show what you have learned

- Connect related examples
- Summarize important details
- Explain how something works
- Interpret what something means

Analyze

characterize	contrast
classify	divide
compare	examine

Break down information

- Divide a whole into its parts
- Group things into categories
- Analyze causes and effects
- Examine similarities and differences

Synthesize

assemble	imagine
combine	invent
construct	link
formulate	

Shape information into a new form

- Bring together a body of evidence
- Blend the old with the new
- Predict or hypothesize
- Construct a new way of looking at something

Evaluate

assess	measure
check	monitor
critique	rank
judge	rate

Determine the worth of information

- Point out a subject's strengths and weaknesses
- Evaluate its clarity, accuracy, logic, value, and so on
- Convince others of its value/worth

Apply

anticipate	propose
choose	select
generate	

Use what you have learned

- Propose a better way of doing something
- Generate a plan of action
- Offer solutions to a problem

Think by using analysis. ■■▪

The word *analyze* literally means "to loosen or undo." When you analyze something, you break it down into parts and examine each part separately. You classify information, compare objects, trace a process, or explain causes.

As you analyze, think about the questions listed below. Note that each type of thinking answers certain kinds of questions. Remember, too, that thinking tasks often require two or more kinds of analysis that support one another.

Composition:	What elements does it contain? What is not part of it?
Categories:	How are things grouped, divided, or classified?
Structures:	What are the parts or elements? How are they related?
Comparisons/ contrasts:	How are things similar? How are they different?
Causes/effects:	Why did this happen? What are the results?
Processes:	How does it work or happen? What are the stages?

Example: Read through the passage below, from "Wayward Cells." In the full essay on pages 217–218, student writer Kerri Mertz explains the process by which healthy body cells become cancerous cells. Note how in this excerpt, the writer develops an overall analysis based on a process but also uses compare-contrast and cause-effect thinking within that structure, as well as informal definition.

The writer explains a cellular process and contrasts healthy and cancerous versions.

Most healthy cells reproduce rather quickly, but their reproduction rate is controlled. For example, your blood cells completely die off and replace themselves within a matter of weeks, but existing cells make only as many new cells as the body needs. The DNA codes in healthy cells tell them how many new cells to produce. However, cancer cells don't have this control, so they reproduce quickly with no stopping point, a characteristic called "autonomy" (Braun 3). What's more, all their "offspring" have the same qualities as their messed-up parent, and the resulting overpopulation produces growths called tumors.

The writer explains the three harmful effects of tumor cells (the cause).

Examples illustrate the analysis.

Tumor cells can hurt the body in a number of ways. First, a tumor can grow so big that it takes up space needed by other organs. Second, some cells may detach from the original tumor and spread throughout the body, creating new tumors elsewhere. This happens with lymphatic cancer—a cancer that's hard to control because it spreads so quickly. A third way that tumor cells can hurt the body is by doing work not called for in their DNA. For example, a gland cell's DNA code may tell the cell to produce a necessary hormone in the endocrine system. However, if cancer damages or distorts that code, sick cells may produce more of the hormone than the body can use—or even tolerate (Braun 4). Cancer cells seem to have minds of their own, and this is why cancer is such a serious disease.

Think by using synthesis. ■■▪■

Synthesis is the opposite of analysis. Where analysis breaks things down into parts, synthesis combines elements into a new whole. In your writing, when you pull together things that are normally separate, you are synthesizing. Common ways of synthesizing include predicting, inventing, redesigning, and imagining a whole new way of looking at something.

Working with synthesis involves both reason and imagination. Start by looking closely at two or more items that you want to synthesize, and then think of fresh ways they can be related. Don't be afraid to see your subjects in a new way. In other words, think "sideways" rather than straight ahead. Ask the following questions:

Applying:	What can I do with both? What will be the outcome?
Bridging:	How can I build a connection between the two?
Combining:	How can I connect, associate, or blend the two?
Conflicting:	Which is good, better, or best? What strength does each offer the other?
Inventing:	What parts could these two play in a drama?
Proposing:	What do I suggest doing with both?
Sequencing:	Which comes first? Is one an extension of the other?
Projecting:	Based on current information, what is the best forecast for what will happen in the near future or the long term?

Example: Read through the passage below, from "In Africa, AIDS Has a Woman's Face," by former United Nations Secretary-General Kofi Annan (see pages 296–297). In the full article, Annan argues that resolving the AIDS crisis in Africa must begin by saving the familial, social, and economic backbones of African cultures—women. In the following passage, Annan synthesizes his discussion by projecting what is necessary for successful solutions.

Pulling together his discussion of the twin tragedies of AIDS and famine in Africa, the writer calls for imaginative, multifaceted solutions.

Because this crisis is different from past famines, we must look beyond relief measures of the past. Merely shipping in food is not enough. Our effort will have to combine food assistance and new approaches to farming with treatment and prevention of H.I.V. and AIDS. It will require creating early-warning and analysis systems that monitor both H.I.V. infection rates and famine indicators. It will require new agricultural techniques, appropriate to a depleted work force. It will require a renewed effort to wipe out H.I.V.-related stigma and silence.

It will require innovative, large-scale ways to care for orphans, with specific measures that enable children in AIDS-affected communities to stay in school. Education and prevention are still the most powerful weapons against the spread of H.I.V. Above all, this new international effort must put women at the center of our strategy to fight AIDS.

Think by using evaluation.

Movies, proposals, arguments—anything can be evaluated. Evaluation measures the value or worth of things. For example, when you express your judgment about an issue or discuss the weak and strong points of what someone else has said, you are evaluating. Many kinds of writing are evaluative.

To evaluate a topic, start by learning as much about it as possible. Then consider which criteria or standards are appropriate. Next, judge how the topic measures up based on those criteria. Support your judgment with concrete details, examples, illustrations, and comparisons. Ask questions like these:

Aspects:	What elements of the topic will I evaluate?
Vantage point:	What are my experience and my point of view?
Criteria:	On which standards will I base my judgment?
Assessment:	How does the topic measure up by those standards?
Comparison:	How does it compare to and contrast with similar things?
Recommendation:	Based on my evaluation, what do I advise?

Example: The passage below is taken from David Blankenhorn's "Fatherless America," on pages 279–283. In the full essay, Blankenhorn examines the causes and effects of the increased fatherlessness within U.S. families—that is, the absence of fathers in many homes. In the following excerpt, he assesses the failures of a society that is losing a healthy sense of fatherhood.

The writer establishes a criterion for evaluating a culture's fatherhood models and practices.

. . . Margaret Mead and others have observed that the supreme test of any civilization is whether it can socialize men by teaching them to be fathers—creating a culture in which men acknowledge their paternity and willingly nurture their offspring. Indeed, if we can equate the essence of the antisocial male with violence, we can equate the essence of the socialized male with being a good father. Thus, at the center of our most important cultural imperative, we find the fatherhood script: the story that describes what it ought to mean for a man to have a child. . . .

After exploring this criterion in depth (not shown), the writer measures U.S. culture and assesses its failures with respect to fatherhood.

The stakes on this issue could hardly be higher. Our society's conspicuous failure to sustain or create compelling norms of fatherhood amounts to a social and personal disaster. Today's story of fatherhood features one-dimensional characters, an unbelievable plot, and an unhappy ending. It reveals in our society both a failure of collective memory and a collapse of moral imagination. It undermines families, neglects children, causes or aggravates our worst social problems, and makes individual adult happiness—both male and female—harder to achieve.

Ultimately, this failure reflects nothing less than a culture gone awry: a culture increasingly unable to establish the boundaries, erect the sign-posts, and fashion the stories that can harmonize individual happiness with collective well-being. In short, it reflects a culture that increasingly fails to "enculture" individual men and women, mothers and fathers.

Think by using application. ■■■

Thinking by using application defines the practical implications of something. It involves using what you know to demonstrate, show, relate, or extend ideas in view of their outcomes. For example, using what you have learned about the ecology of forest fires to examine the effects of a particular fire—that's application in action.

Applying involves moving from ideas to possible action. First, understand the information you have. Second, relate this information to a given situation. Third, select those facts and details that clarify and support the application. Fourth, test the application to see whether it has been reasonable.

> When applying ideas, let questions like these guide your writing:
>
> **Purpose:** What is something designed to be or do?
>
> **Benefits:** What would this idea make clearer, better, or more complete?
>
> **Solutions:** What problems are solved by application of this idea?
>
> **Outcomes:** What results can be expected? Where could we go from there?

Example: Read the paragraphs below, from Anna Quindlen's "Uncle Sam and Aunt Samantha" (pages 312–314). In this essay, Quindlen argues that in the United States, women— as well as men—should be eligible to be drafted for military service. In the passage below, she applies the concept of equal rights to this specific situation.

Using the word "egalitarian" to refer to a key principle, the writer points out the real inequality and argues for a change.	Parents face a series of unique new challenges in this more egalitarian world, not the least of which would be sending a daughter off to war. But parents all over this country are doing that right now, with daughters who enlisted; some have even expressed surprise that young women, in this day and age, are not required to register alongside their brothers and friends. While all involved in this debate over the years have invoked the assumed opposition of the people, even 10 years ago more than half of all Americans polled believed women should be made eligible for the draft. Besides, this is not about comfort but about fairness. My son has to register with the Selective Service this year, and if his sister does not when she turns 18, it makes a mockery not only of the standards of this household but of the standards of this nation.
She backs up her conclusion with historical context and presses readers to agree.	It is possible in Afghanistan for women to be treated like little more than fecund pack animals precisely because gender fear and ignorance and hatred have been codified and permitted to hold sway. In this country, largely because of the concerted efforts of those allied with the women's movement over a century of struggle, much of that bigotry has been beaten back, even buried. Yet in improbable places the creaky old ways surface, the ways suggesting that we women were made of finer stuff. The finer stuff was usually porcelain, decorative and on the shelf, suitable for meals and show. Happily, the finer stuff has been transmuted into the right stuff. But with rights come responsibilities, as teachers like to tell their students . . .

Critical-Thinking and Writing Activities

As directed by your instructor, complete the following critical-thinking and writing activities by yourself or with classmates

1. Northrop Frye has argued that "[n]obody is capable of free speech unless he [or she] knows how to use language, and such knowledge is not a gift: It has to be learned and worked at." How does Frye's claim relate to the discussions of critical reading, viewing, and writing in this chapter?

2. What thinking, reading, viewing, and writing skills are required in your field of study? Reflect on those possibilities.

3. Choose a subject you know something about. Practice thinking about that subject both inductively and deductively. Then write two paragraphs—one developed inductively and the other developed deductively.

4. Select a sample essay from the "Strategies and Models" section. Read the piece carefully and identify where and how the writer uses different thinking modes. Do the same analysis on a recent sample of your own writing, rating your analysis, synthesis, evaluation, and application.

Learning-Outcomes Checklist

_____ I use the SQ3R reading method for important reading assignments for my courses and research projects, thinking about the rhetorical situation. (See pages 4–5.)

_____ I read actively rather than passively by taking thoughtful notes, annotating texts, mapping, and outlining. (See pages 6–9.)

_____ I respond to texts in an honest, fluid, reflective, and selective way. (See page 10.)

_____ I effectively summarize texts, capturing the text's main argument and providing the main supporting details—all in my own words and in a concise form. (See page 11.)

_____ I view images actively instead of passively, thinking about the rhetorical situation. (See pages 12–13.)

_____ I interpret images, asking deeper questions about each part of the rhetorical situation. (See pages 14–15.)

_____ I judge the value of images, considering the purpose of the image and its quality. (See pages 16–17.)

_____ I think critically through writing, analyzing, synthesizing, evaluating, and applying information. (See pages 18–25.)

2 Beginning the Writing Process

The blank page or screen can be daunting for any writer. That's because writing doesn't go from nothing to a masterpiece in one step. Writing is a process, much like painting.

This chapter focuses on beginning that process. It provides numerous concrete strategies for understanding writing assignments, deciding on a topic, and exploring it. The very act of writing generates ideas and creates new connections that will make it easy to fill the blank page.

Learning Outcomes

▸ Understand the writing process.
▸ Understand the rhetorical situation.
▸ Analyze the assignment.
▸ Select a subject.
▸ Collect information.

Video

Web Link

Video

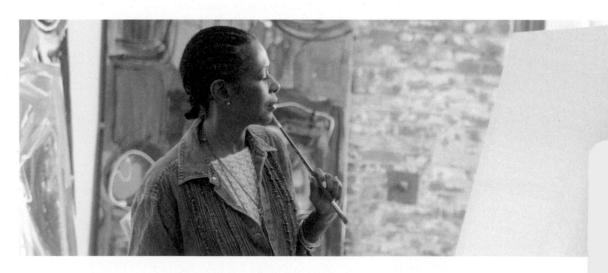

Visually Speaking ▶ Painting is the process of converting infinite possibilities into a single image. How is writing similar? How is it different? What difficulties arise from converting the infinite into the particular?

■ The Writing Process: From Start to Finish

It's easy to feel overwhelmed by a writing project—especially if the form of writing is new to you, the topic is complex, or the paper must be long. However, using the writing process will relieve some of that pressure by breaking down the task into manageable steps. An overview of those steps is shown below, and key principles are addressed on the next page.

Consider the writing process. ■ ˙ ■

The following flowchart maps out the basic steps in the writing process. As you work on your writing project, periodically review this diagram to keep yourself on task.

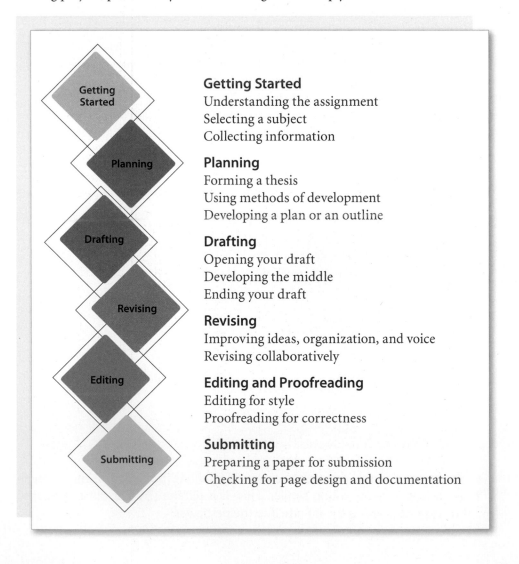

Getting Started
Understanding the assignment
Selecting a subject
Collecting information

Planning
Forming a thesis
Using methods of development
Developing a plan or an outline

Drafting
Opening your draft
Developing the middle
Ending your draft

Revising
Improving ideas, organization, and voice
Revising collaboratively

Editing and Proofreading
Editing for style
Proofreading for correctness

Submitting
Preparing a paper for submission
Checking for page design and documentation

Adapt the process to your project. ■ ■ ■

Video

The writing process shown on the previous page is flexible, not rigid. As a writer, you need to adapt the process to your situation and assignment. To do so, consider these essential principles.

Writing tends not to follow a straight path. While writing begins with an assignment or a need and ends with a reader, the journey in between is often indirect. The steps in the flowchart overlap to show that when you write, you sometimes move back and forth between steps, meaning that the process is recursive. For example, during the revision phase, you may discover that you need to draft a new paragraph or do more research.

Each assignment presents distinct challenges. A personal essay may develop best through clustering or freewriting; a literary analysis through close reading of a story; a lab report through the experimental method; and a position paper through reading of books and journal articles, as well as through careful and balanced reasoning.

Writing can involve collaboration. From using your roommate as a sounding board for your topic choice to working with a group to produce a major report, college writing is not solitary writing. In fact, many colleges have a writing center to help you refine your writing assignments. (See pages 89–91 for more.)

Each writer works differently. Some writers do extensive prewriting before drafting, while others do not. You might develop a detailed outline, whereas someone else might draft a brief list of topics. Experiment with the strategies introduced in chapters 2–7, adopting those that help you.

Good writing can't be rushed. Although some students regard pulling an all-nighter as a badge of honor, good writing takes time. A steady, disciplined approach will generally produce the best results. For example, by brainstorming or reading early in a project, you stimulate your subconscious mind to mull over issues, identify problems, and project solutions—even while your conscious mind is working on other things. Similarly, completing a first draft early enough gives you time to revise objectively.

Different steps call for attention to different writing issues. As you use the writing process, at each stage keep your focus where it belongs:

1. While getting started, planning, and drafting, focus on global issues: ideas, structure, voice, format, and design.

2. During revising, fix big content problems by cutting, adding, and thoroughly reworking material. (Our experience is that students benefit the most from revising—but spend the least time doing it!)

3. While editing and proofreading, pay attention to small, local issues— word choice, sentence smoothness, and grammatical correctness. Worrying about these issues early in the writing process interrupts the flow of drafting and wastes time on material that later is deleted.

■ Understand the Rhetorical Situation

Rhetoric is the art of using language effectively. As Aristotle, Quintilian, and others have explained, your language is effective when all aspects of your message fit the rhetorical situation:

Rhetorical Situation

Think of your role as the writer. ■·■

Are you writing as a concerned citizen, as a student in a class, as a friend relating a story, as a reporter providing news, as a blogger giving an opinion? Your role in writing and otherwise communicating affects the level of language you use, the voice you use, the types of details you include, and so on.

Understand your subject. ■·■

To truly understand your subject, you need to gather and assimilate all relevant details about it, including its history, makeup, function, and impact on people and culture. Knowing those details will help you narrow your focus to a specific thesis and support it well.

> **Writing with Sources:** As you search for information, think about which types of sources are recommended or expected for the assignment. Which should be avoided?

Understand your purpose. ■·■

Key words in an assignment—such as *analyze, explain, defend,* or *describe*—tell you what the purpose of the writing is supposed to be. Understanding why you are writing helps you choose an organizational strategy, such as classification, definition, or process. (See pages 62–66.)

> **Writing with Sources:** Think of the sources that will most help you with your purpose, whether to entertain, compare, inspire, enlighten, and so on.

Understand your audience. ■ ˙ ■

For any writing task, you must understand your audience in order to develop writing that meets their needs. To assess your audience, answer questions like these:

- Who are my readers: instructor? classmates? web users?
- What do they know about my topic, and what do they need to know?
- How well do they understand the terminology involved?
- What are their attitudes toward the topic and toward me?
- How well do they read written English—or visuals such as graphs and charts?
- How will they use my writing (as entertainment or to complete a task)?

Note: Answers to such questions will help you develop meaningful sentences (pages 95–101), choose appropriate words (pages 102–106), and select relevant visuals (page 408).

> **Writing with Sources:** Ask yourself what sources your reader will best understand and most respect. What sources will add to your credibility and authority?

Understand the medium (form). ■ ˙ ■

Many communication options are available for every message. Academic forms include essays, analyses, reports, proposals, research papers, reviews, and so on. It is important to understand the form of the assignment. What works well in a narrative about a past experience would not work as well in a lab report. Also, each of these forms can contain multiple media: written elements, graphics, photos, drawings, videos, audios, links, and so on. Understanding the overall medium and the media within it will help you succeed.

> **Writing with Sources:** Make sure you understand the way that sources are to be cited in the form of communication you are using. (See 491–558 for MLA and APA styles.)

Think about the context. ■ ˙ ■

Think about how this assignment relates to others in the course. Consider these issues:

- **Weight:** Is this an everyday assignment, a weekly or biweekly one, or the *big* one?
- **Assessment:** Find out how the assignment will be graded. What rubric will be used?
- **Intent:** Make certain that you understand the goals of the assignment and understand what your instructor wants you to get out of it.

Note: If the writing you are doing is not in response to an assignment, think about the environment in which the message will be read. What is the history of this issue? What is the current climate like? What might the future be?

> **Writing with Sources:** If you are writing material that will be reviewed and debated by others in your field, think about what sources you would most want your writing to appear in. Make certain you understand the submission guidelines for the source.

■ Understanding the Assignment

Each college instructor has a way of personalizing a writing assignment, but most assignments will spell out (1) the objective, (2) the task, (3) the formal requirements, and (4) suggested approaches and topics. Your first step, therefore, is to read the assignment carefully, noting the options and restrictions that are part of it. The suggestions below will help you do that. (Also see pages 114–117 for one writer's approach.)

Read the assignment. ■ ■

Certain words in the assignment explain what main action you must perform. Here are some words that signal what you are to do:

■ Key Words

Analyze:	Break down a topic into subparts, showing how those parts relate.
Argue:	Defend a claim with logical arguments.
Classify:	Divide a large group into well-defined subgroups.
Compare/contrast:	Point out similarities and/or differences.
Define:	Give a clear, thoughtful definition or meaning of something.
Describe:	Show in detail what something is like.
Evaluate:	Weigh the truth, quality, or usefulness of something.
Explain:	Give reasons, list steps, or discuss the causes of something.
Interpret:	Tell in your own words what something means.
Reflect:	Share your well-considered thoughts about a subject.
Summarize:	Restate someone else's ideas very briefly in your own words.
Synthesize:	Connect facts or ideas to create something new.

■ Options and Restrictions

The assignment often gives you some choice of your topic or approach but may restrict your options to suit the instructor's purpose. Note the options and restrictions in the following short sample assignment:

> Reflect on the way a natural disaster or major historical event has altered your understanding of the past, the present, or the future.

Options:	(1) You may choose any natural disaster or historical event.
	(2) You may focus on the past, present, or future.
	(3) You may examine any kind of alteration.
Restrictions:	(1) You must reflect on a change in your understanding.
	(2) The disaster must be natural.
	(3) The historical event must be major.

Relate the assignment to the goals of the course. ■ ■ ■

1. How much value does the instructor give the assignment? (The value is often expressed as a percentage of the course grade.)
2. What benefit does your instructor want you to receive?
   - Strengthen your comprehension?
   - Improve your research skills?
   - Deepen your ability to explain, prove, or persuade?
   - Expand your style?
   - Increase your creativity?
3. How will this assignment contribute to your overall performance in the course? What course goals (often listed in the syllabus) does it address?

Relate the assignment to other assignments. ■ ■ ■

1. Does it build on previous assignments?
2. Does it prepare you for the next assignment?

Relate the assignment to your own interests. ■ ■ ■

1. Does it connect with a topic that already interests you?
2. Does it connect with work in your other courses?
3. Does it connect with the work you may do in your chosen field?
4. Does it connect with life outside school?

Reflect on the assignment. ■ ■ ■

1. **First impulses:** How did you feel when you first read the assignment?
2. **Approaches:** What's the usual approach for an assignment like this? What's a better way of tackling it?
3. **Quality of performance:** What would it take to produce an excellent piece of writing?
4. **Benefits:** What are the benefits to your education? to you personally? to the class? to society?
5. **Features:** Reflect further on four key features of any writing assignment.
   Purpose: What is the overall purpose of the assignment—to inform, to explain, to analyze, to entertain? What is the desired outcome?
   Audience: Should you address your instructor? your classmates? a general reader? How much does the reader already know about the topic? What type of language should you use?
   Form: What are the requirements concerning length, format, and due date?
   Assessment: How will the assignment be evaluated? How can you be sure that you are completing the assignment correctly?

■ Selecting a Subject

For some assignments, finding a suitable subject (or topic) may require little thinking on your part. If an instructor asks you to summarize an article in a professional journal, you know what you will write about—the article in question. But suppose the instructor asks you to analyze a feature of popular culture in terms of its impact on society. You won't be sure of a specific writing topic until you explore the possibilities. Keep the following points in mind when you conduct a topic search. Your topic must . . .

- meet the requirements of the assignment.
- be limited in scope.
- seem reasonable (that is, be within your means to research).
- genuinely interest you.

Limit the subject area. ■ ■ ■

Many of your writing assignments may relate to general subject areas you are currently studying. Your task, then, is to select a specific topic related to the general area of study—a topic limited enough that you can treat it with some depth in the length allowed for the assignment. The following examples show the difference between general subjects and limited topics:

> **General Subject Area:** Popular culture
> **Limited Topic:** *The Simpsons* TV show
> **General Subject Area:** Energy sources
> **Limited Topic:** Using wind power

Conduct your search. ■ ■ ■

Finding a writing idea that meets the requirements of the assignment should not be difficult, if you know how and where to look. Follow these steps:

1. Check your class notes and handouts for ideas related to the assignment.
2. Search the Internet. Type in a keyword or phrase (the general subject stated in the assignment) and see what you can find. You could also follow a subject tree to narrow a subject. (See page 462.)
3. Consult indexes, guides, and other library references. *The Readers' Guide to Periodical Literature,* for example, lists current articles published on specific topics and where to find them. (See pages 452–457.)
4. Discuss the assignment with your instructor or an information specialist.
5. Use one or more of the prewriting strategies described on the following pages to generate possible writing ideas.

Explore for possible topics. ▰▪▰

You can generate possible writing ideas by using the following strategies. These same strategies can be used when you've chosen a topic and want to develop it further.

■ Journal Writing

Write in a journal on a regular basis. Reflect on your personal feelings, develop your thoughts, and record the happenings of each day. Periodically go back and underline ideas that you would like to explore in writing assignments. In the following journal-writing samples, the writer came up with an idea for a writing assignment about the societal impacts of popular culture.

I read a really disturbing news story this morning. I've been thinking about it all day. In California a little girl was killed when she was struck by a car driven by a man distracted by a billboard ad for lingerie featuring a scantily clothed woman. Not only is it a horrifying thing to happen, but it also seems to me all too symbolic of the way that sexually charged images in the media are putting children, and especially girls, in danger. That reminds me of another news story I read this week about preteen girls wanting to wear the kinds of revealing outfits that they see in music videos, TV shows, and magazines aimed at teenagers. Too many of today's media images give young people the impression that sexuality should begin at an early age. This is definitely a dangerous message.

■ Freewriting

Write nonstop for ten minutes or longer to discover possible writing ideas. Use a key concept related to the assignment as a starting point. You'll soon discover potential writing ideas that might otherwise have never entered your mind. Note in the following example that the writer doesn't stop writing even when he can't think of anything to say. Note also that he doesn't stop to correct typos and other mistakes.

Popular culture. What does that include? Television obviously but thats a pretty boring subject. What else? Movies, pop music, video games. Is there a connection between playing violent video games and acting out violent behavior? Most video players I know would say no but sometimes news reports suggest a connection. Is this something I'd want to write about? Not really. What then? Maybe I could think about this a different way and focus on the positive effects of playing video games. They release tension for one thing and they can really be challenging. Other benefits? They help to kill time, that's for sure, but maybe that's not such a good thing. I would definitely read more if it weren't for video games, tv, etc. Maybe I could write about how all the electronic entertainment that surrounds us today is creating a generation of nonreaders. Or maybe I could focus on whether people aren't getting much physical exercise because of the time they spend with electronic media. Maybe both. At least I have some possibilities to work with.

Quick Guide

Freewriting

Freewriting is the writing you do without having a specific outcome in mind. You simply write down whatever pops into your head as you explore your topic. Freewriting can serve as a starting point for your writing, or it can be combined with any of the other prewriting strategies to help you select, explore, focus, or organize your writing. If you get stuck at any point during the composing process, you can return to freewriting as a way of generating new ideas.

Reminders

- **Freewriting helps you get your thoughts down on paper.** (Thoughts are constantly passing through your mind.)
- **Freewriting helps you develop and organize these thoughts.**
- **Freewriting helps you make sense out of things** that you may be studying or researching.
- **Freewriting may seem awkward at times,** but just stick with it.

The Process

- **Write nonstop and record whatever comes into your mind.** Follow your thoughts instead of trying to direct them.
- **If you have a particular topic or assignment to complete, use it as a starting point.** Otherwise, begin with anything that comes to mind.
- **Don't stop to judge, edit, or correct your writing;** that will come later.
- **Keep writing even when you think you have exhausted all of your ideas.** Switch to another angle or voice, but keep writing.
- **Watch for a promising writing idea to emerge.** Learn to recognize the beginnings of a good idea, and then expand that idea by recording as many specific details as possible.

The Result

- **Review your writing and underline the ideas you like.** These ideas will often serve as the basis for future writings.
- **Determine exactly what you need to write about.** Once you've figured out what you are required to do, you may then decide to do a second freewriting exercise.
- **Listen to and read the freewriting of others;** learn from your peers.

■ Listing

Freely list ideas as they come to mind, beginning with a key concept related to the assignment. (Brainstorming—listing ideas in conjunction with members of a group—is often an effective way to extend your lists.) The following is an example of a student's list of ideas for possible topics on the subject of news reporting:

> **Aspect of popular culture: News reporting**
> Sensationalism
> Sound bites rather than in-depth analysis
> Focus on the negative
> Shock radio
> Shouting matches pretending to be debates
> Press leaks that damage national security, etc.
> Lack of observation of people's privacy
> Bias
> Contradictory health news confusing to readers
> Little focus on "unappealing" issues like poverty
> Celebration of "celebrity"

■ Clustering

To begin the clustering process, write a key word or phrase related to the assignment in the center of your paper. Circle it, and then cluster ideas around it. Circle each idea as you record it, and draw a line connecting it to the closest related idea. Keep going until you run out of ideas and connections. The following is a student's cluster on the subject of sports:

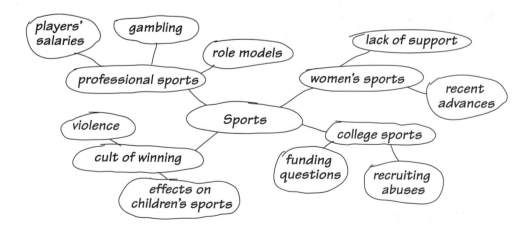

TIP: After four or five minutes of listing or clustering, scan your work for an idea to explore in a freewriting. A writing idea should begin to emerge during this freewriting session. (See pages 35–36.)

■ Collecting Information

Writer and instructor Donald Murray said that "writers write with information. If there is no information, there will be no effective writing." How true! Before you can develop a thoughtful piece of writing, you must gain a thorough understanding of your topic; to do so, you must carry out the necessary reading, reflecting, and researching. Writing becomes a satisfying experience once you can speak with authority about your topic. Use the following guidelines when you start collecting information. (Also see "Research and Writing" in this book.)

- Determine what you already know about your topic. (Use the strategies below this bulleted list.)
- Consider listing questions you would like to answer during your research. (See page 39.)
- Identify and explore possible sources of information. (See page 40.)
- Carry out your research following a logical plan. (See pages 48–53.)

Find out what you already know. ■ ˙ ■

Use one or more of the following strategies to determine what you already know about a writing topic.

1. **Focused freewriting:** At this point, you can focus your freewriting by (1) exploring your limited topic from different angles or (2) approaching your freewriting as if it were a quick draft of the actual paper. A quick version will tell you how much you know about your topic and what you need to find out.

2. **Clustering:** Try clustering with your topic serving as the nucleus word. Your clustering should focus on what you already know. (See page 37.)

3. **Five W's of writing:** Answer the five W's—Who? What? When? Where? and Why?—to identify basic information on your subject. Add How? to the list for better coverage.

4. **Directed writing:** Write whatever comes to mind about your topic, using one of the modes listed below. (Repeat the process as often as you need to, selecting a different mode each time.)

Describe it:	What do you see, hear, feel, smell, and taste?
Compare it:	What is it similar to? What is it different from?
Associate it:	What connections between this topic and others come to mind?
Analyze it:	What parts does it have? How do they work together?
Argue it:	What do you like about the topic? What do you not like about it? What are its strengths and weaknesses?
Apply it:	What can you do with it? How can you use it?

Ask questions. ■■·■

To guide your collecting and researching, you may find it helpful to list questions about your topic that you would like to answer. Alternatively, you can refer to the questions below. These questions address problems, policies, and concepts. Most topics will fall under one of these categories. Use those questions that seem helpful as a guide to your research.

	DESCRIPTION	FUNCTION	HISTORY	VALUE
PROBLEMS	What is the problem? What type of problem is it? What are its parts? What are the signs of the problem?	Who or what is affected by it? What new problems might it cause in the future?	What is the current status of the problem? What or who caused it? What or who contributed to it?	What is its significance? Why? Why is it more (or less) important than other problems? What does it symbolize or illustrate?
POLICIES	What is the policy? How broad is it? What are its parts? What are its most important features?	What is the policy designed to do? What is needed to make it work? What are or will be its effects?	What brought about this policy? What are the alternatives?	Is the policy workable? What are its advantages and disadvantages? Is it practical? Is it a good policy? Why or why not?
CONCEPTS	What is the concept? What are its parts? What is its main feature? Whom or what is it related to?	Who has been influenced by this concept? Why is it important? How does it work?	When did it originate? How has it changed over the years? How might it change in the future?	What practical value does it have? Why is it superior (or inferior) to similar concepts? What is its social worth?

majeczka fr■m shutterstock.com

Identify possible sources. ■ ■ ■

Finding meaningful sources is one of the most important steps you will take as you prepare to write. Listed below are tips that will help you identify good sources:

1. **Give yourself enough time.** Finding good sources of information may be time-consuming. Books and periodicals you need may be checked out, your computer service may be down, and so on.

2. **Be aware of the limits of your resources.** Print material may be out-of-date. Online information may be more current, but it may not always be reliable. (See pages 426–429 for ways to help you evaluate information.)

3. **Use your existing resources to find additional sources of information.** Pay attention to books, articles, and individuals mentioned in reliable initial sources of information.

4. **Ask for help.** The specialists in your school library can help you find information that is reliable and relevant. These people are trained to find information; don't hesitate to ask for their help. (See page 449.)

5. **Bookmark useful websites.** Include reference works and academic resources related to your major.

■ Explore different sources of information.

Of course, books and websites are not the only possible sources of information. Primary sources such as interviews, observations, and surveys may lead you to a more thorough and meaningful understanding of a topic. (See pages 443–445.)

Primary Sources	Secondary Sources
Interviews	Articles
Observations	Reference book entries
Participation	Books
Surveys	Websites

■ Carry out your research.

As you conduct your research, try to use a variety of reliable sources. It's also a good idea to choose an efficient note-taking method before you start. You will want to take good notes on the information you find and record all the publishing information necessary for citing your sources. (See pages 432–435.)

Reserve a special part of a notebook to question, evaluate, and reflect on your research as it develops. The record of your thoughts and actions created during this process will mean a great deal to you—as much as or more than the actual information you uncover. Reflection helps you make sense of new ideas, refocus your thinking, and evaluate your progress.

Track sources. ■·■

Follow these strategies for tracking sources and taking notes.

Track resources in a working bibliography. Once you find a useful book, journal article, news story, or webpage, record identifying information for the source. For more help, see pages 430–431.

Use a note-taking system that respects sources. Essentially, your note-taking system should help you keep an accurate record of useful information and ideas from sources while also allowing you to engage those sources with your own thinking. For a discussion of possible systems, see pages 432–435.

Distinguish summaries, paraphrases, and quotations. As you read sources, you will find material that answers your questions and helps you achieve your writing purpose. At that point, decide whether to summarize, paraphrase, or quote the material:

- A **summary** pulls just the main points out of a passage and puts them in your own words: Summarize source material when it contains relevant ideas and information that you can boil down.
- A **paraphrase** rewrites a passage point by point in your own words: Paraphrase source material when all the information is important but the actual phrasing isn't especially important or memorable.
- A **quotation** records a passage from the source word for word: Quote when the source states something crucial and says it well. **Note:** In your notes, always identify quoted material by putting quotation marks around it.

Summarizing, paraphrasing, and quoting are treated more fully on pages 436–438. Here is a brief example, with the original passage coming from Coral Ann Howells' *Alice Munro*, published in 1998 by Manchester University Press as part of its Contemporary World Writers series.

Original:	"To read Munro's stories is to discover the delights of seeing two worlds at once: an ordinary everyday world and the shadowy map of another imaginary or secret world laid over the real one, so that in reading we slip from one world into the other in an unassuming domestic sort of way."
Summary:	Munro's fiction moves readers from recognizable reality into a hidden world.
Paraphrase:	Reading Munro's fiction gives readers the enjoyment of experiencing a double world: day-to-day reality and on top of that a more mysterious, fantastic world, with the result that readers move smoothly between the worlds in a seamless, ordinary way.
Quotation:	Munro's fiction takes us into "the shadowy map of another imaginary or secret world laid over the real one."

Critical-Thinking and Writing Activities

As directed by your instructor, complete the following critical-thinking and writing activities by yourself or with classmates.

1. Writer Ralph Fletcher shares, "When I write, I am always struck at how magical and unexpected the process turns out to be." Would you describe the writing process you follow as "magical" and "unexpected"? Why or why not?

2. Reread one of your recent essays. Does the writing show that you thoroughly understood your subject, met the needs of your audience, and achieved your purpose?

3. Below is a list of general subject areas. Select one that interests you and do the following: Using the strategies on pages 34–37, brainstorm possible topics and select one. Then use the strategies on pages 38–40 to explore what you know about that topic and what you need to learn.

Arts/music   Environment   Health/medicine   Work/occupation

Learning-Outcomes Checklist

Use this checklist as a guide to help you plan your writing.

_____ I understand the writing process—getting started, planning, drafting, revising, editing and proofreading, and submitting—and I adapt it to fit each project and my own individual style.

_____ I know how to analyze the rhetorical situation:

- My **role**—my position and my goals
- The **subject**—the general area of inquiry
- The **purpose**—to inform, explain, analyze, persuade
- The **form**—essay, narrative, editorial, research paper
- The **audience**—who they are, what they know, what they need
- The **context**—weight, assessment, positioning of the project.

_____ I know how to analyze an assignment, watching for options and restrictions.

_____ I know how to select a subject and explore it through journal writing, freewriting, listing, clustering, and dialogue. I know how to focus the topic to fit the assignment and my interests.

_____ I know how to collect information and track it through note taking and research strategies.

Cross-Curricular Connections

Different academic disciplines require different methods of research note taking. Investigate the styles of research note taking used in your discipline.

3 Planning

Some of us are meticulous planners. We organize our lives in advance and formulate strategies for completing every task. Others of us live more in the moment, believing that whatever needs to get done will get done, with or without a plan.

In writing, author and instructor Ken Macrorie calls for a blend of these two approaches: "Good writing," says Macrorie, "is formed partly through plan and partly through accident." In other words, too much early planning can get in the way of the discovery aspect of writing, while not enough planning can harm the focus and coherence of your writing.

Learning Outcomes

Video

▸ Take stock of the rhetorical situation.

▸ Develop a focused thesis statement.

▸ Pattern your writing from your thesis.

▸ Organize your research.

Visually Speaking ▶ Consider the photo above. In a paragraph or two, explain how planning might play a role in military life. What might be some of its benefits and drawbacks?

■ Revisit the Rhetorical Situation

Use the following planning checklist to help you decide whether to move ahead with your planning or reconsider your topic.

Rhetorical Checklist

Writer
_____ Am I interested in this topic?

_____ How much do I know about this topic, and how much do I need to learn?

Subject
_____ Does the topic fit with the subject requirements of the assignment?

_____ Is the topic the right size—not too general or too specific—for the assignment?

_____ What sources can I use to find out more about this topic?

Purpose
_____ What are the specific goals of the assignment?

_____ Am I writing to entertain, inform, explain, analyze, persuade, reflect?

Form
_____ What form should I create: essay, proposal, report, review?

Audience
_____ Will my readers be interested in this topic? How can I interest them?

_____ What do they know and need to know about it? What opinions do they have?

Context
_____ What weight does this assignment have in terms of my grade?

_____ How will the assignment be assessed?

Working with Sources: For projects that involve research, consider how the rhetorical situation can guide your use of sources:

1. For your **subject**, which sources offer reliable information and analysis that has shaped your thinking and pointed toward a working thesis?

2. To achieve your **purpose** (to entertain, inform, analyze, and/or persuade), which resources/sources should be featured in your writing?

3. Given your **audience**, which resources will help you create credibility with the audience and clarify the topic for them?

Forming Your Thesis Statement

After you have completed enough research and collecting, you may begin to develop a more focused interest in your topic. If all goes well, this narrowed focus will give rise to a thesis for your writing. A thesis statement identifies your central idea. It usually highlights a special condition or feature of the topic, expresses a specific claim about it, or takes a stand.

Web Link

State your thesis in a sentence that effectively expresses what you want to explore or explain in your essay. Sometimes a thesis statement develops early and easily; at other times, the true focus of your writing emerges only after you've written your first draft.

Find a focus.

A general subject area is typically built into your writing assignments. Your task, then, is to find a limited writing topic and examine it from a particular angle or perspective. (You will use this focus to form your thesis statement.)

General Subject	**Limited Topic**	**Specific Focus**
Alternative energy sources	Wind power	Wind power as a viable energy source in the Plains states

State your thesis.

You can use the following formula to write a thesis statement for your essay. A thesis statement sets the tone and direction for your writing. Keep in mind that at this point you're writing a *working thesis statement*—a statement in progress, so to speak. You may change it as your thinking on the topic evolves.

a manageable or limited topic	**+**	**a specific claim or focus**	**=**	**an effective thesis statement**
wind power		provides a viable energy source in the plains states		Wind power provides a viable energy source in the plains states.

Video

Working with Sources: Sometimes your writing can take direction specifically from your sources. You may consider making your thesis a response to a specific source. For example, if one source is especially strong or especially contrary to your own thinking, you could shape your thesis as an affirmation of the strong source's authority or as a rebuttal to the contrary source's claims.

■ Using a Thesis to Pattern Your Writing

An organizing pattern for your essay may be built into your assignment. For example, you may be asked to develop an argument or to write a process paper. When a pattern is not apparent, one may still evolve naturally during the research and information-collecting steps. If this doesn't happen, take a careful look at your thesis statement.

Let your thesis guide you. ■ ·■

An effective thesis will often suggest an organizing pattern. Notice how the thesis statements below direct and shape the writing to follow. (Also see page 21.)

■ Thesis (Focus) for a Personal Narrative

Writers of personal narratives do not always state a thesis directly, but they will generally have in mind an implied theme or main idea that governs the way they develop their writing. The thesis below focuses the reader's attention on a less-than-perfect day in the life of a perfect flight attendant. (See pages 151–152.)

> From the first day Northwest hired me in Minneapolis in 1969, I tried to be a model flight attendant, to develop the qualities my operations manual demanded: poise, good judgment, initiative, adaptability and a spotless appearance. But one time I slipped up: I fell asleep.

■ Thesis for a Cause-and-Effect Essay

A cause-and-effect essay usually begins with one or more causes followed by an explanation of the effects, or with a primary effect followed by an explanation of the causes. In the thesis below, the writer credits team sports with helping to advance women into leadership roles in major corporations. (See pages 170–172.)

> While most of America's corporations are still commanded by male chief executives, women are gaining ground, winning vice-presidential and top management slots and, in a few cases, the highest leadership roles. Many of these young female executives say playing team sports helped them get ahead.

■ Thesis for an Essay of Comparison

Some comparisons treat one subject before the other (subject by subject), others discuss the subjects point by point, and some treat similarities and then differences. The writer of the thesis below introduces her comparison and contrast of two different views of Islamic dress—both of which she holds. (See pages 186–188.)

> To wear *hijab*—Islamic covering—is to invite contradiction. Sometimes I hate it. Sometimes I value it.

■ Thesis for an Essay of Classification

An essay of classification identifies the main parts or categories of a topic and then examines each one. In the thesis below, the writer identifies four ways to discuss literature, and he examines each one in turn. (See pages 206–207.)

> There are four main perspectives, or approaches, that readers can use to converse about literature.

■ Thesis for a Process Essay

Process essays are organized chronologically. As indicated in the thesis below, the writer of this essay will explain how cancer cells multiply and affect the body. (See pages 217–218.)

> When a cell begins to function abnormally, it can initiate a process that results in cancer.

■ Thesis for a Position Essay

A position paper first introduces a topic and then states a position in its thesis. The thesis statement below defines the writer's position on fatherlessness. (See pages 279–283.)

> Fatherlessness is the most harmful demographic trend of this generation. Yet, despite its scale and social consequences, fatherlessness is a problem that is frequently ignored or denied.

■ Thesis for an Essay of Definition

An essay of definition explores the denotation, connotation, and history of a term. In the following thesis statement, the writer names the two words he will explore—*deft* and *daft*—and provides an overview of the definition essay. (See page 235.)

> Let me see if I can explain the original meaning and also how *daft* and *deft* came to part company.

■ Thesis for an Essay Proposing a Solution

A problem-solution essay usually begins with a discussion of the problem and its causes and then examines possible solutions. In the following thesis statement, the writer points to a problem in the supposedly gender-equal society of the United States. After explaining the problem, she offers and argues for a specific solution. (See pages 312–314.)

> While women are represented today in virtually all fields, including the armed forces, only men are required to register for the military draft that would be used in the event of a national-security crisis.

■ Developing a Plan or an Outline

After writing a working thesis and reviewing the methods of development (pages 45–47), you should be ready to organize the information you have collected. Remember, organizing your research and background information *before* you start writing can make the drafting stage less of a hassle. Here are five strategies for effective organizing, starting with the basic list.

Quick List	A brief listing of main points (See below.)
Topic Outline	A more formal plan, including main points and essential details (See page 49.)
Sentence Outline	A formal plan, including main points and essential details, written as complete sentences (See page 50.)
Writing Blueprints	Basic organizational strategies preferred for different forms of writing (See page 51.)
Graphic Organizer	An arrangement of main points and essential details in an appropriate chart or diagram (See pages 52–53.)

Quick Lists ■ ▪ ■

Though listing is the simplest of all the methods of organization, it can help you take stock of your main ideas and get a sense of what further research or planning needs to be done. There is no right or wrong way to go about listing. The key is to come up with a system that works best for you. Here are two examples that you may consider: **the basic bulleted list**, which briefly lists the main points you will discuss, and a **T Chart,** which lists the main points on one side and a supporting detail on the other side.

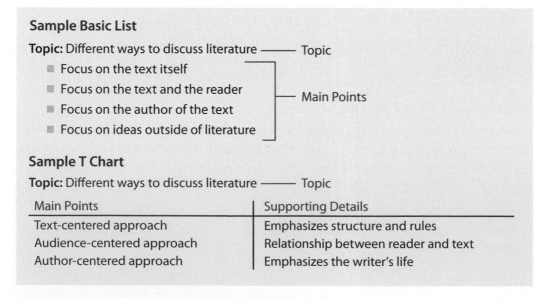

Sample Basic List

Topic: Different ways to discuss literature ——— Topic

- ■ Focus on the text itself
- ■ Focus on the text and the reader
- ■ Focus on the author of the text
- ■ Focus on ideas outside of literature

——— Main Points

Sample T Chart

Topic: Different ways to discuss literature ——— Topic

Main Points	Supporting Details
Text-centered approach	Emphasizes structure and rules
Audience-centered approach	Relationship between reader and text
Author-centered approach	Emphasizes the writer's life

Topic Outline

If you have a good deal of information to sort and arrange, you may want to use a **topic outline** for your planning. In a topic outline, you state each main point and essential detail as a word or phrase. Before you start constructing your outline, write your working thesis statement at the top of your paper to help keep you focused on the subject. (Do not attempt to outline your opening and closing paragraphs unless you are specifically asked to do so.)

An effective topic outline is parallel in structure, meaning the main points (I, II, III) and essential details (A, B, C) are stated in the same way. Notice how the sample outline below uses a parallel structure, making it easy to follow.

Sample Topic Outline

Thesis: There are four main perspectives, or approaches, that ———— Thesis
readers can use to converse about literature.

    I. Text-centered approaches ———————————————— Main Point
      a. Also called formalist criticism
      b. Emphasis on structure of text and rules of genre ——— Supporting
      c. Importance placed on key literary elements   Details

   II. Audience-centered approaches
      a. Also called rhetorical or reader-response criticism
      b. Emphasis on interaction between reader and text

  III. Author-centered approaches
      a. Emphasis on writer's life
      b. Importance placed on historical perspective
      c. Connections made between texts

  IV. Ideological approaches
      a. Psychological analysis of text
      b. Myth or archetype criticism
      c. Moral criticism
      d. Sociological analysis

INSIGHT: Planning is adaptable. Some writers prefer to generate an outline before they begin writing, while others prefer to make a more detailed outline after having written a draft. In the latter strategy, an outline can serve as a tool for evaluating the logic and completeness of the paper's organization.

Sentence Outline ■ ▪ ▪

A **sentence outline** uses complete sentences to explain the main points and essential details in the order that they will be covered in the main part of your essay. Such an outline can help you develop your ideas when writing the paper.

Sample Sentence Outline

Thesis: There are four main perspectives, or approaches, that readers   — Thesis
can use to converse about literature.

   I. A text-centered approach focuses on the literary piece itself.   — Main Point
      a. This approach is often called formalist criticism.
      b. This method of criticism examines text structure and the   — Supporting
         rules of the genre.   Details
      c. A formalist critic determines how key literary elements
         reinforce meaning.
  II. An audience-centered approach focuses on the "transaction"
     between text and reader.
      a. This approach is often called rhetorical or reader-response
         criticism.
      b. A rhetorical critic sees the text as an activity that is different
         for each reader.
 III. An author-centered approach focuses on the origin of a text.
      a. An author-centered critic examines the writer's life.
      b. This method of criticism may include a historical look at a text.
      c. Connections may be made between the text and related works.
 IV. The ideological approach applies ideas outside of literature.
      a. Some critics apply psychological theories to a literary work.
      b. Myth or archetype criticism applies anthropology and classical
         studies to a text.
      c. Moral criticism explores the moral dilemmas in literature.
      d. Sociological approaches include Marxist, feminist, and minority
         criticism.

Working with Sources: When your writing project involves sources, the planning phase will include a great deal of sorting through material. Outlining can help you organize your primary and secondary sources to best support your thesis. As you organize your research in your outline, ask these questions:

- Where and how should I work with primary sources—interviews, surveys, analyses, observations, experiments, and other data I have collected?
- Where and how should I bring in secondary sources—scholarly books, journal articles, and the like?

Writing Blueprints

The writing blueprints on this page lay out basic organizational strategies for different forms of writing. The blueprints may help you arrange the details of your essay or even find holes in your research.

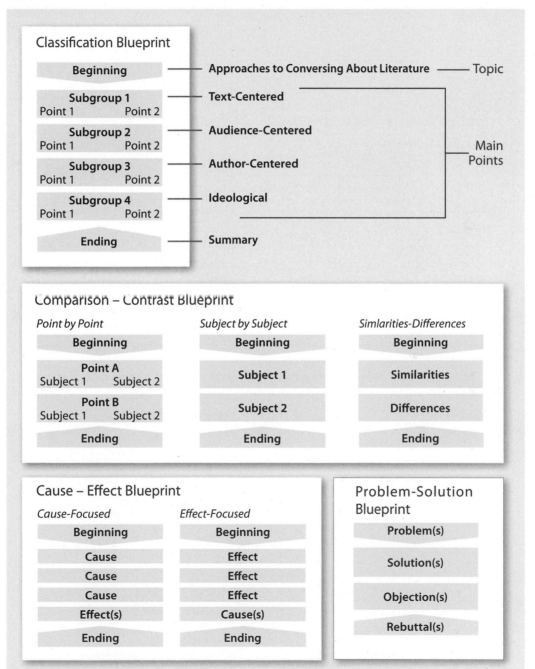

Classification Blueprint

| Beginning | —— Approaches to Conversing About Literature —— Topic |

| Subgroup 1 | —— Text-Centered |
| Point 1   Point 2 | |

| Subgroup 2 | —— Audience-Centered |
| Point 1   Point 2 | |

| Subgroup 3 | —— Author-Centered |
| Point 1   Point 2 | |

| Subgroup 4 | —— Ideological |
| Point 1   Point 2 | |

Main Points

| Ending | —— Summary |

Comparison – Contrast Blueprint

Point by Point

Beginning

Point A
Subject 1   Subject 2

Point B
Subject 1   Subject 2

Ending

Subject by Subject

Beginning

Subject 1

Subject 2

Ending

Similarities-Differences

Beginning

Similarities

Differences

Ending

Cause – Effect Blueprint

Cause-Focused

Beginning

Cause

Cause

Cause

Effect(s)

Ending

Effect-Focused

Beginning

Effect

Effect

Effect

Cause(s)

Ending

Problem-Solution Blueprint

Problem(s)

Solution(s)

Objection(s)

Rebuttal(s)

Graphic Organizers ▪▪▪

If you are a visual person, you might prefer a graphic organizer when it comes to arranging your ideas for an essay or a report. Graphic organizers can help you map out ideas and illustrate relationships among them. The following organizers are related to the methods of development discussed on pages 46–47. Each will help you collect and organize your information. Adapt the organizers as necessary to fit your particular needs or personal style.

Note how the line diagram breaks out the topic, main ideas, and supporting details for use in building an essay of classification.

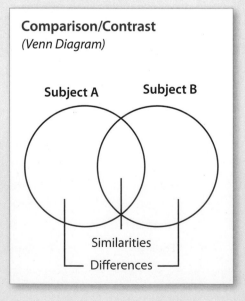

Comparison

Qualities	Subject A	Subject B

Process Analysis

Subject: _____

(Chronological Order)

Problem/Solution

Definition

Critical-Thinking and Writing Activities

As directed by your instructor, complete the following activities.

1. Author Ken Macrorie claims that "good writing is formed partly through plan and partly through accident." Do you agree? Why or why not? Relate Macrorie's idea to your own writing experiences. How carefully do you plan? How much do you leave to accident?

2. A number of organizational patterns are discussed on pages 46–47. Choose one of these patterns and select a model essay from chapters 10–19 that follows the pattern. Read the essay, note the thesis, and explain how the writer develops it.

Learning-Outcomes Checklist

Use this checklist as a guide to help you plan your writing.

_____ I have taken stock of the rhetorical situation.
  - I have reviewed the information I have collected so far.
  - My planning and research fully address my subject, purpose, and audience.

_____ I have developed a focused thesis statement.
  - My thesis statement reflects a limited topic.
  - My thesis statement clearly states the specific idea I plan to develop.
  - The thesis is supported by the information I have gathered.

_____ I have patterned my writing from my thesis.
  - The thesis suggests a pattern of organization for my essay.

_____ I have organized my research.
  - I have organized my support in a list, an outline, or a graphic organizer.
  - I have arranged my source material under my main supporting points.

Cross-Curricular Connections

In most disciplines, it is common practice early in the paper to "survey the literature" on the topic. In a literary analysis, you might survey common interpretations of a key concept before you relay your view.

1. Identify the studies that should be included in the review.

2. Categorize studies by approach or arrange them chronologically.

4 Drafting

French novelist Anatole France once said that his first drafts could have been written by a schoolboy, his next draft by a bright college student, his third draft by a superior graduate, and his final draft "only by Anatole France." Think in those terms as you write your first draft. Your main objective is to get ideas down; you'll have a chance later to improve your writing.

This chapter provides information and advice about drafting a college-level essay. You'll find specific advice for creating the three main parts and arranging information.

Learning Outcomes

Video

▶ Reconsider the rhetorical situation.
▶ Understand essay structure.
▶ Create a strong opening.
▶ Develop the middle.
▶ Create an effective closing.
▶ Understand how to use sources in a draft.

Visually Speaking ▶ How is drafting like sketching? Note the blurred hand with the pencil. What does it suggest about the process of drafting?

■ Reconsider the Rhetorical Situation

As you prepare to write, think about the parts of the rhetorical situation:

Think about your role. ■ ▪ ■

Are you writing as a student, a citizen, a friend, a member of a scholarly community or discipline? Use a voice that represents you well.

Focus on your subject. ■ ▪ ■

As you develop your first draft, these strategies can help you keep your subject in focus.

- Use your outline or writing plan as a general guide. Try to develop your main points, but allow new ideas to emerge naturally.
- Write freely without being too concerned about neatness and correctness. Concentrate on developing your ideas, not on producing a final copy.
- Include as much detail as possible, continuing until you reach a logical stopping point.
- Use your writing plan or any charts, lists, or diagrams you've produced, but don't feel absolutely bound by them.
- Complete your first draft in one or two sittings.
- Use the most natural voice you can so that the writing will flow smoothly. If your voice is too formal during drafting, you'll be tempted to stop and edit your words.
- Quote sources accurately by using your word-processing program's copy-and-paste features or by handwriting or typing quotations carefully.

Reconsider your purpose. ■ ▪ ■

Briefly review (1) what you want your writing to do (your task), (2) what you want it to say (your thesis), and (3) how you want to say it (list of ideas or outline).

Reconsider your audience. ■ ▪ ■

Review who your readers are, including their knowledge of and attitude toward your topic. Then get ready to talk with them, person to person.

Review the form and context. ■ ▪ ■

Make sure you understand the type of writing you should do, the weight of the assignment, and any assessment issues.

> **Writing with Sources:** Use sources that aid your purpose and connect to your audience. Also, make sure your sources do not crowd out your own reasoning and thinking—your role in the assignment.

Basic Essay Structure: Major Moves

The following chart lists the main writing moves that occur during the development of a piece of writing. Use it as a general guide for all of your drafting. Remember to keep your purpose and audience in mind throughout the drafting process.

Opening

Engage your reader.
Stimulate and direct the reader's attention.

Establish your direction.
Identify the topic and put it in perspective.

Get to the point.
Narrow your focus and state your thesis.

Middle

Advance your thesis.
Provide background information and cover your main points.

Test your ideas.
Raise questions and consider alternatives.

Support your main points.
Add substance and build interest.

Build a coherent structure.
Start new paragraphs and arrange the support.

Use different levels of detail.
Clarify and complete each main point.

Ending

Reassert the main point.
Remind the reader of the purpose and rephrase the thesis.

Urge the reader.
Gain the reader's acceptance and look ahead.

■ Opening Your Draft

Video

The opening paragraph is one of the most important elements in any composition. It should accomplish at least three essential things: (1) engage the reader; (2) establish your direction, tone, and level of language; and (3) introduce your line of thought.

> **Advice:** The conventional way of approaching the first paragraph is to view it as a kind of "funnel" that draws a reader in and narrows to a main point. Often, the final sentence explicitly states your thesis.
>
> **Cautions:** ■ Don't feel bound by the conventional pattern, which may sound stale if not handled well.
>
> ■ Don't let the importance of the first paragraph paralyze you. Relax and write.

The information on the next two pages will help you develop your opening. You can refer to the sample essays in the handbook for ideas.

Engage your reader. ■■·■

Your reader will be preoccupied with other thoughts until you seize, stimulate, and direct his or her attention. Here are some effective ways to "hook" the reader:

- Mention little-known facts about the topic.

  Beads may have been what separated human ancestors from their Neanderthal cousins. Yes, beads.

- Pose a challenging question.

  Why would human ancestors spend days carving something as frivolous as beads while Neanderthals spent days hunting mammoths?

- Offer a thought-provoking quotation.

  "The key thing in human evolution is when people start devoting just ridiculous amounts of time to making these [beads]," says archeologist John Shea of Stonybrook University.

- Tell a brief, illuminating story.

  When I walked into the room, I had only to show my hand to be accepted in the group of strangers there. The Phi Delta Kappa ring on my finger—and on all of our fingers—bound us across space and time as a group. Our ancestors discovered the power of such ornamentation forty thousand years ago.

Establish your direction. ■■·■

Web Link

The direction of your line of thought should become clear in the opening part of your writing. Here are some moves you might make to set the right course:

- Identify the topic (issue). Show a problem, a need, or an opportunity.
- Deepen the issue. Connect the topic, showing its importance.
- Acknowledge other views. Tell what others say or think about the topic.

Get to the point. ■·■

You may choose to state your main point up front, or you may wait until later to introduce your thesis. For example, you could work inductively by establishing an issue, a problem, or a question in your opening and then build toward the answer—your thesis—in your conclusion. (See page 20 for more on inductive reasoning.) Sometimes, in fact, your thesis may simply be implied. In any case, the opening should at least hint at the central issue or thesis of your paper. Here are three ways to get to the point:

1. Narrow your focus. Point to what interests you about the topic.

2. Raise a question. Answer the question in the rest of the essay.

3. State your thesis. If appropriate, craft a sentence that boils down your thinking to a central claim. You can use the thesis sentence as a "map" for the organization of the rest of the essay. (See pages 45–47, 114–117, and 416–417.)

■ Weak Opening

Although the opening below introduces the topic, the writing lacks interesting details and establishes no clear focus for the essay.

> I would like to tell you about the TV show *The Simpsons*. It's about this weird family of five people who look kind of strange and act even stranger. In fact, the characters aren't even real—they're just cartoons.

■ Strong Opening

In the essay opener below, the writer uses his first paragraph to get his readers' attention and describe his subject. He uses the second paragraph to raise a question that leads him to a statement of his thesis (underlined).

> The Simpsons, stars of the TV show by the same name, are a typical American family, or at least a parody of one. Homer, Marge, Bart, Lisa, and Maggie Simpson live in Springfield, U.S.A. Homer, the father, is a boorish, obese oaf who works in a nuclear power plant. Marge is an overprotective, nagging mother with an outrageous blue hairdo. Ten-year-old Bart is an obnoxious, "spiky-haired demon." Lisa is eight and a prodigy on the tenor saxophone and in class. The infant Maggie never speaks but only sucks on her pacifier.
>
> What is the attraction of this yellow-skinned family that stars on a show in which all of the characters have pronounced overbites and only four fingers on each hand? Viewers see a little bit of themselves in everything the Simpsons do. The world of Springfield is a parody of the viewer's world, and Americans can't get enough of it. Viewers experience this parody in the show's explanations of family, education, workplace, and politics.

INSIGHT: Note how, after stating the thesis, the writer forecasts the method of supporting that thesis.

■ Developing the Middle

The middle of an essay is where you do the "heavy lifting." In this part you develop the main points that support your thesis statement.

Advice: As you write, you will likely make choices that were unforeseen when you began. Use "scratch outlines" (temporary jottings) along the way to show where your new ideas may take you.

Cautions:
- Writing that lacks effective detail gives only a vague image of the writer's intent.
- Writing that wanders loses its hold on the essay's purpose.

For both of these reasons, always keep your thesis in mind when you develop the main part of your writing. Refer to the guidelines on the next two pages for help. You can refer to the sample essays in this book for ideas.

Advance your thesis. ■▪■

If you stated a thesis in the opening, you can advance it in the middle paragraphs by covering your main points and supporting them in these ways.

Explain: Provide important facts, details, and examples.

Narrate: Share a brief story or re-create an experience to illustrate an idea.

Describe: Tell in detail how someone appears or how something works.

Define: Identify or clarify the meaning of a specific term or idea.

Analyze: Examine the parts of something to better understand the whole.

Compare: Provide examples to show how two things are alike or different.

Argue: Use logic and evidence to prove that something is true.

Reflect: Express your thoughts or feelings about something.

Cite authorities: Add expert analysis or personal commentary.

Test your ideas. ■▪■

When you write a first draft, you're testing your initial thinking about your topic. You're determining whether your thesis is valid and whether you have enough compelling information to support it. Here are ways to test your line of thinking as you write:

Raise questions. Try to anticipate your readers' questions.

Consider alternatives. Look at your ideas from different angles; weigh various options; reevaluate your thesis.

Answer objections. Directly or indirectly deal with possible problems that a skeptical reader might point out.

Build a coherent structure. ▪ ▪ ▪

Design paragraphs as units of thought that develop and advance your thesis clearly and logically. For example, look at the brief essay below, noting how each body paragraph presents ideas with supporting details that build on and deepen the main idea.

Seeing the Light

The writer introduces the topic and states his thesis.

All lightbulbs make light, so they're all the same, right? Not quite. You have many *1* choices regarding how to light up your life. Two types of bulbs are the traditional incandescent and the newer, more compact fluorescent. <u>By checking out how they're different, you can better choose which one to buy.</u>

The writer starts with a basic explanation of how the two types of lightbulbs function differently.

While either incandescent or compact fluorescent bulbs can help you read or *2* find the bathroom at night, each bulb makes light differently. In an incandescent bulb, electricity heats up a tungsten filament (thin wire) to 450 degrees, causing it to glow with a warm, yellow light. A compact fluorescent is a glass tube filled with mercury vapor and argon gas. Electricity causes the mercury to give off ultraviolet radiation. That radiation then causes phosphors coating the inside of the tube to give off light.

The writer shifts his attention to weaknesses of compact bulbs.

Both types of bulbs come in many shapes, sizes, and brightnesses, but compacts *3* have some restrictions. Because of their odd shape, compacts may not fit in a lamp well. Compacts also may not work well in very cold temperatures, and they can't be used with a dimmer switch.

He next explains the strengths of compacts.

On the other hand, while compact fluorescents are less flexible than incandescents, *4* compacts are four times more efficient. For example, a 15-watt compact produces as many lumens of light as a 60-watt incandescent! Why? Incandescents turn only about 5 percent of electricity into light and give off the other 95 percent as heat.

He acknowledges that compacts cost more, but he justifies the cost.

But are compacts less expensive than incandescents? In the short run, no. A *5* compact costs about $15 while an incandescent costs only a dollar. However, because compacts burn less electricity—and last 7 to 10 times longer—in the long run, compacts are less expensive.

The writer rephrases his thesis as a challenge.

Now that you're no longer in the dark about lightbulbs, take a look at the lamp *6* you're using to read this essay. Think about the watts (electricity used), lumens (light produced), efficiency, purchase price, and lamplife. Then decide how to light up your life in the future.

Arrange supporting details. ■·■

Video

Organizing information in a logical pattern within a paragraph strengthens its coherence. The following pages explain and illustrate organizational strategies, providing suggested transitions to go with them. (See also page 481.)

■ Definition

A definition provides the denotation (dictionary meaning) and connotation (feeling) of a given term. It often provides examples, gives anecdotes, and offers negative definitions— what the thing is not. In the paragraph below, the writer begins his definition by posing a question.

> First of all, what is the grotesque—in visual art and in literature? A term originally applied to Roman cave art that distorted the normal, the grotesque presents the body and mind so that they appear abnormal— different from the bodies and minds that we think belong in our world. Both spiritual and physical, bizarre and familiar, ugly and alluring, the grotesque shocks us, and we respond with laughter and fear. We laugh because the grotesque seems bizarre enough to belong only outside our world; we fear because it feels familiar enough to be part of it. Seeing the grotesque version of life as it is portrayed in art stretches our vision of reality. As Bernard McElroy argues, "The grotesque transforms the world from what we 'know' it to be to what we fear it might be. It distorts and exaggerates the surface of reality in order to tell a qualitative truth about it."
>
> —John Van Rys

■ Illustration

An illustration supports a general idea with specific reasons, facts, and details.

> As the years passed, my obsession grew. Every fiber and cell of my body was obsessed with the number on the scale and how much fat I could pinch on my thigh. No matter how thin I was, I thought I could never be thin enough. I fought my sisters for control of the TV and VCR to do my exercise programs and videos. The cupboards were stacked with cans of diet mixes, the refrigerator full of diet drinks. Hidden in my underwear drawer were stacks of diet pills that I popped along with my vitamins. At my worst, I would quietly excuse myself from family activities to turn on the bathroom faucet full blast and vomit into the toilet. Every day I stood in front of the mirror, a ritual not unlike brushing my teeth, and scrutinized my body. My face, arms, stomach, buttocks, hips, and thighs could never be small enough.
>
> —Paula Treick

Video

Illustration/Elaboration

additionally	another	for instance	other
again	as well	in addition	that is
along with	besides	in other words	
also	finally	moreover	
and	for example	next	

■ Analogy

An analogy is a comparison that a writer uses to explain a complex or unfamiliar phenomenon (how the immune system works) in terms of a familiar one (how mall security works).

> The human body is like a mall, and the immune system is like mall security. Because the mall has hundreds of employees and thousands of customers, security guards must rely on photo IDs, name tags, and uniforms to decide who should be allowed to open cash registers and who should have access to the vault. In the same way, white blood cells and antibodies need to use DNA cues to recognize which cells belong in a body and which do not. Occasionally security guards make mistakes, wrestling Kookie the Klown to the ground while DVD players "walk" out of the service entrance, but these problems amount only to allergic reactions or little infections. If security guards become hypervigilant, detaining every customer and employee, the situation is akin to leukemia, in which white blood cells attack healthy cells. If security guards become corrupt, letting thieves take a "five-finger discount," the situation is akin to AIDS. Both systems—mall security and human immunity—work by correctly differentiating friend from foe.
>
> —Rob King

■ Cause and Effect

Cause-and-effect organization shows how events are linked to their results. If you start with effects, follow with specific causes; if you begin with causes, follow with specific effects. The example below discusses the effects of hypothermia on the human body.

> Even a slight drop in the normal human body temperature of 98.6 degrees Fahrenheit causes hypothermia. Often produced by accidental or prolonged exposure to cold, the condition forces all bodily functions to slow down. The heart rate and blood pressure decrease. Breathing becomes slower and shallower. As the body temperature drops, these effects become even more dramatic until it reaches somewhere between 86 and 82 degrees Fahrenheit and the person lapses into unconsciousness. When the temperature reaches between 65 and 59 degrees Fahrenheit, heart action, blood flow, and electrical brain activity stop. Normally such a condition would be fatal. However, as the body cools down, the need for oxygen also slows down. A person can survive in a deep hypothermic state for an hour or longer and be revived without serious complications.
>
> —Laura Black

Cause and Effect

as a result	resulting in
because	since
consequently	therefore
due to the fact that	
every time that	
inevitably	

■ Narration

In the paragraph below, the writer uses narration and chronological order to relate an anecdote—a short, illustrative story.

> When I was six or seven years old, growing up in Pittsburgh, I used to take a precious penny of my own and hide it for someone else to find. It was a curious compulsion; sadly, I've never been seized by it since. For some reason I always "hid" the penny along the same stretch of sidewalk up the street. I would cradle it at the roots of a sycamore, say, or in a hole left by a chipped-off piece of sidewalk. Then I would take a piece of chalk, and, starting at either end of the block, draw huge arrows leading up to the penny from both directions. After I learned to write I labeled the arrows: surprise ahead or money this way. I was greatly excited, during all this arrow-drawing, at the thought of the first lucky passer-by who would receive in this way, regardless of merit, a free gift from the universe. But I never lurked about. I would go straight home and not give the matter another thought, until, some months later, I would be gripped again by the impulse to hide another penny.
>
> —Annie Dillard, *Pilgrim at Tinker Creek*

■ Process

In the paragraph that follows, a student writer describes the process of entering the "tube," or "green room," while surfing.

> At this point you are slightly ahead of the barreling part of the wave, and you need to "stall," or slow yourself, to get into the tube. There are three methods of stalling used in different situations. If you are slightly ahead of the tube, you can drag your inside hand along the water to stall. If you are a couple of feet in front of the barrel, apply all your weight onto your back foot and sink the tail of the board into the water. This is known as a "tail stall" for obvious reasons, and its purpose is to decrease your board speed. If you are moving faster than the wave is breaking, you need to do what is called a "wrap-around." To accomplish this maneuver, lean back away from the wave while applying pressure on the tail. This shifts your forward momentum away from the wave and slows you down. When the wave comes, turn toward the wave and place yourself in the barrel.
>
> —Luke Sunukjian, "Entering the Green Room"

Narration/Process/Chronological

a day before	before	meanwhile	tomorrow
about	during	next	until
after	finally	second	yesterday
afterward	first	soon	
as soon as	in the end	then	
at	later	today	

■ Chronological Order

Chronological (time) order helps you tell a story or present steps in a process. For example, the following paragraph describes how cement is made. Notice how the writer explains every step and uses transitional words to lead readers through the process.

> The production of cement is a complicated process. The raw materials that go into cement consist of about 60 percent lime, 25 percent silica, and 5 percent alumina. The remaining 10 percent is a varying combination of gypsum and iron oxide (because the amount of gypsum determines the drying time of the cement). First, this mixture is ground up into very fine particles and fed into a kiln. Cement kilns, the largest pieces of moving machinery used by any industry, are colossal steel cylinders lined with firebricks. They can be 25 feet in diameter and up to 750 feet long. The kiln is built at a slant and turns slowly as the cement mix makes its way down from the top end. A flame at the bottom heats the kiln to temperatures of up to 3,000 degrees Fahrenheit. When the melted cement compound emerges from the kiln, it cools into little marble-like balls called clinker. Finally, the clinker is ground to a consistency finer than flour and packaged as cement.
>
> —Kevin Maas

■ Classification

When classifying a subject, place the subject in its appropriate category and then show how this subject is different from other subjects in the same category. In the following paragraph, a student writer uses classification to describe the theory of temperament.

> Medieval doctors believed that "four temperaments rule mankind wholly." According to this theory, each person has a distinctive temperament or personality (sanguine, phlegmatic, melancholy, or choleric) based on the balance of four elements in the body, a balance peculiar to the individual. The theory was built on Galen's and Hippocrates' notion of "humors," which stated that the body contains blood, phlegm, black bile, and yellow bile—four fluids that maintain the balance within the body. The sanguine person was dominated by blood, associated with fire: Blood was hot and moist, and the person was fat and prone to laughter. The phlegmatic person was dominated by phlegm (associated with earth) and was squarish and slothful—a sleepy type. The melancholy person was dominated by cold, black bile (connected with the element of water) and as a result was pensive, peevish, and solitary. The choleric person was dominated by hot, yellow bile (air) and thus was inclined to anger.
>
> —Jessica Radsma

Classification

a typical type	in one category	the third variety
another kind	one type	the most common
a second variety	rarest of all	the most popular

■ Climax

Climax is a method in which you first present details and then provide a general climactic statement or conclusion drawn from the details.

> As I walked home, I glanced across the road to see a troubling scene unfold. A burly man strode along the curb, shoulders rounded and face clenched in anger or grief. Behind him, a slim little girl sat on her heels on the sidewalk, hands in her lap and tears streaming down white cheeks. I glanced back at that brute, who climbed into his big black truck and started up the engine. I almost ran across the road to stop him, to set right whatever he'd done. But then I spotted the little dog lying very still in the gutter. The man in the truck must have hit the poor creature, stopped to see if he could help, realized he couldn't, apologized, and left the little girl to grieve. There was nothing I could do, either. Face clenched, I looked back to my side of the street and walked on.
>
> —Jamal Kendal

■ Compare-Contrast

To compare and contrast, show how two or more subjects are similar and different.

> The old man behind the counter is no doubt Pappy, after which Pappy's Grocery is named. He leans on the glass display case, world weary and watchful, tracking the youth by the snack display. The folds deepen around Pappy's intense eyes as the young customer picks lightly at a bag of potato chips, lifts a can of cashews, runs lithe fingers over the packs of gum. He crouches for a better look at the snack cakes, his pants sliding below colorful boxers. Pappy hitches his own belt higher over his tucked-in shirt. "You gonna buy anything?" The young customer startles, looks up with a smooth face and wide eyes, stands, and walks from Pappy's Grocery.
>
> —Tina Jacobs

Comparison/Contrast

as	even though	on the one hand
also	however	on the other hand
although	in the same way	otherwise
both	like	similarly
but	likewise	still
by contrast	one way	yet

Writing with Sources: Advance and deepen your thesis with reliable reasons and evidence. A typical supporting paragraph starts with a topic sentence and elaborates it with detailed evidence and careful reasoning. Make sure to smoothly integrate quotations into the flow of the writing. Also, avoid dropping in quotations without setting them up and explaining them.

■ Ending Your Draft

Closing paragraphs can be important for tying up loose ends, clarifying key points, or signing off with the reader. In a sense, the entire essay is a preparation for an effective ending; the ending helps the reader look back over the essay with new understanding and appreciation. Many endings leave the reader with fresh food for thought.

Web Link

> **Advice:** Because the ending can be so important, draft a variety of possible endings. Choose the one that flows best from a sense of the whole.
>
> **Cautions:** ■ If your thesis is weak or unclear, you will have a difficult time writing a satisfactory ending. To strengthen the ending, strengthen the thesis.
>
> ■ You may have heard this formula for writing an essay: "Say what you're going to say, say it, then say what you've just said." Remember, though, if you need to "say what you've just said," say it in new words.

The information on the next two pages will help you develop your ending. You can refer to the sample essays elsewhere in this book for ideas.

Reassert the main point. ■ ■ ■

If an essay is complicated, the reader may need reclarification at the end. Show that you are fulfilling the promises you made in the beginning.

Remind the reader. Recall what you first set out to do; check off the key points you've covered; or answer any questions left unanswered.

Rephrase the thesis. Restate your thesis in light of the most important support you've given. Deepen and expand your original thesis.

Urge the reader. ■ ■ ■

Your reader may still be reluctant to accept your ideas or argument. The ending is your last chance to gain the reader's acceptance. Here are some possible strategies:

Show the implications. Follow further possibilities raised by your train of thought; be reasonable and convincing.

Look ahead. Suggest other possible connections.

List the benefits. Show the reader the benefits of accepting or applying the things you've said.

INSIGHT: When your writing comes to an effective stopping point, conclude the essay. Don't tack on another idea.

Complete and unify your message. ▪▪▪

Your final paragraphs are your last opportunity to refocus, unify, and otherwise reinforce your message. Draft the closing carefully, not merely to finish the essay but to further advance your purpose and thesis.

▪ Weak Ending

The ending below does not focus on and show commitment to the essay's main idea. Rather than reinforcing this idea, the writing leads off in a new direction.

> I realize I've got to catch my bus. I've spent too much time talking to this woman whose life is a wreck. I give her some spare change and then head off. She doesn't follow me. It's kind of a relief. Toronto is a great city, but sometimes you have weird experiences there. Once a street vendor gave me a free falafel. I didn't want to eat it because maybe something was wrong with it. What a weird city!

▪ Strong Endings

Below are final paragraphs from two essays in this book. Listen to their tone, watch how they reconsider the essay's ideas, and note how they offer further food for thought. (The first example is a revision of the weak paragraph above.)

> I tell her I need to get going. She should go, too, or she'll be late for the hearing. Before getting up, I reach into my wallet and give her two TTC passes and some spare change. I walk her to the street and point her toward Old City Hall. She never thanks me, only looks at me one last time with immense vulnerability and helplessness. Then she walks away.
>
> I wonder as I hurry towards the station if she'll be okay, if her boyfriend really will get out of jail, and if her grandmother will ever take her back. Either way, I think as I cross Bay Street, what more can I do? I have a bus to catch.

(See the full essay on pages 148–150.)

> Passion and power permeate all of Latin America's music. The four major types of music—indigenous, Iberian and Mestizo folk, Afro-American, and popular urban— are as diverse as the people of Latin America, and each style serves a valued need or function in Latinos' everyday lives. As a result, those listening to Latin American music—whether it is a Peruvian Indian's chant, a Venezuelan farmer's whistled tune, a Cuban mambo drummer's vivacious beat, or the Bogotá rock concert's compelling rhythms—are hearing much more than music. They are hearing the passion and power of the Latin American people.

> **Writing with Sources:** Save the best for last. Consider using an especially thought-provoking statement, quotation, or detail in your conclusion. Doing so can help you clinch your point.

Working with Sources: If you are using sources, take care not to overwhelm your draft with source material. Keep the focus on your own ideas:

- Avoid strings of references and chunks of source material with no discussion, explanation, or interpretation on your part in between.
- Don't offer entire paragraphs of material from a source (whether paraphrased or quoted) with a single in-text citation at the end. When you do so, your thinking disappears.
- Be careful not to overload your draft with complex information and dense data lacking explanation.
- Resist the urge to simply copy and paste big chunks from sources. Even if you document the sources, your paper will quickly become a patchwork of source material with a few weak stitches (your contribution) holding it together.
- Note the careful use of source material in the following paragraph.

Sample Paragraph Showing Integration of Source Material

Topic sentence: idea elaborating and supporting thesis

Development of idea through reasoning

Support of idea through reference to source material

Concluding statement of idea

Antibiotics are effective only against infections caused by bacteria and should never be used against infections caused by viruses. Using an antibiotic against a viral infection is like throwing water on a grease fire—water may normally put out fires but will only worsen the situation for a grease fire. In the same way, antibiotics fight infections, but they cause the body harm only when they are used to fight infections caused by viruses. Viruses cause the common cold, the flu, and most sore throats, sinus infections, coughs, and bronchitis. Yet antibiotics are commonly prescribed for these viral infections. The New England Journal of Medicine reports that 22.7 million kilograms (25,000 tons) of antibiotics is prescribed each year in the United States alone (Wenzel and Edmond, 1962). Meanwhile, the CDC reports that approximately 50 percent of those prescriptions are completely unnecessary ("Antibiotic Overuse" 25). "Every year, tens of millions of prescriptions for antibiotics are written to treat viral illnesses for which these antibiotics offer no benefits," says the CDC's antimicrobial resistance director David Bell, M.D. (qtd. in Bren 30). Such mis-prescribing is simply bad medical practice that contributes to the problem of growing bacterial infection.

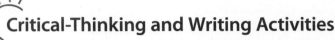

Critical-Thinking and Writing Activities

As directed by your instructor, complete the following critical-thinking and writing activities by yourself or with classmates.

1. Patricia T. O'Connor says, "All writing begins life as a first draft, and first drafts are never any good. They're not supposed to be." Is this claim true? Why or why not? What do you hope to accomplish with a first draft?

2. Study the chart on page 57. Based on other material you have read or written, add another writing move for each of the three main parts of the essay: opening, middle, and ending. Name the move, explain it, and tell what types of writing it might appear in.

3. Read the final paragraphs of any three essays included in this book. Write a brief analysis of each ending based on the information on pages 67–68.

4. Imagine that you are a journalist who has been asked to write an article about a wedding, a funeral, or another significant event you have experienced. Choose an event and sketch out a plan for your article. Include the main writing moves and the type of information at each stage of your writing.

Learning-Outcomes Checklist

_____ I have reconsidered the rhetorical situation, thinking about my role, the subject, my purpose, my audience, the medium, and the context.

_____ I understand the essay structure—opening, middle, and closing.

_____ I have created a strong opening.
  - The opening engages the reader.
  - The opening establishes a focus and states a main point.

_____ I have developed the ideas in the middle of my essay.
  - The middle advances my thesis by developing and testing ideas.
  - The middle orders supporting details in a clear, logical way.

_____ I have created an effective closing.
  - The closing reasserts the main point and completes the message.

_____ I understand how to use sources to best effect in a draft.

Cross-Curricular Connections

When next you write a paper in one of your content-area classes, use the tips in this chapter. Afterward, indicate which tip was most helpful and why.

5 Revising

The word *revising* means "taking another look," so revising is best done after a brief break. Set aside your writing and return to it later with fresh eyes. Also, enlist the fresh eyes of another reader, whether a roommate, a classmate, or someone at the writing center. Revising is all about getting perspective.

Of course, once you have perspective, you need to figure out how to make improvements. This chapter provides numerous strategies for focusing on the global traits of your writing—ideas, organization, and voice. The changes you make should improve the work significantly, perhaps even reshaping it.

Learning Outcomes

Video

▶ Think about your overall approach.
▶ Think about the global traits.
▶ Revise for ideas and organization.
▶ Revise for voice and style.
▶ Address paragraph issues.
▶ Revise collaboratively.
▶ Use the writing center.

Visually Speaking ▶ The hands in the photo above are shaping a blob of clay into a piece of pottery. How is revising similar to this process? How is it different?

■ Consider Whole-Paper Issues

Video

When revising, first look at the big picture. Take it all in. Determine whether the content is interesting, informative, and worth sharing. Note any gaps or soft spots in your line of thinking. Ask yourself how you can improve what you have done so far. The information that follows will help you address whole-paper issues such as these.

Revisit the rhetorical situation. ■ ˙ ■

Just as the rhetorical situation helped you to set your direction in writing, it can help you make course corrections. Think about each part of the rhetorical situation.

Consider your role. How are you coming across in this draft? Do you sound authoritative, engaged, knowledgeable, confident? How do you want to come across?

Think about your subject. Have you stated a clear focus? Have you supported it with a variety of details? Have you explored the subject fully?

Remember your purpose. Are you trying to analyze, describe, explain, propose? Does the writing succeed? Do the ideas promote your purpose? Does your organization support the purpose? Is your writing voice helpful in achieving your purpose?

Check the form. Have you created writing that matches the form that your instructor requested? Have you taken best advantage of the form, including graphics or other media, if appropriate?

Consider your audience. Have you captured their attention and interest? Have you provided them the information they need to understand your writing? Have you considered their values, needs, and opinions, and used them to connect?

Think about the context. Is this piece of writing the correct length and level of seriousness for the assignment? Is it on schedule? How does it match up to what others are doing?

Writing with Sources: Make sure that your sources work well for each part of the rhetorical situation. Choose sources that

- reflect well on you, showing that you understand and care about the topic.
- illuminate the subject with accurate, precise, substantial information.
- help you achieve your purpose, whether to inform, persuade, or reflect.
- work well within the form and can be appropriately credited.
- are seen as authoritative by the audience.
- are timely and credible in the context.

Consider your overall approach. ■ ▪ ■

Video

Sometimes it's better to start fresh if your writing contains stretches of uninspired ideas. Consider a fresh start if your first draft shows one of these problems:

The topic is worn-out. An essay titled "Lead Poisoning" may not sound very interesting. Unless you can approach it with a new twist ("Get the Lead Out!"), consider cutting your losses and finding a fresh topic.

The approach is stale. If you've been writing primarily to get a good grade, finish the assignment, or sound cool, start again. Try writing to learn something, prompt real thinking in readers, or touch a chord.

Your voice is predictable or fake. Avoid the bland "A good time was had by all" or the phony academic "When one studies this significant problem in considerable depth . . . " Be real. Be honest.

The draft sounds boring. Maybe it's boring because you pay an equal amount of attention to everything and hence stress nothing. Try condensing less important material and expanding what's important.

The essay is formulaic. In other words, it follows the "five-paragraph" format. This handy organizing frame may prevent you from doing justice to your topic and thinking. If your draft is dragged down by rigid adherence to a formula, try a more original approach.

Writing with Sources: Test the balance of reasoning and sources. Make sure your draft is not thin on source material, but also make sure that the source material does not dominate the conversation. Use these tips for balancing reasoning and sources:

1. Before diving into source material within a paragraph or section of your paper, flesh out your thinking more fully. Offer reasoning that elaborates the claim and effectively leads into the evidence.

2. As you present evidence from source material, build on it by explaining what it means. Evidence doesn't typically speak for itself: through analysis, synthesis, illustration, contrast, and other means, you need to show how or why your sources advance your thesis.

3. After you have presented evidence that elaborates on and supports your idea, extend your thoughts by addressing the reader's "So what?" or "Why does this matter?" skepticism.

Revising Your First Draft

Revising helps you turn your first draft into a more complete, thoughtful piece of writing. The following information will help you do that.

Prepare to revise.

Once you've finished a first draft, set it aside (ideally for a few days) until you can look at the draft objectively and make needed changes. If you drafted on paper, photocopy the draft. If you drafted on a computer, print your paper (double-spaced). Then make changes with a good pencil or colored pen. If you prefer revising on the computer, consider using your software editing program. In all cases, save your first draft for reference.

Think globally.

When revising, focus on the big picture—the overall strength of the ideas, organization, and voice.

Ideas: Check your thesis, focus, or theme. Has your thinking on your topic changed? Also think about your readers' most pressing questions concerning this topic. Have you answered these questions? Finally, consider your reasoning and support. Are both complete and sound?

Organization: Check the overall design of your writing, making sure that ideas move smoothly and logically from one point to the next. Does your essay build effectively? Do you shift directions cleanly? Fix structural problems in one of these ways:

- Reorder material to improve the sequence.
- Cut information that doesn't support the thesis.
- Add details where the draft is thin.
- Rewrite parts that seem unclear.
- Improve links between points by using transitions.

Voice: Voice is your personal presence on the page, the tone and attitude that others hear when reading your work. In other words, voice is the between-the-lines message your readers get (whether you want them to or not). When revising, make sure that the tone of your message matches your purpose, whether it is serious, playful, or satiric.

INSIGHT: Don't pay undue attention to spelling, grammar, and punctuation at this early stage in the process. Otherwise, you may become distracted from the task at hand: improving the content of your writing. Editing and proofreading come later.

■ Revising for Ideas and Organization

As you review your draft for content, make sure the ideas are fully developed and the organization is clear. From your main claim or thesis to your reasoning and your evidence, strengthen your thinking and sequencing.

Web Link

Examine your ideas. ■ ▪ ▪

Review the ideas in your writing, making sure that each point is logical, complete, and clear. To test the logic in your writing, see pages 257–260.

■ Complete Thinking

Have you answered readers' basic questions? Have you supported the thesis? The original passage below is too general; the revision is clearly more complete.

> **Original Passage** (Too general)
>
> As soon as you receive a minor cut, the body's healing process begins to work. Blood from tiny vessels fills the wound and begins to clot. In less than 24 hours, a scab forms.
>
> **Revised Version** (More specific)
>
> As soon as you receive a minor cut, the body's healing process begins to work. In a simple wound, the first and second layers of skin are severed along with tiny blood vessels called capillaries. As these vessels bleed into the wound, minute structures called platelets help stop the bleeding by sticking to the edges of the cut and to one another, forming a plug. The platelets then release chemicals that react with certain proteins in the blood to form a clot. The blood clot, with its fiber network, begins to join the edges of the wound together. As the clot dries out, a scab forms, usually in less than 24 hours.

■ Clear Thesis

Make sure that your writing centers on one main issue or thesis. Although this next original passage lacks a thesis, the revision has a clear one.

> **Original Passage** (Lacks a thesis)
>
> Teen magazines are popular with young girls. These magazines contain a lot of how-to articles about self-image, fashion, and boy-girl relationships. Girls read them to get advice on how to act and how to look. Girls who don't really know what they want are the most eager readers.
>
> **Revised Version** (Identifies a specific thesis statement)
>
> Adolescent girls often see teen magazines as handbooks on how to be teenagers. These magazines influence the ways they act and the ways they look. For girls who are unsure of themselves, these magazines can exert an enormous amount of influence. Unfortunately, the advice these magazines give about self-image, fashion, and boys may do more harm than good.

Examine your organization. ◼ ▪ ▪

Good writing has structure. It leads readers logically and clearly from one point to the next. When revising for organization, consider four areas: the overall plan, the opening, the flow of ideas, and the closing.

◼ Overall Plan

Look closely at the sequence of ideas or events that you share. Does that sequence advance your thesis? Do the points build effectively? Are there gaps in the support or points that stray from your original purpose? If you find such problems, consider the following actions:

- Refine the focus or emphasis by rearranging material within the text.
- Fill in the gaps with new material. Go back to your planning notes.
- Delete material that wanders away from your purpose.
- Use an additional (or different) method of organization. For example, if you are comparing two subjects, add depth to your analysis by contrasting them as well. If you are describing a complex subject, show the subject more clearly and fully by distinguishing and classifying its parts. (See pages 62–69 for more on organizational methods.)

INSIGHT: What is the best method of organization for your essay? The writing you are doing will usually determine the choice. As you know, a personal narrative is often organized by time. Typically, however, you combine and customize methods to develop a writing idea. For example, within a comparison essay you may do some describing or classifying. See pages 46–47 and 117 for more on the common methods of development.

◼ Opening Ideas

Reread your opening paragraph(s). Is the opening organized effectively? Does it engage readers, establish a direction for your writing, and express your thesis or focus? The original opening below doesn't build to a compelling thesis statement, but the revised version engages the reader and leads to the thesis.

Original Opening (Lacks interest and direction)

The lack of student motivation is a common subject in the news. Educators want to know how to get students to learn. Today's higher standards mean that students will be expected to learn even more. Another problem in urban areas is that large numbers of students are dropping out. How to interest students is a challenge.

Revised Version (Effectively leads readers into the essay)

How can we motivate students to learn? How can we get them to meet today's rising standards of excellence? How can we, in fact, keep students in school long enough to learn? The answer to these problems is quite simple. Give them money. Pay students to study and learn and stay in school.

■ Flow of Ideas

Look closely at the beginnings and endings of each paragraph. Have you connected your thoughts clearly? (See page 86 for a list of transition words.) The original opening words of the paragraph sequence below, from an essay of description, offer no links for readers. The revised versions use strong transitions indicating spatial organization (order by location).

Original First Words in the Four Middle Paragraphs

There was a huge, steep hill . . .
Buffalo Creek ran . . .
A dense "jungle" covering . . .
Within walking distance from my house . . .

Revised Versions (Words and phrases connect ideas)

Behind the house, there was a huge, steep hill . . .
Across the road from the house, Buffalo Creek ran . . .
On the far side of the creek bank was a dense "jungle" covering . . .
Up the road, within walking distance from my house . . .

INSIGHT: Review "Supporting Your Claims" (pages 254–256) and use those strategies to strengthen weak or unconvincing passages.

■ Closing Ideas

Reread your closing paragraph(s). Do you offer an effective summary, reassert your main point in a fresh way, and provide readers with food for thought as they leave your writing? Or is your ending abrupt, repetitive, or directionless? The original ending below is uninspiring; it adds little to the main part of the writing. The revision summarizes the main points in the essay and then urges the reader to think again about the overall point of writing.

Original Ending (Sketchy and flat)

Native Son deals with a young man's struggle against racism. It shows the effects of prejudice. Everyone should read this book.

Revised Version (Effectively ends the writing)

Native Son deals with a young man's struggle in a racist society, but also with so much more. It shows how prejudice affects people, how it closes in on them, and what some people will do to find a way out. Anyone who wants to better understand racism in the United States should read this book.

TIP: To generate fresh ideas for your closing, freewrite answers to questions like these: Why is the topic important to me? What should my readers have learned? Why should this issue matter to readers? What evidence or appeal (pages 262–263) will help readers remember my message and act on it? How does the topic relate to broader issues in society, history, or life?

Web Link

Video

Revising for Voice and Style

Generally, readers more fully trust writing that speaks in an informed voice and a clear, natural style. To develop an informed voice, make sure that your details are correct and complete; to develop a clear style, make sure that your writing is well organized and unpretentious. Check the issues below. (For a definition of voice, see page 74.)

Check the level of commitment.

Consider how and to what degree your writing shows that you care about the topic and reader. For example, note how the original passage below lacks a personal voice, revealing nothing about the writer's connection to—or interest in—the topic. In contrast, the revision shows that the writer cares about the topic.

> **Original Passage** (Lacks voice)
>
> Cemeteries can teach us a lot about history. They make history seem more real. There is an old grave of a Revolutionary War veteran in the Union Grove Cemetery. . . .
>
> **Revised Version** (Personal, sincere voice)
>
> I've always had a special feeling for cemeteries. It's hard to explain any further than that, except to say history never seems quite as real as it does when I walk among many old gravestones. One day I discovered the grave of a Revolutionary War veteran. . . .

Check the intensity of your writing.

All writing—including academic writing—is enriched by an appropriate level of intensity, or even passion. In the original passage below, the writer's concern for the topic is unclear because the piece sounds neutral. In contrast, the revised version exudes energy.

> **Original Passage** (Lacks feeling and energy)
>
> The Dream Act could make a difference for people. It just takes a long time to get any bill through Congress. This bill probably will never get approved. Instead of passing the Dream Act, the country will probably just deport high school students from other countries.
>
> **Revised Passage** (Expresses real feelings)
>
> Given such debates, it might be a long time before the bill becomes law, thereby dashing the dreams of nearly 65,000 high school students like Maria who can't wait another year because they may already be in deportation proceedings. We need to step up and educate our representatives and senators about the importance of passing the Dream Act on its own instead of including the bill along with CIR. We need to urge them to debate and approve the Dream Act now, thereby making Maria's dreams—and the dreams of thousands of students like her—a reality!

Develop an academic style.

Most college writing requires an academic style. Such a style isn't stuffy; you're not trying to impress readers with ten-dollar words. Rather, you are using language that facilitates a thoughtful, engaged discussion of the topic. To choose the best words for such a conversation, consider the issues that follow.

Video

■ Personal Pronouns

In some academic writing, personal pronouns are acceptable. Such is the case in informal writing, such as reading responses, personal essays involving narration, description, and reflection, and opinion-editorial essays written for a broad audience. In addition, *I* is correctly used in academic writing rooted in personal research, sometimes called an *I-search paper.*

Generally, however, avoid using *I, we,* and *you* in traditional academic writing. The concept, instead, is to focus on the topic itself and let your attitude be revealed indirectly. As E. B. White puts it, "To achieve style, begin by affecting none—that is, begin by placing yourself in the background."

> **No:** I really think that the problem of the homeless in Chicago is serious, given the number of people who are dying, as I know from my experience where I grew up.
>
> **Yes:** Homelessness in Chicago often leads to death. This fact demands the attention of more than lawmakers and social workers; all citizens must address the problems of their suffering neighbors.

TIP: Use the pronoun *one* carefully in academic prose. When it means "a person," *one* can lead to a stilted style if overused. In addition, the pronoun *their* (a plural pronoun) should not be used with *one* (a singular pronoun).

■ Technical Terms and Jargon

Technical terms and jargon—"insider" words—can be the specialized vocabulary of a subject, a discipline, a profession, or a social group. As such, jargon can be difficult to read for "outsiders." Follow these guidelines:

- Use technical terms to communicate with people within the profession or discipline as a kind of shorthand. However, be careful that such jargon doesn't devolve into meaningless buzzwords and catchphrases.
- Avoid jargon when writing for readers outside the profession or discipline. Use simpler terms and define technical terms that must be used.

> **Technical:** Bin's Douser power washer delivers 2200 psi p.r., runs off standard a.c. lines, comes with 100 ft. h.d. synthetic-rubber tubing, and features variable pulsation options through three adjustable s.s. tips.
>
> **Simple:** Bin's Douser power washer has a pressure rating of 2200 psi (pounds per square inch), runs off a common 200-volt electrical circuit, comes with 100 feet of hose, and includes three nozzles.

■ Level of Formality

Most academic writing (especially research papers, literary analyses, lab reports, and argumentative essays) should meet the standards of formal English. **Formal English** is characterized by a serious tone; careful attention to word choice; longer and more complex sentences reflecting complex thinking; strict adherence to traditional conventions of grammar, mechanics, and punctuation; and avoidance of contractions.

> Formal English, modeled in this sentence, is worded correctly and carefully so that it can withstand repeated readings without seeming tiresome, sloppy, or cute.

You may write other papers (personal essays, commentaries, journals, and reviews) in which informal English is appropriate. **Informal English** is characterized by a personal tone, the occasional use of popular expressions, shorter sentences with slightly looser syntax, contractions, and personal references (*I, we, you*), but it still adheres to basic conventions.

> Informal English sounds like one person talking to another person (in a somewhat relaxed setting). It's the type of language that you're reading now. It sounds comfortable and real, not affected or breezy.

TIP: In academic writing, generally avoid slang—words considered outside standard English because they are faddish, familiar to few people, and sometimes insulting.

■ Unnecessary Qualifiers

Using qualifiers (such as *mostly, often, likely,* or *tends to*) is an appropriate strategy for developing defendable claims in argumentative writing. (See pages 252–253.) However, when you "overqualify" your ideas or add intensifiers (*really, truly*), the result is insecurity—the impression that you lack confidence in your ideas. The cure? Say what you mean, and mean what you say.

> **Insecure:** I totally and completely agree with the new security measures at sporting events, but that's only my opinion.
>
> **Secure:** I agree with the new security measures at sporting events.

FYI Each academic discipline has its own vocabulary and its own vocabulary resources. Such resources include dictionaries, glossaries, or handbooks. Check your library for the vocabulary resources in your discipline. Use them regularly to deepen your grasp of that vocabulary.

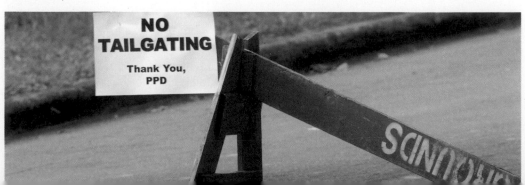

Know when to use the passive voice.

Most verbs can be in either the active or the passive voice. When a verb is active, the sentence's subject performs the action. When the verb is passive, the subject is acted upon.

Active:	If you *can't attend* the meeting, *notify* Richard by Thursday.
Passive:	If a meeting *can't be attended* by you, Richard *must be notified* by Thursday.

Weaknesses of Passive Voice: The passive voice tends to be wordy and sluggish because the verb's action is directed backward, not ahead. In addition, passive constructions tend to be impersonal, making people disappear.

Passive:	The sound system *can* now *be used* to listen in on sessions in the therapy room. Parents *can be helped* by having constructive one-on-one communication methods with children modeled by therapists.
Active:	Parents *can* now *use* the sound system to listen in on sessions in the therapy room. Therapists *can help* parents by modeling constructive one-on-one communication methods with children.

Strengths of Passive Voice: Using the passive voice isn't wrong. In fact, the passive voice has some important uses: (1) when you need to be tactful (say, in a bad-news letter), (2) if you wish to stress the object or person acted upon, and (3) if the actual actor is understood, unknown, or unimportant.

Active:	Our engineers determined that you bent the bar at the midpoint.
Passive:	Our engineers determined that the bar had been bent at the midpoint. (tactful)
Active:	Congratulations! We *have approved* your scholarship for $2,500.
Passive:	Congratulations! Your scholarship for $2,500 *has been approved.* (emphasis on receiver; actor understood)

TIP: Avoid using the passive voice unethically to hide responsibility. For example, an instructor who says, "Your assignments could not be graded because of scheduling difficulties," might be trying to evade the truth: "I did not finish grading your assignments because I was watching *CSI.*"

Writing with Sources: Academic writing must be free of plagiarism. Check that you have clearly indicated which material in your draft is summarized, paraphrased, or quoted from another source. (For more help, see pages 436–438.)

■ Addressing Paragraph Issues

While drafting, you may have constructed paragraphs that are loosely held together, poorly developed, or unclear. When you revise, take a close look at your paragraphs for focus, unity, and coherence (pages 83–85).

Remember the basics. ■ ▪ ■

A paragraph should be a concise unit of thought. Revise a paragraph until it . . .
- is organized around a controlling idea—often stated in a topic sentence.
- consists of supporting sentences that develop the controlling idea.
- concludes with a sentence that summarizes the main point and prepares readers for the next paragraph or main point.
- serves a specific function in a piece of writing—opening, supporting, developing, illustrating, countering, describing, or closing.

Sample Paragraph

Topic sentence	Tumor cells can hurt the body in a number of ways. First, a tumor can grow so big that it takes up space needed by other organs. Second, some cells may detach from the original tumor and spread throughout the body, creating new tumors elsewhere. This happens with lymphatic cancer—a cancer that's hard to control because it spreads so
Supporting sentences	quickly. A third way that tumor cells can hurt the body is by doing work not called for in their DNA. For example, a gland cell's DNA code may tell the cell to produce a necessary hormone in the endocrine system. However, if cancer damages or distorts that code, sick cells may produce more of the hormone than the body can use—or
Closing sentence	even tolerate (Braun 4). Cancer cells seem to have minds of their own, and this is why cancer is such a serious disease.

Keep the purpose in mind. ■ ▪ ■

Use these questions to evaluate the purpose and function of each paragraph:
- What function does the paragraph fulfill? How does it add to your line of reasoning or the development of your thesis?
- Would the paragraph work better if it were divided in two—or combined with another paragraph?
- Does the paragraph flow smoothly from the previous paragraph, and does it lead effectively into the next one?

Check for unity. ■ ■ ■

A unified paragraph is one in which all the details help to develop a single main topic or achieve a single main effect. Test for unity by following these guidelines.

■ Topic Sentence

Very often the topic of a paragraph is stated in a single sentence called a "topic sentence." Check whether your paragraph needs a topic sentence. If the paragraph has a topic sentence, determine whether it is clear, specific, and well focused. Here is a formula for writing good topic sentences:

Formula: A topic sentence = a limited topic + a specific feeling or thought about it.

Example: The fear that Americans feel (limited topic) comes partly from the uncertainty related to this attack (a specific thought).

■ Placement of the Topic Sentence

Normally the topic sentence is the first sentence in the paragraph. However, it can appear elsewhere in a paragraph.

Middle Placement: Place a topic sentence in the middle when you want to build up to and then lead away from the key idea.

During the making of *Apocalypse Now,* Eleanor Coppola created a documentary about the filming called *Hearts of Darkness: A Filmmaker's Apocalypse.* In the first film, the insane Colonel Kurtz has disappeared into the Cambodian jungle. As Captain Willard searches for Kurtz, the screen fills with horror. **However, as *Hearts of Darkness* relates, the horror portrayed in the fictional movie was being lived out by the production company.** For example, in the documentary, actor Larry Fishburne shockingly says, "War is fun. . . . Vietnam must have been so much fun." Then toward the end of the filming, actor Martin Sheen suffered a heart attack. When an assistant informed investors, the director exploded, "He's not dead unless I say he's dead."

End Placement: Place a topic sentence at the end when you want to build to a climax, as in a passage of narration or persuasion.

When sportsmen stop to reflect on why they find fishing so enjoyable, most realize that what they love is the feel of a fish on the end of the line, not necessarily the weight of the fillets in their coolers. Fishing has undergone a slow evolution over the last century. While fishing used to be a way of putting food on the table, most of today's fishermen do so only for the relaxation that it provides. The barbed hook was invented to increase the quantity of fish a man could land so that he could better feed his family. **This need no longer exists, so barbed hooks are no longer necessary.**

■ Supporting Sentences

All the sentences in the body of a paragraph should support the topic sentence. The closing sentence, for instance, will often summarize the paragraph's main point or emphasize a key detail. If any sentences shift the focus away from the topic, revise the paragraph in one of the following ways:

- Delete the material from the paragraph.
- Rewrite the material so that it clearly supports the topic sentence.
- Create a separate paragraph based on the odd-man-out material.
- Revise the topic sentence so that it relates more closely to the support.

■ Consistent Focus

Examine the following paragraph about fishing hooks. The original topic sentence focuses on the point that some anglers prefer smooth hooks. However, the writer leaves this initial idea unfinished and turns to the issue of the cost of new hooks. In the revised version, unity is restored: The first paragraph completes the point about anglers who prefer smooth hooks; the second paragraph addresses the issue of replacement costs.

Original Paragraph (Lacks unity)

According to some anglers who do use smooth hooks, their lures perform better than barbed lures as long as they maintain a constant tension on the line. Smooth hooks can bite deeper than barbed hooks, actually providing a stronger hold on the fish. Some people have argued that replacing all of the barbed hooks in their tackle would be a costly operation.

Revised Version (Unified)

According to some anglers who do use smooth hooks, their lures perform better than barbed lures as long as the anglers maintain a constant tension on the line. Smooth hooks can bite deeper than barbed hooks, actually providing a stronger hold on the fish. These anglers testify that switching from barbed hooks has not noticeably reduced the number of fish that they are able to land. In their experience, and in my own, enjoyment of the sport is actually heightened by adding another challenge to playing the fish (maintaining line tension).

Some people have argued that replacing all of the barbed hooks in their tackle would be a costly operation. While this is certainly a concern, barbed hooks do not necessarily require replacement. With a simple set of pliers, the barbs on most conventional hooks can be bent down, providing a cost-free method of modifying one's existing tackle. . . .

 Paragraphs that contain unrelated ideas lack unity and are hard to follow. As you review each paragraph for unity, ask yourself these questions: Is the topic of the paragraph clear? Does each sentence relate to the topic? Are the sentences organized in the best possible order?

Check for coherence. ■ ▪ ■

When a paragraph is coherent, the parts stay together. A coherent paragraph flows smoothly because each sentence is connected to others by patterns in the language such as repetition and transitions. To strengthen the coherence in your paragraphs, check for the issues discussed below.

■ Effective Repetition

To achieve coherence in your paragraphs, consider using repetition—repeating words or synonyms where necessary to remind readers of what you have already said. You can also use parallelism—repeating phrase or sentence structures to show the relationships among ideas. At the same time, you will add a unifying rhythm to your writing.

> **Ineffective:** The floor was littered with discarded soda cans, newspapers that were crumpled, and wrinkled clothes.
>
> **Effective:** **The floor was littered with discarded soda cans, crumpled newspapers, and wrinkled clothes.** (Three parallel phrases are used.)
>
> **Ineffective:** Reading the book was enjoyable; to write the critique was difficult.
>
> **Effective:** **Reading the book was enjoyable; writing the critique was difficult.** (Two similar structures are repeated.)

■ Clear Transitions

Linking words and phrases like "next," "on the other hand," and "in addition" connect ideas by showing the relationship among them. There are transitions that show location and time, compare and contrast things, emphasize a point, conclude or summarize, and add or clarify information. (See page 86 for a list of linking words and phrases.) Note the use of transitions in the following examples:

> The paradox of Scotland is that violence had long been the norm in this now-peaceful land. In fact, the country was born, bred, and came of age in war.
> (The transition is used to emphasize a point.)
>
> The production of cement is a complicated process. First, the mixture of lime, silica, alumina, and gypsum is ground into very fine particles.
> (The transition is used to show time or order.)

INSIGHT: Another way to achieve coherence in your paragraphs is to use pronouns effectively. A pronoun forms a link to the noun it replaces and ties that noun (idea) to the ideas that follow. As always, don't overuse pronouns or rely too heavily on them in establishing coherence in your paragraphs.

■ Transitions and Linking Words

The words and phrases below can help you tie together words, phrases, sentences, and paragraphs.

Words used to show location:

above	behind	down	on top of
across	below	in back of	onto
against	beneath	in front of	outside
along	beside	inside	over
among	between	into	throughout
around	beyond	near	to the right
away from	by	off	under

Words used to show time:

about	during	next	today
after	finally	next week	tomorrow
afterward	first	second	until
as soon as	immediately	soon	when
at	later	then	yesterday
before	meanwhile	third	

Words used to compare things (show similarities):

also	in the same way	likewise
as	like	similarly

Words used to contrast things (show differences):

although	even though	on the other hand	still
but	however	otherwise	yet

Words used to emphasize a point:

again	for this reason	particularly	to repeat
even	in fact	to emphasize	truly

Words used to conclude or summarize:

all in all	finally	in summary	therefore
as a result	in conclusion	last	to sum up

Words used to add information:

additionally	and	equally important	in addition
again	another	finally	likewise
along with	as well	for example	next
also	besides	for instance	second

Words used to clarify:

for instance	in other words	put another way	that is

Note: Use transitions to link, expand, or intensify an idea, but don't add elements carelessly, creating run-on or rambling sentences (pages 662–664).

Check for completeness. ■▪▪

The sentences in a paragraph should support and expand on the main point. If your paragraph does not seem complete, you will need to add information.

Supporting Details

If some of your paragraphs are incomplete, they may lack details. There are numerous kinds of details, including the following:

facts	anecdotes	analyses	paraphrases
statistics	quotations	explanations	comparisons
examples	definitions	summaries	analogies

Add details based on the type of writing you are engaged in.

Describing: Add details that help readers see, smell, taste, touch, or hear it.
Narrating: Add details that help readers understand the events and actions.
Explaining: Add details that help readers understand what it means, how it works, or what it does.
Persuading: Add details that strengthen the logic of your argument.

Specific Details

The original paragraph below fails to answer fully the question posed by the topic sentence. In the revised paragraph, the writer uses an anecdote to answer the question.

Original Paragraph (Lacks completeness)

So what is stress? Actually, the physiological characteristics of stress are some of the body's potentially good self-defense mechanisms. People experience stress when they are in danger. In fact, stress can be healthy.

Revised Version (Full development)

So what is stress? Actually, the physiological characteristics of stress are some of the body's potentially good self-defense mechanisms. Take, for example, a man who is crossing a busy intersection when he spots an oncoming car. Immediately his brain releases a flood of adrenaline into his bloodstream. As a result, his muscles contract, his eyes dilate, his heart pounds faster, his breathing quickens, and his blood clots more readily. Each one of these responses helps the man leap out of the car's path. His muscles contract to give him exceptional strength. His eyes dilate so that he can see more clearly. His heart pumps more blood and his lungs exchange more air—both to increase his metabolism. If the man were injured, his blood would clot faster, ensuring a smaller amount of blood loss. In this situation and many more like it, stress symptoms are good (Curtis 25–26).

INSIGHT: If a paragraph is getting long, divide it at a natural stopping point. The topic sentence can then function as the thesis for that part of your essay or paper.

Working with Sources: Test your evidence to make certain that it provides the support you need.

- **accurate:** The information is all correct.
- **precise:** The data are concrete and specific, not vague and general.
- **substantial:** The amount of evidence reaches a critical mass—enough to convey the idea and convince readers of its validity.
- **authoritative:** The evidence comes from a reliable source. Moreover, the information is as close to the origin as possible; it is not a report conveying thirdhand or fourthhand information.
- **representative:** The information fairly represents the range of data on the issue. Your presentation of evidence is balanced.
- **fitting:** Given your purpose, the topic, and your reader, the evidence is appropriate and relevant for the question or issue you are discussing.

The reference page below comes from the APA paper, "Our Roots Go Back to Roanoke (see pages 547–557)." Note how student writer Renee Danielle Singh used a variety of sources that meet the criteria listed above.

Our Roots   12

References

Journal article

Beltrane, T., & McQueen, D. V. (1979). Urban and rural Indian drinking patterns: The special case of the Lumbee. *International Journal of the Addictions, 14*(4), 533–548.

Book

Blu, K. I. (1980). *The Lumbee problem: The making of an American Indian People.* Cambridge: Cambridge University Press.

Bryant, A., Goins, R. T., Bell, R., Herrell, R., Manson, S. M., & Buchwald, D. (2004). Health differences among Lumbee Indians using public and private sources of care. *Journal of Rural Health, 20*(3), 231–236.

Bryant, A., & LaFromboise, T. D. (2005). The racial identity and cultural orientation of Lumbee American Indian high school students. *Cultural Diversity & Ethnic Minority Psychology, 11*(1), 82–89.

Proceedings feature

Grier, J. O., Ruderman, R. J., & Johnson, A. H. (1979). HLA profile in the Lumbee Indians of North Carolina. *Transplant Proceedings, 11*(4), 1767–1769.

Revising Collaboratively

Every writer can benefit from feedback from an interested audience, especially one that offers constructive and honest advice during a writing project. Members of an existing writing group already know how valuable it is for writers to share their work. Others might want to start a writing group to experience the benefits. Your group might collaborate online or in person. In either case, the information on the next two pages will help you get started.

Web Link

Video

Know your role.

Writers and reviewers should know their roles and fulfill their responsibilities during revising sessions. Essentially, the writer should briefly introduce the draft and solicit honest responses. Reviewers should make constructive comments in response to the writing.

Provide appropriate feedback.

Feedback can take many forms, including the three approaches described here.

Basic Description: In this simple response, the reviewer listens or reads attentively and then simply describes what she or he hears or sees happening in the piece. The reviewer offers no criticism of the writing.

> **Ineffective:** "That was interesting. The piece was informative."
>
> **Effective:** "First, the essay introduced the challenge of your birth defect and how you have had to cope with it. Then in the next part you . . ."

Summary Evaluation: Here the reviewer reads or listens to the piece and then provides a specific evaluation of the draft.

> **Ineffective:** "Gee, I really liked it!" or "It was boring."
>
> **Effective:** "Your story at the beginning really pulled me in, and the middle explained the issue strongly, but the ending felt a bit flat."

Thorough Critique: The reviewer assesses the ideas, organization, and voice in the writing. Feedback should be detailed and constructive. Such a critique may also be completed with the aid of a review sheet or checklist. As a reviewer, be prepared to share specific responses, suggestions, and questions. But also be sure to focus your comments on the writing, rather than the writer.

> **Ineffective:** "You really need to fix that opening! What were you thinking?"
>
> **Effective:** "Let's look closely at the opening. Could you rewrite the first sentence so it grabs the reader's attention? Also, I'm somewhat confused about the thesis statement. Could you rephrase it so it states your position more clearly?"

Respond according to a plan.

Using a specific plan or scheme like the following will help you give clear, helpful, and complete feedback.

OAQS Method: Use this simple four-step scheme—**Observe, Appreciate, Question,** and **Suggest**—to respond to your peers' writing.

1. **Observe** means to notice what another person's essay is designed to do and say something about its design or purpose. For example, you might say, "Even though you are writing about your boyfriend, it appears that you are trying to get a message across to your parents."

2. **Appreciate** means to praise something in the writing that impresses or pleases you. You can find something to appreciate in any piece of writing. For example, you might say, "You make a very convincing point" or "With your description, I can actually see his broken tooth."

3. **Question** means to ask whatever you want to know after you've read the essay. You might ask for background information, a definition, an interpretation, or an explanation. For example, you might say, "Can you tell us what happened when you got to the emergency room?"

4. **Suggest** means to give helpful advice about possible changes. For example, you might say, "With a little more physical detail—especially more sounds and smells—your third paragraph could be the highlight of the whole essay. What do you think?"

Asking the Writer Questions

Reviewers should ask the following types of questions while reviewing a piece of writing:

- **To help writers reflect on their purpose and audience . . .**
  Why are you writing this?
  Who will read this, and what do they need to know?

- **To help writers focus their thoughts . . .**
  What message are you trying to get across?
  Do you have more than one main point?
  What are the most important examples?

- **To help writers think about their information . . .**
  What do you know about the subject?
  Does this part say enough?
  Does your writing cover all of the basics (*Who? What? Where? When? Why?* and *How?*)?

- **To help writers with their openings and closings . . .**
  What are you trying to say in the opening?
  How else could you start your writing?
  How do you want your readers to feel at the end?

■ Using the Writing Center

A college writing center or lab is a place where a trained adviser will help you develop and strengthen a piece of writing. You can expect the writing center adviser to do certain things; other things only you can do. For quick reference, refer to the chart below.

Web Link

Adviser's Job	Your Job
Make you feel at home	Be respectful
Discuss your needs	Be ready to work
Help you choose a topic	Decide on a topic
Discuss your purpose and audience	Know your purpose and audience
Help you generate ideas	Embrace the best ideas
Help you develop your logic	Consider other points of view; stretch your own perspective
Help you understand how to research your material	Do the research
Read your draft	Share your writing
Identify problems in organization, logic, expression, and format	Recognize and fix problems
Teach ways to correct weaknesses	Learn important principles
Help you with grammar, usage, diction, vocabulary, and mechanics	Correct all errors

TIPS for getting the most out of the writing center

- Visit the center at least several days before your paper is due.
- Take your assignment sheet with you to each advising session.
- Read your work aloud, slowly.
- Expect to rethink your writing from scratch.
- Do not defend your wording—if it needs defense, it needs revision.
- Ask questions. (No question is "too dumb.")
- Request clarification of anything you don't understand.
- Ask for examples or illustrations of important points.
- Write down all practical suggestions.
- Ask the adviser to summarize his or her remarks.
- Rewrite as soon as possible after—or even during—the advising session.
- Return to the writing center for a response to your revisions.

Critical-Thinking and Writing Activities

As directed by your instructor, complete the following critical-thinking and writing activities by yourself or with classmates.

1. Doris Lessing has stated that when it comes to writing, "The more a thing cooks, the better." In what sense is revision a crucial stage in that cooking process? Using Lessing's cooking metaphor as a starting point, explore how revision should function in your own writing.

2. Review the opening and closing paragraphs of one of your essays. Then come up with fresh and different approaches for those paragraphs using the information on pages 76–77 as a guide.

3. For your current writing assignment, ask a peer to provide detailed feedback using the information in this chapter as a guide. Then take a fresh copy of your paper to the writing center and work through your draft with an adviser. Revise the draft as needed.

Learning-Outcomes Checklist

_____ I have thought about my overall approach, reconsidering the rhetorical situation—my role, subject, purpose, form, audience, and context.

_____ I have thought about the three global traits: ideas, organization, and voice.

_____ I have revised for ideas and organization.
   - **Ideas:** I have a clear thesis and have provided excellent support.
   - **Organization:** I have an opening, a middle, and a closing, and I use a consistent pattern of organization.

_____ I have revised for voice and style.
   - **Voice:** My voice works well for all parts of the rhetorical situation.

_____ I have made sure paragraphs are unified, coherent, and complete.

_____ I have gotten a peer review and have helped others revise.

_____ I have made use of the writing center as needed.

Cross-Curricular Connections

As you write papers for your major, make sure to use types of evidence and methods of analysis that the discipline accepts and values.

6 Editing and Proofreading

Editing and proofreading allow you to fine-tune your writing, making it ready to hand in. When you edit, look first for words, phrases, and sentences that sound awkward, uninteresting, or unclear. When you proofread, check your writing for spelling, mechanics, usage, and grammar errors. Ask one of your writing peers to help you.

The guidelines and strategies given in this chapter will help you edit your writing for style and clarity and proofread it for errors.

Learning Outcomes

Video

▸ Understand editing.
▸ Combine short, simplistic sentences.
▸ Expand sentences to create a more expressive style.
▸ Improve sentence style.
▸ Use effective words.
▸ Proofread your writing.

Visually Speaking ▶ How does the image above connote editing and proofreading? What tools could a writer use for this phase of the writing process?

■ Editing Your Revised Draft

When you have thoroughly revised your writing, you need to edit it so as to make it clear and concise enough to present to readers. Use the editing guidelines below to check your revised draft.

Review the overall style of your writing. ■ ■ ■

1. **Read your revised writing aloud.** Better yet, have a writing peer read it aloud to you. Highlight any writing that doesn't read smoothly and naturally.

2. **Check that your style fits the rhetorical situation.**

> **Goal:** Does your writing sound as if you wrote it with a clear aim in mind? Do the sentence style and word choice match the goal?
>
> **Reader:** Is the tone sincere? Does the writing sound authentic and honest?
>
> **Subject:** Does the writing suit the subject and your treatment of it in terms of seriousness or playfulness, complexity or simplicity?

3. **Examine your sentences.** Check them for clarity, conciseness, and variety. Replace sentences that are wordy or rambling; combine or expand sentences that are short and choppy. Also, vary the beginnings of your sentences and avoid sentence patterns that are too predictable. (See pages 95–101.)

Consider word choice. ■ ■ ■

1. **Avoid redundancy.** Be alert for words or phrases that are used together but mean nearly the same thing.

> repeat again   red in color   refer back

2. **Watch for repetition.** When used appropriately, repetition can add rhythm and coherence to your writing. When used ineffectively, however, it can be a real distraction.

> **The man** looked as if he were in his late seventies. **The man** was dressed in an old suit. I soon realized that **the man** was homeless. . . .

3. **Look for general nouns, verbs, and modifiers.** Specific words are much more effective than general ones. (See page 102.)

> The girl moved on the bench. (general)
> Rosie slid quietly to the end of the park bench. (specific)

4. **Avoid highly technical terms.** Check for jargon or technical terms that your readers will not know or that you haven't adequately explained. (See page 103.)

> As the **capillaries** bleed, **platelets** work with **fibrinogens** to form a clot.

5. **Use fair language.** Replace words or phrases that are biased or demeaning. (See pages 104–106.)

Combining Sentences

Effective sentences often contain several basic ideas that work together to show relationships and make connections. Here are five basic ideas followed by seven examples of how the ideas can be combined into effective sentences.

1. The longest and largest construction project in history was the Great Wall of China.
2. The project took 1,700 years to complete.
3. The Great Wall of China is 1,400 miles long.
4. It is between 18 and 30 feet high.
5. It is up to 32 feet wide.

Edit short, simplistic sentences.

Combine your short, simplistic sentences into longer, more detailed sentences. Sentence combining is generally carried out in the following ways:

- Use a **series** to combine three or more similar ideas.
  The Great Wall of China is **1,400 miles long,** between **18 and 30 feet high,** and up to **32 feet wide.**

- Use a **relative pronoun** (*who, whose, that, which*) to introduce subordinate (less important) ideas.
  The Great Wall of China, **which is 1,400 miles long and between 18 and 30 feet high,** took 1,700 years to complete.

- Use an **introductory phrase** or **clause.**
  Having taken 1,700 years to complete, the Great Wall of China was the longest construction project in history.

- Use a **semicolon** (and a conjunctive adverb if appropriate).
  The Great Wall took 1,700 years to complete; it is 1,400 miles long and up to 30 feet high and 32 feet wide.

- Repeat a **key word** or phrase to emphasize an idea.
  The Great Wall of China was the longest construction **project** in history, a **project** that took 1,700 years to complete.

- Use **correlative conjunctions** (*either, or; not only, but also*) to compare or contrast two ideas in a sentence.
  The Great Wall of China is **not only** up to 30 feet high and 32 feet wide, **but also** 1,400 miles long.

- Use an **appositive** (a word or phrase that renames) to emphasize an idea.
  The Great Wall of China—**the largest construction project in history**—is 1,400 miles long, 32 feet wide, and up to 30 feet high.

Expanding Sentences

Expand sentences when you edit so as to connect related ideas and make room for new information. Length has no value in and of itself: The best sentence is still the shortest one that says all it has to say. An expanded sentence, however, is capable of saying more—and saying it more expressively.

Use cumulative sentences.

Modern writers often use an expressive sentence form called the cumulative sentence. A cumulative sentence is made of a general "base clause" that is expanded by adding modifying words, phrases, or clauses. In such a sentence, details are added before and after the main clause, creating an image-rich thought. Here's an example of a cumulative sentence, with the base clause or main idea in boldface:

> In preparation for her Spanish exam, **Julie was studying** at the kitchen table, completely focused, memorizing a list of vocabulary words.

Discussion: Notice how each new modifier adds to the richness of the final sentence. Also notice that each of these modifying phrases is set off by a comma. Here's another sample sentence:

> With his hands on his face, **Tony was laughing** halfheartedly, looking puzzled and embarrassed.

Discussion: Such a cumulative sentence provides a way to write description that is rich in detail, without rambling. Notice how each modifier changes the flow or rhythm of the sentence.

Expand with details.

Here are seven basic ways to expand a main idea:

1. with **adjectives and adverbs:** *halfheartedly, once again*
2. with **prepositional phrases:** *with his hands on his face*
3. with **absolute phrases:** *his head tilted to one side*
4. with **participial (ing or ed) phrases:** *looking puzzled*
5. with **infinitive phrases:** *to hide his embarrassment*
6. with **subordinate clauses:** *while his friend talks*
7. with **relative clauses:** *who isn't laughing at all*

INSIGHT: To edit sentences for more expressive style, it is best to (1) know your grammar and punctuation (especially commas); (2) practice tightening, combining, and expanding sentences using the guidelines in this chapter; and (3) read carefully, looking for models of well-constructed sentences.

Checking for Sentence Style

Writer E. B. White advised young writers to "approach sentence style by way of simplicity, plainness, orderliness, and sincerity." That's good advice from a writer steeped in style. It's also important to know what to look for when editing your sentences. The information on this page and the following four pages will help you edit your sentences for style and correctness.

Avoid these sentence problems.

Always check for and correct the following types of sentence problems. Turn to the pages listed below for guidelines and examples when attempting to fix problems in your sentences.

Short, Choppy Sentences: Combine or expand any short, choppy sentences; use the examples and guidelines on page 95.

Flat, Predictable Sentences: Rewrite any sentences that sound predictable and uninteresting by varying their structures and expanding them with modifying words, phrases, and clauses. (See pages 98–100.)

Incorrect Sentences: Look carefully for fragments, run-ons, and comma splices and correct them accordingly.

Unclear Sentences: Edit any sentences that contain unclear wording, misplaced modifiers, dangling modifiers, or incomplete comparisons.

Unacceptable Sentences: Change sentences that include nonstandard language, double negatives, or unparallel construction.

Unnatural Sentences: Rewrite sentences that contain jargon, clichés, or flowery language. (See page 103.)

Review your writing for sentence variety.

Use the following strategy to review your writing for variety in terms of sentence beginnings, lengths, and types.

- In one column on a piece of paper, list the opening words in each of your sentences. Then decide if you need to vary some of your sentence beginnings.
- In another column, identify the number of words in each sentence. Then decide if you need to change the lengths of some of your sentences.
- In a third column, list the kinds of sentences used (exclamatory, declarative, interrogative, and so on). Then, based on your analysis, use the instructions on the next two pages to edit your sentences as needed.

Writing with Sources: When you integrate a quotation into the flow of text, make sure that the quotation works with the material around it. Either make the quotation a grammatical part of the sentence, or introduce the quotation with a complete sentence followed by a colon.

Vary sentence structures. ■■"■

To energize your sentences, vary their structures using one or more of the methods shown on this page and the next.

1. **Vary sentence openings.** Move a modifying word, phrase, or clause to the front of the sentence to stress that modifier. However, avoid creating dangling or misplaced modifiers.

> **The norm:** We apologize for the inconvenience this may have caused you.
>
> **Variation:** For the inconvenience this may have caused you, we apologize.

2. **Vary sentence lengths.** Short sentences (ten words or fewer) are ideal for making points crisply. Medium sentences (ten to twenty words) should carry the bulk of your information. When well crafted, occasional long sentences (more than twenty words) can develop and expand your ideas.

> **Short:** Welcome back to Magnolia Suites!
>
> **Medium:** Unfortunately, your confirmed room was unavailable last night when you arrived. For the inconvenience this may have caused you, we apologize.
>
> **Long:** Because several guests did not depart as scheduled, we were forced to provide you with accommodations elsewhere; however, for your trouble, we were happy to cover the cost of last night's lodging.

3. **Vary sentence kinds.** The most common sentence is declarative—it states a point. For variety, try exclamatory, imperative, interrogative, and conditional statements.

> **Exclamatory:** Our goal is providing you with outstanding service!
>
> **Declarative:** To that end, we have upgraded your room at no expense.
>
> **Imperative:** Please accept, as well, this box of chocolates as a gift to sweeten your stay.
>
> **Interrogative:** Do you need further assistance?
>
> **Conditional:** If you do, we are ready to fulfill your requests.

INSIGHT: In creative writing (stories, novels, plays), writers occasionally use fragments to vary the rhythm of their prose, emphasize a point, or create dialogue. Avoid fragments in academic or business writing.

Writing with Sources: When you refer to ideas from a source, use the "historical present tense." That is, refer to the person and her or his work in the present tense—"Einstein **writes** that relativity . . ." Use past tense only if you want to emphasize the pastness of the source.

4. **Vary sentence arrangements.** Where do you want to place the main point of your sentence? You make that choice by arranging sentence parts into loose, periodic, balanced, or cumulative patterns. Each pattern creates a specific effect.

■ **Loose Sentence**

The Travel Center offers an attractive flight-reservation plan for students, one that allows you to collect bonus miles and receive $150,000 in life insurance per flight.

Analysis: This pattern is direct. It states the main point immediately (bold), and then tacks on extra information.

■ **Periodic Sentence**

Although this plan requires that you join the Travel Center's Student-Flight Club and pay the $10 admission fee, **in the long run you will save money!**

Analysis: This pattern postpones the main point (bold) until the end. The sentence builds to the point, creating an indirect, dramatic effect.

■ **Balanced Sentence**

Joining the club in your freshman year will save you money over your entire college career; in addition, **accruing bonus miles over four years will earn you a free trip to Europe!**

Analysis: This pattern gives equal weight to complementary or contrasting points (bold); the balance is often signaled by a comma and a conjunction (*and, but*) or by a semicolon. Often a conjunctive adverb (*however, nevertheless*) or a transitional phrase (*in addition, even so*) will follow the semicolon to further clarify the relationship.

■ **Cumulative Sentence**

Because the club membership is in your name, **you can retain its benefits** as long as you are a student, even if you transfer to a different college or go on to graduate school.

Analysis: This pattern puts the main idea (bold) in the middle of the sentence, surrounding it with modifying words, phrases, and clauses.

5. **Use positive repetition.** Although you should avoid needless repetition, you might use emphatic repetition to repeat a key word to stress a point.

■ **Repetitive Sentence**

Each year, more than a million young people who read poorly leave high school unable to read well, functionally illiterate.

■ **Emphatic Sentence**

Each year, more than a million young people leave high school functionally illiterate, so **illiterate** that they can't read daily newspapers, job ads, or safety instructions.

Use parallel structure. ◼ ◾ ▪

Coordinated sentence elements should be parallel—that is, they should be written in the same grammatical forms. Parallel structures save words, clarify relationships, and present the information in the correct sequence. Follow these guidelines.

1. **For words, phrases, or clauses in a series,** keep elements consistent.

   Not parallel: I have tutored students in Biology 101, also Chemistry 102, not to mention my familiarity with Physics 200.

   Parallel: I have tutored students in *Biology 101, Chemistry 102,* and *Physics 200.*

   Not parallel: I have volunteered as a hospital receptionist, have been a hospice volunteer, and as an emergency medical technician.

   Parallel: I have done volunteer work as *a hospital receptionist, a hospice counselor,* and *an emergency medical technician.*

2. **Use both parts of correlative conjunctions** (*either, or; neither, nor; not only, but also; as, so; whether, so; both, and*) so that both segments of the sentence are balanced.

   Not parallel: *Not only* did Blake College turn 20 this year. Its enrollment grew by 16 percent.

   Parallel: *Not only* did Blake College turn 20 this year, *but* its enrollment *also* grew by 16 percent.

3. **Place a modifier correctly** so that it clearly indicates the word or words to which it refers.

   Confusing: MADD promotes *severely* punishing and eliminating drunk driving because this offense leads to a *great number* of deaths and sorrow.

   Parallel: MADD promotes eliminating and *severely* punishing drunk driving because this offense leads to *many* deaths and *untold* sorrow.

4. **Place contrasting details in parallel structures** (words, phrases, or clauses) to stress a contrast.

   Weak contrast: The average child watches 24 hours of television a week and reads for 36 minutes.

   Strong contrast: Each week, the average child *watches television for 24 hours but reads for only about half an hour.*

Writing with Sources: When using sources, smoothly integrate text references to those sources. (For guidelines, see pages 491–528 for MLA and pages 529–558 for APA.)

Avoid weak constructions. ■ ▪ ▪

Avoid constructions (like those below) that weaken your writing.

■ Nominal Constructions

The nominal construction is both sluggish and wordy. Avoid it by changing the noun form of a verb (*description or instructions*) to a verb (*describe or instruct*). At the same time, delete the weak verb that preceded the noun.

NOMINAL CONSTRUCTIONS (noun form underlined)	**STRONG VERBS**
Tim gave a <u>description</u> . . .	Tim *described* . . .
Lydia provided <u>instructions</u> . . .	Lydia *instructed* . . .

Sluggish: John *had a discussion* with the tutors regarding the incident. They gave him their *confirmation* that similar developments had occurred before, but they had not *provided* submissions of their reports.

Energetic: John *discussed* the incident with the tutors. They *confirmed* that similar problems had developed before, but they hadn't *submitted* their reports.

■ Expletives

Expletives such as "it is" and "there is" are fillers that serve no purpose in most sentences—except to make them wordy and unnatural.

Sluggish: *It is* likely that Nathan will attend the Communication Department's Honors Banquet. *There is* a journalism scholarship that he might win.

Energetic: Nathan will likely attend the Communication Department's Honors Banquet and might win a journalism scholarship.

■ Negative Constructions

Sentences constructed upon the negatives *no, not, neither/nor* can be wordy and difficult to understand. It's simpler to state what *is* the case.

Negative: During my four years on the newspaper staff, *I have not been* behind in making significant contributions. My editorial skills *have* certainly *not deteriorated,* as I have *never failed* to tackle challenging assignments.

Positive: During my four years on the newspaper staff, *I have made* significant contributions. My editorial skills have steadily *developed* as I *have tackled* difficult assignments.

Avoiding Imprecise, Misleading, and Biased Words

Web Link

As you edit your writing, check your choice of words carefully. The information on the next five pages will help you edit for word choice.

Substitute specific words.

Replace vague nouns and verbs with words that generate clarity and energy.

Specific Nouns

Make it a habit to use specific nouns for subjects. General nouns (*woman, school*) give the reader a vague, uninteresting picture. More specific nouns (*actress, university*) give the reader a better picture. Finally, very specific nouns (*Meryl Streep, Notre Dame*) are the type that can make your writing clear and colorful.

GENERAL TO SPECIFIC NOUNS

Person	Place	Thing	Idea
woman	school	book	theory
actor	university	novel	scientific theory
Meryl Streep	Notre Dame	*Pride and Prejudice*	relativity

Vivid Verbs

Like nouns, verbs can be too general to create a vivid word picture. For example, the verb *looked* does not say the same thing as *stared, glared, glanced,* or *peeked.*

- Whenever possible, use a verb that is strong enough to stand alone without the help of an adverb.

  Verb and adverb: John fell down in the student lounge.

  Vivid verb: John **collapsed** in the student lounge.

- Avoid overusing the "be" verbs (*is, are, was, were*) and helping verbs. Often a main verb can be made from another word in the same sentence.

  A "be" verb: Cole is someone who follows international news.

  A stronger verb: Cole **follows** international news.

- Use active rather than passive verbs. (Use passive verbs only if you want to downplay who is performing the action in a sentence. See page 81.)

  Passive verb: Another provocative essay was submitted by Kim.

  Active verb: Kim **submitted** another provocative essay.

- Use verbs that show rather than tell.

  A verb that tells: Dr. Lewis is very thorough.

  A verb that shows: Dr. Lewis **prepares** detailed, interactive lectures.

Replace jargon and clichés. ■ ▪ ▪

Replace language that is overly technical or difficult to understand. Also replace overused, worn-out words.

■ Understandable Language

Jargon is language used in a certain profession or by a particular group of people. It may be acceptable to use if your audience is that group of people, but to most ears jargon will sound technical and unnatural.

> **Jargon:** The bottom line is that our output is not within our game plan.
> **Clear:** Production is not on schedule.
> **Jargon:** I'm having conceptual difficulty with these academic queries.
> **Clear:** I don't understand these review questions.
> **Jargon:** Pursuant to our conversation, I have forwarded you a remittance attached herewith.
> **Clear:** As we discussed, I am mailing you the check.

■ Fresh and Original Writing

Clichés are overused words or phrases. They give the reader no fresh view and no concrete picture. Because clichés spring quickly to mind (for both the writer and the reader), they are easy to write and often remain unedited.

an axe to grind	piece of cake
as good as dead	planting the seed
beat around the bush	rearing its ugly head
between a rock and a hard place	stick your neck out
burning bridges	throwing your weight around
easy as pie	up a creek

■ Purpose and Voice

Other aspects of your writing may also be tired and overworked. Be alert to the two types of clichés described below.

Clichés of Purpose:

- Sentimental papers gushing about an ideal friend or family member, or droning on about a moving experience
- Overused topics with recycled information and predictable examples

Clichés of Voice:

- Writing that assumes a false sense of authority: "I have determined that there are three basic types of newspapers. My preference is for the third."
- Writing that speaks with little or no sense of authority: "I flipped when I saw *Viewpoints*."
- Writing that is pretentious: "Because I have researched the topic thoroughly, readers should not question my conclusion."

Change biased words. ■ ▪ ■

When depicting individuals or groups according to their differences, use language that implies equal value and respect for all people.

■ Words Referring to Ethnicity

ACCEPTABLE GENERAL TERMS	ACCEPTABLE SPECIFIC TERMS
American Indians, Native Americans	Cherokee people, Inuit people, and so forth
Asian Americans (not Orientals)	Chinese Americans, Japanese Americans, and so forth
Latinos, Latinas, Hispanics	Mexican Americans, Cubans Americans, and so forth

African Americans, blacks
"African American" has come into wide acceptance, though the term "black" is preferred by some individuals.

Anglo Americans (English ancestry), **European Americans**
Use these terms to avoid the notion that "American," used alone, means "white."

Additional References

NOT RECOMMENDED	PREFERRED
Eurasian, mulatto	person of mixed ancestry
nonwhite	person of color
Caucasian	white
American (to mean U.S. citizen)	U.S. citizen

■ Words Referring to Age

AGE GROUP	ACCEPTABLE TERMS
up to age 13 or 14	boys, girls
between 13 and 19	youth, young people, young men, young women
late teens and 20s	young adults, young women, young men
30s to age 60	adults, men, women
60 and older	older adults, older people (not elderly)
65 and older	seniors (senior citizens also acceptable)

INSIGHT: Whenever you write about a person with a disability, an impairment, or other special condition, give the person and your readers the utmost respect. Nothing is more distracting to a reader than an insensitive or outdated reference.

■ Words Referring to Disabilities or Impairments

In the recent past, some writers were choosing alternatives to the term *disabled*, including *physically challenged*, *exceptional*, or *special*. However, it is not generally held that these new terms are precise enough to serve those who live with disabilities. Of course, degrading labels such as *crippled*, *invalid*, and *maimed*, as well as overly negative terminology, must be avoided.

NOT RECOMMENDED	PREFERRED
handicapped	disabled
birth defect	congenital disability
stutter, stammer, lisp	speech impairment
an AIDS victim	person with AIDS
suffering from cancer	person who has cancer
mechanical foot	prosthetic foot
false teeth	dentures

■ Words Referring to Conditions

People with various disabilities and conditions have sometimes been referred to as though they were their condition (quadriplegics, depressives, epileptics) instead of people who happen to have a particular disability. As much as possible, remember to refer to the person first, the disability second.

NOT RECOMMENDED	PREFERRED
the disabled	people with disabilities
cripples	people who have difficulty walking
the retarded	people with a developmental disability
dyslexics	students with dyslexia
neurotics	patients with neuroses
subjects, cases	participants, patients
quadriplegics	people who are quadriplegic
wheelchair users	people who use wheelchairs

■ Additional Terms

Make sure you understand the following terms that address specific impairments:

hearing impairment	=	partial hearing loss, hard of hearing (not deaf, which is total loss of hearing)
visual impairment	=	partially sighted (not blind, which is total loss of vision)
communicative disorder	=	speech, hearing, and learning disabilities affecting communication

■ Words Referring to Gender

- Use parallel language for both sexes:

  The **men** and the **women** rebuilt the school together.
  Hank and **Marie**
  Mr. Robert Gumble, Mrs. Joy Gumble

  Note: The courtesy titles *Mr., Ms., Mrs.,* and *Miss* ought to be used according to the person's preference.

- Use nonsexist alternatives to words with masculine connotations:

  humanity (not *mankind*)   **synthetic** (not *man-made*)
  artisan (not *craftsman*)

- Do not use masculine-only or feminine-only pronouns (*he, she, his, her*) when you want to refer to a human being in general:

  A politician can kiss privacy good-bye when **he** runs for office.
  (not recommended)

  Instead, use *he or she,* change the sentence to plural, or eliminate the pronoun:

  A politician can kiss privacy good-bye when **he or she** runs for office.
  Politicians can kiss privacy good-bye when **they** run for office.
  A politician can kiss privacy good-bye when running for office.

- Do not use gender-specific references in the salutation of a business letter when you don't know the person's name:

  Dear Sir: Dear Gentlemen: (neither is recommended)

  Instead, address a position:

  Dear Personnel Officer:
  Dear Members of the Economic Committee:

■ Occupational Issues

NOT RECOMMENDED	PREFERRED
chairman	**chair, presiding officer, moderator**
salesman	**sales representative, salesperson**
clergyman	**minister, priest, rabbi**
male/female nurse	**nurse**
male/female doctor	**doctor, physician**
mailman	**mail carrier, postal worker, letter carrier**
insurance man	**insurance agent**
fireman	**firefighter**
businessman	**executive, manager, businessperson**
congressman	**member of Congress, representative, senator**
steward, stewardess	**flight attendant**
policeman, policewoman	**police officer**

Proofreading Your Writing

The following guidelines will help you check your revised writing for spelling, mechanics, usage, grammar, and form.

Web Link

Review punctuation and mechanics. ■ ·■

1. **Check for proper use of commas** before coordinating conjunctions in compound sentences, after introductory clauses and long introductory phrases, between items in a series, and so on.
2. **Look for apostrophes** in contractions, plurals, and possessive nouns.
3. **Examine quotation marks** in quoted information, titles, or dialogue.
4. **Watch for proper use of capital letters** for first words in written conversation and for proper names of people, places, and things.

Look for usage and grammar errors. ■ ·■

1. **Look for words that writers commonly misuse:** *there/their/they're; accept/except.*
2. **Check for verb use.** Subjects and verbs should agree in number: Singular subjects go with singular verbs; plural subjects go with plural verbs. Verb tenses should be consistent throughout.
3. **Review for pronoun/antecedent agreement problems.** A pronoun and its antecedent must agree in number.

Check for spelling errors. ■ ·■

1. **Use a spell checker.** Your spell checker will catch most errors.
2. **Check each spelling you are unsure of.** Especially check those proper names and other special words your spell checker won't know.
3. **Consult a handbook.** Refer to a list of commonly misspelled words, as well as an up-to-date dictionary.

Check the writing for form and presentation. ■ ·■

1. **Note the title.** A title should be appropriate and lead into the writing.
2. **Examine any quoted or cited material.** Are all sources of information properly presented and documented? (See pages 491–528 and 529–558.)
3. **Look over the finished copy of your writing.** Does it meet the requirements for a final manuscript? (See page 130.)

Critical-Thinking and Writing Activities

As directed by your instructor, complete the following activities.

1. The nineteenth-century British writer Matthew Arnold offers this advice to writers about refining their writing: "Have something to say and say it as clearly as you can. That is the only secret of style." Does your own writing clearly communicate a meaningful message? Explain why or why not.

2. Choose a writing assignment that you have recently completed. Edit the sentences in this writing for style and correctness using pages 94–101 as a guide. Then use pages 102–106 in this chapter to edit the piece of writing for vague words, jargon, clichés, and biased language.

3. Combine some of the following ideas into longer, more mature sentences. Write at least four sentences, using page 95 as a guide.

   > Dogs can be difficult to train. The necessary supplies include a leash and treats. Patience is also a necessity. Dogs like to please their owners. Training is not a chore for dogs. A well-trained dog is a pleasure to its owner.

Learning-Outcomes Checklist

_____ I understand that editing involves checking overall sentence style and word choice.

_____ I have combined short, simplistic sentences.

_____ I have expanded sentences, where appropriate, to create a more expressive style.

_____ I have avoided sentence problems and improved sentence style.
  - Varying sentence structures
  - Varying sentence arrangements
  - Using parallel structure
  - Avoiding weak constructions

_____ I have made sure that I use strong, effective words.
  - Using specific nouns and vivid verbs
  - Replacing jargon and clichés
  - Changing biased words

_____ I have proofread my writing, checking punctuation, mechanics, usage, grammar, and spelling—as well as form and presentation.

Cross-Curricular Connections

Different disciplines have different documentation systems, each with its own conventions, formats, and punctuation practices. For MLA style, see pages 491–528, and for APA style, see pages 529–558.

7 Submitting Writing and Creating Portfolios

Submitting you writing might be as simple as handing it in to your instructor or posting it to a class wiki, or it might be as involved as submitting it to a journal in your area of study or assembling it with your other works to publish in a portfolio. Whatever the case, sharing your writing makes all the work you have done worthwhile. As writer Tom Liner states, "You learn ways to improve your writing by seeing its effect on others."

This chapter will help you prepare your writing for submission and sharing. When you make your writing public—in whatever form—you are *publishing* it.

Learning Outcomes

▶ Format your writing.
▶ Submit writing, perhaps in a portfolio.

Video

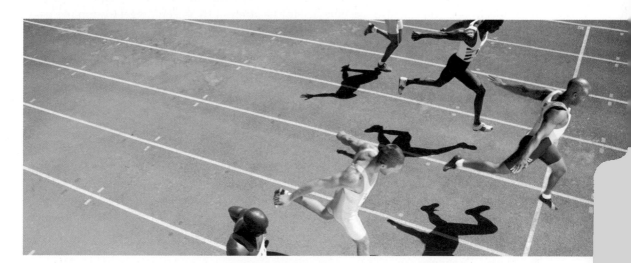

Visually Speaking ▶ How does the image above relate to submitting your writing? How is writing like running a race?

◼ Formatting Your Writing

A good page design makes your writing clear and easy to follow. Keep that in mind when you produce a final copy of your writing.

Strive for clarity in page design. ◼ ▪ ◼

Examine the following design elements, making sure that each is appropriate and clear in your project and in your writing.

◼ Format and Documentation

Keep the design clear and uncluttered. Aim for a sharp, polished look in all your assigned writing.

Use the designated documentation form. Follow all the requirements outlined in the MLA (pages 491–528) or APA (pages 529–558) style guides.

◼ Typography

Use an easy-to-read serif font for the main text. Serif type, **like this,** has "tails" at the tops and bottoms of the letters. For most types of writing, use a 10- or 12-point type size.

Consider using a sans serif font for the title and headings. Sans serif type, **like this,** does not have "tails." Use larger, perhaps 18-point, type for your title and 14-point type for any headings. You can also use boldface for headings if they seem to get lost on the page. (Follow your instructor's formatting guidelines.)

 Because most people find a sans serif font easier to read on screen, consider a sans serif font for the body and a serif font for the titles and headings in any writing you publish online.

◼ Spacing

Follow all requirements for indents and margins. This usually means indenting the first line of each paragraph five spaces, maintaining a one-inch margin around each page, and double-spacing throughout the paper.

Avoid widows and orphans. Avoid leaving headings, hyphenated words, or single lines (widows) of new paragraphs alone at the bottom of a page. Also avoid single words (orphans) at the bottom of a page or carried over to the top of a new page.

◼ Graphic Devices

Create bulleted or numbered lists to highlight individual items in a list. But, be selective, using traditional paragraphs when they help you more effectively communicate your message. Writing should not include too many lists.

Include charts or other graphics. Graphics should be neither so small that they get lost on the page, nor so large that they overpower the page.

■ Submitting Writing and Creating Portfolios

Once you have formatted and proofread your final draft, you should be ready to share your writing. For college assignments, you will often simply turn in your paper to your instructor. However, you should also think about sharing your writing with other audiences, including those who will want to see your writing portfolio.

Consider potential audiences. ■▪■

You could receive helpful feedback by taking any of the following steps:

- Share your writing with peers or family members.
- Submit your work to a local publication or an online journal.
- Post your writing on an appropriate website, including your own.
- Turn in your writing to your instructor.

Select appropriate submission methods. ■▪■

There are two basic methods for submitting your work.

- **Paper submission:** Print an error-free copy on quality paper.
- **Electronic submission:** If allowed, send your writing as an e-mail attachment.

Use a writing portfolio. ■▪■

There are two basic types of writing portfolios: (1) *a working portfolio* in which you store documents at various stages of development, and (2) *a showcase portfolio* with which you share appropriate finished work. For example, you could submit a portfolio to complete course requirements or to apply for a scholarship, graduate program, or job. The documents below are commonly included in a showcase portfolio:

- A table of contents listing the pieces included in your portfolio
- An opening essay or letter detailing the story behind your portfolio (how you compiled it and why it features the qualities expected by the intended reader)
- A specified number of—and types of—finished pieces
- A cover sheet attached to each piece of writing, discussing the reason for its selection, the amount of work that went into it, and so on
- Evaluation sheets or checklists charting the progress or experience you want to show related to issues of interest to the reader

Critical-Thinking and Writing Activities

As directed by your instructor, complete the following critical-thinking and writing activities by yourself or with classmates.

1. Catherine Drinker Bowen has argued the following: "Writing is not apart from living. Writing is a kind of double living." As you think about sharing your own writing and adding it to your writing portfolio, does this claim ring true? Why or why not?

2. Choose one of your recent writing assignments and use the instructions on page 110 to assess the quality of your formatting and page design. Edit and redesign the paper as needed.

3. For the class in which you are using this book, begin two working portfolios: (1) an electronic portfolio on your computer and (2) a paper portfolio in a sturdy folder or binder. In the electronic portfolio, store all drafts of your assignments, as well as all related electronic correspondence with your instructor. In your paper portfolio, store all printed drafts of your work, including copies that show your instructor's notations and grades.

Learning-Outcomes Checklist

_____ I have formatted my writing according to assignment and submission guidelines.
  - Using appropriate headings, layout, margins, typography, and documentation

_____ I have submitted my writing in an appropriate way.
  - Fitting my assignment, program, and career goals

_____ I have added my writing to my portfolio.
  - Demonstrating an appropriate level of scholarship and research
  - Using appropriate voice and style
  - Including an attractive design

Cross-Curricular Connections

How does writing a paper in your discipline establish your position in the research community? How does adding a paper to your portfolio establish your position in your writing career?

8 One Writer's Process

An essay is an attempt to understand a topic more deeply and clearly. That's one of the reasons this basic form of writing is essential in many college courses. It's a tool for both discovering and communicating.

How do you move from an assignment to a finished, polished essay? The best strategy is to take matters one step at a time, from understanding the assignment to submitting the final draft. Don't try to churn out the essay the night before it's due.

This chapter shows how student writer Angela Franco followed the writing process outlined in chapters 2 through 7.

Learning Outcomes

Audio

▸ Understand the assignment and select a topic.

▸ Research the topic and plan the writing.

▸ Write a first draft.

▸ Complete an initial revision.

▸ Get a peer response and complete a second revision.

▸ Edit the draft.

▸ Proofread the draft.

Visually Speaking ▶ How does the image above relate to a writer's process? What does the brightly colored umbrella say about the walker's personal style?

Angela's Assignment and Response

Video

In this chapter, you will follow student Angela Franco as she writes an assigned essay for her Environmental Policies class. Start by carefully reading the assignment and discussion below, noting how she thinks through the rhetorical situation.

Audio

Angela examined the assignment. ■ ■ ■

Angela carefully read her assignment and responded with the notes below.

> "Explain in a two- to three-page essay how a local environmental issue is relevant to the world community. Using *The College Writer* as your guide, format the paper and document sources in APA style, but omit the title page and abstract. You may seek revising help from a classmate or from the writing center."

■ Role

- *I'm writing as a student in Environmental Policies, and as a resident of Ontario.*

■ Subject

- *The subject is a recent environmental issue.*

■ Purpose

- *My purpose is to explain how the issue is relevant to all people. That means I must show how this issue affects my audience—both positively and negatively.*

■ Form

- *I need to write a two- to three-page essay—that sounds formal.*
- *I'll need to include a thesis statement, as well as references to my sources using APA style.*

■ Audience

- *My audience will be people like me—neighbors, classmates, and community members.*
- *I'll need to keep in mind what they already know and what they need to know.*

■ Context

- *I'll use the guidelines and checklists in <u>The College Writer</u> to evaluate and revise my writing.*
- *I'll get editing feedback from Jeanie and from the writing center.*

TIP: For each step in the writing process, choose strategies that fit your writing situation. For example, a personal essay in an English class might require significant time getting started, whereas a lab report in a chemistry class might require little or none.

Angela explored and narrowed her assignment. ■▪■

Angela explored her assignment and narrowed its focus by clustering and freewriting.

■ Angela's Cluster

When she considered environmental issues, Angela first thought of water pollution as a possible topic for her essay. After writing the phrase in the center of her page, she drew from memories, experiences, and readings to list related ideas and details. Notice how she used three different-colored inks to distinguish the topic (blue) from ideas (red) and details (green).

Video

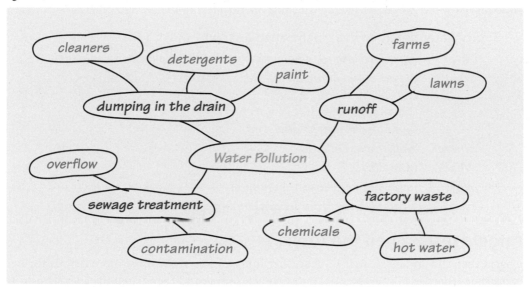

■ Angela's Freewriting

Angela decided to freewrite about the water pollution caused a few years earlier by improper sewage treatment in a small Canadian town.

> *I remember reading an article about problems in a small Canadian town. People actually died. The water they drank was contaminated. This is becoming a problem in developed countries like ours. I thought for a long time this was a problem only in developing countries. So who is responsible for sewage treatment? Who guarantees the safety of our drinking water? How does water get contaminated? Are there solutions for every kind of contamination: mercury, PCBs, sewage?*

■ Angela's Narrowed Assignment

Based on her freewriting, Angela rephrased her assignment to narrow its focus.

> *Explain in a two- to three-page essay how a recent water pollution problem in a small Canadian town is relevant to the world community.*

Angela's Planning

Audio

Video

Angela reviewed her narrowed assignment and reassessed her topic.

■ Narrowed Writing Assignment

Explain in a two- to three-page essay how a recent water pollution problem in a small Canadian town is relevant to the world community.

Angela focused her topic. ■ ■ ■

To focus her topic, Angela answered the journalistic questions (five Ws and H).

> **Topic: Water pollution in a small Canadian town**
>
> *Who?* - Farm operators, wastewater officials, Walkerton residents
>
> *What?* - Water supply contaminated
> - Spread bacteria (E. coli)
> - Caused disease
> - Clean, fresh water depleted
>
> *Where?* - Walkerton, Ontario
>
> *When?* - May 2000
>
> *Why?* - Improper regulation; human error
>
> *How?* - Groundwater from irrigation, untreated sewage, and runoff

Angela researched the topic. ■ ■ ■

Angela then did some research to check her information and collect more details for her paper. She recorded all the essential data on each source and then listed the specific details related to her topic. Here's one source:

> *CBC News. (2010, May 17) "Inside Walkerton: Canada's worst ever E. coli contamination." CBC News.*
>
> - *May 15—water sampled*
> - *May 17—first patients with flu-like symptoms*
> - *May 18—Lab confirms E. coli contamination in water, but Public Utilities Commission (PUC) does not report information.*
> - *May 19—Medical Health Office (MHO) discovers E. coli outbreak, but is assured by the PUC that the water is safe.*
> - *May 20—At least 40 people treated at hospital with bloody diarrhea, but PUC says twice that water is safe.*
> - *May 21—MHO tells people not to drink water, runs their own test.*
> - *May 23—MHO finds E. coli, learns of May 18 memo, and that chlorinator not working for some time.*
> - *May 24—Three adults and a baby die of E. coli.*

Video

Angela decided how to organize her writing. ▪ ▪ ▪

With a focus selected, Angela used the three guidelines below to choose the best organizational pattern for her writing.

■ **Guidelines**

1. **Review your assignment and record your response.**

> **Assignment:** Explain in a two- to three-page essay how a recent environmental issue is relevant to the world community.
>
> **Response:** *My assignment clearly states that I need to explain my topic, so I have a general idea of how my paper will be organized.*

2. **Decide on your thesis statement and think about your essay's possible content and organization.**

Video

> **Thesis Statement:** The water pollution incident in Walkerton, Ontario, had a devastating effect that every town should learn from.
>
> **Reflection:** *After reading my thesis statement, it's obvious that I'm going to be writing about a problem and its causes.*

3. **Choose an overall method and reflect on its potential effectiveness.**

> **Reflection:** *Looking at the list of methods, I see that I can use cause/ effect or problem/solution. After making two quick lists of my main points using both approaches, I decided to use a problem/ solution approach. I will still talk about causes and effects in my essay—they just won't be front and center.*
>
> *With problem/solution, I need to first present the problem clearly so that readers can fully understand it and see why it's important. Then I need to explore solutions to the problem—maybe what they did in Walkerton and what we all need to do to make water safe.*

TIP: Many essays you write will be organized according to one basic method or approach. However, within that basic structure you may want to include other methods. For example, while developing a comparison essay you may do some describing or classifying. In other words, you should choose methods of development that (1) help you understand the topic and (2) help your readers understand your message.

Video

Angela's First Draft

After composing her opening, middle, and closing paragraphs, Angela put together her first draft. She then added a working title.

Audio

Video

Video

The writer uses a series of images to get the reader's attention.

The thesis statement (boldfaced) introduces the subject.

The writer describes the cause of the problem.

The writer indicates some of her source material with a citation.

Water Woes

It's a hot day. Several people just finished mowing their
lawns. A group of bicyclists—more than 3,000—have been
passing through your picturesque town all afternoon. Dozens of
Little Leaguers are batting, running, and sweating. What do all
these people have in common? They all drinks lots of tap water,
especially on hot summer days. They also take for granted that
the water is clean and safe. But in reality, the water they drink
could be contaminated and pose a serious health risk. **That's just
what happened in Walkerton, Ontario, where a water pollution
incident had a devastating effect that every town can learn from.**

What happened in Walkerton Ontario? Heavy rains fell on
May 12. It wasn't until May 21 that the townspeople were
advised to boil their drinking water. The rains washed cattle
manure into the town well. The manure contained E coli, a type
of bacteria. E coli is harmless to cattle. It can make people sick.
Seven days after the heavy rains, people began calling public
health officials. The warning came too late. Two people had
already died (Wickens, 2000).

Once Walkerton's problem was identified, the solutions were
known. The government acted quickly to help the community
and to clean the water supply. One Canadian newspaper reported
that a $100,000 emergency fund was set up to help families
with expenses. Bottled water for drinking and containers
of bleach for sanitizing and cleaning were donated by local
businesses.

1

2

3

Video

So what messed up Walkerton? Basically, people screwed *4*
up! According to one news story, a flaw in the water treatment
system allowed the bacteria-infested water to enter the well.
The manure washed into the well, but the chlorine should have
killed the deadly bacteria. In Walkerton, the PUC group fell
asleep at the wheel.

> The writer covers the solutions that were used to resolve the problem.

At last, the Provincial Clean Water Agency restored the main *5*
water and sewage systems by flushing out all of the town's
pipes and wells. The ban on drinking Walkerton's water was
finally lifted seven months after the water became contaminated.

> The concluding paragraph stresses the importance of public awareness.

Could any good come from Walkerton's tragedy? Does it *6*
have a silver lining? It is possible that more people are aware
that water may be contaminated. Today people are beginning to
take responsibility for the purity of the water they and their
families drink. In the end, more and more people will know
about the dangers of contaminated water—without learning it
the hard way.

Angela kept a working bibliography. ■ ■ ■

As she researched her topic, Angela kept a working bibliography—a list of resources that she thought might offer information helpful to her essay. During the writing process, she deleted some resources, added others, and edited the document that became the references page on page 129.

Working References

CBC News. (2010, May 17). "Inside Walkerton: Canada's worst
ever E.coli contamination." *CBC News.*

Phone interview with Alex Johnson, Walkerton Police
Department, 23 September 2007.

Blackwell, Thomas (2001, January 9). Walkerton doctor defends
response. *The Edmonton Journal.*
http://edmontonjournal.com.

■ Angela's First Revision

Video

Audio

After finishing the first draft, Angela set it aside. When she was ready to revise it, she looked carefully at global issues—ideas, organization, and voice. She wrote notes to herself to help keep her thoughts together.

Angela's comments

I need to give my opening more energy.

Does my thesis still fit the paper?— Yes.

Using time sequence, put this paragraph in better order.

Move this paragraph —it interrupts the discussion of causes.

Water Woes

an unusually   Saturday afternoon ⊙
        It's ^a hot ~~day.~~ Several people just finished mowing their
pedal up the street ⊙
lawns. A group of bicyclists, ~~more than 3,000—have been~~
~~passing through your picturesque town all afternoon.~~ Dozens of
Little Leaguers are batting, running, and sweating. What do all
these people have in common? They all drink lots of tap water,
especially on hot summer days. They also take for granted that
the water is clean and safe. But in reality, the water they drink
could be contaminated and pose a serious health risk. That's just
what happened in Walkerton, Ontario, where a water pollution
incident had a devastating effect that every town can learn from.

        What happened in Walkerton, Ontario? Heavy rains fell on
May 12. [It wasn't until May 21 that the townspeople were
advised to boil their drinking water.] The rains washed cattle
manure into the town well. The manure contained E coli, a type
of bacteria. E coli is harmless to cattle. It can make people sick.
Seven days after the heavy rains, people began calling public
health officials. The warning came too late. Two people had
already died (Wickens, 2000).

        Once Walkerton's problem was identified, the solutions were
known. The government acted quickly to help the community
and to clean the water supply. One Canadian newspaper reported
that a $100,000 emergency fund was set up to help families
with expenses. Bottled water for drinking and containers of
bleach for sanitizing and cleaning were donated
by local businesses.

1

2

3

My voice here is too informal.

went wrong in   Human error was a critical factor.
So what ^ ~~messed up~~ Walkerton? ^ ~~Basically, people screwed~~

g First,
~~up!~~ ^ According to one news story, a flaw in the water treatment
Even after
system allowed the bacteria-infested water to enter the well. ^ The

manure washed into the well, ~~but~~ the chlorine should have killed

the deadly bacteria. In Walkerton, the ~~PUC group fell asleep at~~

~~the wheel.~~

Explain "fell asleep." Move paragraph three here and combine.

In addition
~~At last,~~ the Provincial Clean Water Agency restored the

main water and sewage systems by flushing out all of the

town's pipes and wells. The ban on drinking Walkerton's

water was finally lifted seven months after the water became

contaminated.

Cut the clichés.

Could any good come from Walkerton's tragedy? ~~Does it~~

~~have a silver lining?~~ It is possible that more people are aware

that water may be contaminated. Today people are beginning to

take responsibility for the purity of the water they and their

families drink. In the end, more and more people will know

about the dangers of contaminated water—without learning it

the hard way.

*Public Utilities Commission was responsible for overseeing
the testing and treating of the town's water, but they
failed to monitor it properly. Apparently, shortcuts were
taken when tracking the water's chlorine level, and as a
result, some of the water samples were mislabeled. There
was also a significant delay between the time that the
contamination was identified and the time it was reported.*

4

5

6

Video

Angela's Second Revision

Next, Angela asked a peer to review her work. His comments are in the margin. Angela used them to make additional changes, including writing a new opening and closing.

Reviewer's comments	Angela's changes

Water Woes

WARNING: City tap water is polluted with animal waste. Using the 1
water for drinking, cooking, or bathing could cause sickness or death.

Could you make the opening more relevant and urgent?

According to the Seirra Club, run-off pollutants from farm cites are 2
steadily seeping into our streams, lakes, reservoirs and wells. Because
much of our drinking water comes from these resources, warnings like
the one above are already posted in a number of U.S. and Canadian
communities, and many more postings will be needed (Sierra Club, 2005).
As the Seirra Club argues, the pollution and related warnings are serious,
and failure to take them seriously could be deadly. For example, a few
years ago the citizens of Walkerton Ontario learned that the water that
they believed to be clean was actually poisoned.

Could you clarify your focus on the topic?

The events   *began*
~~What happened~~ in Walkerton, ~~Ontario? Heavy rains fell~~ 3
                    , 2000, when heavy rains
on May 12, ~~The rains~~ washed cattle manure into the town well.
The manure contained E coli, a type of bacteria. E coli is
harmless to cattle. It can make people sick. Seven days after
                    to complain of nausea and diarrhea
the heavy rains, people began calling public health officials. It
wasn't until May 21 that the townspeople were advised to boil
their drinking water. The warning came too late. Two people had
         , and more than 2,000 were ill
already died (Wickens, 2000).

Add the year and other specific details.

Several factors contributed to the terrible tragedy in Walkerton, 4
~~So what went wrong in Walkerton? Human error was a~~
including human error.   *The Edmonton Journal*
~~critical factor.~~ First, according to ~~one news story~~, a flaw in the
water treatment system allowed the bacteria-infested water to
         (Blackwell, 2001)
enter the well. Even after the manure washed into the well, the

Make sure you document all source material—you have just one citation in your draft.

chlorine should have killed the deadly bacteria. In Walkerton, the
Public Utilities Commission was responsible for overseeing

the testing and treating of the town's water, but it failed to monitor it properly. Apparently, shortcuts were taken when tracking the water's chlorine level, and as a result, some of the water samples were mislabeled. There was also a significant delay between the time that the contamination was identified and the time it was reported.

Once Walkerton's problem was identified, ~~the solutions were known.~~ The government acted quickly to help the community ~~and to clean the water supply.~~ *The Edmonton Journal* ~~One Canadian newspaper~~ reported a $100,000 emergency fund was set up to help families with expenses. *Local businesses donated* Bottled water for drinking and containers of bleach for basic sanitizing and cleaning ~~were donated by local businesses.~~ In addition, the Provincial Clean Water Agency restored the main water and sewage systems by flushing out all of the town's pipes and wells. The ban on drinking Walkerton's water was finally lifted seven months after the water became contaminated.

4

As the Sierra Club warned and the citizens of Walkerton learned, water purity is a life-and-death issue. Fortunately, both the United States and Canada have been addressing the problem. For example, since 2001, more states and provinces are tightening their clean-water standards, more communities have begun monitoring their water quality, and more individuals have been using water-filtration systems, bottled water, or boiled tap water. However, a tragedy like that in Walkerton could happen again. To avoid such horror, all of us must get involved by demanding clean tap water in our communities and by promoting the polices and procedures needed to achieve that goal.

5

Use active voice.

Consider adding details—maybe an entire paragraph—calling readers to action, and stating your thesis clearly.

■ Angela's Edited Draft

When Angela began editing, she read each of her sentences aloud to check for clarity and smoothness. **The first page of Angela's edited copy is shown below.**

Video

Audio

The writer revises the title.

in Walkerton
Water Woes ∧

> *Warning: City tap water is polluted with animal waste. Using the water for drinking, cooking, or bathing could cause sickness or death.*

According to the Seirra Club, run-off pollutants from farm cites are steadily seeping into our streams, lakes, reservoirs ∧ and wells. Because much of our drinking water comes from these resources, warnings like the one above are already posted in a number of U.S. and Canadian communities, and many more

might   in the future

postings ~~will~~ be needed ∧ (Sierra Club, 2005). As the Seirra Club argues, the pollution and related warnings are serious, and failure to take them seriously could be deadly. For example, a few years ago the citizens of Walkerton Ontario learned that the

tragically

water that they believed to be clean was ∧ ~~actually~~ poisoned.

She qualifies her statement, replacing "will" with "might."

The events in Walkerton began on May 12, 2000, when heavy rains washed cattle manure into the town well. The manure

commonly called   While E coli

contained ~~E coli~~ a bacteria ∧ E coli ∧ is harmless to cattle ∧ It can make people sick. Seven days after the heavy rains, people began calling public health officials to complain of nausea and diarrhea. It wasn't until May 21 that the townspeople were advised to boil their drinking water. The warning came too late. Two people had already died, and more than 2,000 were ill (Wickens, 2000).

She rewrites and combines several choppy sentences.

Several factors contributed to the ~~terrible~~ tragedy in Walkerton, including human error. First, according to *The Edmonton Journal*, a flaw in the water treatment system allowed the ~~bacteria~~-infested water to enter the well (Blackwell, 2001). Even after the manure washed into the well, the chlorine . . .

Angela deletes unnecessary words.

1

2

3

▮ Angela's Proofread Draft

Angela reviewed her edited copy for punctuation, agreement issues, and spelling. **The first page of Angela's proofread essay is shown below.**

Video

Water Woes in Walkerton

> *Warning: City tap water is polluted with animal waste. Using the water for drinking, cooking, or bathing could cause sickness or death.*

The writer corrects errors that the spell checker did not pick up.

According to the Sierra Club, run-off pollutants from farm sites are steadily seeping into our streams, lakes, reservoirs, and wells. Because much of our drinking water comes from these resources, warnings like the one above are already posted in a number of U.S. and Canadian communities, and many more postings might be needed in the future (Sierra Club, 2005). As the Sierra Club argues, the pollution and related warnings are serious, and failure to take them seriously could be deadly.

She adds a comma between the city and province.

For example, a few years ago the citizens of Walkerton, Ontario, learned that the water that they believed to be clean was tragically poisoned.

She adds periods and italicizes "E. coli" to show that it is a scientific term.

The events in Walkerton began on May 12, 2000, when heavy rains washed cattle manure into the town well. The manure contained bacteria commonly called *E. coli*. While *E. coli* is harmless to cattle, it can make people sick. Seven days after the heavy rains, people began calling public health officials to complain of nausea and diarrhea. It wasn't until May 21 that the townspeople were advised to boil their drinking water. The warning came too late. Two people had already died, and more than 2,000 were ill (Wickens, 2000).

She adds a word for clarity.

Several factors contributed to the tragedy in Walkerton, including human error. First, according to *The Edmonton Journal*, a flaw in the water treatment system allowed the infested water to enter Walkerton's well (Blackwell, 2001). Even after the manure washed ~~into the well~~ *into Walkerton's well*, the chlorine should have . . .

1

2

3

Angela's Finished Essay

Video

Audio

After proofreading and formatting her essay, Angela added a heading and page numbers. She also added more documentation and a references page at the end. As assigned, she omitted the title page and abstract.

Running Head: CLEAN WATER IS EVERYONE'S BUSINESS   1

Angela Franco

Professor Kim Van Es

English 101

October 18, 2010

Clean Water Is Everyone's Business

> Warning: City tap water is polluted with animal waste. Using the water for drinking, cooking, or bathing could cause sickness or death.

According to the Sierra Club, run-off pollutants from farm sites are steadily seeping into our streams, lakes, reservoirs, and wells. Because much of our drinking water comes from these resources, warnings like the one above are already posted in a number of U.S. and Canadian communities, and many more postings might be needed in the future (Sierra Club, 2005). As the Sierra Club argues, the pollution and related warnings are serious, and failure to take them seriously could be deadly. For example, a few years ago the citizens of Walkerton, Ontario, learned that the water that they believed to be clean was tragically poisoned.

The events in Walkerton began on May 12, 2000, when heavy rains washed cattle manure into the town well. The

The writer revises the title.

The title is changed. The warning is emphasized with red print.

An appropriate font and type size are used.

CLEAN WATER IS EVERYONE'S BUSINESS   2

manure contained the bacteria commonly called *E. coli*. While *E. coli* is harmless to cattle, it can make people sick. Seven days after the heavy rains, people began calling public health officials to complain of nausea and diarrhea. It wasn't until May 21 that the townspeople were advised to boil their drinking water. The warning came too late. Two people had already died, and more than 2,000 were ill (Wickens, 2000).

Several factors contributed to the tragedy in Walkerton, including human error. First, according to *The Edmonton Journal*, a flaw in the water treatment system allowed the infested water to enter Walkerton's well (Blackwell, 2001). Even after the manure washed into Walkerton's well, the chlorine should have killed the deadly bacteria. In Walkerton, the Public Utilities Commission was responsible for overseeing the testing and treating of the town's water, but it failed to monitor the procedure properly ("Walkerton's water-safety," 2000). Apparently, shortcuts were taken when tracking the water's chlorine level, and as a result, some of the water samples were mislabeled. There was also a significant delay between the time that the contamination was identified and the time it was reported.

Once Walkerton's problem was identified, the government acted quickly to help the community. In its December 7, 2000, edition, *The Edmonton Journal* reported that a $100,000 emergency fund was set up to help families with expenses. Local businesses donated bottled water for drinking and containers of bleach for basic sanitizing and cleaning. In addition, the Provincial

Clean Water Agency restored the main water and sewage systems by flushing out all of the town's pipes and wells. Seven months after the water became contaminated, the ban on drinking Walkerton's water was finally lifted.

As the Sierra Club warns and the citizens of Walkerton learned, water purity is a life-and-death issue. Fortunately, both the United States and Canada have been addressing the problem. For example, since 2001, more states and provinces have been tightening their clean-water standards, more communities have been monitoring their water quality, and more individuals have been using water-filtration systems, bottled water, or boiled tap water. However, a tragedy like that in Walkerton could happen again. To avoid such horror, all of us must get involved by demanding clean tap water in our communities and by promoting the policies and procedures needed to achieve that goal.

5

The writer restates her thesis in the last sentence.

CLEAN WATER IS EVERYONE'S BUSINESS   4

References

Sources used are listed correctly, in alphabetical order.

Blackwell, T. (2001, January 9). Walkerton doctor defends response. *The Edmonton Journal*. Retrieved September 22, 2010, from <http://edmontonjournal.com>.

Sierra Club. (n.d.) Water sentinels: Keeping it clean around the U.S.A. Retrieved September 24, 2008, from <http://sierraclub.org/watersentinels/>.

Each entry follows APA rules for content, format, and punctuation.

Walkerton's water-safety tests falsified regularly, utility official admits. (2000, December 7). *The Edmonton Journal*. Retrieved April 2, 2005, from <http://edmontonjournal.com>.

Wickens, D. (2000, June 5). Tragedy in Walkerton. *Maclean's*, *113*(23), 34–36.

Critical-Thinking and Writing Activities

Complete these activities by yourself or with classmates.

1. Scott Russell Sanders suggests that "essays are experiments in making sense of things." Does Sanders' statement ring true? What makes such experiments flop or succeed? What kinds of "sense" do essays create?

2. Review Angela's writing process. How does it compare with your own writing process on a recent assignment?

3. Review the peer-editing instructions in "Revising Collaboratively" (pages 89–90). Then reread the reviewer's comments in the margins of Angela's second revision (pages 122–123). Do the comments reflect the instructions? Explain.

Cross-Curricular Connections

Angela used APA style, which is standard for the social sciences: psychology, sociology, political science, and education. MLA style is standard for English and humanities. Make sure to find out what documentation style your instructor requires.

Learning-Outcomes Checklist

_____ I understand how to analyze an assignment and select a topic.

- I read assignments closely, noting key words.
- I think about the rhetorical situation—role, subject, purpose, form, audience, and context.
- I explore topics, using graphic organizers, and I narrow the topic by writing a thesis statement.

_____ I understand how to research my topic and plan my writing.

- I gather information from a variety of sources and take notes to track the sources.
- I organize my writing by revisiting the assignment, the thesis statement, and the likely method of organization I will use.

_____ I understand how to write a first draft.

- I write an opening that gets the reader's attention and introduce my thesis.
- I create a middle that develops my thesis, organizing details according to my plan.
- I draft an ending that wraps up the essay in a meaningful way.

_____ I understand how to revise my material.

- I think in terms of the global traits—ideas, organization, and voice.
- I add, cut, reorganize, and rewrite material to make it work better.

_____ I understand how to get a peer response and complete a second revision.

- I provide my draft to a reviewer and ask for specific suggestions for improvement of ideas, organization, and voice.
- I weigh each suggestion and make more changes to address the issues.

_____ I understand how to edit the revised draft.

- I focus on word choice, using specific nouns and vivid verbs and avoiding weak wording.
- I focus on sentences, creating effective style through sentence variety and avoiding sentence errors.

_____ I understand how to proofread the draft.

- I check the conventions of punctuation, mechanics, spelling, and usage.
- I ask another person to help me find errors.

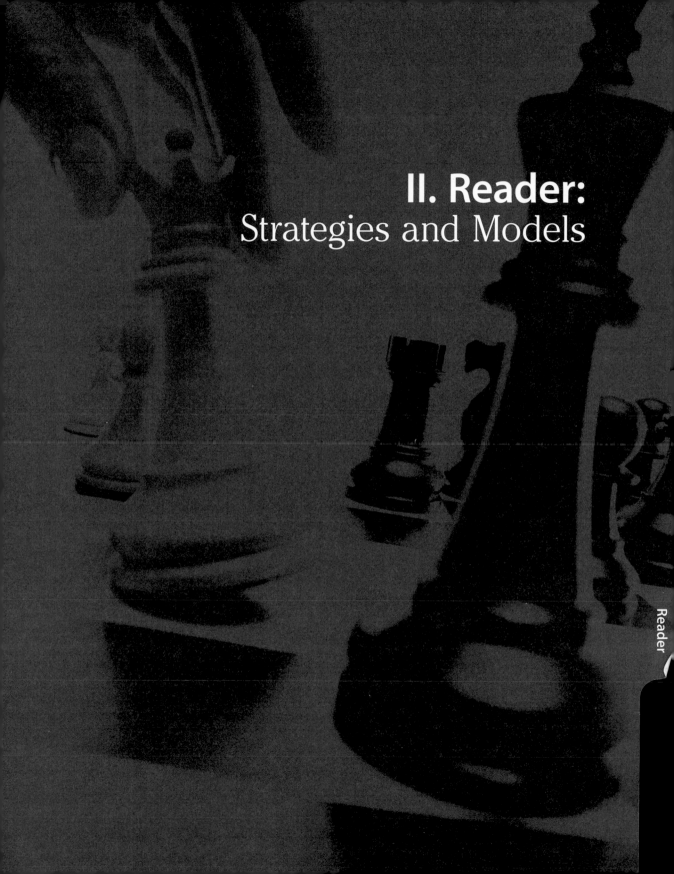

II. Reader:
Strategies and Models

Writing Across the Curriculum

9 Forms of College Writing

In college, professors in nearly all departments give writing assignments. Why? Because they know that writing helps you learn course material today and use that information in subsequent college courses and in the workplace.

The chapter begins by showing the big picture: the three divisions into which most college curricula are divided, and the academic departments that constitute each division. The chapter then presents more specific information about academic departments, including the topics students study, the forms of writing teachers assign, and the traits of those forms.

Learning Outcomes

Video

▶ Understand how a college curriculum and faculty are organized.

▶ Understand what kind of writing you can expect to do in your courses.

▶ Understand how writing and thinking skills are connected throughout the curriculum.

Visually Speaking ▶ What does the photograph above suggest about the forms of writing assigned in college courses?

■ Three Curricular Divisions

Based on each department's area of study, the college curriculum is generally divided into three groups: humanities, social sciences, and natural and applied sciences. These groups are then subdivided into specific departments, such as biology, chemistry, and physics. Below you will find an explanation of each division, along with its common departments.

Humanities ■"■

Scholars within this division study human culture, both past and present. They examine topics such as the history of civilization, cultural institutions and trends, religious beliefs and practices, languages and their use, and artwork and performance skills. Some departments in this division include the following:

Archeology	Ethnic Studies	Modern Languages	Theater Arts
Asian Studies	Film Studies	Music	Theology
Dance	Graphic Design	Philosophy	Visual Arts
English	History	Religion	Women's Studies

Social Sciences ■"■

Scholars in this division study human behavior and societies using research strategies adapted from the natural sciences. For example, a researcher may develop a hypothesis regarding a topic or phenomenon, and then devise an experiment to test that hypothesis. Students study economic systems, correctional programs, and personality disorders. Departments in this division include the following:

Anthropology	Economics	Geophysics	Psychology
Business	Education	Government	Social Work
Communication	Genetics	Health & Phys. Ed.	Sociology
Criminology	Geography	Political Science	Urban Planning

Natural and Applied Sciences ■"■

The natural sciences (such as biology, zoology, and chemistry) focus on specific aspects of nature, such as animal life, plant life, and molecular structures. In contrast, the applied sciences (such as mathematics, computer science, and engineering) consider how to use science-based information to understand concepts and develop artifacts. Here are some of the departments in this division:

Agriculture	Biology	Environment	Physics
Agronomy	Botany	Forestry	Physiology
Anatomy	Chemistry	Mathematics	Public Health
Architecture	Computer Science	Nutrition	Space Science
Astronomy	Engineering	Oceanography	Zoology

■ Types of Writing in Each Division

Listed below are the types of writing commonly assigned in the three academic divisions. Often instructors in different divisions will assign the same type of essay—but with a different purpose, audience, or focus. When an assigned form differs from the one shown in the book, adapt the guidelines in the book to the form stated in the assignment.

Humanities ■ ▪ ▪

Anecdotes (143)
Application Writing (382–388)
Cause and Effect (163–180)
Classification (201–214)
Comparison and Contrast (181–200)
Definition (231–246)
Describing a Process (215–230)
Essay Test (365–375)
Interview Report (325–332)
Literary Analysis (349–364)

Narration, Description, and Reflection (141–160)
Oral Presentations (401–410)
Personal Essay (141–160)
Persuading Readers to Act (287–304)
Proposing a Solution (305–322)
Research Paper (491–528)
Taking a Position (265–286)
Test Taking (365–375)
Web Writing (389–400)

Social Sciences ■ ▪ ▪

Abstracts/Summaries (436–438, 547)
Application Writing (382–388)
Cause and Effect (163–180)
Classification (201–214)
Comparison and Contrast (181–200)
Definition (231–246)
Describing a Process (215–230)
Field Report (341–343)
Interview Report (325–332)
Oral Presentations (401–410)

Personal Essay (141–160)
Persuading Readers to Act (287–304)
Proposing a Solution (305–322)
Research Paper (529–558)
Research Proposal (420–421)
Surveys (444–445)
Taking a Position (265–286)
Test Taking (365–375)
Web Writing (389–400)

Natural and Applied Sciences ■ ▪ ▪

Abstracts/Summaries (436–438, 547)
Application Writing (382–388)
Cause and Effect (163–180)
Classification (201–214)
Comparison and Contrast (181–200)
Definition (231–246)
Describing a Process (215–230)
Experiment Report (335–340)
Field Report (341–343)
Interview Report (325–332)

Lab Report (334–340)
Personal Essay (141–160)
Persuading Readers to Act (287–304)
Proposing a Solution (305–322)
Research Paper (529–558)
Research Proposal (420–421)
Surveys (444–445)
Test Taking (365–375)
Web Writing (389–400)

Traits of Writing Across the Curriculum

Listed below are the more common writing tasks in each of the three divisions, along with seven traits that distinguish good writing for each task.

Humanities

Idea:	**Personal writing:** Explores the writer's ideas, experiences, and feelings
Organization:	Usually chronological
Voice:	Engaging, fits the story, honest, direct
Word Choice:	Words are precise and fit the writer's topic, purpose, audience, and characters
Sentences:	Appropriate for dialogue and description; others use varied forms
Correctness:	Documentation (where necessary) follows MLA or CMS style
Design:	Designed as an essay with proper formatting and typeface

Idea:	**Analysis of a work of art:** Describes the work and analyzes its parts and how they function
Organization:	Appropriate for the work and the writer's focus
Voice:	Objective appraisal and analysis, supported by evidence
Word Choice:	Appropriate for the art form; technical terms explained
Sentences:	Varied in length and structure, with clear transitions
Correctness:	Documentation follows MLA or CMS style
Design:	Designed as an essay with proper formatting and typeface

Idea:	**Argument supporting a claim:** Persuades reader regarding the point's meaning, importance, and truth
Organization:	Order fits the topic and purpose: cause/effect, compare/contrast, and so on
Voice:	Informed, impartial, inviting
Word Choice:	Precise, with scholarly terms used in the discipline
Sentences:	Tend to be longer; complexity fits the topic and audience
Correctness:	Documentation follows MLA or CMS style
Design:	Designed as an essay with proper formatting and typeface

Idea:	**Analysis of a phenomenon:** Explains its meaning in relation to its historical, social, and/or natural context (e.g., Marxism)
Organization:	Often combines cause/effect, compare/contrast, and examples
Voice:	Scholarly, fair, informed, balanced
Word Choice:	Precise, often including scholarly terms used in the discipline
Sentences:	Tend to be longer; complexity fits the topic and audience
Correctness:	Documentation follows MLA or CMS style
Design:	Designed as an essay with proper formatting, typeface, and graphics

Social Sciences ■▪■

Idea:	**Case study:** Describes and analyzes the topic, identifies methodology, gives results
Organization:	Gives overview, presents steps chronologically, analyzes outcome
Voice:	Impartial reporting; respectful, thoughtful analysis
Word Choice:	Precise statistics and discipline-related terms
Sentences:	Medium-length sentences with clear transitions
Correctness:	Documentation follows APA or CMS style
Design:	Formatted as a report for easy reading and in accordance with the discipline's or department's style guide

Idea:	**Literature review:** Summarizes and evaluates journal articles (usually research based) on a topic
Organization:	Each article discussed separately followed by conclusions
Voice:	Unbiased reporting, formal tone, logical analysis
Word Choice:	Includes precise technical terms and statistics
Sentences:	Shorter sentences and paragraphs with clear transitions
Correctness:	Documentation follows APA or CMS style
Design:	Formatted as a report for easy reading and in accordance with the discipline's or department's style guide

Idea:	**Policy or project analysis:** Analyzes the topic, its history, and its effects
Organization:	Analysis often uses cause/effect, classification, and compare/contrast
Voice:	Impartial, informed, concerned, thoughtful
Word Choice:	Includes precise technical terms and statistics
Sentences:	Sentences are varied in length and structure, with clear transitions
Correctness:	Documentation follows APA or CMS style
Design:	Formatted as a report for easy reading and in accordance with the discipline's or department's style guide

Idea:	**Process description:** Describes materials, steps in the process, and the importance of the process
Organization:	Usually states topic and outcome, gives steps chronologically
Voice:	Objective, yet concerned about effectiveness and safety
Word Choice:	Precise, often including technical terms
Sentences:	Description of a process—sentences tend to be short, direct, and in parallel form
Correctness:	Documentation follows APA or CMS style
Design:	Formatted as a report for easy reading and in accordance with the discipline's or department's style guide, or as workplace instructions with numbered steps and graphics

Natural and Applied Sciences ■▪▪

Idea: **Lab or experiment report:** Includes clear data, logical analysis, unbiased reporting

Organization: States issues and hypothesis, methods with procedure, results with data, discusses results

Voice: Interested, curious, impartial, logical, meticulous

Word Choice: Precise, often including scientific and technical terms

Sentences: Medium length, logical, passive voice only when needed

Correctness: Documentation and format follow CSE or APA style

Design: Formatted as a report in accordance with the discipline's style guide; graphics (such as tables, charts) are clear

---

Idea: **Field report:** Includes clear data and unbiased reporting

Organization: States focus and issues, methods with procedure, results with data, discusses results

Voice: Interested, curious, logical, meticulous

Word Choice: Precise, often including scientific and technical terms

Sentences: Medium length, logical, passive voice only when needed

Correctness: Documentation and format follow CSE or APA style

Design: Formatted as a report in accordance with the discipline's style guide; graphics (such as tables, photos) are strong

---

Idea: **Literature review:** Summarizes and compares journal articles (usually research based)

Organization: Each article discussed separately, followed by conclusions

Voice: Equitable reporting, formal tone, logical, clear analysis

Word Choice: Includes technical scientific words and concepts; first person rarely used

Sentences: Shorter sentences and paragraphs with clear transitions

Correctness: Documentation and format follow CSE or APA style

Design: Formatted as a report with proper spacing and typeface

---

Idea: **Process explanation:** Describes each step in a process

Organization: Usually states topic, gives steps chronologically, closes

Voice: Impartial, concerned about effectiveness and safety

Word Choice: Precise, often including scientific and technical terms

Sentences: Description of a process—sentences vary depending on the form; instructions—short, direct

Correctness: Documentation follows CSE or APA style

Design: Formatted as an essay or workplace instructions

---

fyi

Research and Documentation Websites

MLA Modern Language Association **www.mla.org**

APA American Psychological Association **www.apa.org**

CMS Chicago Manual of Style **www.press.uchicago.edu**

CSE Council of Science Editors **councilscienceeditors.org**

Note: CSE has replaced CBE *(Council of Biology Editors)*

Narrative, Descriptive, and Reflective Writing

Chapter 10 offers instruction in writing personal essays, pieces that focus on experience, especially the writer's experience—whether of places, people, or events—with the goal of vividly sharing that experience with readers. To that end, personal essays tend to be informal in voice and style, freely using personal pronouns such as "I" and "we." Note, too, that such writing depends on strategies of narration, description, and reflection.

As with all forms of writing, you should develop your personal essays using whatever strategies fit your writing situation: your subject, audience, and purpose. For examples, watch how the authors of the essays in chapter 10 use not only the strategies for narration, description, and reflection (commonly associated with personal writing), but also the strategies for cause/effect, compare/contrast, and definition (often associated with analytical writing).

Narrative, Descriptive, and Reflective Writing

Narration, Description, and Reflection

Personal narratives tell stories—not ones that the writers made up, but ones that they lived. Whatever the topics, the stories should help readers see, hear, touch, and taste those details that make the experiences come alive. To do that, writers must carefully describe key aspects of the experience. But they might also reflect on why the experiences are important—exploring their personal and shared meanings.

When reading such personal essays, do so with an open mind—seeking to go where writers guide you, to experience what they carefully describe, and to analyze how they craft their work.

As you prepare to write your own story, get ready to relive it yourself—to reexperience all that you felt, thought, or sensed during the event. In addition, be ready to learn something new about the experience, about others, and even about yourself.

Learning Outcomes

▶ Understand the elements of narrative writing: setting, character, plot, dialogue, and theme.

▶ Understand the nature and use of anecdotes.

▶ Know the traits and functions of reflective writing.

▶ Know the traits and functions of descriptive writing.

▶ Use strategies like these to write a personal essay.

Audio

Video

Video

Video

Visually Speaking ▶ Study the photograph above. Can you imagine a story associated with this image? How might a photograph of your own inspire a personal narrative?

Web Link

Reading Personal Essays

The strategies below will help you read personal essays—writing that blends narration, description, and reflection.

Consider the rhetorical situation. ▪▪▪

Think about the writer's purpose, audience, and topic, and how these might be linked.

- **Purpose:** Writers develop personal essays to explore meaningful aspects of life— people, experiences, and things that they care for and are shaped by.
- **Audience:** Most personal essays are written for a general audience, with the writer hoping that readers will empathize with and connect to the writer's experience.
- **Topic:** In personal essays, writers address any topics that they find meaningful and worth exploring through the lens of personal experience and reflection.

Consider the writer's strategies. ▪▪▪

For personal essays, writers primarily use **narration**, **description**, and **reflection**, but they often combine these strategies with others such as compare/contrast and definition.

- **Narration:** Well-written narratives are stories that include the following:

> **Characters** who are well-developed, often complex, and engaging
>
> **Dialogue** that indicates who characters are and what they think and say about themselves, others, and life itself
>
> **Action** that includes conflicts and shows what characters do; usually it is organized chronologically, though it may start in the middle or flash back; often the action reveals that characters are not who they think or say they are
>
> **Settings** that often influence—and sometimes reflect—the characters and action; time and place anchor the experience naturally and culturally

Video

- **Description:** Effective descriptive passages offer precise details that help readers sensually and thoughtfully experience the topic. In addition, figurative language such as metaphors, similes, and symbols commonly enrich the text.
- **Reflection:** Strong reflective passages relay the writers' observations and insights regarding the nature, impact, and value of their experiences.

Reader's Checklist

_____ Why does the writer care about the topic, and how is he or she affected by it?

_____ What ideas or themes evolve from the story? Explain.

_____ Are the characters' actions and dialogue believable and consistent?

_____ Is the description concise, precise, informing, and engaging?

■ Brief Narratives: Anecdotes

A common narrative is the anecdote—a brief story that enlivens your writing while introducing a topic or illustrating an idea. Read the anecdotes below, along with the essays from which they are taken. Then assess the anecdotes' effectiveness.

Video

Anecdote Introducing a Topic ■ ▪ ▪

> The other day, my wife, watching our son-in-law with his large hands gracefully tie the shoelaces of his little daughter, remarked, "You really are deft." Ever the cynic, I remarked, "He's not only deft, he's daft." I talk that sort of nonsense frequently, but as I said this, I began to wonder. What if *deft* and *daft* come from the same root and once meant the same thing? A quick trip to the dictionary showed that, indeed, they did once mean the same thing (though my wife thought me daft when I first suggested it).
>
> From "Deft or Daft," page 235

Anecdote Illustrating a Point ■ ▪ ▪

> LAST week, the Senate majority leader, Harry Reid, found himself in trouble for once suggesting that Barack Obama had a political edge over other African-American candidates because he was "light-skinned" and had "no Negro dialect, unless he wanted to have one." Mr. Reid was not expressing sadness but a gleeful opportunism that Americans were still judging one another by the color of their skin, rather than—as the Rev. Dr. Martin Luther King Jr., whose legacy we commemorated on Monday, dreamed—by the content of their character.
>
> From "Shades of Prejudice," page 189

Anecdote Illustrating a Trait ■ ▪ ▪

> Jackie Thomas, Nike's associate director of sports marketing, usually spends her lunch hour on the sports-shoe company's basketball courts charging for the basket, always outnumbered by male colleagues. "I hold my own," boasts the 33-year-old executive.
>
> She also does well playing the corporate game back inside the headquarter's offices. Thomas, a former University of California—Berkeley college basketball point guard, says her success is due in large part to the lessons she learned growing up playing competitive team sports. "It's taught me that if you lose a game, you go back afterward and figure out what went wrong and how to overcome it the next time," says the former tomboy from Kingston, Jamaica.
>
> While most of America's corporations are still commanded by male chief executives, women are gaining ground, winning vice-presidential and top management slots and, in a few cases, the highest leadership roles. Many of these young female executives say playing team sports helped them get ahead.
>
> From "If You Let Me Play . . . ," page 170

Narration, Description, and Reflection ■ ▪ ■

In this essay, student writer Robert Minto recalls a series of events through which he learned something about his community, himself, and the nature of life. Note that following his introduction, Minto uses chronological order to organize his narrative.

Essay Outline

Introduction: Setting, key characters, and conflict: moths (such as Ryan) vs. spiders (such as Old Jack)

1. Narrator goes to Ryan's house.
2. They stop at narrator's house, pass church, arrive at cemetery.
3. They explore cemetery and discuss spirits.
4. They hear moaning and move toward it.
5. They see Old Jack's grandson and a girl.
6. They return to bikes and ride past church to Ryan's house.

Closing: Narrator tells Old Jack about grandson and girl and then reflects on the moth/spider conflict.

The title forecasts a study of insects.

Introduction: setting, key characters, and conflict: moths (such as Ryan) vs. spiders (such as Old Jack)

Ryan, a moth

The Entomology of Village Life

Buddy didn't know that we were clichés. I knew. I liked it that way. We spent our days together—me too inquisitive and his tail always wagging. My neighbor, Old Jack, who was forever pulling weeds in his garden, self-exiled from a sharp-tongued wife, was a cliché too. So was the grange on the other side of my house. Most of the men in Naymari, Pennsylvania, never missed a grange meeting, mainly to supervise the village's one employee, Pedro, who mowed the grass in the park. Within this small web of places and personalities, life abounded. Some people were the moths, tied down and struggling; some were the spiders, growing fat on gossip.

One of the moths lived across the street. He was my friend Ryan. Ryan lived in the dirtiest house I've ever seen. His mother cared for him and for two younger, mentally disabled boys as well. She had a big heart but too few hands and no husband. In the winter, they all huddled around a kerosene heater, wearing most of the clothing they owned, the two youngest boys often licking the snot that dripped from their cold noses. They couldn't afford oil. Through a government program, Ryan had received an old IBM computer. He spent most of his time playing Tetris on it in his room. Sometimes when Buddy and I got up early in the morning to roam the village, we'd stop outside Ryan's window, and I'd toss pebbles at it. (His mother and I had this understanding that I could get him up to play, but because she slept in later than we did, I couldn't yell.) Soon his bleary eyes would peer over the sill. Eventually he'd come out, and I'd lead him off on

1

2

some adventure.

Old Jack, on the other hand, was one of Naymeri's spiders. His garden wasn't merely a refuge from his wife, but it was also the epicenter of his web. At the slightest hint of gossip, he'd scurry down the street with a twine-wrapped bundle of asparagus, his specialty, to gain entry into whatever home promised the best information. With most people, me included, Jack gossiped on a strictly business model. He'd tell me his latest and juiciest stories and in return, I'd offer him—as keeper of the town's skeleton closet—whatever my wandering uncovered. It was Jack who told me, with relish, the acrimonious story of how Ryan's family had broken apart. He enjoyed the telling. *3*

Old Jack also hated abortion, but not because of religion—he hated that too. One time, standing in his asparagus and gesturing with a weed, he told me why. *4*

"You seen those hooded graves?" he asked. *5*

"What graves?" I said, holding Buddy so he wouldn't pee on Jack's onions. *6*

"You haven't seen 'em? The graves with cages across the way at the Methodist church?" *7*

"Oh, *those*. Sure, I've seen 'em." *8*

"Do you know why they got cages?" *9*

"Why?" *10*

Jack shook his weed again, and a little shower of dirt crumbled off it. "Because," he said, "if you go over there at night and listen, you can hear the spirits of aborted children screaming to get out and hurt the people who killed 'em!" *11*

I shivered. Buddy licked my face. *12*

A few minutes later I was tossing pebbles at Ryan's window. Eventually he staggered out of the house. *13*

"Hey Ryan," I said quietly, "want an adventure?" *14*

Ryan thought that was a good idea, but he wanted to know if he should bring anything. Last adventure we got all wet in a stream, and he wished he'd brought some boots. *15*

"Nah," I told him, "we're just gonna listen to some spirits." *16*

We stopped by my house to get a paper bag filled with Swiss-and-ham-on-rye and a smoked pig's ear for Buddy. Then we grabbed our bikes and headed east toward the park, the cemetery, and the Methodist church. We left our bikes in the gravel parking lot by the church. We could see the pastor in the big glass window of his study. He had his head on his arms, sleeping. *17*

The hooded graves were at the far edge of the cemetery, right beside the woods that harbored our park. The unmowed grass beside these graves suggested that they might not be part of the cemetery. Ryan and I waded through the grass and peered past the wire mesh that caged the white stones. Because they were worn smooth by rain, any carved writing on the stones was long gone. I tugged on one of the cages until Ryan nervously told me to stop. He needn't have—I couldn't *18*

Marginal annotations:

Old Jack, a spider

1 Narrator goes to Ryan's house.

2 They stop at narrator's house, pass the church, and arrive at cemetery.

3 They explore cemetery and discuss spirits.

budge it. It was firmly planted in the hard earth.

"When do we hear the spirits?" asked Ryan.   *19*

"When the sun goes down," I told him, "I think." We walked over to a big *20* oak tree on the edge of the woods where we could see the graves better. The tree had several nice boles to sit in. I told Ryan the rest of what Jack had told me. We agreed that the children's spirits might want to get even, but Ryan doubted that the spirits could really do that.

"Don't you believe in spirits?" I asked. Of course he did—he went to the *21* Presbyterian church.

"I've *seen* one, too!" said Ryan. "I was in my room when we lived in Florida. *22* That was before we left my dad. I slept upstairs in the attic there, just like here. I was laying in bed when I heard something coming up the stairs and scratching at the door. Then the door opened and a big white thing came in and stood by the bed. I closed my eyes and prayed, and when I opened 'em the thing was gone."

I told him it was probably just his dad. Or maybe his mom.   *23*

"No," he said, "because I got really cold when it came in, and I felt like I *24* couldn't move." We were silent, me imagining, him remembering.

"Then why don't you believe that we'll hear the spirits?" I asked.   *25*

"Why don't you believe in the ghost I saw?" he replied.   *26*

I saw his point. But somehow his story just didn't seem as vivid as Old *27* Jack's story about children's spirits out for revenge. Now *that* one would give me nightmares!

4 They hear moaning and move toward it.

Suddenly I noticed that I couldn't hear Buddy. He'd been nosing around *28* the trees, scratching at the dirt, sniffing at mole-holes, snapping at dandelions. I looked around and saw him standing, stiff. He was staring into the woods. As I turned to follow his gaze I heard a moan.

Ryan jumped. We looked at each other. The moan again. We looked at the *29* hooded graves, but there was nothing to see.

"Did you let it out when you pulled on the cage?" asked Ryan. Then he added, *30* "But didn't you say we wouldn't hear 'em til the sun went *down*?"

The moan again. It seemed to be coming from the grove of trees at our *31* back. We turned toward the sound, and I started to worm forward on my belly into the trees. "Stay," I told Buddy. Ryan obeyed the command as well for about ten seconds, and then he started worming forward too, grumbling quietly. The damp earth was covered with crunchy leaves, but we were small and had practice sneaking.

As we neared the sound, it became more frequent, and then we heard a sort of *32* ragged breathing joining in, like a duet. But it didn't sound like spirits.

5 They see Old Jack's grandson and a girl.

Then we came to a place where we could see something through the trees. It *33* was a zebra-striped car with spinners on the wheels. On top of the car, awkwardly straddling a dark-haired girl, Old Jack's grandson, Jim, was doing his best to make her moan louder. The ragged breathing was his. He jerked up and down, and I could see the silver flash of the car's antenna between them each time they separated. Me and Ryan froze for a few seconds before comprehension struck. Glancing wildly at each other, we squirmed away.

6 They return to bikes and ride past church to Ryan's house.

When we reached the edge of the wood, we stood up and made our way back *34* to our bikes. Somehow, waiting for the spirits had lost its appeal. I glanced at the Methodist church and saw the pastor was awake, waving at us through the window. We pedaled quietly back to town. I imagined that even Buddy seemed subdued. When we reached Ryan's house, he stopped and laid his bike on the grass. We could hear his mom inside, talking to his brothers.

Ryan began to walk up the lawn, back to his Tetris. Then he stopped, turned *35* around and asked, "What are you gonna do?"

I thought for a moment. Then I told him. *36*

About an hour later, I finished telling Old Jack what we'd seen. He was *37* watering his tomatoes, and as I talked, I noticed that one of the plants was nearly floating even though he was staring right at it. I finished up, and he went right on watering that same plant.

Closing: Narrator tells Old Jack about grandson and girl and then reflects on the moth/spider conflict.

Then he glanced over at me and said, "That's very interesting." He *38* contemplated the drowning plant again and added, "But this isn't something to get around town, you know. You wouldn't tell anybody else, would ya?"

I thought for a moment. Then I smiled. *39*

Somewhere, a spider was about to become a moth. *40*

Reading for Better Writing

Working by yourself or with a group, answer these questions:

1. Review the title, "The Entomology of Village Life." Then explain what *entomology* is and why it is (or is not) a good choice for this essay.

2. In the opening paragraph, the writer refers to himself and other village residents as *clichés*. Define *cliché* and explain why the writer might use this term. Does the essay show the characters to be clichés? Explain.

3. In the second paragraph, the writer refers to village residents as moths and spiders. Explain what he might mean by these metaphors and the effect of his using them to open and close the essay.

4. Identify a narrative passage, a descriptive passage, and a reflective passage that you consider well written. Explain why.

5. What is the essay's main idea or theme? How does the writer introduce the idea and develop it?

6. Re-read the essay's last sentence and explain why it is (or is not) an effective closing.

Narration, Description, and Reflection ■■·■

"Spare Change" is the first part of student writer Teresa Zsuffa's "A Diary of Chance Encounters," an essay that explores her experiences of living in Toronto. The piece below recounts a challenging encounter with the face of poverty. For Teresa's full essay, go to **www.thecollegewriter.com/4e.**

"Spare Change"

The writer describes an urban setting and a common situation.

This grime is infectious. The smell of old cigarettes and expired perfume is constricting my throat and turning my stomach. But here I am again on the underground subway platform, changing trains at Bloor-Yonge in Toronto, the weight of my backpack thrusting me forward with the Friday morning rush hour crowd. When the subway doors open I hurry inside and look around frantically, as usual. There is an empty seat to my left, but everyone is keeping a safe four-foot distance, as if the seat will suck them in and destroy them if they sit down. Or at least destroy the facade put on with a Ralph Lauren suit, a Coach handbag, or a pair of authentic Gucci sunglasses. Not like the fake five-dollar ones I picked up from a Chinatown vendor just yesterday. The others keep their starry distance; when I sit down, I see why. *1*

She introduces the central person through concrete details, her words, and the reactions of others (including the writer's own mixed feelings).

She must be about twenty-nine. Her orange track-pants are worn and faded, her T-shirt is far too big, and her powder blue sweatshirt is tied around her waist. Her face and teeth are stained, hair greasy and unkempt. A part of me feels sorry for her. Another part follows the crowd and is careful not to make eye contact. *2*

"Excuse me," she says, perching on the edge of her seat, leaning forward and clasping the metal pole with two hands. No one turns. "Excuse me, which stop do I take to the Old City Hall?" One man shrugs and shakes his head while pretending to check his phone. I feel guilt, but it's easily subdued. After all, she wasn't asking me. *3*

I am deeply engrossed in my Nicholas Sparks novel by the time the driver announces "Dundas Station." As I stuff the book back into my purse and make my way towards the doorway, I'm irritated to see that she also stands up—one stop early for Old City Hall. Doesn't she know she should stay on until Queen? Oh well, she'll figure it out, I reason. The Toronto Transit Commission officers can help her. *4*

I let her off the subway before me. Finally I'm free. *5*

The writer narrates the events and dialogue that lead her to offer help.

But then she stops on the platform and turns her head, like a puppy making sure her owner is following close behind. No eye contact, I remind myself, and try to walk past but she falls into step with me. *6*

"Can I help you carry your bag?" *7*

I may look like a tourist, but I'm smarter. "No, thanks," I reply. *8*

"Well it just looks pretty heavy." We reach the escalator and the staircase and I take the left side, where I can climb the steps and go up twice as fast as those just standing there on the right and enjoying the ride. But it doesn't work; the woman is still at my heels. *9*

"Are you going somewhere?" she asks.   *10*

"Yeah, I have to get to the Greyhound station, I'm going out of town."   *11*

"Oh." Now we are standing in front of the underground entrance to the   *12*
Eaton Center. The Atrium on Bay is to my right, on the other side of which is the
bus station and my ticket out of this alien city that is now my home. The woman
stands frozen and looks around trying to get her bearings. I start to walk away
but hesitate. Looking back, I see her blinking and flinching as people shove past
her. She reminds me of a small child lost at a summer carnival.

I check my watch—quarter past eight. I just missed an express shuttle, and   *13*
the next bus to Niagara Falls, where my father lives, won't be leaving for another
forty-five minutes. Something pulls me back to the woman, and against all sworn
Torontonian rules, I ask if she needs help.

Her dull brown eyes light up. "I need to find the Old City Hall."   *14*

"Okay," I nod. "I'll take you." I lead her through the glass doors into the city's   *15*
busiest mall. It's the fastest way from Dundas to Queen Street, and from there she
will need to walk only a few blocks west. As we're walking, I'm aware of the stares
I'm getting from people I'll never see again.

"So where are you from?" I ask.   *16*

"Sudbury." And I'm instantly speechless. What is this woman doing so far   *17*
from home? How did she get here? I ask why she's in the city.

"My boyfriend. He's in jail, and they're letting him go today. I came to take   *18*
him back home with me after his hearing."

While we walk past Mexx, Aritzia, and Abercrombie, I learn that she had   *19*
taken a bus from Sudbury the day before and spent the night on a park bench.
Her boyfriend is forty-two years old and has been in jail for the past ten months.
I don't ask why. She proudly tells me she was a crack addict and that she's been
clean for three months.

"I just got out of rehab," she says. "Now maybe my grandma will take me   *20*
back in."

"Back in?"   *21*

"Yeah, she kicked me out. She told me I wasn't allowed to be a hooker   *22*
anymore, but I got caught bringing someone home once."

I have no idea how to talk to a prostitute, never mind one who is so open   *23*
about everything she's done, but this woman seems to like me and trust me. The
next thing I know, I'm offering to buy her breakfast before she meets up with her
boyfriend.

There's a McDonald's at the southernmost side of the Eaton Centre,   *24*
overlooking the Queen Street entrance. I tell her she can have anything she wants.
An Egg McMuffin? Fruit and yogurt? But all she wants is Coke and a hash-brown.
I order her two.

We sit down at a freshly wiped table by the window. Beside us, two men in   *25*
grey suits sip coffee over an array of files and spreadsheets. They pause in their
conversation to stare at us—the student traveler and the bedraggled prostitute. I

tell the woman a little about my life, and ask more about hers and her grandmother. She says that they used to go to church together, when she was little, but she hasn't been since. She takes another bite of her hash-brown and tells me she's now twenty-one. Only twenty-one, and her boyfriend is forty-two. She talks about the drugs and the providence of God.

"I know that he helped me stop," she says. "I've been clean for three months, 26 can you believe that? That's a miracle! It has to be a miracle."

At this point all I can do is smile.   27

"I wish I could get my boyfriend to quit," she says, staring off. Then she 28 suddenly leans forward and asks, "Do you know how hard it is? Have you ever done crack?"

"No."   29

"Pot, at least?"   30

[margin note] The writer acknowledges her own inexperience and confusion.

"No. Sorry." I'm not sure why I'm apologizing for never having tried drugs, 31 but the way her face drops and she shifts her eyes makes me feel guilty. As though I can never fully understand her because I've never experienced the things she has.

"Well you should try it," she urges. "It's really good."   32

"Maybe one day." I glance at my watch. It's now quarter-to, and I still need 33 to stand in line to buy my ticket and get to the right platform. I wonder why I'm not panicking yet.

[margin note] The writer offers spare change, a gift that is cited in the title and that symbolizes the women's distanced relationship.

I tell her I need to get going. She should go, too, or she'll be late for the hearing. 34 Before getting up, I reach into my wallet and give her two TTC passes and some spare change. I walk her to the street and point her toward Old City Hall. She never thanks me, only looks at me one last time with immense vulnerability and helplessness. Then she walks away.

I wonder as I hurry towards the station if she'll be okay, if her boyfriend really 35 will get out of jail, and if her grandmother will ever take her back. Either way, I think as I cross Bay Street, what more can I do? I have a bus to catch.

Reading for Better Writing

Working by yourself or with a group, answer these questions:

1. Teresa's essay focuses on an urban setting. What does she evoke about the city, and what descriptions create that feeling?

2. The central character in the essay is presented primarily through description, comparisons, and dialogue. Identify such passages, exploring what they communicate about the woman and how effectively they work.

3. One focus of the essay is the writer's experience of the city and of her encounter with the prostitute. Describe Teresa's thoughts and feelings about both. How does she communicate these? Identify and analyze specific passages, sentences, and phrases.

Narration, Description, and Reflection ■ ■˙ ■

Elizabeth Fuller writes this essay to describe her one-time experience as a stowaway flight attendant—an experience that she enjoys describing but likely does not want to relive.

When Dreams Take Flight

A playful title forecasts what will happen.

In my 20s I was a flight attendant for Northwest Airlines, and I remember the holiday season as the most exhausting of the year. But I loved my job. From the first day Northwest hired me in Minneapolis in 1969, I tried to be a model flight attendant, to develop the qualities my operations manual demanded: poise, good judgment, initiative, adaptability and a spotless appearance.   *1*

The writer describes herself.

But one time I slipped up: I fell asleep. It happened one dreary morning around Thanksgiving. We'd just landed in Washington and I was dog-tired. The crew had disembarked for breakfast; the new passengers wouldn't board for two hours. For some reason, my eye drifted toward the overhead racks. Back then, the racks in Boeing 727's had no doors and were used only for storing pillows, blankets and passengers' coats and hats. I looked at all the little pillows up there, snuggled next to the blankets. And then I climbed up.   *2*

A transition and short clause introduce the action.

This was not easy in a pencil skirt and regulation red half-slip. But I did it. And it was heaven. I lay back on the mountain of pillows and pulled a blanket up over my head. Just before I drifted off, the thought crossed my mind that I ought to set my portable alarm clock — but it was too late.   *3*

A dash and short clause forecast trouble.

I certainly wasn't worrying about our operations manual, though I knew, of course, that flight attendants caught sleeping on duty could lose their wings. But I wasn't on duty, not in the strict sense. What's more, I was exhibiting initiative and adaptability, some of those attributes most cherished by Northwest Airlines.   *4*

She reflects on and rationalizes her choice.

It was a sound sleep. Suddenly I woke to a voice on the public address system: "Morning, folks. This is your captain speaking. We're No. 4 for takeoff, up near the end of the runway. So if you'll just sit back and relax, we'll be taking off in a few minutes. The flight attendants will do the best they can for you this morning, even though they are one short in the second cabin."   *5*

The quotation builds tension and tells what is happening.

I opened my eyes and gasped. The passengers and crew had boarded, and no one had checked my overhead bunk. If only someone had tried to store a coat up there or grab a blanket! I should have been down on the cabin floor, on duty and with my one-inch grosgrain ribbon tying my hair in place, my gold logo centered on the front of my hat. Instead, I was up on that rack, breaking into a cold sweat.   *6*

A series of short sentences suggest her thoughts and fears.

If I ever needed that Northwest Airlines initiative, it was then. I poked my head out and down. The cabin was packed with businessmen reading the financial   *7*

She describes her cautious and embarrassing descent.

papers. I hitched up my skirt — hemmed precisely one and three-quarter inches above the knee — and lowered a leg. This snagged the attention of the last 10 rows, as well as my pantyhose. Then I lowered my other leg. By this time, the rows in front had turned around and were watching too. Luckily, no one laughed.

She summarizes her excuse and notes his suspicion.

I swung down and planted my navy blue pump half on a passenger's armrest 8 and half on his pinstriped leg. My hat was in the overhead rack, I told him, and I had been digging around for a long time trying to find it. I pointed out that I had to wear my hat, or I would be fired.

He cleared his throat but didn't say anything. I thanked him for his 9 understanding and walked up the aisle toward my two fellow flight attendants, who were howling with laughter. We were sobered only by the realization that somebody had to notify the captain.

Mention of the captain sets up the conclusion.

As the plane rose to cruising altitude, the senior flight attendant went to the 10 cockpit and explained that I was back in the cabin. Meanwhile, I put on my smock and began pouring coffee, trying to avoid the rows near my overhead bunk. As I headed back to the galley to refill my coffeepot, I found the captain waiting for me with a stern and unforgiving look. I was getting ready to try to explain when he snapped the galley curtain closed and doubled over with laughter. "All's well that ends well," he said with a wink.

The captain responds by quoting Shakespeare.

Reading for Better Writing

Working by yourself or with a group, answer these questions:

1. Review the title and explain why it is (or is not) a good choice.

2. Re-read the opening paragraph and note what the writer says about her age, employer, the season, her employer's expectations, and her desire to excel. Then explain how each of these details helps set up the story, build interest in the action, and create humor.

3. Cite a descriptive passage that you find particularly engaging and explain why.

4. Compare what the captain says in paragraph 5 with what he says in paragraph 10. What does each statement tell you about his personality, role on the plane, and relationship with the crew? Would paraphrasing the captain have been more effective than quoting him? Why?

5. Review paragraphs 7-9 in which the writer describes her descent from the luggage bin, the passenger whom she steps on, her excuse, and his response. Do the details she offers adequately describe her action and his response? Explain.

6. Do you find the story funny? Why or why not?

Narration, Description, and Reflection ■▪▪

Mary Seymour reflects on her experience with bipolar disorder, which is sometimes called manic depression.

Call Me Crazy, But I Have to Be Myself

The writer labels herself "mentally ill."

Nearly every day, without thinking, I say things like "So-and-so is driving me crazy" or "That's nuts!" Sometimes I catch myself and realize that I'm not being sensitive toward people with mental illness. Then I remember I'm one of the mentally ill. If I can't throw those words around, who can?

Being a functional member of society and having a mental disorder is an intricate balancing act. Every morning I send my son to junior high school, put on professional garb, and drive off to my job as alumni-magazine editor at a prep school, where I've worked for six years. Only a few people at work know I'm manic-depressive, or bipolar, as it's sometimes called.

An example illustrates the extent of the illness.

Sometimes I'm not sure myself what I am. I blend in easily with "normal" people. You'd never know that seven years ago, fueled by the stress of a failing marriage and fanned by the genetic inheritance of a manic-depressive grandfather, I had a psychotic break. To look at me, you'd never guess I once ran naked through my yard or shuffled down the hallways of a psychiatric ward. To hear me, you'd never guess God channeled messages to me through my computer. After my breakdown at 36, I was diagnosed as bipolar, a condition marked by moods that swing between elation and despair.

More examples show the difficulties the writer faces.

It took a second, less-severe psychotic episode in 1997, followed by a period of deep depression, to convince me I truly was bipolar. Admitting I had a disorder that I'd have to manage for life was the hardest thing I've ever done. Since then, a combination of therapy, visits to a psychiatrist, medication, and inner calibration have helped me find an even keel. Now I manage my moods with the vigilance of a mother hen, nudging them back to center whenever they wander too far. Eating wisely, sleeping well, and exercising regularly keep me balanced from day to day. Ironically, my disorder has taught me to be healthier and happier than I was before.

Most of the time, I feel lucky to blend in with the crowd. Things that most people grumble about—paying bills, maintaining a car, working 9 to 5—strike me as incredible privileges. I'll never forget gazing through the barred windows of the psychiatric ward into the parking lot, watching people come and go effortlessly, wondering if I'd ever be like them again. There's nothing like a stint in a locked ward to make one grateful for the freedoms and burdens of full citizenship.

Each sentence begins with a similar phrase that reveals the writer's feelings.

Yet sometimes I feel like an impostor. Sometimes I wish I could sit at the lunch table and talk about lithium and Celexa instead of *Will & Grace*. While everyone talks about her fitness routine, I want to brag how it took five orderlies to hold me down and shoot me full of sedatives when I was admitted to the hospital, and how for a brief moment I knew the answers to every infinite mystery of the blazingly bright universe.

I yearn for people to know me—the real me—in all my complexity, but I'm afraid it would scare the bejesus out of them.

Every now and then, I feel like I'm truly being myself. Like the time the school 7 chaplain, in whom I'd confided my past, asked me to help counsel a severely bipolar student. This young woman had tried to commit suicide, had been hospitalized many times, and sometimes locked herself in her dorm room to keep the "voices" from overwhelming her. I walked and talked with her, sharing stories about medication and psychosis. I hoped to show by example that manic-depression did not necessarily mean a diminished life. At commencement, I watched her proudly accept her diploma; despite ongoing struggles with her illness, she's continuing her education.

> An extended example illustrates the point.

I'm able to be fully myself with my closest friends, all of whom have similar 8 schisms between private and public selves. We didn't set out to befriend each other—we just all speak the same language, of hardship and spiritual discovery and psychological awareness.

What I yearn for most is to integrate both sides of myself. I want to be part of the 9 normal world but I also want to own my identity as bipolar. I want people to know what I've been through so I can help those traveling a similar path. Fear has kept me from telling my story: fear of being stigmatized, of making people uncomfortable, of being reduced to a label. But hiding the truth has become more uncomfortable than letting it out. It's time for me to own up to who I am, complicated psychiatric history and all. Call me crazy, but I think it's the right thing to do.

> The final line echoes the title.

Reading for Better Writing

Working by yourself or with a group, answer these questions:

1. What purpose does Seymour identify for writing the essay? What other purposes might be served by publishing this piece for *Newsweek's* readers?

2. The writer starts with one category label for herself ("mentally ill") and then quickly adds another ("functional member of society"). How does the second label redefine the first?

3. Description is used to support many other kinds of writing, including the types of analytical and persuasive writing outlined here in *The College Writer*. In what other chapters could this essay have been included, and how do you know?

4. Review the "Editing and Proofreading" chapter of this book (pages 93–108), especially the portion on biased words. Why does Seymour use the phrase "call me crazy"? Is her use of the word biased or insulting? Explain.

Narration, Description, and Reflection ■▪■

The following essay by Barbara Kingsolver is taken from her book, *High Tide in Tucson*. In the essay, she describes her brief experience as a bodybuilding wannabe, and she reflects on how she "outgrew" her need to buff up.

As you read the essay, use this column to record your observations and questions.

The Muscle Mystique

The baby-sitter surely thought I was having an affair. Years ago, for a period of three whole months, I would dash in to pick up my daughter after "work" with my cheeks flushed, my heart pounding, my hair damp from a quick shower. I'm loath to admit where I'd really been for that last hour of the afternoon. But it's time to come clean.   *1*

I joined a health club.   *2*

I went downtown and sweated with the masses. I rode a bike that goes nowhere at the rate of five hundred calories per hour. I even pumped a little iron. I can't deny the place was a lekking ground: guys stalking around the weight room like prairie chickens, nervously eying each other's pectorals. Over by the abdominal machines I heard some of the frankest pickup lines since eighth grade ("You've got real defined deltoids for a girl"). A truck perpetually parked out front had vanity plates that read: LFT WTS. Another one, PRSS 250, I didn't recognize as a vanity plate until I understood the prestige of bench pressing 250 pounds.   *3*

I personally couldn't bench press a fully loaded steam iron. I didn't join the health club to lose weight, or to meet the young Adonis who admired my (dubiously defined) deltoids. I am content with my lot in life, save for one irksome affliction: I am what's known in comic-book jargon as the ninety-eight-pound weakling. I finally tipped the scales into three digits my last year of high school, but "weakling" I've remained, pretty much since birth. In polite terminology I'm cerebral; the muscles between my ears are what I get by on. The last great body in my family was my Grandfather Henry. He wore muscle shirts in the days when they were known as BVDs, under his cotton work shirt, and his bronze tan stopped midbiceps. He got those biceps by hauling floor joists and hammering up roof beams every day of his life, including his last. How he would have guffawed to see a roomful of nearly naked bankers and attorneys, pale as plucked geese, heads down, eyes fixed on a horizon beyond the water cooler, pedaling like bats out of hell on bolted-down bicycles. I expect he'd offer us all a job. If we'd pay our thirty dollars a month to *him*, we could come out to the construction site and run up and down ladders bringing him nails. That's why I'm embarrassed about all this. I'm afraid I share his opinion of unproductive sweat.   *4*

Actually, he'd be more amazed than scornful. His idea of fun was watching Ed Sullivan or snoozing in a recliner, or ideally, both at once. Why work like a maniac on your day off? To keep your heart and lungs in shape. Of Course. But I haven't noticed any vanity plates that say GD LNGS. The operative word here is vanity.   *5*

Standards of beauty in every era are things that advertise, usually falsely: "I'm   6
rich and I don't have to work." How could you be a useful farmhand, or even an
efficient clerk-typist, if you have long, painted fingernails? Four-inch high heels, like
the bound feet of Chinese aristocrats, suggest you don't have to do *anything* efficiently,
except maybe put up your tootsies on an ottoman and eat bonbons. (And I'll point
out here that aristocratic *men* wore the first high heels.) In my grandmother's day,
women of all classes lived in dread of getting a tan, since that betrayed a field worker's
station in life. But now that the field hand's station is occupied by the office worker, a
tan, I suppose, advertises that Florida and Maui are within your reach. Fat is another
peculiar cultural flip-flop: in places where food is scarce, beauty is three inches of
subcutaneous fat deep. But here and now, jobs are sedentary and calories are relatively
cheap, while the luxury of time to work them off is very dear. It still gives me pause
to see an ad for a weight-loss program that boldly enlists: "First ten pounds come off
free!" But that is about the size of it, in the strange food-drenched land of ours. After
those first ten, it gets expensive.

As a writer I could probably do my job fine with no deltoids at all, or biceps or   7
triceps, so long as you left me those vermicelli-sized muscles that lift the fingers to
the keyboard. (My vermicellis are *very* well defined.) So when I've writ my piece, off I
should merrily go to build a body that says I don't really have a financial obligation to
sit here in video-terminal bondage.

Well, yes. But to tell the truth, the leisure body and even the GD LNGS are not   8
really what I was after when I signed up at Pecs-R-Us. What I craved, and long for
still, is to be *strong*. I've never been strong. In childhood, team sports were my most
reliable source of humiliation. I've been knocked breathless to the ground by softballs,
basketballs, volleyballs, and once, during a wildly out-of-hand game of Red Rover, a
sneaker. In every case I knew my teammates were counting on me for a volley or a
double play or anyhow something more than clutching my stomach and rolling upon
the grass. By the time I reached junior high I wasn't even the last one picked anymore.
I'd slunk away long before they got to the bottom of the barrel.

Even now, the great mortification of my life is that visitors to my home sometimes   9
screw the mustard and pickle jar lids back on so tightly *I can't get them open!* (The
visitors probably think they are just closing them enough to keep the bugs out.) Sure, I
can use a pipe wrench, but it's embarrassing. Once, my front gate stuck, and for several
days I could only leave home by clambering furtively through the bougainvilleas and
over the garden wall. When a young man knocked on my door to deliver flowers one
sunny morning, I threw my arms around him. He thought that was pretty emotional,
for florists' mums. He had no idea he'd just casually pushed open the Berlin Wall.

My inspiration down at the health club was a woman fire-fighter who could have   10
knocked down my garden gate with a karate chop. I still dream about her triceps.
But I've mostly gotten over my brief fit of muscle envy. Oh, I still make my ongoing,
creative stabs at bodybuilding: I do "girl pushups," and some of the low-impact

things from Jane Fonda's pregnant-lady workout book, even if I'm not. I love to run, because it always seems like there's a chance you might actually get somewhere, so I'll sometimes cover a familiar mile or so of our county road after I see my daughter onto the school bus. (The driver confessed that for weeks he thought I was chasing him; he never stopped.) And finally, my friends have given me an official item of exercise equipment that looks like a glob of blue putty, which you're supposed to squeeze a million times daily to improve your grip. That's my current program. The so-called noncompetitive atmosphere of the health club whipped me, hands down. Realistically, I've always known I was born to be a "before" picture. So I won't be seen driving around with plates that boast: PRSS 250.

Maybe: OPN JRS.   *11*

Reading for Better Writing

Working by yourself or with a group, answer these questions:

1. Kingsolver entitles her essay, "The Muscle Mystique." What does "mystique" mean and in what sense are muscles or bodybuilding a "mystique"?

2. Review the opening few paragraphs and explain how the writer introduces her subject and sets the tone for the essay. Cite words and phrases that you find interesting, engaging, or funny.

3. In the third paragraph, Kingsolver describes the health club as a "lekking ground." What does "lekking" mean, and what does it suggest about the "muscle mystique"?

4. Re-read paragraph four in which the writer compares her own physique with that of her grandfather's. Cite details that help you envision each.

5. Kingsolver contrasts (1) current bodybuilders' focus on playful lekking with (2) her fit grandfather's focus on hard work. What's her point? And how does this point relate to what she says in paragraph 6 about the "standards of beauty" in her time vs. "standards of beauty" in her grandmother's time?

6. Define "self-deprecating humor" and cite examples in paragraphs 7-11. Would these passages be as funny if the writer were describing others' foibles rather than her own?

7. Find two or three passages that you consider reflective writing and explain how they enrich the text.

8. Re-read Kingsolver's last sentence in which she suggests a license-plate inscription that relays her bodybuilding goal. Then work with a classmate to create comic inscriptions that relay your goals.

Writing Guidelines

Model

Planning

1. **Select a topic.** The most promising topics are experiences that gave you insights into yourself, and possibly into others as well. To identify such topics, consider the categories below and then list whatever experiences come to mind:

   - Times when you felt *secure, hopeful, distraught, appreciated, confident, frightened, exploited,* or *misunderstood.*
   - Times when you made a decision about *lifestyles, careers, education,* or *religion.*
   - Events that tested your *will, patience, self-concept,* or *goals.*
   - Events that changed or confirmed your assessment of a *person, a group,* or *an institution.*

TIP: List topics in response to the following statement: *Reflect on times when you first discovered that the world was strange, wonderful, complex, frightening, small, full, or empty.* How did these experiences affect you?

2. **Get the big picture.** Once you have chosen a topic, gather your thoughts by brainstorming or freewriting in response to questions like these:

   - Where did the experience take place and what specific sights, sounds, and smells distinguish the place?
   - Who else was involved, and what did they look like, act like, do, and say?
   - What were the key or pivotal points in your experiences and why?
   - What led to these key moments and what resulted from them?
   - How did your or others' comments or actions affect what happened?
   - What did others learn from this experience—and what did you learn?
   - Did the experience end as you had hoped? Why or why not?
   - What themes, conflicts, and insights arose from the experience?
   - How do your feelings now differ from your feelings then? Why?

TIP: To find out more details about the event or people involved, sort through photo albums and home videos to trigger memories; talk to someone who shared your experiences; consult your journal, old letters, and saved e-mail.

3. **Probe the topic and reveal what you find.** The mind-searching aspect of writing this essay happens while asking so-why questions: *So why does this picture still make me smile?* or *Why does his comment still hurt?* or *Why did I do that when I knew better—or Did I know better?* Your readers need to experience what you experienced, so don't hide what's embarrassing, or painful, or still unclear.

4. **Get organized.** Review your brainstorming or freewriting, and highlight key details, quotations, or episodes. Then list the main events in chronological order, or use a cluster to help you gather details related to your experiences.

Drafting

5. **Write the first draft.** Rough out the first draft. Then test your narration and description by asking whether the quotations, details, and events are accurate and clear. Test your reflection by asking whether it explains how the experience affected you.

Revising

6. **Review the draft.** After taking a break, read your essay for truthfulness and completeness. Does it include needed details and questions?

7. **Get feedback.** Ask a classmate to read your paper and respond to it.

8. **Improve the ideas, organization, and voice.** Use your own review and peer review to address these issues:

   ____ **Ideas:** Does the essay offer readers an engaging, informative look into your life, personality, and perspective?

   ____ **Organization:** Does the essay include (1) an inviting opening that pictures the setting, introduces the characters, and forecasts the themes; (2) a rich middle that develops a clear series of events, nuanced characters, and descriptions; and (3) a satisfying closing that completes the experience and unifies the essay's ideas?

   ____ **Voice:** Is the tone fair, and does it fit the experience? Is your voice genuine, thoughtful, and inviting?

Editing

9. **Edit and proofread your essay.** Polish your writing by addressing these items:

   ____ **Words:** The words in descriptive and narrative passages *show* instead of *tell about*; they are precise and rich, helping readers imagine the setting, envision the characters, and vicariously experience the action. The words in reflective passages are insightful and measured.

   ____ **Sentences:** The sentences in descriptive and reflective passages are clear, varied in structure, and smooth. The sentences in dialogue accurately reflect the characters' personalities, regional diction, and current idioms.

   ____ **Correctness:** The copy includes no errors in spelling, mechanics, punctuation, or grammar.

   ____ **Page Design:** The design is attractive and follows assigned guidelines.

Publishing

10. **Publish your writing** by sharing your essay with friends and family, posting it on a website, or submitting it to a journal or newspaper.

Critical-Thinking and Writing Activities

As directed by your instructor, complete the following critical-thinking and writing activities by yourself or with classmates.

Interactive

1. Review "The Entomology of Village Life," noting how the essay centers on what the writer and his friend witness. Think about what it means to be a witness—to a crime, a tragedy, a triumph, a performance, an encounter, and so on. Then write an essay in which you explore a time that you were a witness.

2. In "Spare Change," Teresa Zsuffa describes her encounter with someone whose qualities, experiences, and values are different from her own. Write a personal essay in which you explore such an encounter in your life.

3. Elizabeth Fuller in "When Dreams Take Flight" and Barbara Kingsolver in "The Muscle Mystique" write about themselves with self-deprecating humor. As readers, we laugh with them because we also have had experiences in which we made mistakes, did something silly, or found that we didn't measure up to our own or others' goals or standards. Choose such an experience that you feel comfortable sharing with others. Then write an essay in which you describe what happened, reflect on its impact, and share the mirth.

Learning-Outcomes Checklist

After reading the essays in this chapter, developing your own personal essay, and getting feedback from classmates and your instructor, use this checklist to assess how effectively you achieved the learning outcomes for this chapter:

_____ I understand how different techniques of narrative writing are crafted: setting, character, plot, dialogue, and theme.

_____ I understand when and how to use anecdotes in different writing forms and for different writing occasions.

_____ I understand what makes for good reflection in personal writing, as well as where and how to do it within an essay.

_____ I understand what makes for engaging and vivid description, as well as how word choice, sensory appeals, and interesting comparisons create such description.

_____ I have effectively blended techniques of narration, description, and reflection to craft a personal essay that shares with readers something of my particular experiences in such a way that readers can understand and relate to the broader significance of that experience.

Analytical Writing

Chapters 11 through 15 introduce the traditional modes of analytical writing: cause-effect, comparison-contrast, classification, process, and definition. All of these modes are analytical in the sense that they involve mentally "breaking down" a topic in an effort to reveal structures and logical relationships. Often called expository writing, such modes seek to clearly explain to readers the logical workings of a given topic, from interracial tensions to character traits to types of music.

Note, however, that virtually any piece of analytical writing blends these distinctive modes. For example, you might use compare-contrast as the primary organizational strategy for an entire essay, but you also might use another mode (such as definition) to organize a specific paragraph within that essay. In all of your writing, you should choose the writing strategy that best fits your subject, audience, and purpose.

Analytical Writing

11 ▶ Cause and Effect

Now, why did that happen? We ask this question every day at home, in college, and on the job in order to understand and cope with things that happen in our lives. For example, knowing why a computer crashed will help us avoid that problem, and knowing the causes and effects of a disease such as diabetes can help us control the condition. In other words, cause and effect reasoning helps us deal with everyday issues, whether large or small.

In a cause and effect essay, the writer develops the thesis through cause and effect reasoning. That is, she or he analyzes and explains the causes, the effects, or both the causes and the effects of a phenomenon. This chapter includes instructions and models that will help you read and write cause-effect analyses.

Learning Outcomes

▶ Understand cause-effect reasoning.

 Audio

▶ Identify and correct related logical fallacies.

▶ Support cause-effect reasoning with detailed, reliable evidence.

 Video

▶ Use transitional words to clarify cause-effect relationships.

 Video

▶ Write, revise, and edit a cause-effect essay.

Visually Speaking ▶ What cause-effect relationship is implied in the photograph above? What research and writing strategies could you use to analyze the phenomenon pictured above.

■ Reading Cause-Effect Writing

When reading cause-effect reasoning, note the writer's rhetorical situation and logic.

Consider the rhetorical situation. ■ ■ ■

Assess how the writer's purpose, audience, and topic affect his or her writing strategies.

- **Purpose.** Writers use cause-effect analysis to deepen understanding about how specific forces work to bring about particular results. In academia and the workplace, cause-effect logic operates in many forms of writing—from persuasive essays and lab reports to project proposals and market analyses. In each situation, writers use cause-effect thinking to explain a phenomenon or to prove a point.

- **Audience.** The audience for cause-effect writing is typically made up of people who may have a basic understanding of the topic but want or need a deeper understanding of the forces operating within it—understanding that may help them make decisions about or take positions on the issue.

- **Topic.** Cause-effect topics are phenomena—events, occurrences, developments, processes, problems, conditions, and so on—that need to be more fully explained in terms of their operating forces.

Consider the analytical logic. ■ ■ ■

As you read each essay, identify the problem or phenomenon addressed and look for the following elements of strong cause-effect logic.

- **Clear Reasoning:** The thesis clearly identifies a cause-effect idea, and the essay's body carefully and systematically explores and supports this idea. The writer also distinguishes between primary and secondary causes and effects.

- **Supporting Details:** Claims identifying causes, effects, and the links between causes and effects are fully supported with reliable, detailed evidence.

- **Logical Analyses:** The reasoning is transparent, unified, and free of logical fallacies such as Bare Assertion (see 257), False Cause (see 259), Slippery Slope (see 259), and False Analogy (see 260).

Reader's Checklist

_____ Is the writer's rationale for writing informed, reasonable, and convincing?

_____ Who is the intended audience, and does the essay present all the information that they need to understand and respond to the analysis?

_____ Is the topic clearly identified and explored as a phenomenon?

_____ Is the thesis clear, and is the argument free of logical fallacies?

_____ What claims does the writer make regarding causes and effects, and are the statements sufficiently limited, focused, and logical?

_____ Are supporting details well researched, relevant, and strong?

Cause and Effect ■·■

Student writer Brittany Korver wrote the following essay in 2008. In the paper, she analyzes how the increasing number of Muslim residents in the Netherlands is impacting Dutch culture and raising tension within a society known for its diversity and tolerance.

Video

> ### Essay Outline
> *Introduction:* Dutch symbols and ethnic tensions
>   **1.** Social changes brought about by immigration: history
>   **2.** Impact of Dutch and Muslim cultures on each other
>   **3.** Secondary differences between Dutch and Muslim cultures: demographics, education, economics
>   **4.** Major differences: cultural practices and world view
>   • Development of us vs. them mentality
>   • Fear of extremism, terrorism, and assassination
> *Conclusion:* Tensions lead to fear and alienation that cannot be overcome without learning to live with differences.

Dutch Discord

The title identifies the phenomenon.

When people outside the Netherlands think of the Dutch, what do they   *1*
envision? Some may picture stoic windmills, grass-covered dykes, and tidy row houses. Others may see barge-filled canals, gay parades, and red-light districts. Still others may envision the Free University in Amsterdam, the harbor in Rotterdam, and the International Court of Justice in The Hague. But when people inside the Netherlands think of common sites in their country, they likely also picture the growing number of domed mosques in Dutch city skylines, veiled faces in the streets, or scarf-covered heads in the classrooms. The fact is, these images are increasingly common in the Netherlands as its Muslim population continues to grow and spread ("One Million Muslims"). More importantly, however, this diffusion appears to have increased tension between the progressive ethnic Dutch—long known for tolerating cultural differences—and their new neighbors.

Introduction: Dutch symbols and ethnic tensions

1 Social changes brought about by immigration: history

The first, most notable influx of Muslims was drawn to the Netherlands   *2*
after World War II by job offers (Shadid 10). The Dutch, looking for cheap labor, recruited large numbers of unskilled laborers from poorer countries (10). These immigrants were typically guest workers who expected to stay temporarily and then return to their homelands, as many of them did (Sunier 318).

By 1973, an economic crisis hit Europe, and the Netherlands no longer needed   *3*
extra workers (Van Amersfoort 179). Many Muslims, however, decided to stay
because the economic conditions in their home countries were even less desirable
than conditions in the Netherlands (Ketner 146). Numerous immigrants became
permanent residents and were joined by their families. When the Dutch finally
tightened restrictions by lowering quotas and raising standards for refugees,
marriages continued between Dutch-Muslim citizens and Muslim foreigners.
Since family reunification is a Dutch migration priority, these spouses continued
to flow into the Netherlands (Van Amersfoort 179). In addition, the Netherlands
experienced increased illegal immigration (179).

However, while legal and illegal immigrants increased the Netherlands'   *4*
Muslim population significantly, the population swelled even more because
of Muslims' relatively high fertility rates (Kent). For example, as of 2004, CBS
(the Netherlands' statistics bureau) reported 945 thousand Muslims living in
the country, a jump of over 339 thousand from ten years earlier ("One Million
Muslims"). They currently account for at least 5.8 percent of the population,
which makes Muslims the fourth largest religious group in the Netherlands,
trailing just behind Dutch Calvinists ("As many Muslims as Calvinists"). While
Muslims are distributed quite sparsely in some provinces (e.g., less than 3 percent
in Friesland), they make up as much as one third of the population in cities such
as Amsterdam (Rawstome 30).

2 Impact of Dutch and Muslim cultures on each other

Not surprisingly, this growing minority is   *5*
both affecting and being affected by Dutch culture.
Ethnic foods are increasingly available in stores and
restaurants (Wagensveld). New shops and market
stands accommodate the demand for folk clothing
(Wagensveld). Private Islamic schools are available, and
mosques dot the landscape (Landman 1125). Coverage
of Turk and Moroccan culture, including their religious
festivals, fill many pages in the Netherlands' souvenir
books (DeRooi 107). In addition, businesses cater to
their new consumers by including dark-haired people

> *Not surprisingly, this growing minority is both affecting and being affected by Dutch culture.*

in their ads and abandoning potentially offensive practices, such as distributing
piggy-banks (Charter 40).

Dutch culture also leaves its mark on this new community. For example, many Muslims find themselves forgetting Islamic holidays because they are too busy or do not know the Arabic calendar ("Time and Migration" 387). Many have adjusted to the Dutch view of time, making their lives faster paced. Some save religious prayers for after work, disrupting the normal prayer schedule (390). In fact, even some mosques encourage change by offering immigrants Dutch language classes, computer courses, and bicycle lessons (Van Amersfoort 185–186).   *6*

3 Secondary differences between Dutch and Muslim cultures

Though assimilation between most cultural groups in the Netherlands is common, the ethnic Dutch and those who trace their roots to Muslim countries retain conspicuous differences, sometimes leading to tensions between them. For example, fertility runs higher among these immigrants, prompting some ethnic Dutch to fear that they will eventually become a minority (Kent). Muslims still have lower education levels, high levels of unemployment, and poorer housing than most other residents. And among second generation Muslims, dropout rates and delinquencies run high (Mamadouh 198).   *7*

4 Major differences: cultural practices and world view

However, the chief challenges that ethnic Dutch have in relating to their Muslim neighbors have little to do with demographic characteristics or economic standing, and more to do with cultural practices and worldviews. For example, ethnic Dutch have difficulty accepting or respecting traditional Muslim views regarding women's roles in society and homosexual lifestyles, as well as resident Muslims' high crime rate and violent Islamic extremism ("Veils and Wooden Clogs" 230). The ethnic Dutch are repulsed by stories of wife beating, arranged marriages, women forbidden to hold jobs, homosexuals put to death in the immigrants' home countries, terrorist attacks in Western countries, and violent crimes committed by immigrants in the Netherlands (230). This cultural clash has led the Netherlands to re-evaluate and in some ways re-direct its pursuit of a multi-cultural state and return to the nation-state model as the ideal (198 Mamadouh).   *8*

In some cases, tensions have evolved into an "us" vs. "them" mentality that includes covert and overt racism and hostility.

(a) us vs. them mentality

In some cases, tensions have evolved into an "us" vs. "them" mentality that includes covert and overt racism and hostility (Shadid16). In the journal *European Education,* Wasif A. Shadid makes this point   *9* by comparing some attitudes in Holland with what appear to be parallel attitudes in South Africa's Apartheid system. Examples of these tensions or attitudes include increasing differentiation between the native Dutch and immigrant groups, politicians speaking negatively of Muslim residents (11-16), and sometimes violent acts between Muslims and non-Muslims (Esman 12).

(b) fear of extremism, terrorism, and assassinations

Since the turn of the millennium, the ethnic Dutch fear of Islamic extremism *10* has also increased, brought on in part by international events such as the September 11, 2001 attacks in the United States, and the subsequent strikes in Madrid and London. This fear was further intensified when two well-known anti-Islam Dutch politicians were assassinated inside the Netherlands. The first was Pim Fortuyn, who was shot in 2002 (Shadid 17). Fortuyn had his own political party, which called for "stopping all immigration" and a "cold war against Islam" (Esman 12). His assassination created a stir because the Dutch suddenly found their freedom of speech jeopardized, thereby widening the rift between the Dutch and Muslim cultures (Wagensveld).

The second Dutch politician assassinated was Theo Van Gogh in 2004, and *11* this event is often referred to as the September 11 of the Netherlands (Esman 12). Like Fortuyn, Van Gogh was very outspoken. He also used offensive language, gained many young followers (Margaronis 6), and went on to make the movie *Submission* with ex-Muslim and screen writer, Ayaan Hirsi Ali, a film that exposed Dutch-Muslim domestic abuse (6). Van Gogh was shot and stabbed to death, resulting in a martyr-like legacy for his cause (Rawstome 30).

The most recent tension-building event was the March 2008 release of the controversial movie *Fitna* (Arabic for strife), directed by Dutch MP Geert Wilders (Rawstome 30). The short movie displays graphic and disturbing images of terrorism and abuse, and it uses quotes from the Koran and Islamic leaders, suggesting that both sources support these violent actions (*Fitna*). The movie is so controversial that fear of violent repercussions is widespread, and many Netherlanders think that Wilders was irresponsible for releasing it (Rawstome 30). Wilders received six hundred death threats by late March, has six body guards, and at times he and his wife live in prison cells for safety (30).

12

> *Wilders received six hundred death threats by late March, has six body guards, and at times he and his wife live in prison cells for safety.*

Conclusion: Tensions lead to fear and alienation.

As events like these suggest, the growth of the Muslim community in the Netherlands appears to have increased the tension between the ethnic Dutch and Muslims. As a result, many ethnic Dutch feel disconcerted, and many Dutch Muslims feel alienated (Shadid 20). Whether those who built windmills and those who build mosques will ever live together in unity remains unclear. But what is clear is that such unity never will happen until the two groups learn to live with the differences that now separate them.   *13*

Note: The Works Cited page is not shown. For sample pages, see MLA (pages 526–527) and APA (page 557).

Reading for Better Writing

Working by yourself or with a group, answer these questions:

1. Do the title and opening paragraph effectively get your attention and introduce the topic? Explain.

2. Brittany Korver wrote this essay expecting that it would be read by other college students and her professor. Review her topic, thesis, and core argument; then explain why they are or are not fitting choices for her audience.

3. In paragraphs 2–4, Brittany uses chronological order to explain how the Muslim population in the Netherlands increased. Review those paragraphs and explain whether her organization and details adequately describe the increase.

4. In the opening sentence of paragraph 5, Brittany says, "[T]his growing minority is both affecting and being affected by Dutch culture." Review paragraphs five and six and explain whether they adequately develop the quotation above.

5. Note how the writer builds paragraphs 7–9 by opening each with a topic sentence and following with documented supporting details. Then explain why these choices do or do not strengthen her argument.

6. In paragraphs 10–12, the writer describes three violent events that transpired since 2002. Explain why she might cite these events and whether she uses them effectively to develop her thesis.

7. Review the opening and closing paragraphs and explain why they do or do not help unify the essay.

Cause and Effect ■ ▪ ■

In the essay below, Mary Brophy Marcus describes successful businesswomen and argues that the skills they learned from organized sports helped them achieve that success. The essay was first published in *US News & World Report*.

If You Let Me Play . . .

The writer uses an anecdote to introduce the topic and focus the essay.

Jackie Thomas, Nike's associate director of sports marketing, usually spends her lunch hour on the sports-shoe company's basketball courts charging for the basket, always outnumbered by male colleagues. "I hold my own," boasts the 33-year-old executive.   *1*

She also does well playing the corporate game back inside the headquarters' offices. Thomas, a former University of California–Berkeley college basketball point guard, says her success is due in large part to the lessons she learned growing up playing competitive team sports. "It's taught me that if you lose a game, you go back afterward and figure out what went wrong and how to overcome it the next time," says the former tomboy from Kingston, Jamaica.   *2*

A dependent clause links the second and third paragraphs.

While most of America's corporations are still commanded by male chief executives, women are gaining ground, winning vice-presidential and top management slots and, in a few cases, the highest leadership roles. Many of these young female executives say playing team sports helped them get ahead. A University of Virginia study conducted in the late 1980s showed that 80 percent of key female leaders from *Fortune* 500 companies said they participated in sports and considered themselves tomboys.   *3*

The writer describes events (or causes) that helped women gain valuable skills in sports.

A lot of credit, female executives say, has to go to Title IX, part of the Federal Education Amendments Act of 1972. It mandated that federally funded schools give women's sports the same treatment as men's games receive. That meant that in schools and colleges across the United States, for every boy's varsity soccer team, there must be a girl's varsity soccer team; for every male basketball scholarship, there must be a female basketball scholarship of equal dollars. Since the early 1970s, the law has increased money for new equipment, coaches, and travel for women's teams. More college scholarships have translated into more diplomas and better jobs for women. Thomas earned a partial academic scholarship when she applied to Berkeley, one of the country's top universities, but without an additional basketball scholarship awarded in her junior and senior years, she would have had a hard time paying for the education.   *4*

Using statistical evidence, she cites effects of the causes described in the previous paragraph.

Girls' participation in high school sports has spiked from about 300,000 in 1971 to 2.4 million in 1996. At the college level, where competition is tougher, the number of female athletes has increased to 123,832 from 80,040 in 1982, says the National Collegiate Athletic Association.   *5*

"No other experience I know of can prepare you for the high-level competition of business," says Anh Ngyuen, 25, a former Carnegie Mellon University varsity soccer star. She should know. Now she battles Microsoft as a product manager for Netscape Communications. "My colleagues can't believe how aggressive I am," she says.   *6*

Sports helped these women master the interpersonal skills, like teamwork, that many men take for granted. "I've seen firsthand hundreds and hundreds of times that one person can't win a soccer or softball game," says Maria Murnane, a 28-year-old senior account executive for a San Francisco public-relations firm. "Same goes for work. You have to learn to trust the people on your team, let them run with projects," the former Northwestern soccer center midfielder says. Her boss, William Harris, the president of Strategy Associates, agrees: "We don't want Lone Rangers. She's a team player—a captain and cheerleader."   *7*

Playing team sports helps with the little things, too. Women learn to speak in sports metaphors as many men do. Lisa Delpy, professor of sports management at George Washington University in Washington, D.C., also notes that in many companies a lot of business is conducted on the golf course, at ballgames, or at other sports events. Women who know the difference between a slide tackle and a sweeper at a World Cup soccer match can fit right in.   *8*

Stephanie Delaney, now 31, captained the varsity soccer team at Franklin and Marshall College in Lancaster, Pennsylvania, when it won the Mid-Atlantic Conference championship her senior year. Now the sales manager for the Caribbean and Latin American division of ConAgra's Lamb-Weston, one of the world's largest frozen-french-fry producers, she was the only woman to play a game of basketball with potential clients at a big food conference last year in Jamaica. "I was the high scorer," she notes.   *9*

And yes, it helped sell french fries. "I didn't close the deal on the court, but afterward when we were hanging out drinking water and shooting the breeze, they agreed to test my product. Now we have Kentucky Fried Chicken's business in Jamaica," says Delaney.   *10*

Female executives say that Title IX had another subtle, but important, effect. For the first time, many boys, coaches, and parents opened their eyes to the fact that their sisters and daughters could be just as strong, fast, and nimble on the field as their brothers and sons. Likewise, girls whose talents had formerly gone unnoticed under driveway basketball nets and on back lots began realizing their own power—that they could compete with boys and win. "When my girlfriends and I formed a softball team back in college, we were dreadful—like the Keystone Kops," recalls Penny Cate, 45, now a vice president at Quaker Oats. "There'd be four of us in the outfield and the ball would go through our legs. But after a few years, we became very good. It built my confidence, made me realize I could accomplish anything in sports or out," she says.   *11*

A quotation supports the writer's thesis: Skills learned in sports help one succeed in business.

The writer supports her thesis with an anecdote.

A lively quotation offers interesting details.

The dash links the word *power* to the defining clause that follows.

That point is repeatedly brought home when Nike executives ask schoolgirls what 12 they think of one of the company's TV ads. The ad begins with the voice of a young girl saying, "If you let me play . . . ." The phrase is finished by other little girls saying things like, "I will have greater self-confidence" or "I will be more likely to stay in school."

The girls often reply, in a tone of genuine befuddlement, "If who lets me play?" 13 They don't see any barriers between themselves and America's playing fields. Twenty years from now, might they say, "*What* glass ceiling?"

Reading for Better Writing

Working by yourself or with a group, answer these questions:

1. Review the writer's title and her reference to it late in the essay. How does the writer use the title to introduce and advance her thesis?

2. Mary Brophy Marcus is a journalist who wrote this essay and many others for publications such as *US News & World Report* and *USA Today*. Review three or four paragraphs from the essay and explain how her word choice, sentence structure, and use of quotations are or are not appropriate for readers of periodicals like these.

3. Review the qualities of an academic style as discussed on pages 79–80. Then explain why Marcus's essay does or does not reflect this style. Cite specific passages to support your answer.

4. Marcus uses cause-effect reasoning to argue that (1) women's participation in sports produces valuable skills and (2) these skills help women succeed in business. Examine three points, along with the evidence (data, quotations, and other elements), that Marcus uses to support either of these claims. Finally, explain why each supporting point and its related evidence are or are not convincing.

5. Marcus concludes her essay with the question, "*What* glass ceiling?" Explain why the quotation does or does not (1) advance her thesis and (2) close the essay effectively.

6. Working with a classmate, review the checklist under Step 8, "Revise the essay," found on page 179. Then analyze to what degree Marcus accomplishes each task in this checklist.

Cause and Effect ■ ▪ ■

Christy Haubegger is the founder of *Latina* magazine. This essay was originally published in the July 12, 1999, issue of *Newsweek* magazine.

Video

The Legacy of Generation Ñ

About 20 years ago, some mainstream observers declared the 1980s the "decade of the Hispanic." The Latino population was nearing 15 million! (It's since doubled.) However, our decade was postponed—a managerial oversight, no doubt—and eventually rescheduled for the '90s. What happens to a decade deferred? It earns compounded interest and becomes the next hundred years. The United States of the 21st century will be undeniably ours. Again. *1*

A metaphor helps to make the writer's point.

It's Manifest Destino. After all, Latinos are true Americans, some of the original residents of the Américas. Spanish was the first European language spoken on this continent. Which is why we live in places like Los Angeles, Colorado, and Florida rather than The Angels, Colored, and Flowered. Now my generation is about to put a Latin stamp on the rest of the culture—and that will ultimately be the Ñ legacy. *2*

The writer lists examples that illustrate her claim.

We are not only numerous; we are also growing at a rate seven times that of the general population. Conservative political ads notwithstanding, this growth is driven by natural increase (births over deaths) rather than immigration. At 30, I may be the oldest childless Latina in the United States. More important, however, while our preceding generation felt pressure to assimilate, America has now generously agreed to meet us in the middle. Just as we become more American, America is simultaneously becoming more Latino. *3*

Examples from pop culture connect with readers and help to make the writer's ideas memorable.

This quiet revolución can perhaps be traced back to the bloodless coup of 1992, when salsa outsold ketchup for the first time. Having toppled the leadership in the condiment category, we set our sights even higher. Fairly soon, there was a congresswoman named Sanchez representing Orange County, a taco-shilling Chihuahua became a national icon, and now everyone is loca for Ricky Martin. *4*

We are just getting started. Our geographic concentration and reputation for family values are making us every politician's dream constituency. How long can New Hampshire, with just four Electoral College votes—and probably an equal number of Hispanic residents—continue to get so much attention from presidential candidates? Advertisers will also soon be begging for our attention. With a median age of 26 (eight years younger than the general market), Latinos hardly exist outside their coveted 18–34 demographic. Remember, we may only be 11 percent of the country, but we buy 16 percent of the lipliner. *5*

The writer transitions to the anticipated effects of the population growth she has described.

The media will change as well, especially television, where we now appear 6 to be rapidly approaching extinction. Of the 26 new comedies and dramas appearing this fall [1999] on the four major networks, not one has a Latino in a leading role. The Screen Actors Guild released employment statistics for 1998 showing that the percentage of roles going to Hispanic actors actually declined from the previous year. But, pretty soon, the cast of "Friends" will need to find some amigos. Seeing as they live in New York City, and there's almost 2 million of us in the metropolitan area, this shouldn't prove too difficult.

Present-tense verbs indicate that the writer is describing current events.

Face it: This is going to be a bilingual country. Back in 1849, the California 7 Constitution was written in both Spanish and English, and we're headed that way again. If our children speak two languages instead of just one, how can that not be a benefit to us all? The re-Latinization of this country will pay off in other ways as well. I, for one, look forward to that pivotal moment in our history when all American men finally know how to dance. Latin music will no longer be found in record stores under "Foreign," and romance will bloom again. Our children will ask us what it was like to dance without a partner.

"American food" will mean low-fat enchiladas and hamburgers served with 8 rice and beans. As a result, the American standard of beauty will necessarily expand to include a female size 12, and anorexia will be found only in medical-history books. Finally, just in time for the baby boomers' senescence, living with extended family will become hip again. Simpsons fans of the next decade will see Grandpa moving back home. We'll all go back to church together.

The paragraph begins with the word *dawn* and ends with *mañana* and *morning*.

At the dawn of a new millennium, America knows Latinos as entertainers and 9 athletes. But, someday very soon, all American children can dream of growing up to be writers like Sandra Cisneros, astronauts like Ellen Ochoa, or judges like Jose Cabranes of the Second Circuit Court of Appeals. To put a Latin spin on a famous Anglo phrase: It is truly mañana in America. For those of you who don't know it (yet), that word doesn't just mean tomorrow; mañana also means morning.

Reading for Better Writing

Working by yourself or with a group, answer these questions:

1. In one sentence, summarize the cause(s) and effect(s) of the changes described in this essay.

2. Writers must make their claims using words that convey an appropriate level of certainty. Is Haubegger's use of "will" (versus "may") appropriate in paragraphs 7 and 8? Why?

3. Review paragraph 9. What is the writer's point? Do you agree?

4. The writer published this essay in 1999. Cite examples showing that the changes she described are continuing.

Cause and Effect ■ ˙ ■

Steven Pinker teaches in the Department of Psychology at Harvard University where he also conducts research on language and cognition. He writes regularly for publications such as *Time* and *The New Republic*, and he is the author of seven books, including *The Language Instinct, How the Mind Works, Words and Rules, The Blank Slate,* and *The Stuff of Thought: Language as a Window into Human Nature.* In the essay below, published in the *New York Times* on June 10, 2010, Pinker analyses how our current use of electronic technologies affects our ability to think deeply and process information.

Mind Over Mass Media

Use a pen to identify Pinker's key points and to record your response.

NEW forms of media have always caused moral panics: the printing press, newspapers, paperbacks and television were all once denounced as threats to their consumers' brainpower and moral fiber. *1*

So too with electronic technologies. PowerPoint, we're told, is reducing discourse to bullet points. Search engines lower our intelligence, encouraging us to skim on the surface of knowledge rather than dive to its depths. Twitter is shrinking our attention spans. *2*

But such panics often fail basic reality checks. When comic books were accused of turning juveniles into delinquents in the 1950s, crime was falling to record lows, just as the denunciations of video games in the 1990s coincided with the great American crime decline. The decades of television, transistor radios and rock videos were also decades in which I.Q. scores rose continuously. *3*

For a reality check today, take the state of science, which demands high levels of brainwork and is measured by clear benchmarks of discovery. These days scientists are never far from their e-mail, rarely touch paper and cannot lecture without PowerPoint. If electronic media were hazardous to intelligence, the quality of science would be plummeting. Yet discoveries are multiplying like fruit flies, and progress is dizzying. Other activities in the life of the mind, like philosophy, history and cultural criticism, are likewise flourishing, as anyone who has lost a morning of work to the Web site *Arts & Letters Daily* can attest. *4*

Critics of new media sometimes use science itself to press their case, citing research that shows how "experience can change the brain." But cognitive neuroscientists roll their eyes at such talk. Yes, every time we learn a fact or skill the wiring of the brain changes; it's not as if the information is stored in the pancreas. *5*

But the existence of neural plasticity does not mean the brain is a blob of clay pounded into shape by experience.

Experience does not revamp the basic information-processing capacities of the   *6* brain. Speed-reading programs have long claimed to do just that, but the verdict was rendered by Woody Allen after he read *War and Peace* in one sitting: "It was about Russia." Genuine multitasking, too, has been exposed as a myth, not just by laboratory studies but by the familiar sight of an S.U.V. undulating between lanes as the driver cuts deals on his cellphone.

Moreover, as the psychologists Christopher Chabris and Daniel Simons show   *7* in their new book *The Invisible Gorilla: And Other Ways Our Intuitions Deceive Us,* the effects of experience are highly specific to the experiences themselves. If you train people to do one thing (recognize shapes, solve math puzzles, find hidden words), they get better at doing that thing, but almost nothing else. Music doesn't make you better at math, conjugating Latin doesn't make you more logical, brain-training games don't make you smarter. Accomplished people don't bulk up their brains with intellectual calisthenics; they immerse themselves in their fields. Novelists read lots of novels, scientists read lots of science.

The effects of consuming electronic media are also likely to be far more limited   *8* than the panic implies. Media critics write as if the brain takes on the qualities of whatever it consumes, the informational equivalent of "you are what you eat." As with primitive peoples who believe that eating fierce animals will make them fierce, they assume that watching quick cuts in rock videos turns your mental life into quick cuts or that reading bullet points and Twitter postings turns your thoughts into bullet points and Twitter postings.

Yes, the constant arrival of information packets can be distracting or addictive,   *9* especially to people with attention deficit disorder. But distraction is not a new phenomenon. The solution is not to bemoan technology but to develop strategies of self-control, as we do with every other temptation in life. Turn off e-mail or Twitter when you work, put away your Blackberry at dinner time, ask your spouse to call you to bed at a designated hour.

And to encourage intellectual depth, don't rail at PowerPoint or Google. It's not   *10* as if habits of deep reflection, thorough research and rigorous reasoning ever came naturally to people. They must be acquired in special institutions, which we call universities, and maintained with constant upkeep, which we call analysis, criticism and debate. They are not granted by propping a heavy encyclopedia on your lap, nor are they taken away by efficient access to information on the Internet.

The new media have caught on for a reason. Knowledge is increasing exponentially; human brainpower and waking hours are not. Fortunately, the Internet and information technologies are helping us manage, search and retrieve our collective intellectual output at different scales, from Twitter and previews to e-books and online encyclopedias. Far from making us stupid, these technologies are the only things that will keep us smart.

Reading for Better Writing

Working by yourself or with a group, answer these questions:

1. Review Pinker's opening paragraph in which he introduces his topic by suggesting that current allegations regarding the negative impact of electronic technologies are similar to past allegations regarding the impact of the printing press, newspapers, paperbacks, and television. Paraphrase his claim, explain why you do or do not agree, and explain whether the opening is or is not effective.

2. The essay is organized as a series of critics' arguments asserting the negative impact of new media, followed by Pinker's counterarguments. Identify three of these exchanges and explain how the point-counterpoint format clarifies both sides of the argument while also making Pinker's position more convincing.

3. Note that Pinker uses cause-effect logic to identify weaknesses in others' claims and to assert the value of his own claims. Identify an example of each that you find persuasive and explain why.

4. Pinker is a scholar aiming to analyze an academic topic with thoughtful, well-researched arguments in an informed, academic tone. Cite passages that illustrate this voice.

5. However, Pinker is also a writer aiming to engage and inform readers who have likely not studied the topic themselves. Identify passages in which his examples and word choice illustrate his effort to connect with these readers.

Writing Guidelines

Model

Planning

1. **Select a topic.** Begin by thinking about categories such as those listed below and listing phenomena related to each category. From this list, choose a topic and analyze its causes, its effects, or both.

   - **Family Life:** adult children living with parents, more stay-at-home dads, families simplifying their lifestyles, adults squeezed by needs of children and parents
   - **Politics:** fewer student voters, increasing support for green-energy production, increased interest in third-party politics, tension between political-action groups
   - **Society:** nursing shortage, doctor shortage, terrorist threats, increasing immigrant-advocacy efforts, shifting ethnic ratios, decreasing number of newspapers
   - **Environment:** common water pollutants, new water-purification technology, decreasing U.S. space exploration, increasing number of nuclear power plants

2. **Narrow and research the topic.** State your topic and below it, list related causes and effects in two columns. Next, do preliminary research to expand the list and distinguish primary causes and effects from secondary ones. Revise your topic as needed to address only primary causes and/or effects that research links to a specific phenomenon.

Cause/Effect Topic: _____

Causes (Because of)	Effects (this results)
1. _____	1. _____
2. _____	2. _____
3. _____	3. _____

3. **Draft and test your thesis.** Based on your preliminary research, draft a working thesis (you may revise it later) that introduces the topic, along with the causes and/or effects you intend to discuss. Limit your argument to only those points you can prove.

4. **Gather and analyze information.** Research your topic, looking for clear evidence that links specific causes to specific effects. As you study the phenomenon, distinguish between primary and secondary causes (main and contributing), direct and indirect results, short-term and long-term effects, and so on. At the same time, test your analysis to avoid mistaking a coincidence for a cause/effect relationship. Use the list of logical fallacies (see pages 257–260) to weed out common errors in logic. For example, finding chemical pollutants in a stream running beside a chemical plant does not "prove" that the plant caused the pollutants.

5. **Get organized.** Develop an outline that lays out your thesis and argument in a clear pattern. Under each main point asserting a cause/effect connection, list details from your research that support the connection.

Thesis: _____

Point #1	Point #2	Point #3
■ Supporting details	■ Supporting details	■ Supporting details
■ Supporting details	■ Supporting details	■ Supporting details

Drafting

6. Use your outline to draft the essay. Try to rough out the essay's overall argument before you attempt to revise it. As you write, show how each specific cause led to each specific effect, citing examples as needed. To show those cause-effect relationships, use transitional words like the following:

▪ accordingly	▪ for this purpose	▪ since	▪ therefore
▪ as a result	▪ for this reason	▪ so	▪ thus
▪ because	▪ hence	▪ such as	▪ to illustrate
▪ consequently	▪ just as	▪ thereby	▪ whereas

Revising

7. Get feedback. Ask a peer reviewer or someone from the college's writing center to read your essay for an engaging opening, a thoughtful cause-effect thesis, clear and convincing reasoning that links specific causes to specific effects, and a closing that deepens and extends the cause-effect analysis of the phenomenon.

8. Revise the essay. Whether your essay presents causes, effects, or both, use the checklist below to trace and refine your argument.

____ **Ideas:** The essay explains the causes and/or effects of the topic in a clear, well-reasoned analysis. The analysis is supported by credible information and free of logical fallacies.

____ **Organization:** The structure helps clarify the cause-effect relationships through a well traced line of thinking, and the links between the main points, supporting points, and evidence are clear.

____ **Voice:** The tone is informed, polite, logical and measured.

Editing and Proofreading

9. Edit the essay for clarity and correctness. Check for the following:

____ **Words:** The diction is precise and clear, and technical or scientific terms are defined. Causes are linked to effects with transitional words and phrases.

____ **Sentences:** Structures are clear, varied, and smooth.

____ **Correctness:** The writing is correct in terms of grammar, punctuation, mechanics, usage, and spelling.

____ **Design:** The format, layout, and typography adhere to expectation; any visuals used enhance the written analysis and clarify the paper's cause-effect reasoning.

Publishing

12. Publish your essay. Share your writing by submitting it to your instructor, posting it on the class's or department's website, or turning it into a presentation.

Critical-Thinking and Writing Activities

As directed by your instructor, complete the following critical-thinking and writing activities by yourself or with classmates.

1. In "Dutch Discord," Brittany Korver analyzes the causes and effects of a shift in the Netherlands' immigration practices. Identify a similar shift in the policies or practices of a city, state, or country that interests you. Then write an essay in which you analyze the causes and effects of this shift.

2. In "If You Let Me Play . . . ," Mary Brophy Marcus uses cause-effect reasoning to analyze how Jackie Thomas's experience in college athletics helped her prepare for a successful business career. Identify experiences that will help you prepare for your career. Then write an essay in which you use cause-effect reasoning to prove your claim.

3. While "The Legacy of Generation Ñ" focuses on cultural changes, "Mind Over Mass Media" analyzes changes wrought by technology. Identify a social change or a technological change that has impacted your life; then analyze the causes or effects of that change.

4. Scan editorials in two or three newspapers, looking for arguments based on cause-effect reasoning. Then examine the arguments for logical fallacies such as false-cause or slippery-slope claims (for help, see page 259). Present your findings to the class.

5. List the kinds of documents written by workers in your planned career and identify which ones are likely based on cause-effect reasoning. Then find examples of two or three of these documents, analyze the quality of the writing, and share your findings with the class.

Learning-Outcomes Checklist

After reading the essays in this chapter, developing your own cause-effect essay, and getting feedback from classmates and your instructor, use this checklist to assess how effectively you achieved the learning outcomes for this chapter:

_____ I understand cause-effect reasoning.

_____ I am able to identify and correct logical fallacies related to cause-effect thinking.

_____ I understand how to support cause-effect reasoning with reliable, detailed evidence.

_____ I can effectively use transitional words and phrases to clarify cause-effect relationships.

_____ I have effectively planned, drafted, revised, and polished a cause-effect essay.

12 Comparison and Contrast

In his plays, William Shakespeare creates characters, families, and even plot lines that mirror each other. As a result, we see Hamlet in relation to Laertes and the Montagues in relation to the Capulets. In the process, we do precisely what the writer wants us to do—we compare and contrast the subjects. The result is clarity and insight: by thinking about both subjects in relation to each other, we understand each one more clearly.

But writers in college and in the workplace also use comparison/contrast as an analytical strategy. To help you read and write such documents, the following pages include instructions and four model essays.

Learning Outcomes

 Audio

 Video

▶ Understand how to read carefully for compare-contrast strategies in essays.

▶ Structure subject-by-subject and trait-by-trait comparisons.

▶ Use details and transitional words to support and clarify compare-contrast claims.

▶ Practice revision and editing strategies that strengthen compare-contrast writing.

▶ Develop an essay that effectively uses compare-contrast strategies.

Visually Speaking ▶ Look closely at the photograph above. What does it suggest about how comparing and contrasting help explain a topic?

■ Reading Comparison-Contrast Writing

When writers use compare-contrast, what should you as a reader look for? The instruction below will help you read essays like those that follow.

Consider the rhetorical situation. ■ ▪ ■

Think about how a writer might use comparison-contrast to achieve her or his purpose, address an audience, and analyze a topic.

- **Purpose:** Writers compare and contrast subjects in order to understand their similarities and differences. Their purpose may be to stress the similarities between seemingly dissimilar things or the differences between things that seem quite similar.
- **Audience:** A compare-contrast writer may have virtually any reader in mind—the instructor for a student essay or potential clients for a marketing document. Whatever the situation, the writer sees readers as people whose understanding of a topic, an issue, or a phenomenon can be deepened with comparative analysis.
- **Topics:** Writers address a wide range of topics through compare-contrast: people, events, phenomena, technologies, problems, products, stories, and so on. The writer simply thinks through what aspects of the topic may be illuminated through comparison and/or contrast.

Consider the compare-contrast practices used. ■ ▪ ■

As you read an essay using compare-contrast, look for the following:

- **Criteria Used for Comparison:** Writers anchor their analyses in specific points of comparison. For example, a comparison of two characters in a play might focus on their backgrounds, their actions in the play, their psychology, their fate, and so on. As you read, trace the features compared, thinking through the writer's choices.
- **Organization of the Comparison:** Such writing is generally structured either subject by subject (first dealing with one topic fully and then the other) or trait by trait (holding up the topics side by side, feature by feature).
- **The Point of the Comparison:** Writers use comparison to illuminate topics through a key idea about connections and distinctions. Identify the essential insight of the comparison, whether the writer states it at the beginning or leaves it to the end.

Reader's Checklist

_____ Why is the writer comparing these topics? Is the goal to stress similarities, differences, or both? How does the comparison speak to specific readers?

_____ What features or traits of the topics are compared? Why?

_____ How does the writer present the topics and the criteria for comparison?

_____ What conclusion does the writer develop through analysis?

Comparison and Contrast ▪▪▪▪

In the essay below, student writer Rachel De Smith analyzes characters from two novels by comparing and contrasting their history, cultures, experiences, and personalities.

Essay Outline

Introduction: Sethe and Orleanna as surprisingly similar characters
1. Living and isolation and loneliness
2. Haunted by the past
3. Grueling journeys of escape

Conclusion: Sethe and Orleanna as suffering but strong women

The title identifies the topics compared and the traits examined.

Introduction: two seemingly different characters share similar lives.

1 Both women live in isolation and loneliness.

(a) Sethe

(b) Orleanna

Sethe in *Beloved* and Orleanna in *Poisonwood Bible:* Isolation, Children, and Getting Out

Toni Morrison's Sethe and Barbara Kingsolver's Orleanna Price seem to be vastly different women, living in different times and cultures, descended from different races. One has had a faithful spouse forced away from her by circumstances; the other lives in a devastating marriage. One is a former slave, while the other is a comparatively well-off minister's wife. However, these two women are more alike than they first appear. Both live in isolation and loneliness, both are haunted by the past, both risk everything to get their children out of devastating circumstances—and both reap the consequences of such risks.

Sethe lives in house number 124, a house generally believed to be haunted, "full of a baby's venom" (Morrison 3). The child's ghost inhabiting the house throws things around, makes spots of colored light appear, shakes floors, and stomps up the stairs. The people of the surrounding community—remembering Sethe's past, fearing ghostly retribution, and resenting the long-ago extravagance of Sethe's mother-in-law, Baby Suggs—diligently avoid the house and its residents. Sethe's one remaining daughter, Denver, will not leave the yard (Morrison 205). The two of them live with the ghost, ostracized.

Orleanna lives in a less malignant but equally isolated situation. When she and her daughters follow her husband on his zealous missionary trip to the Congo, she is the only white woman in a village of people with whom she shares nothing, not even a word of their language. Preoccupied with the troubles in her own house, she remains separated from the villagers by a gulf of cultural misunderstanding—from how to behave in the marketplace to where to get her drinking water (Kingsolver 89, 172). Even when she returns to the United States, Orleanna lives in isolation, hidden among her flower gardens, set apart by the stigma of her past (Kingsolver 407).

The cause of all this isolation, for both women, is the past. When Sethe saw a slave catcher coming for her, she attempted to kill all four of her young children in order

2 Isolation for both women is rooted in a haunting past.

(a) Sethe

(b) Orleanna

to prevent them from becoming slaves (Morrison 149, 163). She succeeded in killing only her second-youngest, known as Beloved. No one went back to the plantation; Sethe went to jail instead. Years later, her two oldest children (sons) run off, unable to face the specter of their dead sister knocking over jars and leaving handprints in cakes. Beloved's death is thus the defining moment not only for Sethe's haunted life but also for Denver's, Baby Suggs', and, in many ways, the entire community's.

Orleanna, like Sethe, has lost a child, though not by her own hand. Her youngest daughter, Ruth May, died of snakebite after an ugly disagreement (involving much shouting and plenty of voodoo) between the Price family and the rest of the village. Orleanna is not immediately responsible for Ruth May's death—in fact, she has recently brought the girl miraculously through a bout with malaria (Kingsolver 276). However, Orleanna still feels tremendous guilt about Ruth May's death, and even about being in Africa at all. In much of Orleanna's narration, she attempts to move past this guilt, periodically asking her absent daughter's forgiveness. Sethe, also hoping for reconciliation, explains herself in a similar way to Beloved. But Beloved seems to feed off of Sethe's remorse, whereas Ruth May, as portrayed in the final chapter of the novel, bears no such ill-will. Ruth May says, "Mother, you can still hold on but forgive, forgive . . . I forgive you, Mother" (Kingsolver 537, 543). Beloved continually punishes Sethe for leaving her behind, but Ruth May is willing to forgive. 5

3 Both women take journeys to escape.

(a) Sethe

Both Sethe and Orleanna endure grueling journeys of escape, though the journeys begin very differently. Sethe has spent a long time planning an escape with her fellow slaves. When the opportunity finally comes, Sethe sends her children on ahead and then follows, pausing on the way to give birth to Denver. Oddly enough, the final stage of her journey to "freedom" seems to be her time in jail, an episode that kept her from going back to the Sweet Home plantation. However, even after Sethe leaves jail and begins a life free from the degradations of the plantation, she cannot escape the stigma of her past, particularly Beloved's violent death. 6

(b) Orleanna

Orleanna's journey, though also long-anticipated or at least long-desired, is a spontaneous event. Following Ruth May's tragic death (the impetus for her journey), Orleanna simply walks away: her daughter Leah recalls that "Mother never once turned around to look over her shoulder" (Kinsolver 389). Their unplanned journey ends up as a fiasco, culminating in malaria during the rainy season somewhere in the depths of the Congo, but all of Orleanna's remaining daughters survive. Though obvious differences exist between the deaths of Ruth May and Beloved, both deaths allow their families some form of escape. In addition, Orleanna, like Sethe, is willing to give up her children in order for them to escape; she sends Rachel with Eeben Axelroot and leaves Leah with Anatole when she and Adah leave the country for good. Orleanna's actions parallel Sethe's, as Sethe sends her children ahead of her (in escape or death) in order for them to leave the plantation. Orleanna sees very little of Rachel and Leah for the rest of her life, but they have escaped the devastation of their lives in the Congo, or at least their lives under Nathan Price, and that is—or must be—enough for her. 7

Conclusion: these two haunted characters are strong women who eventually move beyond guilt.

Sethe and Orleanna are both haunted women. The deaths of their daughters and estrangement from their remaining children prevent these women from finding peace. Both are haunted by guilt—Sethe for her own actions in the murder of Beloved, and Orleanna for her complicity both in Ruth May's death and in the chaos that enveloped the Congo at the same time. Both women are also isolated and lonely, distanced by distrust and misunderstanding from the people around them. And both women, in the long run, risk everything to gain freedom for their children. Distrust, rage, fear, and bad dreams accompany that risk, but both women keep their children from the evil awaiting them—a plantation, a father's oppression. Paul D. questions Sethe on this point, wondering if other circumstances might be even worse than the plantation. Sethe responds, "It ain't my job to know what's worse. It's my job to know what is and to keep them away from what I know is terrible" (Morrison 165). Sethe is never able to achieve true reconciliation with Beloved, but her relationships with Denver and Paul D. help to make up for this loss, while Orleanna is forgiven by Ruth May and eventually reunited (albeit briefly) with her other children. Despite the attendant circumstances, both Sethe and Orleanna are revealed to be strong women, and both eventually move past their paralyzing guilt in their efforts to "walk forward into the light" (Kingsolver 543).

Note: The Works Cited page is not shown. For sample pages, see MLA (pages 526–527 and APA (page 557).

8

Reading for Better Writing

Working by yourself or with a group, do the following:

1. Review the title and opening paragraph, describe how the writer focuses her essay, and explain why you do or do not find that introduction well written.

2. A thesis is a type of contract in which the writers states what he or she will do in the essay. Review the writer's thesis and explain whether she does what she promises.

3. Select two paragraphs and explain why they do or do not clarify the topic and develop the thesis.

4. Based on your reading of this essay, explain why you think that compare-contrast reasoning is or is not an effective strategy for analyzing literature.

5. Explain why the writer's voice is or is not appropriate for this essay. For example is the voice informed or uninformed, objective or manipulative, respectful or disrespectful? Cite passages that support your assessment.

6. Explain how you could use compare-contrast reasoning to complete specific writing assignments in your major, and describe why the strategy would be effective.

Comparison and Contrast ■■·■

Video

Gelareh Asayesh grew up in Iran before moving to Florida. She writes about her experiences in *Saffron Sky: A Life Between Iran and America*. The article below appeared in the *New York Times* in November 2001.

Shrouded in Contradiction

> **Two contrasting scenes appear in the first sentence.**

I grew up wearing the miniskirt to school, the veil to the mosque. In the Tehran of my childhood, women in bright sundresses shared the sidewalk with women swathed in black. The tension between the two ways of life was palpable. As a schoolgirl, I often cringed when my bare legs got leering or contemptuous glances. Yet, at times, I long for the days when I could walk the streets of my country with the wind in my hair. When clothes were clothes. In today's Iran, whatever I wear sends a message. If it's a chador, it embarrasses my Westernized relatives. If it's a skimpy scarf, I risk being accused of stepping on the blood of the martyrs who died in the war with Iraq. Each time I return to Tehran, I wait until the last possible moment, when my plane lands on the tarmac, to don the scarf and long jacket that many Iranian women

As a schoolgirl, I often cringed when my bare legs got leering or contemptuous glances.

> **Italics distinguish *hijab* as a non-English word.**

wear in lieu of a veil. To wear *hijab*—Islamic covering—is to invite contradiction. Sometimes I hate it. Sometimes I value it. 1

Most of the time, I don't even notice it. It's annoying, but so is wearing pantyhose to work. It ruins my hair, but so does the humidity in Florida, where I live. For many women, the veil is neither a symbol nor a statement. It's simply what they wear, as their mothers did before them. Something to dry your face with after your ablutions before prayer. A place for a toddler to hide when he's feeling shy. Even for a woman like me, who wears it with a hint of rebellion, *hijab* is just not that big a deal. 2

> **Notice the one-sentence paragraph.**

Except when it is. 3

"Sister, what kind of get-up is this?" a woman in black, one of a pair, asks me one summer day on the Caspian shore. I am standing in line to ride a gondola up a mountain, where I'll savor some ice cream along with vistas of sea and forest. Women in chadors stand wilting in the heat, faces gleaming with sweat. Women in makeup and clunky heels wear knee-length jackets with pants, their hair daringly 4 exposed beneath sheer scarves.

None have been more daring than I. I've wound my scarf into a turban, 5 leaving my neck bare to the breeze. The woman in black is a government employee paid to police public morals. "Fix your scarf at once!" she snaps.

"But I'm hot," I say. 6

"You're hot?" she exclaims. "Don't you think we all are?" 7

I start unwinding my makeshift turban. "The men aren't hot," I mutter. 8

Her companion looks at me in shocked reproach. "Sister, this isn't about men 9 and women," she says, shaking her head. "This is about Islam."

I want to argue. I feel like a child. Defiant, but 10 powerless. Burning with injustice, but also with a hint of shame. I do as I am told, feeling acutely conscious of the bare skin I am covering. In policing my sexuality, these women have made me more aware of it.

The veil masks erotic freedom, but its advocates 11 believe *hijab* transcends the erotic—or expands it. In the West, we think of passion as a fever of the body, not the soul. In the East, Sufi poets used earthly passion as a metaphor; the beloved they celebrated was God. Where I come from, people are more likely to find delirious passion in the mosque than in the bedroom.

> *The veil masks erotic freedom, but its advocates believe "hijab" transcends the erotic—or expands it.*

There are times when I feel a hint of this passion. A few years after my 12 encounter on the Caspian, I go to the wake of a family friend. Sitting in a mosque in Mashhad, I grip a slippery black veil with one hand and a prayer book with the other. In the center of the hall, there's a stack of Koranic texts decorated with green-and-black calligraphy, a vase of white gladioluses and a large photograph of the dearly departed. Along the walls, women wait quietly.

From the men's side of the mosque, the mullah's voice rises in lament. His voice 13 is deep and plaintive, oddly compelling. I bow my head, sequestered in my veil while at my side a community of women pray and weep with increasing abandon. I remember from girlhood this sense of being exquisitely alone in the company of others. Sometimes I have cried as well, free to weep without having to offer an explanation. Perhaps they are right, those mystics who believe that physical love is an obstacle to spiritual love; those architects of mosques who abstained from images of earthly life, decorating their work with geometric shapes that they

Contradictory feelings are pushed together in a compact list.

The writer offers definitions of passion reflecting three different perspectives.

The writer uses terms of limited certainty, such as *perhaps* and *all I know*.

believed freed the soul to slip from its worldly moorings. I do not aspire to such lofty sentiments. All I know is that such moments of passionate abandon, within the circle of invisibility created by the veil, offer an emotional catharsis every bit as potent as any sexual release.

Outside, the rain pours from a sullen sky. I make my farewells and walk   14 toward the car, where my driver waits. My veil is wicking muddy water from the sidewalk. I gather up the wet and grimy folds with distaste, longing to be home, where I can cast off this curtain of cloth that gives with one hand, takes away with the other.

The final line summarizes the contradictions described in the essay.

Reading for Better Writing

Working by yourself or with a group, answer these questions:

1. Sometimes writers use comparison-contrast organization to take a position on an issue—in some cases to show that one side is better than the other, but in others, to show the difficulty of choosing one side over the other. What do you think is Asayesh's position on *hijab*, and why?

2. Find Asayesh's one-sentence paragraph (paragraph 3). Why might the writer have constructed the paragraph in this way? How would this excerpt differ if that sentence had been part of either the preceding or the following paragraph?

3. What contrasts are listed in paragraph 4? How does the writer use sentence structure and punctuation to mark the contrasts?

4. In paragraph 13, Asayesh uses words that indicate limited certainty, such as *perhaps* and *all I know.* How do these phrases temper her claims?

5. In what ways are the opening and closing sentences alike? How are these similarities significant for readers?

Comparison and Contrast ■■˙■

Shankar Vedantam is a Nieman Fellow at Harvard University, a science reporter for *The Washington Post,* and the author of the recent book, *The Hidden Brain: How Our Unconscious Minds Elect Presidents, Control Markets, Wage Wars and Save Our Lives.* In this essay, Vedantam analyzes how people judge others based on the shade of their skin. (The essay was published in the *New York Times* on January 18, 2010.)

Shades of Prejudice

The writer uses an anecdote to introduce and illustrate his thesis.

LAST week, the Senate majority leader, Harry Reid, found himself in trouble for once suggesting that Barack Obama had a political edge over other African-American candidates because he was "light-skinned" and had "no Negro dialect, unless he wanted to have one." Mr. Reid was not expressing sadness but a gleeful opportunism that Americans were still judging one another by the color of their skin, rather than—as the Rev. Dr. Martin Luther King Jr., whose legacy we commemorated on Monday, dreamed—by the content of their character.

He asserts that research supports his thesis, but he cites no sources.

The Senate leader's choice of words was flawed, but positing that black candidates who look "less black" have a leg up is hardly more controversial than saying wealthy people have an advantage in elections. Dozens of research studies have shown that skin tone and other racial features play powerful roles in who gets ahead and who does not. These factors regularly determine who gets hired, who gets convicted and who gets elected.

He offers examples.

Consider: Lighter-skinned Latinos in the United States make $5,000 more on average than darker-skinned Latinos. The education test-score gap between light-skinned and dark-skinned African-Americans is nearly as large as the gap between whites and blacks.

He supports his point by referring to his colleague's research.

The Harvard neuroscientist Allen Counter has found that in Arizona, California and Texas, hundreds of Mexican-American women have suffered mercury poisoning as a result of the use of skin-whitening creams. In India, where I was born, a best-selling line of women's cosmetics called Fair and Lovely has recently been supplemented by a product aimed at men called Fair and Handsome.

The writer distinguishes racism and colorism by comparing and contrasting the nature and effects of each.

This isn't racism, per se: it's colorism, an unconscious prejudice that isn't focused on a single group like blacks so much as on blackness itself. Our brains, shaped by culture and history, create intricate caste hierarchies that privilege those who are physically and culturally whiter and punish those who are darker.

Colorism is an intraracial problem as well as an interracial problem. Racial minorities who are alert to white-black or white-brown issues often remain silent about a colorism that asks "how black" or "how brown" someone is within their own communities.

6

To support his claim, he gives an example and cites a study.

If colorism lives underground, its effects are very real. Darker-skinned African-American defendants are more than twice as likely to receive the death penalty as lighter-skinned African-American defendants for crimes of equivalent seriousness involving white victims. This was proven in rigorous, peer-reviewed research into hundreds of capital punishment-worthy cases by the Stanford psychologist Jennifer Eberhardt.

7

Take, for instance, two of Dr. Eberhadt's murder cases, in Philadelphia, involving black defendants—one light-skinned, the other dark. The lighter-skinned defendant, Arthur Hawthorne, ransacked a drug store for money and narcotics. The pharmacist had complied with every demand, yet Mr. Hawthorne shot him when he was lying face down. Mr. Hawthorne was independently identified as the killer by multiple witnesses, a family member and an accomplice.

8

The writer compares and contrasts how people are treated by the legal system.

The darker-skinned defendant, Ernest Porter, pleaded not guilty to the murder of a beautician, a crime that he was linked to only through a circuitous chain of evidence. A central witness later said that prosecutors forced him to finger Mr. Porter even though he was sure that he was the wrong man. Two people who provided an alibi for Mr. Porter were mysteriously never called to testify. During his trial, Mr. Porter revealed that the police had even gotten his name wrong—his real name was Theodore Wilson—but the court stuck to the wrong name in the interest of convenience.

9

He cites a similarity and a difference.

Both men were convicted. But the lighter-skinned Mr. Hawthorne was given a life sentence, while the dark-skinned Mr. Porter has spent more than a quarter-century on Pennsylvania's death row.

10

He compares colorism in the legal system with colorism in politics.

To support his claim, he offers an example.

Colorism also influenced the 2008 presidential race. In an experiment that fall, Drew Westen, a psychologist at Emory, and other researchers shot different versions of a political advertisement in support of Mr. Obama. One version showed a light-skinned black family. Another version had the same script, but used a darker-skinned black family. Voters, at an unconscious level, were less inclined to support Mr. Obama after watching the ad featuring the darker-skinned family than were those who watched the ad with the lighter-skinned family.

11

Political operatives are certainly aware of this dynamic. During the 12 campaign, a conservative group created attack ads linking Mr. Obama with Kwame Kilpatrick, the disgraced former mayor of Detroit, which darkened Mr. Kilpatrick's skin to have a more persuasive effect. Though there can be little doubt that as a candidate Mr. Obama faced voters' conscious and unconscious prejudices, it is simultaneously true that unconscious colorism subtly advantaged him over darker-skinned politicians.

> To restate his thesis and unify his essay, the writer refers to the anecdote used in the opening.

In highlighting how Mr. Obama benefited from his links to whiteness, Harry 13 Reid punctured the myth that Mr. Obama's election signaled the completion of the Rev. King's dream. Americans may like to believe that we are now color-blind, that we can consciously choose not to use race when making judgments about other people. It remains a worthy aspiration. But this belief rests on a profound misunderstanding about how our minds work and perversely limits our ability to discuss prejudice honestly.

Reading for Better Writing

Working by yourself or with a group, answer these questions:

1. Describe how Shankar Vedantam uses an anecdote to open and close his essay. Then explain why you do or do not find that strategy effective.

2. The writer asserts that (a) colorism and racism are different and that (b) colorism is both an intraracial problem and an interracial problem. Explain what he means by each assertion and why you do or do not agree.

3. Review paragraphs 7–10 in which the writer compares and contrasts penalties meted out by the legal system. Then explain why these passages do or do not develop his thesis.

4. Note how the writer uses dashes in paragraphs 8 and 9, and then explain why that use is or is not correct.

5. In January 18, 2010, the writer published this essay in the *New York Times*. Cite words or sentences showing that his voice is or is not appropriate for his subject and audience.

Comparison and Contrast ■■▪

Peter Baldwin, a history professor at the University of California at Los Angeles, has written a number of books, including *The Narcissism of Minor Differences: How America and Europe Are Alike.* In the essay below, adapted from that text, he compares and contrasts Europe and America. As you read the essay, use underlining or highlighting, as well as notes in the margin, to trace and respond to Baldwin's compare-contrast thinking and writing.

The Likeness Across the Atlantic

As you read the essay, use this column to record your observations and questions.

1   The Atlantic gets ever wider. Not just in a physical sense, as oceans rise and coastlines recede, but also in ideological terms. Europe and America appear to be pitted against each other as never before. On one shore, capitalist markets, untempered by proper social policies, allow unbridled competition, poverty, pollution, violence, class divides, and social anomie. On the other side, Europe nurtures a social approach, a regulated labor market, and elaborate welfare networks. Possibly it has a less dynamic economy, but it is a more solidaristic and harmonious society. "Our social model," the voice of British left-liberalism, *The Guardian,* describes the European way, as opposed to "feral capitalism" in the United States.

2   That major differences separate the United States from Europe is scarcely a new idea. But it has become more menacingly Manichaean over the past decade. Foreign-policy disagreements fuel it: Iraq, Iran, Israel, North Korea. So does the more general question of what role the world's one remaining superpower should play while it still remains unchallenged. Robert Kagan, a senior associate at the Carnegie Endowment for International Peace, has famously suggested that, when it comes to foreign policy, Americans and Europeans call different planets home. Americans wield hard power and face the nasty choices that follow. Europeans, sheltered now from most geopolitical strife, enjoy the luxury of approaching conflict in a more conciliatory way: Martian unilateralism confronts Venusian multilateralism. But the dispute goes beyond diplomatic and military strategy. It touches on the nature of these two societies. Does having the strongest battalions change the country that possesses them? After all, America is not just militarily strong. It is also—compared with Europe—harsh, violent, and sharp-elbowed. Or so goes the argument.

The idea that the North Atlantic is socioculturally parted is elaborated   *3*
in both Europe and America for reasons that are as connected to domestic
political needs and tactics as they are to any actual differences. American
criticism of Europe, when it can be heard at all, typically concerns foreign
policy or trade issues. American conservatives occasionally make the old
continent a symbol for what they see as the excesses of the welfare state and
statutory regulation. But the longstanding European criticism of America has
become more vehement and widespread and is now shared by right and left
alike. Europeans are keen to define an alternative to American hegemony,
now that Europe no longer needs the protection of the United States in a post-
cold-war world. Beset with internal fractures and disagreements, they have
rediscovered the truism that nothing unites like a common enemy.

A small library of books has been published over the past few years debating   *4*
whether a sociocultural chasm separates (continental) Europe from the
(Anglo-) American barbarians. America's unregulated capitalism is a danger
to Europe, warns the French historian and sociologist Emmanuel Todd. The
notion of a unified West has lost whatever meaning it once had, adds Claus
Offe, a professor of political sociology at the Hertie School of Governance, in
Berlin. A recent letter-writer to the *Financial Times* agrees, although placing
Britain on the side of the Continentals. A common language should not, this
writer claims, obscure the distance between Britain and the United States:
Americans carry guns, execute prisoners, go bankrupt, drive large cars, and
live in large houses. Their men are circumcised and their working class is poor.
The humanist and secular Europeans, by contrast, enjoy socialist hospitals,
schools, and welfare systems. They pay high taxes, live longer, and take the
train. One ponders what unspoken motives inspire such letters. Andrei S.
Markovits, a professor of comparative politics and German studies at the
University of Michigan at Ann Arbor and author of one of the most interesting
recent books on the subject, *Uncouth Nation: Why Europe Dislikes America*
(Princeton University Press, 2007), suggests that anti-Americanism helps fire
the engines of pan-European nationalism. Europeans have less in common
than the aspiring empire builders of the European Union would like. But at
least they can agree on being different from the Americans. Or can they?

Polemic and vituperation abound in the discussion of trans-Atlantic   5
difference; caricature, rather than portrait, is the dominant genre. It is time
to examine more closely what it is we do know. It is time, in other words, to
bring a little empirical meat to the table.

The evidence shows two things. First, Europe is not a coherent or unified   6
continent. The spectrum of difference within even Western Europe is much
broader than normally appreciated. Second, with a few exceptions, the United
States fits into the average range of most quantifiable measures that I have
been able to find. We may therefore conclude either that there is no coherent
European identity, or—if there is one—that the United States is as much a
European country as the usual candidates are. We might rephrase this by
saying that both Europe and the United States are, in fact, parts of a common,
big-tent grouping—call it the West, the Atlantic community, the developed
world, or what you will. America is not Sweden, for sure. But nor is Italy
Sweden, nor France, nor even Germany. And who says that Sweden is Europe,
any more than Vermont is America?

Consider the following examples:

Social welfare: As a portion of the total economy, American public social   7
expenditures narrowly make it into the European norm, sneaking in above
Ireland. But because the American gross domestic product is greater than
those of most European nations, the per capita spending is higher than
this rank suggests. In terms of how much money is paid out on average for
each person, the United States ranks in the lower middle of the European
spectrum, above most of the Mediterranean countries and Iceland and in the
same league as Britain, the Netherlands, and Finland.

Beyond that, a complete accounting of welfare efforts cannot focus only   8
on what the state does through social policy. Other avenues of redistribution
are also important: voluntary efforts, private but legally mandated benefits,
and taxes. If we include all those, the American welfare state is more extensive
than is often realized. By taking account of all these components of social
welfare—public, voluntary, and mandatory—the total effort made in the
United States falls into the middle of the European spectrum.

Foreign travel: Americans are often thought to take little interest in the world   9
around them, except perhaps when invading it. The paucity of Americans
with passports is often held up as an indication of uninterest. Eighty-five

percent of American tourism and travel is domestic. If it follows that 15 percent is international, then Americans join the company of the Greeks, Spaniards, and French, among whom, respectively, 12, 13, and 17 percent of holidays are taken abroad. And that does not take into account the distance needed to travel before the Great Abroad begins. That more than 99 percent of Luxembourgeois vacations of four nights or more were enjoyed outside the nation's borders does not surprise; where else could they possibly have been taken? Assuming that for a European to leave Europe is an effort roughly analogous to that of an American leaving the United States, the figures become more comparable. In 2006, 9.7 million Western Europeans visited the United States, and 13 million Americans visited Europe. Thus, in the realm of travel, Americans were proportionally more interested in Europeans than the other way around. The same year, significantly more Americans (30 million) traveled overseas (other than to Mexico and Canada) than overseas visitors came to the United States (22 million).

Reading, writing, and culture: Americans do not need to read, Simone 10
de Beauvoir was convinced, because they do not think. Thinking is hard to quantify, reading less so. And read the Americans do. There are more newspapers per head in the United States than anywhere in Europe outside Scandinavia, Switzerland, and Luxembourg. The circulation of American newspapers is higher per capita than in most of the Mediterranean countries and in Ireland and Belgium. The United States is also well equipped with libraries. The long tradition of municipally supported public libraries in the United States means that average American readers are better supplied with library books than their peers in Germany, Britain, France, Holland, Austria, and all the Mediterranean nations. Americans also make better use of those public-library books than most Europeans do. Average Americans borrowed 6.4 books each in 2001, more than their peers in Germany, Austria, Norway, Ireland, Luxembourg, France, and throughout the Mediterranean. And with America's amply endowed universities, it is no surprise that the supply of books per capita in college libraries is higher than in any European country other than Finland, Denmark, and Iceland. Not content with borrowing, Americans also buy more books per head than any European population for which we have numbers. Proportionately more Americans claim to read a book per month than anyone but the Swiss, Swedes, Germans, and Irish. And

Americans write more books. Per capita, they come in at the high end of the European spectrum as authors, measured in terms of volumes in print.

It is true that the American government spends less as a percentage of 11 gross domestic product than almost any European government on what the Organization for Economic Cooperation and Development defines as "recreation and culture," though not less than Greece and only a bit less than Britain and Ireland. Those figures, it should be noted, include government payments to Europe's established churches. American households spend more on recreation and culture privately than any Europeans but the Icelanders, the Austrians, and the British. Add state and private money together, and total American outlays on the finer things in life fall in the upper half of the European middle ground.

In short, for most of the quantifiable measures of socioeconomic reality, 12 the divergence within Europe is greater than that between Europe and the United States. Hand on heart, which cities more resemble each other: Stockholm and Minneapolis or Helsinki and Thessaloniki? And as the European Union widens eastward—possibly even to accept Turkey, a Muslim country mostly in Asia—the most recent newcomers (many from regions once called European Turkey, which were part of the Ottoman Empire) efface many of the issues that do distinguish the United States from Europe. These new arrivals, along with Europe's many recent immigrants from Asia and Africa, are very religious, skeptical of a strong state, unenthusiastic about voting, and allergic to high taxes. From the vantage of old Europe, they are, in other words, more like Americans. How odd, really, that Europeans seek to identify an enemy in a culture with which they have so much in common, just at the moment when they are being joined by ones with whom they actually share even less. How odd to turn their backs on a country which, like their own continent, espouses the Reformation, the Scientific Revolution, the Enlightenment, democracy, liberalism, free but appropriately regulated markets, and religious toleration.

Even a few minutes watching the Eurovision Song Contest strengthens 13 both a belief in the continued vitality of relations that span the Atlantic and a belief in a hugely variegated Europe, diverse to the point of incoherence. This must be the nightmare that keeps the empire builders in Brussels awake at night: a vastly expanded Europe, stretching from Kamchatka to the Azores, from the North Pole (now festooned with Danish flags and Russian submarines) to the Dead Sea, with its pidgin English lingua franca and droning, generic, ritual Europol incantations of "Hello Europe" even as the voting descends into unabashed tribalism. Imagine now that Europe's voters were given a choice also between the Australians and the Serbs. With whom would, say, the Norwegians cast their lot? Place your bets, ladies and gentlemen.

Of course, this choice will never be on offer. The world is too complicated   *14* a place for the binary clumpishness of all-or-nothing alternatives between America and Europe. Both sides of this particular divide would do well to consider how proximate and similar the two slopes of their supposed conceptual chasm in fact are. Whether American conservatives or Europeans, each enamored of their own reflection, unless we break this spell of self-enchantment, we risk suffering the fate of Narcissus. Readers will recall that Ovid's ill-fated hero dies of thirst, for fear that kissing the water's surface will disrupt the image that has so enthralled him.

Reading for Better Writing

Working by yourself or with a group, answer these questions:

1. First describe how Baldwin introduces his topic and thesis, and then explain why the opening is or is not engaging and clear.

2. In the opening 4 paragraphs, the writer focuses on differences between Europe and the U.S; in paragraph 5, he builds a transition; and in the remaining paragraphs, he focuses on similarities. Review these organizational choices and then explain why they do or do not help the writer develop his thesis.

3. Review paragraph 6 and explain how it (a) re-focuses the writer's argument and (b) introduces the claims in the remaining paragraphs.

4. Review paragraphs 8-10, noting how the writer classifies "examples" of similarities into three types, each introduced by a boldfaced title. Then explain why his classification strategy does or does not help him develop his argument.

5. Cite examples from the essay to prove or disprove that Baldwin's document is written in an academic style. (For information about an academic style, see pages 79–80.)

Writing Guidelines

Model

Planning

1. **Select a topic.** List subjects that are similar and/or different in ways that you find interesting, perplexing, disgusting, infuriating, charming, or informing. Then choose two subjects whose comparison and/or contrast gives the reader some insight into who or what they are. *Note:* Make sure that the items have a solid *basis* for comparison. Comparable items are types of the same thing (e.g., two rivers, two characters, two films, two mental illnesses, two banking regulations, two search engines, two theories).

2. **Get the big picture.** Using a computer or a paper and pen, create three columns as shown below. Brainstorm a list of traits under each heading. (Also see the Venn diagram on page 52.)

Features Peculiar to Subject #1	Shared Features	Features Peculiar to Subject #2

3. **Gather information.** Review your list of features, highlighting those that could provide insight into one or both subjects. Research the subjects, using hands-on analysis when possible. Consider writing your research notes in the three-column format shown above.

4. **Draft a working thesis.** Review your expanded list of features and eliminate those that now seem unimportant. Write a sentence stating the core of what you learned about the subjects: what essential insight have you reached about the similarities and/or differences between the topics? If you're stuck, try completing the sentence below. (Switch around the terms "similar" and "different" if you wish to stress similarities.)

   Whereas _____ and _____ seem similar, they are different in several ways, and the differences are important because _____ .

5. **Get organized.** Decide how to organize your essay. Generally, *subject by subject* works better for short, simple comparisons. *Trait by trait* works better for longer, more complex comparisons, in that you hold up the topics side by side, trait by trait. Consider, as well, the order in which you will discuss the topics and arrange the traits, choices that depend on what you want to feature and how you want to build and deepen the comparison.

Subject by Subject:	Trait by Trait:
Introduction	Introduction
Subject #1	Trait A
■ Trait A	■ Subject #1
■ Trait B	■ Subject #2
Subject #2	Trait B
■ Trait A	■ Subject #1
■ Trait B	■ Subject #2

Drafting

6. Write your first draft. Review your outline and draft the paper.

> **Subject-by-subject pattern:**
> - **Opening:** get readers' attention, introduce the subjects, and offer a thesis.
> - **Middle:** discuss the first subject, then analyze the second subject, discussing traits parallel to those you addressed with the first subject.
> - **Conclusion:** summarize similarities, differences, and implications.
>
> **Trait-by-trait pattern:**
> - **Opening:** get readers' attention, introduce the subjects, and offer a thesis.
> - **Middle:** compare and/or contrast the two subjects trait by trait; include transitions that help readers look back and forth between the two subjects.
> - **Conclusion:** summarize the key relationships and note their significance.

Revising

7. Get feedback. Ask someone to read your paper, looking for a clear thesis, an engaging introduction, a middle that compares and/or contrasts parallel traits in a logical order, and a unifying closing.

8. Rework your draft. Based on feedback, revise for the following issues:

_____ **Ideas:** The points made and conclusions drawn from comparing and contrasting provide insight into both subjects.

_____ **Organization:** The structure, whether subject by subject or trait by trait, helps readers grasp the similarities and differences between the subjects.

_____ **Voice:** The tone is informed, involved, and genuine.

Editing and Proofreading

9. Carefully edit your essay. Look for the following issues:

_____ **Words** are precise, clear, and defined as needed.

_____ **Sentences** are clear, well reasoned, varied in structure, and smooth.

_____ The **copy** is **correct**, clean, and properly formatted. Graphics are well-placed.

_____ **Page design** is attractive and follows MLA or APA guidelines.

Publishing

10. Publish your essay. Share your writing by submitting it to your instructor, posting it on a website, sharing it with friends and family who might be interested in the topic, crafting a presentation or demonstration, or reshaping your comparison as a blog.

Interactive

Critical-Thinking and Writing Activities

As directed by your instructor, complete the following activities.

1. Review Rachel De Smith's analysis of Toni Morrison's Sethe and Barbara Kingsolver's Orleanna Price. Then choose two characters from other literary works and write an analysis of them using compare and/or contrast organization.

2. Review Gelareh Asayesh's article "Shrouded in Contradiction," noting how she uses comparison-contrast strategies in order to take a position. Draft or revise an essay in which you use comparison-contrast to develop or support your thesis.

3. Re-examine how Shankar Vedantam opens and closes "Shades of Prejudice" with an anecdote (or a news story) that was current when he wrote the essay. Revise one of your recent essays by selecting a recent news story that you can use to develop your thesis. For example, you might use the story to get readers' attention or to compare the story with a parallel situation addressed in your paper.

4. Re-read Peter Baldwin's "The Likeness Across the Atlantic" in which he analyzes Europeans' and Americans' differences and similarities. Choose two other collectives (e.g., countries, cities, states, colleges, or groups of people) and write an essay in which you compare and contrast characteristics that distinguish these communities.

5. Write an essay in which you compare and contrast two people, using subject-by-subject organization. Then revise the essay using trait-by-trait organization. Finally, discuss the essays with a classmate to determine which piece is better.

Learning-Outcomes Checklist

After reading the essays in this chapter, developing your own comparison-contrast essay, and getting feedback from classmates and your instructor, use this checklist to assess how effectively you achieved the learning outcomes for this chapter:

_____ I understand comparison-contrast reasoning, both as a reader and a writer.

_____ I am able to structure compare-contrast writing either subject by subject or trait by trait, and I understand when to use which pattern.

_____ I know how to support compare-contrast reasoning with concrete and precise details, as well as with transitional words that clarify similarities and differences.

_____ I can strengthen compare-contrast writing by using effective revising and editing strategies.

_____ I have effectively planned, drafted, revised, and polished a compare-contrast essay.

13 Classification

Classification is an organizational strategy that helps writers make sense of large or complex sets of things. A writer using this strategy breaks the topic into individual items or members that can be sorted into clearly distinguishable groups or categories. For example, if writing about the types of residents who live in assisted-care facilities, a nursing student might classify them according to various physical and/or mental limitations.

By sorting residents in this way, the writer can discuss them as individuals, as representatives of a group, or as members of the body as a whole. By using an additional strategy such as compare-contrast, she or he can show both similarities and differences between individuals within a group, or between one group and another.

Learning Outcomes

▸ Create and test classification schemes that order items into distinct groups.

▸ Align classification with your writing purpose, audience, and topic.

▸ Assess and use these classification principles: consistency, exclusivity, and completeness.

▸ Create and use a classification grid.

▸ Write, revise, and edit a classification essay.

Audio

Video

Visually Speaking ▶ To learn more about reading and writing classification essays, look again at the photograph above and consider what it suggests about the challenges and benefits of classifying things.

Web Link

Reading Classification Writing

Use the information that follows as a basic guide when reading and analyzing the classification essays in this chapter.

Consider the rhetorical situation.

When reading classification essays, examine the writers' classification schemes—how they break their subjects into groups and why they sort them as they do. Explore whether the classification schemes fit the writer's purpose, audience, and topic.

- **Purpose:** Writers classify a body of information to explain its order, to clarify relationships, and to "locate" specific items within a larger structure. For example, in her essay, "Latin American Music . . ." (pages 203–205), Kathleen Kropp wants to explain how the music reflects Latinos' cultural identity and impacts social change.

- **Audience:** While readership can vary greatly, writers using classification are seeking to illuminate the deeper order of a topic, either to enhance readers' understanding or to support an argument. For example, Kropp's criteria instruct her college-student audience about the history and diversity of Latin American music.

- **Topic:** Writers typically use classification with topics that include a complex body of individual items or members. For example, Kropp's classification takes the large body of Latin American music (made up of many individual songs) and makes sense of it all through four categories that clarify music's role in Latino culture.

Consider classification principles.

The principles that follow help writers sort items into unified and distinct categories.

- **Consistency:** The same criteria should be used in the same way when one sorts items into groups. For example, John Van Rys sorts approaches to literary criticism based on one criterion: the critic's focus when reading (see "Four Ways . . . ," pages 206–207).

- **Exclusivity:** Groups should be distinct. For example, Van Rys identifies four main approaches to literary criticism, and whereas they do share some traits, yet each approach is substantially different from the others.

- **Completeness:** All individual items or members of the larger body should fit into a category with no items left over. For example, any common approach to literary criticism will fit into one of Van Rys's four categories.

Reader's Checklist

_____ Does the writer's classification scheme effectively explain the order of this topic for the target audience?

_____ Are the categories consistent, exclusive, and complete?

_____ Do the writer's classification strategies help you understand the subject?

Classification ■ ■ ■

In the essay below, student writer Kathleen Kropp uses classification strategies to describe the nature of Latin American music and to explain how the music both reflects and affects Latin American culture.

Essay Outline

Introduction: Latin American music's unifying power
   1. Category 1: indigenous music
   2. Category 2: Iberian and Mestizo folk music
   3. Category 3: Afro-American music
   4. Category 4: urban popular music
Conclusion: These diverse types together express the passion and power of Latin American people.

Title: the larger topic and the classification theme

Introduction: Latin American music's unifying power

1 Indigenous music

Latin American Music: A Diverse and Unifying Force

On September 20, 2009, Latin pop, rock, and salsa rhythms danced through the air in Havana's Plaza de la Revolución as more than one million people gathered to witness Paz Sin Fronteras II (Peace Without Borders II). These benefit concerts brought together performers from Cuba, Puerto Rico, Ecuador, and Venezuela. Juanes, a popular Colombian singer who headlined the concerts, explained the event's passion and power like this: "Music becomes an excuse to send a message that we're all here together building peace, that we are here as citizens and this is what we want, and we have to be heard" (Hispanic 17). His statement demonstrates Latinos' belief that their music has the power to unify Latin American people, synthesize their cultural activities, and address their diverse needs. To understand how the music (which is as diverse as Latin America's people) can do this, it is helpful to sort the many forms of music into four major types and consider what each type contributes to Latin American society.

One type is indigenous music, a group of musical forms that connect the human and the spiritual. Archeological evidence indicates that indigenous musical cultures of the Americas began over 30,000 years ago. Over time the first instruments, which were stone and clay sound-producing objects, evolved into wind instruments such as flutes and windpipes. An example of indigenous music connecting the human and spiritual is found among Aymara-speaking musicians in the Lake Titicaca Region of Peru. The people of this region use music to mesh pre-Columbian agricultural rites with current Catholic practices. For instance, during feasts such as the annual Fiesta de la Candelaria (Candlemas Feast), celebrants use Sicus (panpipes), pincullos (vertical duct flutes), cajas (drums),

1

2

chants, dances, and costumes—in combination with Catholic symbolism—to celebrate the gift of staple crops such as corn and potatoes (Indigenous 328, 330).

2 Iberian and Mestizo (mixed) folk music

A second type, Iberian and Mestizo (mixed) folk music, enrich Latinos' *3* everyday lives in a variety of forms, including liturgical music, working songs, and mariachi tunes. For example, whereas the traditional Catholic mass featured organ music, more recent Catholic services such as the Nicaraguan Peasant Mass use the acoustic guitar along with the colorful sounds of the marimba, maracas, and melodies from popular festivals. As a result, worshipers find the music inviting and the passionate lyrics (like those that follow, translated by Mike Yoder, October 2, 1989) socially relevant:

You are the God of the poor, the simple and human God, the God who sweats *4* in the street;

You eat food scrapings there in the park. I've seen you in a corner grocery *5* working behind the counter.

Another form of folk music known as tonadas (or tunes) are used as serenades *6* and working songs. For example, in Venezuela, workers might whistle or sing tonadas while milking, plowing, or fishing (Tonadas). These vocal duets, which also can be accompanied by guitar, have pleasant harmonies, two main melodies, and faster tempos ("Iberian and mestizo folk music" 338, 341).

The mariachi band, a final form of folk music, adds festivity to Mexicans' many *7* celebrations. With its six to eight violins, two trumpets, and a guitar, the band creates a vibrant, engaging sound. During birthdays or feast days, these bands commonly set up on streets and below windows where they awaken the residents above to the sounds of "Las Mañ Anitas," the traditional song for such days. Mariachis are also hired for baptisms, weddings, quinceañeras (the fifteenth birthday for a Mexican girl), patriotic holidays, and funerals (History of the Mariachi).

3 Afro-American music

Afro-American music, the third type of Latin American music, infuses *8* passion and power in its percussion-driven dances and complex rhythm structures. These songs and dances, performed throughout the Caribbean, function as an entertaining, unifying force among Latin people ("Afro-American" 345-6). The energy of Afro-American music is clear in genres such as the mambo and the rumba dances. The rumba, an Afro-Caribbean dance, is highly improvisational and exciting. The quinto (a high-pitched drum) establishes a dialogue with a solo voice and challenges the male dancer, while the tumbadora and palitos (sticks on woodblock) provide a contrast with regular, unchanging rhythm patterns.

The mambo, an Afro-Cuban dance, became popular in Havana, Cuba. In *9* the 1940s, nightclubs throughout Latin America caught the energy of this fast tempo song and dance. Arsenio Rodríguez' "Bruca Managuá" exemplifies this form. Because of the song's sound and lyrics, many black Cubans consider the piece to be an anthem of Afro-Cuban pride and resistance:

I am Calabrí, black by birth/nation, *10*

Without freedom, I can't live, *11*

Too much abuse, the body is going to die. *12*

(*Oxford Encyclopedia for Latinos and Latinas in the United States.* 218)

4 Urban popular music

Urban popular music, the fourth type of Latin American music, combines a dynamic sound with poignant appeals for social change, appeals that resonate with many listeners. The styles of this type of music include rock, heavy metal, punk, hip-hop, jazz, reggae, and R&B. During the September 20, 2009 Paz Sin Fronteras II concerts described earlier, urban popular music was common fare. As U.S. representative Jim McGovern observed, the message of the concerts was to "circumvent politics . . . using the medium of music to speak directly to young people, to change their way of thinking, and leave behind the old politics, hatred, prejudices, and national enmities that have locked too many people in patterns of conflict, violence, poverty, and despair. It is an attempt to break down barriers and ask people to join in common purpose" (Paz Sin Fronteras II). Popular urban musicians such as Juanes utilize music not only to entertain but also to unite Latinos in a universal cause.

Conclusion: passion and power of Latin American music and culture

Passion and power permeate all of Latin America's music. The four major types of music—indigenous, Iberian and Mestizo folk, Afro-American, and popular urban—are as diverse as the people of Latin America, and each style serves a valued need or function in Latinos' everyday lives. As a result, those listening to Latin American music—whether it is a Peruvian Indian's chant, a Venezuelan farmer's whistled tune, a Cuban mambo drummer's vivacious beat, or the Bogotá rock concert's compelling rhythms—are hearing much more than music. They are hearing the passion and power of the Latin American people.

Note: The Works Cited page is not shown. For sample pages, see MLA (pages 526–527) and APA (page 557).

Reading for Better Writing

Working by yourself or with a group, do the following:

1. Review the opening in which Kropp introduces her topic, thesis, and choice to sort the music into four categories. Then explain (a) why the passage is clear or unclear and (b) whether sorting forms into categories seems necessary or helpful.

2. Cite three strategies that Kropp uses to distinguish the four types of music and the various forms within those groups. Are the strategies effective? Why?

3. Identify language that Kropp uses to help you imagine the tone and tenor of the music. Is the word choice helpful? Why?

4 In the last sentence, Kropp re-states—and re-phrases—her thesis. Review the sentence: Is it an effective closing? Why or why not?

Classification ◼▪▪

In this essay John Van Rys, a college professor, classifies four basic approaches to literary criticism. His essay is intended to help college freshmen interpret literature.

Four Ways to Talk About Literature

The writer introduces the topic and criterion for creating four subgroups.

Have you ever been in a conversation in which you suddenly felt lost—out of the loop? Perhaps you feel that way in your literature class. You may think a poem or short story means one thing, and then your instructor suddenly pulls out the "hidden meaning." Joining the conversation about literature—in class or in an essay—may indeed seem daunting, but you can do it if you know what to look for and what to talk about. There are four main perspectives, or approaches, that you can use to converse about literature.   *1*

He describes the first subgroup and gives an example.

Text-centered approaches focus on the literary piece itself. Often called *formalist criticism,* such approaches claim that the structure of a work and the rules of its genre are crucial to its meaning. The formalist critic determines how various elements (plot, character, language, and so on) reinforce the meaning and unify the work. For example, the formalist may ask the following questions concerning Robert Browning's poem "My Last Duchess": How do the main elements in the poem—irony, symbolism, and verse form—help develop the main theme (deception)? How does Browning use the dramatic monologue genre in this poem?   *2*

He describes the second subgroup and gives an example.

Audience-centered approaches focus on the "transaction" between text and reader—the dynamic way the reader interacts with the text. Often called *rhetorical* or *reader-response criticism,* these approaches see the text not as an object to be analyzed, but as an activity that is different for each reader. A reader-response critic might ask these questions of "My Last Duchess": How does the reader become aware of the duke's true nature if it's never actually stated? Do men and women read the poem differently? Who were Browning's original readers?   *3*

He describes the third subgroup and gives examples.

Author-centered approaches focus on the origins of a text (the writer and the historical background). For example, an author-centered study examines the writer's life—showing connections, contrasts, and conflicts between his or her life and the writing. Broader historical studies explore social and intellectual currents, showing links between an author's work and the ideas, events, and institutions of that period. Finally, the literary historian may make connections between the text in question and earlier and later literary works. The author-centered critic might ask these questions of "My Last Duchess": What were Browning's views of marriage, men and women, art, class, and wealth? As an institution, what was marriage like in Victorian England (Browning's era) or Renaissance Italy (the duke's era)? Who was the historical Duke of Ferrara?   *4*

He describes the fourth approach and gives examples of each subgroup in it.

The fourth approach to criticism applies ideas outside of literature to literary works. Because literature mirrors life, argue these critics, disciplines that explore human life can help us understand literature. Some critics, for example, apply psychological theories to literary works by exploring dreams, symbolic meanings, and motivation. Myth or archetype criticism uses insights from psychology, cultural anthropology, and classical studies to explore a text's universal appeal. Moral criticism, rooted in religious studies and ethics, explores the moral dilemmas literary works raise. Marxist, feminist, and minority criticism are, broadly speaking, sociological approaches to interpretation. While the Marxist examines the themes of class struggle, economic power, and social justice in texts, the feminist critic explores the just and unjust treatment of women as well as the effect of gender on language, reading, and the literary canon. The critic interested in race and ethnic identity explores similar issues, with the focus shifted to a specific cultural group.

5

He cites sample questions.

Such ideological criticism might ask a wide variety of questions about "My Last Duchess": What does the poem reveal about the duke's psychological state and his personality? How does the reference to Neptune deepen the poem? What does the poem suggest about the nature of evil and injustice? In what ways are the duke's motives class-based and economic? How does the poem present the duke's power and the duchess's weakness? What is the status of women in this society?

6

The closing presents qualities shared by all four approaches.

If you look at the variety of questions critics might ask about "My Last Duchess," you see both the diversity of critical approaches and the common ground between them. In fact, interpretive methods actually share important characteristics: (1) a close attention to literary elements such as character, plot, symbolism, and metaphor; (2) a desire not to distort the work; and (3) a sincere concern for increasing interest and understanding in a text. In actual practice, critics may develop a hybrid approach to criticism, one that matches their individual questions and concerns about a text. Now that you're familiar with some of the questions defining literary criticism, exercise your own curiosity (and join the ongoing literary dialogue) by discussing a text that genuinely interests you.

7

Reading for Better Writing

Working by yourself or with a group, do the following:

1. Explain how the writer introduces the subject and attempts to engage the reader. Is this strategy effective? Why or why not?

2. The writer uses one poem to illustrate how each of the four critical approaches works. Explain why this strategy is or is not effective.

3. Review the last paragraph and explain why it does or does not unify the essay.

Classification ■▪▫

Stewart Brand, author of *Whole Earth Discipline: An Ecopragmatist Manifesto,* published this essay in December 2009. In the piece, he argues that the climate-change debate is better understood as advocating four main perspectives—not two.

Four Sides to Every Story

The writer introduces his topic and thesis.

He distinguishes the four viewpoints with descriptive names.

A hyperlink helps readers access the speech.

The writer names and describes the second group.

He offers examples illustrating the group's viewpoint.

The quotation relays the speaker's argument and tone.

The writer names and describes the group.

1 Climate talks have been going on in Copenhagen for a week now, and it appears to be a two-sided debate between alarmists and skeptics. But there are actually *four* different views of global warming. A taxonomy of the four:

2 **DENIALISTS** They are loud, sure and political. Their view is that climatologists and their fellow travelers are engaged in a vast conspiracy to panic the public into following an agenda that is political and pernicious. Senator James Inhofe of Oklahoma and the columnist George Will wave the banner for the hoax-callers.

3 "The claim that global warming is caused by man-made emissions is simply untrue and not based on sound science," Mr. Inhofe <u>declared in a 2003 speech to the Senate</u> about the Kyoto accord that remains emblematic of his position. "CO2 does not cause catastrophic disasters—actually it would be beneficial to our environment and our economy. . . . The motives for Kyoto are economic, not environmental—that is, proponents favor handicapping the American economy through carbon taxes and more regulations."

4 **SKEPTICS** This group is most interested in the limitations of climate science so far: they like to examine in detail the contradictions and shortcomings in climate data and models, and they are wary about any "consensus" in science. To the skeptics' discomfort, their arguments are frequently quoted by the denialists.

5 In this mode, Roger Pielke, a climate scientist at the University of Colorado, argues that the scenarios presented by the United Nations Intergovernmental Panel on Climate Change are overstated and underpredictive. Another prominent skeptic is the physicist Freeman Dyson, <u>who wrote in 2007</u>: "I am opposing the holy brotherhood of climate model experts and the crowd of deluded citizens who believe the numbers predicted by the computer models. . . . I have studied the climate models and I know what they can do. The models solve the equations of fluid dynamics, and they do a very good job of describing the fluid motions of the atmosphere and the oceans. They do a very poor job of describing the clouds, the dust, the chemistry and the biology of fields and farms and forests."

6 **WARNERS** These are the climatologists who see the trends in climate headed toward planetary disaster, and they blame human production of greenhouse gases as the primary culprit. Leaders in this category are the scientists James Hansen, Stephen Schneider and James Lovelock. (This is the group that most persuades me and whose views I promote.)

A hyperlink helps readers access the paper.	"If humanity wishes to preserve a planet similar to that on which civilization developed and to which life on earth is adapted," Mr. Hansen wrote as the lead author of <u>an influential 2008 paper</u>, then the concentration of carbon dioxide in the atmosphere would have to be reduced from 395 parts per million to "at most 350 p.p.m." *7*

CALAMATISTS There are many environmentalists who believe that industrial civilization has committed crimes against nature, and retribution is coming. They quote the warners in apocalyptic terms, and they view denialists as deeply evil. The technology critic Jeremy Rifkin speaks in this manner, and the writer-turned-activist Bill McKibben is a (fairly gentle) leader in this category.   *8*

The writer identifies the fourth group.

In his 2006 introduction for *The End of Nature,* his famed 1989 book, Mr. McKibben wrote of climate change in religious terms: "We are no longer able to think of ourselves as a species tossed about by larger forces—now we *are* those larger forces. Hurricanes and thunderstorms and tornadoes become not acts of God but acts of man. That was what I meant by the 'end of nature.'"   *9*

He quotes McKibben and cites the source.

The calamatists and denialists are primarily political figures, with firm ideological loyalties, whereas the warners and skeptics are primarily scientists, guided by ever-changing evidence. That distinction between ideology and science not only helps clarify the strengths and weaknesses of the four stances, it can also be used to predict how they might respond to future climate developments.   *10*

He compares two groups and contrasts them with two others.

If climate change were to suddenly reverse itself (because of some yet undiscovered mechanism of balance in our climate system), my guess is that the denialists would be triumphant, the skeptics would be skeptical this time of the apparent good news, the warners would be relieved, and the calamatists would seek out some other doom to proclaim.   *11*

The writer distinguishes the groups by projecting how they might respond to good news or bad news.

If climate change keeps getting worse, then I would expect denialists to grasp at stranger straws, many skeptics to become warners, the warners to start pushing geoengineering schemes like sulfur dust in the stratosphere, and the calamatists to push liberal political agendas—just as the denialists said they would.   *12*

Reading for Better Writing

Working by yourself or with a group, do the following:

1. Identify Brand's thesis. How does his classification thinking make sense of the topic?

2. Cite three strategies that he uses to distinguish the four viewpoints. Do you find these strategies effective? Why or why not?

3. Identify two of Brand's claims, describe how he supports each claim, and then explain why that support is or is not convincing (for information about claims, see pages 252–256).

Classification ■ ▪ ▪

Jessica Seigel is an award-winning, widely published journalist who has written on diverse subjects, including TV journalism, rock climbing, Cameron Diaz, bonobo apes, and archeological research in Israel. In the essay below, she explains how readers should respond to nuanced literary devices such as symbols, themes, and allegories.

The Lion, the Witch and the Metaphor

Use this margin to record your observations regarding how Seigel uses classification to develop her analysis.

1 THOUGH it's fashionable nowadays to come out of the closet, lately folks are piling in—into the wardrobe, that is, to battle over who owns Narnia: secular or Christian lovers of C. S. Lewis's stories.

2 Children, of course, have been slipping through the magic cupboard into the mythical land for 50 years without assistance from pundits or preachers (though fauns and talking badgers have been helpful). But now that the chronicles' first book, *The Lion, the Witch and the Wardrobe,* has been made into a Disney movie, adults are fighting to claim the action. And that means analyzing it. Or not.

3 The 7-year-old who sat next to me during a recent showing said, "This is really scary." It was scary when the White Witch kills the lion Aslan, who dies to save the loathsome Edmund before rising to help him and his siblings vanquish evil. But adults reducing the story to one note—their own—are even scarier. One side dismisses the hidden Jesus figure as silly or trivial, while the other insists the lion is Jesus in a story meant to proselytize. They're both wrong.

4 As a child, I never knew that Aslan was "Jesus." And that's a good thing. My mother recently remarked that if she'd known the stories were Christian, she wouldn't have given me the books—which are among my dearest childhood memories.

5 But parents today will not be innocent of the religious subtext, considering the drumbeat of news coverage and Disney's huge campaign to remind churchgoing audiences of the film's religious themes. The marketing is so intense that the religious Web site HollywoodJesus.com even worried that ham-fisted promotion might ruin it for non-Christians.

6 But a brief foray into Criticism 101 shows that the wardrobe is big enough for everyone. Symbolism, for example, is when one thing stands for another but is not the thing itself. Psychoanalysts, for instance, have interpreted "The Wonderful Wizard of Oz" as Dorothy's quest for a penis—that is, retrieving the witch's broomstick. Does that symbolism—if you buy it—make Dorothy a pervert? No, because it's hidden. That's the point. Overt and covert meaning can exist independently.

7 Those with a fiduciary, rather than phallic bent, might prefer the theory that L. Frank Baum's Oz stories are a Populist manifesto, with the yellow brick road as the gold standard, the Tin Man as alienated labor, Scarecrow as oppressed farmers, and so on. (And surely some Jungian theory about the collective unconscious explains why both Oz and Narnia are populated by four heroic characters fighting an evil witch.)

Yes, it's allegory land, a place that strings symbols together to create levels of 8
meaning, which a determined scholar has actually quantified as ranging from two
to seven layers. (No word on why not eight.) Allegory, the oldest narrative technique,
often involves talking animals, from Aesop's fox with the grapes to Dr. Seuss's Yertle
the Turtle, supposedly a Hitler figure.

Does that twist the Seuss tale into a political treatise on fascism? No, it adds 9
another level for adults, it teaches morals (even the meekest can unseat the powerful,
etc.), and it's fun—when plain little Mack burps, he shakes the bad king Yertle from
his throne built on turtles.

But which layer is more important—the surface or beneath? Deep thinkers 10
specialize in hidden meanings (building demand, of course, for their interpretive
expertise). An Oxford English professor, Lewis himself explored the depths in his
scholarly books. But he also defended the literal, lamenting in his essay "On Stories"
how modern criticism denigrates the pleasures of a good yarn—and that was 50 years
ago.

While critics today call it "fallacy" to interpret a work by citing the author's 11
intentions, Lewis left a road map for us marked with special instructions for not
annoying children. In his essay "Sometimes Fairy Stories May Say Best What's to Be
Said," he denounced as "moonshine" the idea that he wrote the Narnia chronicles to
proselytize the young. The lion Aslan, he wrote, bounded into his imagination from
his experience as a Christian, coming to him naturally as should all good writing.

"Let the pictures tell you their own moral," he advised in "On Three Ways of 12
Writing for Children." "If they don't show you a moral, don't put one in."

In keeping with that advice, the Narnia chronicles don't beat you on the head— 13
nor does the faithful movie adaptation. If everyone stays on his own level—the
surface for adventurers, and the depths for believers—we can all enjoy, so long as the
advertisers stay out of the way.

Reading for Better Writing

Working by yourself or with a group, do the following:

1. Identify the two conflicting groups (or viewpoints) in this article and describe
   characteristics of each.

2. Summarize Seigel's thesis and explain why you do or do not agree.

3. In the final paragraph, Seigel differentiates the two categories as "adventurers" and
   "believers." Are her subgroups **consistent, exclusive,** and **distinct**? For example,
   could a reader be both an adventurer and a believer? How might a third (or fourth)
   category affect Seigel's argument?

Writing Guidelines

Planning

1. **Select a topic.** Start by writing a few general headings like the academic headings below; then list two or three related topics under each heading. Finally, pick a topic that is characterized by a larger set of items or members that can best be explained by ordering them into categories.

Engineering	Biology	Social Work	Education
Machines	Whales	Child welfare	Learning styles
Bridges	Fruits	Organizations	Testing methods

2. **Look at the big picture.** Do preliminary research to get an overview of your topic. Review your purpose (to explain, persuade, inform, and so on), and consider which classification criteria will help you divide the subject's content into distinct, understandable categories.

3. **Choose and test your criterion.** Choose a criterion for creating categories. Make sure it produces groups that are *consistent* (the same criterion are used throughout the sorting process), *exclusive* (groups are distinct—no member fits into more than one group), and *complete* (each member fits into a subgroup with no member left over).

4. **Gather and organize information.** Gather information from reliable sources. To organize your information, take notes, possibly using a classification grid like the one shown below or the one on page 52. Set up the grid by listing the classification criteria down the left column and listing the groups in the top row of the columns. Then fill in the grid with appropriate details. (The grid below lists the classification criterion and groups discussed in "Four Ways to Talk About Literature," pages 206–207.)

Classification Criteria	Group #1	Group #2	Group #3	Group #4
	Text-centered approach	Audience-centered approach	Author-centered approach	Ideas outside literature
focus of the critical approach	• Trait #1 • Trait #2 • Trait #3	• Trait #1 • Trait #2 • Trait #3	• Trait #1 • Trait #2 • Trait #3	• Trait #1 • Trait #2 • Trait #3

Note: If you do not use a grid, consider using an outline to organize your thoughts.

5. **Draft a thesis.** Draft a working thesis (you can revise it later as needed) that states your topic and identifies your classification scheme. Include language introducing your criteria for classifying groups.

Drafting

6. **Draft the essay.** Write your first draft, using organization planned earlier.

- ■ **Opening:** Get the readers' attention, introduce the subject and thesis, and give your criteria for dividing the subject into categories.
- ■ **Middle:** Develop the thesis by discussing each category, explaining its traits, and showing how it is distinct from the other groups. For example, in the middle section of "Four Ways to Talk About Literature," the writer first shows the unique focus of each of the four approaches to literary criticism, and then illustrates each approach by applying it to the same poem, "My Last Duchess" (see pages 206–207).
- ■ **Closing:** Reflect on and tie together the classification scheme. While the opening and middle of the essay separate the subject into distinct categories, the closing may bring the groups back together. For example, Van Rys closes by identifying characteristics that the four subgroups have in common (see page 207).

Revising

7. **Improve the ideas, organization, and voice.** Ask a classmate or someone from the writing center to read your essay, looking for the following:

- ____ **Ideas:** Are the classification criteria logical and clear, resulting in categories that are consistent, exclusive, and complete? Does the discussion include appropriate examples that clarify the nature and function of each group?
- ____ **Organization:** Does the essay include (1) an engaging opening that introduces the subject, thesis, and criteria for classification, (2) a well-organized middle that distinguishes groups, shows why each group is unique, and supports these claims with evidence, and (3) a unifying conclusion that restates the main idea and its relevance?
- ____ **Voice:** Is the tone informed, courteous, and rational?

Editing

8. **Edit the essay.** Polish your writing by addressing these issues:

- ____ **Words:** The words distinguishing classifications are used uniformly.
- ____ **Sentences:** The sentences and paragraphs are complete, varied, and clear.
- ____ **Correctness:** The usage, grammar, and mechanics are correct.
- ____ **Page Design:** The design follows MLA, APA, CMS, or CSE formatting rules.

Publishing

9. **Publish the essay** by sharing it with your instructor and classmates, publishing it on your website, or submitting it to a print or online journal.

Interactive

Critical-Thinking and Writing Activities

As directed by your instructor, complete the following activities.

1. In "Latin American Music: A Diverse and Unifying Force," Kathleen Kropp uses classification to analyze the nature and impact of an art form. Choose an art form that interests you, research the topic, and write an essay that uses classification to explain the art form's historical development and social impact.

2. "Four Ways to Talk About Literature" examines four approaches to reading and understanding a piece of literature. Identify a similar group of approaches to analysis or problem solving in your program or major. Write an essay in which you break your topic into categories, sort the groups, and explain the topic to the reader.

3. In "Four Sides to Every Story," Steward Brand uses classification to show that the climate-change debate is more complex than a two-position argument. Select an argument in the news or in your major that is erroneously presented as a two-option issue. Then research the topic and write a classification essay that accurately addresses the topic.

4. Find an article in a newspaper or an academic journal that uses classification to develop a thesis. Note the writer's criteria for sorting elements of the topic into categories. Then write a brief essay explaining why the criteria do or do not lead to groups that are consistent, exclusive, and complete. Share your writing with the class.

Learning-Outcomes Checklist

After reading the essays in this chapter, developing your own classification essay, and getting feedback from classmates and your instructor, use this checklist to assess how effectively you achieved the learning outcomes for this chapter.

_____ I know how to assess a writer's classification scheme and to develop a classification scheme for my own writing, especially as such a scheme relates to purpose, audience, and topic.

_____ I understand the nature, value, and function of these classification principles: *consistency, exclusivity,* and *completeness.*

_____ I can use the principles to evaluate whether a writer effectively divides a subject into categories and sorts the individual items into these groups.

_____ I can create and use a classification grid to organize and develop my writing.

_____ I can write an effective classification essay that breaks the subject into distinct categories, sorts individual items into clearly distinguishable groups, and uses the classification to develop my thesis.

14 Process

Process writing helps us understand ourselves and the world around us by answering interesting questions like these: How does cancer spread? How do you download photographs from a camera? or What does Barack Obama's presidency indicate about America's progress toward racial reconciliation?

Writing that answers questions like these analyzes a process by breaking it down into steps, often grouped into stages or phases. Sometimes, the analysis also explains the process's causes and effects.

The two basic forms of process writing are a process essay and instructions. This chapter includes guidelines and models that will help you read and write both forms.

Learning Outcomes

▶ Understand how process essays and instructions are organized and used.

▶ Read and evaluate each form.

▶ Write each form.

▶ Structure the process analysis chronologically with needed transitions.

▶ Read and use signal terms in instructions.

▶ Find regulatory standards for use of signal terms.

Audio

Video

Visually Speaking ▶ The photograph above captures a moment in a process. What is the process, and what writing strategies would you use to explain how to do the process?

■ Reading Process Writing

Process writing is analytical prose in which authors break a process into a clear series of steps (often organized into phases or stages) and then explain how and why those steps lead to a specific outcome. As you read process analyses, note how writers both describe and analyze the process, often using cause-effect reasoning.

Consider the rhetorical situation. ■■·■

Depending on the writer's purpose, audience, and topic, process writing usually takes one of two forms: an essay that describes and analyzes the nature and function of a process, or a set of instructions that tells readers precisely how to do the process.

- **Purpose:** If the writer intends to explain the topic, he or she writes an essay. The essay first offers an overview of the process and then explains how each step leads logically to the next, and how all the steps together complete the process. If the writer wants to help readers work through a process themselves, he or she writes instructions. These documents begin with a list of materials, and then follow with a detailed list of directives, often including precise signal terms such as **"Warning!" "CAUTION!"** or **"DANGER!"**
- **Audience:** Whether the form is an essay or a set of instructions, the text should meet the needs of all its readers, including those who know the least about the topic. To do this, writers should (1) include all the information that readers need, (2) use language that they understand, and (3) define unfamiliar or technical terms.
- **Topic:** Topics addressed in academic process writing are usually course-related phenomena that interest the writer and offer readers insight into their discipline. For an example, see Kerry Mertz's essay, "Wayward Cells" (pages 217–218). Topics addressed in professional publications should interest and educate their readers.

Note signal terms. ■■·■

In instructions, writers use signal terms (like those cited above) to help users complete a process safely and successfully. Three organizations—the American National Standards Institute (ANSI), the International Organization for Standardization (ISO), and the U.S. military (MILSPEC)—set the standards for how signal terms must be used in instructions for these and other businesses. To learn more about how these organizations define, design, and use signal terms and related icons, check their websites.

Reader's Checklist

_____ Does the essay clearly identify the process, outline its stages, explain individual steps, and (if appropriate) discuss causes and effects?

_____ Do the instructions clearly and accurately explain the process, the tools and parts needed, the steps required, and the necessary precautions?

_____ Does the document use clear, precise language and define unfamiliar terms?

Process ■ ▪ ■

Student writer Kerri Mertz wrote this essay to explain how cancer cells affect the body.

Video

> **Outline:**
> *Introduction:* analogy of workers in room as cells in body
>   **1.** First step of cancer development: cell undifferentiating
>   **2.** Second step: reproduction of cancer cells, "autonomy"
>   **3.** Third step: varieties of damage to the body
>   **4.** The development of promising treatments
> *Conclusion:* restate analogy—wayward cells as wayward workers

Title:
metaphor for
process

Wayward Cells

Imagine a room containing a large group of people all working hard toward the same goal. Each person knows his or her job, does it carefully, and cooperates with other group members. Together, they function smoothly—like a well-oiled machine.

Introduction:
cells-workers
analogy

Then something goes wrong. One guy suddenly drops his task, steps into another person's workstation, grabs the material that she's working with, and begins something very different—he uses the material to make little reproductions of himself, thousands of them. These look-alikes imitate him—grabbing material and making reproductions of themselves. Soon the bunch gets so big that they spill into other people's workstations, getting in their way, and interrupting their work. As the number of look-alikes grows, the work group's activity slows, stutters, and finally stops.

A human body is like this room, and the body's cells are like these workers. If the body is healthy, each cell has a necessary job and does it correctly. For example, right now red blood cells are running throughout your body carrying oxygen to each body part. Other cells are digesting that steak sandwich that you had for lunch, and others are patching up that cut on your left hand. Each cell knows what to do because its genetic code—or DNA—tells it what to do. When a cell begins to function abnormally, it can initiate a process that results in cancer.

1 Cancer starts
with cell
undifferenti-
ating.

The problem starts when one cell "forgets" what it should do. Scientists call this "undifferentiating"—meaning that the cell loses its identity within the body (Pierce 75). Just like the guy in the group who decided to do his own thing, the cell forgets its job. Why this happens is somewhat unclear.

The problem could be caused by a defect in the cell's DNA code or by something in the environment, such as cigarette smoke or asbestos (German 21). Causes from inside the body are called genetic, whereas causes from outside the body are called carcinogens, meaning "any substance that causes cancer" (Neufeldt and Sparks 90). In either case, an undifferentiated cell can disrupt the function of healthy cells in two ways: by not doing its job as specified in its DNA and by not reproducing at the rate noted in its DNA.

1

2

3

4

5

2 Cancer cells reproduce autonomously.

Most healthy cells reproduce rather quickly, but their reproduction rate is   6
controlled. For example, your blood cells completely die off and replace themselves
within a matter of weeks, but existing cells make only as many new cells as the body
needs. The DNA codes in healthy cells tell them how many new cells to produce.
However, cancer cells don't have this control, so they reproduce quickly with no
stopping point, a characteristic called "autonomy" (Braun 3). What's more, all their
"offspring" have the same qualities as their messed-up parent, and the resulting
overpopulation produces growths called tumors.

3 Tumors damage the body.

Tumor cells can hurt the body in a number of ways. First, a tumor can grow so big   7
that it takes up space needed by other organs. Second, some cells may detach from the
original tumor and spread throughout the body, creating new tumors elsewhere. This
happens with lymphatic cancer—a cancer that's hard to control because it spreads so
quickly. A third way that tumor cells can hurt the body is by doing work not called
for in their DNA. For example, a gland cell's DNA code may tell the cell to produce a
necessary hormone in the endocrine system. However, if cancer damages or distorts
that code, sick cells may produce more of the hormone than the body can use—or
even tolerate (Braun 4). Cancer cells seem to have minds of their own, and this is why
cancer is such a serious disease.

4 Promising treatments offer hope.

Fortunately, there is hope. Scientific research is already helping doctors do   8
amazing things for people suffering with cancer. One treatment that has been used
for some time is chemotherapy, or the use of chemicals to kill off all fast-growing
cells, including cancer cells. (Unfortunately, chemotherapy can't distinguish between
healthy and unhealthy cells, so it may cause negative side effects such as damaging
fast-growing hair follicles, resulting in hair loss.) Another common treatment is
radiation, or the use of light rays to kill cancer cells. One of the newest and most
promising treatments is gene therapy—an effort to identify and treat chromosomes
that carry a "wrong code" in their DNA. A treatment like gene therapy is promising
because it treats the cause of cancer, not just the effect. Year by year, research is helping
doctors better understand what cancer is and how to treat it.

Conclusion: wayward cells as wayward workers

Note: The Works Cited page is not shown.

Much of life involves dealing with problems like wayward workers, broken   9
machines, or dysfunctional organizations. Dealing with wayward cells is just another
problem. While the problem is painful and deadly, there is hope. Medical specialists
and other scientists are making progress, and some day they will help us win our
battle against wayward cells.

Reading for Better Writing

Working by yourself or with a group, do the following:

1. Explain why the analogy in the opening and closing is or is not effective.

2. Explain how transitions are used to lead into and out of each step.

3. Explain how the essay both describes and analyzes the process.

Process ■ ˙ ■

Nicholas D. Kristof, a Pulitzer Prize-winning journalist, describes how interracial marriages have become common in the United States.

Love and Race

The writer uses a contrast to introduce the thesis.

1   In a world brimming with bad news, here's one of the happiest trends. Instead of preying on people of different races, young Americans are falling in love with them.

2   Whites and blacks can be found strolling together as couples even at the University of Mississippi, once a symbol of racial confrontation.

3   "I will say that they are always given a second glance," acknowledges C. J. Rhodes, a black student at Ole Miss. He adds that there are still misgivings about interracial dating, particularly among black women and a formidable number of "white Southerners who view this race-mixing as abnormal, frozen by fear to see Sarah Beth bring home a brotha."

4   Mixed-race marriages in the U.S. now number 1.5 million and are roughly doubling each decade. About 40 percent of Asian-Americans and 6 percent of blacks have married whites in recent years.

Statistics ground the main point.

5   Still more striking, one survey found that 40 percent of Americans had dated someone of another race.

6   In a country where racial divisions remain deep, all this love is an enormously hopeful sign of progress in bridging barriers. Scientists who study the human genome say that race is mostly a bogus distinction reflecting very little genetic difference, perhaps one-hundredth of 1 percent of our DNA.

7   Skin color differences are recent, arising over only the last 100,000 years or so, a twinkling of an evolutionary eye. That's too short a period for substantial genetic differences to emerge, and so there is perhaps 10 times more genetic differences within a race than there is between races. Thus we should welcome any trend that makes a superficial issue like color less central to how we categorize each other.

An anecdote demonstrates how much the situation has changed.

8   The rise in interracial marriage reflects a revolution in attitudes. As recently as 1958, a white mother in Monroe, N.C., called the police after her little girl kissed a black playmate on the cheek; the boy, Hanover Thompson, 9, was then sentenced to 14 years in prison for attempted rape. (His appeals failed, but he was released later after an outcry.)

9   In 1963, 59 percent of Americans believed that marriage between blacks and whites should be illegal. At one time or another 42 states banned interracial marriages, although the Supreme Court finally invalidated these laws in 1967.

10   Typically, the miscegenation laws voided any interracial marriages, making the children illegitimate, and some states included penalties such as enslavement,

life imprisonment, and whippings. My wife is Chinese-American, and our relationship would once have been felonious.

At every juncture from the 19th century on, the segregationists warned that *11* granting rights to blacks would mean the start of a slippery slope, ending with black men marrying white women. The racists were prophetic.

A quotation makes an ironic point.

"They were absolutely right," notes Randall Kennedy, the Harvard Law *12* School professor and author of a dazzling new book, *Interracial Intimacies*. . . . "I do think [interracial marriage] is a good thing. It's a welcome sign of thoroughgoing desegregation. We talk about desegregation in the public sphere; here's desegregation in the most intimate sphere."

These days, interracial romance can be seen on the big screen, on TV shows, *13* and in the lives of some prominent Americans. Former Defense Secretary William Cohen has a black wife, as does Peter Norton, the software guru. The Supreme Court justice Clarence Thomas has a white wife.

The writer puts himself in the article.

I find the surge in intermarriage to be one of the most positive fronts in *14* American race relations today, building bridges and empathy. But it's still in its infancy.

I was excited to track down interracial couples at Ole Miss, thinking they *15* would be perfect to make my point about this hopeful trend: But none were willing to talk about the issue on record.

"Even if people wanted to marry [interracially], I think they'd keep it kind of *16* quiet," explained a minister on campus.

The writer sums up the main point.

For centuries, racists warned that racial equality would lead to the *17* "mongrelization" of America. Perhaps they were right in a sense, for we're increasingly going to see a blurring of racial distinctions. But these distinctions acquired enormous social resonance without ever having much basis in biology.

Reading for Better Writing

Working by yourself or with a group, do the following:

1. Review the opening paragraph and explain why the passage does or does not effectively introduce the topic and focus the essay.

2. Kristof argues that the popularity of interracial marriages is a process that has developed over time. Cite key events or stages in that process and explain why they indicate progress.

3. "Love and Race" was written for a broad audience. How might the content and style of the essay be different if it were written as a research paper for a college course in sociology?

4. Review the last paragraph and explain why you do or do not find it a strong closing.

Process

Gerald L. Early is an award-winning writer and a professor of African and African-American studies at Washington University. In the essay below, published in *The Chronicle of Higher Education* one month before Barack Obama was elected president, Early analyzes the process that has led him and others to ask whether Obama's presidency marks the end of race as we know it.

Video

The End of Race as We Know It

"And could politics ever be an expression of love?"
Ralph Ellison, *Invisible Man* (1952)

Use this column to record your own observations about the essay.

The controversial *New Yorker* cover of July 21, 2008—showing the Democratic presidential nominee, Barack Obama, as a Muslim jihadist and his wife, Michelle, as a gun-toting, Afro-wearing black militant—actually missed its target. It was funny as a kind of political and cultural satire, but only if you view the Obamas as channeling the first generation of black students to attend elite, white universities.   1

That was my generation—we're about 10 to 15 years older. We started attending college in 1970, almost as soon as black-studies programs, special black dorms, and special black admissions were instituted. Many of us were secretly, in our imagination, Muslim back in those days, or we adopted certain superficial Muslim pieties. We didn't eat pork, castigating it as slave food, and we sometimes called God "Allah." Among our heroes were the late, martyred Malcolm X and the living but also martyred Muhammad Ali, both Muslims. Ali himself kept the image of holy war alive in popular culture in the way he promoted many of his fights: as a cosmic battle between the good Muslim and the reprobate, pork-eating, Uncle Tom Christian. He did this especially against black opponents like Floyd Patterson, Joe Frazier, and George Foreman. *The Autobiography of Malcolm X* was the central book of our generation, the story of how true Islam spiritually and politically reawakened an African-American. The basketball great Lew Alcindor became Kareem Abdul-Jabbar in 1971. The Nation of Islam was highly respected, even highly feared by some. Amiri Baraka, our poet laureate and leading agitprop dramatist, was publishing work with the alternative Jihad Press, based in Newark, N.J., his hometown, and his form of cultural nationalism gave a respectful nod to Islam. The jazz pianist Doug Carn wrote a tune, "Jihad," that appeared on his popular (with black college students) 1973 album, *Revelation*. Other hip black-college-student music of the period: The tenor saxophonist Pharoah Sanders and the singer Leon Thomas recorded a tune called "Hum-Allah-Hum-Allah-Hum-Allah" on their 1969 album, *Jewels of Thought*. A 1966 album of Sanders was called *Tauhid*, an Islamic theological term.   2

In our bull sessions, some of us would talk about jihad, or righteous war, against the whites. (It was all talk.) Some of us actually became Muslims (very   3 few—we were Christians to the bone, despite our chatter about "the white man's religion") or joined some Eastern religious sect and adopted certain garb and mannerisms. Many of us wore wild Afros, making them wilder with blowout kits, and thought we were revolutionaries of a sort. After all, some of the black upperclassmen among us had seized buildings in protest, and a few even brandished weapons during the sieges.

Looking at *The New Yorker* cover as a middle-aged, black baby boomer, far removed from any of the Orientalism and racial and political romanticism of my youth, reminded me of a certain kind of silliness, but it also, strangely, moved me deeply. The cover told the story of a rite of African-American passage that occurred at a particular time for the generation of blacks who would become the most successful in the history of the group, and the most integrated. The relatively difficult years that my generation endured integrating white institutions—difficult not in any material sense, but in the sense that we were not very well prepared academically or emotionally to cope with our surroundings (we were given more than we knew what to do with, so much that one felt simultaneously intoxicated by the riches and stressed to the breaking point by how alien it all felt)—made us clutch at any sort of feeble identity protection we could muster. We had to "act black" because, after all, that is why we were at the university in the first place: to provide diversity in the only way we knew how. 4

Basically, entrapped in our excessive and youthful self-consciousness, our special sort of juvenile insecurity, we were trying, ironically, to show that we belonged, to protect ourselves from being considered "dumb niggers," or, even worse, "charity cases," the ragtag tail end of the American bourgeois elite. Some succeeded (by graduating). Many didn't. It is a modern story about integration in America—not the bloody civil-rights struggle of gaining access, but rather how people can sometimes be killed by kindness, paddled by paternalism, undone by philanthropy. I think back on it all as a remarkable form of self-hazing. 5

In looking at that *New Yorker* cover, it occurred to me that an important dimension of black identity politics was the memory of being something you never were but that you needed to think you might have been. Middle-aged black yuppies, like me—we, the generation of the Talented Tenth, the recipients of the gifts of the civil-rights struggle, those to whom much was given—see a great deal of ourselves in the Obamas. Whether we are elitists is unclear (many of us probably are—there is no shortage of black snobs), but we were surely educated to be an elite, a professional cadre for the race, gate-crashers turned gatekeepers—guardians who ensure diversity at predominantly white institutions rather than exult in and maintain the precarious, tarnished glory of black, "shadow" institutions. 6

The *New Yorker* cover reminds me how much we have, as integrationists, tried to fit in and how much we may secretly feel (or hope) we haven't. But the cover not only reminds me how much this group has done to make whites feel comfortable around us by adopting "secret identities" (the exotic nature of which were meant 7 to nonplus and annoy whites, while titillating their sense of romantic racialism). It also posed an important question: How comfortable are we with ourselves? Did we, in our desperation, ask race to do more work, support more of a psychological burden, than such a limited concept could ever hope to do because, alas, it was all we had: white people's crazy, self-serving idea of what human difference means? As Kwame Anthony Appiah wrote: "There is nothing in the world that can do all we ask race to do for us." We even hoped it would make us Americans while it would protect us from America.

As black people know better than many, it is, as Henry James acknowledged, a complex fate to be an American, especially to pose as being an American against one's will, the forever skeptical quasi-American, as most of us did. Anti-Americanism—not saluting the flag, ignoring the playing of the national anthem, decrying the United States and its policies at any and every opportunity—was common among black college students at the time, particularly those with any intellectual pretension. As influenced as we were by black cultural nationalism and trickle-down Marxism, this is hardly surprising.   8

But the irony of our anti-Americanism was that it masked our yearning for inclusion, which is why we were attending white colleges and universities in the first place. We grasped an identity of "blackness," of the superficially non-Western, in our confused hunt to fit into somebody's scheme and our reflexive fear that we would certainly not fit into a Western or white scheme. We did not want to be, in James Baldwin's words, "bastards of the West," but the very nature of our identity quest was propelled by the fact that we knew, inescapably, we were just that. It was the West, America, that we knew and by which we measured and understood reality. We had a complicated, uncertain place in the American scheme, a scheme we desired but that did not desire us. Suppose one day our place would become more assured in the scheme, suppose one day we could be unconditionally loyal to the scheme. Would we recognize that day, or would we be so historically conditioned that we would not know when history had finally turned a page, ended a chapter, entered a new phase of its unfolding?   9

Dinesh D'Souza's controversial 1995 book, *The End of Racism,* proposed that if racism has a historical beginning (which it does), then it must be reasonable to think it would have a historical end. The book then proposes: Suppose there is sufficient evidence to show that we have now reached that endpoint? The end of racism would mean that blacks can live their lives as fully as whites can, that any existing racism is residual and has no impact on the quality of black life. Thus the end of racism means the end of the claim of black victimization. But how would we know when we have reached it? What sign would show that we have arrived at, in effect, the end of America's racial history?   10

Considering the vociferous responses by black intellectuals and leftists to D'Souza, we had not unambiguously arrived at that point in 1995. Apparently,   11 for many black leaders, pundits, and scholars, the signs were not the success of Bill Cosby or Oprah Winfrey, not the Nobel Prize of Toni Morrison or the career of Spike Lee, not the crossover achievement of Serena and Venus Williams and Tiger Woods, not the political careers of Condoleezza Rice or Colin Powell, not the stardom of Will Smith and Morgan Freeman, not the Ivy League college presidency of Ruth Simmons or the arrival of such black public intellectuals as Henry Louis Gates Jr., Michael Eric Dyson, Orlando Patterson, and Cornel West.

None of those have been the tipping point. The accomplishments of those 12 people and thousands more did not indicate to many African-Americans that America had advanced beyond racism and that blacks had transcended their victimization. We had the anxiety of the paranoid: Whites are always out to get us, no matter how much we might succeed. In fact, they are out to get you all the more if you do succeed. We had the self-deprecating, cynical view of our elite status that spoke of guilt because of our lack of solidarity (we kill each other at an alarming clip) and our continuing need for white philanthropy (our dependency undermines our sense of power as a group): Successful blacks are nothing more than social and political tranquilizers that mask the continued existence of racism and the brutal victimization of black people. The thought crosses my mind from time to time: Am I doing good by doing well?

Might the presidency of Barack Obama be the tipping point? Blacks may become famous authors, film directors, diplomats, CEO's, fashion models, 13 entertainers, and physicists. But the presidency of the country, the most powerful person in the world, is the ultimate—to have authority that all whites, everyone in the world, would be bound to respect. What could mean more to a people who have endured a history of powerlessness? Black people were convinced that no black would become president of the United States during the lifetime of the baby-boom generation, not in the lifetime of any African-American adult currently living. That may change in a matter of weeks. My mother, who is 79 years old, summed it up: "I never thought I would live to see the day when I could vote for a black man for president and he actually has a chance to win." My mother says this as if that fact signifies the end of America's racial history, or at least the end of race as we once knew it.

The presidential campaign of Barack Obama has raised the question of what happens to the black American meta-narrative of heroic or noble victimization if 14 he wins. (Presumably nothing happens to it if he loses; the loss can be blamed on racism, as it will, in fact, be another example of victimization. White folks will always find a way to cut down a successful black man, to not let him get too far, is the common belief. That sort of black cynicism, expressed in different political and aesthetic modalities, underscores both the blues and rap. If Obama loses, he becomes, in black folklore, John Henry, the "natural" man with the courage to go up against the political machine. The moral of the tale, in politics as in life, is that the machine always wins.)

The author Charles Johnson, in an essay that appeared in the summer 2008 *15* issue of *The American Scholar,* argued that the black American narrative of victimization has already reached its end: "It simply is no longer the case that the essence of black American life is racial victimization and disenfranchisement, a curse and a condemnation, a destiny based on color in which the meaning of one's life is thinghood, created even before one is born." Perhaps black conservatism, the first sustained attempt by blacks to de-emphasize racism as a factor in black life, arose in the 1970s and 1980s as a way around the victimization narrative, as a way to move beyond civil rights. Perhaps it was the beginning of victimization fatigue. Afrocentrism re-energized the victim narrative in the 1990s by designating the achievements and destruction of Africanity as the core reality of Western civilization.

Many of us black professionals, members of the black elite, keep the embers *16* of our victimization burning for opportunistic reasons: to leverage white patronage, to maintain our own sense of identity and tradition. In some respects, this narrative has something of the power in its endurance that original sin does for Christians. In fact, our narrative of victimization is America's original sin, or what we want to serve as the country's original sin, which may be why we refuse to give it up.

We have used it shamelessly—especially those who are least entitled to do so, *17* as we have suffered the least—hustled it to get over on whites, to milk their guilt, to excuse our excesses and failures. Being the victim justifies all ethical lapses, as the victim becomes morally reprehensible in the guise of being morally outraged. Being the victim has turned into a sucker's game, the only possible game that the weak can play against the strong with any chance of winning. Nonetheless, the narrative does a kind of cultural work that serves our purposes in some profound ways, and it may be good for the country as a whole in reminding everyone about the costs of American democracy, its fragile foundation, its historically based hypocrisy. The conservatives are right: Freedom isn't free, and the black victim narrative reminds us all of that.

In the end, black people chose to see themselves as America's exceptionalist *18* people, the only ones who came to the land of freedom as perpetually unfree, who came to the land that welcomed the exile and the outcast against their will and who remained in that land as exiles and outcasts. In the grand scheme of American exceptionalism, the God-designed empire meant to do good, were African-Americans who troubled the waters with their own exceptionalist claims that went counter to the story of American triumphalist history. How could the country claim to be good and do good when it so mistreated blacks? The African-American story, perforce, had to be the tale of America's tragedy.

But of course that is not quite the case: The black American story of *19* victimization, our exceptionalism, was meant to be a triumphalist story of its own sort. Black Americans have survived, persevered, and even thrived despite the enormous obstacles thrown in our way. In a way, the black American narrative revealed American hypocrisy but simultaneously reinscribed American greatness, for blacks were heroic victims, and only in America could the heroism of the weak win a victory able to humble a nation into recognition of its wrongs.

The black narrative of victimization may have outlived its historical need 20 and its psychological urgency, but it still may have a kind of cultural work to do as a tale of redemption and an example of salvation history. If we are the shining city on a hill, part of that city must be the quarters of bondage, the world the slaves made, and America's true greatness might be that it is the only nation that symbolizes itself in this way, the grand city as the uplift of all people, even those it has enslaved. In the tale of heroism in adversity, perhaps best exemplified in spirituals, black-American Christianity, and the secular humanism of the blues, the narrative of victimization reminds all Americans of the need, from time to time, to lift every voice and sing in tribute to who we are, however inadequate, and to what we hope we can be when we arrive at that day when, as Martin Luther King Jr. prophesied in his vision of America as a beloved community, politics becomes an expression of love.

Reading for Better Writing

Working by yourself or with a group, do the following:

1. In this essay, Gerald L. Early describes and analyzes a process. What is the process, and how does he introduce it?

2. In paragraphs 1, 4, 6, and 7, Early refers to the July 21, 2008 front cover of *The New Yorker*. Describe the cover, find an image of it online, and explain how Early uses it to introduce and develop his thesis.

3. In paragraph 9, Early says, "But the irony of our anti-Americanism was that it masked our yearning for inclusion." What is *irony* and how is "our anti-Americanism" ironic?

4. In paragraphs 12 and 13, Early uses the phrase, "tipping point." Explain what the phrase means and how he uses it to develop his thesis.

5. In paragraph 19, Early says, "In a way, the black American narrative revealed American hypocrisy but simultaneously reinscribed American greatness." Explain what the sentence means and why you do or do not agree.

6. Review Early's final paragraph. In what ways does it bring his process analysis to a conclusion?

Instructions ■▪▪

These instruction, like those for many technical devices, include both written and visual elements.

Opening:
Use a descriptive title. Note or list materials needed.

Downloading Photographs from the MC-150 Digital Camera

Note: MC-150 software must be loaded on your computer to download photographs from the camera.

Middle:
State steps in chronological order and parallel form.

1. Turn your computer on.

2. Plug the camera's USB cable into your computer.

Add graphics (such as the arrow) to create a quick visual cue.

3. Turn the camera's mode dial to the **data transfer setting** (Figure 1).

4. Open the camera's flash-card door and plug the other end of the USB cable into the **camera port** (Figure 2).

Boldface words that need special attention.

Figure 1: Data Transfer Setting

5. Select USB transfer from the camera screen menu. The MC-150 software will then launch on your computer.

To show an object's size, use a reference (such as the fingers).

6. Follow the instructions on the computer screen to download all of your photos or specific photos.

7. When your download is complete, turn the camera off and unplug the USB cable from the camera and the computer.

Use only well-focused photographs.

Figure 2: Camera Port

Closing:
Note common problems.

Note: If the MC-150 software doesn't launch, disconnect the camera (step 7), and then restart the computer and continue on from step 2.

Writing Guidelines

Model

Planning

1. **Select a topic.** Use prompts like those below to generate a list of topics.

   - A course-related process
   - A process in nature
   - A process in the news
   - A process that helps you get a job

2. **Review the process.** Use your knowledge of the topic to fill out an organizer like the one on the right. List the subject at the top, each of the steps in chronological order, and the outcome at the bottom. For a complex process, break it down into stages or phases first; then outline the steps within each phase.

   > Process Analysis
   > Subject:
   >   - Step #1
   >   - Step #2
   >   - Step #3
   > Outcome:

3. **Research as needed.** Find information that helps you explain the process: what it is, what steps are required, what order the steps follow, how the steps are done, what outcome the process produces, and what safety precautions are needed. If possible, observe the process or perform it yourself. Carefully record correct names, materials, tools, and safety or legal issues.

4. **Organize information.** Revise the organizer as needed. Then develop an outline, including steps listed in the organizer, as well as supporting details from your research.

Drafting

5. **Draft the document.** Write the document using the guidelines below.

Describing and Explaining a Process

- **Opening:** Introduce the topic; give an overview of the process, possibly forecasting its main stages; and explain why the process is important.
- **Middle:** Order the process into phases if necessary, clearly describe each step in the process, and link steps with transitions such as *first, second, next, finally,* and *while.* Explain the importance of each step, and how it is linked to other steps in the process. Describe the overall outcome of the process and explain its relevance.
- **Closing:** Summarize the process and restate key points as needed; if appropriate, explain follow-up activity.

Writing Instructions

- **Opening:** Name the process in the title, summarize the process's goal, and list any materials and tools needed.
- **Middle:** Present each step in a separate—usually one- or two-sentence—paragraph. Number the steps and state each clearly, using firm commands directed to the reader. Where appropriate, include signal terms indicating **Caution! WARNING!** or **DANGER!**
- **Closing:** In a short paragraph, explain how and when follow-up action should be completed.

Note: To state instructions as direct commands, use action verbs in the imperative mood. The *mood* of a verb indicates the tone or attitude it conveys.

Revising

6. **Improve the ideas, organization, and voice.** Ask a classmate or someone from the writing center to evaluate the following:

____ **Ideas:** Is the process presented as a unified phenomenon that includes a logical series of stages and steps? If causes and effects are addressed, are the claims clear and supported with well-researched details?

____ **Organization:** Does the *process essay* include an opening that introduces the process and thesis; a middle that describes stages and steps clearly and correctly; and a closing that unifies the essay by accenting key points?

____ Do the *instructions* include an opening that correctly names the process and lists materials needed; a middle that states each step (or directive) correctly and in the required order; and a closing that specifies follow-up action?

____ **Voice:** Is the tone informed, concerned, and objective? Are *instructions* stated as firm, direct commands using action verbs in the imperative mood?

TIP: Test instructions by using them to perform the process.

Editing

7. **Edit the essay.** Polish your writing by addressing the following:

____ **Words:** The words are precise, clear, and correct.
  - Technical terms are correct, used uniformly, and defined.
  - Transitions link steps, and a consistent verb tense is used.

____ **Sentences:** The sentences are smooth, varied in structure, and engaging. In instructions, sentences are shaped as clear, brief commands formatted in accordance with standards set by regulatory agencies such as the American National Standards Institute (ANSI), the International Organization for Standardization (ISO), or the U.S. military (MILSPEC).

____ **Correctness:** The finished copy includes correct usage, grammar, punctuation, and spelling.

____ **Page Design:** The design features steps in the process. In instructions, signal terms and symbols conform to standards set by ANSI, ISO, or MILSPEC.

Publishing

8. **Publish the essay** by offering it to instructors, students, and nonprofit agencies working with the process. Also consider posting the writing on a suitable website.

Critical-Thinking and Writing Activities

As directed by your instructor, complete the following activities by yourself or in a group.

Interactive

1. Reread the topics that you listed under "Select a Topic" on page 228. Choose a topic and write about it as an essay or as a set of instructions.

2. Review "Wayward Cells," the essay that analyzes what cancer is and how it progresses. Then choose another natural or social science process that interests you and write an essay describing and analyzing that process. Conversely, think of a process within the arts and humanities (e.g., a historical movement, a cultural change, a plot pattern in fiction or film, an artistic method).

3. Review the instructions "Downloading Photographs from the MC-150 Digital Camera," considering how the written and visual elements on the page work together. Draft or revise a process document in which visual elements are essential to effectively communicate your ideas. Integrate relevant, high-quality visuals (photos, illustrations, diagrams) that will help readers to better understand the process.

4. In his essay, "The End of Race as We Know It," Gerald L. Early analyzes a process through which he came to a new and deeper understanding of himself and others. Think about a time or phase in your own life during which you came to know yourself more fully. (Conversely, look at a transition in the lives of other people, whether an individual or an identifiable group.) Then write an essay in which you analyze the transition, identify related stages and steps, explain their causes and effects, and address the overall impact of the experience.

Learning-Outcomes Checklist

Use this checklist to assess what you have learned about process writing:

_____ I understand what process essays are, why they are written, and how they are organized chronologically with needed transitions.

_____ I understand what instructions are, why they are written, and how they are organized.

_____ I can read the content and evaluate the quality of process essays and instructions.

_____ I can read and respond to signal terms in instructions.

_____ I know how to access technical-writing standards set by the American National Standards Institute (ANSI), the International Organization for Standardization (ISO), and the U.S. military (MILSPEC).

_____ I can draft, revise, edit, design, and publish both a process essay and a set of instructions.

15 Definition

Most forms of academic and workplace writing—from essays and reports to proposals and literature reviews—include brief (one- or two-sentence) definitions of terms. Although this chapter will help you read and write those (see pages 233–235), its main purpose is to help you understand and write longer, essay-length pieces sometimes called extended definitions.

Such definitions clarify, and deepen readers' understanding of a term—whether the term refers to something concrete or abstract. When reading such essays, consider how the writers "extend" your understanding of their topics, often using examples and stories to do so.

Learning Outcomes

Audio

▸ Understand how the writing situation informs definition writing.

▸ Parse a word's root, prefix, suffix, denotations, connotations, and etymology.

▸ Read and evaluate brief and extended definitions.

▸ Research and write brief and extended definitions.

▸ Use anecdotes, quotations, comparisons, and contrasts.

Visually Speaking ▶ To learn more about reading and writing definition essays, look again at the photograph above and consider what it suggests about why we need definitions, write them, and use them.

Web Link

Reading Definition Writing

To effectively read extended definitions, consider the essays' rhetorical situation and the specific definition strategies the writers use—and why.

Consider the rhetorical situation.

To understand a definition, consider the writer's purpose, audience, and topic.

- **Purpose:** Writers compose definitions for many reasons—to correctly define a misunderstood term, to deepen or re-direct its meaning, to plumb a term's history, or to entertain readers. Look for the point of the definition.
- **Audience:** People who read definition essays do so for different reasons, but all seek to learn something. For some readers, the term may be new; while for others, the term may be familiar but misunderstood. Determine the target audience and think through its relationship to the term being defined.
- **Topic:** For any definition, the topic is a term. But what terms do writers typically focus on? Terms may be technical, unusual, complex, comical, or new. They may have changed through time. They may be crucial to a larger analysis or argument. As you read a definition, ask "Why this term?"

Consider definition-writing strategies.

To understand a definition, identify the writer's strategies. Consider, for example, what the writer conveys about the term's **denotative** (or literal) meaning, its **connotative** (or suggested) meaning, and its **etymological** (or historical) meaning. Examine, as well, the use of anecdotes, comparisons, and contrasts. For example, the writers whose essays are included in this chapter make the following choices:

- Shon Bogar defines his topic (human trafficking) in part by distinguishing it from related practices. In other words, he explains what the practice is by showing what it *is not*.
- David Schelhaas explains the meanings of *deft* and *daft* by sharing a funny anecdote and analyzing the words' etymologies—or historical development.
- In "On *Excellence*," Cynthia Ozick distinguishes her mother's personality from her own by offering two distinct extended definitions of *excellence*, each illustrated with engaging anecdotes and clarified with keen observations.
- In his extended definition entitled "Wikipedia and the Meaning of *Truth*," Simon L Garfinkle shares anecdotes and cites historical phenomena to explain how we determine what is—or *is not—truth*.

Reader's Checklist

_____ Precisely what does the writer claim about the term's meaning?

_____ Is the definition current, relevant, complete, and clear?

_____ Is the definition accurate in terms of its past and current usage?

Definition ■■▪

The excerpt below comes from a research paper by student writer Shon Bogar. The paper focuses on the problems of human trafficking and slavery as phenomena associated with current trends in globalization. After reviewing global economic trends since the end of the Cold War, Bogar defines the key terms that readers must understand if they are to appreciate the problem. (For more on research writing, see chapters 27–32.)

Video

Economic Disparities Fuel Human Trafficking

At the end of the introduction, the writer transitions to the extended definition.

. . . . These great economic disparities, from extreme poverty to fabulous wealth, have helped fuel the international trade in human cargo, as those people with nothing seek a better life serving those with excess.   *1*

An informal definition of the broader concept of slavery prefaces the extended definition.

The buying, selling, and forced exploitation of people—slavery—is not a new phenomenon. Most nations and most cultures have, at one time or another, enslaved others and been themselves enslaved in turn. The pattern continues today; in fact, slavery exists far beyond the developing world and reaches into the comfortable First World of the United States, Europe, Japan, and Australia. However, examining current trends in the trade of human cargo shows that trafficking and slavery are extremely difficult to define and understand, and that they coexist with and are codependent upon each other. These problems, moreover, have a variety of complex causes and too few solutions that offer a realistic possibility of ending this global abomination.   *2*

The main term is distinguished from related terms using reliable source material.

Human trafficking, in particular, is a term that is difficult to define properly, but it must first be clarified if the problem itself is to be addressed. To begin, migration, human smuggling, and human trafficking are distinct but related phenomena, and incorrect definitions would put different groups of people in the wrong category, with potentially dire consequences. For example, the Trafficking Victims Prevention Act (TVPA), which came into law in 2000, requires the U.S. government to ensure that victims of trafficking are not jailed or "otherwise penalized solely for unlawful acts as a direct result of being trafficked" (U.S. Department of State, 2004), whereas illegal immigrants are still subject to deportation and criminal proceedings. The U.S. State Department recognizes the potentially "confusing" difference between smuggling and human trafficking, so it defines human smuggling as "the procurement or transport for profit of a person for illegal entry in a country" (2004). However, even if the smuggling involves "dangerous or degrading conditions," the act is still considered smuggling, not human trafficking, and so smuggling is considered an immigration matter, not necessarily a human rights issue (2004).   *3*

The writer offers a formal definition of the key term "human trafficking" by going to official sources.

What distinguishes trafficking from smuggling is the element of exploitation, including but not limited to "fraud, force, or coercion" (U.S. Department of State, 2004). With this distinction in mind, the United Nations Convention Against Transnational Organized Crime has developed this standard definition of human   *4* trafficking: "the recruitment, transportation, transfer, harbouring or receipt of persons, by means of the threat or use of force or other forms of coercion, of abduction, of fraud, of deception, of the abuse of power, or of a position of vulnerability or of the giving or receiving of payments or benefits to achieve the consent of a person having control over another person, for the purpose of exploitation" (U.N. Resolution 25, 2001). To unravel the U.N. legalese, human trafficking involves any use of force, coercion, fraud, or deception by those with power so as to exploit people, primarily by moving them into some form of slavery. Under this definition, smuggling can become trafficking if the smugglers have used any means of deception. Unfortunately, the requirement that the smuggler/trafficker be aware of the "victim's final circumstances" makes distinguishing between smuggling and trafficking an inexact science (U.S. Department of State, 2004), and it creates a new set of problems in combating trafficking apart from smuggling. Nevertheless, this definition of human trafficking is a helpful starting point from which the United Nations and governments around the globe can start to fight the trafficking and eventual enslavement of people.

> The writer restates a complex legal definition in terms readers will understand.

> While admitting a difficulty in the definition, the writer stresses the definition's usefulness.

All difficulties of definition aside, human trafficking and slavery are real   5
problems—historical problems that have taken new shapes due to globalization. In fact, today human trafficking is linked to millions of people experiencing multiple forms of slavery, from traditional "chattel slavery" to sexual slavery to debt bondage. . . .

Reading for Better Writing

Working by yourself or with a group, answer these questions:

1. Without looking back at the model, define "human trafficking" in a sentence or two.

2. Examine each of the three main paragraphs of Bogar's extended definition. What does each paragraph accomplish? How do the paragraphs build on each other?

3. Identify the strategies that the author uses to argue that the definition is necessary. Is the reasoning compelling? Why or why not?

4. Look again at the sources that the writer uses to develop the necessary definitions. Why are these sources appropriate for the terms in question? Which other types of sources might be useful?

5. Examine how the writer transitions into and out of the extended definition. Are these transitions effective? Why or why not?

Definition ■ ▪ ▪

Professor David Schelhaas delivered the following definition on his weekly radio program, *What's the Good Word*?

Deft or Daft

The writer introduces the topic with an anecdote.

The other day, my wife, watching our son-in-law with his large hands gracefully tie the shoelaces of his little daughter, remarked, "You really are deft." Ever the cynic, I remarked, "He's not only deft, he's daft." I talk that sort of nonsense frequently, but as I said this, I began to wonder. What if *deft* and *daft* come from the same root and once meant the same thing? A quick trip to the dictionary showed that, indeed, they did once mean the same thing (though my wife thought me daft when I first suggested it).   *1*

He describes the history of *daft*.

Let me see if I can explain the original meaning and also how *daft* and *deft* came to part company. *Daft* originally meant mild or gentle. The Middle English *dafte* comes from the Old English *gadaefte,* which has as its underlying sense fit or suitable. Quite likely, mild or gentle people were seen as behaving in a way that was fit and suitable.   *2*

Gradually, however, the mild, gentle meaning descended in connotation to mean crazy or foolish. First, animals were described as daft—that is, without reason and eventually people also. The word *silly*, which once meant happy or blessed, slid down the same slope. So that explains where *daft* got its present meaning.   *3*

He compares and contrasts the two words.

But how does *deft*, meaning skillful or dexterous, fit into the picture? Again, if we start with the Old English meaning of *fit* or *suitable*, we can see a connection to skillful. In fact, the root of *gadaefte*, which is *dhabh*, to fit, carries with it the sense of a joiner or an artisan, someone who skillfully made the ends or corners of a cupboard or piece of furniture fit neatly together. From *fit* to *skillful* to *dexterous*. Thus we see how one root word meaning *fit* or *suitable* went in two different directions—one meaning crazy, the other meaning skillful.   *4*

He closes with a reflection and his usual sign-off.

These days it is usually considered much better to be deft than to be daft. But don't be too sure. It is good to remind ourselves that one person's deftness might very well appear as daftness to another.   *5*

This is David Schelhaas asking, "What's the Good Word?"   *6*

Reading for Better Writing

Working by yourself or with a group, answer these guidelines:

1. Explain how the opening attempts to engage the reader. In what ways does it succeed?

2. Describe how the writer shows that the meanings of the words have changed. Is his explanation clear? Why or why not?

3. Describe the writer's tone. Is it effective for a radio program? Explain.

Definition ▪▪▪

Cynthia Ozick is an American writer known for her fiction, poetry, and essays on Jewish American life. In 2005, she was nominated for the Man Booker International Prize for lifetime achievement in literature.

On *Excellence*

In my Depression childhood, whenever I had a new dress, my cousin Sarah would get suspicious. The nicer the dress was, and especially the more expensive it looked, the more suspicious she would get. Finally she would lift the hem and check the seams. This was to see if the dress had been bought or if my mother had sewed it. Sarah could always tell. My mother's sewing had elegant outsides, but there was something catch-as-catch-can about the insides. Sarah's sewing, by contrast, was as impeccably finished inside as out; not one stray thread dangled.

My uncle Jake built meticulous grandfather clocks out of rosewood; he was a perfectionist and sent to England for the clockworks. My mother built serviceable radiator covers and a serviceable cabinet, with hinged doors, for the pantry. She built a pair of bookcases for the living room. Once, after I was grown and in a house of my own, she fixed the sewer pipe. She painted ceilings, and also landscapes; she reupholstered chairs. One summer she planted a whole yard of tall corn. She thought herself capable of doing anything, and did everything she imagined. But nothing was perfect. There was always some clear flaw, never visible head-on. You had to look underneath where the seams were. The corn thrived, though not in rows. The stalks elbowed one another like gossips in a dense little village.

"Miss Brrrrroooobaker," my mother used to mock, rolling her Russian r's, whenever I crossed a *t* she had left uncrossed, or corrected a word she had misspelled, or became impatient with a *v* that had tangled itself up in a *w* in her speech. ("Vvventriloquist," I would say. "Vventriloquist," she would obediently repeat. And the next time it would come out "wiolinist.") Miss Brubaker was my high school English teacher, and my mother invoked her name as an emblem of raging finical obsession. "Miss Brrrrroooobaker," my mother's voice hoots at me down the years, as I go on casting and recasting sentences in a tiny handwriting on monomaniacally uniform paper. The loops of my mother's handwriting—it was the Palmer Method—were as big as hoops, spilling generous splashy ebullience. She could pull off, at five minutes' notice, a satisfying dinner for ten concocted out of nothing more than originality and panache. But the napkin would be folded a little off-center, and the spoon might be on the wrong side of the knife. She was an optimist who ignored trifles; for her, God was not in the details but in the intent. And all these culinary and agricultural efflorescences were extracurricular, accomplished in the crevices and niches of a fourteen-hour business day. When she scribbled out her family memoirs, in heaps of dog-eared notebooks or on the backs of old bills or on the margins of last year's calendar, I would resist typing them; in the speed of the chase she often omitted words like "the," "and," "will." The same flashing and bountiful hand fashioned and fired ceramic pots, and painted brilliant autumn views and vases of imaginary flowers and ferns, and decorated ordinary Woolworth platters with lavish enameled gardens. But bits of the painted petals would chip away.

Lavish: my mother was as lavish as nature. She woke early and saturated the hours with work and inventiveness, and read late into the night. She was all profusion, abundance, fabrication. Angry at her children, she would run after us whirling the cord of the electric iron, like a lasso or a whip; but she never caught us. When, in the seventh grade, I was afraid of failing the Music Appreciation final exam because I could not tell the difference between "To a Wild Rose" and "Barcarolle," she got the idea of sending me to school with a gauze sling rigged up on my writing arm, and an explanatory note that was purest fiction. But the sling kept slipping off. My mother gave advice like mad—she boiled over with so much passion for the predicaments of strangers that they turned into permanent cronies. She told intimate stories about people I had never heard of.

Despite the gargantuan Palmer loops (or possibly because of them), I have always known that my mother's was a life of—intricately abashing word!—excellence: insofar as excellence means ripe generosity. She burgeoned, she proliferated; she was endlessly leafy and flowering. She wore red hats and called herself a gypsy. In her girlhood she marched with the suffragettes and for Margaret Sanger and called herself a Red. She made me laugh, she was so varied: like a tree on which lemons, pomegranates, and prickly pears absurdly all hang together. She had the comedy of prodigality.

My own way is a thousand times more confined. I am a pinched perfectionist, the ultimate fruition of Miss Brubaker; I attend to crabbed minutiae and am self-trammeled through taking pains. I am a kind of human snail, locked in and condemned by my own nature. The ancients believed that the moist track left by the snail as it crept was the snail's own essence, depleting its body little by little; the farther the snail toiled, the smaller it became, until it finally rubbed itself out. That is how perfectionists are. Say to us "Excellence," and we will show you how we use up our substance and wear ourselves away, while making scarcely any progress at all. The fact that I am an exacting perfectionist in a narrow strait only, and nowhere else, is hardly to the point, since nothing matters to me so much as a comely and muscular sentence. It is my narrow strait, this snail's road: the track of the sentence I am writing now; and when I have eked out the wet substance, ink or blood, that is its mark, I will begin the next sentence. Only in reading out sentences am I perfectionist; but then there is nothing else I know how to do, or take much interest in. I miter every pair of abutting sentences as scrupulously

4

5

6

Lavish is introduced as a word that is a synonym of *excellence*.

One definition of *excellence* is offered.

The writer offers herself as a contrast to her mother's excellence.

as Uncle Jake fitted one strip of rosewood against another. My mother's worldly and bountiful hand has escaped me. The sentence I am writing is my cabin and my shell, compact, self-sufficient. It is the burnished horizon—a merciless planet where flawlessness is the single standard, where even the inmost seams, however hidden from a laxer eye, must meet perfection. Here "excellence" is not strewn casually from a tipped cornucopia, here disorder does not account for charm, here trifles rule like tyrants.

The writer contrasts lavish excellence with the excellence of perfectionism.

I measure my life in sentences, and my sentences are superior to my mother's, 7 pressed out, line by line, like the lustrous ooze on the underside of the snail, the snail's secret open seam, its wound, leaking attar. My mother was too mettlesome to feel the force of a comma. She scorned minutiae. She measured her life according to what poured from the horn of plenty, which was her ample, cascading, elastic, susceptible, inexact heart. My narrower heart rides between the tiny horns of the snail, dwindling as it goes.

And out of this thinnest thread, this ink-wet line of words, must rise a visionary 8 fog, a mist, a smoke, forging cities, histories, sorrows, quagmires, entanglements, lives of sinners, even the life of my furnace-hearted mother: so much wilderness, waywardness, plentitude on the head of the precise and impeccable snail, between the horns.

A poetic closing sums up the definition.

Reading for Better Writing

Working by yourself or with a group, answer these questions:

1. What words and phrases does Ozick use to define *excellence?* How does contrasting her mother's life with her own enable Ozick to further define *excellence?* What point(s) is she making about *excellence?*

2. One way to write a definition is to use words and phrases that have similar meanings to the word you wish to define. What other techniques does Ozick use to define *excellence?* What additional strategies could be used to define a term?

3. Writing a good definition is challenging because it requires the use of precise words to shed light on the meaning of another word that has its own precise meaning(s). Find instances where Ozick lists one term or idea after another to build precision into a definition. How would her meaning change if she had used only one word from the list?

4. Find examples of words that have especially positive or negative connotations. How do these connotations help Ozick to make her main point(s)?

Definition ■·■

Simson L. Garfinkle is a contributing editor to *Technology Review;* an associate professor at the Naval Postgraduate School in Monterey, California; and an associate of the School of Engineering and Applied Sciences at Harvard. In the following essay, published in 2008, he analyzes how the nature and use of Wikipedia affect how we discern what is true.

Wikipedia and the Meaning of *Truth*

Why the online encyclopedia's epistemology should worry those who care about traditional notions of accuracy.

As you read this essay, annotate it and take notes—identifying strategies the writer uses to develop an extended definition

With little notice from the outside world, the community-written encyclopedia Wikipedia has redefined the commonly accepted use of the word "truth." 1

Why should we care? Because Wikipedia's articles are the first- or second-ranked results for most Internet searches. Type "iron" into Google, and Wikipedia's article on the element is the top-ranked result; likewise, its article on the Iron Cross is first when the search words are "iron cross." Google's search algorithms rank a story in part by how many times it has been linked to; people are linking to Wikipedia articles a lot. 2

This means that the content of these articles really matters. Wikipedia's standards of inclusion—what's in and what's not—affect the work of journalists, who routinely read Wikipedia articles and then repeat the wikiclaims as "background" without bothering to cite them. These standards affect students, whose research on many topics starts (and often ends) with Wikipedia. And since I used Wikipedia to research large parts of this article, these standards are affecting you, dear reader, at this very moment. 3

Many people, especially academic experts, have argued that Wikipedia's articles can't be trusted, because they are written and edited by volunteers who have never been vetted. Nevertheless, studies have found that the articles are remarkably accurate. The reason is that Wikipedia's community of more than seven million registered users has organically evolved a set of policies and procedures for removing untruths. This also explains Wikipedia's explosive growth: if the stuff in Wikipedia didn't seem "true enough" to most readers, they wouldn't keep coming back to the website. 4

These policies have become the social contract for Wikipedia's army of apparently insomniac volunteers. Thanks to them, incorrect information generally disappears quite quickly. 5

So how do the Wikipedians decide what's true and what's not? On what is their epistemology based? 6

Unlike the laws of mathematics or science, wikitruth isn't based on principles such as consistency or observability. It's not even based on common sense or firsthand experience. Wikipedia has evolved a radically different set of epistemological standards—standards that aren't especially surprising given that the site is rooted in a Web-based community, but that should concern those of us who are interested in traditional notions of truth and accuracy. On Wikipedia, 7 objective truth isn't all that important, actually. What makes a fact or statement fit for inclusion is that it appeared in some other publication—ideally, one that is in English and is available free online. "The threshold for inclusion in Wikipedia is verifiability, not truth," states Wikipedia's official policy on the subject.

Verifiability is one of Wikipedia's three core content policies; it was codified   8 back in August 2003. The two others are "no original research" (December 2003) and "neutral point of view," which the Wikipedia project inherited from Nupedia, an earlier volunteer-written Web-based free encyclopedia that existed from March 2000 to September 2003 (Wikipedia's own NPOV policy was codified in December 2001). These policies have made Wikipedia a kind of academic agora where people on both sides of politically charged subjects can rationally discuss their positions, find common ground, and unemotionally document their differences. Wikipedia is successful because these policies have worked.

Unlike Wikipedia's articles, Nupedia's were written and vetted by experts.   9 But few experts were motivated to contribute. Well, some wanted to write about their own research, but Larry Sanger, Nupedia's editor in chief, immediately put an end to that practice.

"I said, 'If it hasn't been vetted by the relevant experts, then basically we   10 are setting ourselves up as a frontline source of new, original information, and we aren't set up to do that,'" Sanger (who is himself, ironically or not, a former philosophy instructor and by training an epistemologist) recalls telling his fellow Nupedians.

With experts barred from writing about their own work and having no   11 incentive to write about anything else, Nupedia struggled. Then Sanger and Jimmy Wales, Nupedia's founder, decided to try a different policy on a new site, which they launched on January 15, 2001. They adopted the newly invented "wiki" technology, allowing anybody to contribute to any article—or create a new one—on any topic, simply by clicking "Edit this page."

Soon the promoters of oddball hypotheses and outlandish ideas were all   12 over Wikipedia, causing the new site's volunteers to spend a good deal of time repairing damage—not all of it the innocent work of the misguided or deluded. (A study recently published in Communications of the Association for Computing Machinery found that 11 percent of Wikipedia articles have been vandalized at least once.) But how could Wikipedia's volunteer editors tell if something was true? The solution was to add references and footnotes to the articles, "not in order to help the reader, but in order to establish a point to the satisfaction of the [other] contributors," says Sanger, who left Wikipedia before the verifiability policy was formally adopted. (Sanger and Wales, now the chairman emeritus of the Wikimedia Foundation, fell out about the scale of Sanger's role in the creation of Wikipedia. Today, Sanger is the creator and editor in chief of Citizendium, an alternative to Wikipedia that is intended to address the inadequacy of its "reliability and quality.")

Verifiability is really an appeal to authority—not the authority of truth, but   13 the authority of other publications. Any other publication, really. These days, information that's added to Wikipedia without an appropriate reference is likely to be slapped with a "citation needed" badge by one of Wikipedia's self-appointed editors. Remove the badge and somebody else will put it back. Keep it up and you might find yourself face to face with another kind of authority—one of the English-language Wikipedia's 1,500 administrators, who have the ability to place increasingly restrictive protections on contentious pages when the policies are ignored.

To be fair, Wikipedia's verifiability policy states that "articles should rely on 14 reliable, third-party published sources" that themselves adhere to Wikipedia's NPOV policy. Self-published articles should generally be avoided, and non-English sources are discouraged if English articles are available, because many people who read, write, and edit En.Wikipedia (the English-language version) can read only English.

Mob Rules

In a May 2006 essay on the technology and culture website Edge.org, futurist 15 Jaron Lanier called Wikipedia an example of "digital Maoism"—the closest humanity has come to a functioning mob rule.

Lanier was moved to write about Wikipedia because someone kept editing 16 his Wikipedia entry to say that he was a film director. Lanier describes himself as a "computer scientist, composer, visual artist, and author." He is good at all those things, but he is no director. According to his essay, he made one short experimental film in the 1990s, and it was "awful."

"I have attempted to retire from directing films in the alternative universe 17 that is the Wikipedia a number of times, but somebody always overrules me," Lanier wrote. "Every time my Wikipedia entry is corrected, within a day I'm turned into a film director again."

Since Lanier's attempted edits to his own Wikipedia entry were based on 18 firsthand knowledge of his own career, he was in direct violation of Wikipedia's three core policies. He has a point of view; he was writing on the basis of his own original research; and what he wrote couldn't be verified by following a link to some kind of legitimate, authoritative, and verifiable publication.

Wikipedia's standard for "truth" makes good technical and legal sense, given 19 that anyone can edit its articles. There was no way for Wikipedia, as a community, to know whether the person revising the article about Jaron Lanier was really Jaron Lanier or a vandal. So it's safer not to take people at their word, and instead to require an appeal to the authority of another publication from everybody who contributes, expert or not.

An interesting thing happens when you try to understand Wikipedia: the 20 deeper you go, the more convoluted it becomes. Consider the verifiability policy. Wikipedia considers the "most reliable sources" to be "peer-reviewed journals and books published in university presses," followed by "university-level textbooks," then magazines, journals, "books published by respected publishing houses," and finally "mainstream newspapers" (but not the opinion pages of newspapers).

Once again, this makes sense, given Wikipedia's inability to vet the real-world identities of authors. Lanier's complaints when his Wikipedia page claimed that he was a film director couldn't be taken seriously by Wikipedia's "contributors" until Lanier persuaded the editors at Edge to print his article bemoaning the claim. This Edge article by Lanier was enough to convince the Wikipedians that the Wikipedia article about Lanier was incorrect—after all, there was a clickable link! Presumably the editors at Edge did their fact checking, so the wikiworld could now be corrected. *21*

As fate would have it, Lanier was subsequently criticized for engaging in the wikisin of editing his own wikientry. The same criticism was leveled against me when I corrected a number of obvious errors in my own Wikipedia entry. *22*

"Criticism" is actually a mild word for the kind of wikijustice meted out to people who are foolish enough to get caught editing their own Wikipedia entries: the entries get slapped with a banner headline that says "A major contributor to this article, or its creator, may have a conflict of interest regarding its subject matter." The banner is accompanied by a little picture showing the scales of justice tilted to the left. Wikipedia's "Autobiography" policy explains in great detail how drawing on your own knowledge to edit the Wikipedia entry about yourself violates all three of the site's cornerstone policies—and illustrates the point with yet another appeal to authority, a quotation from The Hitchhiker's Guide to the Galaxy. *23*

But there is a problem with appealing to the authority of other people's written words: many publications don't do any fact checking at all, and many of those that do simply call up the subject of the article and ask if the writer got the facts wrong or right. For instance, Dun and Bradstreet gets the information for its small-business information reports in part by asking those very same small businesses to fill out questionnaires about themselves. *24*

"No Original Research"

What all this means is hard to say. I am infrequently troubled by Wiki's unreliability. (The quality of the writing is a different subject.) As a computer scientist, I find myself using Wikipedia on a daily basis. Its discussions of algorithms, architectures, microprocessors, and other technical subjects are generally excellent. When they aren't excellent and I know better, I just fix them. And when they're wrong and I don't know better—well, I don't know any better, do I? *25*

I've also spent quite a bit of time reviewing Wikipedia's articles about such things as the "Singularity Scalpel," the "Treaty of Algeron," and "Number Six." Search for these terms and you'll be directed to Wikipedia articles with the titles "List of Torchwood items" and "List of treaties in Star Trek," and to one about a Cylon robot played by Canadian actress Tricia Helfer. These articles all hang their wikiexistence upon scholarly references to original episodes of Dr. Who, Torchwood, Star Trek, and Battlestar Galactica—popular television shows that *26* the Wikipedia contributors dignify with the word "canon."

I enjoy using these articles as sticks to poke at Wikipedia, but they represent 27 a tiny percentage of Wikipedia's overall content. On the other hand, they've been an important part of Wikipedia culture from the beginning. Sanger says that early on, Wikipedia made a commitment to having a wide variety of articles: "There's plenty of disk space, and as long as there are people out there who are able to write a decent article about a subject, why not let them? . . . I thought it was kind of funny and cool that people were writing articles about every character in *The Lord of the Rings*. I didn't regard it as a problem the way some people do now."

What's wrong with the articles about fantastical worlds is that they are at 28 odds with Wikipedia's "no original research" rule, since almost all of them draw their "references" from the fictions themselves and not from the allegedly more reliable secondary sources. I haven't nominated these articles for speedy deletion because Wikipedia makes an exception for fiction—and because, truth be told, I enjoy reading them. And these days, most such entries are labeled as referring to fictional universes.

So what is Truth? According to Wikipedia's entry on the subject, "the term 29 has no single definition about which the majority of professional philosophers and scholars agree." But in practice, Wikipedia's standard for inclusion has become its de facto standard for truth, and since Wikipedia is the most widely read online reference on the planet, it's the standard of truth that most people are implicitly using when they type a search term into Google or Yahoo. On Wikipedia, truth is received truth: the consensus view of a subject.

That standard is simple: something is true if it was published in a newspaper 30 article, a magazine or journal, or a book published by a university press—or if it appeared on Dr. Who.

Reading for Better Writing

Working by yourself or with a group, answer these questions:

1. What does Garfinkle's subtitle convey about his essay and his purpose?

2. Garfinkle says that wiki readers "repeat the wikiclaims as 'background' without bothering to cite them." Is he correct, and is the practice a problem? Explain.

3. Review Garfinkle's subheadings "Mob Rules" and "No Original Research." Then explain what they mean and why they do or do not help readers understand his argument.

4. Review paragraph 29 in which the writer quotes Wikipedia's definition of truth and then says, "On Wikipedia, truth is received truth: the consensus view of a subject." Explain what he means, and whether this issue is a serious one.

Writing Guidelines

Model

Planning

1. Select a topic. Beneath headings like these, list words that you'd like to explore:

Words related to an art or sport:	Words that are (or should be) in the news:	Words that are overused, un-used, or abused:	Words that make you laugh or worry:	Words that do (or don't) describe you:

TIP: The best topics are abstract nouns (*truth, individualism*), complex terms (*code blue, dementia*), or words connected to a personal experience (*excellence, deft, daft*).

2. Identify what you know. To discern what you already know about the topic, write freely about the word, letting your writing go where it chooses. Explore both your personal and your academic connections with the word.

3. Gather information. To find information about the word's history, usage, and grammatical form, use strategies such as these:

- Consult a general dictionary, preferably an unabridged dictionary; list both denotative (literal) and connotative (associated) meanings for the word.
- Consult specialized dictionaries that define words from specific disciplines or occupations: music, literature, law, medicine, and so on.
- If helpful, interview experts on your topic.
- Check reference books such as *Bartlett's Familiar Quotations* to see how famous speakers and writers have used the word.
- Research the word's etymology and usage by consulting appropriate Web sources such as dictionary.com, m-w.com, or xrefer.com.
- Do a general search on the web to see where the word pops up in titles of songs, books, or films; company names, products, and ads; nonprofit organizations' names, campaigns, and programs; and topics in the news.
- List synonyms (words meaning the same—or nearly the same) and antonyms (words meaning the opposite).

4. Compress what you know. Based on your freewriting and research, try writing a formal, one-sentence definition that satisfies the following equation:

> **Equation:** Term = larger class + distinguishing characteristics
> **Examples:** Swedish pimple = fishing lure + silver surface, tubular body, three hooks
> melodrama = stage play + flat characters, contrived plot, moralistic theme
> Alzheimer's = dementia + increasing loss of memory, hygiene, social skills

5. Get organized. To organize the information that you have, and to identify details that you may want to add, fill out a graphic organizer like the one on page 53.

Drafting

6. **Draft the essay.** Review your outline as needed to write the first draft.
   - **Opening:** Get the reader's attention and introduce the term. If you are organizing the essay from general to specific, consider using an anecdote, an illustration, or a quotation to set the context. If you are organizing the essay from specific to general, consider including an interesting detail from the word's history or usage. When using a dictionary definition, avoid the dusty phrase "According to *Webster* . . ."
   - **Middle:** Show your readers precisely what the word means. Build the definition in paragraphs that address distinct aspects of the word: common definitions, etymology, usage by professional writers, and so on. Link paragraphs so that the essay unfolds the word's meaning layer by layer.
   - **Closing:** Review your main point and close your essay. (You might, for example, conclude by encouraging readers to use—or not use—the word.)

Revising

7. **Improve the ideas, organization, and voice.** Ask a classmate or someone from the college's writing center to read your essay for the following:
   - **Ideas:** Is each facet of the definition **clear**, showing precisely what the word does and does not mean? Is the definition **complete**, telling the reader all that she or he needs to know in order to understand and use the word?
   - **Organization:** Does the **opening** identify the word and set the context for what follows? Are the **middle** paragraphs cohesive, each offering a unit of meaningful information? Does the **closing** wrap up the message and refocus on the word's core meaning?
   - **Voice:** Is the voice informed, engaging, instructive, and courteous?

Editing

8. **Edit the essay by addressing these issues:**
   - **Words:** The words are precise and clear to the essay's audience.
   - **Sentences:** The sentences are complete, varied in structure, and readable.
   - **Correctness:** The copy includes no errors in spelling, usage, punctuation, grammar, or mechanics.
   - **Design:** The page design is correctly formatted and attractive.

Publishing

9. **Publish the essay.** Share your writing with interested readers, including friends, family, and classmates. Submit the essay to your instructor. If appropriate, use what you learned to edit a wiki article on your topic.

Critical-Thinking and Writing Activities

As directed by your instructor, complete the following activities.

1. In the passage excerpted from "Economic Disparities Fuel Human Trafficking" (pages 233–234), student writer Shon Bogar defines terms that readers must grasp in order to understand the rest of his essay. Choose an essay (your own or someone else's) that includes a word or concept needing clarification. Define the topic and insert the definitions into the text, along with transitions that smoothly lead the reader into and out of the definition.

2. Review "Deft or Daft" and choose a pair of words that similarly mirror each other's meaning. Research the words, and write an essay comparing and contrasting their etymologies and meanings.

3. Review "On *Excellence*" by Cynthia Ozick, focusing on how she uses lists of words, phrases, and ideas to build precise definitions. Experiment with this definition strategy as you draft or revise an essay.

4. In her essay, Ozick defines *excellence* by comparing and contrasting herself and her mother. Choose two people in your life and select a word or concept that distinguishes how they are similar and different. Then write an essay that defines the word or concept while describing the two people.

5. "Wikipedia and the Meaning of *Truth*" explores how a relatively new phenomenon challenges a traditional concept. Write an extended definition exploring how a similar phenomenon has challenged a traditional term (e.g., reality TV, eBooks, digital natives, smart phones).

6. Write an essay defining a word or phrase that is understood by people in a particular field of study but not by "outsiders." Write for the audience of outsiders.

Learning-Outcomes Checklist

Use the checklist below to assess your grasp of the learning outcomes.

_____ I understand how an author's consideration of his or her situation (purpose, audience, and topic) strengthens the person's definition writing.

_____ I know how to research and analyze a word's root, prefix, suffix, denotations, connotations, and etymology.

_____ I can read and evaluate the quality of brief and extended definitions.

_____ I can research and write brief and extended definitions.

_____ I can find and use anecdotes, quotations, comparisons, and contrasts to develop an extended definition.

Persuasive Writing

"Convince me!" is the reader's cry that lies behind all persuasive writing. Whether you are taking a position on an issue (chapter 17), persuading readers to take action (chapter 18), or proposing a solution to a vexing problem (chapter 19), you are arguing a point in an attempt to persuade readers to accept your claims, with the result that they change their own thinking and perhaps even their actions. In other words, even though each of these forms has a distinctive rhetorical emphasis, all three rely on foundational strategies for argumentation and persuasion (chapter 16): from making and supporting claims effectively to avoiding logical fallacies.

Carefully study the four chapters in this section, noting the strategies discussed in each. Then, when you're writing a persuasive essay, use those strategies that best address your writing situation: your subject, audience, and purpose.

Persuasive Writing

Strategies for Argumentation and Persuasion

16

"I wasn't convinced." "I just didn't buy it." Maybe you've said something similar while watching a political debate, viewing a TV ad, or discussing an issue in class or at work. You simply didn't find the argument logical or convincing.

College is a place where big issues get argued out—in class and out. To participate in that dialogue, you must be able to read and listen to others' arguments, analyze them, and build your own.

This chapter will help you do that. It explains what argumentation is, how to identify weak arguments, and how to construct strong ones. The three ensuing chapters then explain and model three forms of written argumentation: taking a position, persuading readers to act, and proposing a solution.

Learning Outcomes

▶ Understand how to build an argument.

▶ Distinguish and develop three types of claims.

▶ Use evidence to qualify and support claims.

▶ Assess and use nine types of evidence.

▶ Identify and correct logical fallacies.

▶ Make needed concessions, develop rebuttals, and use appropriate appeals.

Audio

Video

Video

Visually Speaking ▶ Study the photograph above. What does it suggest about how to build a convincing argument?

Building Persuasive Arguments

Web Link

Video

What is an argument? Formally, an *argument* is a series of statements arranged in a logical sequence, supported with sound evidence, and expressed powerfully so as to sway your reader or listener. Arguments appear in a variety of places:

- A research paper about e-mail surveillance by the FBI.
- An analysis of "Good Country People" (short story) or *Poisonwood Bible* (novel).
- A debate about the ethics of transferring copyrighted music over the Internet.

Follow these steps.

Step 1: Prepare your argument.

- **Identify your audience and purpose.** Who is your audience and what is your goal? Do you want to take a position, persuade readers to act, or offer a solution?
- **Generate ideas and gather solid evidence.** You can't base an argument on opinions. Find accurate, pertinent information about the issue and uncover all viewpoints on it.
- **Develop a line of reasoning.** To be effective, you need to link your ideas in a clear, logical sequence.

Step 2: Make and qualify your claim.

- **Draw reasonable conclusions from the evidence.** State your claim (a debatable idea) as the central point for which you will argue. For example, you might assert that something is true, has value, or should be done.
- **Add qualifiers.** Words such as "typically" and "sometimes" soften your claim, making it more reasonable and acceptable.

Step 3: Support your claim.

- **Support each point** in your claim with solid evidence.
- **Identify logical fallacies.** Test your thinking for errors in logic. (See pages 257–260.)

Step 4: Engage the opposition.

- **Make concessions,** if needed, by granting points to the opposition.
- **Develop rebuttals** that expose the weaknesses of the opposition's position, whenever possible.
- **Use appropriate appeals**—emotional "tugs" that ethically and logically help readers see your argument as convincing.

■ Preparing Your Argument

An argument is a reason or chain of reasons used to support a claim. To use argumentation well, you need to know how to draw logical conclusions from sound evidence. Preparing an effective argument involves a number of specific steps, starting with those discussed below.

Video

Consider the situation. ■ ◦ ▪

- **Clearly identify your purpose and audience.** This step is essential for all writing, but especially true when building an argument. (See pages 30–31.)
- **Consider a range of ideas** to broaden your understanding of the issue and to help focus your thinking on a particular viewpoint. (See pages 44–45.)
- **Gather sound evidence** to support your viewpoint. (See pages 254–256.)

Develop a line of reasoning. ■ ◦ ▪

Argumentative writing requires a clear line of reasoning with each point logically supporting your argument. Develop the line of reasoning as you study the issue, or use either of the following outlines as a guide.

Sample Argumentative Outlines

Outline 1: **Present your supporting arguments, then address counterarguments, and conclude with the strongest argument.**
Introduction: question, concern, or claim
1. Strong argument-supporting claim
   - Discussion and support
2. Other argument-supporting claims
   - Discussion of and support for each argument
3. Objections, concerns, and counterarguments
   - Discussion, concessions, answers, and rebuttals
4. Strongest argument-supporting claim
   - Discussion and support
Conclusion: argument consolidated—claim reinforced

Outline 2: **Address the arguments and counterarguments point by point.**
Introduction: question, concern, or claim
1. Strong argument-supporting claim
   - Discussion and support
   - Counterarguments, concessions, and rebuttals
2. Other argument-supporting claims
   - For each argument, discussion and support
   - For each argument, counterarguments, concessions, and rebuttals
3. Strongest argument-supporting claim
   - Discussion and support
   - Counterarguments, concessions, and rebuttals
Conclusion: argument consolidated—claim reinforced

Making and Qualifying Claims

Video

An argument centers on a claim—a debatable statement. That claim is the thesis, or key point you wish to explain and defend so well that readers agree with it. A strong claim has the following traits:

- **It's clearly arguable**—it can be vigorously debated.
- **It's defendable**—it can be supported with sufficient arguments and evidence.
- **It's responsible**—it takes an ethically sound position.
- **It's understandable**—it uses clear terms and defines key words.
- **It's interesting**—it is challenging and worth discussing, not bland and easily accepted.

Distinguish claims from facts and opinions.

A claim is a conclusion drawn from logical thought and reliable evidence. A fact, in contrast, is a statement that can be checked for accuracy. An opinion is a personally held taste or attitude. A claim can be debated, but a fact or an opinion cannot.

Fact: *The Fellowship of the Ring* is the first book in J. R. R. Tolkien's trilogy *The Lord of the Rings*.

Opinion: I liked the movie almost as much as the book.

Claim: While the film version of *The Fellowship of the Ring* does not completely follow the novel's plot, the film does faithfully capture the spirit of Tolkien's novel.

Note: While the fact's accuracy can easily be checked, the opinion statement simply offers a personal feeling. Conversely, the claim states an idea that can be supported with reasoning and evidence.

Distinguish three types of claims.

Truth, value, and policy—these types of claims are made in an argument. The differences among them are important because each type has a distinct goal.

- **Claims of truth** state that something is or is not the case. As a writer, you want readers to accept your claim as trustworthy.

  The Arctic ice cap will begin to disappear as early as 2050.

  The cholesterol in eggs is not as dangerous as previously feared.

Comment: Avoid statements that are (1) obviously true or (2) impossible to prove. Also, truth claims must be argued carefully because accepting them (or not) can have serious consequences.

Sample Essay: "Ah, the Power of Women," pages 267–269.

■ **Claims of value** state that something does or does not have worth. As a writer, you want readers to accept your judgment.

> Volunteer reading tutors provide a valuable service.
>
> Many music videos fail to present positive images of women.

Comment: Claims of value must be supported by referring to a known standard or by establishing an agreed-upon standard. To avoid a bias, base your judgments on the known standard, not on your feelings.

Sample Essay: "Our Wealth: Where Is It Taking Us?" pages 289–291

■ **Claims of policy** state that something ought or ought not to be done. As a writer, you want readers to approve your course of action.

> Special taxes should be placed on gas-guzzling SUVs.
>
> The developer should not be allowed to fill in the pond where the endangered tiger salamander lives.

Comment: Policy claims focus on action. To arrive at them, you must often first establish certain truths and values; thus an argument over policy may include both truth and value claims.

Sample Essay: "Uncle Sam and Aunt Samantha," pages 312–314

Develop a supportable claim. ■ ■ ■

Video

An effective claim balances confidence with common sense. Follow these tips:

■ **Avoid all-or-nothing, extreme claims.** Propositions using words that are overly positive or negative—such as *all, best, never,* and *worst*—may be difficult to support. Statements that leave no room for exceptions are easy to attack.

> **Extreme:** All people charged even once for DUI should never be allowed to drive again.

■ **Make a truly meaningful claim.** Avoid claims that are obvious, trivial, or unsupportable. None is worth the energy needed to argue the point.

> **Obvious:** College athletes sometimes receive special treatment.
>
> **Trivial:** The College Rec Center is a good place to get fit.
>
> **Unsupportable:** Athletics are irrelevant to college life.

■ **Use qualifiers to temper your claims.** Qualifiers are words or phrases that make claims more reasonable. Notice the difference between these two claims:

> **Unqualified:** Star athletes take far too many academic shortcuts.
>
> **Qualified:** Some star athletes take improper academic shortcuts.

Note: The "qualified" claim is easier to defend because it narrows the focus and leaves room for exceptions. Use qualifier words like these:

almost	many	often	tends to
frequently	maybe	probably	typically
likely	might	some	usually

■ Supporting Your Claims

A claim stands or falls on its support. It's not the popular strength of your claim that matters, but rather the strength of your reasoning and evidence. To develop strong support, consider how to select and use evidence.

Gather evidence. ■▪■

Video

Several types of evidence can support claims. To make good choices, review each type, as well as its strengths and weaknesses.

■ **Observations and anecdotes** share what people (including you) have seen, heard, smelled, touched, tasted, and experienced. Such evidence offers an "eyewitness" perspective shaped by the observer's viewpoint, which can be powerful but may also prove narrow and subjective.

> Most of us have closets full of clothes: jeans, sweaters, khakis, T-shirts, and shoes for every occasion.

Video

■ **Statistics** offer concrete numbers about a topic. Numbers don't "speak for themselves," however. They need to be interpreted and compared properly—not slanted or taken out of context. They also need to be up-to-date, relevant, and accurate.

> Pennsylvania spends $30 million annually in deer-related costs.
>
> Wisconsin has an estimated annual loss of $37 million for crop damage alone.

■ **Tests and experiments** provide hard data developed through the scientific method, data that must nevertheless be carefully studied and properly interpreted.

> According to the two scientists, the rats with unlimited access to the functional running wheel ran each day and gradually increased the amount of running; in addition, they started to eat less.

■ **Graphics** provide information in visual form—from simple tables to more complex charts, maps, drawings, and photographs. When poorly done, however, graphics can distort the truth. See the bar graphs in the experiment report on pages 335–340 and the photographs in "Downloading Photographs . . ." on page 227.

■ **Analogies** compare two things, creating clarity by drawing parallels. However, every analogy breaks down if pushed too far.

> It is obvious today that America has defaulted on this promissory note insofar as her citizens of color are concerned. Instead of honoring this sacred obligation, America has given the Negro people a bad check; a check which has come back marked "insufficient funds." But we refuse to believe that the bank of justice is bankrupt.
>
> —Martin Luther King, Jr.

- **Expert testimony** offers insights from an authority on the topic. Such testimony always has limits: Experts don't know it all, and they work from distinct perspectives, which means that they can disagree.

> One specialist opposed to drilling is David Klein, a professor at the Institute of Arctic Biology at the University of Alaska–Fairbanks. Klein argues that if the oil industry opens up the ANWR for drilling, the number of caribou will likely decrease because the calving locations will change.

- **Illustrations, examples, and demonstrations** support general claims with specific instances, making such statements seem concrete and observable. Of course, an example may not be your best support if it isn't familiar.

> Think about how differently one can frame Rosa Parks' historic action. In prevailing myth, Parks—a holy innocent—acts almost on whim. . . . The real story is more empowering: It suggests that change is the product of deliberate, incremental action.

- **Analyses** examine parts of a topic through thought patterns—cause/effect, compare/contrast, classification, process, or definition. Such analysis helps make sense of a topic's complexity, but muddles the topic when poorly done.

> If colorism lives underground, its effects are very real. Darker-skinned African-American defendants are more than twice as likely to receive the death penalty as lighter-skinned African-American defendants for crimes of equivalent seriousness. . . .

- **Predictions** offer insights into possible outcomes or consequences by forecasting what might happen under certain conditions. Like weather forecasting, predicting can be tricky. To be plausible, a prediction must be rooted in a logical analysis of present facts.

> While agroterrorist diseases would have little direct effect on people's health, they would be devastating to the agricultural economy, in part because of the many different diseases that could be used in an attack.

Use evidence. ■ ▪ ■

Finding evidence is one thing; using it well is another. To marshal evidence in support of your claim, follow three guidelines:

1. **Go for quality and variety, not just quantity.** More evidence is not necessarily better. Instead, support your points with sound evidence in different forms. Quality evidence is . . .

   - *accurate:* correct and verifiable in each detail.
   - *complete:* filled with pertinent facts.
   - *concrete:* filled with specifics.
   - *relevant:* clearly related to the claim.
   - *current:* reliably up-to-date.
   - *authoritative:* backed by expertise, training, and knowledge.
   - *appealing:* able to influence readers.

2. **Use inductive and deductive patterns of logic.** Depending on your purpose, use inductive or deductive reasoning. (See page 20.)

Induction: Inductive reasoning works from the particular toward general conclusions. In a persuasive essay using induction, look at facts first, find a pattern in them, and then lead the reader to your conclusion.

> For example, in "Nuclear Is Not the Answer," Alyssa Woudstra first examines the benefits and liabilities of nuclear energy versus fossil fuels before asserting her claim that using the latter is a better choice. (See pages 270–272.)

Deduction: Deductive reasoning—the opposite of inductive reasoning—starts from accepted truths and applies them to a new situation so as to reach a conclusion about it. For deduction to be sound, be sure the starting principles or facts are true, the new situation is accurately described, and the application is logical.

> For example, Martin Luther King opened his 1963 "I Have a Dream" speech by noting that more than one hundred years earlier, the Emancipation Proclamation promised African Americans justice and freedom. He then described the continuing unjust treatment of African Americans, deducing that the promises in the Proclamation remained unfulfilled. (See pages 292–295.)

3. **Reason using valid warrants.** To make sense, claims and their supporting reasons must have a logical connection. That connection is called the *warrant*—the often unspoken thinking used to relate the reasoning to the claim. If warrants are good, arguments hold water; if warrants are faulty, then arguments break down. In other words, beware of faulty assumptions.

Check the short argument outlined below. Which of the warrants seem reasonable and strong, and which seem weak? Where does the argument fail?

> **Reasoning:** If current trends in water usage continue, the reservoir will be empty in two years.

> **Claim:** Therefore, Emeryville should immediately shut down its public swimming pools.

Unstated Warrants or Assumptions:

> It is not good for the reservoir to be empty.
> The swimming pools draw significant amounts of water from the reservoir.
> Emptying the pools would help raise the level of the reservoir.
> No other action would better prevent the reservoir from emptying.
> It is worse to have an empty reservoir than an empty swimming pool.

INSIGHT: Because an argument is no stronger than its warrants, you must make sure that your reasoning clearly and logically supports your claims.

Identifying Logical Fallacies

Fallacies are false arguments—that is, bits of fuzzy, dishonest, or incomplete thinking. They may crop up in your own thinking, in your opposition's thinking, or in such public "arguments" as ads, political appeals, and talk shows. Because fallacies may sway an unsuspecting audience, they are dangerously persuasive. By learning to recognize fallacies, however, you may identify them in opposing arguments and eliminate them from your own writing. In this section, logical fallacies are grouped according to how they falsify an argument.

Distorting the Issue

The following fallacies falsify an argument by twisting the logical framework.

■ **Bare Assertion** The most basic way to distort an issue is to deny that it exists. This fallacy claims, "That's just how it is."

> The private ownership of handguns is a constitutional right. (*Objection:* The claim shuts off discussion of the U.S. Constitution or the reasons for regulation.)

■ **Begging the Question** Also known as circular reasoning, this fallacy arises from assuming in the basis of your argument the very point you need to prove.

> We don't need a useless film series when every third student owns a DVD player or VCR. (*Objection:* There may be uses for a public film series that private video viewing can't provide. The word "useless" begs the question.)

■ **Oversimplification** This fallacy reduces complexity to simplicity. Beware of phrases like "It's a simple question of." Serious issues are rarely simple.

> Capital punishment is a simple question of protecting society.

■ **Either/Or Thinking** Also known as black-and-white thinking, this fallacy reduces all options to two extremes. Frequently, it derives from a clear bias.

> Either this community develops light-rail transportation or the community will not grow in the future. (*Objection:* The claim ignores the possibility that growth may occur through other means.)

■ **Complex Question** Sometimes by phrasing a question a certain way, a person ignores or covers up a more basic question.

> Why can't we bring down the prices that corrupt gas stations are charging? (*Objection:* This question ignores a more basic question—"Are gas stations really corrupt?")

■ **Straw Man** In this fallacy, the writer argues against a claim that is easily refuted. Typically, such a claim exaggerates or misrepresents the opponents' position.

> Those who oppose euthanasia must believe that the terminally ill deserve to suffer.

Sabotaging the Argument ■·■

These fallacies falsify the argument by twisting it. They destroy reason and replace it with something hollow or misleading.

■ **Red Herring** This strange term comes from the practice of dragging a stinky fish across a trail to throw tracking dogs off the scent. When a person puts forth a volatile idea that pulls readers away from the real issue, readers become distracted. Suppose the argument addresses drilling for oil in the Arctic National Wildlife Refuge (ANWR) of Alaska, and the writer begins with this statement:

> In 1989, the infamous oil spill of the *Exxon Valdez* led to massive animal deaths and enormous environmental degradation of the coastline. (*Objection:* Introducing this notorious oil spill distracts from the real issue—how oil drilling will affect the ANWR.)

■ **Misuse of Humor** Jokes, satire, and irony can lighten the mood and highlight a truth; when humor distracts or mocks, however, it undercuts the argument. What effect would the mocking tone of this statement have in an argument about tanning beds in health clubs?

> People who use tanning beds will just turn into wrinkled old prunes or leathery sun-dried tomatoes!

■ **Appeal to Pity** This fallacy engages in a misleading tug on the heartstrings. Instead of using a measured emotional appeal, an appeal to pity seeks to manipulate the audience into agreement.

> Affirmative action policies ruined this young man's life. Because of them, he was denied admission to Centerville College.

■ **Use of Threats** A simple but unethical way of sabotaging an argument is to threaten opponents. More often than not, a threat is merely implied: "If you don't accept my argument, you'll regret it."

> If we don't immediately start drilling for oil in the ANWR, you will soon face hour-long lines at gas stations from New York to California.

■ **Bandwagon Mentality** Someone implies that a claim cannot be true because a majority of people are opposed to it, or it must be true because a majority support it. (History shows that people in the minority have often had the better argument.) At its worst, such an appeal manipulates people's desire to belong or be accepted.

> It's obvious to intelligent people that cockroaches live only in the apartments of dirty people. (*Objection:* Based on popular opinion, the claim appeals to a kind of prejudice and ignores scientific evidence about cockroaches.)

■ **Appeal to Popular Sentiment** This fallacy consists of associating your position with something popularly loved: the American flag, baseball, apple pie. Appeals to popular sentiment sidestep thought to play on feelings.

> Anyone who has seen *Bambi* could never condone hunting deer.

Drawing Faulty Conclusions from the Evidence

This group of fallacies falsifies the argument by short-circuiting proper logic in favor of assumptions or faulty thinking.

■ **Appeal to Ignorance** This fallacy suggests that because no one has proven a particular claim, it must be false; or, because no one has disproven a claim, it must be true. Appeals to ignorance unfairly shift the burden of proof onto someone else.

> Flying saucers are real. No scientific explanation has ruled them out.

■ **Hasty or Broad Generalization** Such a claim is based on too little evidence or allows no exceptions. In jumping to a conclusion, the writer may use intensifiers such as *all, every,* or *never.*

> Today's voters spend too little time reading and too much time being taken in by 30-second sound bites. (*Objection:* Quite a few voters may, in fact, spend too little time reading about the issues, but it is unfair to suggest that this is true of everyone.)

■ **False Cause** This well-known fallacy confuses sequence with causation: If *A* comes before *B*, *A* must have caused *B*. However, *A* may be one of several causes, or *A* and *B* may be only loosely related, or the connection between *A* and *B* may be entirely coincidental.

> Since that new school opened, drug use among young people has skyrocketed. Better that the school had never been built.

■ **Slippery Slope** This fallacy argues that a single step will start an unstoppable chain of events. While such a slide may occur, the prediction lacks evidence.

> If we legalize marijuana, it's only a matter of time before hard drugs follow and America becomes a nation of junkies and addicts.

Misusing Evidence

These fallacies falsify the argument by abusing or distorting the evidence.

■ **Impressing with Numbers** In this case, the writer drowns readers in statistics and numbers that overwhelm them into agreement. In addition, the numbers haven't been properly interpreted.

> At 35 ppm, CO levels factory-wide are only 10 ppm above the OSHA recommendation, which is 25 ppm. Clearly, that 10 ppm is insignificant in the big picture, and the occasional readings in some areas of between 40 and 80 ppm are aberrations that can safely be ignored. (*Objection:* The 10 ppm may be significant, and higher readings may indicate real danger.)

■ **Half-Truths** A half-truth contains part of but not the whole truth. Because it leaves out "the rest of the story," it is both true and false simultaneously.

> The new welfare bill is good because it will get people off the public dole. (*Objection:* This may be true, but the bill may also cause undue suffering for some truly needy individuals.)

- **Unreliable Testimonial** An appeal to authority has force only if the authority is qualified in the proper field. If he or she is not, the testimony is irrelevant. Note that fame is not the same thing as authority.

    On her talk show, Alberta Magnus recently claimed that most pork sold in the United States is tainted. (*Objection:* Although Magnus may be an articulate talk show host, she is not an expert on food safety.)

- **Attack Against the Person** This fallacy directs attention to a person's character, lifestyle, or beliefs rather than to the issue.

    Would you accept the opinion of a candidate who experimented with drugs in college?

- **Hypothesis Contrary to Fact** This fallacy relies on "if only" thinking. It bases the claim on an assumption of what would have happened if something else had, or had not, happened. Being pure speculation, such a claim cannot be tested.

    If only multiculturalists hadn't pushed through affirmative action, the United States would be a united nation.

- **False Analogy** Sometimes a person will argue that X is good (or bad) because it is like Y. Such an analogy may be valid, but it weakens the argument if the grounds for the comparison are vague or unrelated.

    Don't bother voting in this election; it's a stinking quagmire. (*Objection:* Comparing the election to a "stinking quagmire" is unclear and exaggerated.)

Misusing Language ■■·■

Essentially, all logical fallacies misuse language. However, three fallacies falsify the argument, especially by the misleading use of words.

- **Obfuscation** This fallacy involves using fuzzy terms like *throughput* and *downlink* to muddy the issue. These words may make simple ideas sound more profound than they really are, or they may make false ideas sound true.

    Through the fully functional developmental process of a streamlined target-refractory system, the U.S. military will successfully reprioritize its data throughputs. (*Objection:* What does this sentence mean?)

- **Ambiguity** Ambiguous statements can be interpreted in two or more opposite ways. Although ambiguity can result from unintentional careless thinking, writers sometimes use ambiguity to obscure a position.

    Many women need to work to support their children through school, but they would be better off at home. (*Objection:* Does *they* refer to *children* or *women*? What does *better off* mean? These words and phrases can be interpreted in opposite ways.)

- **Slanted Language** By choosing words with strong positive or negative connotations, a writer can draw readers away from the true logic of the argument. Here is an example of three synonyms for the word *stubborn* that the philosopher Bertrand Russell once used to illustrate the bias in slanted language:

    I am firm. You are obstinate. He is pigheaded.

Video

Engaging the Opposition

Think of an argument as an intelligent, lively dialogue with readers. Anticipate their questions, concerns, objections, and counterarguments. Then follow these guidelines.

Make concessions.

By offering concessions—recognizing points scored by the other side—you acknowledge your argument's limits and the truth of other positions. Paradoxically, such concessions strengthen your overall argument by making it seem more credible. Concede your points graciously, using words such as the following:

Admittedly	Granted	I agree that	I cannot argue with
It is true that	You're right	I accept	No doubt
Of course	I concede that	Perhaps	Certainly it's the case

> While foot-and-mouth disease is not dangerous to humans, other animal diseases are.

Develop rebuttals.

Even when you concede a point, you can often answer that objection by rebutting it. A good rebuttal is a small, tactful argument aimed at a weak spot in the opposing argument. Try these strategies:

1. **Point out the counterargument's limits** by putting the opposing point in a larger context. Show that the counterargument leaves something important out of the picture.
2. **Tell the other side of the story.** Offer an opposing interpretation of the evidence, or counter with stronger, more reliable, more convincing evidence.
3. **Address logical fallacies in the counterargument.** Check for faulty reasoning or emotional manipulation. For example, if the counterargument presents a half-truth, offer information that presents "the rest of the story."

> It is true that Chernobyl occurred more than twenty years ago, so safety measures for nuclear reactors have been greatly improved. However, that single accident is still affecting millions of people who were exposed to the radiation.

Consolidate your claim.

After making concessions and rebutting objections, you may need to regroup. Restate your claim so carefully that the weight of your whole argument can rest on it.

> One of these is bovine spongiform encephalopathy, better known as mad-cow disease.

■ Using Appropriate Appeals

Video

For your argument to be persuasive, it must not only be logical, but also "feel right." It must treat readers as real people by appealing to their common sense, hopes, pride, and notion of right and wrong. How do you appeal to all these concerns? Do the following: (1) build credibility, (2) make logical appeals, and (3) focus on readers' needs.

Build credibility. ■▪▪

Video

A persuasive argument is credible—so trustworthy that readers can change their minds painlessly. To build credibility, observe these rules:

- **Be thoroughly honest.** Demonstrate integrity toward the topic—don't falsify data, spin evidence, or ignore facts. Document your sources and cite them wherever appropriate.
- **Make realistic claims, projections, and promises.** Avoid emotionally charged statements, pie-in-the-sky forecasts, and undeliverable deals.
- **Develop and maintain trust.** From your first word to your last, develop trust—in your attitude toward the topic, your treatment of readers, and your respect for opposing viewpoints.

Make logical appeals. ■▪▪

Arguments stand or fall on their logical strength, but your readers' acceptance of those arguments is often affected more by the emotional appeal of your ideas and evidence. To avoid overly emotional appeals, follow these guidelines:

- **Engage readers positively.** Appeal to their better natures—to their sense of honor, justice, social commitment, altruism, and enlightened self-interest. Avoid appeals geared toward ignorance, prejudice, selfishness, or fear.
- **Use a fitting tone.** Use a tone that is appropriate for the topic, purpose, situation, and audience.
- **Aim to motivate, not manipulate, readers.** While you do want them to accept your viewpoint, it's not a win-at-all-costs situation. Avoid bullying, guilt-tripping, and exaggerated tugs on heartstrings.
- **Don't trash-talk the opposition.** Show tact, respect, and understanding. Focus on issues, not personalities.
- **Use arguments and evidence that readers can understand and appreciate.** If readers find your thinking too complex, too simple, or too strange, you've lost them.

INSIGHT: Remember the adage: The best argument is so clear and convincing that it sounds like an explanation.

Focus on readers' needs.

Instead of playing on readers' emotions, connect your argument with readers' needs and values. Follow these guidelines:

- **Know your real readers.** Who are they—peers, professors, or fellow citizens? What are their allegiances, their worries, their dreams?

- **Picture readers as resistant.** Accept that your readers, including those inclined to agree with you, need convincing. Think of them as alert, cautious, and demanding—but also interested.

- **Use appeals that match needs and values.** Your argument may support or challenge readers' needs and values. To understand those needs, study the table below, which is based loosely on the thinking of psychologist Abraham Maslow. Maslow's hierarchy ranks people's needs on a scale from the most basic to the most complex. The table begins at the bottom with *having necessities* (a basic need) and ends at the top with *helping others* (a more complex need). For example, if you're writing to argue for more affordable housing for the elderly, you'd argue differently to legislators (whose focus is on *helping others*) than to the elderly who need the housing (whose focus is on *having necessities*). Follow these guidelines:

  - Use appeals that match the foremost needs and values of your readers.
  - If appropriate, constructively challenge those needs and values.
  - Whenever possible, phrase your appeals in positive terms.
  - After analyzing your readers' needs, choose a persuasive theme for your argument—a positive benefit, advantage, or outcome that readers can expect if they accept your claim. Use this theme to help readers to care about your claims.

Reader needs . . .	Use persuasive appeals to . . .
To make the world better by helping others	values and social obligations
To achieve by being good at something getting recognition	self-fulfillment, status appreciation
To belong by being part of a group	group identity, acceptance
To survive by avoiding threats having necessities	safety, security physical needs

Video

Critical-Thinking and Writing Activities

Interactive

As directed by your instructor, complete the following critical-thinking and writing activities by yourself or with classmates.

1. Select an essay from chapters 17–19, "Taking a Position," "Persuading Readers to Act," or "Proposing a Solution." Read the essay carefully. Then describe and evaluate the essay's argumentative strategies by answering the questions below:

   ■ What is the main claim the writer makes? Is it a claim of truth, value, or policy?

   ■ Is the claim arguable—that is, is it supportable, appropriately qualified, and effectively phrased?

   ■ What arguments does the writer develop in support of the claim? Are these arguments logical?

   ■ What types of evidence does the writer provide to support his or her discussion?

   ■ Is the evidence valid, sufficient, and accurate?

   ■ Does the writer effectively address questions, alternatives, objections, and counterarguments?

2. Review the essay that you read for the first activity, and then answer the following questions:

   ■ Describe the writer's tone. Does it effectively engage readers?

   ■ Does the argument seem credible and authoritative? Explain.

   ■ Identify ways that the writer connects with readers' needs and values. How does he or she develop a persuasive theme that appeals to those needs and stresses reader benefits?

3. Find a quality article in a respected journal in your major. Read the article and then answer these questions: What forms of reasoning, appeals, and evidence does the author use? What forms does he or she avoid? Is the reasoning convincing? Why?

Learning-Outcomes Checklist

Use this checklist to assess your grasp of argumentative and persuasive strategies.

_____ I understand how to build an argument, starting with situation analysis and developing a line of reasoning.

_____ I can distinguish and develop three types of claims.

_____ I can use evidence to qualify and support claims.

_____ I understand the strengths and weaknesses of nine types of evidence.

_____ I can identify and correct logical fallacies.

_____ I can make needed concessions, develop rebuttals, and use appropriate appeals.

17 Taking a Position

Sometimes you just have to take a stand. An issue comes up that upsets you or challenges your thinking, and in response, you say, "Okay, this is what I believe, and this is why I believe it."

Learning to read and write position papers enables you to do this. The reading skills help you analyze others' positions, recognize their strengths, and identify their weaknesses. The writing skills help you probe a topic, refine your own perspective on the issues, educate others about the topic, and convince them that your position has value.

This chapter will help you refine both skills. In addition, because both skills are used across the college curriculum and at work, learning this chapter's writing skills and strategies will help you succeed in the classroom today and in the workplace throughout your career.

Learning Outcomes

Audio

Video

▶ Read and assess position papers for clarity and logic.

▶ Identify logical fallacies: oversimplification, either/ or thinking, straw-man and red-herring claims, appeals to pity, personal attacks.

▶ Make concessions and rebut arguments.

▶ Develop claims with reliable evidence.

▶ Write a logical position paper in a measured, rational voice.

Visually Speaking ▶ Study the photograph above. What does it suggest about how or why people take a position on an issue? What written argument might articulate the position pictured in the photograph?

■ Reading Position Writing

How should you read a position paper? The instructions below will guide you.

Consider the rhetorical situation. ■■■

Think first about how the writer uses persuasion to achieve a specific purpose, affect a particular audience, and address a given topic.

- **Purpose:** In most cases, writers produce position papers in order to educate and to persuade: they want (1) to inform you about the nature and relevance of a topic and (2) to persuade you that their position on the topic is the best, most reasonable option.
- **Audience:** A writer may address a variety of readers: people opposed to the writer's position, people uncertain of what position to take, people unaware that an issue exists, or even people who agree with the writer's position but are looking for sensible reasons. Good writers shape the content, organization, and tone of position essays to effectively address such intended readers.
- **Topic:** The topics addressed in meaningful position papers are debatable issues about which informed people can reasonably disagree. Therefore, as a reader, you will learn more about a paper's topic by focusing not only on the writer's position, but also on the reasoning that she or he uses to develop that position, including her or his attention to alternative positions.

Consider qualities of strong arguments. ■■■

When reading a position paper, look for the following:

- **Informed Writing:** The writer has researched the topic thoroughly and understands it fully, including positions other than his or her own.
- **Logical Writing:** The writer presents the topic objectively, describes alternative positions fairly, and takes the position supported by the best evidence and strongest logic. The writing avoids logical fallacies such as oversimplification, either/or thinking, straw-man claims, red-herring assertions, appeals to pity, or attacks against opponents. (For information on these and other fallacies, see pages 257–260.)
- **Engaging Writing:** Rather than quarreling or pontificating, the writer converses with readers making reasonable concessions, rebutting opposing arguments, and consolidating or refocusing claims. (For details on these strategies, see page 261.)

Reader's Checklist

_____ What is the topic, and is it debatable, stated fairly, and addressed fully?

_____ What are the writer's claims, and are they supported by reliable evidence?

_____ Is the overall argument clear, unified, and free of logical fallacies?

_____ Is the tone measured, reasonable, and free of manipulative language?

Taking a Position ■ ■ ■

Student writer Aleah Stenberg wrote the following essay to explain and promote her interpretation of (or position on) the characters and themes in Louise Erdrich's *Love Medicine*.

Outline

Introduction: Erdrich's *Love Medicine* presents women as the stronger, controlling gender in Chippewa culture.

1. The novel shows that Chippewa culture respects women.
2. Marie and Lulu exemplify this power/control.
3. They learn of power from elders/tribal customs.
4. Sexual power garners social/political clout.
5. Culture, power, and prominence generate conflict.

Conclusion: Erdrich's setting warrants her characterization and ideas.

Title introduces theme.

Introduction: Erdrich's setting warrants her depicting women as the dominant gender.

1 Characters refer to and support women's dominant role.

Ah, the Power of Women

While most American literature commonly portrays a negative view of women, Louise Erdrich's Native American novel, *Love Medicine,* does just the opposite. Her female characters are the catalyst around which the action of the book revolves. The two strongest women, Lulu Lamartine and Marie Kashpaw, create the dissonant nucleoli that give rise to the conflict in the novel and also trump the men in most forms of power. The matriarchal Native American culture depicted by Erdrich provides a setting in which these women can roar. 1

The culture of the Chippewa highly regards mothers in particular and women in general. As a child, Lulu learns this lesson by noting the respect allotted her mother. Lulu acknowledges, "I never grew from the curve of my mother's arms" (Erdrich 68), and finds in nature manifestations of her connection to her mother's person and power. This mother/daughter bond is impenetrable for men. While Lulu mourns her mother's passing, she never mentions a father. The closest father figure she has is Uncle Nanapush, but even when conversing about his death ceremony, she does so by referencing her feelings for her mother: "I couldn't bear to think of losing him the way I had lost my mother" (71). The oldest clan matron, Rushes Bear, also alludes to the matriarchal culture of the tribe as she laments about Nector Kashpaw: "My son is marrying one of that lowlife family that insulted me. Those Lazarres breed fast and die young. I hope I'll outlive her tough bread and Nector Kashpaw will once again respect his mother" (72). Nector's actions don't insult his father or his family in a European sense; instead, he disgraces his mother. By recognizing mothers as the beating heart of the family, the Chippewa respect them accordingly. 2

In light of the reverence for women in Chippewa society, Erdrich's strongest, most prominent characters are Marie Kashpaw and Lulu Lamartine. These two are 3

2 Marie and Lulu, like less prominent female characters, control males.

3 The women learn about their power by listening to elders and observing Chippewa culture.

4 Through their sexual power, they garner social and political influence.

5 Culture, power, and prominence generate conflict.

in charge of the house and rule over their husbands. Other female characters are also strong, although they play lesser roles. Rushes Bear and Sister Leopolda are strongly influential but in different times or spheres; for example, Sister Leopolda rules with a cruel hand at the Sacred Heart Convent. Erdrich's male characters have less prominent roles, and their main purpose—many times—is to be subordinated by domineering females.

The women in *Love Medicine* have supremacy over the men in many aspects.   4 Sexual power over males guides much of the story in both Lulu and Marie's lives. Lulu, particularly, has many affairs; she knows what she wants, gets it, and then does away with what she doesn't like. Each of her boys and daughter is symbolic of her conquering another man. At a young age, Lulu learned about sexual power while listening to older women. Lulu remembers, "Rushes Bear always said that a man has to enter and enter, repeatedly, as if in punishment for having ever left the woman's body. She said that the woman is complete. Men must come through us to live" (82). The idea that men are incomplete because they left the woman's body gives females the edge in sexual relations. The man needs her; the woman is not dependant on the man; on the contrary, she has command of the relationship. This same idea also points to the reverence of women in Chippewa culture. The mother is the creator of new life and the sustainer of the men she beds (whether her husband or not), and as such, she is given great honor.

The sexual power of women in *Love Medicine* also gives them political and social   5 clout. Lulu wields her political power when she denounces the proposed tomahawk factory which would require moving her house: "Before I'd move the Lamartine household I'd hit the tribe with a fistful of paternity suits that would make their heads spin. Some of them had forgotten until then that I'd even had their son. Still others must have wondered. I could see the back neck hair on the wives all over that room prickle" (285). Lulu's sexual power gives her a platform to preside over political decisions. Because of women's power sexually, they also are given social influence. One of the examples in Lulu's life is deciding which Lamartine to marry. She tells Beverly, "I am a woman of detachable parts. You should know by now. You simply weren't playing in your league with strip poker" (115). And she adds, "It was after I won your shorts with my pair of deuces and Henry's with my eights, and you were naked except for your hat, that I decided which one to marry" (115). So many men are sexually attracted to Lulu that she can pick and choose whom she wants. In the culture the novel describes, women are venerated for their sexuality. They can then use that given power to gain influence in tribal society and politics.

Matriarchal Chippewa culture; the sexual, political, and social power given to   6 women; and Erdrich's use of strong female characters culminate in Lulu and Marie forming the central conflict of the piece. Both these women are strong and at odds, the nuclei of opposing forces, two different pressure systems raging over North Dakota. Nector Kashpaw is a main object of competition for these two. Like the arms race of the Cold War, Marie and Lulu also engage in a race to have the most children. Lulu has many children, all by different fathers. Marie, after two of her and Nector's offspring die in childhood, rapidly adopts children and takes in young family members. These women are constantly vying for supremacy over each other. Even when they become friends, Lyman Lamartine notes, "Their statures had to be completely equal. . . . They each needed territory to control. . . . Their friendship, if that's what you'd call it, was hard to figure. Set free by Nector's death, they couldn't get enough of their own differences. They argued unceasingly about the past, and didn't agree on the present either" (311). In addition to these battles within their friendship, all other conflicts in *Love Medicine* stem from Lulu and Marie's on-going war or are in some way linked to it.

Conclusion: Erdrich's setting warrants her depicting women as the stronger, controlling gender.

Erdrich gives women center stage in *Love Medicine*. By choosing the matriarchal   *7* Chippewa tribe as her setting, she is able to create powerful female characters with dissonant relationships. Writing against the typical, American, male-dominated social order, Erdrich constructs a world in which women are in charge. Even though the female characters in the book are mothers who do laundry, cook meals, and finish long "to-do" lists, they are not held to this position. They have the power to rise above and take jurisdiction. Full of strong females, *Love Medicine* asserts a positive feminist message: women—hear them roar.

Note: The Works Cited page is not shown. For sample pages, see MLA (pages 526–527) and APA (page 557).

Reading for Better Writing

Working by yourself or with a group, do the following:

1. Stenberg's essay is a literature review in which she introduces a novel (her topic) and describes and analyzes its setting, characters, and themes. Describe how she uses the title and opening paragraphs to introduce this topic.

2. Stenberg's paper is also a persuasive essay in which she explains and advocates her interpretation of—or position on—one issue in the novel. Explain how the writer uses the title and opening sentences to introduce and focus her argument.

3. In your own words, state her core argument or claim—her position on the novel.

4. Review paragraphs 2-6, identify the supporting claim developed in each paragraph, and explain how Stenberg uses these points to support and clarify her main claim.

5. Describe how the writer uses her closing paragraph to refine and clarify her position. Does the paragraph accomplish these goals? Explain.

Taking a Position ■■■

Student writer Alyssa Woudstra wrote the following essay to take a position on an environmental issue—energy production.

The title partly declares the position.	**Nuclear Is Not the Answer**

In recent years, it has become popular to be "green" in all areas of life. Celebrities and corporations constantly advertise natural cleaning products, fuel-efficient cars, and energy-efficient light bulbs. Governments offer home-improvement grants to people who renovate their homes to include low-flush toilets, weather-proof windows, and additional insulation. Due to climate change and pollution, concern for the environment is rising. One major issue centers on which type of energy production is best for the environment. Nuclear power and fossil fuels are two major methods for energy production, and nuclear power could be seen as the "greener" option. However, the risks of nuclear power far outweigh its benefits, making fossil fuels the safer and more environmentally responsible option.

Alyssa starts with common ground and narrows to her position on energy production.

As a significant method of energy production, nuclear power does offer distinct advantages. The Nuclear Energy Institute's statistics show that nuclear energy accounted for fourteen percent of the world's electricity production in 2008, and that as of September 2009, thirty countries were using nuclear power ("Around the World"). This popularity speaks to nuclear power's advantages over fossil fuels. First, nuclear power plants do not release the harmful emissions that coal-burning plants do, so nuclear power does not contribute greatly to global warming (Evans 115). Second, a single nuclear power plant can produce a large amount of energy, making nuclear an efficient source ("Pros and Cons"). In fact, according to Robert Evans, "The amount of thermal energy released from just one kilogram of U235 undergoing fission is equivalent to that obtained by burning some 2.5 million kilograms, or 2500 tonnes, of coal" (116).

She examines the positives of what she actually opposes.

Nevertheless, these advantages of nuclear power are outweighed by its disadvantages. Nuclear power plants produce radioactive waste, which is an enormous health and safety concern. The waste cannot simply be disposed of but must be carefully stored for hundreds of generations. The isotopes used in nuclear reactions have half-lives of thousands of years. For example, plutonium-239 has a half-life of around 24,000 years (American Assembly 24). This radioactive waste must be stored safely to prevent radiation poisoning, but it would be nearly impossible to do so for that long.

She turns to the disadvantages of nuclear energy: its risks and dangers.

A further danger of nuclear power is that while every safety precaution might be in place, it is possible for terrible accidents to happen. The most famous nuclear accident took place on April 26, 1986, when reactor number four at the Chernobyl Nuclear Power Plant in the Ukraine, which was then part of the Soviet Union, exploded after a power excursion. That explosion then caused the rest of

The writer reminds readers of a historical illustration.

the plant to explode (Hawks et. al. 98-102). This accident released one hundred times more radiation than the bombing of Hiroshima and Nagasaki combined ("No More Chernobyls"). Chernobyl's radiation spread all over Europe, affecting people as far away as Romania and Bulgaria, exposing more than 600,000 to the effects of radiation poisoning (Medvedev 194-216). More than twenty years after Chernobyl, people are still dying from cancer that was likely caused by the disaster.

It is true that Chernobyl occurred more than twenty years ago, so safety 5 measures for nuclear reactors have since been greatly improved. However, that single accident is still affecting millions of people who were exposed to the radiation. Moreover, the accident had a devastating impact on the environment: even now, vegetation in the area around Chernobyl is practically non-existent. If more nuclear power plants are built, the risk of similar accidents will rise.

Beyond accidents, however, is the possibility of deliberate sabotage in 6 the form of terrorism ("Pros and Cons"). If terrorists wanted to cause mass devastation, they could attack a nuclear power plant or become employees that purposely cause errors to create an explosion. On September 11, 2001, millions of people were affected at once. If a power plant were attacked, it would also affect millions, since it would cause the loss of not only many jobs but also many lives. Moreover, the risk of terrorism also surrounds the nuclear waste left behind after the reactions. Easier to obtain than pure uranium, such waste could be used to build "dirty bombs" (Evans 133).

Beyond the risks and dangers of nuclear power, still another argument 7 against it is that it is nonrenewable. Fossil fuels are also nonrenewable, but nuclear power is not an alternative in this way. In their reactors, nuclear power plants use uranium, a rare element. It is estimated that the Earth's supply of Uranium will last only thirty to sixty years, depending on how much is actually used in reactors ("Pros and Cons").

But is energy from fossil fuels really better than nuclear power? The burning 8 of fossil fuels (including coal, oil, and natural gas) is the most common method of energy production. Like nuclear, fossil fuels are nonrenewable. However, burning fossil fuels, for the time being is a better option than using nuclear energy. It is true that using fossil fuels has a negative effect on the environment. In order to obtain fossil fuels, much damage is caused to the environment by drilling for oil or mining for coal. Also, burning fossil fuels produces gases that can aggravate respiratory conditions like asthma and emits greenhouse gases that damage the atmosphere. Moreover, particles emitted from smokestacks collect in clouds, causing acid rain (Sweet 25). With oil, spills can contaminate groundwater and surface water, creating risks to animals, plants, and humans.

Despite the fact that using fossil fuels involves many risks, it has some 9 advantages over nuclear energy. Significantly, fossil fuels are much less expensive than uranium. Although it is still expensive to access fossil fuels, it is drastically

Alyssa concedes and rebuts a concern.

With a question, she turns to her own position, acknowledging its problems.

cheaper than the cost of nuclear energy. In addition, if large deposits of coal or oil are found, it will not be necessary to excavate in as many places to retrieve them. Although a larger area would be disturbed, fewer sites would be affected. Also, while fossil fuels are nonrenewable, they may be used wisely, conserving them until a better energy source can be established (Heron).

However, perhaps the biggest advantage of fossil fuel energy over nuclear   *10* energy lies in the possibility of progress to make current methods more environmentally friendly. At this time, burning coal for power uses only one-third of its potential energy (Heron). If scientists study more efficient uses of the coal, this waste, as well as many health and environmental concerns, could be prevented. For example, burning coal can be made cleaner through electrostatic precipitators. Also known as "smokestack scrubbers," these filters can be used in smokestacks to prevent soot particles from getting into the air. As the soot-filled air passes through the smokestack, it goes through a set of wires that negatively charge the soot particles. As the air continues through the pipe, it passes through positively charged metal plates. The negatively charged soot particles, which are made up mostly of unburned carbon, "stick" to the positively charged plates, and the particle-free air continues out the smokestack. The stuck particles are then either manually scraped or automatically shaken off by the machine itself ("Static Electricity"). If more factories used electrostatic precipitators, a large amount of air pollution would be prevented.

Although it is not ideal, burning fossil fuels is still a better option than   *11* nuclear power until renewable energy sources such as wind, solar, and geothermal power become more available. Clearly, society must continue to work toward greater conservation and use of renewable energy. As stewards of the Earth, all humans should be concerned about the environment. If people continue to use nuclear power, the risks related to accidents, sabotage, and radioactive waste will not only be their responsibility but will also impact their descendants for many generations.

Note: The Works Cited page is not shown. For examples, see MLA (pages 526–527) and APA (page 557).

Reading for Better Writing

Working by yourself or with a group, answer the following:

1. Alyssa begins her essay by examining extensively an opposing position—support for nuclear energy. How effective is this strategy?

2. Review how Alyssa supports her position on energy from fossil fuels. How complete and compelling is this support?

3. Alyssa wrote her position paper prior to the BP oil spill in the Gulf of Mexico. How might acknowledging this environmental disaster change her essay?

Contrary Positions ▪▪▪

Sometimes, a writer takes a position in response to another writer, as shown in the following essays by Gary Steiner and Natalie Angier. Steiner, a professor of philosophy at Bucknell University and author of *Animals and the Moral Community,* advocates a pure vegan lifestyle in "Animal, Vegetable, Miserable" below. Angier's essay (pages 276–278), "Sorry, Vegans: Brussel Sprouts Like to Live, Too," responds in part to Steiner. Both pieces were published in 2009 in *The New York Times.*

The writer introduces the topic.	## Animal, Vegetable, Miserable

LATELY more people have begun to express an interest in where the meat they *1* eat comes from and how it was raised. Were the animals humanely treated? Did they have a good quality of life before the death that turned them into someone's dinner?

Some of these questions, which reach a fever pitch in the days leading up to Thanksgiving, pertain to the ways in which animals are treated. (Did your turkey get to live outdoors?) Others focus on the question of how eating the animals in question will affect the consumer's health and well-being. (Was it given hormones and antibiotics?)

He states the core issue and identifies his own position.

None of these questions, however, make any consideration of whether it is wrong *2* to kill animals for human consumption. And even when people ask this question, they almost always find a variety of resourceful answers that purport to justify the killing and consumption of animals in the name of human welfare. Strict ethical vegans, of which I am one, are customarily excoriated for equating our society's treatment of animals with mass murder. Can anyone seriously consider animal suffering even remotely comparable to human suffering? Those who answer with a resounding no typically argue in one of two ways.

He summarizes opposing positions and offers an example.

Some suggest that human beings but not animals are made in God's image and *3* hence stand in much closer proximity to the divine than any non-human animal; according to this line of thought, animals were made expressly for the sake of humans and may be used without scruple to satisfy their needs and desires. There is ample support in the Bible and in the writings of Christian thinkers like Augustine and Thomas Aquinas for this pointedly anthropocentric way of devaluing animals.

He offers a second example.

Others argue that the human capacity for abstract thought makes us capable of *4* suffering that both qualitatively and quantitatively exceeds the suffering of any non-human animal. Philosophers like Jeremy Bentham, who is famous for having based moral status not on linguistic or rational capacities but rather on the capacity to suffer, argue that because animals are incapable of abstract thought, they are imprisoned in an eternal present, have no sense of the extended future and hence cannot be said to have an interest in continued existence.

The most penetrating and iconoclastic response to this sort of reasoning came *5* from the writer Isaac Bashevis Singer in his story "The Letter Writer," in which he called the slaughter of animals the "eternal Treblinka."

He uses an anecdote to present a counter-argument.

The story depicts an encounter between a man and a mouse. The man, Herman 6
Gombiner, contemplates his place in the cosmic scheme of things and concludes that
there is an essential connection between his own existence as "a child of God" and the
"holy creature" scuffling about on the floor in front of him.

Steiner states the story's theme and explains its relevance.

Surely, he reflects, the mouse has some capacity for thought; Gombiner even thinks 7
that the mouse has the capacity to share love and gratitude with him. Not merely a
means for the satisfaction of human desires, nor a mere nuisance to be exterminated,
this tiny creature possesses the same dignity that any conscious being possesses. In the
face of that inherent dignity, Gombiner concludes, the human practice of delivering
animals to the table in the form of food is abhorrent and inexcusable.

He castigates "free-range" arguments.

Many of the people who denounce the ways in which we treat animals in the 8
course of raising them for human consumption never stop to think about this
profound contradiction. Instead, they make impassioned calls for more "humanely"
raised meat. Many people soothe their consciences by purchasing only free-range
fowl and eggs, blissfully ignorant that "free range" has very little if any practical
significance. Chickens may be labeled free-range even if they've never been outside
or seen a speck of daylight in their entire lives. And that Thanksgiving turkey? Even
if it is raised "free range," it still lives a life of pain and confinement that ends with
the butcher's knife.

He identifies his opponents' "real" reason for inaction as "not caring."

How can intelligent people who purport to be deeply concerned with animal 9
welfare and respectful of life turn a blind eye to such practices? And how can people
continue to eat meat when they become aware that nearly 53 billion land animals
are slaughtered every year for human consumption? The simple answer is that most
people just don't care about the lives or fortunes of animals. If they did care, they
would learn as much as possible about the ways in which our society systematically
abuses animals, and they would make what is at once a very simple and a very difficult
choice: to forswear the consumption of animal products of all kinds.

He offers one acceptable solution.

The easy part of this consists in seeing clearly what ethics requires and then just 10
plain doing it. The difficult part: You just haven't lived until you've tried to function
as a strict vegan in a meat-crazed society. What were once the most straightforward
activities become a constant ordeal. You might think that it's as simple as just removing
meat, eggs and dairy products from your diet, but it goes a lot deeper than that.

He defines and advocates a pure vegan lifestyle.

To be a really strict vegan is to strive to avoid all animal products, and this 11
includes materials like leather, silk and wool, as well as a panoply of cosmetics and
medications. The more you dig, the more you learn about products you would never
stop to think might contain or involve animal products in their production—like
wine and beer (isinglass, a kind of gelatin derived from fish bladders, is often used
to "fine," or purify, these beverages), refined sugar (bone char is sometimes used to
bleach it) or Band-Aids (animal products in the adhesive). Just last week I was told
that those little comfort strips on most razor blades contain animal fat.

To go down this road is to stare headlong into an abyss that, to paraphrase 12
Nietzsche, will ultimately stare back at you.

The challenges faced by a vegan don't end with the nuts and bolts of material 13
existence. You face quite a few social difficulties as well, perhaps the chief one being
how one should feel about spending time with people who are not vegans.

Is it O.K. to eat dinner with people who are eating meat? What do you say when 14
a dining companion says, "I'm really a vegetarian—I don't eat red meat at home."
(I've heard it lots of times, always without any prompting from me.) What do you do
when someone starts to grill you (so to speak) about your vegan ethics during dinner?
(Wise vegans always defer until food isn't around.) Or when someone starts to lodge
accusations to the effect that you consider yourself morally superior to others, or
that it is ridiculous to worry so much about animals when there is so much human
suffering in the world? (Smile politely and ask them to pass the seitan.)

Let me be candid: By and large, meat-eaters are a self-righteous bunch. The 15
number of vegans I know personally is . . . five. And I have been a vegan for almost 15
years, having been a vegetarian for almost 15 before that.

Five. I have lost more friends than this over arguments about animal ethics. 16
One lapidary conclusion to be drawn here is that people take deadly seriously the
prerogative to use animals as sources of satisfaction. Not only for food, but as beasts
of burden, as raw materials and as sources of captive entertainment—which is the way
animals are used in zoos, circuses and the like.

These uses of animals are so institutionalized, so normalized in our society that 17
it is difficult to find the critical distance needed to see them as the horrors that they
are: so many forms of subjection, servitude and—in the case of killing animals for
human consumption and other purposes—outright murder.

People who are ethical vegans believe that differences in intelligence between 18
human and non-human animals have no moral significance whatsoever. The fact that
my cat can't appreciate Schubert's late symphonies and can't perform syllogistic logic
does not mean that I am entitled to use him as an organic toy, as if I were somehow
not only morally superior to him but virtually entitled to treat him as a commodity
with minuscule market value.

We have been trained by a history of thinking of which we are scarcely aware to 19
view non-human animals as resources we are entitled to employ in whatever ways we
see fit in order to satisfy our needs and desires. Yes, there are animal welfare laws. But
these laws have been formulated by, and are enforced by, people who proceed from
the proposition that animals are fundamentally inferior to human beings. At best,
these laws make living conditions for animals marginally better than they would be
otherwise—right up to the point when we send them to the slaughterhouse.

Think about that when you're picking out your free-range turkey, which has 20
absolutely nothing to be thankful for on Thanksgiving. All it ever had was a short and
miserable life, thanks to us intelligent, compassionate humans.

> Steiner acknowledges the challenges of his position.

> He concludes by stating that the core problem is humans' belief that they are fundamentally superior to animals.

Questions on this and the following essay are on page 278.

Sorry, Vegans: Brussels Sprouts Like to Live, Too

The title introduces the topic and sets a playful tone.

I stopped eating pork about eight years ago, after a scientist happened to 1 mention that the animal whose teeth most closely resemble our own is the pig. Unable to shake the image of a perky little pig flashing me a brilliant George Clooney smile, I decided it was easier to forgo the Christmas ham. A couple of years later, I gave up on all mammalian meat, period. I still eat fish and poultry, however, and pour eggnog in my coffee. My dietary decisions are arbitrary and inconsistent, and when friends ask why I'm willing to try the duck but not the lamb, I don't have a good answer. Food choices are often like that: difficult to articulate yet strongly held. And lately, debates over food choices have flared with particular vehemence.

Angier describes her position on meat eating as personal and arbitrary vs. strict and ideological.

In his new book, *Eating Animals,* the novelist Jonathan Safran Foer describes 2 his gradual transformation from omnivorous, oblivious slacker who "waffled among any number of diets" to "committed vegetarian." Last month, Gary Steiner, a philosopher at Bucknell University, argued on the Op-Ed page of *The New York Times* that people should strive to be "strict ethical vegans" like himself, avoiding all products derived from animals, including wool and silk. Killing animals for human food and finery is nothing less than "outright murder," he said, Isaac Bashevis Singer's "eternal Treblinka."

She describes Steiner's position.

But before we cede the entire moral penthouse to "committed vegetarians" 3 and "strong ethical vegans," we might consider that plants no more aspire to being stir-fried in a wok than a hog aspires to being peppercorn-studded in my Christmas clay pot. This is not meant as a trite argument or a chuckled aside. Plants are lively and seek to keep it that way. The more that scientists learn about the complexity of plants—their keen sensitivity to the environment, the speed with which they react to changes in the environment, and the extraordinary number of tricks that plants will rally to fight off attackers and solicit help from afar—the more impressed researchers become, and the less easily we can dismiss plants as so much fiberfill backdrop, passive sunlight collectors on which deer, antelope and vegans can conveniently graze. It's time for a green revolution, a reseeding of our stubborn animal minds.

She suggests his logic (approves eating plants but disapproves eating meat) is logically inconsistent.

When plant biologists speak of their subjects, they use active verbs and vivid 4 images. Plants "forage" for resources like light and soil nutrients and "anticipate" rough spots and opportunities. By analyzing the ratio of red light and far red light falling on their leaves, for example, they can sense the presence of other chlorophyllated competitors nearby and try to grow the other way. Their roots ride the underground "rhizosphere" and engage in cross-cultural and microbial trade.

Angier explains animal-plant parallels.

"Plants are not static or silly," said Monika Hilker of the Institute of Biology 5 at the Free University of Berlin. "They respond to tactile cues, they recognize different wavelengths of light, they listen to chemical signals, they can even talk" through chemical signals. Touch, sight, hearing, speech. "These are sensory modalities and abilities we normally think of as only being in animals," Dr. Hilker said.

Plants can't run away from a threat but they can stand their ground. "They are very good at avoiding getting eaten," said Linda Walling of the University of California, Riverside. "It's an unusual situation where insects can overcome those defenses." At the smallest nip to its leaves, specialized cells on the plant's surface release chemicals to irritate the predator or sticky goo to entrap it. Genes in the plant's DNA are activated to wage systemwide chemical warfare, the plant's version of an immune response. We need terpenes, alkaloids, phenolics—let's move.

"I'm amazed at how fast some of these things happen," said Consuelo M. De Moraes of Pennsylvania State University. Dr. De Moraes and her colleagues did labeling experiments to clock a plant's systemic response time and found that, in less than 20 minutes from the moment the caterpillar had begun feeding on its leaves, the plant had plucked carbon from the air and forged defensive compounds from scratch.

Just because we humans can't hear them doesn't mean plants don't howl. Some of the compounds that plants generate in response to insect mastication— their feedback, you might say—are volatile chemicals that serve as cries for help. Such airborne alarm calls have been shown to attract both large predatory insects like dragon flies, which delight in caterpillar meat, and tiny parasitic insects, which can infect a caterpillar and destroy it from within.

Enemies of the plant's enemies are not the only ones to tune into the emergency broadcast. "Some of these cues, some of these volatiles that are released when a focal plant is damaged," said Richard Karban of the University of California, Davis, "cause other plants of the same species, or even of another species, to likewise become more resistant to herbivores."

Yes, it's best to nip trouble in the bud.

Dr. Hilker and her colleagues, as well as other research teams, have found that certain plants can sense when insect eggs have been deposited on their leaves and will act immediately to rid themselves of the incubating menace. They may sprout carpets of tumorlike neoplasms to knock the eggs off, or secrete ovicides to kill them, or sound the S O S. Reporting in The Proceedings of the National Academy of Sciences, Dr. Hilker and her coworkers determined that when a female cabbage butterfly lays her eggs on a brussels sprout plant and attaches her treasures to the leaves with tiny dabs of glue, the vigilant vegetable detects the presence of a simple additive in the glue, benzyl cyanide. Cued by the additive, the plant swiftly alters the chemistry of its leaf surface to beckon female parasitic wasps. Spying the anchored bounty, the female wasps in turn inject their eggs inside, the gestating wasps feed on the gestating butterflies, and the plant's problem is solved.

6

7

8

9

10

She supports her assertions by quoting several experts.

She compares plants and humans.

Angier quotes an expert and playfully supports his opinion.

She describes how plants communicate with insects.

She playfully labels and describes the process.

Here's the lurid Edgar Allan Poetry of it: that benzyl cyanide tip-off had been donated to the female butterfly by the male during mating. "It's an anti-aphrodisiac pheromone, so that the female wouldn't mate anymore," Dr. Hilker said. "The male is trying to ensure his paternity, but he ends up endangering his own offspring." 11

Plants eavesdrop on one another benignly and malignly. As they described in *Science* and other journals, Dr. De Moraes and her colleagues have discovered that seedlings of the dodder plant, a parasitic weed related to morning glory, can detect volatile chemicals released by potential host plants like the tomato. The young dodder then grows inexorably toward the host, until it can encircle the victim's stem and begin sucking the life phloem right out of it. The parasite can even distinguish between the scents of healthier and weaker tomato plants and then head for the hale one. 12

In closing, Angier notes that to live, all animals must kill and eat something.

"Even if you have quite a bit of knowledge about plants," Dr. De Moraes said, "it's still surprising to see how sophisticated they can be." 13

It's a small daily tragedy that we animals must kill to stay alive. Plants are the ethical autotrophs here, the ones that wrest their meals from the sun. Don't expect them to boast: they're too busy fighting to survive. 14

Reading for Better Writing

Working by yourself or with a group, do the following:

1. On a sheet of paper, create two columns. In the left column, paraphrase Gary Steiner's core argument and list his supporting claims; and in the right column, paraphrase Natalie Angier's core argument and list her supporting claims. Explain how the positions are similar and different, and assess the strength of each writer's reasoning, taking into account the supporting claims and the evidence offered.

2. Describe each writer's voice and cite words or phrases exemplifying that voice. Then explain how each writer's voice colors his or her argument.

3. Examine each argument for logical fallacies such as either/or thinking (page 257), appeal to pity (page 258), and attack against the person (page 260). If you find examples, explain how they affect the writer's argument.

Video

Taking a Position ■▪■

In the essay below, David Blankenhorn argues that America is losing its understanding of and appreciation for fatherhood.

Fatherless America

Use this column to record your observations about the essay.

The United States is becoming an increasingly fatherless society. A generation ago, an American child could reasonably expect to grow up with his or her father. Today, an American child can reasonably expect not to. Fatherlessness is now approaching a rough parity with fatherhood as a defining feature of American childhood. *1*

This astonishing fact is reflected in many statistics, but here are the two most important. Tonight, about 40 percent of American children will go to sleep in homes in which their fathers do not live. Before they reach the age of eighteen, more than half of our nation's children are likely to spend at least a significant portion of their childhoods living apart from their fathers. Never before in this country have so many children been voluntarily abandoned by their fathers. Never before have so many children grown up without knowing what it means to have a father. *2*

Fatherlessness is the most harmful demographic trend of this generation. It is the leading cause of declining child well-being in our society. It is also the engine driving our most urgent social problems, from crime to adolescent pregnancy to child abuse to domestic violence against women. Yet, despite its scale and social consequences, fatherlessness is a problem that is frequently ignored or denied. Especially within our elite discourse, it remains largely a problem with no name. *3*

If this trend continues, fatherlessness is likely to change the shape of our society. Consider this prediction. After the year 2000, as people born after 1970 emerge as a large proportion of our working-age adult population, the United States will be a nation divided into two groups, separate and unequal. The two groups will work in the same economy, speak a common language, and remember the same national history. But they will live fundamentally divergent lives. One group will receive basic benefits—psychological, social, economic, educational, and moral—that are denied to the other group. *4*

The primary fault line dividing the two groups will not be race, religion, class, education, or gender. It will be patrimony. One group will consist of those adults who grew up with the daily presence and provision of fathers. The other group will consist of those who did not. By the early years of the next [twenty-first] century, these two groups will be roughly the same size. *5*

Surely a crisis of this scale merits a response. At a minimum, it requires a serious debate. Why is fatherhood declining? What can be done about it? Can our *6* society find ways to invigorate effective fatherhood as a norm of male behavior? Yet, to date, the public discussion on this topic has been remarkably weak and defeatist. There is a prevailing belief that not much can—or even should—be done to reverse the trend.

When the crime rate jumps, politicians promise to do something about it. 7
When the unemployment rate rises, task forces assemble to address the problem. As random shootings increase, public health officials worry about the preponderance of guns. But when it comes to the mass defection of men from family life, not much happens.

There is debate, even alarm, about specific social problems. Divorce. Out-of- 8
wedlock childbearing. Children growing up in poverty. Youth violence. Unsafe neighborhoods. Domestic violence. The weakening of parental authority. But in these discussions, we seldom acknowledge the underlying phenomenon that binds together these otherwise disparate issues: the flight of males from their children's lives. In fact, we seem to go out of our way to avoid the connection between our most pressing social problems and the trend of fatherlessness.

We avoid this connection because, as a society, we are changing our minds about 9
the role of men in family life. As a cultural idea, our inherited understanding of fatherhood is under siege. Men in general, and fathers in particular, are increasingly viewed as superfluous to family life: either as expendable or as part of the problem. Masculinity itself, understood as anything other than a rejection of what it has traditionally meant to be male, is typically treated with suspicion and even hostility in our cultural discourse. Consequently, our society is now manifestly unable to sustain, or even find reason to believe in, fatherhood as a distinctive domain of male activity.

The core question is simple: Does every child need a father? Increasingly, our 10
society's answer is "no" or at least "not necessarily." Few idea shifts in this century are as consequential as this one. At stake is nothing less than what it means to be a man, who our children will be, and what kind of society we will become.

This [essay] is a criticism not simply of fatherlessness but of a culture of 11
fatherlessness. For, in addition to losing fathers, we are losing something larger: our idea of fatherhood. Unlike earlier periods of father absence in our history, we now face more than a physical loss affecting some homes. We face a cultural loss affecting every home. For this reason, the most important absence our society must confront is not the absence of fathers but the absence of our belief in fathers.

In a larger sense, this [essay] is a cultural criticism because fatherhood, much 12
more than motherhood, is a cultural invention. Its meaning for the individual man is shaped less by biology than by cultural script or story—a societal code that

guides, and at times pressures, him into certain ways of acting and of understanding himself as a man.

Like motherhood, fatherhood is made up of both a biological and a social 13 dimension. Yet in societies across the world, mothers are far more successful than fathers at fusing these two dimensions into a coherent parental identity. Is the nursing mother playing a biological or social role? Is she feeding or bonding? We can hardly separate the two, so seamlessly are they woven together.

But fatherhood is a different matter. A father makes his sole biological 14 contribution at the moment of conception—nine months before the infant enters the world. Because social paternity is only indirectly linked to biological paternity, the connection between the two cannot be assumed. The phrase "to father a child" usually refers only to the act of insemination, not to the responsibility for raising a child. What fathers contribute to their offspring after conception is largely a matter of cultural devising.

Moreover, despite their other virtues, men are not ideally suited to responsible 15 fatherhood. Although they certainly have the capacity for fathering, men are inclined to sexual promiscuity and paternal waywardness. Anthropologically, human fatherhood constitutes what might be termed a necessary problem. It is necessary because, in all societies, child well-being and societal success hinge largely upon a high level of paternal investment: the willingness of adult males to devote energy and resources to the care of their offspring. It is a problem because adult males are frequently—indeed, increasingly—unwilling or unable to make that vital investment.

Because fatherhood is universally problematic in human societies, cultures 16 must mobilize to devise and enforce the father role for men, coaxing and guiding them into fatherhood through a set of legal and extralegal pressures that require them to maintain a close alliance with their children's mother and to invest in their children. Because men do not volunteer for fatherhood as much as they are conscripted into it by the surrounding culture, only an authoritative cultural story of fatherhood can fuse biological and social paternity into a coherent male identity.

For exactly this reason, Margaret Mead and others have observed that the 17 supreme test of any civilization is whether it can socialize men by teaching them to be fathers—creating a culture in which men acknowledge their paternity and willingly nurture their offspring. Indeed, if we can equate the essence of the antisocial male with violence, we can equate the essence of the socialized male with being a good father. Thus, at the center of our most important cultural imperative, we find the fatherhood script: the story that describes what it ought to mean for a man to have a child.

Just as the fatherhood script advances the social goal of harnessing male 18 behavior to collective needs, it also reflects an individual purpose. That purpose, in a word, is happiness. Anthropologists have long understood that the genius of an effective culture is its capacity to reconcile individual happiness with collective well-being. By situating individual lives within a social narrative, culture endows private behavior with larger meaning. By linking the self to moral purposes larger than the self, an effective culture tells us a story in which individual fulfillment transcends selfishness, and personal satisfaction transcends narcissism.

In this respect, our cultural script is not simply a set of imported moralisms, 19 exterior to the individual and designed only to compel self-sacrifice. It is also a pathway—indeed, our only pathway—to what the founders of the American experiment called the pursuit of happiness.

The stakes on this issue could hardly be higher. Our society's conspicuous 20 failure to sustain or create compelling norms of fatherhood amounts to a social and personal disaster. Today's story of fatherhood features one-dimensional characters, an unbelievable plot, and an unhappy ending. It reveals in our society both a failure of collective memory and a collapse of moral imagination. It undermines families, neglects children, causes or aggravates our worst social problems, and makes individual adult happiness—both male and female—harder to achieve.

Ultimately, this failure reflects nothing less than a culture gone awry: a culture 21 increasingly unable to establish the boundaries, erect the sign-posts, and fashion the stories that can harmonize individual happiness with collective well-being. In short, it reflects a culture that increasingly fails to "enculture" individual men and women, mothers and fathers.

In personal terms, the end result of this process, the final residue from what 22 David Gutmann calls the "deculturation" of paternity, is narcissism: a me-first egotism that is hostile not only to any societal goal or larger moral purpose but also to any save the most puerile understanding of personal happiness. In social terms, the primary results of decultured paternity are a decline in children's well-being and a rise in male violence, especially against women. In a larger sense, the most significant result is our society's steady fragmentation into atomized individuals, isolated from one another and estranged from the aspirations and realities of common membership in a family, a community, a nation, bound by mutual commitment and shared memory.

[A good father] is a cultural model, or what Max Weber calls an ideal social 23 type—an anthropomorphized composite of cultural ideas about the meaning of paternity. I call him the Good Family Man. As described by one of the fathers [I] interviewed . . . , a good family man "puts his family first."

A good society celebrates the ideal of the man who puts his family first. Because *24* our society is now lurching in the opposite direction, I see the Good Family Man as the principal casualty of today's weakening fatherhood script. And because I cannot imagine a good society without him, I offer him as the protagonist in the stronger script that I believe is both necessary and possible.

Reading for Better Writing

Working by yourself or with a group, do the following:

1. What is Blankenhorn's position (thesis), and how does he introduce this idea? Which claim seems to be the most significant and when does it appear in the essay?

2. Choose five paragraphs and analyze their structure (e.g., topic sentence, supporting details, sentence structure, and transitions linking paragraphs). Then explain how these elements do or do not help present a clear message.

3. Working with a classmate, choose seven logical fallacies explained on pages 257–260. Then discuss why you believe that Blankenhorn's argument does or does not include these fallacies. Share your ideas with the class.

4. In paragraph 9, Blankenhorn makes the following claim: "Masculinity itself, understood as anything other than a rejection of what it has traditionally meant to be male, is typically treated with suspicion and even hostility in our cultural discourse." Explain what he means and why you find it a strong or weak claim.

5. Analyze three passages in which the writer uses data to support a point. Then explain why that use of data is or is not effective.

6. In paragraph 17, Blankenhorn says, "Margaret Mead and others have observed that the supreme test of any civilization is whether it can socialize men by teaching them to be fathers—creating a culture in which men acknowledge their paternity and willingly nurture their offspring." Explain what the quotation means and why it does or does not support the writer's thesis.

7. In paragraph 22, the writer says, "In personal terms, the end result of this process, the final residue from what David Gutmann calls the 'deculturation' of paternity, is narcissism." Define narcissism and explain how Blankenhorn's use of the term does or does not develop his argument.

Writing Guidelines

Note: For in-depth help on developing persuasive arguments, see pages 249–264.

Planning

1. **Select a debatable topic.** Review the list below and add topics as needed.
   - **Current Affairs:** Explore recent trends, new laws, and emerging controversies discussed in the news media, blogs, or online discussion groups.
   - **Burning Issues:** What issues related to family, work, education, recreation, technology, the environment, or popular culture do you care about?
   - **Dividing Lines:** What issues divide your communities? Religion, gender, politics, regionalism, nationalism? Choose a topic and freewrite to clarify your position.
   - **Fresh Fare:** Avoid tired issues unless you take a fresh perspective.

2. **Take stock.** Before you dig into your topic, assess your starting point. What is your current position on the topic? Why? What evidence do you have?

3. **Get inside the issue.** To take a defensible position, study the issue carefully:
   - Investigate all possible positions on the issue and research as needed.
   - Do firsthand research that produces current, relevant information,
   - Write your position at the top of a page. Below it, set up "Pro" and "Con" columns. List arguments in each column.
   - Develop reasoning that supports your position and test it for the following: (a) no logical fallacies, such as slanted language, oversimplification, either/or thinking, straw-man and red-herring claims, appeals to pity, and personal attacks (see pages 257–260); and (b) an effective range of support: statistics, observations, expert testimony, comparisons, experiences, and analysis (see pages 254–256).

4. **Refine your position.** By now, you may have sharpened or radically changed your initial position on the topic. Before you organize and draft your essay, reflect on those changes. If it helps, use this formula:
   I believe this to be true about _____.

5. **Organize your argument and support.** Now you've committed yourself to a position. Before drafting, review these organizational options:
   - **Traditional Pattern:** Introduce the issue, state your position, support it, address and refute opposition, and restate your position.
   - **Blatant Confession:** Place your position statement in the first sentence.
   - **Delayed Gratification:** Describe various positions on the topic, compare and contrast them, and then take and defend your position.
   - **Changed Mind:** If your research changed your mind, explain how and why.
   - **Winning Over:** If readers oppose your position, address their concerns by anticipating and answering each objection or question

Drafting

6. Write your first draft. Using freewriting and/or your notes, draft the paper.

- **Opening:** Seize the reader's attention, possibly with a bold title—or raise concern for the issue with a dramatic story, a pointed example, a vivid picture, a thought-provoking question, or a personal confession. Supply background information that readers need to understand the issue.

- **Development:** Deepen, clarify, and support your position statement, using solid logic and reliable support. Address opposing views fairly as part of a clear, well-reasoned argument that helps readers understand and accept your position.

- **Closing:** End on a lively, thoughtful note that stresses your commitment. If appropriate, make a direct or indirect plea to readers to adopt your position.

Revising

7. Improve the ideas, organization, and voice. Ask a classmate or someone from the college's writing center to read your position paper for the following:

____ **Ideas:** Does the writing effectively establish and defend a stand on a debatable issue? Is the position clearly stated and effectively qualified and refined? Do the reasoning and support help the reader understand and appreciate the position?

____ **Organization:** Does the opening effectively raise the issue? Does the middle offer a carefully sequenced development and defense of the position? Does the closing successfully drive home the position?

____ **Voice:** Is the voice thoughtful, measured, committed, and convincing?

Editing

8. Edit and proofread the essay by addressing these issues:

____ **Words:** Language is precise, concrete, and lively—no jargon, clichés, or insults.

____ **Sentences:** Constructions vary in length and flow smoothly.

____ **Correctness:** The copy includes no errors in spelling, usage, punctuation, grammar, or mechanics.

____ **Design:** The page design is correctly formatted and attractive; information is properly documented according to the required system (e.g., MLA, APA).

Publishing

9. Publish your essay. Submit your position paper according to your instructor's requirements. In addition, seek a forum for your position—with peers in a discussion group, with relatives, or online.

Critical-Thinking and Writing Activities

Interactive

As directed by your instructor, complete the following critical-thinking and writing activities by yourself or with classmates.

1. Reflect on hot topics in your major—check textbooks, talk to professors or experts, and review journals in the field. Then write a position paper on a controversial issue.

2. Review Alyssa Woudstra's essay, "Nuclear Is Not the Answer." Then research this or another energy-related topic and write an essay in which you take a clear, well-reasoned position on one or more key issues.

3. Review Gary Steiner's and Natalie Angier's essays on what we should or should not eat. Then research the topic and develop your own argument in which you address relevant issues that they raise, as well as other issues that you think are relevant. Seek to state your position clearly and support your claims with reliable evidence.

4. Review David Blankenhorn's essay, "Fatherless America," paying special attention to the way he builds his argument with clear, well-documented claims. Then write your own position paper in which you oppose or support a claim about the family in society.

5. Draft or revise a position paper that addresses a controversial issue that exists within a community to which you belong (e.g., city, neighborhood, generation, race or ethnic group, gender, consumer group, online network) by respectfully describing opposing ideas and showing how each view is reasonable and acceptable.

Learning-Outcomes Checklist

Use the checklist below to assess what you have learned about taking a position in writing.

_____ I can read and evaluate a position paper for clarity and logic.

_____ I can identify these logical fallacies in others' writing and correct them in my own writing: oversimplification, either/or thinking, straw-man and red-herring claims, appeals to pity, personal attacks.

_____ I can strengthen my argument by answering opponents' questions, making reasonable concessions, and rebutting opposing arguments.

_____ I can develop logical claims supported with reliable evidence.

_____ I can write a well-reasoned position paper in a measured but compelling voice.

Persuading Readers to Act

18

Persuading people to do something is challenging, requiring that you convince them to believe you, to rethink their own perspectives, and to take a concrete step. In the end, you need to change people's minds in order to change their actions.

Writers achieve this goal with sound logic, reliable support, and fitting appeals. Every day, persuasive writing like this appears in newsletters, editorials, marketing documents, business proposals, academic journals, white papers, and traditional essays.

Because the form is so common, you can expect to read and write versions of it in college and in the workplace. As you read the essays in this chapter, carefully analyze how writers develop convincing appeals for action. Then when you write your own essay, try these same strategies.

Learning Outcomes

► Read and assess a call-to-action paper for a rational, convincing argument.

 Audio

► Use as evidence appropriate anecdotes, tests, experiments, analogies, and expert testimony.

 Video

► Develop reasonable, vs. extreme, trivial, or unqualified claims.

 Video

► Identify logical fallacies: half-truths, unreliable testimonials, personal attacks, false analogies.

► Write a compelling, persuasive paper in a mature, informed voice.

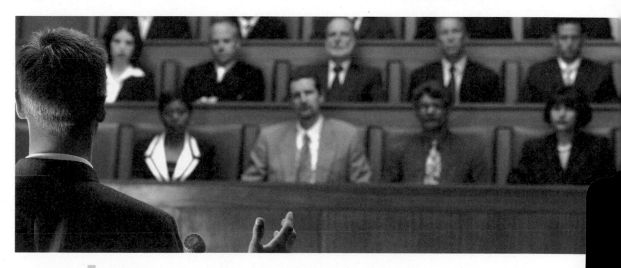

Visually Speaking ► Review the photograph above. What does it suggest about how or why people persuade others to act on an issue?

■ Reading Persuasive Writing

How should you read a paper that urges you to act on an issue? The instructions below offer helpful instructions.

Consider the rhetorical situation. ■▪■

When reading an appeal to act, anticipate what the writer wants people to do, what audience he or she has in mind, and how the topic is treated.

- **Purpose:** Whether in academics, the workplace, or public life, writers call for action because they believe change is needed. Something is not right. Something needs to be improved or fixed. The writer's goal is to convince readers to care about the issue strongly enough to take a concrete step.
- **Audience:** The intended readers are people whom the writer believes need to be pressed to act. Readers may be unaware of the issue, may feel overwhelmed by it, may have an interest in not acting, or may not care enough about the issue to actually act. The writer thus educates and urges such readers.
- **Topic:** In academics, the topics addressed might be related to a specific discipline (e.g., educational mentoring campaign, expanding an arts program), a political or social issue (e.g., shelter for abused women, Special Olympics program), or a general humanitarian concern (e.g., help for victims of an epidemic, a flood, or a war).

Look for convincing qualities. ■▪■

When reading an appeal to act, look for the following:

- **Compelling Argument:** The writer accurately describes the issue, convinces readers of its importance, and calls for a doable and effective action. The writer's claims are fact based and reasonable, not extreme, trivial, or unqualified (see pages 252–253).
- **Logical Argument:** The argument is based on reliable evidence such as appropriate anecdotes, tests, experiments, analogies, and expert testimony (see pages 254–255); and the argument avoids logical fallacies such as half-truths, unreliable testimonials, attacks against a person, and false analogies (see pages 257–260).
- **Mature Voice:** The writing sounds informed and genuine; it includes no manipulative appeals, quarrelsome language, or demeaning accusations.

Reader's Checklist

_____ What is the issue, and what action is requested to address it?

_____ Who are the intended readers, and what capacity to act do they have?

_____ Are the writer's claims accurate, compelling, and logical?

_____ Is the argument's tone informed, genuine, and respectful?

_____ Is the writing convincing—does it move readers to do what the writer requests?

Persuading Readers to Act ▪▪▪

Student writer Henry Veldboom, a mature student with children of his own, wrote this essay to call North American readers to reconsider what they value.

Video

> ## Outline
> *Introduction:* the issue of North American wealth and its real cost
> **1.** Modern capitalism is based on harmful consumerism.
> **2.** Consumers must consider the results of their consumption.
> **3.** People must examine especially how consumerism impacts children.
> *Conclusion:* individual consumer change necessary for social change

Title: issue and central question

Our Wealth: Where Is It Taking Us?

Introduction: North American wealth and its real cost

North America's wealth and the lifestyle it affords are known throughout the world. This knowledge has created a belief that wealth and happiness are synonymous, which in turn has perpetuated the dreams of people around the globe who hope to achieve the same successes witnessed here in the West. Is there truth to the idea that wealth and happiness coexist? Ask North Americans if they would willingly trade life here for that in a struggling country and they would likely say "No." Their wealth has made their lives quite comfortable. Most would admit to enjoying the lifestyle such wealth allows; few would want to give it up. But what is this wealth really costing North Americans—especially children?

1 Modern capitalism is based on harmful consumerism.

While North American wealth grew out of the capitalism that culminated in the nineteenth-century Industrial Revolution, today's capitalism is a system largely based on consumerism—an attitude that values the incessant acquisition of goods in the belief that it is necessary and beneficial. The goal, then, of a modern capitalist economy is to produce many goods as cheaply as possible and have these goods purchased on a continual basis. The forces behind capitalism—business owners at the demand of stockholders—employ an ever-expanding array of marketing techniques to accomplish the goal of selling products. Expert on marketing George Barna defines marketing as the process of directing "goods and services from the producer to the consumer, to satisfy the needs and desires of the consumer and the goals of the producer" (41). On the receiving end of today's capitalism are consumers whose needs are in general self-serving and based on self-actualization. Corporations promote this way of thinking and capitalize on it through marketing techniques. Social commentator Benjamin Barber describes this modern interaction in the following way: "[This thinking] serves capitalist consumerism directly by nurturing a culture of impetuous consumption necessary to selling puerile goods in a developed world that has few genuine needs" (81).

2 Consumers must consider the results of their consumption.

Admittedly, deciphering genuine needs from superfluous wants is not an easy task. However, putting debates about materialism aside, people must consider the results of their consumption. The 2008-2009 economic upheaval still lingers in people's minds despite the recent upward trend in the North American economy. When such financial turmoil happens, the typical response is to lay blame. Some people are quick to accuse corporations of causing the turmoil and governments of allowing corporations to operate as they do. Noted journalist and anti-establishment advocate Linda McQuaig comments on the shift in the 1970s that gave individuals more freedoms; in turn, corporations accommodated the lax attitudes of government to themselves and were "ensured freedom from their restraints on their profit-making" (22). Do North American corporations and governments share the responsibility to properly use wealth and direct the economy? Yes, they most certainly do. However, individuals must also examine their own fiscal responsibility. McQuaig addresses this issue as well, highlighting "the power and centrality of greed in our culture" (23). She raises a word that no one wants to be labeled with—greed. When people begin discussing their financial woes in relation to individual greed, the blame rests squarely on each member of society.

3 People must examine how consumerism harms children

The behavior that has led to the current financial crisis is not only impacting   4
adults but also putting children at risk. Deceptive marketing tactics make use of psychological knowledge and social patterning research to convince consumers to purchase particular products. Adults who possess the mental capacity to discern motives and detect subversion are being effectively manipulated by cunning advertising techniques, resulting in massive debt loads, addiction, and bankruptcy. However, the greater concern with these marketing practices is that they are being aimed at children who have less ability to defend themselves. Psychiatrist Susan Linn describes the marketing aimed at children as "precisely targeted, refined by scientific

(a) marketing manipulation

method, and honed by child psychologists . . ." (5). It isn't the case that children are getting caught in marketing traps set for adults; rather, kids are being targeted. Linn remarks that developmental psychology which was once used solely for treating children's mental health is now used to determine "weaknesses" in children's thinking in order to exploit these weaknesses (24). The weaknesses are due to children's brains not having reached full cognitive development, resulting in unstable patterns of thinking in areas such as reasoning, memory, and problem solving (Weiten 47). At such a disadvantage, children are unable to withstand the marketing ploys aimed at them.

(b) influence on parental spending

Knowing that children are the targets of aggressive mass marketing is all the   5
more serious when the scope of the situation is considered. Much research has been done on purchasing patterns, and while the fact that North Americans spend large amounts of money on goods may not be surprising, when children are added to the equation the picture changes. Expert on consumerism, economics, and family studies Juliet Schor has done a considerable amount of convincing research in this area. She comments on the purchasing influence of children and notes that children aged four to twelve influenced an estimated $670 billion of adult purchasing in 2004 (23). Children having influence on such large amounts of money being spent catches the attention of producers who consequently aim their marketing at kids in order to sell adult products. Schor also notes the results of a Nickelodeon (an entertainment

company) study that states when it comes to recognizing brands, "the average ten year old has memorized 300 to 400 brands" (25). Kids know the products and they know what they want; the dollar amount parents are spending in response to their children reflects this.

(c) physical and mental health problems

The effects of aggressive marketing and consumerism on North American children 6 are exhibited in a wide range of health problems. At first glance, the relationship between consumerism and children's health may appear to be coincidental. However, much research shows a direct link between marketing to children and their health. Having done her own research and examined other studies, Juliet Schor concludes that "the more [children] buy into the commercial and materialist messages, the worse they feel about themselves, the more depressed they are, and the more they are beset by anxiety, headaches, stomach-aches, and boredom" (173). (On a related note, the time spent by children sitting in front of televisions and computers is an important factor in this outcome. These media are the prime vehicles for advertising and are contributing to sedentary lifestyles, which in turn cause health problems.) Materialism is having an effect not only on adults but also on youth. When children are asked what they aspire to be, the top answer is "to be rich" (37). The health of the minds and bodies of North American children is deteriorating as a result of consumerism and the new capitalism.

Conclusion: Individual consumers must change if society is to change.

Having examined the current state of North American society in terms of the 7 economic and personal health related to the new capitalism, one begins to see that society is in a situation that is neither beneficial nor sustainable. Changes must be made. If the response is to look for someone or something to blame, everyone must stop and take a look in the mirror. Changing habits and attitudes must start with the individual. While adopting a particular economic ideology is not the point, North Americans must take a hard look at their society and decide if this is how they want to live. If this society carries on unchanged, what future will its children have? North America has an abundance of wealth; the decision of where to go with it must be made: time is running out.

Note: The Works Cited pages is not shown. For sample pages, see MLA (pages 526–527) and APA (page 557).

Reading for Better Writing

Working by yourself or with a group, answer these questions:

1. In his title, Veldboom identifies the issue as wealth. How does he clarify and deepen the issue in the essay's opening paragraphs?

2. While acknowledging economic and social systems, Veldboom stresses individual values and responsibilities. How effective is this emphasis?

3. What action does the essay call for? Do you find the action practical and compelling? Why or why not?

Persuading Readers to Act ■▪■

Video

Dr. Martin Luther King, Jr., was a leader in the Civil Rights Movement during the 1950s and 1960s. On August 28, 1963, he delivered this persuasive speech to a crowd of 250,000 people gathered at the Lincoln Memorial in Washington, D.C.

I Have a Dream

King starts with a tragic contrast.

1 Five score years ago, a great American, in whose symbolic shadow we stand, signed the Emancipation Proclamation. This momentous decree came as a great beacon light of hope to millions of Negro slaves who had been seared in the flames of withering injustice. It came as a joyous daybreak to end the long night of captivity.

He uses figurative language to describe the present situation.

2 But one hundred years later, we must face the tragic fact that the Negro is still not free. One hundred years later, the life of the Negro is still sadly crippled by the manacles of segregation and the chains of discrimination. One hundred years later, the Negro lives on a lonely island of poverty in the midst of a vast ocean of material prosperity. One hundred years later, the Negro is still languishing in the corners of American society and finds himself an exile in his own land. So we have come here today to dramatize an appalling condition.

An analogy clarifies the problem.

3 In a sense we have come to our nation's Capitol to cash a check. When the architects of our republic wrote the magnificent words of the Constitution and the Declaration of Independence, they were signing a promissory note to which every American was to fall heir. This note was a promise that all men would be guaranteed the unalienable rights of life, liberty, and the pursuit of happiness.

4 It is obvious today that America has defaulted on this promissory note insofar as her citizens of color are concerned. Instead of honoring this sacred obligation, America has given the Negro people a bad check; a check which has come back marked "insufficient funds." But we refuse to believe that the bank of justice is bankrupt. We refuse to believe that there are insufficient funds in the great vaults of opportunity of this nation. So we have come to cash this check—a check that will give us upon demand the riches of freedom and the security of justice. We have

Repeated words and phrases create urgency.

also come to this hallowed spot to remind America of the fierce urgency of now. This is no time to engage in the luxury of cooling off or to take the tranquilizing drug of gradualism. Now is the time to make real the promises of Democracy. Now is the time to rise from the dark and desolate valley of segregation to the sunlit path of racial justice. Now is the time to open the doors of opportunity to all of God's children. Now is the time to lift our nation from the quicksands of racial injustice to the solid rock of brotherhood.

5 It would be fatal for the nation to overlook the urgency of the moment and to underestimate the determination of the Negro. This sweltering summer of the Negro's legitimate discontent will not pass until there is an invigorating autumn

of freedom and equality. 1963 is not an end, but a beginning. Those who hope that the Negro needed to blow off steam and will now be content will have a rude awakening if the nation returns to business as usual. There will be neither rest nor tranquility in America until the Negro is granted his citizenship rights. The whirlwinds of revolt will continue to shake the foundations of our nation until the bright day of justice emerges.

King addresses specific audiences in turn.

But there is something I must say to my people who stand on the warm 6 threshold which leads into the palace of justice. In the process of gaining our rightful place we must not be guilty of wrongful deeds. Let us not seek to satisfy our thirst for freedom by drinking from the cup of bitterness and hatred. We must forever conduct our struggle on the high plane of dignity and discipline. We must not allow our creative protest to degenerate into physical violence. Again and again we must rise to the majestic heights of meeting physical force with soul force. The marvelous new militancy which has engulfed the Negro community must not lead us to a distrust of all white people, for many of our white brothers, as evidenced by their presence here today, have come to realize that their destiny is tied up with our destiny and their freedom is inextricably bound to our freedom. We cannot walk alone.

He responds to the arguments of opponents.

And as we talk, we must make the pledge that we shall march ahead. We 7 cannot turn back. There are those who are asking the devotees of civil rights, "When will you be satisfied?" We can never be satisfied as long as the Negro is the victim of the unspeakable horrors of police brutality. We can never be satisfied as long as our bodies, heaving with the fatigue of travel, cannot gain lodging in the motels of the highways and the hotels of the cities. We cannot be satisfied as long as the Negro's basic mobility is from a smaller ghetto to a larger one. We can never be satisfied as long as a Negro in Mississippi cannot vote and a Negro in New York believes he has nothing for which to vote. No, no, we are not satisfied, and we will not be satisfied until justice rolls down like waters and righteousness like a mighty stream.

Appropriate emotional appeals are used in the context of suffering.

I am not unmindful that some of you have come here out of great trials and 8 tribulations. Some of you have come fresh from narrow jail cells. Some of you have come from areas where your quest for freedom left you battered by the storms of persecution and staggered by the winds of police brutality. You have been the veterans of creative suffering. Continue to work with the faith that unearned suffering is redemptive.

Go back to Mississippi, go back to Alabama, go back to South Carolina, go 9 back to Georgia, go back to Louisiana, go back to the slums and ghettos of our northern cities, knowing that somehow this situation can and will be changed. Let us not wallow in the valley of despair.

I say to you today, my friends, that in spite of the difficulties and frustrations 10 of the moment I still have a dream. It is a dream deeply rooted in the American dream.

I have a dream that one day this nation will rise up and live out the true *11* meaning of its creed: "We hold these truths to be self-evident; that all men are created equal."

I have a dream that one day on the red hills of Georgia the sons of former *12* slaves and the sons of former slaveowners will be able to sit down together at the table of brotherhood.

I have a dream that the state of Mississippi, a desert state sweltering with the *13* heat of injustice and oppression, will be transformed into an oasis of freedom and justice.

I have a dream that my four little children will one day live in a nation where *14* they will not be judged by the color of their skin but by the content of their character.

I have a dream today. *15*

I have a dream that the state of Alabama, whose governor's lips are presently *16* dripping with the words of interposition and nullification, will be transformed into a situation where little black boys and black girls will be able to join hands with little white boys and girls and walk together as sisters and brothers.

I have a dream today.

I have a dream that one day every valley shall be exalted, every hill and *17* mountain shall be made low, the rough places will be made plain, and the crooked *18* places will be made straight, and the glory of the Lord shall be revealed, and all flesh shall see it together.

This is our hope. This is the faith with which I return to the South. With *19* this faith we will be able to hew out of the mountain of despair a stone of hope. With this faith we will be able to transform the jangling discords of our nation into a beautiful symphony of brotherhood. With this faith we will be able to work together, to pray together, to struggle together, to go to jail together, to stand up for freedom together, knowing that we will be free one day.

This will be the day when all God's children will be able to sing with new *20* meaning.

> *My country 'tis of thee*   *21*
> *Sweet land of liberty,*
> *Of thee I sing,*
> *Land where my fathers died,*
> *Land of the pilgrims' pride,*
> *From every mountainside*
> *Let freedom ring.*

And if America is to be a great nation this must become true. So let freedom *22* ring from the prodigious hilltops of New Hampshire. Let freedom ring from

---

The repetition of key phrases becomes a persuasive refrain.

King's vision offers hope and motivates readers to change society.

He appeals to ideals and to humanity's better nature, ending with a vision of a just society.

the mighty mountains of New York. Let freedom ring from the heightening Alleghenies of Pennsylvania!

Let freedom ring from the snow-capped Rockies of Colorado! 23

Let freedom ring from the curvaceous peaks of California! 24

But not only that; let freedom ring from Stone Mountain of Georgia! 25

Let freedom ring from Lookout Mountain of Tennessee! 26

Let freedom ring from every hill and molehill of Mississippi! From every 27 mountainside, let freedom ring.

When we let freedom ring, when we let it ring from every village and every 28 hamlet, from every state and every city, we will be able to speed up that day when all of God's children, black men and white men, Jews and Gentiles, Protestants and Catholics, will be able to join hands and sing in the words of the old Negro spiritual, "Free at last! Free at last! Thank God almighty, we are free at last!"

The closing urges readers to work for a better future.

Reading for Better Writing

Working by yourself or with a group, answer these questions:

1. King is actually speaking to several audiences at the same time. Who are these different audiences? How does King address each?

2. For what specific changes does King call? What does he want his listeners to do?

3. Explore the writer's style. How does he use religious imagery, comparisons, and analogies? How does repetition function as a persuasive technique?

4. In a sense, King's speech addresses a gap between reality and an ideal. How does he present this gap?

Persuading Readers to Act ■■▪

Kofi Annan, the former Secretary General of the United Nations, wrote the essay below in order to urge readers worldwide to help address AIDS and famine in Africa.

In Africa, AIDS Has a Woman's Face

The title and introduction aim to create urgency about the issue.

A combination of famine and AIDS is threatening the backbone of Africa—the women who keep African societies going and whose work makes up the economic foundation of rural communities. For decades, we have known that the best way for Africa to thrive is to ensure that its women have the freedom, power, and knowledge to make decisions affecting their own lives and those of their families and communities. At the United Nations, we have always understood that our work for development depends on building a successful partnership with the African farmer and her husband.

Study after study has shown that there is no effective development strategy in which women do not play a central role. When women are fully involved, the benefits can be seen immediately: families are healthier; they are better fed; their income, savings and reinvestment go up. And, what is true of families is true of communities and, eventually, of whole countries.

Stressing the importance of women in African societies, Annan outlines the double catastrophe happening.

But today, millions of African women are threatened by two simultaneous catastrophes: famine and AIDS. More than 30 million people are now at risk of starvation in southern Africa and the Horn of Africa. All of these predominantly agricultural societies are also battling serious AIDS epidemics. This is no coincidence: AIDS and famine are directly linked.

Because of AIDS, farming skills are being lost, agricultural development efforts are declining, rural livelihoods are disintegrating, productive capacity to work the land is dropping, and household earnings are shrinking—all while the cost of caring for the ill is rising exponentially. At the same time, H.I.V. infection and AIDS are spreading dramatically and disproportionately among women. A United Nations report released last month shows that women now make up 50 percent of those infected with H.I.V. worldwide—and in Africa that figure is now 59 percent. Today, AIDS has a woman's face.

AIDS has already caused immense suffering by killing almost 2.5 million Africans this year alone. It has left 11 million African children orphaned since the epidemic began. Now it is attacking the capacity of these countries to resist famine by eroding those mechanisms that enable populations to fight back—the coping abilities provided by women.

In famines before the AIDS crisis, women proved more resilient than men. Their survival rate was higher, and their coping skills were stronger. Women were the ones who found alternative foods that could sustain their children in time of drought. Because droughts happened once a decade or so, women who had experienced previous droughts were able to pass on survival techniques to younger women. Women are the ones who nurture social networks that can help spread the burden in times of famine.

Annan contrasts women's situation before and after the arrival of AIDS.

But today, as AIDS is eroding the health of Africa's women, it is eroding the   7
skills, experience and networks that keep their families and communities going.
Even before falling ill, a woman will often have to care for a sick husband, thereby
reducing the time she can devote to planting, harvesting and marketing crops. When
her husband dies, she is often deprived of credit, distribution networks or land rights.
When she dies, the household will risk collapsing completely, leaving children to fend
for themselves. The older ones, especially girls, will be taken out of school to work in
the home or the farm. These girls, deprived of education and opportunities, will be
even less able to protect themselves against AIDS.

He presses for a new combination of necessary, related actions.

Because this crisis is different from past famines, we must look beyond relief   8
measures of the past. Merely shipping in food is not enough. Our effort will have
to combine food assistance and new approaches to farming with treatment and
prevention of H.I.V. and AIDS. It will require creating early-warning and analysis
systems that monitor both H.I.V. infection rates and famine indicators. It will require
new agricultural techniques, appropriate to a depleted work force. It will require a
renewed effort to wipe out H.I.V.-related stigma and silence.

It will require innovative, large-scale ways to care for orphans, with specific   9
measures that enable children in AIDS-affected communities to stay in school.
Education and prevention are still the most powerful weapons against the spread of
H.I.V. Above all, this new international effort must put women at the center of our
strategy to fight AIDS.

He points to hopeful signs and cases as a way of convincing readers that change can happen.

Experience suggests that there is reason to hope. The recent United Nations   10
report shows that H.I.V. infection rates in Uganda continue to decline. In South
Africa, infection rates for women under 20 have started to decrease. In Zambia, H.I.V.
rates show signs of dropping among women in urban areas and younger women in
rural areas. In Ethiopia, infection levels have fallen among young women in the center
of Addis Ababa.

We can and must build on those successes and replicate them elsewhere. For that,   11
we need leadership, partnership, and imagination from the international community
and African governments. If we want to save Africa from two catastrophes, we would
do well to focus on saving Africa's women.

Reading for Better Writing

Working by yourself or with a group, answer these questions:

1. How does the writer introduce the topic and focus the essay? Explain.

2. What does Annan ask readers to do? Is his request clear and convincing? Why?

3. Choose a paragraph that you find particularly convincing and explain why.

Persuading Readers to Act ■ ■ ■

In the following essay, published in August 2009, Barbara Ehrenreich argues that whereas America's poor citizens sometimes loiter, trespass, or panhandle, most do these things because they're poor—not because they're criminals. In response to such behavior, she urges readers to show compassion and to act on behalf of the poor.

Is It Now a Crime to Be Poor?

As you read, highlight strategies and take marginal notes exploring how Ehrenreich raises the issue and calls for action.

It's too bad so many people are falling into poverty at a time when it's almost   1
illegal to be poor. You won't be arrested for shopping in a Dollar Store, but if you are truly, deeply, in-the-streets poor, you're well advised not to engage in any of the biological necessities of life—like sitting, sleeping, lying down, or loitering. City officials boast that there is nothing discriminatory about the ordinances that afflict the destitute, most of which go back to the dawn of gentrification in the '80s and '90s. "If you're lying on a sidewalk, whether you're homeless or a millionaire, you're in violation of the ordinance," a city attorney in St. Petersburg, Fla., said in June, echoing Anatole France's immortal observation that "the law, in its majestic equality, forbids the rich as well as the poor to sleep under bridges."

In defiance of all reason and compassion, the criminalization of poverty has   2
actually been intensifying as the recession generates ever more poverty. So concludes a new study from the National Law Center on Homelessness and Poverty, which found that the number of ordinances against the publicly poor has been rising since 2006, along with ticketing and arrests for more "neutral" infractions like jaywalking, littering or carrying an open container of alcohol. [See Homes Not Handcuffs: The Criminalization of Homelessness in U.S. Cities.]

The report lists America's 10 "meanest" cities—the largest of which are Honolulu,   3
Los Angeles and San Francisco—but new contestants are springing up every day. The City Council in Grand Junction, Colo., has been considering a ban on begging, and at the end of June, Tempe, Ariz., carried out a four-day crackdown on the indigent. How do you know when someone is indigent? As a Las Vegas statute puts it, "An indigent person is a person whom a reasonable ordinary person would believe to be entitled to apply for or receive" public assistance.

That could be me before the blow-drying and eyeliner, and it's definitely Al   4
Szekely at any time of day. A grizzled 62-year-old, he inhabits a wheelchair and is often found on G Street in Washington—the city that is ultimately responsible for the bullet he took in the spine in Fu Bai, Vietnam, in 1972. He had been enjoying the luxury of an indoor bed until last December, when the police swept through the shelter in the middle of the night looking for men with outstanding warrants.

It turned out that Mr. Szekely, who is an ordained minister and does not drink,   5
do drugs or curse in front of ladies, did indeed have a warrant—for not appearing in court to face a charge of "criminal trespassing" (for sleeping on a sidewalk in a

Washington suburb). So he was dragged out of the shelter and put in jail. "Can you imagine?" asked Eric Sheptock, the homeless advocate (himself a shelter resident) who introduced me to Mr. Szekely. "They arrested a homeless man in a shelter for being homeless."

The viciousness of the official animus toward the indigent can be breathtaking. A few years ago, a group called Food Not Bombs started handing out free vegan food to hungry people in public parks around the nation. A number of cities, led by Las Vegas, passed ordinances forbidding the sharing of food with the indigent in public places, and several members of the group were arrested. A federal judge just overturned the anti-sharing law in Orlando, Fla., but the city is appealing. And now Middletown, Conn., is cracking down on food sharing.

If poverty tends to criminalize people, it is also true that criminalization inexorably impoverishes them. Scott Lovell, another homeless man I interviewed in Washington, earned his record by committing a significant crime—by participating in the armed robbery of a steakhouse when he was 15. Although Mr. Lovell dresses and speaks more like a summer tourist from Ohio than a felon, his criminal record has made it extremely difficult for him to find a job.

For Al Szekely, the arrest for trespassing meant a further descent down the circles of hell. While in jail, he lost his slot in the shelter and now sleeps outside the Verizon Center sports arena, where the big problem, in addition to the security guards, is mosquitoes. His stick thin arms are covered with pink crusty sores, which he treats with a regimen of frantic scratching.

For the not-yet homeless, there are two main paths to criminalization—one involving debt, and the other skin color. Anyone of any color or pre-recession financial status can fall into debt, and although we pride ourselves on the abolition of debtors' prison, in at least one state, Texas, people who can't afford to pay their traffic fines may be made to "sit out their tickets" in jail.

Often the path to legal trouble begins when one of your creditors has a court issue a summons for you, which you fail to honor for one reason or another. (Maybe your address has changed or you never received it.) Now you're in contempt of court. Or suppose you miss a payment and, before you realize it, your car insurance lapses; then you're stopped for something like a broken headlight. Depending on the state, you may have your car impounded or face a steep fine—again, exposing you to a possible summons. "There's just no end to it once the cycle starts," said Robert Solomon of Yale Law School. "It just keeps accelerating."

By far the most reliable way to be criminalized by poverty is to have the wrong-color skin. Indignation runs high when a celebrity professor encounters racial profiling, but for decades whole communities have been effectively "profiled" for the suspicious combination of being both dark-skinned and poor, thanks to the "broken windows" or "zero tolerance" theory of policing popularized by Rudy Giuliani, when he was mayor of New York City, and his police chief William Bratton.

Flick a cigarette in a heavily patrolled community of color and you're littering;   *12*
wear the wrong color T-shirt and you're displaying gang allegiance. Just strolling
around in a dodgy neighborhood can mark you as a potential suspect, according to
Let's Get Free: A Hip-Hop Theory of Justice, an eye-opening new book by Paul Butler, a
former federal prosecutor in Washington. If you seem at all evasive, which I suppose
is like looking "overly anxious" in an airport, Mr. Butler writes, the police "can force
you to stop just to investigate why you don't want to talk to them." And don't get
grumpy about it or you could be "resisting arrest."

There's no minimum age for being sucked into what the Children's Defense Fund   *13*
calls "the cradle-to-prison pipeline." In New York City, a teenager caught in public
housing without an ID—say, while visiting a friend or relative—can be charged with
criminal trespassing and wind up in juvenile detention, Mishi Faruqee, the director
of youth justice programs for the Children's Defense Fund of New York, told me.
In just the past few months, a growing number of cities have taken to ticketing and
sometimes handcuffing teenagers found on the streets during school hours.

In Los Angeles, the fine for truancy is $250; in Dallas, it can be as much as   *14*
$500—crushing amounts for people living near the poverty level. According to the
Los Angeles Bus Riders Union, an advocacy group, 12,000 students were ticketed for
truancy in 2008.

Why does the Bus Riders Union care? Because it estimates that 80 percent of the   *15*
"truants," especially those who are black or Latino, are merely late for school, thanks
to the way that over-filled buses whiz by them without stopping. I met people in Los
Angeles who told me they keep their children home if there's the slightest chance of
their being late. It's an ingenious anti-truancy policy that discourages parents from
sending their youngsters to school.

The pattern is to curtail financing for services that might help the poor while   *16*
ramping up law enforcement: starve school and public transportation budgets,
then make truancy illegal. Shut down public housing, then make it a crime to be
homeless. Be sure to harass street vendors when there are few other opportunities for
employment. The experience of the poor, and especially poor minorities, comes to
resemble that of a rat in a cage scrambling to avoid erratically administered electric
shocks.

And if you should make the mistake of trying to escape via a brief marijuana-   *17*
induced high, it's "gotcha" all over again, because that of course is illegal too. One
result is our staggering level of incarceration, the highest in the world. Today the same
number of Americans—2.3 million—reside in prison as in public housing.

Meanwhile, the public housing that remains has become ever more prisonlike,   *18*
with residents subjected to drug testing and random police sweeps. The safety net, or
what's left of it, has been transformed into a dragnet.

Some of the community organizers I've talked to around the country think   *19*
they know why "zero tolerance" policing has ratcheted up since the recession began.

Leonardo Vilchis of the Union de Vecinos, a community organization in Los Angeles, suspects that "poor people have become a source of revenue" for recession-starved cities, and that the police can always find a violation leading to a fine. If so, this is a singularly demented fund-raising strategy. At a Congressional hearing in June, the president of the National Association of Criminal Defense Lawyers testified about the pervasive "overcriminalization of crimes that are not a risk to public safety," like sleeping in a cardboard box or jumping turnstiles, which leads to expensively clogged courts and prisons.

A Pew Center study released in March found states spending a record $51.7 billion   *20* on corrections, an amount that the center judged, with an excess of moderation, to be "too much."

But will it be enough—the collision of rising prison populations that we can't   *21* afford and the criminalization of poverty—to force us to break the mad cycle of poverty and punishment? With the number of people in poverty increasing (some estimates suggest it's up to 45 million to 50 million, from 37 million in 2007) several states are beginning to ease up on the criminalization of poverty—for example, by sending drug offenders to treatment rather than jail, shortening probation and reducing the number of people locked up for technical violations like missed court appointments. But others are tightening the screws: not only increasing the number of "crimes" but also charging prisoners for their room and board—assuring that they'll be released with potentially criminalizing levels of debt.

Maybe we can't afford the measures that would begin to alleviate America's   *22* growing poverty—affordable housing, good schools, reliable public transportation and so forth. I would argue otherwise, but for now I'd be content with a consensus that, if we can't afford to truly help the poor, neither can we afford to go on tormenting them.

Reading for Better Writing

Working by yourself or with a group, answer these questions:

1. Note how Ehrenreich uses the title, opening sentence, and opening paragraph to introduce her topic and focus her argument. Are these strategies effective?

2. Identity two passages in which the writer makes a claim and then supports it by citing a study or an academic authority. Is this strategy convincing?

3. Cite two passages in which the writer uses an anecdote or illustration to support a claim. Do these strategies strengthen her argument?

4. Precisely what does the writer want her readers to do? Why might she have published this appeal in *The New York Times*?

Writing Guidelines

Note: For in-depth help on developing persuasive arguments, see pages 249–264.

Planning

1. **Select a topic.** List issues about which you feel passionately such as community problems, international issues, disaster-relief efforts, educational outreach programs, environmental clean-up efforts, or social or political campaigns. Then choose a related topic that is debatable, significant, current, and manageable.

Not Debatable	Debatable
Statistics on spending practices	The injustice of consumerism
The existence of racism	Solutions to racism
Recyclables are dumped in landfills	Tax on paper/plastic grocery bags

2. **Choose and analyze your audience.** Think about who your readers are and why they might resist the change that you advocate.

3. **Narrow your focus and determine your purpose.** Should you focus on one aspect of the issue or all of it? What should you and can you try to change? How might you best organize your argument?.

4. **Generate ideas and support.** Use prewriting strategies like those below to develop your thinking and gather support:

   - Set up "opposing viewpoints" columns in which you list arguments accepted by advocates of each position.
   - Research the issue to find current, reliable sources from many perspectives.
   - Research other calls to action on this issue, noting their appeals, supporting evidence, and success.
   - Brainstorm the range of actions that might be taken in response to the issue. For each action, explore how attractive and doable it might be for your readers.
   - Consider what outcomes or results you want.

5. **Organize your thinking.** Consider using the following strategies:

   - Make a sharp claim (like those below) that points toward action:
     On the issue of _____, *I believe* _____.
     Therefore, we must change _____.
   - Review the evidence, and develop your line of reasoning by generating an outline or using a graphic organizer. (See pages 50–53.)
     Simple Outline: Introduction: the issue and initial claim
     　　　Describing the issue and its importance: point 1, 2, etc.
     　　　Explaining possible actions and benefits: point 1, 2, etc.
     Conclusion: call to specific action

Drafting

6. **Write your first draft.** As you write, remember your goal and specific readers:

- **Opening:** Gain the readers' attention, raise the issue, help the readers care about it, and state your claim.
- **Development:** Decide where to place your most persuasive supporting argument: first or last. Anticipate readers' questions and objections, and use appropriate logical and emotional appeals to overcome their resistance to change.
- **Closing:** Restate your claim, summarize your support, and call your readers to act.
- **Title:** Develop a thoughtful, energetic working title that stresses a vision or change. (For ideas, scan the titles of the sample essays in this chapter.)

Revising

7. **Improve the ideas, organization, and voice.** Ask a classmate or someone from the college's writing center to read your call-to-action paper for the following:

- _____ **Ideas:** Does the writing prompt readers to change their thinking and behavior? Does the essay show effective reasoning, good support, and a clear call to action—without logical fallacies such as half-truths, unreliable testimonials, attacks against a person, and false analogies (see pages 257–260)?
- _____ **Organization:** Does the opening engagingly raise the issue? Does the middle carefully press the issue and the need for action? Does the closing successfully call for specific changes and actions?
- _____ **Voice:** Is the tone energetic but controlled, confident but reasonable? Does the writing inspire readers to join your cause and act?

Editing

8. **Edit and proofread the essay by checking issues like these:**

- _____ **Words:** Language is precise, concrete, and easily understood—no jargon, clichés, doublespeak, or loaded terms.
- _____ **Sentences:** Constructions flow smoothly and are varied in structure.
- _____ **Correctness:** The copy includes no errors in grammar, punctuation, usage, or spelling.
- _____ **Design:** The page design is correctly formatted and attractive; information is properly documented according to the required system (e.g., MLA, APA).

Publishing

9. **Prepare and publish your final essay.** Submit the essay to your instructor. If appropriate, solicit feedback from another audience—perhaps on a website, in the school newspaper, at a campus club, or from a community organization.

Critical-Thinking and Writing Activities

As directed by your instructor, complete the following critical-thinking and writing activities by yourself or with classmates.

Interactive

1. The four essays in this chapter address significant social and ethical issues: wealth and poverty, health and famine, racial equality. List topics like these, choose one, narrow the focus to a specific issue, and then write an essay that persuades readers to do something related to the issue.

2. If you are a natural sciences major, consider debatable issues that are central to studying and applying the sciences—environmental, medical, biotechnical, and agricultural issues, for example. If you are a social science or humanities major, do the same brainstorming in your area. Then chose an issue where you see a need for change and write an essay in which you describe the issue and persuade readers to take the action that you recommend.

3. As a service project, visit an administrator at a local nonprofit agency (e.g., school, hospital, church, employment office, YMCA) and offer to write an editorial, news article, or letter in which you describe one of the agency's needs and persuade readers to offer their help.

4. What issues have come up in your job? Contemplate issues such as pay equity, equal opportunity, management policies, and unsafe work conditions. Then write a persuasive report to a decision maker or to fellow employees.

Learning-Outcomes Checklist

Use the checklist below to assess what you have learned about persuading readers to act.

_____ I can understand and evaluate arguments that urge readers to act.

_____ I understand how appropriate anecdotes, tests, experiments, analogies, and expert testimony can be used effectively as supporting evidence in a call-to-action paper.

_____ I can develop an argument based on reasonable rather than extreme, trivial, or unqualified claims.

_____ I can assess the quality of a persuasive essay (including my own writing) by evaluating the argument for these logical fallacies: half-truths, unreliable testimonials, personal attacks, and false analogies.

_____ I can write a compelling call-to-action paper in a mature, informed voice.

19 Proposing a Solution

Proposals are prescriptions for change. As such, they challenge readers to care about a problem, accept a solution, and act on it. A strong proposal offers a logical, practical, and creative argument that leads toward positive change, whether it's helping immigrants acquire citizenship, defending against terrorism, or requiring both men and women to register for the military draft.

Proposal writers argue for such remedies in all areas of life. In your college courses, you'll be challenged to generate solutions to many difficult problems. In your community, you may participate in policy making and civic development. In the workplace, you may write proposals that justify expenditures, sell products, or troubleshoot problems. In each situation, you'll have to clearly explain the problem, offer a solution, argue for adopting it, and possibly also explain how to implement it.

Learning Outcomes

Audio

▶ Read and assess problem/solution essays for clear information, logical claims, and reliable evidence.

▶ Analyze a problem's history, causes, effects.

Video

▶ Analyze a solution's benefits and drawbacks.

▶ Identify logical fallacies such as obfuscation, oversimplification, and slanted language.

▶ Write a convincing essay that logically analyzes a problem and proposes a reasonable solution.

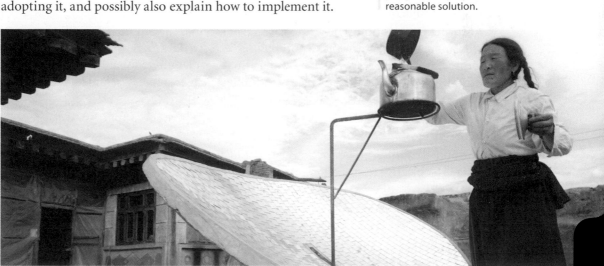

Visually Speaking ▶ Review the photograph above. What does it suggest about problems and solutions? What problem/solution writing might relate to this image?

Reading Problem-Solution Writing

The instructions below will help you understand and use problem/solution logic.

Consider the rhetorical situation.

When reading problem/solution writing, think about its purpose, audience, and topic.

- **Purpose:** Problem/solution writing aims to inform: to describe a problem accurately, to present workable solutions, and to explain the strengths and weaknesses of each. However, such writing also aims to persuade: to convince readers that a problem is urgent, that one solution is better than others, or that readers should implement it.

- **Audience:** Potentially, writers could have four audiences: people responsible for the problem, decision makers with the power to adopt a solution, people affected by the problem, and a public who just want information about the problem. When reading the document, note whether it (1) offers all of its readers the information that they need and (2) communicates in language that they can understand and trust.

- **Topic:** Clearly, problem/solution writing focuses on a problem, but it can be a problem broadly conceived—perhaps as a challenge or an opportunity. Across the college curriculum, such problems are typically discipline-related (e.g., dyslexia in Education, oil spills in Environmental Studies, agoraphobia in Psychology). In the workplace, problem/solution reasoning is used in proposals.

Consider the reasoning.

When reading problem/solution writing, look for the following:

- **Accurate Description:** The writer correctly describes the problem, including relevant details regarding its history, causes, effects, dangers, costs, and direct or indirect impact on readers. The writing also describes all reasonable solutions, including details about their history, side effects, costs, successes, and failures.

- **Thorough Analysis:** The writer carefully analyzes the problem, each solution, and why the recommended solution is the best choice. The writer supports all claims with reliable data and logical reasoning.

- **Rational Argument:** The writer's claims and appeals for action are thoughtful, stated in objective terms, and presented in a measured, informed voice.

Reader's Checklist

_____ What is the problem, what is its history, and why should the problem be resolved?

_____ What is the solution, how does it resolve the problem, and with what side effects?

_____ What action does the writer call for, and is it effective, realistic, and cost effective?

_____ Are persuasive statements reasonable, well-documented, and free of fallacies?

Proposing a Solution ■■▪■

Journalism major Renee Wielenga wrote and published "Dream Act . . ." as a newspaper article. She then revised the piece as an essay, but retained the problem/solution reasoning used in her original article.

Video

> **Outline**
> *Introduction:* (Problem) Students' dreams foiled by immigration laws; (Solution) Dream Act offers route to legal residency.
> **1.** Bill's requirements for residency and citizenship
> **2.** Bill's origin and increasing support
> **3.** Bill's remaining impediments
> *Conclusion:* The Dream Act warrants readers' support.

Title: the problem and solution

Dream Act May Help Local Student Fight for Residency

Introduction: (Problem) Students' dreams foiled by immigration laws

Attending college, joining the military, creating a career path: these are dreams for most U.S. high school graduates. But for Maria Lopez, a senior at San Marshall High School who has lived in the U.S for seven years, there is only one legal option: return to Mexico. She is one of nearly 65,000 high school students each year who do not have the opportunity to pursue their dreams because they arrived in the U.S. illegally. Like many of these students, Maria is highly motivated, hard working, and excited to be involved in her high school. However, Maria's parents brought her to this country without going through the legal immigration process. As a result, by law she is an undocumented alien who has no method to achieve legal residency while living in the U.S.

(Solution) Dream Act offers route to legal residency.

Currently, children like Maria have only one route to legal residency: go back to their country of birth, file the proper paperwork, and then return to the U.S. Unfortunately, attempts to return legally are often difficult, with roadblocks such as a ten-year restriction on re-entering the U.S. However, one piece of proposed federal legislation could help these young people pursue their dreams: The Development, Relief, and Education for Alien Minors Act (S. 729), better known as the Dream Act, is an amendment to the Illegal Immigration Reform and Immigrant Responsibility Act of 1996.

1 Bill's requirements for residency and citizenship

The current version of this bill would grant eligible immigrant students six years of conditional residency during which they could earn full citizenship. To be eligible for conditional residency, a student must: (1) graduate from a U.S. high school or obtain a GED, (2) be of good moral character, (3) have arrived in the U.S. under the age of 16, (4) have proof of residence in the U.S. for at least five consecutive years since the arrival date, and (5) be between the ages of 12 and 35 at the time of the bill's enactment. To gain full citizenship, the student must do one of the following during his or her residency: (1) complete at least two years of work toward a four-year college degree, (2) earn a two-year college degree, or (3) serve in the military for two years. If, within the six-year period, a student does not complete either the college requirement or the military-service requirement, the person would lose his or her temporary residency and be subject to deportation.

2 Bill's origin and increasing support

While the Dream Act was first introduced in 2001, and its progress toward approval has been slow, the bill's popularity has grown each year since then. For example, in March 2009, the bill was re-introduced in the U.S. Senate by Richard Durbin (D-IL) and Richard Lugar (R-IN). Also at that time, Howard Berman (D-CA), Lincoln Diaz-Balart (R-FL), Lucille Roybal-Allard (D-CA), and a number of other legislators introduced the bill in the House of Representatives where the document is called the American Dream Act (H.R. 1751). In addition to these officials, many citizens such as Maria's guidance counselor, Ben Barry, favor the bill, believing that it would give immigrant students a chance to give back to the country that has given so much to them, and the bill would offer those students an opportunity to utilize their hard-earned education and talents.

3 Bill's remaining impediments

However, as of January 2010, the bill remains in the first step in the legislative process—a process in which bills go to committees or "mini congresses" that deliberate, investigate, and revise the bill before it is brought up for general debate in either the Senate or the House of Representatives. The disheartening fact, though, is that the majority of bills never make it out of these committees. Furthermore, supporters of Comprehensive Immigration Reform (CIR) are in favor of including the Dream Act as part of CIR, which could make the Dream Act subject to change yet again.

Conclusion: The Dream Act warrants our support.

Given such debates, it might be a long time before the bill becomes law, thereby dashing the dreams of nearly 65,000 high school students like Maria who can't wait another year because they may already be in deportation proceedings. We need to step up and educate our Representatives and Senators about the importance of passing the Dream Act on its own instead of including the bill along with CIR. We need to urge them to debate and approve the Dream Act now, thereby making Maria's dreams—and the dreams of thousands of students like her—a reality!

Reading for Better Writing

Working by yourself or with a group, answer these questions:

1. What problem does Wielenga address, and how does she get readers to care about it?

2. What solution does she propose, and how does she explain or assert its value?

3. In paragraph 6, Wielenga urges readers to promote her solution. Explain why you do or do not find her rationale for action convincing.

4. As noted in the introduction, Wielenga published an earlier form of this essay in a newspaper. Given its content and tone, explain why you think this version of the piece might be appropriate for a news article, an editorial, or both.

Proposing a Solution ■■˙■

In this essay, student writer Brian Ley defines agroterrorism, predicts that it could become a serious problem, and proposes a multifaceted solution.

Audio

Video

Preparing for Agroterror

The writer opens by illustrating the problem.

An al-Qaeda terrorist in Africa obtains a sample of fluid from a cow infected with foot-and-mouth disease, and he sends the fluid to an accomplice in a small, rural American town. This terrorist takes the sample around the country, stopping at several points to place small amounts of the fluid on objects that animals are likely to touch. When he is finished, he drives to the nearest airport and leaves the country unnoticed.   1

Cows, pigs, and sheep then come into contact with this highly contagious disease. Over the next few days, farmers see blisters on the feet and mouths of their animals. Thinking that the animals have a bacterial infection, the farmers administer antibiotics and wait for improvement. However, because antibiotics can't kill a virus, the animals get sicker. Meanwhile, the virus is spreading by means of wind and the movement of animals and humans. Within a few weeks, the virus is out of control.   2

While the story above is hypothetical, it is also very possible. People used to think of terrorists as men in ski masks blowing up embassies and taking hostages. But after the events of September 11, 2001, and the subsequent anthrax scares, it is clear that more kinds of terrorism are possible.   3

He defines the problem and presents expert testimony.

One type rarely considered is agroterrorism, which involves using diseases as weapons to attack a country's agriculture industry in order to attack the country itself. The agroterrorist's weapons of choice are those diseases that affect plants, animals, and even humans. Professor Peter Chalk of the RAND Corporation, an expert on transnational terrorism, believes that agroterrorism should be a huge concern for Americans because it has many advantages from a terrorist's point of view (37).   4

He analyzes why the problem could become serious.

First of all, an attack on the agricultural sector of the United States would be quite easy. The diseases needed to kill large populations of animals can be obtained with little difficulty; the most devastating ones are ready for use in their natural form. These samples pose little risk to the terrorist because many of the diseases are harmless to humans.   5

In addition, doing agroterrorism is less risky in terms of getting caught and getting punished. Agroterrorism is hard to trace, especially because Americans have assumed that all animal epidemics are natural in origin and that American livestock contract such diseases only by accident. Consequences for those caught inflicting a disease on animals are also less severe than for terrorists who harm   6 humans. In fact, because agroterrorism first affects the health of plants and animals rather than humans, terrorists using this strategy can even escape some guilt for their actions.

Using specific details, he outlines the problem's potential effects.

However, while agroterrorist diseases would have little direct effect on people's health, they would be devastating to the agricultural economy, in part because of the many different diseases that could be used in an attack. One of the most devastating is foot-and-mouth disease. This illness hurts all infected animals by impeding their weight gain, and it hurts dairy cows in particular by decreasing their milk production. Because the disease is highly contagious, all infected animals, along with any cloven-hoofed animals within about 50 miles of the infection site, must be killed.

While foot-and-mouth disease is not dangerous to humans, other animal diseases are. One of these is bovine spongiform encephalopathy, better known as mad-cow disease ("Mad Cow"). This illness is not easily spread, but a few cases in the United States would send people into a panic. Meat consumption would drop sharply, and the agricultural economy would be deeply shaken.

Another disease that could be used as a weapon is West Nile encephalitis. This virus can be spread by insects and can even cross species, affecting horses, birds, pigs, and humans. It is a fatal illness without a vaccination or a cure. These diseases are likely candidates for use in an agroterrorist attack (Smith 249).

The agricultural community is particularly susceptible to a terrorist attack. Unlike "typical" terrorist targets in metropolitan areas, farms do not have sophisticated security systems to protect against intruders. The average farmer's security system includes a mean dog and a shotgun: the dog for humans and the gun for animal pests. If terrorists wanted to infect a dairy, swine operation, or even a large-scale cattle-finishing operation, they would encounter few obstacles. The terrorists merely have to place a piece of infected food in an area with livestock. This single action could start an epidemic.

The writer proposes a multifaceted solution.

Agroterrorism is a threat that demands a response. Several actions can be taken to discourage terrorism as well as to deal with its consequences. One of the first steps is convincing all citizens—farmers and nonfarmers alike—that agroterrorism could happen, and that it could cause horrific consequences. Farmers must realize that they are susceptible to an attack even though they may live far from large metropolitan areas. Nonfarmers must realize how an attack could affect them. If nonfarmers know that an attack could create panic, drive up food prices, and possibly eliminate food sources, they will look out for suspicious activity and report it.

Preventive action on farms is needed to ensure the safety of the food supply. For example, the South Dakota Animal Industry Board recently published a newsletter outlining several precautions that farmers can take. Farms should have better security, especially in areas where animals are kept. These security measures include allowing only authorized persons to have access to farm buildings and animals and keeping all key farm buildings locked ("Precautions").

Farmers also need training to detect the diseases that terrorists might use *13* and to know what actions can contain and decontaminate an infected area. For example, if a farmer discovers that cows have blisters on their tongues and noses, and that they are behaving abnormally, the owner should immediately call a veterinarian to assess the situation. Because the disease might be foot-and-mouth, no cattle should leave the farm until a diagnosis has been made.

In addition, public authorities need a plan for responding to an identified *14* agroterrorism attack. For example, thousands of animals may have to be killed and disposed of—an action with significant environmental concerns. Moreover, public money should be used for continued research of the diseases that may be spread by agroterrorists. Vaccines and treatments may be produced that would stop diseases or limit them from becoming epidemic.

Agroterrorism has not yet been used on a large scale anywhere on the globe. *15* However, its use seems inevitable. The United States is a prime target for terrorism of this sort because the country has the largest, most efficiently raised food supply in the world. Destroying part of this supply would affect not only the United States but also all those countries with whom it trades. Because the United States is a prime target, it must act now to develop its defenses against agroterrorism. If the country waits until an attack happens, people may become ill, the overall economy could be damaged, and the agricultural economy may never recover.

> The closing stresses the problem's seriousness and calls for action.

Note: The Works Cited page is not shown. For sample pages, see MLA (pages 526–527) and APA (page 557).

Reading for Better Writing

Working by yourself or with a group, answer these questions:

1. This essay predicts that a problem may develop. Is the writer's prediction persuasive? Why or why not?

2. What tactics does the writer use to get readers concerned about the problem? Are these strategies successful?

3. The solution proposed is multifaceted. Briefly list who must do what. Is this solution persuasive? Is it workable? Does it get at root causes?

4. A strong proposal provides convincing evidence about both the problem and the solution. Trace the evidence used in this essay. Are the types of evidence convincing? Do any gaps need to be filled?

Proposing a Solution ▪▪▪

Anna Quindlen's *New York Times* column "Public and Private" won the 1992 Pulitzer Prize for commentary. She now writes a regular column for *Newsweek,* where "Uncle Sam and Aunt Samantha" was originally published in 2001.

Uncle Sam and Aunt Samantha

Each of the first five paragraphs is one sentence long.

One out of every five new recruits in the United States military is female.   *1*

The Marines gave the Combat Action Ribbon for service in the Persian Gulf   *2* to 23 women.

Two female soldiers were killed in the bombing of the *USS Cole*.   *3*

The Selective Service registers for the draft all male citizens between the ages   *4* of 18 and 25.

The writer identifies the problem that she wants solved.

What's wrong with this picture?   *5*

As Americans read and realize that the lives of most women in this country   *6* are as different from those of Afghan women as a Cunard cruise is from maximum-security lockdown, there has nonetheless been little attention paid to one persistent gender inequity in U.S. public policy. An astonishing anachronism, really: While women are represented today in virtually all fields, including the armed forces, only men are required to register for the military draft that would be used in the event of a national-security crisis.

She provides background about the source and history of the problem.

Since the nation is as close to such a crisis as it has been in more than sixty   *7* years, it's a good moment to consider how the draft wound up in this particular time warp. It's not the time warp of the Taliban, certainly, stuck in the worst part of the 13th century, forbidding women to attend school or hold jobs or even reveal their arms, forcing them into sex and marriage. Our own time warp is several decades old. The last time the draft was considered seriously was twenty years ago, when registration with the Selective Service was restored by Jimmy Carter after the Soviet invasion of, yep, Afghanistan. The president, as well as the Army chief of staff, asked at the time for the registration of women as well as men.

Amid a welter of arguments—women interfere with esprit de corps, women   *8* don't have the physical strength, women prisoners could be sexually assaulted, women soldiers would distract male soldiers from their mission—Congress shot down the notion of gender-blind registration. So did the Supreme Court, ruling that since women were forbidden to serve in combat positions and the purpose of the draft was to create a combat-ready force, it made sense not to register them.

But that was then, and this is now. Women have indeed served in combat   *9* positions, in the Balkans and the Middle East. More than 40,000 managed to serve in the Persian Gulf without destroying unit cohesion or failing because of upper-body strength. Some are even now taking out targets in Afghanistan from fighter jets, and apparently without any male soldier's falling prey to some predicted excess of chivalry or lust.

Talk about cognitive dissonance. All these military personnel, male and *10* female alike, have come of age at a time when a significant level of parity was taken for granted. Yet they are supposed to accept that only males will be required to defend their country in a time of national emergency. This is insulting to men. And it is insulting to women. Caroline Forell, an expert on women's legal rights and a professor at the University of Oregon School of Law, puts it bluntly: "Failing to require this of women makes us lesser citizens."

Yet they are supposed to accept that only males will be required to defend their country . . .

Neither the left nor the right has been particularly *11* inclined to consider this issue judiciously. Many feminists came from the antiwar movement and have let their distaste for the military in general and the draft in particular mute their response. In 1980 NOW [National Organization for Women] released a resolution that buried support for the registration of women beneath opposition to the draft, despite the fact that the draft had been redesigned to eliminate the vexing inequities of Vietnam, when the sons of the working class served and the sons of the Ivy League did not. Conservatives, meanwhile, used an equal-opportunity draft as the linchpin of opposition to the Equal Rights Amendment, along with the terrifying specter of unisex bathrooms. (I have seen the urinal, and it is benign.) The legislative director of the right-wing group Concerned Women for America once defended the existing regulations by saying that most women "don't want to be included in the draft." All those young men who went to Canada during Vietnam and those who today register with fear and trembling in the face of the Trade Center devastation might be amazed to discover that lack of desire is an affirmative defense.

Parents face a series of unique new challenges in this more egalitarian world, *12* not the least of which would be sending a daughter off to war. But parents all over this country are doing that right now, with daughters who enlisted; some have even expressed surprise that young women, in this day and age, are not required to register alongside their brothers and friends. While all involved in this debate over the years have invoked the assumed opposition of the people, even ten years ago more than half of all Americans polled believed women should be made eligible for the draft. Besides, this is not about comfort but about fairness. My son has to register with the Selective Service this year, and if his sister does not when she turns 18, it makes a mockery not only of the standards of this household but of the standards of this nation.

Margin notes:

A quotation helps to explain why the writer understands the situation to be a problem.

The writer anticipates and addresses counter-arguments to her position.

She supports her position with statistics as well as personal anecdotes and comparisons to other situations.

The writer appeals to the reader's logic and ethics.

It is possible in Afghanistan for women to be treated like little more than 13 fecund pack animals precisely because gender fear and ignorance and hatred have been codified and permitted to hold sway. In this country, largely because of the concerted efforts of those allied with the women's movement over a century of struggle, much of that bigotry has been beaten back, even buried. Yet in improbable places the creaky old ways surface, the ways suggesting that we women were made of finer stuff. The finer stuff was usually porcelain, decorative and on the shelf, suitable for meals and show. Happily, the finer stuff has been transmuted into the right stuff. But with rights come responsibilities, as teachers like to tell their students. This is a responsibility that should fall equally upon all, male and female alike. If the empirical evidence is considered rationally, if the decision is divested of outmoded stereotypes, that's the only possible conclusion to be reached.

> *This is a responsibility that should fall equally upon all, male and female alike.*

Reading for Better Writing

Working by yourself or with a group, answer these questions:

1. Which problem(s) does Quindlen identify? Which solution(s) does she propose? To what extent would the proposed solution(s) solve the problem(s) Quindlen discusses?

2. Review the section in chapter 16 about "Identifying Logical Fallacies" (see pages 257–260). Quindlen's opponents might accuse her of "either/or thinking," pointing out that instead of addressing only two options, she could also have argued to end the draft for everyone. Which other logical fallacies might Quindlen's opponents accuse her of making? Would you agree with them? Why or why not?

3. Which strategies does Quindlen use to try to convince readers that the situation she describes is problematic?

4. Why does the writer acknowledge that there may be opposition to her description of the problem and to her proposed solution? How does she respond to these counterarguments?

5. Why does the essay open with a series of one-sentence paragraphs? How might the effect of the essay differ if these sentences had been combined into one paragraph?

Proposing a Solution ■ ▪ ■

Paul Bignell published the essay below in the December 13, 2009, edition of *The Independent*. In the essay, he describes dying languages across the globe and argues that their loss would significantly diminish world culture. He closes by urging readers to be informed about the problem and to pursue workable solutions.

As you read, take notes about the author's presentation of both the problem and the solution, as well as your response to his argument.

The beckoning silence: Why half of the world's languages are in serious danger of dying out

High up, perched among the remote hilltops of eastern Nepal, sits a shaman, resting on his haunches in long grass. He is dressed simply, in a dark waistcoat and traditional kurta tunic with a Nepalese cap sitting snugly on his head. To his left and right, two men hold recording devices several feet from his face, listening patiently to his precious words. His tongue elicits sounds alien to all but a few people in the world, unfamiliar even to those who inhabit his country. His eyes flicker with all the intensity of a man reciting for the first time to a western audience his tribe's version of the Book of Genesis, its myth of origins. *1*

The shaman's story is centuries old, passed down from one generation to the next through chants, poems, songs, proverbs and plain story-telling. Yet this narrative and, indeed, his entire language have never been recorded in text. And, faced with the onslaught of rapid globalization and social change, they are dying. Whether it be through well-intentioned national education programs in Nepalese, the younger generation leaving for bigger Asian cities or simply the death of elders, the day when no one will speak the ancient tongue of the Rai tribe is fast approaching. *2*

The plight of the shaman's language and that of his community is by no means confined to this small, but beautiful area of Nepal; it is the apparent fate of thousands of communities, societies, and indigenous groups all around the world. But not if Dr. Mark Turin can help it. *3*

The University of Cambridge academic is leading a project that aims to pull thousands of languages back from the brink of extinction by recording and archiving words, poems, chants—anything that can be committed to tape—in a bid to halt their destruction. Languages the majority of us will never know anything about. *4*

Of the world's 6,500 living languages, around half are expected to die out by the end of this century, according to Unesco. Just 11 are spoken by more than half the earth's population, so it is little wonder that those used by only a few are being left behind as we become a more homogenous, global society. In short, 95 percent of the world's languages are spoken by only five per cent of its population—a remarkable level of linguistic diversity stored in tiny pockets of speakers around the world. *5*

In a small office room in the back of Cambridge's Museum of Archaeology & Anthropology—a place in which you almost expect Harrison Ford to walk around the corner at any moment, fedora on head, whip in hand —Turin looks over the contents of a box that arrived earlier in the morning from India. "[The receptionists] *6* are quite used to getting these boxes now," says the 36-year-old anthropologist, who is based at the university. Inside the box, which is covered in dozens of rupee postage stamps, are DVDs representing hours of chants, songs, poems and literature from a tiny Indian community that is desperate for its language to have a voice and be included in Turin's venture.

For many of these communities, the oral tradition is at the heart of their   7
culture. The stories they tell are creative works as well as communicative. Unlike the languages with celebrated written traditions, such as Sanskrit, Hebrew and Ancient Greek, few indigenous communities—from the Kallawaya tribe in Bolivia and the Maka in Paraguay to the Siberian language of Chulym, to India's Arunachal Pradesh state Aka group and the Australian Aboriginal Amurdag community—have recorded their own languages or ever had them recorded. Until now. Turin launched the World Oral Literature Project earlier this year with an aim to document and make accessible endangered languages before they disappear without trace.

He is trying to encourage indigenous communities to collaborate with   8
anthropologists around the world to record what he calls "oral literature" through video cameras, voice recorders and other multimedia tools by awarding grants from a £30,000 pot that the project has secured this year. The idea is to collate this literature in a digital archive that can be accessed on demand and will make the nuts and bolts of lost cultures readily available. As useful as this archive will be for Western academic study—the World Oral Literature Project is convening for its first international workshop in Cambridge this week—Turin believes it is of vital importance that the scheme also be used by the communities he and his researchers are working with.

The project suggested itself when Turin was teaching in Nepal. He wanted to   9
study for a Ph.D. in endangered languages and, while discussing it with his professor at Leiden University in the Netherlands, was drawn to a map on his tutor's wall. The map was full of pins of a variety of colors which represented all the world's languages that were completely undocumented. At random, Turin chose a "pin" to document. It happened to belong to the Thangmi tribe, an indigenous community in the hills east of Kathmandu, the capital of Nepal. "Many of the choices anthropologists and linguists who work on these traditional field-work projects take are quite random," he admits. "There's a lot of serendipity involved."

Continuing his work with the Thangmi community in the 1990s, Turin began   10
to record the language he was hearing, realizing that not only was this language and its culture entirely undocumented, it was known to few outside the tiny community. He set about trying to record their language and myth of origins. "I wrote 1,000 pages of grammar in English that nobody could use—but I realized that wasn't enough. It wasn't enough for me, it wasn't enough for them. It simply wasn't going to work as something for the community. So then I produced this trilingual word list in Thangmi, Nepali and English."

In short, it was the first ever publication of that language. That small dictionary *11* is still sold in local schools for a modest 20 rupees, and used as part of a wider cultural regeneration process to educate children about their heritage and language. The task is no small undertaking: Nepal itself is a country of massive ethnic and linguistic diversity, home to 100 languages from four different language families. What's more, ever fewer ethnic Thangmi speak the Thangmi language. Many of the community members have taken to speaking Nepali, the national language taught in schools and spread through the media, and community elders are dying without passing on their knowledge.

Since the project got under way, along with similar ventures by the National *12* Geographic initiative Enduring Voices, the Hans Rausing Endangered Languages Project and the Arcadia Fund, many more communities around the world have similarly either requested inclusion or responded to the suggestion that their language is in need of recording. (One task involved making recordings of ceremonial chants of the Barasana language, spoken by just 1,890 people in the Vaupés region of Columbia.)

The lexicographer Dr. Sarah Ogilvie worked with the Umagico Aboriginal *13* community at Cape York Peninsula in northern Australia, for example. Like Turin, she developed an entire dictionary of the community's language, Morrobalama—the first time their purely oral language had ever been written and recorded. Living with the community for a year-and-a-half in difficult conditions and being the only non-native person in the group, she began learning the language from scratch, as no one spoke English.

"As a lexicographer, I wanted to look at how we could write better dictionaries *14* of languages that are dying—that not only preserve the language, but can be used as practical tools themselves," says Ogilvie.

After learning Morrobalama orally, she started her dictionary by writing the *15* words down in the International Phonetic Alphabet. Then, by looking for patterns in the sounds, she was able to come up with a unique writing system. "I was lucky in the sense that no one else had tried to record the language before; often for linguists, the situation is made more complex if someone has already attempted to record the language before them—it may have been written badly, yet you can't erase it and the community might have actually become quite attached to it."

Despite Turin's enthusiasm for his subject, he is baffled by many linguists' refusal *16* to engage in the issue he is working on. "Of the 6,500 languages spoken on Earth, many do not have written traditions and many of these spoken forms are endangered," he says. "There are more linguists in universities around the world than there are spoken languages—but most of them aren't working on this issue. To me it's amazing that in this day and age, we still have an entirely incomplete image of the world's linguistic diversity. People do Ph.D.s on the apostrophe in French, yet we still don't know how many languages are spoken.

"When a language becomes endangered, so too does a cultural world view. We 17 want to engage with indigenous people to document their myths and folklore, which can be harder to find funding for if you are based outside Western universities. If you are a Himalayan tribesman, you might not have access to a video camera to record your shaman and elders."

While these languages may seem remote and distant, it is worth remembering 18 that British languages such as Welsh and Gaelic were in danger of becoming extinct not so long ago. In fact, Turin admits that these languages, too, including Cornish, need considerable effort to keep them going. "People often think it's only tribal cultures that are under threat. But all over Europe there are pockets of traditional communities and speech forms that have become extinct. It is the domain of stronger nation states with better resources to look after their own indigenous tongues, through Welsh-language TV, for example, and for those from north-western France, Breton literature."

Similar to the introduction of the Welsh Language Act in 1993, the Scottish 19 Government is moving to protect and promote Gaelic. A new agreement means that Gaelic can now be used formally in meetings between Scottish government ministers and EU officials. An extra £800,000 was also pledged for a project promoting Gaelic in schools, taking the level of funding to £2.15m. Nevertheless, Scottish Gaelic is not one of the EU's list of 23 "official" languages.

Yet, despite the struggles facing initiatives such as the World Oral Literature 20 Project, there are historical examples that point to the possibility that language restoration is no mere academic pipe dream. The revival of a modern form of Hebrew in the 19th century is often cited as one of the best proofs that languages long dead, belonging to small communities, can be resurrected and embraced by a large number of people. By the 20th century, Hebrew was well on its way to becoming the main language of the Jewish population of both Ottoman and British Palestine. It is now spoken by more than seven million people in Israel.

Turin's projects receive a tiny fraction of the amounts spent in the UK on 21 promoting language, but he believes there is much more at stake than even language and culture in the communities he works with: their extinction hints at dangers for the very biodiversity of their homelands, too. Experts now agree that there is a correlation between areas of cultural, linguistic and biological diversity. The mountain ranges, rivers and gorges that might isolate a human community and lead to the development of their specific native tongue are often the same geographical features that give rise to specialized ecosystems.

"The more flora and fauna you have, the more you can eat, therefore the less 22 people have to trade, minimizing the effects of interaction with other outside influences," he says. "In parts of Papua New Guinea, for example, five minutes away from your house you have everything you need to survive. Places that are diverse in species are diverse in languages and cultures." In other words, if the locals start speaking other languages, it is indicative of a growing outside influence—and that can be bad news for the ecology.

Yet, despite the difficulties these communities face in saving their languages, 23 Dr. Turin believes that the fate of the world's endangered languages is not sealed, and globalization is not necessarily the nefarious perpetrator of evil it is often presented to be. "I call it the globalization paradox: on the one hand globalization and rapid socio-economic change are the things that are eroding and challenging diversity. But on the other, globalization is providing us with new and very exciting tools and facilities to get to places to document those things that globalization is eroding. Also, the communities at the coal-face of change are excited by what globalization has to offer."

In the meantime, the race is on to collect and protect as many of the languages 24 as possible, so that the Rai Shaman in eastern Nepal and those in the generations that follow him, can continue their traditions and have a sense of identity. And it certainly is a race: Turin knows his project's limits and believes it inevitable that a large number of those languages will disappear. "We have to be wholly realistic. A project like ours is in no position, and was not designed, to keep languages alive. The only people who can help languages survive are the people in those communities themselves. They need to be reminded that it's good to speak their own language and I think we can help them do that—becoming modern doesn't mean you have to lose your language."

[For more information visit the Hans Rausing Endangered Languages Project, www. hrelp.org and the World Oral Literature Project, www.oralliterature.org]

Reading for Better Writing

Working by yourself or with a group, answer the following questions:

1. Describe the problem that Bignell addresses, cite two or three examples, and explain why he thinks that situation should be resolved.

2. The writer uses anecdotes, quotations, and data to show that the demise of languages is a problem worth solving. Cite three passages that you find effective and explain why.

3. Identify two efforts or solutions that the writer suggests might help resolve the problem. Describe the efforts and assess their potential effectiveness.

4. Has the writer convinced you that the problem is real and warrants solving? Explain.

Writing Guidelines

Model

Planning

1. **Select and narrow a topic.** Brainstorm possibilities from this list:
   - **People Problems:** Consider generations—your own or a relative's. What problems face this generation? Why, and how can they be solved?
   - **College Problems:** List problems faced by college students. In your major, what problems are experts trying to solve?
   - **Social Problems:** What problems do our communities and country face? Where do you see suffering, injustice, inequity, waste, or harm?
   - **Workplace Problems:** What job-related problems have you experienced or might you experience?

   Then test your topic:
   - Is the problem real, serious, and currently—or potentially—harmful?
   - Do you care about this problem and believe that it must be solved? Why?
   - Can you offer a workable solution—or should you focus on part of the problem?

2. **Identify and analyze your audience.** You could have four audiences: people responsible for the problem, decision makers with the power to deliver change, people affected by the problem, and a public that wants to learn about it.
   - What do readers know about the problem? What are their questions or concerns?
   - Why might they accept or resist change? What solution might they prefer?
   - What arguments and evidence would convince them to acknowledge the problem, to care about it, and to take action?

3. **Probe the problem.** If helpful, use the graphic organizer on page 53.
   - **Define the problem.** What is it, exactly? What are its parts or dimensions?
   - **Determine the problem's seriousness.** Why should it be fixed? Who is affected and how? What are its immediate, long-term, and potential effects?
   - **Analyze causes.** What are its root causes and contributing factors?
   - **Explore context.** What is the problem's background, history, and connection to other problems? What solutions have been tried in the past? Who, if anyone, benefits from the problem's existence?
   - **Think creatively.** Look at the problem from other perspectives—other states and countries, both genders, different races and ethnic groups, and so on.

4. **Choose the best solution.** List all imaginable solutions—both modest and radical fixes. Then evaluate the alternatives:
   - List criteria that any solution should meet.
   - List solutions and analyze their strengths, weaknesses, costs, and so on.
   - Choose the best solution and gather evidence supporting your choice.

Drafting

5. Outline your proposal and complete a first draft. Describe the problem, offer a solution, and defend it using strategies that fit your purpose and audience.

■ **The problem:** Inform and/or persuade readers about the problem by using appropriate background information, cause/effect analysis, examples, analogies, parallel cases, visuals, and expert testimony.

■ **The solution:** If necessary, first argue against alternative solutions. Then present your solution, stating what should happen, who should be involved, and why.

■ **The support:** Show how the solution solves the problem. Use facts and analysis to argue that your solution is feasible and to address objections. If appropriate, use visuals such as photographs, drawings, or graphics to help readers grasp the nature and impact of the problem.

Revising

6. Improve the ideas, organization, and voice. Ask a classmate or someone from the college's writing center to read your call-to-action paper for the following:

_____ **Ideas:** Does the solution fit the problem? Is the proposal precise, well researched, and well reasoned—free from oversimplification and obfuscation?

_____ **Organization:** Does the writing move convincingly from problem to solution, using fitting compare/contrast, cause/effect, and process structures?

_____ **Voice:** Is the tone positive, confident, objective, and sensitive to opposing viewpoints—and appropriate to the problem's seriousness.

Editing

7. Edit and proofread the essay. Look for these issues:

_____ **Words:** Words are precise, effectively defined, and clear.

_____ **Sentences:** Sentences are smooth, energetic, and varied in structure.

_____ **Correctness:** The copy has correct grammar, spelling, usage, and mechanics.

_____ **Design:** The design includes proper formatting and documentation.

Publishing

8. Prepare and share your final essay. Submit your proposal to your instructor, but also consider sharing it with audiences who have a stake in solving the problem.

Critical-Thinking and Writing Activities

As directed by your instructor, complete the following critical-thinking and writing activities by yourself or with classmates.

Interactive

1. Note that Renee Wielenga initially wrote her essay in journalistic style and published the piece in a regional newspaper. Select a problem in your community, research the problem, and then write a news article or an editorial on the topic. Use problem/solution reasoning and submit the piece to your college or community newspaper.

2. "Preparing for Agroterror" predicts that a problem might develop. Thinking about current conditions and trends, forecast a problem, and write a proposal explaining how to prepare for or prevent it.

3. Review the section in chapter 16 about "Engaging the Opposition" (pages 261–263). Also review how Anna Quindlen engages her opposition in "Uncle Sam and Aunt Samantha." Then consider a persuasive piece that you are drafting or revising. How might you engage the opposition in a dialogue about your arguments? Revise your writing as needed.

4. Review the section in chapter 16 about "Identifying Logical Fallacies" (pages 257–260). Write a humorous problem/solution essay in which you make an argument that includes a number of obvious logical fallacies. Share your writing with the class.

5. What are some challenges facing the planet Earth and the human race in the foreseeable future? Find a focused challenge and write a proposal that addresses it.

Learning-Outcomes Checklist

Use the checklist below to identify what you have learned from this chapter and what you should review.

_____ I can read and evaluate problem/solution essays for clear information, logical claims, and reliable evidence.

_____ I can analyze a problem's history, causes, effects, and impact on my intended readers.

_____ I can analyze potential solutions, evaluate their strengths and weaknesses, select the best solution, and rationally explain my choice.

_____ I can identify and correct logical fallacies such as obfuscation, oversimplification, and slanted language.

_____ I can write a convincing essay that rationally analyzes a problem, proposes a reasonable solution, and advocates its implementation.

Report Writing

It's tempting to suggest that the contents of reports include "just the facts." Whether they focus on interviews (chapter 20) or scientific research (chapter 21), reports at first glance seek only to share with readers the objective results of primary research. However, a more careful reading of reports reveals that they do much more. For example, the reports in this section not only describe their topics, but also use analytical strategies (such as cause-effect) to interpret or explain the activities that they describe.

As you read the various types of reports in this section, note both the research methods and organizational strategies used by each writer. Then, as you write your own report, choose research methods and writing strategies that fit your rhetorical situation: your audience, your purpose, and your subject.

Report Writing

20 Interview Report

An interview is a question-and-answer session with someone—an expert on a topic, a client, or a case-study subject—to gain insight into the topic and/or person. You might use what you learn as primary-source information, or you might use the interview as an entire piece of writing, such as an interview report.

Conducting a productive interview and writing a good report requires careful planning. Planning gives you background information and helps you develop questions that produce solid data, vivid details, and lively quotations—the qualities that engage readers and create memorable reading.

Learning Outcomes

 Read and evaluate interview reports.

 Plan and schedule an interview.

 Write both open and closed questions.

 Conduct the interview and take accurate notes.

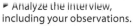 Analyze the interview, including your observations.

▶ Write the report with effective quotations, summaries, paraphrases, and a unifying theme.

Audio

Video

Visually Speaking ▶ Review the photograph above. What does it suggest about conducting interviews and writing interview reports?

■ Reading Interview Reports

The instructions below will help you read and evaluate interview reports.

Consider the rhetorical situation. ■▪■

When reading an interview report, think about how the writer's purpose, audience, and topic influence the questions asked and the answers offered.

- **Purpose:** A good writer interviews a person to get reliable, primary-source information that reveals the individual's insights, reflections, and feelings about the topic. The writer then uses that information respectfully to write a report with correct details and quotations, and accurate analysis of what the interviewee said and did.

- **Audience:** Interview reports written within an organization (e.g., college or business) usually address topics important to the organization and are intended for readers within the organization. However, interview reports in magazines such as *People, Sports Illustrated,* or *Business Weekly* address topics that interest the publication's readers.

- **Topic:** If the purpose for writing is to describe or analyze the interviewee, then the person interviewed is the topic. However, if the purpose is to gain the interviewee's insights or ideas about someone or something else, then the interviewee is a source for information about the topic. For example, in the report on pages 327–329, the mortuary business is the topic, and the mortician interviewed is a source.

Consider the interview process. ■▪■

When reading interview reports, note how successful writers do the following:

- **Ask clear, relevant questions.** Getting quality information depends on the art of interviewing—planning relevant questions, listening well, taking good notes, following up with sensible responses, and being open to surprises.

- **Respect the interviewee's ideas, feelings, and voice.** Good writers seek to understand the interviewee's story, values, and personality. These interviewers listen much more than talk. They communicate their subject's words, ideas, and voice through accurate description, summaries, paraphrases, and quotations.

- **Analyze and synthesize the results.** Analysis helps a writer understand pieces of information, and synthesis helps the person show how the pieces are related. A good writer does both in order to develop a unified essay with a meaningful theme.

Reader's Checklist

_____ Does the opening introduce the interview's setting, subject, and context?

_____ Are the questions clear and do they evoke interesting, meaningful information?

_____ Does the writer effectively use summaries, paraphrases, and quotations to communicate the person's ideas, feelings, and personality?

Interview Report

Because of a disturbing childhood experience, college student Benjamin Meyer toured a funeral home and interviewed the director. In the following essay, Benjamin reports on what he learned.

The Dead Business

"You're going to tour a what?"   1

"A funeral home."   2

My friends were shocked. They laughed while describing scenes from *Night*   3
of the Living Dead and *The Shining*.

But their stories didn't frighten me—I feared something else. When I was ten,   4
my grandmother died, and my family drove to the funeral home to view the body.
As we entered the place, I noticed the funeral director standing in the corner,
looking like a too-eager-to-please salesman who'd made a deal he didn't deserve.
The guy's thin-lipped smile seemed unnatural—almost glib. Like a ghoul in a
business suit, he didn't seem to care that a stroke had stopped my grandmother's
beating heart midway through the doxology that concluded the Sunday-evening
church service. He didn't seem to care that she and I would share no more cookies,
no more coloring books, no more Rook games, no more laughing, no more. I was
ten, very sad, and he didn't seem to care.

Now a college student, I wanted to tour a different funeral home to work   5
through my earlier experience. While I no longer feared ghouls, I was still nervous
while driving to the Vander Ploeg Furniture Store/Funeral Home. I remembered
the thin-lipped smile.

I walked inside not knowing what to expect. Suddenly, a man from behind a   6
desk hopped out of his chair and said, "Hi, I'm Howard Beernink."

I looked at the tall, smiling guy, paused a moment, and glanced back at the   7
door. His partner had stepped in front of the exit while scribbling on tags that
dangled from Lazy Boy rockers. I realized that this interview was something I had
to do . . . like getting a tetanus shot.

Howard led me into a room full of furniture where he found a soft, purple   8
couch. We sat down, and he described how the business started.

In 1892, pioneers established the town of Sioux Center, Iowa. Winter storms   9
and disease pummeled the tiny community, and soon residents needed someone
to bury the dead. A funeral director wasn't available, but a furniture maker
was. The furniture maker was the only person with the tools, hardwood, and
knowledge to build coffins. As a result, the Vander Ploeg Furniture Store/Funeral
Home was born.

Marginal notes:

The writer starts with background information that creates a personal theme.

Freely using "I," the writer tells the story of his visit and interview.

He describes the setting.

He relates the early history of the business.

Today, starting a funeral home isn't that easy. For example, a funeral home *10*
requires the services of an embalmer, and an embalmer must be certified by the
state. To get a certificate, the person must complete two years of college, one year
of embalming school, and one year of apprentice work. After that, the individual
must pass a state exam every year to retain certification.

"But why a funeral home director?" I was baffled. Why would anyone embalm *11*
dead bodies for a living?

"Because it's a family business." Howard smiled as if he expected my question. *12*
"Vander Ploegs and Beerninks have run this place for generations. Today it's
difficult to start a funeral home because there are so many of them with long
histories and good reputations."

After he answered the rest of my questions, Howard asked if I wanted to see *13*
the embalming room.

"Okay," I said, tentatively. *14*

He led me through doors, down hallways, up a staircase, and into a well- *15*
lighted display room containing several coffins. Finally, we entered a small, cold
room containing a row of cupboards, a large ceramic table, and a small machine
that resembled a bottled-water cooler.

"We like to keep the room cold when we're not using it," Howard said. *16*

"What is all this stuff?" I asked. *17*

Howard described why embalming is done and what it involves. The purpose *18*
of embalming is to extend the period for viewing the body, and the process
includes replacing body fluids with embalming fluid. He opened a cupboard,
pulled out a bottle of fluid and said, "Here . . . smell."

"Smells like Pepto-Bismol," I replied. *19*

After he embalms the body, Howard applies makeup so the face appears *20*
"more natural." He gets his cosmetics (common powders and tints) from the local
Avon lady.

"But sometimes we also have to use this," Howard said, pulling out another *21*
bottle.

"Tissue builder?" I asked, squinting at the label. *22*

"It's like silicon implants," he answered. "We inject it into sunken cheeks, like *23*
the cheeks of cancer victims."

When the body is ready for burial, the funeral director must show a price list *24*
to the family of the deceased. The Funeral Rule, adopted in 1984 by the Federal
Trade Commission, requires that a price list be shown to the family before they see
caskets, cement boxes, and vaults. The purpose of the Funeral Rule is to prevent
unethical funeral directors from manipulating customers with comments like,

"But that's a pauper's casket; you don't want to bury your mother in that. Bury her in this beauty over here." Unfortunately, only a third of the country's 22,000 funeral homes abide by the Funeral Rule.

"After showing customers where the caskets are, I step away so they can talk 25 among themselves," said Howard. "It's unethical to bother the family at this difficult time."

Before burying a casket, Howard and his partner place it in either a cement 26 box or a vault. A cement box is a container that's neither sealed nor waterproofed, whereas a vault is both sealed and waterproofed. Howard explained, "Years ago, cemeteries began to sink and cave in on spots, so state authorities demanded containers. Containers make the cemetery look nicer."

After the tour, I asked Howard, "How has this job affected your life?" 27

He glanced at the ceiling, smiled, and said, "It's very fulfilling. My partner 28 and I comfort people during a stressful time in their lives, and it strengthens our bond with them."

> He ends the report with a strong quotation and personal reflection.

As I drove back to the college, I thought again about Howard's comment, and 29 about my childhood fear. Howard was right. He doesn't exploit people. Instead, he comforts them and helps them move on. And while I still fear the pain of saying good-bye to someone I love, I don't fear funeral directors anymore. They're just people who provide services that a community needs.

Reading for Better Writing

Working by yourself or with a group, answer these questions:

1. This report centers on the writer's own story, reflections, and needs. Discuss how these elements are woven into the report. Are they effective? Why or why not?

2. Examine the opening and the closing of the essay. Do they work well together? Do they effectively share a theme for the report? Explain.

3. Describe how the writer organizes the interview's results. Is the organization effective? Explain.

4. Look carefully at the writer's use of summary and paraphrase on the one hand and quotation on the other hand. Are the strategies effective? Explain.

Writing Guidelines

Model

Planning

1. **Choose a topic and a person to interview.** If your purpose is to write about a specific person, choose someone intriguing. However, if your purpose is to use the interviewee as a resource, interview someone who is an authority or has special experience with the topic.

2. **Plan the interview.** As soon as possible, take care of the details:
   - Determine your goal—what you want the interview to accomplish and what information and insights you want to gather.
   - Choose a recording method (pen and paper, recorder) and a medium (face-to-face, telephone, e-mail, video conference).
   - Research the topic and interviewee and draft questions to evoke information.
   - Contact the interviewee and politely request an interview. Explain who you are, why you need the interview, and how you will use it. Schedule a time and place convenient for the interviewee. To record the interview, ask permission.
   - Gather and test tools and equipment: a notebook, pens, and perhaps recording equipment (tape, video, digital camera).

3. **Prepare questions.** Do the following to help you structure the interview:
   - Consider types of questions to ask—the five W's and H.
   - Understand open and closed questions. Closed questions ask for simple, factual answers; open questions ask for detailed explanations.
        Closed: How many months did you spend in Vietnam?
        Open: Can you describe your most vivid memory of Vietnam?
   - Avoid slanted questions that pressure a person to give a specific answer.
        Slanted: Aren't you really angry that draft dodgers didn't do their duty?
        Neutral: How do you feel about those who avoided the draft?
   - Think about specific topics to cover and write questions for each one. Start with simple questions that establish rapport and follow with key questions.
   - List questions on the left side of the page with room for notes on the right. Rehearse your questions, visualizing how the interview should go.

4. **Conduct the interview.** Arrive on time and be professional:
   - Introduce yourself, reminding the interviewee why you've come.
   - If you have permission to record the interview, set up equipment off to the side so that it doesn't interfere with the conversation. Take notes on key facts.
   - Listen actively by including nods and eye contact. Pay attention to the interviewee's body language.
   - Be flexible. If the person looks puzzled by a question, rephrase it or ask another. If the person avoids a question, politely rephrase it. Don't react negatively or forcefully invade the interviewee's private territory.

- Ask one of these questions if an answer needs to be amplified:
  - **Clarifying:** "Do you mean this or that?"
  - **Explanatory:** "What do you mean by that?"
  - **Detailing:** "What happened exactly? Can you describe that?"
  - **Analytical:** "What were the causes? The outcomes?"
  - **Probing:** "What do you think that meant?"
  - **Comparative:** "Did that remind you of anything?"
  - **Contextual:** "What else was going on then? Who else was involved?"
  - **Summarizing:** "Overall, what was your response? What was the net effect?"
- Listen "between the lines" for what the interviewee seems to want to say.
- Give the interviewee a chance to add any final thoughts.

5. **Follow up.** As soon as possible, review your notes and fill in the blanks. By phone or in writing, clarify points and thank the interviewee.

Drafting

6. **Organize and draft the report.** Shape the opening to seize interest, the middle to sustain interest, and the closing to reward interest:
   - Analyze and interpret the interview results. Locate the heart or theme of your report, and then develop an outline supporting the theme.
   - Start with background, along with a point that grabs readers' interest.
   - Summarize and paraphrase material from the interview. (See pages 436–438.) Use quotations selectively to share the interviewee's voice or stress a point.
   - If appropriate, weave your thoughts and reflections into the report.

Revising

7. **Improve the ideas, organization, and voice.** On your own or with help from a classmate or writing-center tutor, review these issues in your draft:
   - ____ **Ideas:** Does the report supply complete, satisfying insights?
   - ____ **Organization:** Does the draft have an engaging opening and closing?
   - ____ **Voice:** Is the writing lively, fair, and respectful?

Editing

8. **Edit and proofread.** Review your report for precise **word choice, smooth sentences, correct grammar,** and **reader-friendly design**. Make sure especially that quotations are integrated smoothly.

Publishing

9. **Prepare a final copy.** Submit a clean copy to your instructor (and perhaps the interviewee), but also look for ways to publish your report.

Critical-Thinking and Writing Activities

As directed by your instructor, complete the following activities.

1. Generate a list of people who understand the challenges and opportunities related to the career you want to pursue. Then select a person, interview her or him, and write a report.

2. "The Dead Business" recounts the writer's exploration of a topic that caused him discomfort and sadness. What similar issues affect you? Would an interview help you work through an issue? Write your own reflective interview report.

3. Do you know someone who has led a fascinating life? Someone who on the surface seems to have led an ordinary life? Someone serving others in inspiring ways? Interview that person and write his or her story in an extended interview report.

4. Is there a particular issue in your community that concerns you—a public debate, a college problem, a program being cut back? Who has insights into the issue? Who holds opposing views? Whose lives are affected? Who has the power to change things? Select one or more people to interview, and then write a report on the issue.

5. Read an interview report in a popular journal and analyze how the writer asks questions and uses the interviewee's answers. Then write a paper in which you explain why the writer's interview and report do or do not illustrate the standards discussed in this chapter.

Learning-Outcomes Checklist

Use the checklist below to assess and review what you have learned about reading and writing interview reports.

_____ I can read and evaluate interview reports for organization, details, clarity, and voice.

_____ I can plan, schedule, and conduct an interview in an honest, professional manner.

_____ I can write both open and closed questions that are neutral vs. slanted.

_____ I can conduct an interview in a professional manner and take accurate notes.

_____ I can analyze the interview, including the interviewee's comments and demeanor, to discern his or her meaning.

_____ I can write an interview report that captures the writer's voice; includes correct quotes, summaries, and paraphrases; portrays the person accurately; and develops a unifying theme.

21 Lab, Experiment, and Field Report

Good science writing is rooted in good science—the careful study of phenomena through observation and experiment. Social scientists seek to understand human behavior and societies, whereas natural scientists investigate the physical world.

As a student, you may be asked to read science articles and to conduct scientific research in a range of courses. In classes, you may write literature reviews to summarize and assess what research has been done on an issue. In labs and in the field, you may perform experiments, gather data, and interpret results, and then share your insights with others.

This chapter will help you put your science research into writing—and your good writing into science.

Learning Outcomes

Audio

Video

▸ Read and evaluate science writing for logic and clarity.

▸ Understand and follow the scientific method.

▸ Utilize scientific style appropriately: objective tone, fitting use of passive voice.

▸ Structure science writing using IMRAD: introduction, methods, results, and discussion.

▸ Write an experiment or field report in APA or CSE style.

Visually Speaking ▸ Review the photograph above. What does it suggest about science, the scientific method, and science writing?

Web Link

Reading Science Writing

In order to read and do science writing effectively, you need to understand certain principles of science. Follow the guidelines below.

Consider the rhetorical situation.

When reading a scientific article (scholarly or popular), consider the rhetorical situation. When doing your own writing, perform a similar analysis.

- **Purpose:** Typically, the goal is to report experimental and observational results. However, sometimes it is to summarize several studies on a topic so to disseminate scientific knowledge to a broad audience.
- **Audience:** Most readers are experts—scientists interested in the topic addressed, seeking to debate and build knowledge (typically in scholarly journals). Other readers may be laypeople—non-experts nevertheless interested in the topic (typically reading trade or popular magazines).
- **Topic:** Scientists study phenomena, seeking to understand, for example, the cause-effect forces at work. Virtually any natural or social phenomenon is a potential topic.

Consider science-writing strategies.

Sound science writing depends on these principles: the scientific method, the IMRAD format, and careful distinctions.

- **The Scientific Method:** Science focuses on measured observations aimed at understanding. Experiments are set up to test hypotheses about why things happen. However, experiments don't prove hypotheses correct: Experimental results can merely "agree with" or disprove a hypothesis. Overall, the method moves from observation to explanation as you do the following:

    1. Observe something interesting (often while looking for something else).
    2. Check whether other scientists have explained the same observation.
    3. Summarize your observations and turn that generalization into a testable hypothesis—a working theory explaining the phenomenon.
    4. Design research to test the hypothesis, paying attention to variables and controls.
    5. Based on the results of your experiment, accept, reject, or modify your hypothesis.
    6. Repeat steps 3 through 5 until you understand the phenomenon. Then write up your research so that others can respond to your work.

- **IMRAD Format:** To model scientific thinking, lab and field reports include an *introduction* establishing the problem, a *methods* section detailing procedures, a *results* section providing the data, *and* a *discussion* that interprets the data: IMRAD.

Experiment Report ■■'■

In this report, student writers Dana Kleckner, Brittany Korver, Nicolette Storm, and Adam Verhoef share the results of an experiment in which they tested a hypothesis about the impact of an invasive plant species, Eastern Red Cedar, on Midwestern native species.

> ## Outline
> *Introduction:* allelopathy and Eastern Red Cedar hypothesis
> *Method:* growing Black-Eyed Susans and Poppies in soil samples
> *Results:* no significant differences between cedar and non-cedar soil samples
> *Discussion:* Eastern Red Cedar does not negatively affect germination of native species.

The title contains key terms identifying the experiment's cause-effect focus.

The Effects of the Eastern Red Cedar on Seedlings and Implications for Allelopathy

Abstract

The abstract summarizes the experiment and its findings.

The Eastern Red Cedar *(Juniperus virginiana)* is an invasive species that threatens native tall-grass prairies in much of the Midwest (Norris *et al* 2001). In an effort to learn more about its invasive characteristics, we decided to test for possible allelopathic properties. Allelopathy refers to the growth inhibition of one species by another species releasing toxins from its tissues (Simberloff 1995). In this study, the germination and survival of Black-Eyed Susans *(Rudbeckia hirta)* and Poppies *(Papaver orientale)* were examined. Seeds were planted in soil gathered from under three Eastern Red Cedar trees at Oak Grove State Park (Northwestern Iowa) and in soil from three non-cedar locations at this park. Germination and survival of the seedlings in controlled conditions were documented over thirty-two days. We found no significant difference between germination and survival proportions of the two seed types between the cedar and non-cedar soil. This led us to conclude that the Eastern Red Cedar does not negatively affect the germination and survival of the selected seed types.

1

Introduction

The introduction offers background and surveys past research.

Several factors can give a plant dominance in an area. One of these factors is the production of allelopathic chemicals. Allelopathy is the secretion of chemicals by one plant that suppresses the growth of other nearby plants (Simberloff 1995). This phenomenon reduces competition for limited resources. One possible method of allelopathy is the secreting of chemicals through the roots, directly into the soil. The chemicals can also be stored in the leaves, flowers, fruits, and seeds, releasing chemicals into the soil as they decompose (Norris *et al* 2007).

2

These allelopathic properties are present in several invasive species, such as the Japanese Red Pine (Node *et al* 2003).

3   The object in this experiment was to test for allelopathic capabilities of the Eastern Red Cedar *(Juniperus virginiana)*. The Eastern Red Cedar is a pioneer invader in the Midwest, quickly populating disturbed land (Norris *et al* 2001). This invasion is problematic in certain areas of the Midwest, as it often changes the native ecology of the area it invades, namely tall-grass prairies (Norris *et al* 2001). In the effort to preserve native ecosystems, a correct understanding of the characteristics of invaders is useful. The knowledge of the allelopathic properties of this species could assist in preservation efforts.

4   We predicted that eastern red cedars are allelopathic and that the soil around cedar trees would have a negative effect on the germination and lifespan of other plants. We hypothesized that seeds planted in cedar soil would germinate at a lower frequency and have shorter life spans than those planted in non-cedar soil under the same conditions.

The writers identify the specific problem, explain the value of their research, and state their hypothesis.

Methods

5   The experiment took place from March 19 to April 20, 2009 in the Northwestern College biology lab. Our professors collected soil from Oak Grove State Park near Hawarden, Iowa several months in advance. They gathered soil from three different locations under three different cedars trees and from three nearby non-cedar locations. They placed the soils under sun lamps to dry, and then stored the soil in plastic Ziplock bags.

6   To prepare for this experiment, two rows of evenly spaced holes were drilled into 18 potting trays for drainage. Each tray was labeled with the soil's location number and the soil type (cedar or non-cedar). From each specified location, soil was measured out equally and placed into the trays. In an effort to make the growing conditions realistic, any foreign plant roots, stems, etc. were left in the soil.

The writers detail the experimental procedure using precise terms and steps.

7   Black-Eyed Susans *(Rudbeckia hirta)* and Poppies *(Papaver orientale)* were chosen because of their equal planting depth and equal time for seed germination. Two rows were planted in each tray with 10 evenly spaced Black-Eyed Susan seeds on one side and ten evenly spaced Poppy seeds on the other side (both were planted according to the directions on the packages).

8   On March 19, each tray was placed approximately 35cm. under sun lamps that ran on a 12hrs on/12hrs off cycle. Each day, the trays were watered and rotated so that they received an equal amount of light and warmth. When a seed

They explain choices made during the experiment.

To keep the focus on actions rather than themselves as actors, the writers use passive voice (but mainly in the Methods section).

germinated, the date and the plant location in the tray were documented. If the plant died, the date of the death was recorded. Any foreign species that grew were left so as not to disturb the soil. On April 20, thirty-two days later, the data were compiled. The number of each species that germinated at each location and the number of days each plant survived were recorded.

Using Microsoft Excel, we first ran ANOVAs to see if there were any significant *9* differences in germination rates among the three cedar soil sites or any significant difference in germination rates among the non-cedar sites. Then we ran paired t-tests on germination for each seed type between the cedar and non-cedar soils. To compare the percentage of surviving seedlings between cedar and non-cedar soils, we ran an ANOVA for each seed type.

Results

The results are stated in neutral, precise terms and portrayed in figures.

Figures effectively visualize the experimental data, and are properly titled, numbered, and captioned.

We found no significant differences related to location in germination of Black-Eyed Susan seeds ($ANOVA$: F=2.71, F-crit=5.14, df=8, p-value=0.14) (Fig.1) or Poppy seeds ($ANOVA$: F=0.37, F-crit=5.14, df=8, p-value=0.7) (Fig. 1) among the three cedar sites. We also found that there were no significant differences related to location in the germination of Black-Eyed Susans ($ANOVA$: F=1.63, F-crit=5.14, df=8, p-value=0.27) (Fig. 2) or Poppies ($ANOVA$: F=0.31, F-crit=5.14, df=8, p-value=0.74) (Fig. 2) among the three non-cedar sites. Knowing that there were no significant differences in germination among the sites, we condensed the data into four different groups: Black-Eyed Susan cedar, Black-Eyed Susan non-cedar, Poppy cedar, and Poppy non-cedar.

10

Figure 1. There is no significant difference in seed germination among the three cedar soils for Poppies (p=.7) or Black-Eyed Susans (p=.14). Bars represent standard deviation.

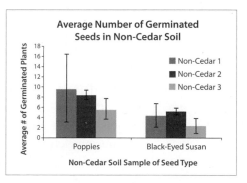

Figure 2. There is no significant difference in seed germination among the three non-cedar soils for Poppies (p=.74) or Black-Eyed Susans (p=.27). Bars represent standard deviation.

The two paired t-tests comparing seed germination in cedar soil versus non-cedar soil showed no significant differences in Black-Eyed Susan germination between the two soil types (t=0.31, p=0.77) (Fig.3) or in Poppy germination between the two soil types (t=-0.78, p=0.46) (Fig.3).

11

12

Figure 3. There is no significant difference in germination between cedar and non-cedar soil for Poppies (p=.48) or Black-Eyed Susans (p=.77). Bars represent standard deviation.

When comparing survivorship of the two seedling types in each soil, we defined surviving plants as those that lived for seven days or more. We ran ANOVAs and found that there was no significant difference between the proportion of seedlings that survived in cedar versus non-cedar soil for Black-Eyed Susans (*ANOVA:* F=0.01, F-crit=4.49, df=1, p=0.92) (Fig. 4) or for Poppies (*ANOVA:* F=0.06, F-crit=4.49, df=1, p=0.82) (Fig. 4).

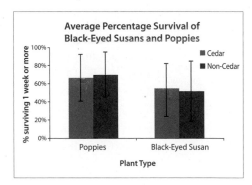

Figure 4. There is no significant difference in seedling survival between cedar and non-cedar soil for Poppies (p=.82) or Black-Eyed Susans (p=.92). Bars represent standard deviation.

Discussion

The writers restate their purpose and hypothesis, and then interpret the results of their experiment.

In this experiment, we sought to discover whether Eastern Red Cedar soil *13* is allelopathic. We predicted that cedar soil was allelopathic and hypothesized that if our prediction were correct, seeds planted in non-cedar soil would show higher germination and higher survival. We tested for significant differences in soil sites, germination of the two seeds types between soil types, and survival percentages of the seed types between soil types. None of these tests yielded a significant difference.

If the Black-Eyed Susans and poppies are good representatives of typically 14 affected plants, then Eastern Red Cedar soil appears not to reduce germination or survival. For those concerned with protecting native ecosystems from these invaders, the implications seem positive. An allelopathic invader would produce more damage than a non-allelopathic invader not only in the secretion of chemicals, but also in those chemicals remaining to harm desirable native species even if that invader is removed (Medley 2007).

They consider the broader implications of their study.

However, even if cedars do not release allelopathic chemicals, a study 15 conducted in the tall grass prairies of Kansas found that the Eastern Red Cedar increased the amount of above-ground biomass and surface-litter nitrogen pools that are linked to the conversion of grassland to forest (Norris *et al* 2007). Though this is not allelopathy, the invasive Eastern Red Cedar still changes the composition of the soil in a manner that could affect the growth of other plants (Norris *et al* 2007).

Also, though the cedar soil appeared not to be allelopathic in our study, 16 we are hesitant to make an assessment of the Eastern Red Cedar's affect on other plant types. Several factors may have confounded our non-allelopathic conclusion. The cedar's chemical may simply not be allelopathic to the types of plants we chose (Medley 2007). We purchased the seeds at a local Bomgaars store, and these seeds are domesticated strains. Domesticated strains may be more resistant to allelopathic chemicals and selected for high germination (Node 2003). If allelopathic chemicals are present, the chemicals may have been affected by the storage period and drying process and consequently have a different effect on seedlings (Norris *et al* 2001).

The writers identify complicating factors and reflect on the experiment's method.

Though we doubt that chemicals affected the outcome of our study, we had 17 several slight complications. In one of our planting boxes, more than ten poppies germinated. This was likely due to accidentally planting more than ten of the tiny seeds. In our statistics, we chose to count them all because excessive seeds were likely accidentally planted in other boxes as well. A recording complication occurred when some poppies germinated outside of their row in their container. The species type of some of the small seedlings was hard to distinguish as they were mixed together.

If we repeated this experiment, we would change both materials and methods. 18 We would grow separate seed types in separate containers so there would be no confusion as to the species. We would also be more attentive to the seeds during the planting process, so none would stick together and distort our data. To see if the drying process was a factor, in addition to planting in dried soil, we would plant in freshly gathered soil. Finally, we would use plant species that are actually threatened by possible cedar allelopathy instead of species to which this possibility is irrelevant in real life. A native tall grass may react much differently to cedar soil and would provide more interesting and relevant application.

Note: The references page is not shown. For more on documentation in the social sciences, see APA on pages 529–558. For more on documentation in the natural sciences, see CSE at **councilscienceeditors.org**.

Reading for Better Writing

Working by yourself or with a group, do the following:

1. Where do the writers discuss the experiment's purpose and value? Are their efforts convincing?

2. In the "Methods" section, what strategies do the writers use to ensure that the experiment can be repeated?

3. In the "Results" section, what is the relationship between the writers' statements and the four figures?

4. In the "Discussion" section, how do the writers interpret the experiment results? Are their interpretations and conclusions sound? Why or why not?

Field Report ■■■

In the following workplace report, a team of writers investigates the causes and effects of cockroach infestation in an apartment complex. In the study, they use their findings to recommend solutions.

SOMMERVILLE DEVELOPMENT CORPORATION

Date: September 20, 2010

To: Bert Richardson, VP of Tenant Relations

From: Hue Nguyen, Cherryhill Complex Manager
Sandra Kao, Building Superintendent
Roger Primgarr, Tenant Relations
Juan Alexander, Tenant Representative

The subject line functions as a title.

Subject: Investigation of Cockroach Infestation at 5690 Cherryhill

The opening clarifies the study's purpose and goals.

During the month of July 2010, 26 tenants of the 400-unit building at 5690 Cherryhill informed the building superintendent that they had found cockroaches in their units. On August 8, the management-tenant committee authorized us to investigate these questions: 1

1. How extensive is the cockroach infestation?
2. How can the cockroach population best be controlled?

We monitored this problem from August 9 to September 8, 2010. This report   2
contains a summary, an overview of our research methods, and findings, conclusions, and recommendations.

SUMMARY

The summary focuses on outcomes.

The 5690 Cherryhill building has a moderate infestation of German   3
cockroaches. Only an integrated control program can manage this infestation. Pesticide fumigations address only the symptoms, not the causes. We recommend that Sommerville adopt a comprehensive program that includes (1) education, (2) cooperation, (3) habitat modification, (4) treatment, and (5) ongoing monitoring.

RESEARCH METHODS AND FINDINGS

Overview of Research

We researched the problem in the following ways:

Research methods are described.

1. Contacted the Department of Agriculture, the Ecology Action Center, and Ecological Agriculture Projects.
2. Consulted three exterminators.
3. Inspected the 5690 Cherryhill building, from ground to roof.
4. Placed pheromone traps in all units to monitor the cockroach population.

The Cockroach Population

Results are categorized logically.

Pheromone traps revealed German cockroaches, a common variety. Of the 400 units, 112 units (28 percent) showed roaches. Based on the numbers, the infestation is rated as moderate.

The German Cockroach

Findings are presented clearly and concisely.

Research shows that these roaches thrive in apartment buildings.

- Populations thrive when food, water, shelter, and migration routes are available. They prefer dark, humid conditions near food sources.
- The cockroach seeks shelter in spaces that allow its back and underside to remain in constant contact with a solid surface.

Methods of Control

Sources we consulted stressed the need for an integrated program of cockroach control involving sanitation, habitat modification, and non-toxic treatments that attack causes. Here are the facts:

- The German cockroach is immune to many chemicals.
- Roaches detect most pesticides before direct contact.
- Spot-spraying simply causes roaches to move to unsprayed units.
- Habitat modification through (1) eliminating food and water sources, (2) caulking cracks and crevices, (3) lowering humidity, and (4) increasing light and airflow makes life difficult for cockroaches.

CONCLUSIONS

Conclusions follow logically from the findings.

Based on our findings, we conclude the following:

1. A single method of treatment, especially chemical, will be ineffective.
2. A comprehensive program of sanitation, habitat modification, and nontoxic treatments will eliminate the German cockroach.

RECOMMENDATIONS

Recommendations apply what was learned in the study.

We recommend that Sommerville Development adopt an Integrated Program of Cockroach Prevention and Control for its 5690 Cherryhill building. Management would assign the following tasks to appropriate personnel: *9*

Education: (1) Give tenants information on sanitation, prevention, and home remedies; and (2) hold tenant meetings to answer questions. *10*

Habitat Modification: Revise the maintenance program and renovation schedule to give priority to the following: *11*
- Apply residual insecticides before sealing cracks.
- Caulk cracks and crevices (baseboards, cupboards, pipes, sinks). Insert steel wool in large cavities (plumbing, electrical columns).
- Repair leaking pipes and faucets. Insulate pipes to eliminate condensation.
- Schedule weekly cleaning of common garbage areas.

Treatment: In addition to improving sanitation and prevention through education, attack the roach population through these methods: *12*
- Use home remedies, traps, and hotels.
- Use borax or boric acid powder formulations as residual, relatively nontoxic pesticides.
- Use chemical controls on an emergency basis.
- Ensure safety by arranging for a Health Department representative to make unannounced visits to the building.

Monitoring: Monitor the cockroach population in the following ways: *13*
1. Every six months, use traps to check on activity in all units.
2. Keep good records on the degree of occurrence, population density, and control methods used.

The closing stresses the value and benefits of the study.

We believe that this comprehensive program will solve the cockroach problem. We recommend that Sommerville adopt this program for 5690 Cherryhill and consider implementing it in all its buildings. *14*

Reading for Better Writing

Working by yourself or with a group, answer these questions:

1. Examine the report's format and organizational strategies. How is this workplace report similar to and different from the experiment report in this chapter?
2. Describe the tone of the report. What does this tone accomplish?
3. This report depends extensively on cause-effect thinking. Where do the writers use cause-effect thinking, and how effective is it?

Writing Guidelines

Model

Planning

1. **Review the lab manual and any handouts.** In most science courses, studies and experiments are assigned through textbooks, manuals, and handouts. Study those materials to understand what you must do and why. Read background information on the topic in textbooks and other sources.

2. **Use a field or lab notebook.** Accurate, complete record keeping is crucial to doing good scientific research. Use the notebook to plan research, record what you do, collect data, make drawings, and reflect on results. For each notebook entry, record the date and your goal.

3. **Plan and complete your study or experiment.** Do the following:
   - Develop your key research questions. If you are conducting an experiment (not just a study), then state your hypotheses and design procedures for testing them.
   - Gather the proper tools, equipment, and materials required.
   - Carefully conduct your tests and perform your observations.
   - Take copious notes, being especially careful to record data accurately, clearly, and completely. If helpful, use a data-collection sheet.

Drafting

4. **Relying on your notebook, draft the report.** Study the data. Were results expected or unexpected? Which factors could explain those results? What further research might be necessary? Then draft the report in the sequence outlined below:
   - **Methods:** Explain what you did to study the topic or test the hypothesis. Supply essential details, factors, and explanations. Be so clear that someone else could repeat the steps you took.
   - **Results:** Using two strategies, present the data you collected. First, share data in graphical forms—as tables, line charts, bar graphs, photographs, and so on. While the correct design of graphics and the proper presentation of statistical data are beyond the scope of this book, follow this basic rule: Make your graphic independent of the written text by giving it a descriptive title, clear headings and labels, units of measurement, and footnotes. Readers should be able to study your graphics and see the "story" of your study. Second, draw attention to the major observations and key trends available in the data. However, do not interpret the data in your results or give your reactions to them.
   - **Discussion:** Interpret the results by relating the data to your original questions and hypotheses, offering conclusions, and supporting each conclusion with details. Essentially, answer the question, "What does it all mean?" Explain which hypotheses were supported, and why. Also explore unexpected results, and suggest possible explanations. Conclude by reemphasizing the value of what you learned.

- **Introduction:** Once you have mapped out the methods, results, and discussion, write an introduction that creates a framework for the report. Explain why you undertook the study, provide background information and any needed definitions, and raise your key questions and/or hypotheses.
- **Summary or abstract:** If required, write a summary of your study's purpose, methods, results, and conclusions. An abstract is a one-paragraph summary that allows readers to (1) get the report in a nutshell and (2) determine whether or not to read the study.
- **Title:** Develop a precise title that captures the "story" of your study. Worry less about the length of the title and more about its clarity.
- **Front and end matter:** If required, add a title page, references page, and appendixes.

Revising

5. **Improve the ideas, organization, and voice.** Review your report, or ask a classmate or someone from the college's writing center to check the following:

_____ **Ideas:** Does the report provide scientifically sound conclusions about accurate data related to a clear hypothesis or issue?

_____ **Organization:** Is the traditional IMRAD structure followed effectively?

_____ **Voice:** Is the tone objective and informed, but also inquisitive?

Editing

6. **Edit and proofread the essay** by checking for these conventions of science writing:

_____ **Words:** The language is precise (not ambiguous), specific (not vague), and concise (not wordy); technical terms are defined as needed.

_____ **Sentences:** Constructions flow smoothly, using the passive voice when needed to focus on the action and the receiver, not the actor. (See page 81.)

_____ **Correctness:** The copy includes no errors in spelling, usage, punctuation, grammar, or mechanics. The writing follows the disciplinary conventions for capitalization, abbreviations, numbers, and symbols.

_____ **Design:** The page design is correctly formatted and attractive, including presentation of graphics; information is properly documented.

Publishing

7. **Prepare and share your report.** Submit a polished report to your instructor. Also consider writing a relevant article, editorial, or blog post on the topic.

Critical-Thinking and Writing Activities

As directed by your instructor, complete the following critical-thinking and writing activities by yourself or with classmates.

1. In your discipline, what are the main objects of study? How does or might the scientific method get followed with this subject matter?

2. The experiment report on the effects of the Eastern Red Cedar tests a hypothesis about a natural phenomenon. Guided by your instructor, develop a hypothesis about a technological or social change (e.g., cell phone habits, online gaming, reality TV shows). Then develop a simple, manageable experiment to test your hypothesis.

3. The field report objectively researches the problem of cockroach infestation. Which campus or community problems could you research in a similar manner? Develop a research plan, get approval from your instructor, and complete your study.

4. In a popular science magazine such as *Nature* or *National Geographic*, read an article about a topic that interests you. Then read an article on the same topic in a scholarly science journal (available typically through your library's databases). Compare and contrast the two articles in terms of purpose, audience, content, and style.

5. Which issues, problems, or puzzles exist in your area of study? With help from an instructor in your major, write a proposal to conduct an experiment or field research. (See pages 420–421 for help with research proposals.)

Learning-Outcomes Checklist

Use the checklist below to assess what you have learned about science writing.

_____ I can read and evaluate science writing (both scholarly and popular) for logic and clarity.

_____ I understand the scientific method, both with respect to experimentation and observation, and can follow that method in my own research.

_____ I know how to write in an appropriate scientific style—with an objective tone that nevertheless conveys curiosity and concern, and with appropriate but limited use of the passive voice of verbs.

_____ I understand the logic behind the IMRAD structure (introduction, methods, results, and discussion), and I can effectively develop that organization in my own writing.

_____ I can effectively write an experiment or field report.

Special Forms
of Writing

Chapters 22 through 26 focus on special writing occasions—or rhetorical situations. These chapters explain how to develop a variety of writing forms: a literary analysis, an essay test, a resumé, a webpage, and an oral presentation.

As you read the model pieces, note each writer's strategies for organizing and presenting her or his message. Analyze how and why those strategies are (or are not) effective for the writer's audience, purpose, and subject. Then consider how you might address a similar writing situation.

Special Forms of Writing

Writing About Literature and the Arts

22

In one way or another, people respond to the arts. Audiences may applaud a dancer, gripe about a film, or praise a poet. Often writers respond more precisely, by analyzing one actor's performance while criticizing another's, or by praising a film's script but questioning camera angles or lighting.

Because the arts are complex, writing about them requires careful listening, reading, and/or viewing. For example, you might analyze a film or play in terms of the acting, the casting, or the directing. Similarly, you might analyze a poem or story by looking at its form, its diction, or the insights it provides. This chapter includes model essays, guidelines, and literary terms to help you respond to and analyze a variety of art forms.

Learning Outcomes

▶ Read and evaluate writing about literature or the arts for clarity, reasoning, and insight.

▶ Understand and use literary and art terms and concepts.

▶ Analyze a literary text or other artwork by addressing specific elements.

▶ Write an analysis with an insightful thesis, clear reasoning, and sound evidence.

Audio

Video

Visually Speaking ▶ Review the photograph above. What does it suggest about the relationship between art and life? How might you write about this image to explain the arts?

Reading About Literature and the Arts

The instructions below will help you read about and respond to the arts.

Consider the rhetorical situation.

To understand art analyses, think about the writer's purpose, audience, and topic.

- **Purpose:** Most writers aim to analyze an artwork: to describe its features, to explain how it impacts an audience, and to understand its essential qualities. However, writers reviewing an artwork focus more on its strengths and weaknesses.
- **Audience:** In college, the primary audience for writing about the arts is students and instructors; off campus, art stories and reviews are written for any community members interested in art events, art-related issues, or reading books.
- **Topic:** The topic might be one artwork (e.g., a sculpture, novel, or film), multiple works created by the same artist (e.g., a series of poems or paintings), a group performance (e.g., a play, an opera, or a symphony), an individual performance (e.g., a pianist, an actor, or a dancer), or critical approaches to an art.

Understand terms used to write about the arts.

As you read, note the terms used to address specific art forms; three examples follow:

- **Plays and Films:** To describe characters, writers use terms such as *antagonist, protagonist,* or *tragic hero;* to discuss plots, they use words like *exposition, rising action,* and *denouement;* or to describe a setting, they might use *stage picture, proscenium arch,* or *thrust stage.*
- **Stories and Novels:** Writers might describe diction with terms like *archaic, colloquial,* or *slang;* describe nuanced language as *antithetical, hyperbolic,* or *understated;* or describe style with terms such as *genre, satire,* or *melodrama.*
- **Poetry:** Writers describe word sounds with terms like *assonance, consonance,* or *alliteration;* they describe rhythmic effects with words such as *iambic, pyrrhic,* or *quatrain;* and they refer to visual allusions as *symbols, images,* or *motifs.* (For definitions of terms like these, see the lists on pages 360–363.)

Note: Essays that analyze artwork are located in this chapter and on pages 183, 203, 206, 210, and 267.

Reader's Checklist

_____ Does the writer understand the elements of the art form, what distinguishes a quality artwork, and how to assess those qualities?

_____ Does the essay explore nuances such as ironies, motifs, symbols, or allusions?

_____ Does the essay have a clear thesis supported by relevant evidence?

_____ Is the tone informed, respectful, and honest?

Writing About a Short Story ■■■

In the essay below, student writer Anya Terekhina analyzes the characters and ideas in Flannery O'Connor's short story "Good Country People."

"Good Country People": Broken Body, Broken Soul

The writer provides background for understanding the characters in O'Connor's stories.

Flannery O'Connor's short stories are filled with characters who are bizarre, *1* freakish, devious, and sometimes even murderous. Every short story, according to O'Connor in *Mystery and Manners: Occasional Prose,* should be "long in depth" and meaning (94). To achieve this, O'Connor develops characters with heavily symbolic attributes and flaws, and "it is clearly evident that boldly outlined inner compulsions are reinforced dramatically by a mutilated exterior self" (Muller 22). In "Good Country People," Joy-Hulga is a typical O'Connor character—grotesque yet real. Her realness comes from her many flaws and, ironically, her flaws are a self-constructed set of illusions. Throughout the story, O'Connor carefully links Joy-Hulga's physical impairments with deeper handicaps of the soul; then, at the closing, she strips Hulga of these physical flaws while helping her realize that her corresponding beliefs are flawed as well.

O'Connor first introduces her character as Joy Hopewell, a name of optimism. *2* However, we soon understand that her chosen name, Hulga, is more fitting. The new name distresses her mother, Mrs. Hopewell, who is "certain that she [Joy] had thought and thought until she had hit upon the ugliest name in any language" (O'Connor 1943). Hulga has connotations of "hull = hulk = huge = ugly" (Grimshaw 51), and all of these are accurate descriptions of her. Far from having a sweet temperament, Hulga stomps and sulks around the farm, "constant outrage . . . [purging] every expression from her face" (1942).

Although Hulga's demeanor could be blamed on her physical impairments, *3* she devises her own rationalizations for behaving as she does. Ironically, each rationale is symbolized by one of her physical disabilities, yet she doesn't recognize the handicaps for what they imply.

The writer begins listing the protagonist's physical disabilities and explains how each one symbolizes a deeper problem in her soul.

One of Hulga's many ailments is her weak heart, which will likely limit her life *4* span. Hulga blames this affliction for keeping her on the Hopewell farm, making it plain that "if it had not been for this condition, she would be far from these red hills and good country people" (1944). Having a Ph.D. in philosophy, Hulga claims to want work as a university professor, lecturing to people at her intellectual level. Hulga's weak heart functions as more than a dream-crusher; it "symbolizes her emotional detachment—and inability to love anyone or anything" (Oliver 233). She exhibits no compassion or love for anything, not even "dogs or cats or birds or flowers or nature or nice young men" (1944–45).

Hulga also suffers from poor vision. Without her eyeglasses, she is helpless. 5
Strangely though, her icy blue eyes have a "look of someone who has achieved
blindness by an act of will and means to keep it" (1942). Her self-induced blindness
symbolizes her blindness to reality. She is indeed intelligent, but she has packed
her brain full of ideas and thoughts that only obscure common sense, let alone
truth. Because of Hulga's extensive education and her focus on philosophical
reasoning, she considers herself superior to everyone around her. For example,
she yells at her mother, "Woman! . . . Do you ever look inside and see what you
are not? God!" (1944).

Hulga's last and most noticeable physical impairment is her missing leg, which 6
was "literally blasted off" (1944) in a hunting accident when she was ten years
old. In *Mystery and Manners,* O'Connor stresses that the wooden leg operates
interdependently at a literal and a symbolic level, which means "the wooden leg
continues to accumulate meaning" throughout the story (99). Hulga's biggest
physical handicap symbolizes her deepest affliction: her belief in nothing.

She points out the root of the protagonist's problems: her lack of belief in anything.

Hulga's philosophical studies did focus on the
study of nothing, particularly on the arguments of the
French philosopher Nicolas Malebranche. O'Connor
describes Hulga as believing "in nothing but her own
belief in nothing" (*Mystery* 99). Over time, Hulga's
belief in nothing develops into more than just academic
study. Her nihilism becomes her religion—suitable for
a woman who considers herself superior and despises
platitudes. As she explains to Manley Pointer, "We
are all damned . . . but some of us have taken off our
blindfolds and see that there's nothing to see. It's a kind
of salvation" (1952). Hulga's religious terms suggest
that she uses faith in nothingness to find the meaning
that she can't find elsewhere.

7

Her nihilism becomes her religion— suitable for a woman who considers herself superior and despises platitudes.

The writer demonstrates how the protagonist's flaws lead her to make distorted judgments.

Hulga's nihilism is symbolized by her wooden leg, which is the only thing 8
she tends to with care: "She took care of it as someone else would his soul, in
private and almost with her own eyes turned away" (1953). This limb is wooden
and corresponds to Hulga's wooden soul. Whereas she believes she worships
Nothing, what she actually worships is an "artificial leg and an artificial belief"
(Oliver 235).

Not realizing that her false leg and false religion cripple her both physically 9
and spiritually, Hulga considers seducing Manley Pointer, the Bible salesman. She

delightfully imagines that she will have to help him deal with his subsequent remorse, and then she will instruct him into a "deeper understanding of life" (1950). Of course, her intellectual blindness keeps her from realizing that her superiority is only an illusion. Instead, she views Manley as "a vulnerable innocent, a naïve Fundamentalist, and she wishes to seduce him to prove that her sophisticated textbook nihilism is superior to his simpleminded faith" (Di Renzo 76).

In classic O'Connor fashion, the characters and situation reverse dramatically *10* at the end of the story. Hulga and Manley are alone in a hayloft and begin embracing. At first, Hulga is pleased with her reaction to kissing as it aligns well with Malebranche's teachings: "it was an unexceptional experience and all a matter of the mind's control" (1951). Soon, however, she realizes that she is enjoying the first human connection of her life. At this point, the *innocent* Bible salesman has already stripped Hulga of her first physical impairment: her weak heart.

11
Hulga hardly notices when Manley takes advantage of her next impairment: "when her glasses got in his way, he took them off of her and slipped them into his pocket" (1952). With her heart opened and her intellectual perspective fuzzy, Hulga swiftly descends into what she despises—platitudes. Hulga and Manley exchange clichéd mumblings of love, and this leads Manley to ask if he can remove her artificial leg. After brief hesitation, Hulga agrees because she feels he has touched and understood a central truth inside her. She considers it a complete surrender, "like losing her own life and finding it again, miraculously, in his" (1953).

> *With her heart opened and her intellectual perspective fuzzy, Hulga swiftly descends into what she despises— platitudes.*
12

She revisits the protagonist's physical disabilities, showing how the Bible salesman exploits each one.

As soon as the artificial leg is off, Manley whips out one of his Bibles, which is hollow. Inside are whiskey, obscene playing cards, and contraceptives. In only moments, Hulga loses control: As each of her physical handicaps is exploited, pieces of her world view crumble, leaving her confused and weak.

The writer reflects on the change in both characters.

In an ironic reversal, Hulga becomes the naïf and Manley becomes the cynic. *13* Hulga pleads in disbelief, "Aren't you . . . just good country people?" (1954). She knows that she has reverted to her mother's platitudes: "If the language is more sophisticated than any at Mrs. Hopewell's command, it is no less trite, and the smug self-deception underlying it . . . is, if anything, greater" (Asals 105). Manley assumes a startling, haughty air, exclaiming, "'I hope you don't think . . . that I believe in that crap! I may sell Bibles but I know which end is up and I wasn't born yesterday and I know where I'm going!'" (1954). Although they exchange roles, both characters use clichés to express their immature, yet authentic, worldviews.

Manley runs off with Hulga's wooden leg, leaving her vulnerable and *14* dependent, two things she previously despised. But "Hulga's artificial self—her mental fantasy of her own perfection—has gone out the door with her artificial limb. She is stuck in the hayloft with her actual self, her body, her physical and emotional incompleteness" (Di Renzo 79).

> The closing explains how Hulga finally acknowledges the truth about herself.

In one brief morning of delusional seduction, Hulga learns more about *15* herself and her world than she learned in all her years of university. Forced to acknowledge her physical, emotional, and spiritual disabilities, Hulga begins to realize what she is not—neither a wise intellectual for whom there is *hope*, nor "good country people" who merely *hope well*.

Note: The Works Cited page is not shown. For sample pages, see MLA (pages 526–527) and APA (page 557).

Reading for Better Writing

Working by yourself or with a group, answer these questions:

1. In her opening paragraph, Terekhina cites Flannery O'Connor's view that every short story should be "long in depth" and meaning. Does Terekhina adequately explore that depth and meaning? Why?

2. In her second paragraph, Terekhina analyzes Hulga Hopewell's first name; in the last paragraph, she comments on the last name. Does Terekhina's attention to names help you understand Hulga's character and the story's themes? How?

3. A writer's thesis is a type of "contract" that he or she makes with readers, spelling out what the essay will do. Review Terekhina's thesis (last sentence, first paragraph) and assess how effectively she fulfills that contract. Cite supporting details.

4. Flannery O'Connor has received strong acclaim for her clearly developed, complex characters. Does Terekhina adequately explore that complexity? Explain.

5. Many praise O'Connor for the challenging philosophical or ethical questions raised in her fiction. What questions does Terekhina identify in "Good Country People," and does she effectively discuss them?

6. What does Terekhina say about the story's plot, symbols, and diction? Does she effectively analyze these elements? Why?

Audio

Writing About a Poem ■▪▪

In the essay on the following two pages, student writer Sherry Van Egdom analyzes the form and meaning of the poem below, "Let Evening Come," by American poet Jane Kenyon. Born in 1947 and raised on a farm near Ann Arbor, Michigan, Kenyon settled in New Hampshire at Eagle Pond Farm after she married fellow poet Donald Hall. During her life, Kenyon struggled with her faith, with depression, and with cancer. At the time of her death in 1995 from leukemia, she was the poet laureate of New Hampshire.

Before you read the student writer's analysis, read the poem aloud to enjoy its sounds, rhythm, images, diction, and comparisons. Then read the piece again to grasp more fully how the poem is structured, what it expresses, and how its ideas might relate to your life. Finally, read Van Egdom's analysis and answer the questions that follow it.

Let Evening Come

Let the light of late afternoon
shine through chinks in the barn, moving
up the bales as the sun moves down.

Let the crickets take up chafing
as a woman takes up her needles
and her yarn. Let evening come.

Let dew collect on the hoe abandoned
in long grass. Let the stars appear
and the moon disclose her silver horn.

Let the fox go back to its sandy den.
Let the wind die down. Let the shed
go black inside. Let evening come.

To the bottle in the ditch, to the scoop
in the oats, to air in the lung
let evening come.

Let it come, as it will, and don't
be afraid. God does not leave us
comfortless, so let evening come.

"Let Evening Come": An Invitation to the Inevitable

by Sherry Van Egdom

The writer introduces the poet and her poetry.

The work of American poet Jane Kenyon is influenced primarily by the circumstances and experiences of her own life. She writes carefully crafted, deceptively simple poems that connect both to her own life and to the lives of her readers. Growing out of her rural roots and her struggles with illness, Kenyon's poetry speaks in a still voice of the ordinary things in life in order to wrestle with issues of faith and mortality (Timmerman 163). One of these poems is "Let Evening Come." In this poem, the poet takes the reader on a journey into the night, but she points to hope in the face of that darkness.

Narrowing her focus to the specific poem, the writer states her thesis.

She begins her analysis by explaining the stanza structure and progression.

That movement toward darkness is captured in the stanza form and in the progression of stanzas. Each three-line stanza offers a self-contained moment in the progress of transition from day to night. The first stanza positions the reader in a simple farm setting. Late afternoon fades into evening without the rumble of highways or the gleam of city lights to distract one's senses from nature, the peace emphasized by the alliteration of "l" in "Let the light of late afternoon." As the sun sinks lower on the horizon, light seeps through cracks in the barn wall, moving up the bales of hay. In the second stanza, the crickets get busy with their nighttime noises. Next, a forgotten farm hoe becomes covered with dew drops, and the silvery stars and moon appear in the sky. In the fourth stanza, complete blackness arrives as a fox returns to its empty den and the silent wind rests at close of day. The alliteration of "d" in "den" and "die down" gives a sinking, settling feeling (Timmerman 176). In the fifth stanza, a bottle and scoop keep still, untouched in their respective places, while sleep comes upon the human body. In the final stanza, Kenyon encourages readers to meet this emerging world of darkness without fear.

The writer shows attention to the poem's fine details and to secondary sources on the poem.

She advances her reading of the poem by exploring images, comparisons, and symbols: the poem's "imaginative logic."

Within this stanza progression, the journey into the night is intensified by strong images, figures of speech, and symbols. The natural rhythm of work and rest on the farm is symbolized by the light that rises and falls in the first stanza (Timmerman 175). The simile comparing the crickets taking up their song to a woman picking up her knitting suggests a homespun energy and conviction. The moon revealing her "silver horn" implies that the moon does not instantly appear with brightness and beauty but rather reveals her majesty slowly as the night comes on. The den, the wind, and the shed in stanza four stress a kind of internal, hidden darkness. Then stanza five focuses on connected objects: the thoughtlessly discarded bottle resting in the ditch, oats and the scoop for feeding, human lungs and the air that fills them. Kenyon mentions the air in the lung *after* the bottle, ditch, scoop, and oats in order to picture humanity taking its position among the established natural rhythm of the farm (Harris 31).

The writer compares possible interpretations of a central, repeated statement in the poem.

The refrain, "let evening come," is a powerful part of the poem's journey toward 4 darkness, though critics interpret the line differently. Judith Harris suggests that it symbolizes an acceptance of the inevitable: Darkness will envelop the world, and night will surely come, just as mortality will certainly take its toll in time. This acceptance, in turn, acts as a release from the confinement of one's pain and trials in life. Rather than wrestle with something that cannot be beaten or worry about things that must be left undone, Kenyon advises herself and her readers to let go (31). Night intrudes upon the work and events of the day, perhaps leaving them undone just as death might cut a life short and leave it seemingly unfinished.

By contrast, John Timmerman argues that "let" is used twelve times in a 5 supplicatory, prayer-like manner (176). The final two lines, in turn, act as a benediction upon the supplications. The comfort of God is as inevitable as the evening, so cling to faith and hope and let evening come. Although the Comforter is mentioned only in the last two lines, that statement of faith encourages readers to find a spiritual comfort in spite of the coming of the night.

In her conclusion, the writer offers the poet's explanation of the poem's origin and then expands on the thesis.

When asked how she came to write "Let Evening Come," Jane Kenyon replied 6 that it was a redemptive poem given to her by the Holy Ghost. When there could be *nothing*—a great darkness and despair, there is a great *mystery* of love, kindness, and beauty (Moyers 238). In the poem's calm journey into the night, Kenyon confronts darkness and suffering with a certain enduring beauty and hope (Timmerman 161). Death will come, but there remains divine comfort. "Let Evening Come" encourages readers to release their grip on the temporary and pay attention to the Comforter who reveals Himself both day *and* night.

Note: The Works Cited page is not shown. For sample pages, see MLA (pages 526–527) and APA (page 557).

Reading for Better Writing

Working by yourself or with a group, answer these questions:

1. Review the opening and closing paragraphs of the essay. How do they create a framework for the writer's analysis of the poem?

2. On which elements of the poem does the writer focus? Does this approach make sense for her analysis? Explain.

3. In her essay, the writer refers to the poet's life and to ideas from secondary sources. Do these references work well with her analysis? Why or why not?

4. Read the essay "Four Ways to Talk About Literature" on pages 206–207. Which approach does the student writer use to analyze Kenyon's poem? Does this approach make sense? How might another approach interpret the poem differently?

Writing Guidelines

Model

Planning

1. **Select a topic.** Choose an art form and artwork with which you are familiar or you are willing to learn about.

2. **Understand the work.** Experience it thoughtfully (two or three times, if possible), looking carefully at its content, form, and overall effect.

   - For plays and films, examine the plot, props, setting, characters, dialogue, lighting, costumes, sound effects, music, acting, and directing.
   - For novels and short stories, focus on point of view, plot, setting, characters, style, diction, symbols, and theme. (See pages 360–362.)
   - For poems, examine diction, tone, sound patterns, figures of speech (e.g., metaphors), symbolism, irony, structure, genre, and theme. (See page 363.)
   - For music, focus on harmonic and rhythmic qualities, dynamics, melodic lines, lyrics, and interpretation.

3. **Develop a focus and approach.** Take notes on what you experience, using the list above to guide you. Seek to understand the whole work before you analyze the parts, exploring your ideas and digging deeply through freewriting and annotating. Select a dimension of the work as a focus, considering what approach to analyzing that element might work. (See "Four Ways to Talk About Literature" on pages 206–207.)

4. **Organize your thoughts.** Review the notes that you took as you analyzed the work. What key insights has your analysis led you to see? Make a key insight your thesis, and then organize supporting points logically in an outline.

Drafting

5. **Write the first draft.**

   Opening: Use ideas like the following to gain your readers' attention, identify your topic, narrow the focus, and state your thesis:

   - Summarize your subject briefly. Include the title, the author or artist, and the literary form or performance.
     Example: In her poem "Let Evening Come," Jane Kenyon points to hope in the face of death.
   - Start with a quotation from the work and then comment on its importance.
   - Explain the artist's purpose and how well she or he achieves it.
   - Open with a general statement about the artist's style or aesthetic process.
     Example: The work of American poet Jane Kenyon is influenced primarily by the circumstances and experiences of her own life.
   - Begin with a general statement about the plot or performance.
     Example: In Stephen Spielberg's movie *War of the Worlds,* Ray Ferrier and his two children flee from their New Jersey home in a stolen minivan.

- Assert your thesis. State the key insight about the work that your analysis has revealed—the insight your essay will seek to support.

Middle: Develop or support your focus by following this pattern:
- State the main points, relating them clearly to the focus of your essay.
- Support each main point with specific details or direct quotations.
- Explain how these details prove your point.

Conclusion: Tie key points together and assert your thesis or evaluation in a fresh way, leaving readers with a sense of the larger significance of your analysis.

Revising

6. Improve the ideas, organization, and voice. Review your draft for its overall content and tone. Ask a classmate or writing-center tutor for help, if appropriate.

_____ **Ideas:** Does the essay show clear and deep insight into specific elements of the text, artwork, or performance? Is that insight effectively developed with specific references to the work itself?

_____ **Organization:** Does the opening effectively engage the reader, introduce the text or artwork, and focus attention on an element or issue? Does the middle carefully work through a "reading" of the work? Does the conclusion reaffirm the insight into the work and expand the reader's understanding?

_____ **Voice:** Does the tone convey a controlled, measured interest in the text or artwork? Is the analytical attitude confident but reasonable?

Editing

7. Edit and proofread the essay by checking issues like these:

_____ **Words:** Language, especially the terminology is precise and clear.

_____ **Sentences:** Constructions flow smoothly and are varied in length and structure; quotations are effectively integrated into sentence syntax.

_____ **Correctness:** The copy includes no errors in spelling, usage, punctuation, grammar, or mechanics.

_____ **Design:** The page design is correctly formatted and attractive; references are properly documented according to the required system (e.g., MLA).

Publishing

8. Publish your essay. Submit your essay to your instructor, but consider other ways of sharing your insights about this work or artist—blogging, submitting a review to a periodical (print or online), or leading classmates in a discussion (e.g., book club, post-performance meeting, exhibition tour).

Literary Terms

Your analysis of novels, poems, plays, and films will be deeper and more sophisticated if you understand the most common literary terms.

Allusion is a reference to a person, a place, or an event in history or literature.

Analogy is a comparison of two or more similar objects, suggesting that if they are alike in certain respects, they will probably be alike in other ways, too.

Anecdote is a short summary of an interesting or humorous, often biographical incident or event.

Antagonist is the person or thing actively working against the protagonist, or hero.

Climax is the turning point, an intense moment characterized by a key event.

Conflict is the problem or struggle in a story that triggers the action. There are five basic types of conflict:

> **Person versus person:** One character in a story is in conflict with one or more of the other characters.
>
> **Person versus society:** A character is in conflict with some element of society: the school, the law, the accepted way of doing things, and so on.
>
> **Person versus self:** A character faces conflicting inner choices.
>
> **Person versus nature:** A character is in conflict with some natural happening: a snowstorm, an avalanche, the bitter cold, or any other element of nature.
>
> **Person versus fate:** A character must battle what seems to be an uncontrollable problem. Whenever the conflict is a strange or unbelievable coincidence, the conflict can be attributed to fate.

Denouement is the outcome of a play or story. See **Resolution**.

Diction is an author's choice of words based on their correctness or effectiveness.

> **Archaic** words are old-fashioned and no longer sound natural when used, such as "I believe thee not" for "I don't believe you."
>
> **Colloquialism** is an expression that is usually accepted in informal situations and certain locations, as in "He really grinds my beans."
>
> **Heightened language** uses vocabulary and sentence constructions that produce a stylized effect unlike that of standard speech or writing, as in much poetry and poetic prose.
>
> **Profanity** is language that shows disrespect for someone or something regarded as holy or sacred.
>
> **Slang** is the everyday language used by group members among themselves.
>
> **Trite** expressions lack depth or originality, or are overworked or not worth mentioning in the first place.
>
> **Vulgarity** is language that is generally considered common, crude, gross, and, at times, offensive. It is sometimes used in fiction, plays, and films to add realism.

Exposition is the introductory section of a story or play. Typically, the setting, main characters, and themes are introduced, and the action is initiated.

Falling action is the action of a play or story that follows the climax and shows the characters dealing with the climactic event or decision.

Figure of speech is a literary device used to create a special effect or to describe something in a fresh way. The most common types are *antithesis, hyperbole, metaphor, metonymy, personification, simile,* and *understatement.*

> **Antithesis** is an opposition, or contrast, of ideas.
>> "It was the best of times, it was the worst of times, it was the age of wisdom, it was the age of foolishness . . ."
>>> — Charles Dickens, *A Tale of Two Cities*
>
> **Hyperbole** (hi-pur´ ba-lee) is an extreme exaggeration or overstatement.
>> "I have seen this river so wide it had only one bank."
>>> —Mark Twain, *Life on the Mississippi*
>
> **Metaphor** is a comparison of two unlike things in which no word of comparison (*as* or *like*) is used: "Life is a banquet."
>
> **Metonymy** (ma-ton´a-mee) is the substituting of one term for another that is closely related to it, but not a literal restatement.
>> "Friends, Romans, countrymen, lend me your ears." (The request is for the attention of those assembled, not literally their ears.)
>
> **Personification** is a device in which the author speaks of or describes an animal, object, or idea as if it were a person: "The rock stubbornly refused to move."
>
> **Simile** is a comparison of two unlike things in which *like* or *as* is used.
>> "She stood in front of the altar, shaking like a freshly caught trout."
>>> —Maya Angelou, *I Know Why the Caged Bird Sings*
>
> **Understatement** is stating an idea with restraint, often for humorous effect. Mark Twain described Aunt Polly as being "prejudiced against snakes." (Because she hated snakes, this way of saying so is *understatement.*)

Video

Genre refers to a category or type of literature based on its style, form, and content. The mystery novel is a literary genre.

Imagery refers to words or phrases that a writer uses to appeal to the reader's senses.
> "The sky was dark and gloomy, the air was damp and raw, the streets were wet and sloppy."
>> —Charles Dickens, *The Pickwick Paper*

Irony is a deliberate discrepancy in meaning or in the way something is understood. There are three kinds of irony:

> **Dramatic irony,** in which the reader or the audience sees a character's mistakes or misunderstandings, but the character does not.
>
> **Verbal irony,** in which the writer says one thing and means another ("The best substitute for experience is being sixteen").
>
> **Irony of situation,** in which there is a great difference between the purpose of a particular action and the result.

Mood is the feeling that a piece of literature arouses in the reader: *happiness, sadness, peacefulness, anxiety,* and so forth.

Paradox is a statement that seems contrary to common sense yet may, in fact, be true: "The coach considered this a good loss."

Plot is the action or sequence of events in a story. It is usually a series of related incidents that build upon one another as the story develops. There are five basic elements in a plot line: *exposition, rising action, climax, falling action,* and *resolution.*

Point of view is the vantage point from which the story unfolds.

> In the **first-person** point of view, the story is told by one of the characters: "I stepped into the darkened room and felt myself go cold."
>
> In the **third-person** point of view, the story is told by someone outside the story: "He stepped into the darkened room and felt himself go cold."
>
> **Third-person** narrations can be *omniscient,* meaning that the narrator has access to the thoughts of all the characters, or *limited,* meaning that the narrator focuses on the inner life of one central character.

Protagonist is the main character or hero of the story.

Resolution (or denouement) is the portion of the play or story in which the problem is solved. The resolution comes after the climax and falling action and is intended to bring the story to a satisfactory end.

Rising action is the series of conflicts or struggles that build a story or play toward a fulfilling climax.

Satire is a literary tone used to ridicule or make fun of human vice or weakness, often with the intent of correcting, or changing, the subject of the satiric attack.

Setting is the time and place in which the action of a literary work occurs.

Structure is the form or organization a writer uses for her or his literary work. A great number of possible forms are used regularly in literature: parable, fable, romance, satire, farce, slapstick, and so on.

Style refers to how the author uses words, phrases, and sentences to form his or her ideas. Style is also thought of as the qualities and characteristics that distinguish one writer's work from the work of others.

Symbol is a person, a place, a thing, or an event used to represent something else. For example, the dove is a symbol of peace.

Theme is the statement about life that a particular work shares with readers. In stories written for children, the theme is often spelled out clearly at the end. In more complex literature, the theme will often be more complex and will be implied, not stated.

Tone is the overall feeling, or effect, created by a writer's use of words. This feeling may be serious, mock-serious, humorous, satiric, and so on.

■ Poetry Terms

Alliteration is the repetition of initial consonant sounds in words such as "rough and ready." An example of alliteration is underlined below:

"Our gang paces the pier like an old myth . . . "

—Anne-Marie Oomen, "Runaway Warning"

Assonance is the repetition of vowel sounds without the repetition of consonants.

"My words like silent rain drops fell . . . "

—Paul Simon, "Sounds of Silence"

Blank verse is an unrhymed form of poetry. Each line normally consists of ten syllables in which every other syllable, beginning with the second, is stressed. As blank verse is often used in very long poems, it may depart from the strict pattern from time to time.

Consonance is the repetition of consonant sounds. Although it is very similar to alliteration, consonance is not limited to the first letters of words:

" . . . and high school girls with clear-skin smiles . . . "

—Janis Ian, "At Seventeen"

Foot is the smallest repeated pattern of stressed and unstressed syllables in a poetic line. (See **Verse**.)

> **Iambic:** an unstressed followed by a stressed syllable (re-peat´)
> **Anapestic:** two unstressed followed by a stressed syllable (in-ter rupt´)
> **Trochaic:** a stressed followed by an unstressed syllable (old´-er)
> **Dactylic:** a stressed followed by two unstressed syllables (o´-pen-ly)
> **Spondaic:** two stressed syllables (heart´-break´)
> **Pyrrhic:** two unstressed syllables (Pyrrhic seldom appears by itself.)

Onomatopoeia is the use of a word whose sound suggests its meaning, as in *clang, buzz,* and *twang*.

Refrain is the repetition of a line or phrase of a poem at regular intervals, especially at the end of each stanza. A song's refrain may be called the *chorus*.

Rhythm is the ordered or free occurrences of sound in poetry. Ordered or regular rhythm is called meter. Free occurrence of sound is called *free verse*.

Stanza is a division of poetry named for the number of lines it contains:

> **Couplet:** two-line stanza   **Sestet:** six-line stanza
> **Triplet:** three-line stanza   **Septet:** seven-line stanza
> **Quatrain:** four-line stanza   **Octave:** eight-line stanza
> **Quintet:** five-line stanza

Verse is a metric line of poetry. It is named according to the kind and number of feet composing it: *iambic pentameter, anapestic tetrameter,* and so on. (See **Foot**.)

> **Monometer:** one foot   **Pentameter:** five feet
> **Dimeter:** two feet   **Hexameter:** six feet
> **Trimeter:** three feet   **Heptameter:** seven feet
> **Tetrameter:** four feet   **Octometer:** eight feet

Critical-Thinking and Writing Activities

As directed by your instructor, complete the following activities.

1. Get a copy of "Good Country People," read the story, write your own analysis, and share the essay with your class.

2. Review "Let Evening Come" and write your own analysis of the poem. Read your essay to the class and discuss how its style and content compare with that of the essay on pages 356–357.

3. Choose a film and watch it critically, preferably twice. Then find two reviews of the film, note their theses and supporting evidence, and write an essay in which you evaluate why the reviews are (or are not) informed, insightful, and fair.

4. Attend a concert with classmates. Afterward, discuss the style of the music, the performance of the singer or group, and the content of the lyrics. Note the age of the audience and discuss how and why it responded as it did. Finally, discuss whether you found the concert worthwhile.

5. Visit an art gallery and examine an exhibit that engages you. Describe what you find appealing or intriguing and explain why. Also explain what value this exhibit might have for your community.

Learning-Outcomes Checklist

Use the checklist below to assess and review what you have learned about reading and writing about the arts.

_____ I can read and evaluate writing about literature and the arts for clarity, reasoning, and insight.

_____ I understand how writers use arts-related terminology to describe, analyze, and critique texts and artworks; I can use this terminology correctly myself.

_____ I can analyze and evaluate a work by addressing relevant issues, looking for appropriate qualities, and using reasonable criteria.

_____ I can write an analysis that has an insightful thesis, clear reasoning, and relevant supporting evidence from the work.

23 Taking Essay Tests

There is nothing more disheartening than sitting down to take a test for which you're not prepared. The results are predictable—and they're not pretty. Conversely, there is nothing more exhilarating than walking out of a classroom after nailing a test. This is especially true in a college setting, where tests count for so much and second chances and extra credit are rare.

Many of the writing skills that you've already developed should serve you well in taking essay tests. Read the instructions for an essay test carefully, and you'll find requests for describing, analyzing, classifying, persuading, and more.

This chapter will help you write better essay answers. As a bonus, it suggests a variety of other helpful ways to improve your test-taking skills.

Learning Outcomes

▶ Use daily/weekly review strategies.

▶ Use study groups and memory guides.

▶ Understand key words in essay questions.

▶ Rephrase questions as topic sentences.

▶ Write clear answers.

▶ Use tips for taking essay and objective tests.

Audio

Video

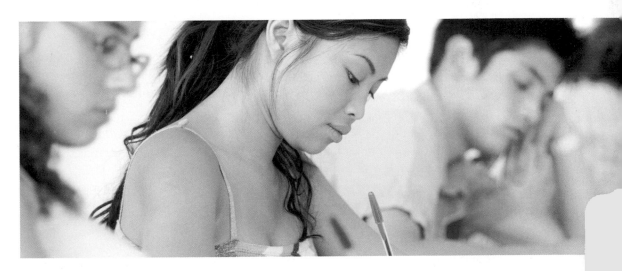

Visually Speaking ▶ Study the photo above. Then list the many ways that focus is crucial to success on essay tests.

Reviewing for Tests

Do you consider yourself a "bad" test taker? Do you know the material, yet somehow perform poorly on tests? Do you feel overwhelmed by all the information you have to cover when studying for a test? Does even the thought of studying so much material make you nervous? What you need is a positive mental attitude—and good study habits. Together they can make the difference between "spacing" during a test and "acing" an exam.

Perform daily reviews. ■■■

Why daily? Begin your reviews on the first day of class; if you miss a day, dust yourself off and keep going. Daily reviews are especially good because you tend to forget new information rapidly. Reviewing while the material is fresh in your mind helps to move it from your short-term memory into your long-term memory.

How much time? Even spending five or ten minutes on your review before or after each class will pay big dividends. Depending on the day's class, you may read through (or talk through) your notes, look over the headings in a reading assignment, skim any summaries you have, or put information into graphic organizers.

What to Do
- Put "Daily review of . . ." on your "To Do" list, calendar, or date book.
- Use the buddy system. Make a pact with a classmate and review together.
- Put your subconscious to work by reviewing material before you go to sleep.

Perform weekly reviews. ■■■

Why weekly? More than anything else, repetition helps anchor memory. You can cram a lot of data into your brain the night before an exam, but a day or two later you won't remember much of anything. And when final exam time comes, you'll have to learn the material all over again.

How much time? Plan to spend about one hour per week for each class. (This review can take place either by yourself or with a study group.) Remember that repetition is the single most important factor in learning anything.

What to Do
- Make mind maps and flash cards of important information.
- Practice answering review questions by saying them aloud and by writing out short answers.
- Test your understanding of a subject by teaching or explaining it to someone else.
- Organize a study group. (See page 367.)
- Create mnemonics. (See page 368.)

Forming a Study Group

A study group can keep you interested in a subject, force you to keep up with classwork, and increase your retention of study material. Group energy can be more powerful than individual energy. You will hear other points of view and other ways to approach a subject that you may never have thought of on your own. If you use a chat room, you can meet via a computer. To get started, follow these guidelines.

1. **Find five to six people.**
   - Consider people who seem highly motivated and collaborative.
   - Ask your instructor to inform the class about the opportunity.

2. **Consider a chat room.**
   - Check first with your instructor and student services about the availability of chat rooms on your campus network.
   - Go to any search engine (Yahoo!, Google, Excite, and so on) and enter the term "chat room." For example, Yahoo! provides both private and public chat rooms ("clubs") free of charge.

3. **Arrange a time and place.**
   - Plan one session. (It may become obvious at the first meeting that your group won't work out.)
   - Agree on a time limit for the initial session.
   - Choose somebody in the group to keep everyone on task (or rotate this duty) and agree to accept any prodding and nudging with good humor.

4. **Set realistic goals and decide on a plan of action.**
   - Discuss what the group needs to accomplish and what your goals are.
   - Agree to practice "people skills" (listening, observing, cooperating, responding, and clarifying).
   - Decide which parts of the coursework you will review (lectures? labs? texts? exam questions?).

5. **Evaluate at the end of the first session.**
   - Honestly and tactfully discuss any problems that arose.
   - Ask who wants to continue.
   - Choose a time (and place) for your next session.
   - Determine an agenda for the next session.
   - Exchange necessary information such as phone numbers, e-mail addresses, chat room passwords, and so forth.

■ Using Mnemonics and Other Memory Guides

Mnemonics is the art of improving memory by using key words, formulas, or other aids to create "file tabs" in your brain that help you pull out hard-to-remember information.

Acronyms Use the first letter in each word to form a new word. Everyone learns a few acronyms during their school years, but feel free to make up your own.

> **HOMES** (the Great Lakes—**H**uron, **O**ntario, **M**ichigan, **E**rie, **S**uperior)

Acrostics Form a phrase or silly sentence in which the first letter of each word helps you remember the items in a series.

> **Z**oe **C**ooks **C**howder **I**n **P**ink **P**ots **I**n **M**iami. (essential minerals—**z**inc, **c**alcium, **c**hromium, **i**ron, **p**otassium, **p**hosphorus, **i**odine, **m**agnesium)

Categories Organize your information into categories for easier recall.

> Types of joints in body
>
> immovable: skull sutures, teeth in sockets . . .
> slightly movable: between vertebrae, junction at front of pelvis . . .
> freely movable: shoulder, elbow, hip, knee, ankle . . .

Peg words Create a chain of associations with objects in a room, a sequence of events, or a pattern with which you are familiar (such as the player positions on a baseball diamond).

> To remember a sequence of Civil War battles, you might "peg" them to the positions on a baseball field—for example, Shiloh to home plate (think of the "high" and "low" balls); the Battle of Bull Run to the pitcher's mound (think of the pitcher's battle for no runs); and so on.

Rhymes Make up rhymes or puns.

> *Brown v. Board of Education* / ended public-school segregation.

TIPS to improve your memory

- ■ **Intend to remember.** Scientists say that our brains never forget anything: It's our recall that is at fault. Who forgets that they have tickets to a concert? We remember the things that are important to us.

- ■ **Link new information** to things you already know.

- ■ **Organize your material.** Understand the big picture and then divide the information you need to know into smaller, more manageable categories.

- ■ **Review new material as soon as possible.** The sooner you review, the more likely you'll remember.

Taking the Essay Test

Your instructors expect you to include all the right information, and they expect you to organize it in a clear, well-thought-out way. In addition, they expect you to evaluate, synthesize, predict, analyze, and write a worthwhile answer.

Look for key words.

Key words help you define your task. Pay special attention to them when you read questions. Key words tell you how to present all the information you'll need to write an essay answer.

Following is a list of key terms, along with a definition and an example of how each is used. Studying these terms carefully is the first step in writing worthwhile answers to essay questions.

Analyze To analyze is to break down a larger problem or situation into separate parts of relationships.

Analyze the major difficulties found at urban housing projects.

Classify To classify is to place persons or things (especially animals and plants) together in a group because they share similar characteristics. Science uses a special classification or group order: phylum, class, order, family, genus, species, and variety.

Classify three kinds of trees found in the rainforests of Costa Rica.

Compare To compare is to use examples to show how things are similar and different, placing the greater emphasis on similarities.

Compare the vegetation in the rainforests of Puerto Rico with the vegetation in the rainforests of Costa Rica.

Contrast To contrast is to use examples to show how things are different in one or more important ways.

Contrast the views of George Washington and Harry S Truman regarding the involvement of the United States in world affairs.

Compare and contrast To compare and contrast is to use examples that show the major similarities and differences between two things (or people, events, ideas, and so forth). In other words, two things are used to clarify each other.

Compare and contrast people-centered leadership with task-centered leadership.

Define To define is to give the meaning for a term. Generally, defining involves identifying the class to which a term belongs and explaining how it differs from other things in that class.

Define the term "emotional intelligence" as it pertains to humans.

Describe To describe is to give a detailed sketch or impression of a topic.

Describe how the Euro tunnel (the Chunnel) was built.

Diagram To diagram is to explain with lines or pictures—a flowchart, map, or other graphic device. Generally, a diagram will label the important points or parts.

Diagram the parts of a DNA molecule.

Discuss To discuss is to review an issue from all sides. A discussion answer must be carefully organized to stay on track.

Discuss how Rosa Parks's refusal to move to the back of the bus affected the civil rights movement.

Evaluate To evaluate is to make a value judgment by giving the pluses and minuses along with supporting evidence.

Evaluate the efforts of midsized cities to improve public transportation services.

Explain To explain is to bring out into the open, to make clear, and to analyze. This term is similar to *discuss* but places more emphasis on cause/effect relationships or step-by-step sequences.

Explain the effects of global warming on a coastal city like New Orleans.

Justify To justify is to tell why a position or point of view is good or right. A justification should be mostly positive—that is, the advantages are stressed over the disadvantages.

Justify the use of antilock brakes in automobiles.

Outline To outline is to organize a set of facts or ideas by listing main points and subpoints. A good outline shows at a glance how topics or ideas fit together or relate to one another.

Outline the events that caused the United States to enter World War II.

Prove To prove is to bring out the truth by giving evidence to back up a point.

Prove that Atticus Finch in *To Kill a Mockingbird* provided an adequate defense for his client.

Review To review is to reexamine or to summarize the key characteristics or major points of the topic. Generally speaking, a review presents material in the order in which it happened or in decreasing order of importance.

Review the events since 1976 that have led to the current hip-hop culture.

State To state is to present a concise statement of a position, fact, or point of view.

State your reasons for voting in the last national election.

Summarize To summarize is to present the main points of an issue in a shortened form. Details, illustrations, and examples are usually omitted.

Summarize the primary responsibilities of a school in a democracy.

Trace To trace is to present—in a step-by-step sequence—a series of facts that are somehow related. Usually the facts are presented in chronological order.

Trace the events that led to the fall of the Union of Soviet Socialist Republics.

Plan and write the essay-test answer. ■ ■ ■

In addition to a basic understanding of the key words, you must understand the process of writing the essay answer.

1. **Reread the question several times.** (Pay special attention to any key words used in the question.)

2. **Rephrase the question into a topic sentence/thesis statement** with a clear point.

   Question: Explain why public housing was built in Chicago in the 1960s.

   Thesis statement: Public housing was built in Chicago because of the Great Migration, the name given to the movement of African Americans from the South to the North.

3. **Outline the main points you plan to cover in your answer.** Time will probably not allow you to include all supporting details in your outline.

4. **Write your essay (or paragraph).** Begin with your thesis statement (or topic sentence). Add whatever background information may be needed, and then follow your outline, writing as clearly as possible.

One-Paragraph Answer

If you feel that only one paragraph is needed to answer the question, use the main points of your outline as supporting details for your thesis statement.

Question: Explain why public housing was built in Chicago in the 1960s.

Topic Sentence	Public housing was built in Chicago because of the Great Migration, the name given to the movement of African Americans from the South to the North. The mechanical cotton picker, introduced in the 1920s, replaced field hands in the cotton fields of the South. At that time Chicago's factories and stockyards were hiring workers. In addition, Jim Crow laws caused hardships and provided reasons for African Americans to move north. Finally, some African Americans had family and
Supporting Details	relatives in Chicago who had migrated earlier and who, it was thought, could provide a home base for the new migrants until they could get work and housing. According to the U.S. Census Reports, there were 109,000 African Americans in Chicago in 1920. By 1960, there were more than 800,000. However, this increase in population could have been handled except that the public wanted to keep the African Americans in the Black Belt, an area in South Chicago. Reluctant lending agencies and realtors made it possible for speculators to operate. Speculators increased the cost of houses
Conclusion	by 75 percent. All of these factors led to a housing shortage for African Americans, which public housing filled.

Multiparagraph Answer

If the question is too complex to be handled in one paragraph, your opening paragraph should include your thesis statement and any essential background information. Begin your second paragraph by rephrasing one of the main points from your outline into a suitable topic sentence. Support this topic sentence with examples, reasons, or other appropriate details. Handle additional paragraphs in the same manner. If time permits, add a summary or concluding paragraph to bring all of your thoughts to a logical close.

Question: Explain the advantages and disadvantages of wind energy.

Thesis: Wind energy has an equal number of advantages and disadvantages.

Outline
I. Advantages of wind energy
   A. Renewable
   B. Economical
   C. Nonpolluting
II. Disadvantages of wind energy
   A. Intermittent
   B. Unsightly
   C. A danger to some wildlife

The introductory paragraph sets up the essay's organization.

Wind energy has an equal number of advantages and disadvantages. It is *1* renewable, economical, and nonpolluting; but it is also intermittent, unsightly, and a danger to the bird population.

Wind energy is renewable. No matter how much wind energy is used today, there *2* will still be a supply tomorrow. As evidence indicates that wind energy was used to propel boats along the Nile River about 5000 B.C.E., it can be said that wind is an eternal, renewable resource.

Wind energy is economical. The fuel (wind) is free, but the initial cost for wind *3* turbines is higher than for fossil-fueled generators. However, wind energy costs do not include fuel purchases and only minimal operating expenses. Wind power reduces the amount of foreign oil the United States imports and reduces health and environmental costs caused by pollution. Is it possible to sell excess power? The Public Utilities Regulatory Policy Act of 1978 (PURPA) states that a local electric company must buy any excess power produced by a qualifying individual. This act encourages the use of wind power.

Each paragraph follows a point in the outline.

Wind energy does not pollute. Whether one wind turbine is used by an individual *4* or a wind farm supplies energy to many people, no air pollutants or greenhouse gases are emitted. California reports that 2.5 billion pounds of carbon dioxide and 15 million pounds of other pollutants have *not* entered the air thanks to wind energy.

How unfortunate is it that wind energy is intermittent? If a wind does not blow, there is little or no electrical power. One way to resolve this dilemma is to store the energy that wind produces in batteries. The word *intermittent* also refers to the fact that wind power is not always available at the places where it is most needed. Often the sites that offer the greatest winds are located in remote locations far from the cities that demand great electrical power.

Specific details explain the main point.

Are wind turbines unsightly? A home-sized wind machine rises about 30 feet with rotors between 8 and 25 feet in diameter. The largest machine in Hawaii stands about 20 stories high with rotors a little longer than the length of a football field. This machine supplies electricity to 1,400 homes. Does a single wind turbine upset the aesthetics of a community as much as a wind farm? The old adage "Beauty is in the eye of the beholder" holds up wherever wind turbines rotate. If ongoing electrical costs are almost nil, that wind turbine may look beautiful.

Questions help the reader understand the issue.

How serious is the issue of bird safety? The main questions are these: (1) Why do birds come near wind turbines? (2) What, if any, are the effects of wind development on bird populations? (3) What can be done to lessen the problem? If even one bird of a protected species is killed, the Endangered Species Act has been violated. If wind turbines kill migratory birds, the Migratory Bird Treaty Act has been violated. As a result, many countries and agencies are studying the problem carefully.

The ending makes a final conclusion.

The advantages of wind energy seem to outweigh the disadvantages. The wind-energy industry has been growing steadily in the United States and around the world. The new wind turbines are reliable and efficient. People's attitudes toward wind energy are mostly positive. Many manufacturers and government agencies are now cooperating to expand wind energy, making it the fastest-growing source of electricity in the world.

Reading for Better Writing

Working by yourself or with a group, answer these questions:

1. How does the writer provide a clear focus and logical organization in the essay answer? How soon are the focus and organization provided? What advantages does this approach offer the writer? The reader?

2. How do the sentences used to introduce the advantages differ from the sentences used to introduce the disadvantages? How does this technique aid the reader?

3. Why must the paragraphs in the body contain specific facts and examples? Which facts and examples does this writer use?

Quick Guide

■ Writing Under Pressure: The Essay Test

Make sure you are ready for the test both mentally and physically.

■ **Carefully listen to or read the instructions.**
  1. How much time do you have to complete the test?
  2. Do all the essay questions count equally?
  3. Can you use any aids, such as a dictionary or handbook?
  4. Are there any corrections, changes, or additions to the test?

■ **Begin the test immediately and watch the time.** Don't spend so much time answering one question that you run out of time before answering the others.

■ **Read all the essay questions carefully,** paying special attention to the key words. (See pages 369–370.)

■ **Ask the instructor for clarification** if you don't understand something.

■ **Rephrase each question into a controlling idea for your essay answer.** (This idea becomes your thesis statement.)

■ **Think before you write.** Jot down all the important information and work it into a brief outline. Do this on the back of the test sheet or on a piece of scrap paper.

■ **Use a logical pattern of organization and a strong topic sentence for each paragraph.** Tie points together with clear, logical transitions.

■ **Write concisely,** but don't use abbreviations or nonstandard language.

■ **Be efficient.** Write about those areas of the subject of which you are most certain first; then work on other areas as time permits.

■ **Keep your test paper neat and use reasonable margins.** Neatness is always important, and readability is a must, especially on an essay exam.

■ **Revise and proofread.** Read through your essay as carefully and completely as time permits.

Note: Also see "Tips for Coping with Test Anxiety," page 376.

Taking an Objective Test

Even though objective tests are generally straightforward and clear, following some tips can help you avoid making foolish mistakes.

True/False Test

- Read the entire question before answering. Often the first half of a statement will be true or false, while the second half is just the opposite. For an answer to be true, the entire statement must be true.
- Read each word and number. Pay special attention to names, dates, and numbers that are similar and could be easily confused.
- Beware of true/false statements that contain words such as *all, every, always,* and *never.* Very often these statements will be false.
- Watch for statements that contain more than one negative word. Remember: Two negatives make a positive. (*Example:* It is unlikely ice will not melt when the temperature rises above 32 degrees F.)

Matching Test

- Read through both lists quickly before you begin answering. Note any descriptions that are similar and pay special attention to the differences.
- When matching a word to a word, determine the part of speech of each word. If the word is a verb, for example, match it with another verb.
- When matching a word to a phrase, read the phrase first and look for the word it describes.
- Cross out each answer as you find it—unless you are told that the answer can be used more than once.
- Use capital letters rather than lowercase letters because they are less likely to be misread by the person correcting the test.

Multiple-Choice Test

- Read the directions to determine whether you are looking for the correct answer or the best answer. Also, check whether some questions can have two (or more) correct answers.
- Read the first part of the question, checking for negative words such as *not, never, except,* and *unless.*
- Try to answer the question in your mind before looking at the choices.
- Read all the choices before selecting your answer. This step is especially important on tests in which you must select the best answer, or on tests where one of your choices is a combination of two or more answers. (*Example:* d. Both a and b / e. All of the above / f. None of the above)

Tips for Coping with Test Anxiety

Consider the following advice:

- **Study smart.** Use a variety of study and memory techniques to help you see your coursework from several different angles.

- **Review with others.**   Join a study group and prepare with the members. Also, ask a classmate or family member to put you to the test.

- **Prepare yourself both physically and mentally.** Get a good night's sleep and eat a healthful, light meal before the test (doughnuts and coffee are *not* a healthful, light meal).

- **Get some exercise.** Aerobic exercise (running, swimming, walking, aerobics) is a great way to relieve stress, and exercise has been proven to help you think more quickly and more clearly.

- **Hit the shower.** Hot water is relaxing, cold water is stimulating, and warm water is soothing. Take your pick.

- **Get to class early . . . but not too early!** Hurrying increases anxiety, but so does waiting.

- **Relax.** Take a few deep breaths, close your eyes, and think positive thoughts. The more relaxed you are, the better your memory will serve you.

- **Glance through the entire test.** Then plan your time, and pace yourself accordingly. You don't want to discover with only 5 minutes of class time left that the last question is an essay that counts for 50 percent of your grade.

- **Begin by filling in all the answers you know.** This process relieves anxiety and helps to trigger answers for other questions that you may not know immediately. Also, jot down important facts and formulas that you know you will need later on.

- **Don't panic.** If other people start handing in their papers long before you are finished, don't worry. They may have given up or rushed through the exam. The best students often finish last.

BOTTOM LINE

The better you prepare for a test—mentally and physically—the less likely you'll be to suffer serious test anxiety.

Writing for the Workplace

24

One thing you already know about writing in college life is that you have to do a lot of writing in your courses—and it has to be good. By writing well, you make a positive impression in the classroom. But did you know that life outside the classroom also requires lots of writing?

This chapter will help you write work-related documents. Sample letters and memos will help you communicate effectively with people ranging from the registrar to scholarship committees. The sample application essay and resumés will help you apply for a job, a program, or an internship. In addition, the e-mail writing instructions will help you take care of business with other readers, no matter where in the world they might be.

Learning Outcomes

Audio

▶ Write clear, properly formatted letters, memos, and e-mails.

▶ Write persuasive job-search correspondence.

▶ Write convincing, focused application essays.

▶ Write organized, detailed, and effectively formatted resumés.

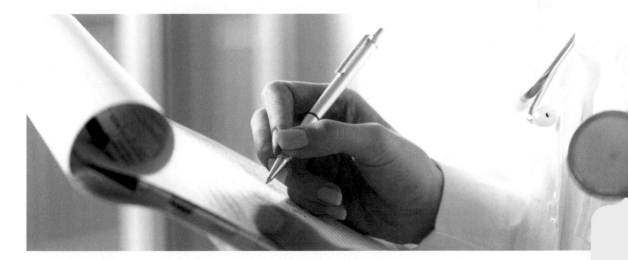

Visually Speaking ▶ What does the photograph above suggest about how and why people write in the workplace?

■ Writing the Business Letter

Business letters do many things—for example, share ideas, promote products, or ask for help. Putting a message in writing gives you time to think about, organize, and edit what you want to say. In addition, a written message serves as a record of important details for both the sender and the recipient.

Parts of the Business Letter ■■·■

1. **Heading** The heading gives the writer's complete address, either in the letterhead (company stationery) or typed out, followed by the date.

2. **Inside Address** The inside address gives the reader's name and address.
   - If you're not sure which person to address or how to spell someone's name, you could call the company or check their website for the information.
   - If the person's title is a single word, place it after the name and a comma (Mary Johnson, President). A longer title goes on a separate line.

3. **Salutation** The salutation begins with *Dear* and ends with a colon, not a comma.
   - Use *Mr.* or *Ms.* plus the person's last name, unless you are well acquainted. Do not guess at *Miss* or *Mrs.*
   - If you can't get the person's name, replace the salutation with *Dear* or *Attention* followed by the title of an appropriate reader. (*Examples:* Dear Dean of Students: or Attention: Personnel Manager)
   Note: See pages 104–106 for a complete list of "unbiased" ways to refer to an individual or a particular group.

4. **Body** The body should consist of single-spaced paragraphs with double-spacing between paragraphs. (Do not indent the paragraphs.)
   - If the body goes to a second page, put the reader's name at the top left, the number 2 in the center, and the date at the right margin.

5. **Complimentary Closing** For the complimentary closing, use *Sincerely, Yours sincerely,* or *Yours truly* followed by a comma; use *Best wishes* if you know the person well.

6. **Signature** The signature includes the writer's name both handwritten and typed.

7. **Initials** When someone types the letter for the writer, that person's initials appear (in lowercase) after the writer's initials (in capitals) and a colon.

8. **Enclosure** If a document (brochure, form, copy, or other form) is enclosed with the letter, the word *Enclosure* or *Encl.* appears below the initials.

9. **Copies** If a copy of the letter is sent elsewhere, type *cc:* beneath the enclosure line, followed by the person's or department's name.

Model Letter

Heading

Box 143
Balliole College
Eugene, OR 97440-5125
August 29, 2010

Four to Seven Spaces

Inside Address

Ms. Ada Overlie
Ogg Hall, Room 222
Balliole College
Eugene, OR 97440-0222

Double Space

Salutation

Dear Ms. Overlie:

Double Space

As the president of the Earth Care Club, I welcome you to Balliole Community College. I hope the year will be a great learning experience both inside and outside the classroom.

Double Space

Body

That learning experience is the reason I'm writing—to encourage you to join the Earth Care Club. As a member, you could participate in the educational and action-oriented mission of the club. The club has most recently been involved in the following:

- Organizing a reduce, reuse, recycle program on campus
- Promoting cloth rather than plastic bag use among students
- Giving input to the college administration on landscaping, renovating, and building for energy efficiency
- Putting together the annual Earth Day celebration

Double Space

Which environmental concerns and activities would you like to focus on? Bring them with you to the Earth Care Club. Simply complete the enclosed form and return it by September 9. Then watch the campus news for details on our first meeting.

Complimentary Closing and Signature

Yours sincerely,

Dave Wetland   **Four Spaces**

Dave Wetland
President

Double Space

Initials Enclosure Copies

DW:kr
Encl. membership form
cc: Esther du Toit, membership committee

Writing Memos and E-Mail

A memorandum is a written message sent from one person to one or more other people within the same organization. As such, a memo is less formal than a letter. A memo can vary in length from a sentence or two to a four- or five-page report, and a memo can be delivered in person, dropped in a mailbox, or sent via e-mail.

Memos are written to create a flow of information within an organization—asking and answering questions, describing procedures and policies, or reminding people about appointments and meetings. Here are some guidelines:

- Write memos only when necessary, and only to those people who need them.
- Distribute them through the appropriate media—mail, fax, bulletin boards, kiosk, intranet, or e-mail.
- Make your subject line precise (a brief summary) so that the topic is clear and the memo is easy to file.
- Get to the point: (1) state the subject, (2) give necessary details, and (3) state the response you want.

Date:　　September 24, 2010

To:　　All Users of the Bascom Hill Writing Lab

From:　　Kerri Kelley, Coordinator

Subject:　New Hours/New Equipment for Writing Lab

The subject line clarifies the memo's purpose.

The main point is stated immediately.

Beginning October 1, the Bascom Hill Writing Lab will expand its weekend hours as follows: Fridays, 7:00 a.m.–11:00 p.m.; Saturdays, 8:00 A.M.–11:00 p.m.

Also, six additional computers will be installed next week, making it easier to get computer time. We hope these changes will help meet the increased demand for time and assistance we've experienced this fall. Remember, it's still a good idea to sign up in advance. To reserve time, call the lab at 462-7722 or leave your request at bhill@madwis.edu.

Readers are asked to take note of a few final facts.

Finally, long-range planners, mark your calendars. The lab will be closed on Thanksgiving Day morning and open from 1:00 p.m. to 11:00 p.m. We will also be closed on Christmas and New Year's Day. We will post our semester-break hours sometime next month.

Sending E-Mail

With e-mail, people can correspond through computer networks around the globe. E-mail allows you to do the following:

- Send, forward, and receive many messages quickly and efficiently, making it ideal for group projects and other forms of collaboration
- Set up mailing lists (specific groups of e-mail addresses) so that you can easily send the same message to several people at the same time
- Organize messages in "folders" for later reference, and reply to messages

TIPS for e-mail

- **Revise and edit messages for clarity and correctness before sending them.** Confusing sentences, grammatical errors, and typos limit your ability to communicate on a computer screen just as they do on paper.
- **Use e-mail responsibly.** Sooner or later you will send e-mail to the wrong person, or a reader will forward your message to another person without your permission. Keep these possibilities in mind at all times, and never write anything that would embarrass you if the wrong party received it.
- **Make messages easy to read and understand.** (1) Provide a clear, complete subject line so readers can scan it and decide whether to read or delete the message. (2) Type short paragraphs.

| Send | Chat | Attach | Address | Fonts | Colors | Save As Draft |

From: "Sherry West" SWEST@stgeorge.edu

To: outreach@stgeorge.edu

Subject: Agenda for Student Outreach Committee Meeting

Please remember that our next meeting is this Wednesday, Sept. 22, at 8:00 p.m. in SUB Room 201. We'll discuss the following agenda items:

1. The minutes of our Sept. 8 meeting
2. A proposal from SADD about Alcohol Awareness Week
3. A progress report on the Habitat for Humanity project

Before the meeting, please review the minutes and the SADD proposal attached to this message.

Applying for a Job

When you apply for some jobs, you have to do nothing more than fill out an application form. With other jobs, it's a different story. You may be required to write a letter of application, gather letters of recommendation, write an application essay, and put together a resumé. The following pages provide models to fit nearly every occasion.

The Letter of Application

Web Link

Your letter of application (or cover letter) introduces you to an employer and often highlights information on an accompanying resumé. Your goal in writing this letter is to convince the employer to invite you for an interview.

Ogg Hall, Room 222
Balliole College
Eugene, OR 97440-0222
September 2, 2010

Address a specific person, if possible.

Professor Edward Mahaffy
Greenhouse Coordinator
Balliole College
Eugene, OR 97440-0316

Dear Professor Mahaffy:

State the desired position and your chief qualification

I recently talked with Ms. Sierra Arbor in the Financial Aid Office about work-study jobs for 2010–2011. She told me about the Greenhouse Assistant position and gave me a job description. As a full-time Balliole student, I'm writing to apply for this position. I believe that my experience qualifies me for the job.

Focus on how your skills meet the reader's needs.

As you can see from my resumé, I spent two summers working in a raspberry operation, doing basic plant care and carrying out quality-control lab tests on the fruit. Also, as I was growing up, I learned a great deal by helping with a large farm garden. In high school and college, I studied botany. Because of my interest in this field, I'm enrolled in the Environmental Studies program at Balliole.

Request an interview and thank the reader.

I am available for an interview. You may phone me any time at 341-3611 (and leave a message on my machine) or e-mail me at dvrl@balliole.edu. Thank you for considering my application.

Yours sincerely,

Ada Overlie

Ada Overlie

Encl. resumé

The Recommendation Request Letter ■·■

When you apply for a job or program, it helps to present references or recommendations to show your fitness for the position. To get the support you need from people familiar with your work (instructors and employers), you need to ask for that support. You can do so in person or by phone, but a courteous and clear letter or e-mail message makes your request official and helps the person complete the recommendation effectively. Here is a suggested outline:

- **Situation:** Remind the reader of your relationship to him or her; then ask the person to write a recommendation or to serve as a reference for you.
- **Explanation:** Describe the work you did for the reader and the type of job, position, or program for which you are applying.
- **Action:** Explain what form the recommendation should take, to whom it should be addressed, and where and when it needs to be sent.

2456 Charles Street
Lexington, KY 40588-8321
March 19, 2010

Dr. Rosa Perez
271 University Boulevard
University of Kentucky
Lexington, KY 40506-1440

Dear Dr. Perez:

The Situation

As we discussed on the phone, I would appreciate your writing a recommendation letter for me. You know the quality of my academic work, my qualities as a person, and my potential for working in the medical field.

The Explanation

As my professor for Biology 201 and 202, you are familiar with my grades and work habits. As my adviser, you know my career plans and understand whether I have the qualities needed to succeed in the medical profession. I am asking you for your recommendation because I am applying for summer employment with the Lexington Ambulance Service. I recently received my Emergency Medical Technician (Basic) license to prepare for such work.

The Action

Please send your letter to Rick Falk, EMT Coordinator, at the University Placement Office by April 8. Thank you for your help. Let me know if you need any other information (phone 231-6700; e-mail jnwllms@ukentucky.edu).

Yours sincerely,

Jon Williams

Jon Williams

The Application Essay ◼▪▪

For some applications, you may be asked to submit an essay, a personal statement, or a response paper. For example, you might be applying for admission to an academic program (social work, engineering, optometry school) or for an internship, a scholarship, or a research grant. Whatever the situation, what you write and how well you write it will be important factors in the success of your application.

On the facing page is a model application essay. Jessy Jezowski wrote this essay as part of her application to a college social work program.

TIPS for an application essay

- **Understand what you are being asked to write and why.** How does the essay fit into the entire application? Who will read your essay? What will they look for?

- **Focus on the instructions for writing the essay.** What type of question is it? What topics are you asked to write about? What hints do the directions give about possible organization, emphasis, style, length, and method of submitting the essay?

- **Be honest with yourself and your readers.** Don't try to write only what you think readers want to hear.

- **Think about your purpose and audience:**
  - What do you want to gain (internship, scholarship, job interview), and how could your writing help you gain it?
  - Who are your readers? What do they know about you? What should they know?

- **Develop your essay using the following organization** (if the instructions allow for it):
  - An introduction with a fresh, interesting opening statement and a clear focus or theme
  - A body that develops the focus or theme clearly and concisely—with some details and examples—in a way appropriate to the instructions
  - A conclusion that stresses a positive point and looks forward to participating in the program, internship, organization, or position

- **Write in a style that is personal but professional.** Use words that fit the subject and the readers. Avoid clichés, and balance generalizations with concrete examples and details.

- **Refine your first draft into a polished piece.** First, get feedback from another student or, if appropriate, a professor, and revise the essay. Second, edit the final version thoroughly: You don't want typos, incorrect names, and grammar errors to derail your application.

Model Application Essay

Audio

February 28, 2010
Jessy Jezowski

Personal Statement

The opening provides a clear focus for the essay.

While growing up in Chicago, I would see people hanging out on street
corners, by grocery stores, and in parks—with no home and barely any belongings.
Poverty and its related problems are all around us, and yet most people walk by
them with blinders on. I have found myself quick to assume that someone else will
help the poor man on the corner, the woman trapped in an abusive relationship,
or the teenager struggling with an eating disorder. But I know in my heart that
all members of society are responsible to and for each other. Social welfare issues
affect every member of society— including me.

1

The writer demonstrates knowledge of the field and explains what she hopes to learn.

Because these issues are serious and difficult to solve, I wish to major in
social work and eventually become a social worker. In the major, I want to gain
the knowledge, skills, and attitudes that will make me part of the solution, not
part of the problem. By studying social work institutions, the practices of social
work, and the theory and history behind social work, I hope to learn how to help
people help themselves. When that pregnant teenager comes to me, I want to have
strong, practical advice—and be part of an effective social work agency that can
help implement that advice.

2

Two concrete examples help back up her general statements.

I am especially interested at this point in working with families and
teenagers, in either a community counseling or school setting. Two experiences
have created this interest. First, a woman in my church who works for an adoption
agency, Ms. Lesage, has modeled for me what it means to care for individuals and
families within a community and around the world. Second, I was involved in
a peer counseling program in high school. As counselors, we received training
in interpersonal relationships and the nature of helping. In a concrete way, I
experienced the complex challenges of helping others.

3

The conclusion summarizes her goals for the future.

I believe strongly in the value of all people and am interested in the well-
being of others. As a social worker, I would strive to make society better (for
individuals, families, and communities) by serving those in need, whatever their
problems.

4

■ Preparing a Resumé

A strong resumé isn't generic—a ho-hum fill-in-the-blanker. Rather, it's a vivid word picture of your skills, knowledge, and past responsibilities. It says exactly who you are by providing the kind of information listed below.

Personal Data: name, address, phone number, e-mail address (enough for the reader to identify you and reach you easily).

Job Objective: the type of position you want and the type of organization for which you want to work.

Skills Summary: the key qualities and skills you bring to a position, listed with supporting details. Here are some skill areas that you might consider for your own resumé:

- Communication
- Organization
- Problem solving
- Computer

- Management (people, money, other resources)
- Working with people, counseling, training
- Sales, marketing, public relations
- Languages

Experience: positions you've held (where and when), and your specific duties and your accomplishments.

Education: degrees, courses, and special projects.

Other Experiences: volunteer work, awards, achievements, tutoring jobs, extra-curricular activities (related to your job objective), licenses, and certifications.

TIPS for resumé writing

- **Design each resumé to fit the particular job.**
- **Be specific—use numbers, dates, and names.**
- **Present information first that is the most impressive** and/or most important to the job for which you are applying. This guideline will help you determine whether to put your experience or your education first.
- **Use everyday language and short, concise phrases.**
- **Be parallel**—list similar items using similar structures.
- **Use boldface type, underlining, white space, and indentations to make your resumé more readable.**
- **Get someone else's reaction;** then revise and proofread.

Sample Resumé

Ada Overlie

Home	**School**
451 Wiser Lake Road	Ogg Hall, Room 222
Ferndale, WA 98248-8941	Balliole College
(360) 354-5916	Eugene, OR 97440-0222
	Phone: (503) 341-3611
	Email: dvrl@balliole.edu

Present contact information and employment objectives.

Job Objective: Part-time assistant in a nursery or greenhouse.

Skills Summary:

Horticultural Skills: Familiar with garden planting, care, and harvesting practices—planning, timing, companion planting, fertilizing.

Lab Skills: Familiar with procedures for taking fruit samples, pureeing them, checking for foreign objects, and testing sugar content.

Feature skills with appropriate headings and lists.

Experience:

Summers 2009 and 2010: Lab Technician.
  Mayberry Farms and Processing Plant, Ferndale, WA.
  Worked in Quality Control testing raspberries to make sure they met company standards.

Summers 2007 and 2008: Camp Counselor.
  Emerald Lake Summer Camp, Hillsboro, WA.
  Supervised 12-year-olds in many camp activities, including nature hikes in which we identified plants and trees.

List work and education chronologically, from most to least current.

Education:

August 2010 to present: Balliole College, Eugene, OR.
  Environmental Studies and Communication major.
  Courses completed and in progress include Environmental Studies and General Botany. First semester GPA 3.7.

August 2006 to June 2010: Ferndale High School, Ferndale, WA.
  Courses included Biology, Agriculture, U.S. Government, and Economics.
  Special Projects: Completed research papers on clean-water legislation and organic farming practices.

Format for paper only; boldface, underlining, bulleted or indented lists, two columns.

References available upon request.

Offer references.

Sample Electronic Resumé

To find employees, companies often use computer programs to search electronic resumés for keywords (especially nouns) found in job descriptions or ads. Anticipating such a search, Jonathan Greenlind identified keywords and inserted them into his job description and resumé.

Present contact information and employment objective.

Jonathan L. Greenlind
806 5th Avenue
Waterloo, Iowa 50701
Telephone: 319.268.6955
E-mail: grnlnd@aol.com

OBJECTIVE
Position as hydraulics supervisor that calls for hydraulics expertise, technical skills, mechanical knowledge, reliability, and enthusiasm

List skills, experiences, and education using many keywords.

SKILLS
Operation and repair specialist in main and auxiliary power systems, subsystems, landing gears, brakes and pneumatic systems, hydraulic motors, reservoirs, actuators, pumps and cylinders from six types of hydraulic systems

Dependable, resourceful, strong leader, team worker

Format for e-mail:
• one column
• bullets
• simple sans serif typeface
• flush-left margin
• no italics, boldface, or underlining
• ASCII or RTF text (readable by all computers)

EXPERIENCE
Aviation Hydraulics Technician
United States Navy (2005–present)
• Repair, test, and maintain basic hydraulics, distribution systems, and aircraft structural hydraulics systems
• Manufacture low-, medium-, and high-pressure rubber and Teflon hydraulic hoses, and aluminum stainless-steel tubing
• Perform preflight, postflight, and other periodic aircraft inspections
• Operate ground-support equipment
• Supervise personnel

Aircraft Mechanic
Sioux Falls International Airport (2003–2005)
Sioux Falls, South Dakota
• Performed fueling, engine overhauls, minor repairs, and tire and oil changes of various aircraft

EDUCATION
• United States Navy (2005–2009)
• Certificate in Hydraulic Technical School "A", GPA 3.8/4.0
• Certificate in Hydraulic, Pneumatic Test Stand School, GPA 3.9/4.0
• Courses in Corrosion Control, Hydraulic Tube Bender, Aviation Structural Mechanics
• Equivalent of 10 semester hours In Hydraulic Systems Maintenance and Structural Repair

Offer references.

References available upon request.

25 Writing for the Web

A strong website depends on well-written, well-organized, and well-designed content. Above all, web content should be concise, focused, and visually appealing. After all, people don't read websites so much as they scan them, so information should be presented in short chunks of text. For that reason, webpages should be brief, designed to minimize scrolling and maximize the use of available screen space.

This chapter addresses the rhetorical fundamentals of creating a strong website, developing strong webpages, and using writing venues such as OWLs, blogs, MUDs, MOOs, and social networking sites.

Learning Outcomes

▶ Understand webpage elements and functions.

Audio

▶ Read and assess webpage contents and designs.

▶ Develop informative webpages and orderly, accessible websites.

Video

▶ Test, refine, and post webpages.

▶ Understand venues like OWLs, blogs, MUDs, MOOs, chat servers, and social media.

Visually Speaking ▶ What does the image above suggest about writing for the web? What subject or scene might you picture instead? Why?

■ Webpage Elements and Functions

To design an effective website and develop dynamic webpages, you need to start with a basic understanding of webpage elements and functions. Because webpages use the same elements as printed pages, many of the same design principles apply. However, unlike printed pages, webpages are fluid (flowing their contents to match screen and browser settings), and they can include both elements and functions, as shown and discussed below and on the pages that follow.

Page Elements ■■■

On the web, page elements are defined primarily by purpose—headings, body text, image, and so forth. Before designing a webpage, it helps to understand the purpose of those elements.

1. **Headings** (also called headers) come in six levels and are used to separate different sections and subsections of web documents. Heading 1 is the largest; heading 6 is the smallest. All are bold black serif font by default.

2. **Body text** is organized into chunks, called paragraphs, which are separated by white space. Unlike printed text, paragraphs on the web do not generally have a first-line indentation. By default, body text is a black serif font roughly the same size as a heading level 4 (though not bold).

3. **Preformatted text** is "monospaced"; it displays all characters at the same width, like typewriter font. It is used primarily to show mathematical formulas, computer code, and the like.

4. **Lists** can be formatted in three types: Ordered lists are numbered, unordered lists are bulleted, and definition lists present pairs of information—usually terms alongside their definitions, which are indented. Because readers can scan them quickly, lists are an efficient way to present information.

5. **Images** can include photographs, clip art, graphs, line drawings, cartoon figures, icons, and animations. These can make a page much slower to display, so use them judiciously. Always be sure you have the legal right to use any images that you include in your pages. (See "Copyright violations," page 479.)

6. **Background color** for a webpage is white by default (medium gray in older browsers), which makes the standard headings and text easily legible.

7. **Tables** are a common tool for webpage layout. Simply put, tables are grids made up of rows and columns. By creating a table with no visible borders, a web designer can gain some control over where elements appear on a page.

Sample Webpage

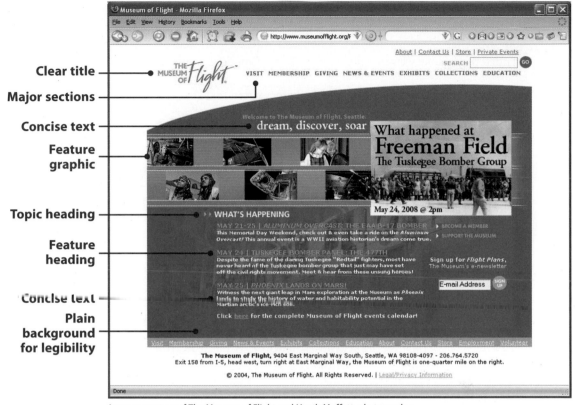

Clear title
Major sections
Concise text
Feature graphic
Topic heading
Feature heading
Concise text
Plain background for legibility

Images courtesy of The Museum of Flight and Heath Moffett, photographer.

fyi As seen above, not all webpages have black serif font on a white background. However, because web browsers are designed to flow content to suit each computer screen, changing the default styles can be problematic. It helps to keep the following tips in mind:

- **Simple is best.** Simple pages display the fastest and have the least chance of breaking. The more graphics you add, the longer a page takes to load. The more you change the default font settings, the more complicated the code becomes and the greater the chance of computer error.

- **Different computers display things differently.** Not every computer has the same font styles installed, and colors look different on different monitors. Always check your work on many different systems.

- **The user is king (or queen).** No matter which font style and size you choose, the reader can change how things display on her or his machine. So focus on useful content and clear organization instead of struggling to control graphic design.

Page Functions ■■■■

Webpage functions set electronic pages apart from printed pages. On the web, readers can browse pages in almost any order, send and receive e-mail, send messages and files, post messages, and join live "chat" sessions. In short, readers can interact with webpages in ways they cannot with printed pages. Like webpage elements, webpage functions should serve your site's purpose.

1. **Hyperlinks** are strings of specially formatted text that enable readers to jump to another spot on the web. Internal hyperlinks (links for short) take you to another section of the same webpage or to another page on the same site. External links lead to pages on other websites. "Mail to" links allow readers to address e-mail to recipients, such as a professor or a classmate.

2. **Menus** offer structured lists of links that operate like a website's table of contents. Menus are typically presented in a column or row at the edge of a webpage. Good websites include a standard site menu on every page so readers don't get lost.

3. **Forms** enable the host of a website to interact with the site's readers. Web forms can be used for questionnaires, surveys, complaints and service requests, job applications, or suggestion boxes.

■ Developing a Website and Webpages

Regardless of the purpose, topic, and audience of your website, you can develop it by following the steps outlined on the next four pages.

Get focused. ■■■■

Create an overview of the project—the purpose, the audience, and the topic. The questions below will help you get focused and develop fitting content for the site.

1. **What is the primary purpose of the website?** Am I creating a library of documents that my audience will reference? Am I going to present information and announcements about myself or my organization? Am I trying to promote a specific product or service?

2. **Who is the site's audience?** Which people will seek out this site? Why? What do they need? How often will they visit the site, and how often should it be updated? How comfortable is my audience with using computers and websites? What level of formality is appropriate for the language? Which graphics, colors, and design will appeal to them?

3. **What is the site's central topic?** What do I already know about the topic? What do I need to learn, and where can I find the information? How will I demonstrate that the information is credible and reliable? What will my audience want to know about the topic? How can I divide the information into brief segments? What visual elements would help present my message? Which other websites address this topic? Should my website link to them?

Establish your central message. ■ ▪ ■

After you've made decisions about your purpose, audience, and topic, write out the main idea you want to communicate. You might call this the theme or "mission statement" of your website.

> The purpose of this website is to inform fellow students and the <u>general public</u> about <u>current research into hybrid-vehicle transportation</u>.

To help you stay on target with your project, post this mission statement in plain sight. Note, too, that you might modify your goal as the site develops, or add secondary goals for the site.

Create a site map. ■ ▪ ■

As you gather content for your site, create a site map. Websites can be as simple as an elementary school bulletin board or as complex as a United States federal government site. Here are four principles to keep in mind:

> 1. **No one will read your entire site.** People curl up with books, not websites. If your audience is not asking for content, don't provide it.
> 2. **Your site will have many small audiences**—not one big audience. A site's audience may include anyone with a computer, an Internet connection, and an interest in your site's topic. Keep all potential readers in mind.
> 3. **Websites are not linear.** A single "home page" or "splash page" introduces the site, which branches out like tree limbs into pages with varied content. Websites "conclude" whenever the reader quits reading.
> 4. **You may need to build the site in phases.** You can add pages to a website after it has been published, so be careful that your site's organization does not limit future additions.

Sample Site Map

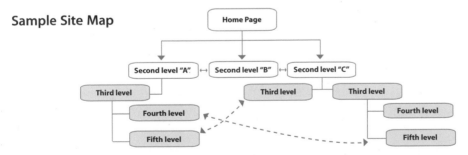

A map for a simple site might include only four items—a home page, page "A," page "B," and page "C" (as shown in white on the diagram). Users can "jump" between any of the secondary-level pages or back to the home page.

A more complex website typically needs more levels (as shown in green on the diagram). Likewise, its menu will offer more navigation choices. Related pages might be connected with links (as represented by the dotted lines).

Study similar sites. ■▪■

Learn from successful sites, especially sites that serve a similar purpose—a campus club site, a department site, a personal job-search site. How do similar sites use elements: headings, body text, preformatted text, background color, lists, images, and tables? How do the sites use functions—links, menus, and forms? The seven traits (see pages 136–137) can also supply helpful benchmarks for evaluating sites.

1. **Ideas:** Does the site present clear ideas and information?
2. **Organization:** Is the content carefully and clearly structured?
3. **Voice:** Is the tone fitting for the audience?
4. **Words:** Is the language understandable? Is the wording concise?
5. **Sentences:** Are the sentences easy to read and generally short?
6. **Correctness:** Does the site avoid distracting errors?
7. **Design:** Are the pages user-friendly? Is the site easy to navigate?

Gather and prioritize content. ■▪■

Brainstorm and research the actual content, with the goal of creating an outline for your site. How many topics will the site address? How wide will your coverage of a topic be? How deep? Your outline can also be used to create the website's table of contents. Based on your research, discussions with others, and the deadlines for the project, select the content, features, and functions your site will offer.

Think about support materials. ■▪■

List the documents (brochures, artworks, instructions, poems, reports) that will be presented on your site and note whether they will be displayed as webpages, made available for readers to download, or both. Construct a grid to keep track of how documents will be used.

List graphics that could make your pages more visual and informative and could help readers grasp the meaning of complex data or processes. Photographs may help "put a face" on your organization. Logos and icons will help brand your pages. Review the list below for electronic files that may be appropriate to your topic, audience, and purpose. (Remember: Use only graphics that are legally available. See the discussion of copyright on page 479.)

Images	Audio	Video
charts	music	animations
drawings	sound effects	film clips
graphs	spoken text	presentations
photographs		webcasts

Design and develop individual pages. ■ ⬝ ■

When you create individual pages for your site, consider both the design and the content—specifically, how to make the two work well together.

Design Principles

Most webpages—and the pages of most other publications—are designed on grids. Look at any newspaper or magazine page, and you should be able to draw horizontal and vertical lines denoting columns and rows of content. Some rows may span multiple columns, and some columns may overrun several rows.

Another fundamental design concept is balance. You might balance light elements with dark ones, text with images, and so forth. The balance of your page design should be driven by the purpose of your website, its audience, and its topic.

Websites may contain a variety of pages—each tailored to different purposes, audiences, and topics—to present some combination of informational and promotional content. Use each page's purpose to guide decisions about which elements and functions to include.

 Webpage design should follow fundamental document-design principles, including strategies for using color effectively. For more information, visit **www. thecollegewriter.com/4e.**

Drafting Principles

1. **Identify the site.** Working from your mission statement, write a brief introduction informing visitors about the site's purpose.
2. **Provide clear links.** Create links for your pages, using clear descriptors such as "Original Poetry." (Avoid phrases such as "Click here for poetry.") If necessary, add a descriptive sentence to further identify the link. Let visitors know precisely where each link will take them.
3. **Introduce each page.** Search sites may deliver some visitors to a page other than your home page. Give each page a brief introduction that clearly identifies it. Also, remember to provide a link back to your home page.
4. **Title each page.** Atop the browser window is a title bar where the current page should be identified. This title is used in browser bookmarks, search engine listings, and the like, so be sure to give every page on your website a descriptive title.
5. **Keep pages uncluttered.** Dense text is even more difficult to read on screen than on paper, so use short paragraphs when you can. Add headings to identify sections, and include visuals to help break up the text.
6. **Save the page as HTML.** To be viewed in a web browser, your pages must be formatted in Hypertext Markup Language (HTML). Your word processor may have a "Save as HTML" or "Save as Webpage" option. Many HTML editing programs are also available on the web.

Test, refine, and post your site. ■▪▪

Most websites are developed through the combined efforts of writers, graphic designers, and programmers. In such an environment, many content and layout ideas might be considered, rejected, and reformulated to produce and launch the site. Of course, the audience ultimately decides a website's success or failure. For that reason, test and refine your site before posting it.

1. **Check the site yourself.** Open your home page from your web browser. Does the site make sense? Can you navigate it easily?

2. **Get peer review.** Ask classmates—both experienced and inexperienced with the website's topic and with Internet searching—to use your site. Watch them navigate it, and take notes about any confusion they have.

3. **Check the text.** Reread all the text on your site. Trim wherever possible (the shorter, the better online), and check all spelling and punctuation.

4. **Check the graphics.** Do images load properly? Do they load quickly? Are menus and page headings in the same place on every page?

5. **Provide a feedback link.** Provide your e-mail address on the site, inviting visitors to contact you with any comments after the site goes "live."

6. **Post the site.** Upload the site to your hosting space. (Check your host's instructions for doing so.) Add the posting date to each page, and update it each time you change a page.

7. **Check for universality.** View the site on several different types of computers, using different browsers. Does the layout display well on all of them? Make any needed changes.

8. **Announce the site.** Advertise your site in e-mails. Submit it to search sites. Consider joining a "web ring" of similar sites to draw more traffic. Let your professors, classmates, friends, and family know about your site.

9. **Monitor the site.** After a site has been launched, its success may be measured by the amount of traffic it receives, feedback submitted by users, and any use of resources or services. (Check with your host for ways to measure traffic.)

10. **Make adjustments and updates.** A website should be a living thing. Update the content when possible to keep it fresh, and make any adjustments needed to adapt to changing technologies.

INSIGHT: Avoid using any features and functions that do not support your overall purpose for writing. If you find yourself distracted by the many bells and whistles of the web, remember that it's better to have a simple website that presents information clearly and effectively than a complex site that does not.

Sample Webpages

On the next two pages, you'll find sample pages from student and academic websites. Study each model for insights about what makes for strong web content and design.

 For further analysis of webpages, including nonprofit and business sites, go to **www.thecollegewriter.com/4e.** There you'll also find tutorials on analyzing and evaluating websites.

Student-Designed Website

The following website was developed by undergraduate students from a Southwestern U.S. university who were studying abroad. Southwest Sojourners is a multiuser site with blogs and chat rooms that allow students to keep in touch with one another and with friends and family back home.

- **Purpose:** This site is a gathering place for undergraduate students studying abroad. It describes itself as a "home away from home" for such students. The tone is light, conversational, and inviting, as befitting the purpose of connecting these students to one another and to the important people in their lives.

- **Audience:** The site is meant for students, friends, and family members. By providing straight news, individualized blogs, and chat rooms and e-mail options, the site allows users to be as passive or as active as they wish. Membership is required for active participation, and members must "sign" a user's agreement before posting material.

- **Format:** The golden background and sun icon visually convey the Southwestern theme, while the minimalist format makes the site easy to navigate. A large four-item toolbar on the left directs users to the linked pages, and brief text on the right gives a clear indication of what lies at the end of each link.

SOUTHWEST SOJOURNERS

Welcome to Southwest Sojourners! This site is meant to be a home away from home for students from Southwestern U.S. universities who are studying abroad. If you are such a student—or a friend or family member of such a student—this is the spot for you! Lurk, if you like, or log in and join the conversation.

Sojourners News
These pages are updated regularly with information about special events on this site—and in reality.

Click here for a list of students who are blogging about their studies abroad.

Student Blogs
For members only: Join the conversation with students in England, Germany, Italy, India, Japan—and elsewhere!

Chat Rooms
Membership is free, but we do need a little information and a digital signature on our posting agreement.

Log In!
Contact the Webmaster at: Webmaster@southsojourn.edu.
Site design: Mikayla Evans and Griffin Jenson

site launched: 29 January 2008
last updated: 29 July 2011

Academic Website

The Massachusetts Institute of Technology's Space Nanotechnology Laboratory website is an academic research site. It contains information about a specialized laboratory in the MIT Kavli Institute for Astrophysics and Space Research.

Courtesy of Space Nanotechnology Laboratory, Massachusetts Institute of Technology.

- **Purpose:** This site aims to inform a very specific audience about a team of professors, graduate research assistants, and staff and their work to develop nanotechnology for space exploration. The site features the laboratory's creation of the "MIT Nanoruler," a device capable of measuring to the billionth of a meter. The site also provides pages that outline the laboratory's mission, history, people, projects, and facilities.

- **Audience:** This website addresses "a consortium of microfabrication facilities with shared interests." In addition to providing articles of interest to this group, the site includes a list of available positions for professionals and students who may wish to join the laboratory. A sponsors page shows that the audience also includes funding agencies such as NASA and the National Science Foundation.

- **Format:** The top of the home page announces the site and university, using iconic images of waveforms and a satellite to convey its central focus. Beneath this masthead, the page features the laboratory's current great achievement: "Home of the MIT Nanoruler" and "Read more about the Nanoruler." A selection of photos highlights work in the lab, and to the left, a list of pages makes navigation transparent.

■ Writing for Different Internet Environments

The Internet is a complex construct made up of much more than webpages. Other writing venues on the Net are described below, with writing tips for each.

OWLs Your university or college probably has a writing lab where you can seek help with your writing assignments. It might also have a web-based OWL (online writing lab) where you can access help. OWLs post answers to questions you may have about writing, and they often allow you to e-mail or send an instant message (see below) to a writing tutor. Before contacting an OWL tutor, carefully read any instructions posted on the site. *Example:* Purdue University OWL, owl.english.purdue.edu

Web Link

MUDs, MOOs, and MUSHes Some instructors hold classes or deliver lectures online in a MUD (multiuser dimension), a text-based "world" that people can share. (MOOs and MUSHes are variants of MUDs.) MUDs have virtual rooms to explore and virtual objects to examine and handle. To use a MUD, you must learn the text commands for interacting with it. Most MUDs require software for a telnet connection, but some are accessible via telnet-enabled webpages. *Example:* Diversity University MOO, www.marshall.edu/commdis/moo

Web Link

Message Boards Many websites have forms that allow visitors to post messages for public display. The messages and any replies are usually listed together so that readers can follow the message "thread."

Web Link

Mailing Lists Mailing lists allow users to send and receive text messages within a specific group of people interested in a particular subject. The software that maintains a mailing list is called a "list server." Some mailing lists are excellent resources of specialized information. *Example:* **QUANTUMTEACHING-NMC <MTEACHING-NMC@ LISTS.MAINE.EDU>**

Web Link

Chat Servers A chat server provides a place on the Net where you can type a message that other people will see instantly. Those people can then respond with text messages of their own. Some teachers and tutors may use a chat room to confer with students or to hold a class discussion online. Although some chat servers require special software, many are available as webpages. *Example:* Yahoo! Chat, chat.yahoo.com

Web Link

Instant Messaging Services Instant messaging (IM) services allow you to send a text message instantaneously to friends and colleagues who use the same software. Most IMs also allow users to send computer files to one another. (Just be careful not to pass on a computer virus this way.) *Example:* ICQ, web.icq.com

Web Link

Blogs A blog (short for "weblog") is basically just an online journal posted to a webpage. In effect, it is a one-person message board (see above). For many people, blogging is more convenient than creating a webpage of their own, because it involves no design issues and requires no uploading of files.

Web Link

Critical-Thinking and Writing Activities

As directed by your instructor, complete the following activities.

1. Research and study the content, style, and design of websites related to your particular major, field, or discipline. Then develop a report on those sites, incorporating three or four screen shots for analysis.

2. Go to the home page of your college or university and review the page elements and functions. Team up with a classmate to discuss how well the page addresses its purpose(s), audience(s), and topic(s). Then imagine you have been hired to revise and refine the page. Print out a copy and mark it up with your changes. Create a "mockup" of a new and improved home page. Draft a one-page overview that explains how your revision is better than the original.

3. Working with classmates, brainstorm a list of campus clubs and associations that currently do not have websites (or at least not quality websites). Using the guidelines from this chapter, develop a website for one of them. As another option, consider a nonprofit organization in your area. Collaborate and conduct research as needed.

Learning-Outcomes Checklist

Use this checklist to review and revise your site and its pages:

_____ The purpose of the website is presented—or evident—on the home page and elsewhere on the site.

_____ The page elements—headlines, body text, preformatted text, background colors, lists, images, and tables—work together and are suited to the page's audience, topic, and purpose.

_____ The page functions, including navigation menus, are logically presented and enable readers to find what they need quickly.

_____ The content collected for the site (from brochures to reports) and support materials (images, audio, and video) are available, approved, accurate, and in the correct format for presentation or download.

_____ The site plan allows information to be presented and cross-referenced in logical and efficient pathways.

_____ The page design incorporates the design principles described on pages 395–396.

_____ The informational and promotional aspects of the site are appropriate to the audience, topic, and purpose.

26 Preparing Oral Presentations

Throughout your career, you will give many oral presentations. In each situation, start by identifying the following:

- **Your purpose:** Am I trying to persuade, inspire, inform, or teach?
- **Your audience:** What are their ages, interests, knowledge of the topic, and attitude toward me?
- **Your topic:** What should I speak about, and where can I find the best information?

This chapter will help you answer these questions and develop a strong speech.

Learning Outcomes

Audio

- ► Accurately assess a speaking situation.

- ► Develop an opening, middle, and closing that fit your speaking situation.

Video

- ► Develop list, outline, and manuscript forms of a speech, complete with cues for audio/visual effects.

- ► Design and use presentation software.

- ► Plan, write, rehearse, and present an effective speech.

Visually Speaking ► What does the photograph above suggest about the nature and impact of public speaking?

■ Organizing Your Presentation

After you've gathered your information, you must organize and develop the message. How? Start by thinking about your presentation as having three distinct parts: (1) an introduction, (2) a body, and (3) a conclusion. The guidelines on this page and the following two pages will help you integrate, organize, and refine all the parts so they communicate the message and achieve your purpose.

Prepare an introduction. ■■■

For any speaking situation, you should develop an introduction that does the following things:

- Greets the audience and grabs their attention
- Communicates your interest in them
- Introduces your topic and main idea
- Shows that you have something worthwhile to say
- Establishes an appropriate tone

You may greet the audience in many ways, including introducing yourself or making appropriate comments about the occasion, the individuals present, or the setting. Following these comments, introduce your topic and main idea as quickly and as clearly as you can. For example, you could open with one of these attention-grabbing strategies:

- A little-known fact or statistic
- A series of questions
- A humorous story or anecdote
- An appropriate quotation
- A description of a serious problem
- A cartoon, picture, or drawing
- A short demonstration
- A statement about the topic's importance
- An eye-catching prop or display
- A video or an audio clip

TIP: As a matter of courtesy, audiences will generally give you their attention—but only for about thirty seconds. After that, you must *earn* it by presenting information that they believe is worth hearing.

Develop the body. ◼▪◾

The body of your presentation should deliver the message—and supporting points—so clearly that the audience understands the presentation after hearing it only once. The key to developing such a clear message is choosing an organizational pattern that fits your purpose.

Before you outline the body, take a moment to review what you want your presentation to do: Explain a problem? Promote an idea? Teach a process? Be sure the organizational pattern will help you do that. For example, if you want to teach a process, the outline should list the process steps in chronological order. If your outline is clear, you may begin to write.

Organizational Patterns

Organizational patterns for explaining a process and other purposes are listed below.

- **Chronological order:** Arrange information according to the time order in which events (or steps in a process) take place.
- **Order of importance:** Arrange information according to its importance—greatest to least or least to greatest.
- **Comparison/contrast:** Give information about subjects by comparing and contrasting them.
- **Cause/effect:** Give information about a situation or problem by showing the causes and the effects.
- **Order of location:** Arrange information about subjects according to where things are located in relation to each other.
- **Problem/solution:** Describe a problem and then present a solution for it.

Writing an Outline or a Manuscript

After deciding how to organize your message, write it out in either outline or manuscript form. For help, see the tips below and the model on pages 405–407.

Body-Building Tips

- Build your presentation around several key ideas. (Don't try to cover too much ground.)
- Write with a personal, natural voice.
- Support your main points with reliable facts and clear examples.
- Present your information in short, easy-to-follow segments.
- Use positive, respectful language. (Avoid jargon.)
- Use graphic aids and handouts.

Come to a conclusion. ■▪▪

A strong introduction and conclusion work like bookends supporting the body of the presentation. The introduction gets the audience's attention, sets the tone, states the main idea, and identifies the key points of the message. Almost in reverse, the conclusion reviews those points, restates the main idea, reinforces the tone, and refocuses the audience on what it should think about or do. Together, those bookends emphasize and clarify the message so that listeners will understand and remember it.

Concluding Strategies

Here are some strategies—which you can use alone or in combination—for concluding a presentation:

- Review your main idea and key points.
- Issue a personal challenge.
- Come "full circle." (State those arguments or details that back up your original point.)
- Recommend a plan of action.
- Suggest additional sources of information.
- Thank the audience and ask for questions.

Hold a Q & A session. ■▪▪

After your presentation, you may want to invite your audience to ask questions. Very often, a Q & A session is the real payoff for participants. They can ask for clarification of points or inquire about how your message applies to their personal situations. Audience members may even offer their own insights or solutions to problems mentioned in the presentation.

Q & A Tips

The following suggestions will help you lead a good Q & A session:

- Listen carefully and think about each part of the question.
- Repeat or paraphrase questions for the benefit of the entire group.
- Answer the questions concisely and clearly.
- Respond honestly when you don't know the answer, and offer to find one.
- Ask for a follow-up question if someone seems confused after your answer.
- Look directly at the group when you answer.
- Be prepared to pose an important question or two if no one asks a question.
- Conclude by thanking the audience for their participation.

Writing Your Presentation

How much of your presentation you actually write out depends on your topic, audience, purpose, and—of course—personal style. The three most common forms to use when making a presentation are a list, an outline, and a manuscript.

List: Use a list for a short, informal speech such as an after-dinner introduction. Think about your purpose and then list the following:

- Your opening sentence (or two)
- A summary phrase for each of your main points
- Your closing sentence

Outline: Use an outline for a more complex or formal topic. You can organize your material in greater detail without tying yourself to a word-for-word presentation. Here's one way you can do it:

- Opening (complete sentences)
- All main points (sentences)
- Supporting points (phrases) quotations (written out) all supporting technical details, statistics, and sources (listed)
- Closing (complete sentences)

Wherever appropriate, include notes on visual aids (in caps or boldface).

Manuscript: Use the guidelines below if you plan to write out your presentation word for word:

- Double-space and number pages (or cards).
- Use complete sentences on a page (do not run sentences from one page to another).
- Mark difficult words for pronunciation.
- Mark the script for interpretation using symbols such as boldface or italics to signal emphasis or vocal color.

List

1. Opening sentence or two
2. Phrase 1
   Phrase 2
   Phrase 3
3. Closing sentence

Outline

I. Opening statement
   A. Point with support
   B. Point (purpose or goal)
      [VISUAL 1]
II. Body (with 3-5 main points)
   A. Main point
      1. Supporting details
      2. Supporting details
   B. Main point
      1. Supporting details
      2. Supporting details
   C. Main point
      1. Supporting details
      2. Supporting details
III. Closing statement
   A. Point, including restatement of purpose
   B. Point, possibly a call to action
      [VISUAL 2]

Student Model ■·■

Interactive

In her formal presentation below, student Burnette Sawyer argues that college students must begin a retirement savings plan today. Notice that she uses italics to mark words needing vocal color and boldface to mark words needing emphasis. She places all visual aid cues in color.

Save Now or Pay Later

Imagine that you've finished school, gotten a job, worked hard all week, and this dollar bill represents your whole paycheck. [hold up dollar bill] As your employer, I'm about to hand you the check when I stop, tear off about 20 percent like this, give it to Uncle Sam, and say, "Here's my employee's income tax." Then I tear off another 30 percent like this, give that to Uncle Sam too, and say, "And here's her Medicare and Social Security tax."   1

Finally, I give you this half and say, "Here, hard worker, this is what's left of your *whole paycheck*."   2

Does that sound like science fiction?   3

Senator Alan Simpson doesn't think so. In the magazine *Modern Maturity,* he says that unless legislation changes the Social Security system, *our generation* will have to pay 20 percent [SLIDE 1] of our paychecks as income tax, and 30 percent [SLIDE 2] as Social Security tax. That means we can keep just **50 percent** [SLIDE 3] of what we earn.   4

But the news gets **worse**. Remember this 30 percent that we paid to Social Security? [hold up piece of dollar bill] Well, that won't be enough money for retired people to live on in the year 2043. Remember that year, 2043—we'll come back to that soon.   5

What's the problem? The Social Security system can't ensure our savings for retirement.   6

What's the solution? We have to start our own savings plans, and the earlier, the better.   7

Ever since the Social Security system started back in 1935 [SLIDE 4], it has never been secure. While the system has been "fixed" a number of times, these fix-it jobs haven't solved the problem. For example, writer Keith Carlson points out that in 1983 [SLIDE 5] Congress raised payroll taxes, extended the retirement age, and said that the system would be in good financial shape until 2056.   8

But then, says Carlson, *just nine years later,* a report came out saying that Congress had been **wrong**. The report [SLIDE 6] said in 1992 that Social Security money wouldn't even last that long—it would run out by 2043. *Remember that year, 2043?* That's before many of us are supposed *to retire at age 67*!   9

Do you think this news is bad? The AARP Bulletin reported on the Bipartisan Commission on Entitlement and Tax Reform. This commission warned that   10

Sidebar annotations:

The speaker begins with an anecdote.

She tears the dollar for emphasis.

The speaker asks questions to involve the audience.

Throughout the speech, she uses 11 slides to give her listeners a clear understanding of the main points.

entitlement programs like Social Security [SLIDE 7] are growing so fast they could "bankrupt the country" by the year 2029—long before we retire!

So what should we do? This fall many of us will vote in a presidential election 11 for the first time. Both Democrats and Republicans say they have a plan to fix Social Security. What if we all vote for the presidential candidate with the best plan? Will that save our retirement funds? **Don't count on it!** As the track record for Social Security shows, one more fix-it job won't fix the system. We have to start *our own* retirement plans—and do it early in our careers.

In fact, in his book *Retirement 101,* Willard Enteman says that we should start 12 a personal savings plan the day we get our first paychecks. In sociology class last week, Mr. Christians made the same point. He gave us this bar graph [SLIDE 8] showing that if our goal is to save $500,000 by age 67, we had better *start early* before saving gets too expensive.

As you can see from the graph, if we start saving when we're 25, we can reach 13 $500,000 by saving just $121 a month. [SLIDE 9] If we wait until we're 35, we'll have to save $282 a month. [SLIDE 10] If we wait until we're 45, we'll have to put away $698 a month. [SLIDE 11] And if we wait until we're 55, we'll need $2,079 a month.

Look at the difference. To reach $500,000 by age 67 would cost $121 a month 14 if we start at 25, and $2,079 a month if we start at 55.

What's my point? The Social Security system *can't promise* us financial 15 security when we retire.

What's the solution? We have to start our own savings plans; and the *earlier* 16 we start, the *easier* it will be to reach our goals.

Note: Sample slides for this presentation are shown on page 408.

> The closing paragraphs help listeners reflect on the subject.

Marking Your Presentation

As you rehearse your presentation, decide which words or phrases to emphasize, where to pause, and where to add visual aids. Then use the symbols and text enhancements below to mark the copy of your presentation.

Italic or boldface. . . . . for additional feeling or emotion

Underlining . . . . for greater volume or emphasis

Dash, diagonal, ellipsis . . . . for a pause—or / a break in the flow

Brackets . . . . for actions or [visual aids]

Use visual aids.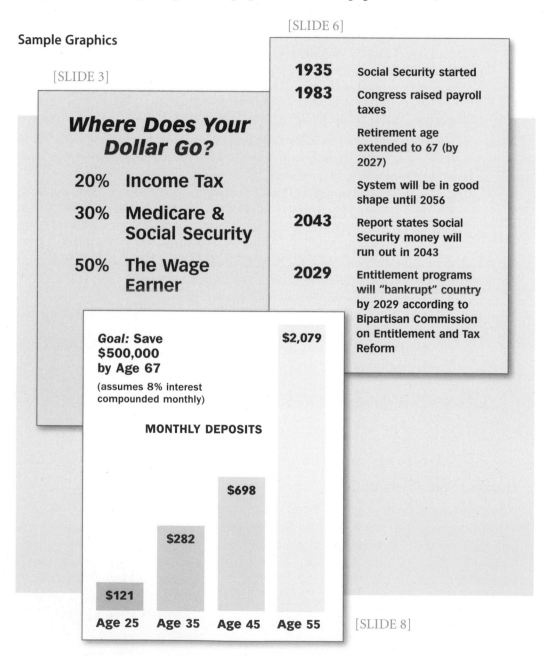

While constructing your presentation, think about visual aids that would grab the audience's attention and help them understand the message. For example, in her speech, Burnette Sawyer used the computer-generated graphics below. (See pages 406–407.)

Sample Graphics

[SLIDE 3]

[SLIDE 6]

Where Does Your Dollar Go?

20% Income Tax

30% Medicare & Social Security

50% The Wage Earner

1935	Social Security started
1983	Congress raised payroll taxes
	Retirement age extended to 67 (by 2027)
	System will be in good shape until 2056
2043	Report states Social Security money will run out in 2043
2029	Entitlement programs will "bankrupt" country by 2029 according to Bipartisan Commission on Entitlement and Tax Reform

Goal: Save $500,000 by Age 67
(assumes 8% interest compounded monthly)

MONTHLY DEPOSITS

$121 Age 25
$282 Age 35
$698 Age 45
$2,079 Age 55

[SLIDE 8]

Developing Computer Presentations

To help you use presentation software effectively, follow the guidelines below.

1. **Develop a design.** Be sure your graphic design fits your topic and your audience—polished for a serious topic, casual for an informal topic.

2. **Create pages.** If a main idea has several parts, present each one on its own page. Each click of the mouse button (or computer key) should reveal a new detail.

3. **Use transitions.** Dissolves, fades, wipes, and other transitional effects refine a computer presentation and keep the audience's attention (as long as the devices don't detract from the message).

4. **Add sound.** Just as graphics and animation can enhance a presentation, so, too, can sound. Music can serve as an introduction or backdrop, and sound effects can add emphasis. Voice recording can add authority and help drive home key points.

TIP for speakers: Text can be animated to appear from off-screen at just the right moment. Graphics can be made to appear one element at a time, and illustrations can change before the viewer's eyes. Remember to use special effects—especially animation—wisely.

5. **Fine-tune your presentation.** Practice delivering your presentation while clicking through your pages. Try it with an audience of fellow students, if possible, and ask for their input.

6. **Check for word choice and style.** Make sure that the words on the screen are key words. Use these words as talking points—don't try to cover any point word for word. Also, check that transitions, animations, and sounds are smooth and not disruptive.

7. **Edit the final version.** Check spelling, punctuation, usage, and other mechanics. Remember: On-screen errors are glaringly obvious to everyone.

8. **Rehearse.** Perform your presentation for a friend or family member. Practice running the equipment until you can use it with confidence.

9. **Make a backup copy.** Protect all the effort you invested in your presentation.

TIP: Choose an easy-to-read font and type-size. In most situations, 36-point headings and 24-point text work well. However, the type-size needed depends on a number of variables, including the screen size, lens type, and audience's distance from the screen.

Overcoming Stage Fright Checklist

While it's okay to feel a little nervous before a presentation (the emotion keeps you alert), stage fright can limit your ability to communicate. The remedy for stage fright is confidence—confidence in what to say and how to say it. To develop that confidence, do the following:

Personal Preparation

_____ Know your subject well.

_____ Rehearse the presentation thoroughly, including the use of visuals.

_____ Schedule your time carefully, making sure to arrive early.

_____ Try to relax before the presentation by stretching or doing a deep-breathing exercise, remembering that your presentation can be successful without being perfect.

The Room and Equipment

_____ See that the room is clean, comfortable, and well lit.

_____ Make sure tables and chairs are set up and arranged correctly.

_____ Check that AV equipment is in place and working.

_____ Test the microphone volume.

_____ Position the screen and displays for good visibility.

Personal Details

_____ Check your clothing and hair.

_____ Arrange for drinking water to be available.

_____ Put your script and handouts in place.

Speaking Strategies

_____ Be confident, positive, and energetic.

_____ Maintain eye contact when speaking or listening.

_____ Use gestures naturally—don't force them.

_____ Provide for audience participation; survey the audience: "How many of you . . . ?"

_____ Maintain a comfortable, erect posture.

_____ Speak up and speak clearly—don't rush.

_____ Reword and clarify when necessary.

_____ After the presentation, ask for questions and answer them clearly.

_____ Thank the audience.

III. Research and Writing

Research and Writing

Getting Started: From Planning Research to Evaluating Sources

27

At first glance, research looks like a dry-as-dust business carried out by obsessed scholars in dim libraries and mad scientists in cluttered laboratories. Research couldn't be further from the reality of your life.

But is it? Consider car tires. Before these were mounted, scientists researched which materials would resist wear and which adhesives would keep treads on steel belts. Sloppy research could cause blowouts; good research builds safe tires.

For you, the rewards of research projects can be great—new insights into a subject that really interests you, a deepened understanding of your major or profession, reliable knowledge to share with others, and sharpened thinking skills. This chapter will help you get started on such a project.

Learning Outcomes

Audio

▶ Understand the rhetorical context of research writing.

▶ Implement a workable process and plan.

▶ Develop research questions and a thesis.

▶ Understand the breadth of resources available and select fitting resources

▶ Engage and evaluate sources.

▶ Develop a working bibliography.

▶ Avoid plagiarism.

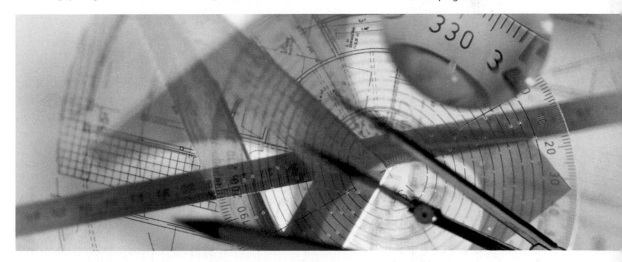

Visually Speaking ▶ Review the photograph above. What does this image suggest to you about research? Does the image help you visualize getting started on a research project?

Quick Guide

Papers with Documented Research

Web Link

When you work on a research project, you ask important questions, look systematically for answers, and share your conclusions with readers. In other words, it's all about curiosity, discovery, and dialogue.

- **Starting Point:** The assignment usually relates to a course concept, so consider what your instructor wants you to learn and how your project will be evaluated. Then take ownership of the project by looking for an angle that makes the writing relevant for you.

- **Purpose:** The project requires you to conduct research and share results. Your main goal is to discover the complex truth about a topic and clarify that discovery for others.

- **Form:** The traditional research paper is a fairly long essay (5 to 15 pages) complete with thesis, supporting paragraphs, integrated sources, and careful documentation. However, you may be asked to shape your research into a field report, a website, or a multimedia presentation.

- **Audience:** Traditionally, research writing addresses "the academic community," a group made up mainly of instructors and students. However, your actual audience may be more specific: addicted smokers, all Floridians, fellow immigrants, and so on.

- **Voice:** The tone is usually formal or semiformal, but check your instructor's expectations. In any research writing, maintain a thoughtful, confidently measured tone. After all, your research has made you somewhat of an authority on the topic.

- **Point of View:** Generally, research writers avoid the pronouns "I" and "you" in an effort to remain properly objective and academic sounding. Unfortunately, this practice can result in an overuse of both the pronoun "one" and the passive voice. Some instructors encourage students to connect research with experience, meaning that you may use the pronouns "I" and "you" occasionally. Be careful, however, to keep the focus where it belongs—on the topic. Bottom line: Follow your instructor's requirements concerning pronoun use. For more on developing a strong academic style for your research writing, see pages 79–80.

INSIGHT: The best research writing centers on your ideas—ideas you develop through thoughtful engagement with sources. In poor research papers, the sources dominate, and the writer's perspective disappears.

■ The Research Process: A Flowchart

The research process involves getting started, planning, conducting the research, and organizing the results. This process is flexible enough to be adapted to diverse research projects. In fact, real research is typically dynamic: You might think during the planning phase that you've nailed down your topic, only to discover a surprising topical detour while conducting research. Generally, however, the research process maps out as shown below. When you get your assignment—whether to write a five-page paper on pasteurization or to develop a website on Middle Eastern political conflicts—review the process and tailor it to the task.

Getting Started
- Review the assignment.
- Consider your resources.
- Choose a subject.

List or cluster your current ideas and opinions.

Talk with others to learn opposing opinions.

Conduct preliminary research in reference works.

Planning Your Research
Narrow the topic, form a research question or working thesis, develop a research plan, and select keyword–searching terms.

Conducting Research

Conduct Primary Research

Take Careful Notes

Conduct Secondary Research

Observe, interview, survey, or experiment.

Reflect in your research journal.

Check books, articles, and websites.

Analyze primary documents and artifacts.

Create and add to a working bibliography.

Search catalogs, indexes, databases, and the Internet.

- Evaluate and take notes from sources.
- Summarize, paraphrase, and quote.

Organizing and Drafting
- Answer your research question or refine your thesis.
- Develop an outline.
- Write the research paper, integrating and documenting sources.

Getting Started: Getting Focused

Video

Early in your project, get focused by narrowing your topic, brainstorming research questions, and developing a working thesis. For help understanding assignments and selecting topics, as well as other prewriting strategies, see pages 32–37.

Establish a narrow, manageable topic.

Video

To do good research, you need an engaging, manageable topic. Once you have a broad topic, narrow your focus to a specific feature or angle that allows for in-depth research. Try these strategies:

- Check your topic in the Library of Congress subject headings, available in your library. Note "narrower terms" listed (see page 424).
- Read about your topic. By consulting specialized reference works, explore background that directs you to subtopics (see page 453).
- Check the Internet. For example, follow a subject directory to see where your topic leads (see pages 462–467).
- Freewrite to discover which aspect of the topic interests you most: a local angle, a connection with a group of people, or a personal concern.

Broad Topic	Manageable Focus
Homelessness	Homeless Families in Los Angeles
Bacteria and Viruses	Bacterial Resistance to Antibiotics
Alternative Energy Sources	Hydrogen Fuel-Cell Vehicles

Brainstorm research questions.

Good research questions help you find meaningful information and ideas about your topic. These questions sharpen your research goal, and the answers will become the focus of your writing. Brainstorm questions by following these guidelines:

List both simple and substantial questions. Basic questions aim for factual answers. More complex questions get at analysis, synthesis, and evaluation.

- **Question of fact:** When did Kim Jong Il gain power in North Korea?
- **Question of interpretation:** How did Kim Jong Il maintain power?

List main and secondary questions. Ask a primary question about your topic—the main issue that you want to get at. Then brainstorm secondary questions that you need to research to answer your primary question.

- **Main Question:** Should consumers buy hydrogen fuel-cell cars?
- **Secondary Questions** *(Who, What, When, Where, Why, How)*: Who has developed hydrogen fuel-cell cars? What is a hydrogen fuel-cell car? When were these cars developed? Where are hydrogen fuel-cell cars currently used? Why are they being developed? How does one work?

Testing Your Main Research Question

_____ Is the question so broad that I can't answer it in the project's time and page limits?

_____ Is the question so narrow that I won't be able to find sources?

_____ Is the question so simple that it will be too easy to answer?

_____ Will the question lead to significant sources and intellectual challenge?

_____ Am I committed to answering this question? Does it interest me?

_____ Will the question and answers interest my readers?

Develop a working thesis.

A working thesis offers a preliminary answer to your main research question. As your initial perspective on the topic, a good working thesis keeps you focused during research, helping you decide whether to carefully read a particular book or just skim it, fully explore a website or quickly skim through it. Make your working thesis a statement that demands "Prove it!" Don't settle for a simple statement of fact about your topic; instead, choose a working thesis that seems debatable or that requires some explanation. Try this formula:

> _Formula:_   Working Thesis =
> **limited topic** + _tentative claim, statement,_ or _hypothesis_
>
> _Examples:_   **E-communication technologies** _are rewiring our brains._
>
> **Downtown revitalization** _will have distinct economic, environmental, and social benefits._
>
> **Internet dating** _is weakening long-term relationships._

Working Thesis Checklist

_____ Does my working thesis focus on a single, limited topic?

_____ Is my working thesis stated in a clear, direct sentence?

_____ Does my working thesis convey my initial perspective about the topic?

_____ Do I have access to enough good information to support this working thesis?

_____ Does my working thesis direct me to write a paper that meets all assignment requirements?

INSIGHT: Your working thesis is written in sand, not stone. It may change as you research the topic because sources may push you in new directions. In fact, such change shows that you are engaging your sources and growing in your thinking.

Developing a Research Plan

Video

It pays to plan your research. In fact, minutes spent planning research can save hours doing research. With your limited topic, main research question, and working thesis in front of you, plan your project more fully.

Choose research methods.

Consider these questions: What do you already know about the topic? What do you need to know? Which resources will help you answer your research question? Which resources does the assignment require? Based on your answers, map out a research plan that draws resources from fitting categories.

Background research: To find information about your topic's context, central concepts, and key terms, take these steps:
- Use the Library of Congress subject headings to find keywords for searching the library catalog, periodical databases, and the Internet (see page 424).
- Conduct a preliminary search of the library catalog, journal databases, and the Internet to confirm that good resources on your topic exist.
- Use specialized reference works to find background information, definitions, facts, and statistics (see page 453).

Field or primary research: If appropriate for your project, conduct field research:
- Use interviews (page 448) or surveys (page 444–445) to get key information from experts or others.
- Conduct observations or experiments (page 443) to obtain hard data.
- Analyze key documents or artifacts (pages 446–447).

Library research: Select important library resources:
- Use scholarly books to get in-depth, reliable material (pages 452–453).
- Use periodical articles (print or electronic) to get current, reliable information (pages 454–456). Select from news sources, popular magazines, scholarly journals, and trade journals.
- Consider other library resources, such as a documentary, recorded interview, pamphlet, marketing study, or government publication.

Internet research: Plan effective Internet searches using the following:
- Search engines and subject guides: Choose tools that will lead you to quality resources (pages 462–465).
- Expert guidance: Select reputable websites that librarians or other experts recommend (page 462).
- Evaluation: Test all web resources for reliability (pages 468–471).
- Limitations: How many web resources are you allowed to use, if any?

Get organized to do research. ■ ■ ■

An organized approach to doing your research will save you time, help you work efficiently, and prevent frustration. Get organized by addressing these issues:

Establishing Priorities for Resources, Time, and Effort

- How much research material do you need?
- What range of resources will give you quality, reliable information?
- Which types of research does the assignment specify? Are you limited, for example, in the number of Internet sources you can use?
- What are the project's priorities: What must you do? Which tasks are secondary in nature?
- What weight does the project carry in the course? How should you match your time and effort with that weight?

INSIGHT: Gather more information than you could ever use in your paper. That richness gives you choices and allows you to sift for crucial information.

Selecting Research Methods and Systems

- Given the resources and technologies available, select methods that help you do research efficiently: signing out hard-copy library holdings or using interlibrary loan; photocopying book sections and journal articles; printing, saving, downloading, bookmarking, or e-mailing digital materials.
- Develop a note-taking system. Choose from the note-card, double-entry notebook, copy-and-annotate, and research-log methods (pages 432–435). In addition, set up a working bibliography (pages 430–431).
- Choose and review a documentation system. It's likely that your instructor will designate a system such as MLA (pages 491–528) or APA (pages 529–558). If he or she doesn't do so, then use a method that suits the subject matter and discipline. Review the system's basic rules and strategies.

Establishing a Schedule

The time frame for completing a research project obviously varies from one assignment to the next. What you have to work with is the time frame between getting the assignment and turning in the project at the deadline, whether that time frame is two weeks or two months, along with any intermediate deadlines set by your instructor for specific phases of the project (e.g., topic selection, project proposal, working bibliography, first draft). Generally, however, you should spend about half your time on research and half on writing. To stay on track, sketch out a preliminary schedule with tentative deadlines for completing each phase of your work.

Web Link: A schedule template is available at <**www.thecollegewriter.com/4e**>.

Writing a Research Proposal

Video

For some research projects, you may need to submit a proposal early in the process. The proposal seeks to explain what you plan to research, why, and how. Such a proposal thus aims to show that the research is valid (makes good scholarly sense), to argue that the research is valuable (will lead to significant knowledge), to communicate your enthusiasm for the project, and to demonstrate that your plan is workable within the constraints of the assignment—all in order to gain your instructor's feedback and approval. Note the parts modeled in the sample proposal.

Understand the parts of a research proposal.

1. **Introduction:** In a brief paragraph, state your research idea, explaining why the topic is important and worth researching. Provide any background information that the instructor may need.

2. **Description:** Discuss your proposed research topic by identifying the central issue or concern about the topic, indicating the main question that you want to answer through research, listing secondary questions that relate to the main question, stating a working thesis or hypothesis in response to the main question, and explaining the research outcomes that you expect from the study.

3. **Plan (methods and procedures):** Explain how you plan to answer your questions, how you plan to research your topic. Include an explanation of your primary research (the "first-hand" investigation), a description of research tools you plan to use (e.g., catalogs, reference works, lab equipment, survey software), and a working bibliography indicating your initial survey of resources.

4. **Schedule:** List deadlines that are part of the assignment and deadlines that you've set for yourself.

5. **Approval Request:** Ask for feedback and approval from your instructor.

Sample Research Proposal

The research proposal below offers a student's plan for analyzing Jane Austen's *Pride and Prejudice,* both novel and film adaptation.

Film Studies 201 Proposal:
Jane Austen's *Pride and Prejudice* as Fiction and Film
Gwendolyn Mackenzie

Nearly 200 years after her death, Jane Austen's novels still captivate readers, filmmakers, and filmgoers—including me. For my research paper, I will explore one aspect of this phenomenon within *Pride and Prejudice* and the 2005 film adaptation directed by Joe Wright.

Description: Specifically, I want to see how the novel and film explore gender prejudice. My main research question is, What sense do these texts make of prejudice as it relates to relationships between men and women? My working thesis is that the 2005 film portrayal of gender inequality in *Pride and Prejudice* highlights and intensifies the issue of gender inequality introduced in the novel.

This study of gender prejudice will allow me (1) to appreciate the treatment of this theme in fiction and in film, (2) to understand film adaptations more fully, and (3) to explain in a small way the Jane Austen phenomenon. As part of the project, I will write a 6-8 page paper.

Plan: My primary research will involve rereading the novel and reviewing the 2005 film adaptation. In terms of secondary research, I have done an initial search of our library's catalog and of EBSCOhost for books and articles. This is my working bibliography:

Primary Sources

Austen, Jane. *Pride and Prejudice: An Authoritative Text, Background and Sources, Criticism*. Ed. Donald J. Gray. New York: Norton, 2001. Print.

Wright, Joe. *Pride and Prejudice*. [U.K.]: Universal Pictures, 2005. Film.

Secondary Sources

Cartmell, Deborah, and Imelda Whelehan. *Adaptations: From Text to Screen, Screen to Text*. London; New York: Routledge, 2004. Print.

Crusie, Jennifer. *Flirting with Pride and Prejudice: Fresh Perspectives on the Original Chick-Lit Masterpiece*. Dallas: BenBella, 2005. Print.

Grandi, Roberta. "The Passion Translated: Literary and Cinematic Rhetoric in *Pride and Prejudice* (2005)." *Literature Film Quarterly* 36.1 (2008): 45-51. Print.

McFarlane, Brian. "Something Old, Something New: 'Pride and Prejudice' on Screen." *Screen Education* (2005): 6-14. Print.

Stovel, Nora Foster. "From Page to Screen: Dancing to the Altar in Recent Film Adaptations of Jane Austen's Novels." *Persuasions: The Jane Austen Journal* (2006): 185-198. EBSCOhost. Web. 6 Nov. 2010.

Sutherland, Kathryn. *Jane Austen's Textual Lives: From Aeschylus to Bollywood*. Oxford: Oxford UP, 2007. Print.

Todd, Janet M. *The Cambridge Introduction to Jane Austen*. Cambridge; New York: Cambridge UP, 2006. NetLibrary. Web. 6 Nov. 2010.

Schedule: Here is my schedule for completing this project:
1. Finish rereading the novel and reviewing the film: November 14.
2. Complete secondary research: November 20.
3. Develop outline for paper: November 23.
4. Finish first draft of paper: November 30.
5. Revise, edit, and proofread paper: December 4.
6. Submit paper: December 6.

Approval Request: Dr. Rajan, I would appreciate your feedback on my proposed project, as well as your approval of my plan.

Exploring Information Resources and Sites

To conduct thorough, creative, but efficient research, you need a sense of which types of resources are available for your project and where to find them. Check the tables that follow.

Consider different information resources.

Examine the range of resources available: Which will give you the best information for your project? While one project (for example, a sociological report on airport behaviors) might require personal, direct sources, another project (for example, the effects of the September 11, 2001, terrorist attacks on the air transportation industry) might depend on government reports, business publications, and journal articles. Generally, a well-rounded research paper relies on a range of quality resources; in particular, it avoids relying on insubstantial web information.

Type of Resource	Examples
Personal, direct resources	Memories, diaries, journals, logs, experiments, tests, observations, interviews, surveys
Reference works (print and electronic)	Dictionaries, thesauruses, encyclopedias, almanacs, yearbooks, atlases, directories, guides, handbooks, indexes, abstracts, catalogs, bibliographies
Books (print and electronic)	Nonfiction, how-to, biographies, fiction, trade books, scholarly and scientific studies
Periodicals and news sources	Print newspapers, magazines, and journals; broadcast news and news magazines; online magazines, news sources, and discussion groups
Audiovisual, digital, and multimedia resources	Graphics (tables, graphs, charts, maps, drawings, photos), audiotapes, CDs, videos, DVDs, webpages, online databases
Government publications	Guides, programs, forms, legislation, regulations, reports, records, statistics
Business and nonprofit publications	Correspondence, reports, newsletters, pamphlets, brochures, ads, catalogs, instructions, handbooks, manuals, policies and procedures, seminar and training materials

Consider different information sites. ▪▪▪

Where do you go to find the resources that you need? Consider the information "sites" listed below, remembering that many resources may be available in different forms in different locations. For example, a journal article may be available in library holdings or in an electronic database.

Information Location	Specific "Sites"
People	Experts (knowledge area, skill, occupation) Population segments or individuals (with representative or unusual experiences)
Libraries	General: public, college, online Specialized: legal, medical, government, business
Computer resources	Computers: software, disks Networks: Internet and other online services (e-mail, limited-access databases, discussion groups, MUDs, chat rooms, websites, blogs, YouTube, image banks, wikis); intranets
Mass media	Radio (AM and FM) Television (network, public, cable, satellite) Print (newspapers, magazines, journals)
Testing, training, meeting, and observation sites	Plants, facilities, field sites, laboratories Research centers, universities, think tanks Conventions, conferences, seminars Museums, galleries, historical sites
Municipal, state, and federal government offices	Elected officials, representatives Offices and agencies, Government Printing Office Websites (GPO, www.gpoaccess.gov)
Business and nonprofit publications	Computer databases, company files Desktop reference materials Bulletin boards (physical and electronic) Company and department websites Departments and offices Associations, professional organizations Consulting, training, and business information services

Conducting Effective Keyword Searches

Web Link

Keyword searching can help you find information in electronic library catalogs, online databases that index periodical articles (for example, Lexis-Nexis, EBSCOhost), print indexes to periodical publications (for example, *Business Periodicals Index*), Internet resources, print books, and e-books.

Choose keywords carefully.

Keywords give you "compass points" for navigating through a sea of information. That's why choosing the best keywords is crucial. Consider these tips:

1. **Brainstorm a list of possible keywords**—topics, titles, and names—based on your current knowledge and/or background reading.

2. **Consult the Library of Congress subject headings.** These books contain the keywords librarians use when classifying materials. For example, if you looked up *immigrants,* you would find the entry below, indicating keywords to use, along with narrower, related, and broader terms. When you are conducting subject searches of catalogs and databases, these are the terms that will get you the best results.

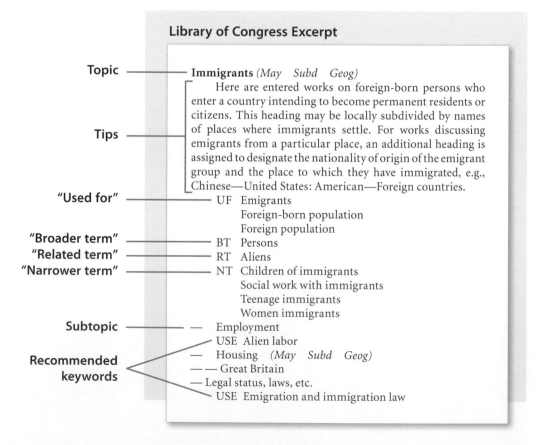

Library of Congress Excerpt

Topic ——————— **Immigrants** *(May   Subd   Geog)*

Tips ——————— Here are entered works on foreign-born persons who enter a country intending to become permanent residents or citizens. This heading may be locally subdivided by names of places where immigrants settle. For works discussing emigrants from a particular place, an additional heading is assigned to designate the nationality of origin of the emigrant group and the place to which they have immigrated, e.g., Chinese—United States: American—Foreign countries.

"Used for" ——————— UF Emigrants
                              Foreign-born population
                              Foreign population

"Broader term" ——————— BT Persons
"Related term" ——————— RT Aliens
"Narrower term" ——————— NT Children of immigrants
                              Social work with immigrants
                              Teenage immigrants
                              Women immigrants

Subtopic ——————— — Employment
                              USE Alien labor

Recommended keywords ——————— — Housing *(May   Subd   Geog)*
                              — — Great Britain
                              — Legal status, laws, etc.
                              USE Emigration and immigration law

Use keyword strategies.

The goal of a keyword search is to find quality research sources. To ensure that you identify the best resources available, follow these strategies:

Get to know the database. Look for answers to these questions:
- What material does the database contain? What time frames?
- What are you searching—authors, titles, subjects, full text?
- What are the search rules? How can you narrow the search?

Use a shotgun approach. Start with the most likely keyword. If you have no "hits," choose a related term. Once you get some hits, check the citations for clues regarding which words to use as you continue searching.

Use Boolean operators to refine your search. When you combine keywords with Boolean operators—such as those below—you will obtain better results.

Video

Boolean Operators

Narrowing a Search **And, +, not, -** Use when one term gives you too many hits, especially irrelevant ones	buffalo and bison *or* buffalo + bison	Searches for citations containing both keywords
	buffalo not water +buffalo –water	Searches for "buffalo" but not "water," so that you eliminate material on water buffalo
Expanding a Search **Or** Combine a term providing few hits with a related word	buffalo or bison	Searches for citations containing either term
Specifying a Phrase **Quotation marks** Indicate that you wish to search for the exact phrase enclosed	"reclamation project"	Searches for the exact phrase "reclamation project"
Sequencing Operations **Parentheses** Indicate that the operation should be performed before other operations in the search string	(buffalo or bison) and ranching	Searches first for citations containing either "buffalo" or "bison" before checking the resulting citations for "ranching"
Finding Variations **Wild card symbols** Depending on the database, symbols such as $, ?, or # can find variations of a word	ethic# ethic$	Searches for terms like *ethics* and *ethical*

Video

Engaging and Evaluating Sources

Using reliable benchmarks, you should test all sources before you rely on them in your writing. After all, credible sources help your own credibility; sources that aren't credible destroy it. The benchmarks on the next four pages will help you test your sources' usefulness and reliability.

Engage your sources.

Engaged reading is the opposite of passive reading—treating all sources equally, swallowing whole what's in the material, or looking only for information that supports your opinion. Full engagement involves these practices:

Test each source to see if it's worth reading. When reviewing source citations and generating a working bibliography, study titles, descriptions, lengths, and publication dates, asking these questions:
- How closely related to my topic is this source?
- Is this source too basic, overly complex, or just right?
- What could this source add to my overall balance of sources?

If you were writing about the International Space Station, for example, you might find a ten-page article in *Scientific American* more valuable and insightful than a brief news article on a specific event onboard or a *Star Trek* fan's blog on the topic.

INSIGHT: Don't reject a source simply because it disagrees with your perspective. Good research engages rather than ignores opposing points of view.

Skim sources before reading in-depth. Consider marking key pages or passages with sticky notes, tabs, or a digital bookmark.
- Review the author biography, preface, and/or introduction to discover the perspective, approach, scope, and research methods.
- Using your keywords, review any outline, abstract, table of contents, index, or home page to get a sense of coverage.

Read with an open but not an empty mind. Carry on a dialogue with the source, asking questions like "Why?" and "So what?"
- Note the purpose and audience. Was the piece written to inform or persuade? Is it aimed at the public, specialists, supporters, or opponents?
- Read to understand the source: What's clear and what's confusing?
- Relate the source to your research question: How does the source affirm or challenge your ideas? Synthesize what you read with what you know.
- Record your reactions to it—what it makes you think, feel, believe.
- Consider how you might use this source in your writing—key facts, important ideas, opposing perspectives, or examples.
- Check footnotes, references, appendices, and links for further leads.

Rate source reliability and depth.

You should judge each source on its own merit. Generally, however, types of sources can be rated for depth and reliability, as shown in the table below, based on their authorship, length, topic treatment, documentation, publication method, review process, distance from primary sources, allegiances, stability, and so on. Use the table to

1. Target sources that fit your project's goals,
2. Assess the approximate quality of the sources you're gathering, and
3. Build a strong bibliography that readers will respect.

Deep, Reliable, Credible Sources

Scholarly Books and Articles: largely based on careful research; written by experts for experts; address topics in depth; involve peer review and careful editing; offer stable discussion of topic

Trade Books and Journal Articles: largely based on careful research; written by experts for educated general audience. *Sample periodicals: The Atlantic, Scientific American, Nature, Orion*

Government Resources: books, reports, webpages, guides, statistics developed by experts at government agencies; provided as service to citizens; relatively objective. *Sample source: Statistical Abstract of the United States*

Reviewed Official Online Documents: Internet resources posted by legitimate institutions—colleges and universities, research institutes, service organizations; although offering a particular perspective, sources tend to be balanced

Reference Works and Textbooks: provide general and specialized information; carefully researched, reviewed, and edited; lack depth for focused research (e.g., general encyclopedia entry)

News and Topical Stories from Quality Sources: provide current affairs coverage (print and online), introduction-level articles of interest to general public; may lack depth and length. *Sample sources: the Washington Post, the New York Times; Time, Psychology Today; NPR's All Things Considered*

Popular Magazine Stories: short, introductory articles often distant from primary sources and without documentation; heavy advertising. *Sample sources: Glamour, Seventeen, Reader's Digest*

Business and Nonprofit Publications: pamphlets, reports, news releases, brochures, manuals; range from informative to sales-focused

List Server Discussions, Usenet Postings, Blog Articles, Talk Radio Discussions: highly open, fluid, undocumented, untested exchanges and publications; unstable resource

Unregulated Web Material: personal sites, joke sites, chat rooms, special-interest sites, advertising and junk e-mail (spam); no review process, little accountability, biased presentation

Shallow, Unreliable, Not Credible Sources

Tabloid Articles (print and web): contain exaggerated and untrue stories written to titillate and exploit. *Sample source: the National Enquirer*

Evaluate print and online sources. ◼ ◼ ◼

Web Link

As you work with a source, you need to test its reliability. The benchmarks that follow apply to both print and online sources; note, however, the additional tests offered for web sources. For more on evaluating material on the web, see pages 468–471.

Credible author An expert is an authority—someone who has mastered a subject area. Is the author an expert on this topic? What are her or his credentials, and can you confirm them? For example, an automotive engineer could be an expert on hydrogen fuel-cell technology, whereas a celebrity in a commercial would not.

> *Web test:* Is an author indicated? If so, are the author's credentials noted and contact information offered (for example, an e-mail address)?

Reliable publication Has the source been published by a scholarly press, a peer-reviewed professional journal, a quality trade-book publisher, or a trusted news source? Did you find this resource through a reliable search tool (for example, a library catalog or database)?

> *Web test:* Which individual or group posted this page? Is the site rated by a subject directory or library organization? How stable is the site—has it been around for a while and does material remain available, or is the site "fly-by-night"? Check the site's home page, and read "About Us" pages and mission statements, looking for evidence of the organization's perspective, history, and trustworthiness.

Unbiased discussion While all sources come from a specific perspective and represent specific commitments, a biased source may be pushing an agenda in an unfair, unbalanced, incomplete manner. Watch for bias toward a certain region, country, political party, industry, gender, race, ethnic group, or religion. Be alert to connections among authors, financial backers, and the points of view shared. For example, if an author has functioned as a consultant to or a lobbyist for a particular industry or group (oil, animal rights), his or her allegiances may lead to a biased presentation of an issue.

> *Web test:* Is the online document one-sided? Is the site nonprofit (.org), government (.gov), commercial (.com), educational (.edu), business (.biz), informational (.info), network-related (.net), or military (.mil)? Is the site U.S. or international? Is this organization pushing a cause, product, service, or belief? How do advertising or special interests affect the site? You might suspect, for example, the scientific claims of a site sponsored by a pro-smoking organization.

Web Link: Beware especially of masquerade sites—those that appear to be legitimate but are joke sites or, worse, propaganda lures. Check, for example, www.dhmo.org.

Current information   A five-year-old book on computers may be outdated, but a forty-year-old book on Abraham Lincoln could still be the best source. Given what you need, is this source's discussion up-to-date?

> *Web test:* When was the material originally posted and last updated? Are links live or dead?

Accurate information   Bad research design, poor reporting, and sloppy documentation can lead to inaccurate information. Check the source for factual errors, statistical flaws, and conclusions that don't add up.

> *Web test:* Is the site information-rich or -poor—filled with helpful, factual materials or fluffy with thin, unsubstantiated opinions? Can you trace and confirm sources by following links or conducting your own search?

Full, logical support   Is the discussion of the topic reasonable, balanced, and complete? Are claims backed up with quality evidence? Does the source avoid faulty assumptions, twisted statistical analysis, logical fallacies, and unfair persuasion tactics? (See pages 257–260, for help.)

> *Web test:* Does the webpage offer well-supported claims and helpful links to additional information?

Quality writing and design   Is the source well written? Is it free of sarcasm, derogatory terms, clichés, catch phrases, mindless slogans, grammar slips, and spelling errors? Generally, poor writing correlates with sloppy thinking.

> *Web test:* Are words neutral ("conservative perspective") or emotionally charged ("fascist agenda")? Are pages well designed—with clear rather than flashy, distracting multimedia elements? Is the site easy to navigate?

Positive relationship with other sources   Does the source disagree with other sources? If yes, is the disagreement about the facts themselves or about how to interpret the facts? Which source seems more credible?

> *Web test:* Is the site's information logically consistent with print sources? Do other reputable sites offer links to this site?

INSIGHT: Engage and evaluate visual resources as thoroughly as verbal materials. For example, ask yourself what tables, graphs, and photos really "say":
- Is the graphic informative or merely decorative?
- Does the graphic create a valid or manipulative central idea? For example, does the image seek to bypass logic by appealing to sexual impulses or to crude stereotypes?
- What does the graphic include and exclude in terms of information?
- Is the graphic well designed and easy to understand, or is it cluttered and distorted?
- Is a reliable source provided?

For more instruction on critical viewing, see pages 12–13.

Creating a Working Bibliography

A working bibliography lists sources you have used and intend to use. It helps you track your research, develop your final bibliography, and avoid plagiarism. Here's what to do:

Choose an orderly method.

Select an efficient approach for your project:

- **Paper note cards:** Use 3×5 inch cards, and record one source per card.
- **Paper notebook:** Use a small, spiral-bound book to record sources.
- **Computer program:** Record source information electronically, either by capturing citation details from online searches or by recording bibliographic information using word-processing software or research software such as TakeNote, EndNote Plus, or Bookends Pro.

Including Identifying Information for Sources

Start by giving each source a code number or letter: Doing so will help you when drafting and documenting your paper. Then include specific details for each kind of source listed below, shown on the facing page.

A. **Books:** author, title and subtitle, publication details (place, publisher, date)

B. **Periodicals:** author, article title, journal name, publication information (volume, number, date), page numbers

C. **Online sources:** author (if available), document title, site sponsor, database name, publication or posting date, access date, other publication information, URL

D. **Primary or field research:** date conducted, name and/or descriptive title of person interviewed, place observed, survey conducted, document analyzed

INSIGHT: Consider recording bibliographic details in the format of the documentation system you are using—MLA (pages 491–528) or APA (pages 529–558), for example. Doing so now will save time later. In addition, some research software allows you to record bibliographic information and then format it according to a specific system.

Adding Locating Information

Because you may need to retrace your research footsteps, include details about your research path:

A. **Books:** Include the Library of Congress or Dewey call number.

B. **Articles:** Note where and how you accessed them (stacks, current periodicals, microfilm, database).

C. **Webpages:** Record the complete URL, not just the broader site address.

D. **Field research:** Include a telephone number or an e-mail address.

Annotating the Source

Add a note about the source's content, focus, reliability, and usefulness.

Sample Working Bibliography Entries

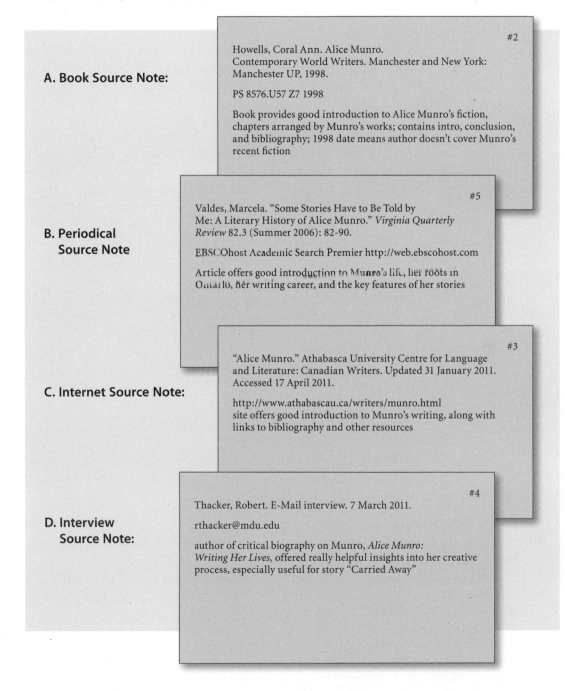

A. Book Source Note:

#2

Howells, Coral Ann. Alice Munro.
Contemporary World Writers. Manchester and New York:
Manchester UP, 1998.

PS 8576.U57 Z7 1998

Book provides good introduction to Alice Munro's fiction,
chapters arranged by Munro's works; contains intro, conclusion,
and bibliography; 1998 date means author doesn't cover Munro's
recent fiction

B. Periodical Source Note

#5

Valdes, Marcela. "Some Stories Have to Be Told by
Me: A Literary History of Alice Munro." *Virginia Quarterly
Review* 82.3 (Summer 2006): 82-90.

EBSCOhost Academic Search Premier http://web.ebscohost.com

Article offers good introduction to Munro's life, her roots in
Ontario, her writing career, and the key features of her stories

C. Internet Source Note:

#3

"Alice Munro." Athabasca University Centre for Language
and Literature: Canadian Writers. Updated 31 January 2011.
Accessed 17 April 2011.

http://www.athabascau.ca/writers/munro.html
site offers good introduction to Munro's writing, along with
links to bibliography and other resources

D. Interview Source Note:

#4

Thacker, Robert. E-Mail interview. 7 March 2011.

rthacker@mdu.edu

author of critical biography on Munro, *Alice Munro:
Writing Her Lives,* offered really helpful insights into her creative
process, especially useful for story "Carried Away"

Developing a Note-Taking System

Video

Accurate, thoughtful notes create a foundation for your research writing. The trick is to practice some sensible strategies and choose an efficient method.

Develop note-taking strategies.

What are you trying to do when you take notes on sources? What you are not doing is (a) collecting quotations to plunk in your project, (b) piling isolated grains of data into a large stack of disconnected facts, or (c) intensively reading and taking notes on every source you find. Instead, use these strategies:

Be selective. Guided by your research questions and working thesis, focus on sources that are central to your project. From these sources, record information clearly related to your limited topic, but also take notes on what surprises or puzzles you. Be selective, avoiding notes that are either too meager or too extensive. Suppose, for example, that you were writing a paper on the engineering problems facing the International Space Station. If you were reading an article on the history and the future of this facility, you might take careful notes on material describing the station's technical details, but not on astronauts' biographies.

Develop accurate, complete records. Your notes should . . .
- Accurately summarize, paraphrase, and quote sources (pages 436–438).
- Clearly show where you got your information.
- Cover all the research you've done—primary research (e.g., interviews, observations), books and periodical articles, and online sources.

Engage your sources. Evaluate what you are reading and develop your own responses. (See pages 4–11.) For example, with an article about the International Space Station, you might test the author's biases, credentials, and logic; and you might respond with knowledge you have gained about other space endeavors.

Take good notes on graphics in sources—tables, line graphs, photographs, maps, and so on. Such graphics are typically packed with information and powerfully convey ideas. (See "Critical Thinking Through Viewing," pages 12–17.)

INSIGHT: Different disciplines use different note-taking practices. In your major, learn these practices through courses that introduce you to the subject matter. Here are two examples:
- In literature studies, students conduct literary analyses by annotating print texts. Students may also take notes through keyword searches of e-books (for example, a Shakespeare play) and reviews of literary criticism.
- In environmental studies, students conduct research by (a) taking notes on published research to develop literature reviews, and (b) using a standard field notebook to collect data, make drawings, and reflect on results.

Note-Taking Systems

A good note-taking system should help you do the following:

- Avoid unintentional plagiarism by developing accurate records, distinguishing among sources, and separating source material from your own ideas.
- Work efficiently at gathering what you need for the project.
- Work flexibly with a wide range of resources—primary and secondary, print and electronic, verbal and visual.
- Engage sources through creative and critical reflection.
- Record summaries, paraphrases, and quotations correctly.
- Be accurate and complete so that you need not reread sources.
- Efficiently develop your paper's outline and first draft.

Four note-taking systems are outlined on the pages that follow. Choose the system that works best for your project, or combine elements to develop your own.

System 1: Paper or electronic note cards. Using paper note cards is the traditional method of note taking; however, note-taking software is now available with most word-processing programs and special programs like TakeNote, EndNote Plus, and Bookends Pro. Here's how a note-card system works:

1. Establish one set of cards (3 × 5 inches, if paper) for your bibliography.
2. On a second set of cards (4 × 6 inches, if paper), take notes on sources:
   - Record one point from one source per card.
   - Clarify the source: List the author's last name, a shortened title, or a code from the matching bibliography card. Include a page number.
   - Provide a topic or heading: Called a slug, the topic helps you categorize and order information.
   - Label the note as a summary, paraphrase, or quotation of the original.
   - Distinguish between the source's information and your own thoughts.

Slug —————————— PROBLEMS WITH INTERNAL-COMBUSTION CARS

Quotation —————————— "In one year, the average gas-powered car produces five tons of carbon dioxide, which as it slowly builds up in the atmosphere causes global warming." (p. 43)

Page Number —————————— -helpful fact about the extent of pollution caused by the traditional i-c engine

Comments —————————— -how does this number compare with what a hybrid produces?

Source —————————— #7

    Upside: Note cards are highly systematic, helping you categorize material and organize it for an outline and a first draft.

Downside: The method can be initially tedious and time-consuming.

System 2: Copy (or save) and annotate. The copy-and-annotate method involves working with photocopies, print versions, or digital texts of sources:

1. Selectively photocopy, print, and/or save important sources. Copy carefully, making sure you have full pages, including the page numbers.

2. As needed, add identifying information on the copy—author, publication details, and date. Each page should be easy to identify and trace. When working with books, simply copy the title and copyright pages and keep them with the rest of your notes.

3. As you read, mark up the copy and highlight key statements. In the margins or digital file, record your ideas:
   - Ask questions. Insert a "?" in the margin, or write out the question.
   - Make connections. Draw arrows to link ideas, or make notes like "see page 36."
   - Add asides. Record what you think and feel while reading.
   - Define terms. Note important words that you need to understand.
   - Create a marginal index. Write keywords to identify themes and main parts.

> **Upside:** Copying, printing, and/or saving helps you record sources accurately; annotating encourages careful reading and thinking.
> **Downside:** Organizing material for drafting is inconvenient; when done poorly, annotating and highlighting involve skimming, not critical thinking.

System 3: The computer notebook or research log. The computer notebook or research log method involves taking notes on a computer or on sheets of paper. Here's how it works:

1. Establish a central location for your notes—a notebook, a file folder, a binder, or an electronic folder.

2. Take notes one source at a time, making sure to identify the source fully. Number your note pages.

3. Using your initials or some other symbol, distinguish your own thoughts from source material.

4. Use codes in your notes to identify which information in the notes relates to which topic in your outline. Then, under each topic in the outline, write the page number in your notes where that information is recorded. With a notebook or log, you may be able to rearrange your notes into an outline by using copy and paste—but don't lose source information in the process!

> **Upside:** Taking notes feels natural without being overly systematic.
> **Downside:** Outlining and drafting may require time-consuming paper shuffling.

System 4: The double-entry notebook. The double-entry notebook involves parallel note taking—notes from sources beside your own brainstorming, reaction, and reflection. Using a notebook or the columns feature of your word-processing program, do the following:

1. Divide pages in half vertically.
2. In the left column, record bibliographic information and take notes on sources.
3. In the right column, write your responses. Think about what the source is saying, why the point is important, whether you agree with it, and how the point relates to other ideas and other sources.

Upside: This method creates accurate source records while encouraging thoughtful responses; also, it can be done on a computer.

Downside: Organizing material for drafting may be a challenge.

Cudworth, Erika. <u>Environment and Society</u>. Routledge Introductions to Environment Series. London and New York: Routledge, 2003.	
Ch. 6 "Society, 'Culture' and 'Nature'—Human Relations with Animals"	*I've actually had a fair bit of personal experience with animals—the horses, ducks, dogs, and cats on our hobby farm. Will this chapter make trouble for my thinking?*
chapter looks at how social scientists have understood historically the relationship between people and animals (158)	
the word *animal* is itself a problem when we remember that people too are animals but the distinction is often sharply made by people themselves (159)	*Yes, what really are the connections and differences between people and animals? Is it a different level of intelligence? Is there something more basic or fundamental? Are we afraid to see ourselves as animals, as creatures?*
"In everyday life, people interact with animals continually." (159)–author gives many common examples	*Many examples—pets, food, TV programs, zoos—apply to me. Hadn't thought about how much my life is integrated with animal life! What does that integration look like? What does it mean for me, for the animals?*

Summarizing, Paraphrasing, and Quoting Source Material

As you work with sources, you must decide what to put in your notes and how to record it—as a summary, a paraphrase, or a quotation. Use these guidelines:

- How relevant is the passage to your research question or working thesis?
- How strong and important is the information offered?
- How unique or memorable is the thinking or phrasing?

The more relevant, the stronger, and the more memorable the material is, the more likely you should note it.

The passage below comes from an article on GM's development of fuel-cell technology. Review the passage; study how the researcher summarizes, paraphrases, and quotes from the source; and then practice these same strategies as you take notes on sources.

> When Karl Benz rolled his Patent Motorcar out of the barn in 1886, he literally set the wheels of change in motion. The advent of the automobile led to dramatic alterations in people's way of life as well as the global economy—transformations that no one expected at the time. The ever-increasing availability of economical personal transportation remade the world into a more accessible place while spawning a complex industrial infrastructure that shaped modern society.
>
> Now another revolution could be sparked by automotive technology: one fueled by hydrogen rather than petroleum. Fuel cells—which cleave hydrogen atoms into protons and electrons that drive electric motors while emitting nothing worse than water vapor—could make the automobile much more environmentally friendly. Not only could cars become cleaner, they could also become safer, more comfortable, more personalized—and even perhaps less expensive. Further, these fuel-cell vehicles could be instrumental in motivating a shift toward a "greener" energy economy based on hydrogen. As that occurs, energy use and production could change significantly. Thus, hydrogen fuel-cell cars and trucks could help ensure a future in which personal mobility—the freedom to travel independently—could be sustained indefinitely, without compromising the environment or depleting the earth's natural resources.
>
> A confluence of factors makes the big change seem increasingly likely. For one, the petroleum-fueled internal-combustion engine (ICE), as highly refined, reliable and economical as it is, is finally reaching its limits. Despite steady improvements, today's ICE vehicles are only 20 to 25 percent efficient in converting the energy content of fuels into drive-wheel power. And although the U.S. auto industry has cut exhaust emissions substantially since the unregulated 1960s—hydrocarbons dropped by 99 percent, carbon monoxide by 96 percent and nitrogen oxides by 95 percent—the continued production of carbon dioxide causes concern because of its potential to change the planet's climate.

Summarize useful passages. ■▪▪

Summarizing condenses in your own words the main points in a passage. Summarize when the source provides relevant ideas and information on your topic.

1. Reread the passage, jotting down a few key words.
2. State the main point in your own words. Add key supporting points, leaving out examples, details, and long explanations. Be objective: Don't mix your reactions with the summary.
3. Check your summary against the original, making sure that you use quotation marks around any exact phrases you borrow.

Sample Summary:

> While the introduction of the car in the late nineteenth century has led to dramatic changes in society and world economics, another dramatic change is now taking place in the shift from gas engines to hydrogen technologies. Fuel cells may make the car "greener," and perhaps even safer, cheaper, and more comfortable. These automotive changes will affect the energy industry by making it more environmentally friendly; as a result, people will continue to enjoy mobility while transportation moves to renewable energy. One factor leading to this technological shift is that the internal-combustion engine has reached the limits of its efficiency, potential, and development—while remaining problematic with respect to emissions, climate change, and health.

INSIGHT: Whenever possible, include a page number, paragraph number, or other locating detail with your paraphrase, summary, or quotation. Such identification at this stage is crucial to avoiding plagiarism down the road (see pages 474–479).

> **From Burns, L. D., McCormick, J. B., and Borroni-Bird, C. E. "Vehicle of Change."** *Scientific American* **287:4 (October 2002): 10 pp.**

Paraphrase key passages. ■▪▪

Paraphrasing puts a whole passage in your own words. Paraphrase passages that present important points, explanations, or arguments but that don't contain memorable or straightforward wording. Follow these steps:

1. Quickly review the passage to get a sense of the whole, and then go through the passage carefully, sentence by sentence.
   - State the ideas in your own words, defining words as needed.
   - If necessary, edit for clarity, but don't change the meaning.
   - If you borrow phrases directly, put them in quotation marks.
2. Check your paraphrase against the original for accurate tone and meaning.

Sample Paraphrase of the Second Paragraph in the Passage:

Automobile technology may lead to another radical economic and social change through the shift from gasoline to hydrogen fuel. By breaking hydrogen into protons and electrons so that the electrons run an electric motor with only the by-product of water vapor, fuel cells could make the car a "green" machine. But this technology could also increase the automobile's safety, comfort, personal tailoring, and affordability. Moreover, this shift to fuel-cell engines in automobiles could lead to drastic, environmentally friendly changes in the broader energy industry, one that will be now tied to hydrogen rather than fossil fuels. The result from this shift will be radical changes in the way we use and produce energy. In other words, the shift to hydrogen-powered vehicles could promise to maintain society's valued mobility, while the clean technology would preserve the environment and its natural resources.

Quote crucial phrases, sentences, and passages. ■ ▪ ▪

Web Link

Quoting records statements or phrases in the original source word for word. Quote nuggets only—statements that are well phrased or authoritative:

1. Note the quotation's context—how it fits in the author's discussion.
2. Copy the passage word for word, enclosing it in quotation marks and checking its accuracy.
3. If you omit words, note that omission with an ellipsis. If you change any word for grammatical reasons, put changes in brackets. (See page 487).

Sample Quotations:

"[H]ydrogen fuel-cell cars and trucks could help ensure a future in which personal mobility . . . could be sustained indefinitely, without compromising the environment or depleting the earth's natural resources."

Note: This sentence captures the authors' main claim about the benefits and future of fuel-cell technology.

"[T]he petroleum-fueled internal-combustion engine (ICE), as highly refined, reliable and economical as it is, is finally reaching its limits."

Note: This quotation offers a well-phrased statement about the essential problem.

INSIGHT: Whether you are summarizing, paraphrasing, or quoting, aim to be true to the source by respecting the context and spirit of the original. Avoid shifting the focus or ripping material out of its context and forcing it into your own. For example, in the sample passage the authors discuss the limits of the internal-combustion engine. If you were to claim that these authors are arguing that the internal-combustion engine was an enormous engineering and environmental mistake, you would be twisting their comments to serve your own writing agenda.

fyi For instruction on effectively integrating quotations, paraphrases, and summaries into your writing, see pages 484–487.

▇ Avoiding Unintentional Plagiarism

Careful note taking helps prevent unintentional plagiarism. Plagiarism—using source material without giving credit—is treated more fully elsewhere (pages 474–479); essentially, however, unintentional plagiarism happens when you accidentally use a source's ideas, phrases, or information without documenting that material. At the planning stage of your project, you can prevent this problem from happening by adhering to principles of ethical research and following some practical guidelines.

Video

Practice the principles of ethical research. ▇�A▪

Because of the nature of information and the many challenges of working with it, conducting ethical research can be very complex and involved. To start with, however, commit to these principles of ethical research:

- Do the research and write the paper yourself.
- Adhere to the research practices approved in your discipline.
- Follow school- and discipline-related guidelines for working with people, resources, and technology.
- Avoid one-sided research that ignores or conceals opposition.
- Present real, accurate data and results—not "fudged" or twisted facts.
- Treat source material fairly in your writing.

Practices That Prevent Unintentional Plagiarism

The principles of ethical research above find expression when you prevent unintentional plagiarism. Do so by following these practices:

- Maintain an accurate working bibliography (pages 430–431).
- When taking notes, distinguish source material from your own reflection by using quotation marks, codes, and/or separate columns or note cards.
- When you draft your paper, transfer source material carefully by coding material that you integrate into your discussion, using quotation marks, double-checking your typing, or using copy and paste to ensure accuracy.
- Take time to do the project right—both research and writing. Avoid pulling an all-nighter during which you can't properly work with sources.

Practices That Prevent Internet Plagiarism

An especially thorny area related to unintentional plagiarism centers on the Internet. As with traditional print sources, Internet sources must be properly credited; in other words, web material cannot simply be transferred to your paper without acknowledgement. So treat web sources like print sources. And if you copy and paste digital material while taking notes and drafting, always track its origins with codes, abbreviations, or separate columns.

Critical-Thinking and Writing Activities

As directed by your instructor, complete the following activities.

1. Write a research report about your major area of study. Discuss the types of knowledge the major explores and the professions to which it leads. Address the paper to students considering this major.

2. For a current research project, find and list fifteen to twenty available sources on your topic. Visit libraries to locate books, articles, and so forth. Use a search engine, directories, and other tools to locate sources on the web. Finally, list any interviews, observations, and surveys that you might do. Shape this list of resources into a working bibliography; then add a commentary to the bibliography in which you explain why you believe this to be good, balanced research for this project.

3. Test the reliability of one of your print sources and one of your Internet sources for a current research project. Refer to the questions on pages 428–429, and see if the two resources pass the test. Are both sources credible enough to strengthen your paper?

4. Choose a short article or a passage from one of your longer sources. Restate (paraphrase) what you have read using your own words. Put quotation marks around key words and phrases that you take directly from the text. Next, use the same materials to create a summary. Reduce what you just read to a few clear and important points using your own words.

5. Using what you have learned in this chapter, develop a research proposal that identifies a topic of interest to you, clarifies the value of the research, maps out research methods, and establishes a workable schedule.

Learning-Outcomes Checklist

Use the checklist below to assess what you have learned about getting started on a research project.

_____ I understand the rhetorical context of my research project.

_____ I can effectively follow the research and writing process, including developing a workable research plan and clarifying my plan in a project proposal.

_____ I can formulate main and secondary research questions, and can respond to the main question in the form of a working thesis or hypothesis.

_____ I can effectively work with a broad range of resources, engage them through critical reading, and evaluate their strength and credibility.

_____ I can effectively build a working bibliography and take notes systematically and accurately so as to avoid unintentional plagiarism.

_____ I avoid plagiarism.

28 Conducting Primary and Library Research

Today, conducting research is both easy and difficult. It's easy because research technology is powerful and many research methods are available. It's difficult because that technology and those methods provide access to so much information—the good, the bad, and the ugly.

How do you meet this challenge and conduct quality research? First, consider whether your project would benefit from primary research. When you engage in primary research, you gather information firsthand by observing sites, interviewing people, and analyzing documents. Second, learn how to use an expert resource—your college library. The library is your gateway to quality print and electronic materials.

Learning Outcomes

Audio

▶ Understand primary and secondary sources.

▶ Plan and conduct primary research.

▶ Use the college library, research tools, and resources.

▶ Locate and work with quality reference works.

▶ Locate and work with quality print books.

▶ Locate and work with quality periodical articles.

Visually Speaking ▶ Review the photograph above. What does this image suggest to you about library research? How does it relate to your own experiences of libraries?

Primary and Secondary Sources

Information sources for your research project can be either primary or secondary. Depending on your assignment, you may be expected to use one or both kinds of sources.

Video

Consider primary sources.

A primary source is an original source, one that gives firsthand information on a topic. This source (such as a diary, a person, or an event) informs you directly about the topic, rather than through another person's explanation or interpretation. The most common forms of primary research are observations, interviews, surveys, experiments, and analyses of original documents and artifacts.

Video

Consider secondary sources.

Secondary sources present secondhand information on your topic—information at least once removed from the original. This information has been compiled, summarized, analyzed, synthesized, interpreted, or evaluated by someone studying primary sources. Journal articles, encyclopedia entries, documentaries, and nonfiction books are typical examples of such secondary sources.

Example: Below are possible primary and secondary sources for a research project exploring hybrid car technology and its viability. Note: Whether a source is primary or secondary depends on what you are studying. For example, if you were studying U.S. attitudes toward hybrid cars (and not hybrid car technology itself), the newspaper editorial and TV roundtable would be primary sources.

Primary Sources	Secondary Sources
E-mail interview with automotive engineer	Journal article discussing the development of hybrid car technology
Fuel-efficiency legislation	Newspaper editorial on fossil fuels
Visit and test-drive a car at a dealership	TV news roundtable discussion of hybrid car advantages and disadvantages
Published statistics about hybrid car sales	Promotional literature for a specific hybrid car

INSIGHT: Some resources are tertiary—that is, thirdhand. They are essentially reports of reports of research and, therefore, are distant from the original information. Examples of tertiary sources would include some articles in popular magazines and entries in Wikipedia. Aside from giving you ideas for focusing your topic, tertiary sources should generally not be used in college research projects and should not appear in works-cited or references lists.

Conducting Primary Research

When published sources can't give you the information that you need, consider conducting primary research. However, you must first weigh all its advantages and disadvantages.

Upside of Primary Research
- It produces information precisely tailored to your research needs.
- It gives you direct, hands-on access to your topic.

Downside of Primary Research
- It can take a lot of time and many resources to complete.
- It can require special skills, such as designing surveys and analyzing statistics and original documents.

Conduct primary research.

You need to choose the method of primary research that best suits your project. For help, review the following descriptions:

1. **Surveys and questionnaires** gather written responses you can review, tabulate, and analyze. These research tools pull together varied information—from simple facts to personal opinions and attitudes. See "Conduct surveys" on pages 444–445.

2. **Interviews** involve consulting two types of people. First, you can interview experts for their insights on your topic. Second, you can interview people whose direct experiences with the topic give you their personal insights. See "Conduct interviews," page 448, and "Interview Report," pages 325–332.

3. **Observations, inspections, and field research** require you to examine and analyze people, places, events, and so on. Whether you rely simply on your five senses or use scientific techniques, observing provides insights into the present state of your subject. For help with observation, field research, and writing reports based on this work, go to **www.thecollegewriter.com/4e**.

4. **Experiments** test hypotheses—predictions about why things do what they do—to arrive at conclusions that can be accepted and acted upon. Such testing often explores cause/effect relationships. See "Lab, Experiment, and Field Reports" on pages 333–346.

5. **Analysis of documents and artifacts** involves studying original reports, statistics, legislation, literature, artwork, and historical records. Such analysis provides unique, close-up interpretations of your topic. See "Analyze texts, documents, records, and artifacts" on pages 446–447, as well as "Writing About Literature and the Arts" on pages 349–364.

Conduct surveys.

One source of primary information that you can use for research projects is a survey or questionnaire. Surveys can collect facts and opinions from a wide range of people about virtually any topic. To get valid information, follow these guidelines:

1. Find a focus.
- Limit the purpose of your survey.
- Target a specific audience.

2. Ask clear questions.
- Phrase questions so they can be easily understood.
- Use words that are objective (not biased or slanted).

3. Match your questions to your purpose.
- Closed questions give respondents easy-answer options, and the answers are easy to tabulate. Closed questions can provide two choices (*yes* or *no, true* or *false*), multiple choices, a rating scale (*poor 1 2 3 excellent*), or a blank to fill.
- Open-ended questions bring in a wide variety of responses and more complex information, but they take time to complete, and the answers can be difficult to summarize.

4. Organize your survey so that it's easy to complete.
- In the introduction, state who you are and why you need the information. Explain how to complete the survey and when and where to return it.
- Guide readers by providing numbers, instructions, and headings.
- Begin with basic questions and end with any complex, open-ended questions that are necessary. Move in a logical order from one topic to the next.

5. Test your survey before using it.
- Ask a friend or classmate to read your survey and help you revise it, if necessary, before printing it.
- Try out your survey with a small test group.

6. Conduct your survey.
- Distribute the survey to a clearly defined group that won't prejudice the sampling (random or cross section).
- Get responses from a good sample of your target group (10 percent if at all possible).
- Tabulate responses carefully and objectively.

Note: To develop statistically valid results, you may need expert help. Check with your instructor.

Sample Survey

Confidential Survey

My name is Cho Lang, and I'm conducting research about the use of training supplements. I'd like to hear from you, Alfred University's athletes. Please answer the questions below by circling or writing out your responses. Return your survey to me, care of the Dept. of Psychology, through campus mail by Friday, April 5. Your responses will remain confidential.

1. Circle your gender.   **Male   Female**

2. Circle your year.
   Freshman   Sophomore   Junior   Senior

3. List the sports that you play.

4. Are you presently using a training supplement?
   Yes   No

   Note: If you circled "no," you may turn in your survey at this point.

5. Describe your supplement use (type, amount, and frequency).

6. Who supervises your use of this training supplement?
   Coach   Trainer   Self   Others

7. How long have you used it?
   Less than 1 month   1–12 months   12+ months

8. How many pounds have you gained while using this supplement?

9. How much has your athletic performance improved?
   None   1   2   3   4   5   Greatly

10. Circle any side effects you've experienced.
    Dehydration   Nausea   Diarrhea

The introduction includes the essential information about the survey.

The survey begins with clear, basic questions.

The survey asks an open-ended question.

The survey covers the topic thoroughly.

Analyze texts, documents, records, and artifacts.

An original document or record is one that relates directly to the event, issue, object, or phenomenon you are researching. Examining original documents and artifacts can involve studying letters, e-mail exchanges, case notes, literary texts, sales records, legislation, and material objects such as tools, sculptures, buildings, and tombs. As you analyze such documents and records, you examine evidence in an effort to understand a topic, arrive at a coherent conclusion about it, and support that judgment. How do you work with such diverse documents, records, and artifacts? Here are some guidelines:

Choose evidence close to your topic. Which texts, documents, records, and artifacts originated from or grew out of the topic you are researching? The closer to the topic, the more primary the source. Select materials that are directly related to your research questions and/or working thesis.

> *Example:* If you were studying English labor riots of the 1830s, you could investigate these primary sources:
>
> - To understand what rioters were demanding, copies of speeches given at demonstrations
> - To know who the rioters were, names from police reports or union membership lists
> - To learn the political response to the riots, political speeches or legislation
> - To get at the attitudes of people from that time, newspaper reports, works of art, or novels from the period
> - To find people's personal stories and private opinions related to the riots, personal letters, diaries, family albums, gravestones, and funeral eulogies

Frame your examination with questions. To make sense of the text, document, record, or artifact, understand what you are looking for and why. List the secondary questions that you want to answer in relation to the main question behind your research project.

> *Example:* To study the legislative background behind the development of cleaner cars, such as the hybrid-fuel vehicle, you could access various documents on the Clean Air Act of 1990 (for example, *The Plain English Guide to the Clean Air Act,* an EPA publication). As you study this legislation, you could frame your reading with these additional questions:
>
> - What are the requirements of the Clean Air Act?
> - Specifically, how do those requirements affect automotive technology?
> - Which private and public research projects will likely influence these requirements?
> - Are schedules for change or deadlines written into the Clean Air Act?

Put the document or artifact in context. So that the material takes on meaning, clarify its external and internal natures. First, consider its external context—the five W's and H: What exactly is it? Who made it, when, where, why, and how? Second, consider its internal nature—what the document means, based on what it can and cannot show you: What does the language mean or refer to? What is the document's structure? What are the artifact's composition and style?

> *Example:* If you were examining Mary Wollstonecraft's *A Vindication of the Rights of Woman* in a history or women's studies course, you would consider the following:
>
> - **External Context:** who Mary Wollstonecraft was; when and why she wrote *A Vindication* and under what conditions; for whom she wrote it and their response; the type of document it is
> - **Internal Context:** Wollstonecraft's essential argument and evidence; the nature of her views, their relationship to her times, and their relevance today

Draw coherent conclusions about meaning. Make sense of the source in relation to your research questions. What connections does the source reveal? What important changes or developments? What cause/effect relationships? What themes?

> *Example:* A study of the Clean Air Act might lead you to a variety of conclusions regarding how environmental legislation relates to the development of hybrid technology—for example, that the United States must produce cleaner cars if it hopes to gain improved air quality.

INSIGHT: Studying primary documents and artifacts is central to many disciplines—history, literature, theology, philosophy, political studies, and archaeology, for example. Good analysis depends on asking research questions appropriate for the discipline. With the English labor riots of the 1830s again as an example, here's what three disciplines might ask:

- **Political science:** What role did political theories, structures, and processes play in the riots—both in causing and in responding to them?
- **Art:** How were the concerns of the rioters embodied in the new "realist" style of the mid-1800s? Did artists sympathize with and address an alienated working-class audience? How did art comment on the social structures of the time?
- **Sociology:** What type and quality of education did most workers have in the 1830s? How did that education affect their economic status and employment opportunities? Did issues related to the riots prompt changes in the English educational system? What changes and why?

With these examples in mind, consider your own major: What questions would this discipline ask of the English labor riots, of Mary Wollstonecraft's *A Vindication of the Rights of Woman,* or of the Clean Air Act of 1990?

Condcut interviews. ■ ■ ■

Video

The purpose of an interview is simple: To get information, you talk with someone who has significant experience or someone who is an expert on your topic. Use the guidelines below whenever you conduct an interview. (See also pages 325–332.)

1. **Before the interview,** do your homework about the topic and the person you are planning to interview.

   - Arrange the interview in a thoughtful way. Explain to the interviewee your purpose and the topics to be covered.

   - Think about the specific ideas you want to cover in the interview and write questions for each. Addressing the 5 W's and H *(Who? What? Where? When? Why? and How?)* is important for good coverage.

   - Organize your questions in a logical order so the interview moves smoothly from one subject to the next.

   - Write the questions on the left side of a page. Leave room for quotations, information, and impressions on the right side.

2. **During the interview,** try to relax so that your conversation is natural and sincere.

   - Provide some background information about yourself, your project, and your plans for using the interview information.

   - Use recording equipment only with the interviewee's permission.

   - Jot down key facts and quotations.

   - Listen actively. Show that you're listening through your body language—eye contact, nods, smiles. Pay attention not only to what the person says, but also to how he or she says it.

   - Be flexible. If the person looks puzzled by a question, rephrase it. If the discussion gets off track, redirect it. Based on the interviewee's responses, ask follow-up questions, and don't limit yourself to your planned questions only.

   > *Based on the interviewee's responses, ask follow-up questions, and don't limit yourself to your planned questions only.*

3. **After the interview,** do the appropriate follow-up work.

   - As soon as possible, review your notes. Fill in responses you remember but couldn't record at the time.

   - Thank the interviewee with a note, an e-mail, or a phone call.

   - If necessary, ask the interviewee to check whether your information and quotations are accurate.

   - Offer to send the interviewee a copy of your writing.

Using the Library

The library door is your gateway to information. Inside, the college library holds a wide range of research resources, from books to periodicals, from reference librarians to electronic databases.

Video

Become familiar with the library.

To improve your ability to succeed at all your research assignments, become familiar with your college library system. Take advantage of tours and orientation sessions to learn its physical layout, resources, and services. Check your library's website for policies, tutorials, and research tools. The college library offers a variety of resources for your research projects.

Librarians: Librarians are information experts:
- Librarians manage the library's materials and guide you to resources.
- They help you perform online searches.

Collections: The library collects and houses a variety of materials:
- **Books and electronic materials**—CD-ROMs, CDs, and DVDs
- **Periodicals**—journals, magazines, and newspapers (print or microform)
- **Reference materials**—directories, indexes, handbooks, encyclopedias, and almanacs
- **Special collections**—government publications, historical documents, and original artifacts

Research tools: The library contains many tools that direct you to materials:
- The online catalog allows you to search everything in the library.
- Print indexes and subscription databases (Lexis-Nexis, EBSCOhost, ProQuest Direct) point you to abstracts and full-text articles.
- Internet access connects you with other library catalogs and online references.

Special services: Special services may also help you to complete research:
- Interlibrary loan allows you to obtain books and articles not available in your library.
- "Hold" allows you to request a book that is currently signed out.
- "Reserve" materials give you access to materials recommended by your instructors or heavily in demand.
- The reference desk can help you find information quickly, point you to the right resources, and help you with a search.
- Photocopiers, CD burners, scanners, and presentation software help you perform and share your research.

Search the catalog.

Library materials are catalogued so they are easy to find. In most college libraries, books, videos, and other holdings are catalogued in an electronic database. To find material, use book titles, author names, and related keyword searching. (See also pages 424–425.)

Sample Electronic Catalog

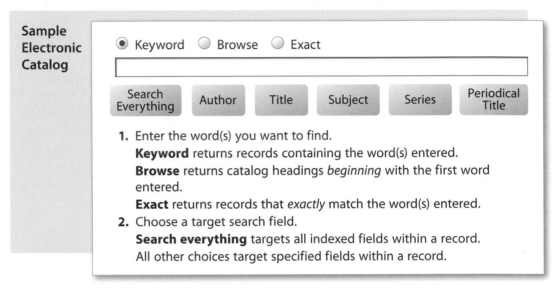

○ Keyword   ○ Browse   ○ Exact

| Search Everything | Author | Title | Subject | Series | Periodical Title |

1. Enter the word(s) you want to find.
   Keyword returns records containing the word(s) entered.
   Browse returns catalog headings *beginning* with the first word entered.
   Exact returns records that *exactly* match the word(s) entered.
2. Choose a target search field.
   Search everything targets all indexed fields within a record. All other choices target specified fields within a record.

When you find a citation for a book or other resource, the result will provide some or all of the following information. Use that information to determine whether the resource is worth exploring further and to figure out other avenues of research. Note that a number of items appearing in blue, underlined type provide links to related books and other resources in the catalog.

Cudworth, Erika, 1966– **1**

2 Title: Environment and Society

3 Publisher: London; New York: Routledge, 2003.

4 Physical descript.: xii, 232 p.: ill.; 24 cm.

5 Subjects: Human ecology [65 rec.]
Nature—Effect of human being on [15 rec.]
Environmental protection [25 rec.]

6 Call number: GF 41 .C83 2003

7 Location: Available—on shelf

1 Author or editor's name

2 Title and subtitle

3 Publisher and copyright date

4 Descriptive information

5 Subject headings (crucial list of topics)

6 Call number

7 Location

Locating Resources by Call Numbers

Library of Congress (LC) call numbers combine letters and numbers to specify a resource's broad subject area, topic, and authorship or title. Finding a book, DVD, or other item involves combining both the alphabetical and the numerical order. Here is a sample call number for *Arctic Refuge: A Vanishing Wilderness?*:

VIDEO QH84.1.A72 1990

subject area **(QH)** topic number **(84)** subtopic number **(1)** cutter number **(A72)**

To find this resource in the library, first note the tab VIDEO. Although not part of the call number, this locator may send you to a specific area of the library. Once there, follow the parts of the call number one at a time:

1. Find the library section on natural history containing videos with the "QH" designation.
2. Follow the numbers until you reach "84."
3. Within the "84" items, find those with the subtopic "1."
4. Use the cutter "A72" to locate the resource alphabetically with "A," and numerically with "72."

Note: In the LC system, pay careful attention to the arrangement of subject area letters, topic numbers, and subtopic numbers: Q98 comes before QH84; QH84 before QH8245; QH84.A72 before QH84.1.A72.

Classification Systems

The LC classification system combines letters and numbers. The Dewey decimal system, which is used in some libraries, uses numbers only. Here is a list of the subject classes for both the LC and Dewey systems.

The Library of Congress and Dewey Decimal Systems

LC Category		Dewey Decimal	LC Category		Dewey Decimal
A	General Works	000–999	K	Law	340–349
B	Philosophy	100–199	L	Education	370–379
	Psychology	150–159	M	Music	780–789
	Religion	200–299	N	Fine Arts	700–799
C	History: Auxiliary Sciences	910–929	P	Language	800–899
D	History: General and			Literature	400–499
	Old World	930–999	Q	Science	500–599
E–F	History: American	970–979	R	Medicine	610–619
G	Geography	910–919	S	Agriculture	630–639
	Anthropology	571–573	T	Technology	600–699
	Recreation	700–799	U	Military Science	355–359, 623
H	Social Sciences	300–399	V	Naval Science	359, 623
J	Political Science	320–329	Z	Bibliography and	010–0199
				Library Science	020–029

Using Books in Research

Your college library contains a whole range of books for you to use, from scholarly studies and reference works to trade books and biographies. Unfortunately, for most research projects you simply don't have time to read an entire book, and rarely do the entire contents relate to your topic. Instead, use the strategy outlined below to refine your research effort.

Approach the book systematically.

1. **Check out front and back information.**
   The title and copyright pages give the book's full title and subtitle; the author's name; and publication information, including publication date and Library of Congress subject headings. The back may contain a note on the author's credentials and other publications.

2. **Scan the table of contents.**
   Examine the contents page to see what the book covers and how it is organized. Ask yourself which chapters are relevant to your project.

3. **Using key words, search the index.**
   Check the index for coverage and page locations of the topics most closely related to your project. Are there plenty of pages, or just a few? Are these pages concentrated or scattered throughout the book?

4. **Skim the preface, foreword, or introduction.**
   Skimming the opening materials will often indicate the book's perspective, explain its origin, and preview its contents.

5. **Check appendices, glossaries, or bibliographies.**
   These special sections may be a good source of tables, graphics, definitions, statistics, and clues for further research.

6. **Carefully read appropriate chapters and sections.**
   Think through the material you've read and take good notes. (See pages 432–435.) Follow references to authors and other works to do further research on the topic. Study footnotes and endnotes for insights and leads.

Consider these options for working productively with books:

- When you find a helpful book, browse nearby shelves for more books.
- To confirm a book's quality, check the Internet, a periodical database, or *Book Review Digest* for a review.
- If your library subscribes to an e-book service such as NetLibrary, you have access to thousands of books in electronic form. You can conduct electronic searches, browse or check out promising books, and read them online.

Check reference works that supply information.

Encyclopedias supply facts and overviews for topics arranged alphabetically.
- General encyclopedias cover many fields of knowledge: *Encyclopedia Britannica, Collier's Encyclopedia*.
- Specialized encyclopedias focus on a single topic: *McGraw-Hill Encyclopedia of Science and Technology, Encyclopedia of American Film Comedy*.

Almanacs, yearbooks, and statistical resources, normally published annually, contain diverse facts.
- *The World Almanac and Book of Facts* presents information on politics, history, religion, business, social programs, education, and sports.
- *Statistical Abstract of the United States* provides data on population, geography, politics, employment, business, science, and industry.

Vocabulary resources supply information on languages.
- General dictionaries, such as *The American Heritage College Dictionary*, supply definitions and histories for a whole range of words.
- Specialized dictionaries define words common to a field, topic, or group: *Dictionary of Engineering, The New Harvard Dictionary of Music*.
- Bilingual dictionaries translate words from one language to another.

Biographical resources supply information about people. General biographies cover a broad range of people. Other biographies focus on people from a specific group. *Examples: Who's Who in America, Dictionary of Scientific Biography, World Artists 1980–1990.*

Directories supply contact information for people, groups, and organizations. *Examples: The National Directory of Addresses and Telephone Numbers, USPS ZIP Code Lookup and Address Information* (online), *Official Congressional Directory.*

Video

Check reference works that are research tools.

Guides and handbooks help readers explore specific topics: *The Handbook of North American Indians, A Guide to Prairie Fauna.*

Indexes point you to useful resources. Some indexes are general, such as *Readers' Guide to Periodical Literature;* others are specific, such as *Environment Index* or *Business Periodicals Index.* (Many are now available online in databases your library subscribes to.)

Bibliographies list resources on a specific topic. A good, current bibliography can be used as an example when you compile your own bibliography on a topic.

Abstracts, like indexes, direct you to articles on a particular topic. But abstracts also summarize those materials so you learn whether a resource is relevant before you invest time in locating and reading it. Abstracts are usually organized into subject areas: Computer Abstracts, Environmental Abstracts, Social Work Abstracts. They are incorporated in many online subscription databases.

Web Link

Finding Periodical Articles

Periodicals are publications or broadcasts produced at regular intervals (daily, weekly, monthly, quarterly). Although some periodicals are broad in their subject matter and audience, as a rule they focus on a narrow range of topics geared toward a particular audience.

- **Daily newspapers and newscasts** provide up-to-date information on current events, opinions, and trends—from politics to natural disasters (*Wall Street Journal, USA Today, The NewsHour*).
- **Weekly and monthly magazines** generally provide more in-depth information on a wide range of topics (*Time, Newsweek, 60 Minutes*).
- **Journals,** generally published quarterly, provide specialized scholarly information for a narrowly focused audience (*English Journal*).

With thousands of periodicals available, how do you find helpful articles? Learn (a) which search tools your library offers, (b) which periodicals it has available in which forms, and (c) how to gain access to those periodicals.

Search online databases.

If your library subscribes to EBSCOhost, Lexis-Nexis, or another database service, use keyword searching (see pages 424–425) to find citations on your topic. You might start with the general version of such databases, such as EBSCOhost's Academic Search Premier, which provides access to more than 4,100 scholarly publications covering all disciplines.

- **Basic Search:** The example below shows an EBSCOhost search screen for a search on hybrid electric cars. Notice how limiters, expanders, and other advanced features help you find the highest-quality materials.

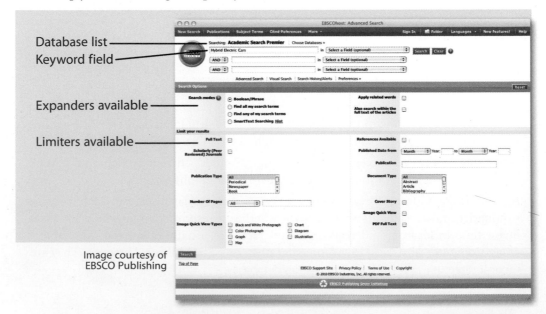

Image courtesy of
EBSCO Publishing

■ **Advanced Search:** A more focused research strategy would involve turning to specialized databases, which are available for virtually every discipline and are often an option within search services such as EBSCOhost (for example, Business Source Elite, PsycINFO, ERIC) and Lexis-Nexis (for example, Legal, Medical, and Business databases). If a basic search turns up little, turn to specialized databases, seeking help from a librarian if necessary. For a list of specialized databases, see page 457.

 Particularly if you need articles published before 1985, you may need to go to the *Readers' Guide to Periodical Literature* or another print index. While databases are converting pre-1985 articles to digital form (for example, the JSTOR database), many excellent periodical articles are available only in print. To use the *Readers' Guide,* consult a librarian.

Generate citation lists of promising articles. ■■·■

Your database search should generate lists of citations, brief descriptions of articles that were flagged through keywords in titles, subject terms, abstracts, and so on. For example, a search focused on hybrid electric cars leads to the results shown below. At this point, study the results and do the following:

■ Refine the search by narrowing or expanding it.
■ Mark specific citations for "capture" or further study.
■ Re-sort the results.
■ Follow links in a specific citation to further information.

Image courtesy of EBSCO Publishing

Study citations and capture identifying information.

By studying citations (especially abstracts), you can determine three things:
- Is this article relevant to your research?
- Is an electronic, full-text version available?
- If not, does the library have this periodical?

To develop your working bibliography (see pages 430–431), you should also "capture" the article's identifying details by using the save, print, or e-mail function, or by recording the periodical's title, the issue and date, and the article's title and page numbers. These functions are shown in the EBSCOhost citation below.

Save options

Source link for more details or full text

Subject links for further research

Summary with keywords highlighted

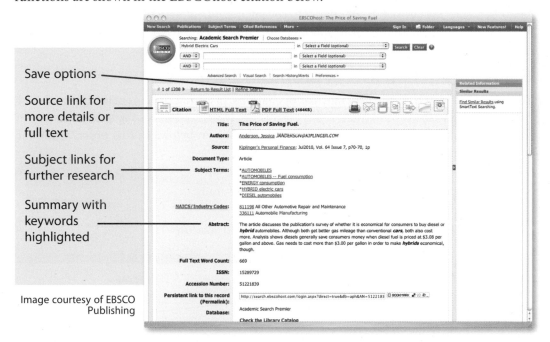

Image courtesy of EBSCO Publishing

Find and retrieve the full text of the article.

When citations indicate that you have promising articles, access those articles efficiently, preferably through a direct link in the citation to an electronic copy. From there you can print, save, or e-mail the article. If the article is not available electronically, track down a print version:

- Check the online citation to see if your library has the article. If necessary, check your library's inventory of periodicals held; this list should be available online and/ or in print. Examine especially closely the issues and dates available, the form (print or microfilm), and the location (bound or current shelves).

- To get the article, follow your library's procedure. You may have to submit a request slip so that a librarian can get the periodical, or you may be able to get it yourself in the current, bound, or microfilm collection. If the article is not available online or in your library, use interlibrary loan.

Databases for Disciplines

Most libraries offer access to databases from a wide range of disciplines. Check your library's website for access to databases like these:

Agricola offers citations from the National Agricultural Library group—with materials focused on issues from animal science to food and nutrition.

ARTbibliographies Modern abstracts articles, books, catalogs, and other resources on modern and contemporary art.

CAIRSS for Music offers bibliographic citations for articles on music-related topics, from music education to music therapy.

Communication & Mass Media Complete offers access to resources on topics like public speaking and TV broadcasting.

Engineering E-journal Search Engine offers free, full-text access to more than 150 online engineering journals.

ERIC offers citations, abstracts, and digests for more than 980 journals in the education field.

First Search, a fee-based information service, offers access to more than 30 scholarly databases in a range of disciplines.

GPO, the Government Printing Office, offers access to records for U.S. government documents (e.g., reports, hearings, judicial rules, addresses, and so on).

Health Source offers access to abstracts, indexing, and full-text material on health-related topics, from nutrition to sports medicine.

Ingenta offers citations for more than 25,000 journals, most in the sciences.

JSTOR offers full-text access to scholarly articles in a full range of disciplines, articles once available only in print.

Math Database offers article citations for international mathematics research.

Medline offers access to journals in medicine and medicine-related disciplines through references, citations, and abstracts.

MLA Bibliography provides bibliographic citations for articles addressing a range of modern-language and literature-related topics.

National Environmental Publications Internet Site (NEPIS) offers access to more than 6,000 EPA documents (full text, online).

PsycINFO offers access to materials in psychology and psychology-related fields (for example, social work, criminology, organizational behavior).

Scirus indexes science resources, citing article titles and authors, source publication information, and lines of text indicating the article's content.

Vocation and Career Collection offers full-text access to more than 400 trade- and industry-related periodicals.

Worldwide Political Science Abstracts offers bibliographic citations in politics-related fields, from public policy to international law.

Critical-Thinking and Writing Activities

As directed by your instructor, complete the following activities.

1. Think about a research project that you have done or are doing now. How might primary research and library research (scholarly books and journals) strengthen your writing? Why not do all your research on the free web using Google and resources like Wikipedia?

2. For the subject "Gender Differences in Toy Preferences," indicate whether the following sources would be considered primary or secondary (P or S):

   _____ a. Observing children in a day-care setting
   _____ b. Journal article about gender-based differences in the brain
   _____ c. Magazine article about a hot new toy
   _____ d. Survey of day-care workers
   _____ e. *Boys' Toys of the Fifties and Sixties* (a book)
   _____ f. Interviews with parents

3. By working with your library's website and its orientation tools, identify where you can physically and/or electronically locate books, reference resources, and journals.

4. Indicate which section of the library would house the following items:

   _____ a. *JAMA (Journal of the American Medical Association)*
   _____ b. *Places Rated Almanac*
   _____ c. *Principles of Corporate Finance (book)*

5. Brainstorm issues related to food production, consumption, or culture. Choosing one focused topic, use your library's catalog and database tools to track down print books and periodical articles. Evaluate the nature, breadth, relevance, and quality of these resources for such a project. Then do a free-web search of the topic, comparing the results.

Learning-Outcomes Checklist

Use the checklist below to assess what you have learned about getting started on a research project.

_____ I understand the differences between primary and secondary sources, and I can make choices about them that fit my research project.

_____ I can plan and conduct primary research such as informal surveys, interviews, observations, and analyses of documents and artifacts.

_____ I have become familiar with my college library: its physical and online dimensions, especially the resources, search tools, and services it offers.

_____ I can effectively find and work with reference works.

_____ I can effectively find and work with books, especially scholarly and trade books.

_____ I can effectively find and work with periodical articles available through library search tools.

29 Conducting Research on the Internet

The image below may look like a child's scribble, but it shows something much more significant: city-to-city Internet connections. The bright tangle of lights on the left is the United States, and the bright tangle on the right is Europe. You'll note, also, jags flying to cities in South America, Africa, India, Australia, and Asia.

Increasingly, the Internet is connecting the world. As you conduct research, you can not only find information from across the globe, but also can connect to the people who provide the information. This chapter helps you get the most out of the Internet as you prepare a research paper.

Learning Outcomes

► Understand the basics of electronic research.

► Use search and metasearch to locate information.

► Use subject trees.

► Understand the strengths and limits of search engines and online resources

► Evaluate the reliability of websites.

► Recognize appropriate and inappropriate sources.

Audio

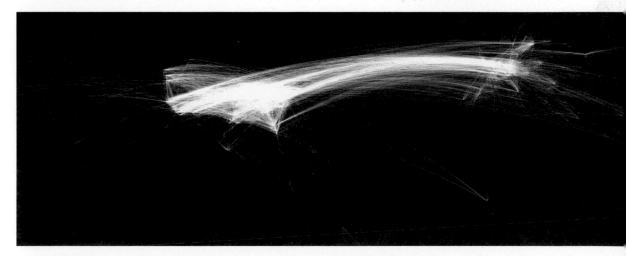

Visually Speaking ► What does the Internet map above tell you about Internet connections in the Western world? What about Internet use elsewhere? What do you think this map will look like in ten years? What does the map tell you about using the Internet for research?

Understanding Internet Basics

Video

Did you know that when you speak on your cell phone or send an e-mail, you are on the Internet? Did you know that the World Wide Web and the Internet are not the same? These two pages provide basic definitions and explanations of the digital world.

The **Internet** is a vast array of interconnected computers and computer networks. It began in 1969 with the ARPANET, a connection of U.S. government computers. Since then, the Internet has expanded into a worldwide system. E-mail, cell phones, and satellites all access and use the Internet, as do people on the World Wide Web.

The **World Wide Web** is a huge collection of websites and pages on the Internet, accessible through the hypertext transfer protocol (HTTP). Put simply, this protocol is a set of rules that allow computers to trade information. The World Wide Web was begun in 1989 by a British engineer named Tim Berners-Lee.

A **uniform resource locator (URL)** is the web address for each page available on the World Wide Web. Just as every home and business has a specific street address, every website has a specific web address that allows other computers to find and access it.

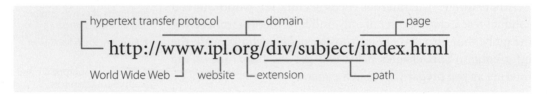

A **domain name** is the website address, often beginning with www and ending with an extension that indicates what type of site it is. Here is a list of common domain types:

.com a commercial or business site
.gov a government site, for federal, state, or local government
.edu an educational site
.org a site for a nonprofit organization
.net a site for an organization that belongs to the Internet's infrastructure
.mil a military site
.biz a business site
.info an information site

A **web browser** is a program on your computer that provides access to the web. Common browsers include Internet Explorer, Safari, and Firefox.

A **webpage** is a specific grouping of information on the web. Webpages often including text, graphics, photographs, videos, and hyperlinks—which are words or graphics that can be clicked to take the user to different webpages.

A **search engine** is a specialized webpage that allows you to find specific terms on sites throughout the web. Here are some popular search engines:

Google   http://www.google.com
Bing   http://www.bing.com
Yahoo   http://www.yahoo.com

A **metasearch engine** is a web page that searches several other search engines at once, compiling the information. Here are some popular metasearch engines:

Ask   http://www.ask.com
Dog Pile   http://www.dogpile.com
Ixquick   http://www.ixquick.com

A **deep-web tool** is an Internet search engine or database that can access materials not available to basic search engines.

Complete Planet   http://www.completeplanet.com

Common Webpage Elements

Using a Subject Guide/Directory

Web Link

A *subject tree,* sometimes called a *subject guide* or *directory,* lists websites that have been organized into categories by experts who have reviewed those sites. As such, a subject tree includes sites selected for reliability and quality.

1. **Search-out the subject trees available to you.** Check whether your library subscribes to a service such as NetFirst, a database in which subject experts have cataloged Internet resources by topic. Here are some other common subject directories:

WWW Virtual Library	http://vlib.org/Overview.html
Ipl2	http://www.ipl.org/
Google Directory	http://www.google.com/dirhp
LookSmart	http://looksmart.com

2. **Follow categories from broad to specific.** A subject tree is arranged from general to specific, so you will need to begin by clicking on a broad category to see a more selective list. Clicking on subcategories will take you to progressively more focused lists. Read the name of a site, review the information beneath the name, check out the domain and extension, and decide if the site is worth exploring. If so, click on it. If not, go back and continue your search.

Common Subject Guide Elements

Using Search and Metasearch

Search and metasearch engines provide quick and powerful access to much of the content of the web. They are invaluable tools for researchers. This page gives tips for getting the most out of your searches, and the next two pages look at search in depth.

Web Link

1. **Select effective keywords:** Keywords are words or phrases that the search engine looks for across the web. The more specific a keyword or phrase is, the more tightly a search will be focused. Here are a set of keywords for the research topic of "games used to simulate real-world scenarios":

General

game	This general term will produce a very unfocused list of millions of websites, ranging from stores selling games to recipes for cooking game.
simulation	This more-specific term will narrow the search considerably, but will show off-topic sites such as suppliers of simulated wood products.
simulation game	This set of keywords is much more specific, but the engine will also find sites using both words but not in combination.
"simulation game"	The quotation marks around this search will turn up only sites that use the exact phrase "simulation game"

Specific

2. **Use Boolean operators:** In addition to using quotation marks, you can use words and symbols to make your search specific. (See also page 425.)

game and **war**	*and* indicates sites with both terms
game + **war**	+ indicates sites with both terms
game not **war**	*not* indicates sites with the first term but not the second
game – **war**	– indicates sites with the first term but not the second
game or **simulation**	*or* indicates sites with either term

3. **Act on search results:** Once a search engine has generated a list of possible sites, you need to survey the results and act on them.

- Read the name of the site and determine how the term is used.
- Review the domain and extension to decide if you will click it.
- Look for information and links.

■ Using Search Engines as Research Tools

Like millions of people, you probably "google it" when you have a question. But how should you use search engines for college research projects? A search engine is a program that automatically scours a large amount of web material using keywords and commands that you submit. In that respect, the search is only as productive as the terms you use, the quality of the search program, and the amount and areas of the web that the engine searches. When you use search engines, be aware of the issues below.

Web Coverage: Even though the largest search engines search billions of web resources, those pages represent just a portion of the web—as little as 20 percent. The point to keep in mind is that any given search engine is not searching the entire web for you and may be focusing on particular kinds of pages and documents. Moreover, a given engine may not be searching each resource in its entirety but only certain portions (e.g., citations) or up to a certain size of the document.

Resource Ranking: A search engine returns results in a ranking of resources based on complex mathematical algorithms—a weighing of a variety of criteria that differ from one engine to the next. One criterion used is the number of times your keywords appear in a given resource. A second criterion might be the number and type of links to a given page—a measure, in other words, of the site's importance or popularity on the web. Moreover, organizations on the web work very hard to make sure that their pages get ranked near the top of searches; some companies hire consultants to help achieve this result or even try to fool the programs. In other words, what you are getting in your search is not necessarily an objective listing of the most relevant and reliable resources for an academic research project.

Search Habits: Using search engines is complicated not just by algorithms but by the habits of users themselves. Studies suggest, for example, that very few users look past the first three hits returned by a search, in fact, that only one percent of searchers go past the first ten hits. (You can understand, then, why some organizations work so hard to get into that top-ten list for specific keyword searches.) Moreover, very few users go on to refine their search after the initial results, supposedly satisfied with what they have found, although studies also suggest that few users can effectively evaluate the returned resources in terms of their quality, authority, objectivity, and timeliness (currency of information). The implications for your college research projects are clear: such search habits rarely lead to quality resources that you can use in an academic project.

Use search engines well.

Given how search engines work, what practices should you follow in using them for an academic research project? Obviously, start by following the assignment's restrictions about using free-web resources. But here are four additional guidelines:

1. **Restrict search-engine use to specific purposes.** Generally, a search engine is useful for college research projects in these circumstances:
   - You have a very narrow topic in mind or an exact question you need answered.
   - You have a highly specific word or phrase to use in your search.
   - You want a large number of results.
   - You are looking for a specific type of Internet file.
   - You have the time to sort the material for reliability.

2. **Learn to do advanced searches.** Basic searches tend to lead to basic results. Most search engines actually allow you to do quite complex searches through advanced-search screens. With these, you can employ Boolean logic to a degree, use limiters and expanders, and refine your results in other ways. Study the search engine's help pages for instructions on how to benefit from these advanced-searching techniques.

3. **Approach results with suspicion.** Given the wide-ranging quality and reliability of material on the free web, it is imperative that you evaluate resources that you find through search engines. See "Evaluating Online Sources" on pages 468-471.

4. **Use search engines that seem to give you more quality results.** Try out a variety of search engines using the same search, and compare the results. While you generally want to choose search engines that cover a large portion of the web, offer quality indexing, and give you high-powered search capabilities, you also want to consider a search-engine's information focus: try out search engines whose goals seem more obviously focused on academics. Below are some suggestions.

- **Internet Public Library:** http://www.ipl.org Offering access to electronic reference resources, to e-books and electronic articles, and to special collections, this site's chief resource is its subject collections of web resources.
- **Infomine:** http://infomine.ucr.edu Subtitled Scholarly Internet Resource Collections, this librarian-built site is designed for college and university faculty and students; the site offers researchers access to databases, electronic journals and books, and more, including government information.
- **LookSmart Find Articles.com:** http://findarticles.com This commercial site can give you citations for articles on your topic, although getting full-text access may involve fees.
- **Google Scholar:** http://scholar.google.com While it indexes just a small portion of all published articles, Google Scholar can help you build citations from a variety of sources, citations you can then find in your library's subscription databases. Moreover, it ranks articles by weighing the full text, the author, the publication, and frequency of citation in other sources.

Understanding the Uses and Limits of Wikipedia

You likely recognize the screen below—an article from Wikipedia. From its beginning in 2001 to today, a large population of volunteer writers and editors has made Wikipedia a top-ten Internet-traffic site. But is Wikipedia acceptable for college-level research? Put simply, Wikipedia is a controversial resource for academic research.

Know Wikipedia's strengths.

Because of its wiki nature, Wikipedia offers researchers a number of advantages.

- **Consensus Model of Knowledge:** Articles represent a collaborative agreement about a topic—a topical knowledge base that is fair and fairly comprehensive. Generally, articles improve over time, offering "open-source" knowledge.
- **Currency of Information:** Because they are web-based, articles are regularly monitored and updated—a distinct advantage over print encyclopedias.
- **Breadth of Information:** With its size and global community, Wikipedia offers articles on a wide range of topics—especially strong in pop culture, current events, computer, and science topics.
- **Links:** Articles are linked throughout so that readers can pursue associated topics, sources, recommended reading, and related categories.

Understand Wikipedia's standards for truth.

Wikipedia applies a different standard of truth than more traditional sources of information. In his revealing article, "Wikipedia and the Meaning of *Truth*," Simson L. Garfinkle provides the following explanation. (See pages 239–243 for the complete essay.)

> Unlike the laws of mathematics or science, wikitruth isn't based on principles such as consistency or observability. It's not even based on common sense or firsthand experience. Wikipedia has evolved a radically different set of epistemological standards—standards that aren't especially surprising given that the site is rooted in a Web-based community, but that should concern those of us who are interested in traditional notions of truth and accuracy. On Wikipedia, objective truth isn't all that important, actually. What makes a fact or statement fit for inclusion is that it appeared in some other publication—ideally, one that is in English and is available free online. "The threshold for inclusion in Wikipedia is verifiability, not truth," states Wikipedia's official policy on the subject.
>
> Verifiability is one of Wikipedia's three core content policies; it was codified back in August 2003. The two others are "no original research" (December 2003) and "neutral point of view," which the Wikipedia project inherited from Nupedia, an earlier volunteer-written Web-based free encyclopedia that existed from March 2000 to September 2003 (Wikipedia's own NPOV policy was codified in December 2001). These policies have made Wikipedia a kind of academic agora where people on both sides of politically charged subjects can rationally discuss their positions, find common ground, and unemotionally document their differences. Wikipedia is successful because these policies have worked.

Know Wikipedia's weaknesses. ■ ■ ■

In some ways, Wikipedia's strengths are closely related to its weaknesses for college-level research. Consider these issues:

- **Popularity Model of Knowledge:** The dynamics of popularity can lead to bias, imbalance, and errors. In some ways, this approach minimizes the value of training, education, and expertise while promoting a kind of democracy of knowledge.
- **Anonymity of Authorship:** Wikipedia allows contributors to remain anonymous. Researchers thus have little way of checking credentials and credibility.
- **Variable Quality of Content:** While many well-established articles are quite stable, balanced, and comprehensive, other articles can be partial, driven by a biased perspective, erroneous, and poorly sourced.
- **Variable Coverage:** Wikipedia's strength in some content areas is matched by gaps and incompleteness in other content areas.
- **Vulnerability to Vandalism:** Wikipedia has a number of processes in place to limit people from harming articles with misinformation, with the result that most vandalism is corrected within hours, but some errors have persisted for months.
- **Tertiary Nature of Information:** For most research projects, Wikipedia articles function as tertiary sources—reports of reports of research. As such, Wikipedia articles are not substantial enough for academic projects.

Use Wikipedia cautiously. ■ ■ ■

Based on Wikipedia's strengths and weaknesses, follow these guidelines:

1. **Respect your assignment.** Instructors may give you varied instruction about using Wikipedia. Respect their guidelines.
2. **Verify Wikipedia information.** If you use information from Wikipedia, also use other more traditional sources to verify that information.
3. **Use Wikipedia as a semi-authoritative reference source.** Generally, the more academic your research assignment, the less you should rely on Wikipedia articles, which are essentially sources of basic and background information.
4. **Use Wikipedia as one starting point.** From a Wikipedia article, you can learn what is considered "open-source" knowledge on your topic, gather ideas for developing a topic, find links to related topics and other resources, and begin to build a bibliography.
5. **Study individual articles to get a sense of their reliability.** When you find a Wikipedia article relevant to your research project, check the article for quality and stability. Use the evaluation criteria on the following pages, but also check the article's history, its discussion page, any tags or icons indicating the article's state, and the "what links here" link in the toolbox at the left of the screen.

Evaluating Online Sources

The Internet contains a wealth of information, but much of it is not suitable for a research report. The information may be incorrect, biased, outdated, plagiarized, or otherwise unreliable. These pages discuss issues to watch for.

Assignment Restrictions

Before engaging any web resources, carefully review your assignment and note any restrictions on what type of sources may be used. If web resources are allowed, abide by the number or percentage indicated in the assignment.

Author/Organization

When using web resources, make sure the sites are sponsored by legitimate, recognizable organizations: government agencies, nonprofit groups, and educational institutions. For most projects, avoid relying on personal or special-interest sites, as well as chat rooms, blogs, news groups, or wikis. (These sources may help you explore a topic, but they do not provide scholarly material suitable for most research reports.)

Balance or Bias

Be aware of the purpose of a site or an article. Editorials and reviews, for example, express the point of view of a given author but are not sources for unbiased information. Unless your purpose is to show the author's point of view or point out two sides of an argument, avoid sources that show a bias toward or against a specific region, country, political party, industry, gender, race, ethnic group, or religion. Also, avoid sites that promote a specific cause, product, service, or belief.

Quality of Information

Test the quality of information on a site. Note whether the information is current (when was it posted/updated last) and check it against other sources for corroboration. Also, favor sites with a depth of information and those that show they truly engage their topic rather than treating it superficially.

Quality of Writing and Design

Avoid sites that show sloppy editing and poor design. These surface flaws can reveal a lack of scholarly rigor or serious commitment on the part of the site's creators.

Evaluation Checklist

Use this checklist to assess the reliability of web sources. The more items you check off, the more reliable the source is.

Assignment Restrictions

_____ **1.** Does the source fit with the type and number allowed in the assignment?

Author/Organization

_____ **2.** Is the person or organization behind the site reliable?

_____ **3.** Is contact information for the person or organization provided?

_____ **4.** Is the site well known and well connected in the field?

_____ **5.** Does the site have a clear "About Us" page and mission statement?

Balance or Bias

_____ **6.** Is the material on the site balanced and unbiased?

_____ **7.** Does the site avoid unfair and inflammatory language?

_____ **8.** Does the site avoid pushing a particular product, cause, service, or belief?

_____ **9.** Does the site provide ample support for its claims?

_____ **10.** Does the site avoid logical fallacies and twisted statistics? (See pages 257–260.)

Quality of Information

_____ **11.** Is the material current?

_____ **12.** Is the website often updated?

_____ **13.** Is the website information-rich?

_____ **14.** Is the information backed up by other reputable print and online sources?

Quality of Writing and Design

_____ **15.** Is the text free of errors in punctuation, spelling, and grammar?

_____ **16.** Is the site effectively and clearly designed?

Sample Evaluations

Reliable

Assignment Restrictions

- The site below would be appropriate for most assignments about the life and work of William Faulkner, as long as free-web sources are allowed.

Author/ Organization

- This site is sponsored by the University of Mississippi, a scholarly source for information, and the article's author, Dr. John B. Padgett, is an authority on Faulkner.

Balance or Bias

- The site clearly extols Faulkner as a great writer but does not shy from showing his shortcomings. The claims are fair and amply supported, without logical fallacies.

Quality of Information

- The website is current, often updated, and information-rich. It is also connected to many other Faulkner resources available on the web.

Quality of Writing and Design

- The site is well designed, with easy navigation, readable text, informative headings, helpful photos, and strong links. The text is well written and well edited.

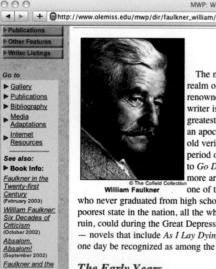

MWP: William Faulkner (1897–1962)

http://www.olemiss.edu/mwp/dir/faulkner_william/   Google

▶Publications
▶Other Features
▶Writer Listings

Go to
▶ Gallery
▶ Publications
▶ Bibliography
▶ Media Adaptations
▶ Internet Resources

See also:
▶ **Book Info:**
Faulkner in the Twenty-first Century
(February 2003)
William Faulkner: Six Decades of Criticism
(October 2002)
Absalom, Absalom!
(September 2002)
Faulkner and the Politics of Reading, by Karl Zender
(August 2002)
Faulkner and Postmodernism, edited by John Duvall and Ann Abadie
(July 2002)
New Orleans Sketches
(June 2002)
The Unvanquished
(Large Print edition)
(April 2002)
Light in August
(April 2002)

William Faulkner

The man himself never stood taller than five feet, six inches tall, but in the realm of American literature, William Faulkner is a giant. More than simply a renowned Mississippi writer, the Nobel Prize-winning novelist and short story writer is acclaimed throughout the world as one of the twentieth century's greatest writers, one who transformed his "postage stamp" of native soil into an apocryphal setting in which he explored, articulated, and challenged "the old verities and truths of the heart." During what is generally considered his period of greatest artistic achievement, from *The Sound and the Fury* in 1929 to *Go Down, Moses* in 1942, Faulkner accomplished in a little over a decade more artistically than most writers accomplish over a lifetime of writing. It is one of the more remarkable feats of American literature, how a young man who never graduated from high school, never received a college degree, living in a small town in the poorest state in the nation, all the while balancing a growing family of dependents and impending financial ruin, could during the Great Depression write a series of novels all set in the same small Southern county — novels that include *As I Lay Dying*, *Light in August*, and above all, *Absalom, Absalom!* — that would one day be recognized as among the greatest novels ever written by an American.

© The Cofield Collection
William Faulkner

The Early Years

William Cuthbert Falkner (as his name was then spelled) was born on September 25, 1897, in New Albany, Mississippi, the first of four sons born to Murry and Maud Butler Falkner. He was named after his great-grandfather, William Clark Falkner, the "Old Colonel," who had been killed eight years earlier in a duel with his former business partner in the streets of Ripley, Mississippi. A lawyer, politician, planter, businessman, Civil War colonel, railroad financier, and finally a best-selling writer (of the novel *The White Rose of Memphis*), the Old Colonel, even in death, loomed as a larger-than-life model of personal and professional success for his male descendants.

A few days before William's fifth birthday, the Falkners moved to Oxford, Mississippi, at the urging of Murry's father, John Wesley Thompson Falkner. Called the "Young Colonel" out of homage to his father rather than to actual military service, the younger Falkner had abruptly decided to sell the railroad begun by his father. Disappointed that he would not inherit the railroad, Murry took a series of jobs in Oxford, most of them with the help of his father. The elder Falkner, meanwhile, founded the First National Bank of Oxford in 1910 with $30,000 in capital.

Related Links & Info

© The Cofield Collection
William Clark Falkner

Unreliable

- As a blog, the made-up website below would not be appropriate for an assignment about the life and work of William Faulkner. A site such as this should be recognized as reflective only of the writer's opinion, not of reliable information or fact.

- There is no author or organization listed for this website. The domain name—myviewsonliterature.wordpress.com—shows that this is a personal opinion blog. Its lack of connection to other websites shows it represents an isolated opinion.

- This blog post shows a strong bias against William Faulkner. The few facts cited inadequately support the writer's main point, and logical fallacies are apparent. The tone of the post is unscholarly, with inflammatory language.

- Though this website is frequently updated, the blog post does not represent current scholarship about William Faulkner. The website is information-poor and is not backed up by any reputable print or online sources.

- The site has an amateurish design and numerous errors, including the persistent misspelling of William Faulkner's name. The writing is slipshod and the editing is poor.

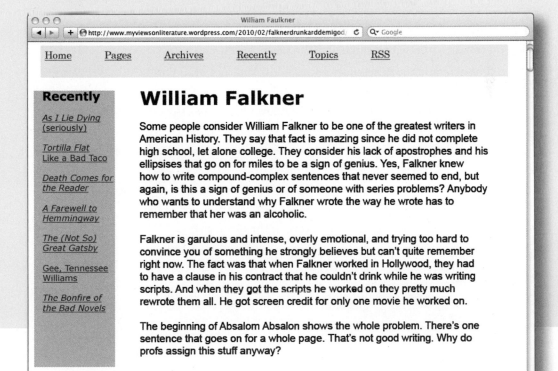

Critical-Thinking and Writing Activities

As directed by your instructor, complete the following activities.

1. Explore your library's handouts and website for information about Internet research. What services, support, and access does the library provide? Explore the various resources with your own major in mind, and draft an informal report to share with your instructor and classmates about the resources available in your discipline.

2. With a current research project in one of your classes as the focus, conduct a search for this project using a search engine listed on page 461. Save useful URLs and articles in the research file. Then use one of the subject trees on page 462 to investigate and evaluate potential websites for the same project. Save useful URLs and articles. Compare and contrast these two processes for finding Internet information.

3. Using the variety of methods outlined in this chapter, work with some classmates
   to search the Internet for information on a controversial topic, event, person, or place. Carefully analyze and evaluate the range of web information you find—the quality, perspective, depth, and reliability. Create a report on your findings for the rest of the class.

Learning-Outcomes Checklist

As you conduct Internet research, use the following checklist:

_____ I understand the differences between the Internet, the World Wide Web, and the deep web.

_____ I know how to use subject trees to discover high-quality, vetted sites for my research.

_____ I understand how to use search and metasearch, selecting effective key terms and using Boolean operators.

_____ I understand the strengths and limits of search engines such as Google and online resources such as Wikipedia; I can use these tools effectively.

_____ I understand the source restrictions on the assignment.

_____ I have carefully evaluated each Internet source for credible authorship, reliable sponsorship, lack of bias, currency, accuracy, logical support, and quality design.

_____ I know the warning signs of unreliable sources.

30 Drafting a Paper with Documented Research

When you write a research paper, you enter a larger conversation about your topic. The paper should center on your own ideas while thoughtfully engaging with the ideas of others. Crediting sources ensures that each voice in the conversation is fairly represented.

This chapter focuses on effective and conscientious use of sources in your writing, with tips for avoiding source abuse and plagiarism. It also helps you write a first draft of your paper.

Learning Outcomes

▶ Understand and avoid plagiarism.

▶ Avoid other source abuses.

▶ Organize and synthesize your findings.

▶ Develop your first draft.

▶ Use source material in your writing.

Visually Speaking ▶ How does the photograph above connote the process of deciding what sources to include in a paper?

Web Link

Video

Avoiding Plagiarism

The road to plagiarism may be paved with the best intentions—or the worst. Either way, the result is still a serious academic offense. As you write your research paper, do everything you can to stay off that road! Start by studying your school's and your instructor's guidelines on plagiarism and other academic offenses. Then study the following pages.

What is plagiarism? ■ ▪ ■

Plagiarism is using someone else's words, ideas, or images (what's called intellectual property) so they appear to be your own. When you plagiarize, you use source material—whether published in print or online—without acknowledging the source. In this sense, plagiarism refers to a range of thefts:

- Submitting a paper you didn't write yourself.
- Pasting large chunks of a source into your paper and passing it off as your own work.
- Using summaries, paraphrases, or quotations without documentation.
- Using the exact phrasing of a source without quotation marks.
- Mixing up source material and your own ideas—failing to distinguish between the two.

Plagiarism refers to more than "word theft." Because plagiarism is really about failing to credit ideas and information, the rules also apply to visual images, tables, graphs, charts, maps, music, videos, and so on.

What does plagiarism look like? ■ ▪ ■

Plagiarism refers to a range of source abuses. What exactly do these violations look like? Read the passage below, and then review the five types of plagiarism that follow, noting how each misuses the source.

> The passage below is from page 87 of "Some Stories Have to Be Told by Me: A Literary History of Alice Munro," by Marcela Valdes, published in the *Virginia Quarterly Review* 82.3 (Summer 2006).
>
> What makes Munro's characters so enthralling is their inconsistency; like real people, at one moment they declare they will cover the house in new siding, at the next, they vomit on their way to the hospital. They fight against and seek refuge in the people they love. The technique that Munro has forged to get at such contradictions is a sort of pointillism, the setting of one bright scene against another, with little regard for chronology.

■ Submitting Another Writer's Paper

The most blatant plagiarism is taking an entire piece of writing and claiming it as your own work. Examples:

- Downloading, reformatting, and submitting an article as your own work.
- Buying a paper from a "paper mill" or taking a "free" paper off the Internet.
- Turning in another student's work as your own (see "Falstaffing" on page 479).

 Just as it's easy to plagiarize using the Internet, it's easy for your professors to recognize and track down plagiarism using Internet tools.

■ Using Copy and Paste

It is unethical to take chunks of material from another source and splice them into your paper without acknowledgment. In the example below, the writer pastes in a sentence from the original article (boldfaced) without using quotation marks or a citation. Even if the writer changed some words, it would still be plagiarism.

> Life typically unfolds mysteriously for Munro's characters, with unexplained events and choices. **Like real people, at one moment they declare they will cover the house in new siding, at the next, they vomit on their way to the hospital.**

■ Failing to Cite a Source

Borrowed material must be documented. Even if you use information accurately and fairly, don't neglect to cite the source. Below, the writer correctly summarizes the passage's idea but offers no citation.

> For the reader, the characters in Munro's stories are interesting because they are so changeable. Munro shows these changes by using a method of placing scenes side by side for contrast, without worrying about the chronological connections.

■ Neglecting Necessary Quotation Marks

Whether it's a paragraph or a phrase, if you use the exact wording of a source, that material must be enclosed in quotation marks. In the example below, the writer cites the source but doesn't use quotation marks around a phrase taken from the original (boldfaced).

> What makes Munro's characters so typically human is that they **fight against and seek refuge in the people they love (Valdes 87).**

■ Confusing Borrowed Material with Your Own Ideas

Through carelessness (often in note taking), you may confuse source material with your own thinking. Below, the writer indicates that he borrowed material in the first sentence, but fails to indicate that he also borrowed the next sentence.

> As Marcela Valdes explains, "[w]hat makes Munro's characters so enthralling is their inconsistency" (87). **To achieve this sense of inconsistency, Munro places brightly lit scenes beside each other in a kind of pointillist technique.**

Why is plagiarism serious?

Perhaps the answer is obvious. But some people operate with the notion that material on the Internet (whether text, graphics, or sound) is "free" and, therefore, fair game for research writing. After all, a lot of stuff on the web doesn't even list an author, so what's the harm? Here's some food for thought:

■ Academic Dishonesty

At its heart, plagiarism is cheating—stealing intellectual property and passing it off as one's own work. Colleges take such dishonesty seriously. Plagiarism, whether intentional or unintentional, will likely be punished in one or more ways:

- A failing grade for the assignment
- A failing grade for the course
- A note on your academic transcript (often seen by potential employers) that failure resulted from academic dishonesty
- Expulsion from college

■ Theft from the Academic Community

The research paper represents your dialogue with other members of the academic community—classmates, the instructor, others in your major, others who have researched the topics, and so on. When you plagiarize, you short-circuit the dialogue:

- You gain an unfair advantage over your classmates who follow the rules and earn their grades.
- You disrespect other writers, researchers, and scholars.
- You disrespect your readers by passing off others' ideas as your own.
- You insult your instructor, a person whose respect you need.
- You harm your college by risking its reputation and its academic integrity.

■ Now and in the Future

Because research projects help you master course-related concepts and writing skills, plagiarism robs you of an opportunity to learn either. Moreover, you rob yourself of your integrity and reputation. After all, as a student you are seeking to build your credibility within the broader academic community, your major, and your future profession.

In addition, research projects often train you for your future work in terms of research, thinking, and writing skills—skills that you will need to succeed in the workplace. If you do not learn the skills now, you will enter the workplace without them—a situation that your employer will, at some point, find out.

One tool to deter plagiarism is Turnitin.com. Students submit their papers for comparison against millions of webpages and other student papers. Students and instructors get reports about originality and matching text. For more on this tool, visit **www.thecollegewriter.com/4e.**

How do I avoid plagiarism? ■ ˙ ■

Preventing plagiarism begins the moment you get an assignment. Essentially, prevention requires your commitment and diligence throughout the project.

Resist temptation. With the Internet, plagiarism is a mouse click away. Avoid last-minute all-nighters that make you desperate; start research projects early. *Note:* It's better to ask for an extension or accept a penalty for lateness than to plagiarize.

Play by the rules. Become familiar with your college's definition, guidelines, and policies regarding plagiarism so that you don't unknowingly violate them. When in doubt, ask your instructor for clarification.

Take orderly, accurate notes. From the start, carefully keep track of source material and distinguish it from your own thinking. Specifically, do the following:

- Maintain an accurate working bibliography (pages 430–431).
- Adopt a decent note-taking system (pages 432–435).
- Accurately summarize, paraphrase, and quote sources in your notes (pages 436–438).

Document borrowed material. Credit information that you have summarized, paraphrased, or quoted from any source, whether that information is statistics, facts, graphics, phrases, or ideas. Readers can then see what's borrowed and what's yours, understand your support, and do their own follow-up research.

> *Common Knowledge Exception:* Common knowledge is information—a basic fact, for instance—that is generally known to readers or easily found in several sources, particularly reference works. Such knowledge need not be cited. However, when you go beyond common knowledge into research findings, interpretations of the facts, theories, explanations, claims, arguments, and graphics, you must document the source. Study the examples below, but whenever you are in doubt, document.
>
> *Examples:*
> - The fact that automakers are developing hybrid-electric cars is common knowledge, whereas the details of GM's AUTOnomy project are not.
> - The fact that Shakespeare wrote *Hamlet* is common knowledge, whereas the details of his sources are not.

Work carefully with source material in your paper. See pages 484–487 for more on integrating and documenting sources, but here, briefly, are your responsibilities:

- Distinguish borrowed material from your own thinking by signaling where source material begins and ends.
- Indicate the source's origin with an attributive phrase and a citation (parenthetical reference or footnote).
- Provide full source information in a works-cited or references page.

■ Avoiding Other Source Abuses

Plagiarism, though the most serious offense, is not the only source abuse to avoid when writing a paper with documented research. Consider these pitfalls, which refer again to the sample passage on page 474.

■ Using Sources Inaccurately

When you get a quotation wrong, botch a summary, paraphrase poorly, or misstate a statistic, you misrepresent the original. In this quotation, the writer carelessly uses several wrong words that change the meaning, as well as adding two words that are not in the original.

> As Marcela Valdes explains, "[w]hat makes Munro's characters so appalling is their consistency. . . . They fight against and seek refuse in the people they say they love" (87).

■ Using Source Material Out of Context

By ripping a statement out of its context and forcing it into yours, you can make a source seem to say something that it didn't really say. This writer uses part of a statement to say the opposite of the original.

> According to Marcela Valdes, while Munro's characters are interesting, Munro's weakness as a fiction writer is that she shows "little regard for chronology" (87).

■ Overusing Source Material

When your paper reads like a string of references, especially quotations, your own thinking disappears. The writer below takes the source passage, chops it up, and splices it together.

> Anyone who has read her stories knows that "[w]hat makes Munro's characters so enthralling is their inconsistency." That is to say, "like real people, at one moment they declare they will cover the house in new siding, at the next, they vomit on their way to the hospital." Moreover, "[t]hey fight against and seek refuge in the people they love." This method "that Munro has forged to get at such contradictions is a sort of pointillism," meaning "the setting of one bright scene against another, with little regard for chronology" (Valdes 87)

■ "Plunking" Quotations

When you "plunk" quotations into your paper by failing to prepare the reader for them and follow them up, the discussion becomes choppy and disconnected. The writer below interrupts the flow of ideas with a quotation "out of the blue." In addition, the quotation hangs at the end of a paragraph with no follow-up.

> Typically, characters such as Del Jordan, Louisa Doud, and Almeda Roth experience a crisis through contact with particular men. "They fight against and seek refuge in the people they love" (Valdes 87).

■ Using "Blanket" Citations

Your reader shouldn't have to guess where borrowed material begins and ends. For example, if you place a parenthetical citation at the end of a paragraph, does that citation cover the whole paragraph or just the final sentence?

■ Relying Heavily on One Source

If your writing is dominated by one source, readers may doubt the depth and integrity of your research. Instead, your writing should show your reliance on a balanced diversity of sources.

■ Failing to Match In-Text Citations to Bibliographic Entries

All in-text citations must clearly refer to accurate entries in the works-cited, references, or endnotes page. Mismatching occurs in the following circumstances:

- An in-text citation refers to a source that is not listed in the bibliography.
- A bibliographic resource is never actually referenced anywhere in the paper.

■ Related Academic Offenses

Beyond plagiarism and related source abuses, steer clear of these academic offenses:

Double-dipping: When you submit one paper in two different classes without permission from both instructors, you take double credit for one project.

Falstaffing: This practice refers to a particular type of plagiarism in which one student submits another student's work. Know that you are guilty of Falstaffing if you let another student submit your paper.

Copyright violations: When you copy, distribute, and/or post in whole or in part any intellectual property without permission from or payment to the copyright holder, you commit a copyright infringement, especially when you profit from this use. To avoid copyright violations in your research projects, do the following:

- **Observe *fair use* guidelines:** Quote small portions of a document for limited purposes, such as education or research. Avoid copying large portions for your own gain.
- **Understand what's in the *public domain:*** You need not obtain permission to copy and use public domain materials—primarily documents created by the government, but also some material posted on the Internet as part of the "copy left" movement.
- **Observe *intellectual property and copyright laws:*** First, know your college's policies on copying documents. Second, realize that copyright protects the expression of ideas in a range of materials—writings, videos, songs, photographs, drawings, computer software, and so on. Always obtain permission to copy and distribute copyrighted materials.
- **Avoid changing a source** (e.g., a photo) without permission of the creator or copyright holder.

◼ Organizing and Synthesizing Your Findings

Your research may generate a mass of notes, printouts, photocopies, electronic files, and more. The challenge is to move from this mass to a coherent structure for the paper you need to write. If you have systematically taken good notes (see pages 432–435), you are well on the way. In addition, the tips below and on the next page will help you move toward order.

Develop your ideas. ◼ ▪ ▪

Good thinking is foundational to good research writing. To develop ideas for your research project, follow these steps:

Refocus on your research questions and working thesis. Has research changed your perspective and position?

Study the evidence. Review your materials once, twice, or more—as long as it takes for ideas to percolate and information to make sense. Consider these questions:

- Is the information complete or at least sufficient for the project?
- Does the information seem reliable and accurate?
- How does the information relate to the topic?
- What connections exist among different pieces of evidence?
- Does the information gathered fall naturally into patterns?

Develop sound conclusions through analysis and synthesis. Practice these strategies (and check pages 18–25 for more on sound thinking):

- Work against personal biases that create blind spots to what the evidence is saying. Be open to different angles provided by all the evidence. Think through both pros and cons.
- Practice logic in your analysis, but also tap into your intuition, creativity, and imagination.
- Interpret statistical data carefully and correctly.
- Logically distinguish between causes and effects; carefully link them.
- If you are comparing, make sure that the items can logically be compared, and make sure that you think through both similarities and differences.
- Avoid either/or and black-and-white thinking, as well as circular arguments, slippery slope claims, and sweeping generalizations. (See logical fallacies at pages 257–260.)
- Check your conclusions against counterarguments, your experience, and common sense. For example, what are the limits of hybrid-vehicle technology? What does your experience with cars and with culture tell you about how technological changes happen and get accepted?

Develop a structure for delivering research results. ■ ■ ■

Using your research questions and conclusions as guides, sift through and order your information. Consider these strategies:

Follow assignment recommendations. A pattern for your paper may be built into the assignment. For example, you may be asked to write a comparison/contrast paper. Shape your outline within that framework.

Clump and split. Using key ideas as main headings, arrange support and evidence under the most fitting heading. Depending on the note-taking system you used, separate and pile note cards, sketch out the structure on paper, use a graphic organizer (see pages 52–53), use a code system, copy and paste material electronically, or cut up your note pages. After categorizing information, decide how best to sequence the key ideas.

Rely on tested patterns. The patterns below offer sound methods for developing your thinking. Each choice offers a basic structure for your paper, but several patterns may be useful within your paper's body.

- **Argumentation** asserts and supports a claim, counters any opposition, and then reasserts the claim (perhaps in a modified form). See pages 249–304.

- **Cause/effect** can (1) explore the factors that led to an event or (2) explore the consequences of a specific event. See pages 163–180.

- **Chronological** order puts items in a sequence (order of events, steps in a process). See pages 215–230.

- **Classification** groups details based on their common traits or qualities. See pages 201–214.

- **Comparison/contrast** shows similarities and/or differences between specific elements of a topic. See pages 181–200.

- **Description** orders details in terms of spatial relationships, color, form, texture, and so on. See pages 141–160.

- **Explanation** clarifies how something works by breaking the object or phenomenon into parts or phases and then showing how they work together. See pages 215–230.

- **Order of importance** arranges items from most to least important, or least to most.

- **Partitioning** breaks down an object, a space, or a location into ordered parts, or a process into steps or phases.

- **Problem/solution** states a problem, explores its causes and effects, and presents solutions. See pages 305–322.

- **Question/answer** moves back and forth from questions to answers in a sequence that logically clarifies a topic

fyi   For more help developing a structure, see pages 48–53.

Developing Your First Draft

Video

As you write your paper, your first goal is to develop and support your ideas—referring to sources, not being dominated by them. The discussion that follows will help you achieve this goal. Your second goal is to respect sources by integrating them naturally and providing correct documentation; that goal is addressed on pages 484–487.

Choose a drafting method.

Before starting your draft, choose a drafting method that makes sense for your project and your writing style. Consider these two options or something in between:

■ Writing Systematically

1. Develop a detailed outline, including supporting evidence.
2. Arrange your notes in precise order.
3. Write methodically, following your thesis, outline, and notes.
4. Cite your sources as you write.

■ Writing Freely

1. Review your working thesis and notes. Then set them aside.
2. If you need to, jot down a brief outline.
3. Write away—get all your research-based thinking down on paper.
4. Going back to your notes, develop your draft further and integrate citations.

Shape your first draft.

Develop the following parts in any order.

Draft an introduction. The introduction should do three things. First, it should say something interesting or surprising to gain your readers' attention. Second, the introduction should focus in on your topic by establishing some common ground. Third, your introduction should identify the issue or challenge related to your topic, and then offer your thesis. Consider these options:

- Begin with a revealing story or quotation.
- Give important background information.
- Offer a series of interesting or surprising facts.
- Cite details showing the topic's relevance.
- Provide important definitions.
- Introduce a problem, an issue, a challenge, a puzzle, or a confusion about your topic.
- Identify the purpose and scope of your research.
- Identify your focus or thesis.
- Forecast how you will develop and support your thesis.

Draft the body. How do you develop a complete and insightful research paper? How do you add dimension and depth to your writing? For starters, you make sure that you have carefully explored and reflected on your specific topic. You also make sure that you have gathered plenty of compelling evidence to support your thesis.

It's in the main part of your paper—in the body—that you develop your thesis. The process usually works in this way: You present each main point supporting your thesis, expand on the points logically, include solid evidence such as facts or examples, and then offer additional analysis or documentation as needed.

Another way to approach your writing is to envision it as a series of paragraph clusters—one cluster of paragraphs for each main point. As you write, you imagine yourself conversing with your readers, telling them what they need to know, and communicating it as clearly and interestingly as you can.

Draft a conclusion. An effective closing adds to the reader's understanding of a research paper. The first part of the closing usually reviews (or ties together) important points in the paper, reinforces or reasserts the thesis, and/or draws a conclusion. The closing's final lines may expand the scope of the text by making a connection between the paper and the reader's experience, or between the paper and life in general.

Create a working title. At any point in the writing process, jot down possible titles that capture your paper's focused topic, research discoveries, and spirit. Consider key words and phrases that hint at your paper's thesis. For some papers, you may want to create a main title and a subtitle, separated by a colon.

TIPS for research writing

- As you draft your paper, keep the focus on your own thoughts. You don't want your paper to read like a strung-together series of references to other sources.

- Present your own ideas honestly and clearly. Although you will be considering the research of others, be sure to analyze this information yourself and relate your sources to one another. Work at offering your personal perspective on the topic.

- Your instructor may want your thesis in a specific location (perhaps in the last sentence of your first paragraph). Follow her or his wishes.

- Don't try to cram everything you've learned into your draft. Select material that is truly needed to develop your thesis.

- Avoid overusing one particular source; also avoid using too many direct quotations.

- To avoid accidental plagiarism, indicate the sources of all borrowed facts as you write your draft. (See "Avoiding Plagiarism," pages 474–477.)

■ Using Source Material in Your Writing

After you've found good sources and taken good notes on them, you want to use that research effectively in your writing. Specifically, you want to show (1) what information you are borrowing and (2) where you got it. By doing so, you create credibility. This section shows you how to develop credibility by integrating and documenting sources so as to avoid plagiarism and other abuses. *Note:* For a full treatment of documentation, see chapter 31 (MLA) and chapter 32 (APA).

Integrate source material carefully. ■ ■ ■

Source material—whether a summary, a paraphrase, or a quotation—should be integrated smoothly into your discussion. Follow these strategies:

■ The Right Reasons

Focus on what you want to say, not on all the source material you've collected. Use sources to do the following:

- Deepen and develop your point with the reasoning offered by a source.
- Support your point and your thinking about it with evidence—with facts, statistics, details, and so on.
- Give credibility to your point with an expert's supporting statement.
- Bring your point to life with an example, an observation, a case study, an anecdote, or an illustration.
- Address a counterargument or an alternative.

■ Quotation Restraint

In most research documents, restrict your quoting to nuggets:

- Key statements by authorities (e.g., the main point that a respected Shakespeare scholar makes about the role of Ophelia in *Hamlet*)
- Well-phrased claims and conclusions (e.g., a powerful conclusion by an ethicist about the problem with the media's coverage of cloning debates and technological developments)
- Passages where careful word-by-word analysis and interpretation are important to your argument (e.g., an excerpt from a speech made by a politician about the International Space Station—a passage that requires a careful analysis for the between-the-lines message)

Quotations, especially long ones, must pull their weight, so generally paraphrase or summarize source material instead.

Primary Document Exception: When a primary text (a novel, a piece of legislation, a speech) is a key piece of evidence or the actual focus of your project, careful analysis of quoted excerpts is required. See pages 446–447 for more.

■ Smooth Integration

When you use quotations, work them into your writing as smoothly as possible. To do so, you need to pay attention to style, punctuation, and syntax. (See pages 486–487.)

Use enough of the quotation to make your point without changing the meaning of the original. Use quotation marks around key phrases taken from the source.

> Ogden, Williams, and Larson also conclude that the hydrogen fuel-cell vehicle is "a strong candidate for becoming the Car of the Future," given the trend toward "tighter environmental constraints" and the "intense efforts underway" by automakers to develop commercially viable versions of such vehicles (25).

Integrate all sources thoughtfully. Fold source material into your discussion by relating it to your own thinking. Let your ideas guide the way, not your sources, by using this pattern:

1. State and explain your idea, creating a context for the source.
2. Identify and introduce the source, linking it to your discussion.
3. Summarize, paraphrase, or quote the source, providing a citation in an appropriate spot.
4. Use the source by explaining, expanding, or refuting it.
5. When appropriate, refer back to a source to further develop the ideas it contains.

Sample Passage. Note the integration of sources in the paragraph below.

Writer's ideas	The motivation and urgency to create and improve hybrid-electric technology comes from a range of complex forces. Some of these forces are economic, others
Attributive phrase	environmental, and still others social. In "Societal Lifestyle Costs of Cars with Alternative Fuels/Engines," Joan Ogden, Robert Williams, and Eric Larson argue
Paraphrase, quotation, or summary	that "[c]ontinued reliance on current transportation fuels and technologies poses serious oil supply insecurity, climate change, and urban air pollution risks" (7).
Citation	Because of the nonrenewable nature of fossil fuels as well as their negative side
Commentary	effects, the transportation industry is confronted with making the most radical changes since the introduction of the internal-combustion automobile more than
Conclusion	100 years ago. Hybrid-electric vehicles are one response to this pressure.

Effectively document your sources. ▪▪▪

Just as you need to integrate source material carefully into your writing, so you must also carefully document where that source material comes from. Readers should recognize which material is yours and which material is not.

Identify clearly where source material begins. Your discussion must offer a smooth transition to source material. Follow the guidelines below:

- For first reference to a source, use an attributive statement that indicates some of the following: author's name and credentials, title of the source, nature of the study or research, and helpful background.

  > **Joan Ogden, Robert Williams, and Eric Larson, members of the Princeton Environmental Institute, explain** that modest improvements in energy efficiency and emissions reductions will not be enough over the next century because of anticipated transportation increases (7).

- For subsequent references to a source, use a simplified attributive phrase, such as the author's last name or a shortened version of the title.

  > **Ogden, Williams, and Larson go on to argue** that "[e]ffectively addressing environmental and oil supply concerns will probably require radical changes in automotive engine/fuel technologies" (7).

- In some situations, such as providing straightforward facts, simply skip the attributive phrase. The parenthetical citation supplies sufficient attribution.

  > Various types of transportation are by far the main consumers of oil (three fourths of world oil imports); moreover, these same technologies are responsible for one fourth of all greenhouse gas sources (Ogden, Williams, and Larson 7).

- The verb you use to introduce source material is key. Use fitting verbs, such as those in the table below. Normally, use the present tense. Use the past tense only to stress the "pastness" of a source.

  > In their 2004 study, "Societal Lifecycle Costs of Cars with Alternative Fuels/ Engines," Ogden, Williams, and Larson present a method for comparing and contrasting alternatives to internal-combustion engines. Earlier, these authors **made** preliminary steps . . .

accepts	considers	explains	rejects	acknowledges
contradicts	highlights	reminds	adds	contrasts
identifies	responds	affirms	criticizes	insists
shares	argues	declares	interprets	shows
asserts	defends	lists	states	believes
denies	maintains	stresses	cautions	describes
outlines	suggests	claims	disagrees	points out
supports	compares	discusses	praises	urges
concludes	emphasizes	proposes	verifies	confirms
enumerates	refutes	warns		

Indicate where source material ends. Closing quotation marks and a citation, as shown below, indicate the end of a source quotation. Generally, place the citation immediately after any quotation, paraphrase, or summary. However, you may also place the citation early in the sentence or at the end if the parenthetical note is obviously obtrusive. When you discuss several details from a page in a source, use an attributive phrase at the beginning of your discussion and a single citation at the end.

> As the "Lifestyle Costs" study concludes, when greenhouse gases, air pollution, and oil insecurity are factored into the analysis, alternative-fuel vehicles "offer lower LCCs than typical new cars" (Ogden, Williams, and Larson 25).

Set off longer quotations. If a quotation is longer than four typed lines, set it off from the main text. Generally, introduce the quotation with a complete sentence and a colon. Indent the quotation one inch (10 spaces) and double-space it, but don't put quotation marks around it. Put the citation outside the final punctuation mark.

> Toward the end of the study, Ogden, Williams, and Larson argue that changes to the fuel-delivery system must be factored into planning:
>
> > In charting a course to the Car of the Future, societal LCC comparisons should be complemented by considerations of fuel infrastructure requirements. Because fuel infrastructure changes are costly, the number of major changes made over time should be minimized. The bifurcated strategy advanced here—of focusing on the H_2 FCV for the long term and advanced liquid hydrocarbon-fueled ICEVs and ICE/HEVs for the near term—would reduce the number of such infrastructure changes to one (an eventual shift to H_2). (25)

Mark changes to quotations.

You may shorten or change a quotation so that it fits smoothly into your sentence—but don't alter the original meaning. Use an ellipsis within square brackets to indicate that you have omitted words from the original. An ellipsis is three periods with spaces between them.

> In their projections of where fuel-cell vehicles are heading, Ogden, Williams, and Larson discuss GM's AUTOnomy vehicle, with its "radical redesign of the entire car. [. . .] In these cars, steering, braking, and other vehicle systems are controlled electronically rather than mechanically" (24).

Use square brackets to indicate a clarification or to change a pronoun or verb tense or to switch around uppercase and lowercase.

> As Ogden, Williams, and Larson explain, "[e]ven if such barriers [the high cost of fuel cells and the lack of an H_2 fuel infrastructure] can be overcome, decades would be required before this embryonic technology could make major contributions in reducing the major externalities that characterize today's cars" (25).

 Chapters 2–7 contain additional tips. See pages 27–42 (Beginning the Writing Process), pages 43–54 (Planning), pages 55–70 (Drafting), pages 71–108 (Revising, Editing), and pages 109–112 (Submitting/Portfolios).

Critical-Thinking and Writing Activities

As directed by your instructor, complete the following critical-thinking and writing activities by yourself or with classmates.

1. With some classmates, debate the seriousness of plagiarism and the use of tools such as Turnitin.com.

2. Closely examine one of your most recent research papers. Have you followed this chapter's guidelines? Where do you need to improve?

3. Review the list of source abuses on pages 478-479. Which of these abuses is most common in research writing? Which abuse is most serious? Write a page focusing on one type of source abuse and explaining its effect on scholarship.

Learning-Outcomes Checklist

Use this checklist as a guide to help you plan your writing.

_____ I understand that plagiarism is the use of someone else's words, ideas, or images so that they appear to be my own.

_____ I understand the seriousness of plagiarism, and I avoid it in all my writing.

_____ I do not submit other writers' writing.

_____ I do not use copy and paste without setting off the material and indicating the source.

_____ I do not confuse borrowed material with my own ideas.

_____ I quote sources accurately, without taking them out of context.

_____ I do not overuse source material, rely too heavily on one source, or use blanket citations.

_____ I do not plunk quotations, dropping them into text without setting them up or explaining them.

_____ My in-text citations match my bibliographic entries.

_____ I avoid double-dipping, Falstaffing, and copyright violations.

_____ I know how to organize and synthesize my findings.

_____ I am comfortable with developing the first draft of my research paper.

_____ I understand how to use source material in my writing, smoothly integrating quotations and documenting my sources.

Documentation and Format Styles

Research-based writing—whether it is done in the humanities, social sciences, or natural and applied sciences—is assigned not only to *show* learning, but also to *share* learning. Careful and correct documentation of sources helps you do both. First, such documentation is a type of road map that *shows* your professor where you have gone and what you have done to learn about your topic and develop your thesis. Second, careful documentation *shares* your research results with all readers, enabling them to retrace your research steps, track the logic of your argument, and possibly study your sources for themselves.

The two chapters that follow will help you document your sources clearly and correctly. Chapter 31 explains how to document sources in accordance with the Modern Language Association's (MLA) style, outlined in the *MLA Handbook for Writers of Research Papers*, Seventh Edition (2009). The chapter includes "I Did *Not* Get My Spahetti-O's," Stevie Jeung's paper illustrating MLA formatting. Chapter 32 explains how to document sources in the American Psychological Association's (APA) style, using the *Publication Manual of the American Psychological Association*, Sixth Edition (2010). This chapter includes "Our Roots Go Back to Roanoke . . . ," Renee Danielle Singh's paper illustrating APA formatting.

Documentation and Format Styles

MLA
31 Documentation Format

In research papers, it is commonly said, "You are commanded to borrow but forbidden to steal." To borrow ideas while avoiding plagiarism (see pages 474–477), you must not only mention the sources you borrow from but also document them completely and accurately. You must follow to the last dot the documentation conventions for papers written in your area.

If you are composing a research paper in the humanities, your instructor will most likely require you to follow the conventions established in the style manual of the Modern Language Association (MLA). This chapter provides you with explanations and examples for citing sources in MLA format.

Learning Outcomes

Audio

► Understand MLA documentation style.

► Understand and use MLA in-text citations.

► Understand and develop MLA works-cited entries.

► Understand and follow MLA format.

Visually **Speaking** ▶ In the image above, what elements of research are imagined?

MLA Research Paper Guidelines

Questions and Answers

Is a separate title page required?	**No.** (unless your instructor requires one, in which case you would format it according to his or her instructions). On the first page of a research paper, type your name, your instructor's name, the course name and number, and the date, one below the other. The title comes next, centered. Then simply begin the text on the next line.
Is the research paper double-spaced?	**Yes.** Double-space everything, even tables, captions, long quotations, or works-cited entries.
What about longer quotations?	Verse quotations of more than three lines should be indented one inch (ten spaces) and double-spaced. Do not add quotation marks. Each line of a poem or play begins a new line of the quotation; do not run the lines together. When you are quoting prose that needs more than four typed lines, indent each line of the quotation one inch (ten spaces) from the left margin and double-space it; do not add quotation marks. To quote two or more paragraphs—in addition to the one inch that you are already indenting for the lengthy quotation—you should indent the first line of each paragraph an extra quarter-inch (three spaces). However, if the first sentence quoted does not begin a paragraph in the source, do not include the additional indent. Indent only the first lines of the successive paragraphs.
Are page numbers required?	**Yes.** Pages should be numbered consecutively in the upper-right corner, one-half inch from the top and flush with the right margin (one inch). Your last name should precede the page number, and no abbreviations or other symbols should be included.
Is an appendix required?	**No.** In MLA style, tables and illustrations are placed as close as possible to the related text.

Is an abstract required?	**No.** An abstract, or summary of your research paper, is not an MLA requirement.
How wide should the margins be?	Top, bottom, left, and right margins should be one inch (except for page numbering). The first word in a paragraph should be indented one-half inch (five spaces). Longer quotations should be set off one inch (ten spaces) from the left margin (see page 492).
Are references placed in the text?	**Yes.** Indicate only page numbers parenthetically if you identify the author in your text. Give the author's last name in a parenthetical reference if it is not mentioned in the text.
Is a list of sources used in the paper required?	**Yes.** Full citations for all sources used (e.g., books, periodicals) are placed in an alphabetized list labeled "Works Cited" at the end of the paper. Whereas in-text parenthetical references generally indicate just the author's last name and a page number for the source material, the works-cited entry provides full publication details.
What about headings?	MLA style does not specify a particular format for headings within the text; normally, headings are used only for separate sections of the paper ("Works Cited" or "Notes," for example).
How do I incorporate reference markers if I submit my paper electronically?	Numbering paragraphs is common in electronic publications. Place the paragraph number in brackets. Follow with a space and begin the paragraph. (For other electronic formatting guidelines, check with your instructor.)
Any other special instructions?	Always ask whether your school, department, or instructor has special requirements that may take precedence over those listed here.

Web Link: For additional questions and answers about MLA format, see the MLA Q&A page at http://www.mla.org/handbook_faq.

Web Link

Guidelines for In-Text Citations

The *MLA Handbook for Writers of Research Papers,* Seventh Edition (2009), suggests giving credit for your sources of information in the body of your research paper. One way to do so is by indicating the author and/or title in the text of your essay, and then putting a page reference in parentheses after the summary, paraphrase, or quotation, as needed. The simplest way to do so is to insert the appropriate information (usually the author and page number) in parentheses after the words or ideas taken from the source. To avoid disrupting your writing, place citations where a pause would naturally occur (usually at the end of a sentence but sometimes within a sentence, before internal punctuation such as a comma or semicolon). These in-text citations (often called "parenthetical references") refer to sources listed on the "Works Cited" page at the end of your paper. (See pages 526–527 for a sample works-cited list.)

Use in-text citations.

As you integrate citations into your paper, follow the guidelines below, referring to the sample citation as needed.

> **Sample In-Text Citation**
>
> As James Cuno, director of the Harvard University Art Museums, points out, the public, which subsidizes museums either directly through donations or indirectly via their status as tax-free nonprofit organizations, expects them to "carry out their duties professionally on its behalf" (164).

- Make sure each in-text citation clearly points to an entry in your list of works cited. The identifying information provided (usually the author's last name) must be the word or words by which the entry is alphabetized in that list.
- Keep citations brief, and integrate them smoothly into your writing.
- When paraphrasing or summarizing rather than quoting, make it clear where your borrowing begins and ends. Use stylistic cues to distinguish the source's thoughts ("Kalmbach points out . . . ," "Some critics argue . . .") from your own ("I believe . . . ," "It seems obvious, however"). See pages 484–487 for more on integrating sources.
- When using a shortened title of a work, begin with the word by which the work is alphabetized in your list of works cited (e.g., "Egyptian, Classical," not "Middle Eastern Art," for "Egyptian, Classical, and Middle Eastern Art").
- For inclusive page numbers larger than ninety-nine, give only the two digits of the second number (346–48, not 346–348).
- When including a parenthetical citation at the end of a sentence, place it before the end punctuation. (Citations for long, indented quotations are an exception. See pages 487, 492, 500, and 501.)

Use sources without traditional authorship and/or pagination. ■ ■ ■

Today many sources, especially electronic ones, have no stated authors and/or no pagination. For such sources, use these in-text citation strategies:

Source Without a Stated Author: In a signal phrase or in the parenthetical reference, identify the source as precisely as possible by indicating the sponsoring agency, the type of document, or the title (shortened in the parenthetical reference). See pages 497–498.

> While the Brooklyn Museum may be best known for the recent controversy over the Sensation exhibition, it does contain a strong collection of contemporary if less controversial art, "ranging from representational to abstract to conceptual" ("Contemporary Art").

Source with No Pagination: If no pagination exists within the document, use paragraph numbers (with the abbreviation *par.*), if the document provides them. If the document includes neither page nor paragraph numbers, cite the entire work. Do not create your own numbering system.

> The Museum's collection of Art of the Americas includes extensive holdings of works by the aboriginal peoples of North, Central, and South America, many of these gathered by archaeologist Herbert Spinden during at least seven expeditions between 1929 and 1950 ("Art of the Americas" par. 3).

Note: Because parenthetical notations are used to signal the end of an attribution, sources with no pagination or paragraph numbers offer a special challenge. When no parenthetical notation is possible, signal a shift back to your own discussion with a source-reflective statement indicating your thinking about the source.

> . . . indicated by his recording the audio tour of the exhibit, his supporting the show financially, and his promoting Sensation at his website. As Welland's discussion of David Bowie's participation indicates, the controversy over the Brooklyn Museum of Art's Sensation exhibit . . .

INSIGHT:

- Stable pagination for many electronic resources is available when you use the ".pdf" rather than the ".html" version of the source.
- For instruction on smoothly integrating source material into your paper, see pages 484–487.
- For cautions about sources without identified authors, see pages 497, 498, 504, and 510.

■ Sample In-Text Citations

The following entries illustrate the most common in-text citations.

■ One Author: A Complete Work

You do not need an in-text citation if you identify the author in your text. (See the first entry below.) However, you must give the author's last name in an in-text citation if it is not mentioned in the text. (See the second entry.) When a source is listed in your works-cited page with an editor, a translator, a speaker, or an artist instead of the author, use that person's name in your citation.

> **With Author in Text:** (This is the preferred way of citing a complete work.)
> In *No Need for Hunger,* Robert Spitzer recommends that the U.S. government develop a new foreign policy to help Third World countries overcome poverty and hunger.
>
> **Without Author in Text:**
> *No Need for Hunger* recommends that the U.S. government develop a new foreign policy to help Third World countries overcome poverty and hunger (Spitzer).

Note: Do not offer page numbers when citing complete works, articles in alphabetized encyclopedias, one-page articles, and unpaginated sources.

■ One Author: Part of a Work

List the necessary page numbers in parentheses if you borrow words or ideas from a particular source. Leave a space between the author's last name and the page reference. No abbreviation or punctuation is needed.

> **With Author in Text:**
> Bullough writes that genetic engineering was dubbed "eugenics" by a cousin of Darwin's, Sir Francis Galton, in 1885 (5).
>
> **Without Author in Text:**
> Genetic engineering was dubbed "eugenics" by a cousin of Darwin's, Sir Francis Galton, in 1885 (Bullough 5).

■ A Work by Two or Three Authors

Give the last names of every author in the same order that they appear in the works-cited section. (The correct order of the authors' names can be found on the title page of the book.)

> Students learned more than a full year's Spanish in ten days using the complete supermemory method (Ostrander and Schroeder 51).

■ A Work by Four or More Authors

Give the first author's last name as it appears in the works-cited section followed by *et al.* (meaning "and others").

> Communication on the job is more than talking; it is "inseparable from your total behavior" (Culligan et al. 111).

Note: You may instead choose to list all of the authors' last names.

■ Two or More Works by the Same Author(s)

In addition to the author's last name(s) and page number(s), include a shortened version of the work's title when you cite two or more works by the same author(s).

> **With Author in Text:**
>
> Wallerstein and Blakeslee claim that divorce creates an enduring identity for children of the marriage (*Unexpected Legacy* 62).
>
> **Without Author in Text:**
>
> They are intensely lonely despite active social lives (Wallerstein and Blakeslee, *Second Chances* 51).

Note: When including both author(s) and title in a parenthetical reference, separate them with a comma, as shown above, but do not put a comma between the title and the page number.

■ Works by Authors with the Same Last Name

When citing different sources by authors with the same last name, it is best to use the authors' full names in the text to avoid confusion. However, if circumstances call for parenthetical references, add each author's first initial. If first initials are the same, use each author's full name.

> Some critics think *Titus Andronicus* too abysmally melodramatic to be a work of Shakespeare (A. Parker 73). Others suggest that Shakespeare meant it as black comedy (D. Parker 486).

■ A Work Authored by an Agency, a Committee, or an Organization

If a book or other work was written by an organization such as an agency, a committee, or a task force, it is said to have a corporate author. (See also page 504.) If the corporate name is long, include it in the text (rather than in parentheses) to avoid disrupting the flow of your writing. After the full name has been used at least once, use a shortened form of the name (common abbreviations are acceptable) in subsequent references. For example, Task Force may be used for *Task Force on Education for Economic Growth*.

> The thesis of the Task Force's report is that economic success depends on our ability to improve large-scale education and training as quickly as possible (113–14).

■ An Anonymous Work

When there is no author listed, give the title or a shortened version of the title as it appears in the works-cited section. (See page 504.)

> Statistics indicate that drinking water can make up 20 percent of a person's total exposure to lead (*Information* 572).

■ Two or More Works Included in One Citation

To cite multiple works within a single parenthetical reference, separate the references with a semicolon.

> In Medieval Europe, Latin translations of the works of Rhazes, a Persian scholar, were a primary source of medical knowledge (Albala 22; Lewis 266).

■ A Series of Citations from a Single Work

If no confusion is possible, it is not necessary to name a source repeatedly when making multiple parenthetical references to that source in a single paragraph. If all references are to the same page, identify that page in a parenthetical note after the last reference. If the references are to different pages within the same work, you need identify the work only once, and then use a parenthetical note with page number alone for the subsequent references.

> Domesticating science meant not only spreading scientific knowledge, but also promoting it as a topic of public conversation (Heilbron 2). One way to enhance its charm was by depicting cherubic putti as "angelic research assistants" in book illustrations (5).

■ A Work Referred to in Another Work

If you must cite an indirect source—that is, information from a source that is quoted from another source—use the abbreviation *qtd. in* (quoted in) before the indirect source in your reference.

> Paton improved the conditions in Diepkloof (a prison) by "removing all the more obvious aids to detention. The dormitories [were] open at night: the great barred gate [was] gone" (qtd. in Callan xviii).

■ A Work Without Page Numbers

If a work has no page numbers or paragraph numbers, treat it as you would a complete work. (See page 496.) This is commonly the case with electronic resources, for example. Do not count pages to create reference numbers of your own.

> Antibiotics become ineffective against such organisms through two natural processes: first, genetic mutation; and second, the subsequent transfer of this mutated genetic material to other organisms (Davies par. 5).

■ A Work in an Anthology or a Collection

When citing the entirety of a work that is part of an anthology or a collection, if it is identified by author in your list of works cited, treat the citation as you would for any other complete work. (See page 496.)

> In "The Canadian Postmodern," Linda Hutcheon offers a clear analysis of the self-reflexive nature of contemporary Canadian fiction.

Similarly, if you are citing particular pages of such a work, follow the directions for citing part of a work. (See page 496.)

> According to Hutcheon, "postmodernism seems to designate cultural practices that are fundamentally self-reflexive, in other words, art that is self-consciously artifice" (18).

(To format this sort of entry in your list of works cited, see pages 504–505.)

■ An Item from a Reference Work

An entry from a reference work such as an encyclopedia or a dictionary should be cited similarly to a work from an anthology or a collection (see above). For a dictionary definition, include the abbreviation *def.* followed by the particular entry designation.

> This message becomes a juggernaut in the truest sense, a belief that "elicits blind devotion or sacrifice" ("Juggernaut," def. 1).

Note: While many such entries are identified only by title (as above), some reference works include an author's name for each entry (as below). Others may identify the entry author by initials, with a list of full names elsewhere in the work.

> The decisions of the International Court of Justice are "based on principles of international law and cannot be appealed" (Pranger).

(See pages 506–507 for guidelines to formatting these entries in your works-cited list.)

■ A Part of a Multivolume Work

When citing only one volume of a multivolume work, if you identify the volume number in the works-cited list, there is no need to include it in your in-text citation. However, if you cite more than one volume of a work, each in-text reference must identify the appropriate volume. Give the volume number followed by page number, separated by a colon and a space.

> "A human being asleep," says Spengler, ". . . is leading only a plantlike existence" (2: 4).

When citing a whole volume, however, either identify the volume number in parentheses with the abbreviation *vol.* (using a comma to separate it from the author's name) or use the full word *volume* in your text.

> The land of Wisconsin has shaped its many inhabitants more significantly than they ever shaped that land (Stephens, vol. 1).

■ A One-Page Work

Cite a one-page work just as you would a complete work. (See page 496.)

> As Samantha Adams argues in her editorial, it is time for NASA "to fully reevaluate the Space Shuttle's long-term viability for sending humans into space."

■ A Sacred Text or Famous Literary Work

Sacred texts and famous literary works are published in many different editions. For that reason, it is helpful to identify sections, parts, chapters, and such instead of or in addition to page numbers. If using page numbers, list them first, followed by an abbreviation for the type of division and the division number.

> The more important a person's role in society—the more apparent power an individual has—the more that person is a slave to the forces of history (Tolstoy 690; bk. 9, ch. 1).

Books of the Bible and other well-known literary works may be abbreviated, if no confusion is possible.

> "A generation goes, and a generation comes, but the earth remains forever" (*The New Oxford Annotated Bible,* Eccles. 1.4).

> As Shakespeare's famous Danish prince observes, "One may smile, and smile, and be a villain" (Ham. 1.5.104).

■ Quoting Prose

To cite prose from fiction (novels, short stories), list more than the page number if the work is available in several editions. Give the page reference first, and then add a chapter, section, or book number in abbreviated form after a semicolon.

> In *The House of the Spirits,* Isabel Allende describes Marcos, "dressed in mechanic's overalls, with huge racer's goggles" (13; ch. 1).

When you are quoting any sort of prose that takes more than four typed lines, indent each line of the quotation one inch (ten spaces) and double-space it; do not add quotation marks. In this case, you put the parenthetical citation (the pages and chapter numbers) outside the end punctuation mark of the quotation itself.

> Allende describes the flying machine that Marcos has assembled:
>
> > The contraption lay with its stomach on terra firma, heavy and sluggish and looking more like a wounded duck than like one of those newfangled airplanes they were starting to produce in the United States. There was nothing in its appearance to suggest that it could move, much less take flight across the snowy peaks. (12; ch. 1)

◼ Quoting Verse

Do not use page numbers when referencing classic verse plays and poems. Instead, cite them by division (act, scene, canto, book, part) and line, using Arabic numerals for the various divisions unless your instructor prefers Roman numerals. Use periods to separate the various numbers.

> In the first act, Hamlet comments, "How weary, stale, flat and unprofitable, / Seem to me all the uses of this world" (1.2.133–34).

Note: A slash, with a space on each side, shows where each new line of verse begins. If you are citing lines only, use the word *line* or *lines* in your first reference and numbers only in additional references.

> At the beginning of the sestet in Robert Frost's "Design," the speaker asks this pointed question: "What had that flower to do with being white, / The wayside blue and innocent heal-all?" (lines 9–10).

Verse quotations of more than three lines should be indented one inch (ten spaces) and double-spaced. Do not add quotation marks. Each line of the poem or play begins a new line of the quotation; do not run the lines together. If a line or lines of poetry are dropped from the quotation, ellipses that extend the width of the stanza should be used to indicate the omission.

> Bin Ramke's poem "A Little Ovid Late in the Day" tells of reading by the last light of a summer day:
>
>> [T]ales of incest, corruption,
>>
>> any big, mythic vice
>>
>> against the color of the sun,
>>
>> the sweetness of the time of day—
>>
>> I know the story,
>>
>> it is the light I care about. (3–8)

◼ Listing an Internet Address

The current (seventh edition) *MLA Handbook* discourages use of Internet addresses, or URLs, as they can so easily change with time. Ideally, you should refer to an entire website by its title, or to a specific article on a site by its author; then, include full reference information in your works-cited list. A URL should be listed in your document or in your works-cited list only when the reader probably cannot locate the source without it, or if your instructor requires it. If that is the case, enclose the address in brackets:

<www.thecollegewriter.com/4e>

Because most word processors will automatically convert the URL to a live hyperlink, you can either turn off the auto-formatting option on your computer or cancel the formatting as soon as it appears. If the instructor allows it, however, you may use live links in electronic versions of your text.

Quick Guide

■ MLA Works Cited

Web Link

The works-cited section lists only the sources you have cited in your text. Begin your list on the page after the text and continue numbering each page. Format your works-cited pages using these guidelines and pages 526–527.

1. Type the page number in the upper-right corner, one-half inch from the top of the page, with your last name before it.

2. Center the title *Works Cited* (not in italics, in quotation marks, or underlined) one inch from the top; then double-space before the first entry.

3. Begin each entry flush with the left margin. If the entry runs more than one line, indent additional lines one-half inch (five spaces) or use the hanging indent function on your computer.

4. End each element of the entry with a period. (Elements are separated by periods in most cases unless only a space is sufficient.) Use a single space after all punctuation.

5. Double-space lines within each entry and between entries.

6. List each entry alphabetically by the author's last name. If there is no author, use the first word of the title (disregard *A, An,* or *The* as the first word). If there are multiple authors, alphabetize them according to which author is listed first in the publication.

7. The *MLA Handbook,* Seventh Edition, requires that each source be identified as print, web, or other (such as television or DVD). For print sources, this information is included after the publisher and date. For web publications, include *Web.* after the date of publication or updating of the site, and before the date you accessed the site.

8. A basic entry for a book would be as follows:

   Black, Naomi. *Virginia Woolf as Feminist.* Ithaca: Cornell UP, 2004. Print.

9. A basic entry for a journal or magazine would be as follows:

   Stelmach, Kathryn. "From Text to Tableau: Ekphrastic Enchantment in *Mrs. Dalloway* and *To the Lighthouse.*" *Studies in the Novel* 38.3 (Fall 2006): 304–26. Print.

10. A basic entry for an online source would be as follows. Note that the URL is included only if the reader probably cannot locate the source without it, or when your instructor requires it. (See page 512.)

    Clarke, S. N. "Virginia Woolf (1882-1941): A Short Biography." *Virginia Woolf Society of Great Britain.* 2000. Web. 12 March 2008.

■ Works-Cited Entries: Nonperiodical Print Publications

■ Components

The entries that follow illustrate the information needed to cite books, sections of a book, pamphlets, and government publications published in print format. The possible components of these entries are listed in order below:

1. Author's name
2. Title of a part of the book (an article in the book or a foreword)
3. Title of the book, italicized
4. Name of editor or translator
5. Edition
6. Number of volume
7. Name of series
8. Place of publication, publisher, year of publication
9. Page numbers, if citation is to only a part (For page spans, use a hyphen; if clarity is maintained, for pages above 100 you may also drop a digit from the second number—for example, 234–41, 234–332.)
10. Medium of publication (Print)

Note: In general, if any of these components do not apply, they are not included in the works-cited entry. However, in the rare instance that a book does not state publication information, use the following abbreviations in place of information you cannot supply:

N.p.	No place of publication given
N.p.	No publisher given
N.d.	No date of publication given
N. pag.	No pagination given

■ Additional Guidelines

- List only the city for the place of publication if the city is in the United States. For cities outside the United States, add an abbreviation for the country if necessary for clarity. If several cities are listed, give only the first.
- Publishers' names should be shortened by omitting articles (*a, an, the*), business abbreviations (*Co., Inc.*), and descriptive words (*Books, Press*). For publishing houses that consist of the names of more than one person, cite only the first of the surnames. Abbreviate *University Press* as *UP*. Also use standard abbreviations whenever possible.

■ A Book by One Author

> Green, Christopher. *Picasso: Architecture and Vertigo*. New Haven: Yale UP, 2005.
> Print.

■ Two or More Books by the Same Author

List the books alphabetically according to title. After the first entry, substitute three hyphens for the author's name.

> Dershowitz, Alan M. *Rights from Wrongs*. New York: Basic Books, 2005. Print.
>
> - - - . *Supreme Injustice: How the High Court Hijacked Election 2000*.
> Oxford: Oxford UP, 2001. Print.

■ A Work by Two or Three Authors

> Bystydzienski, Jill M., and Estelle P. Resnik. *Women in Cross-Cultural Transitions*.
> Bloomington: Phi Delta Kappa Educational Foundation, 1994. Print.

Note: List authors in title-page order. Reverse only the first author's name.

■ A Work by Four or More Authors

> Schulte-Peevers, Andrea, et al. *Germany*. Victoria, Austral.: Lonely Planet, 2000.
> Print.

■ A Work Authored by an Agency, a Committee, or an Organization

> Exxon Mobil Corporation. *Great Plains 2000*. Lincolnwood: Publications Intl., 2001.
> Print.

■ An Anonymous Book

> *Chase's Calendar of Events 2002*. Chicago: Contemporary, 2002. Print.

■ A Single Work from an Anthology

> Mitchell, Joseph. "The Bottom of the Harbor." *American Sea Writing*. Ed. Peter Neill.
> New York: Lib. of America, 2000. 584–608. Print.

■ A Complete Anthology

If you cite a complete anthology, begin the entry with the editor(s).

> Neill, Peter, ed. *American Sea Writing*. New York: Lib. of America, 2000. Print.
>
> Smith, Rochelle, and Sharon L. Jones, eds. *The Prentice Hall Anthology of African
> American Literature*. Upper Saddle River: Prentice, 2000. Print.

■ Two or More Works from an Anthology or a Collection

To avoid unnecessary repetition when citing two or more entries from a larger collection, you may cite the collection once with complete publication information (see Rothfield, below). The individual entries (see Becker and Cuno, below) can then be cross-referenced by listing the author, title of the piece, editor of the collection, and page numbers.

> Becker, Carol. "The Brooklyn Controversy: A View from the Bridge." Rothfield
> 15–21.
>
> Cuno, James. "Sensation and the Ethics of Funding Exhibitions." Rothfield 162–170.
>
> Rothfield, Lawrence, Ed. *Unsettling Sensation: Arts-Policy Lessons from the Brooklyn
> Museum of Art Controversy.* Rutgers Series on the Public Life of the Arts. New
> Brunswick: Rutgers UP, 2001. Print.

■ One Volume of a Multivolume Work

> Cooke, Jacob Ernest, and Milton M. Klein, eds. *North America in Colonial Times.*
> Vol. 2. New York: Scribner's, 1998. Print.

Note: If you cite two or more volumes in a multivolume work, give the total number of volumes after each title. Offer specific references to volume and page numbers in the parenthetical reference in your text, like this: (3: 112–114).

> Salzman, Jack, David Lionel Smith, and Cornel West. *Encyclopedia of
> African-American Culture and History.* 5 vols. New York: Simon, 1996. Print.

■ An Introduction, a Preface, a Foreword, or an Afterword

To cite the introduction, preface, foreword, or afterword of a book, list the author of the part first. Then identify the part by type, with no quotation marks or underlining, followed by the book title. Next, identify the author of the work, using the word *by.* (If the book's author and the part's author are the same person, give just the last name after *by.*) For a book that gives cover credit to an editor instead of an author, identify the editor as usual. List any page numbers for the part cited.

> Barry, Anne. Afterword. *Making Room for Students.* By Celia Oyler. New York:
> Teachers College, 1996. 139–140. Print.
>
> Proulx, Annie. Introduction. *Dance of the Happy Shades.* By Alice Munro. Toronto:
> Penguin Canada, 2005. Print.
>
> Shaw, Randy. "Preface to the Paperback Edition." Preface. *The Activist's Handbook:
> A Primer.* By Shaw. Berkley: U of California, 1996. ix–xiii. Print.

■ A Republished Book (Reprint)

Give the original publication date after the title.

> Atwood, Margaret. *Surfacing.* 1972. New York: Doubleday, 1998. Print.

Note: After the original publication facts, cite new material added: Introd. C. Becker.

■ A Book with Multiple Publishers

When a book lists more than one publisher (not just different offices of the same publisher), include all of them in the order given on the book's title page, separated by a semicolon.

> Wells, H. G. *The Complete Short Stories of H. G. Wells.* New York: St. Martin's;
>   London: A. & C. Black, 1987. Print.

■ Second and Subsequent Editions

An edition refers to the particular publication you are citing, as in the third (3rd) edition.

> Joss, Molly W. *Looking Good in Presentations.* 3rd ed. Scottsdale: Coriolis, 1999.
>   Print.

■ An Edition with Author and Editor

The abbreviation *ed.* also refers to the work of one or more persons that is prepared by another person, an editor.

> Shakespeare, William. *A Midsummer Night's Dream.* Ed. Jane Bachman.
>   Lincolnwood: NTC, 1994. Print.

■ A Translation

> Lebert, Stephan, and Norbert Lebert. *My Father's Keeper.* Trans. Julian Evans.
>   Boston: Little, 2001. Print.

■ An Article in a Familiar Reference Book

It is not necessary to give full publication information for familiar reference works (encyclopedias and dictionaries). For these titles, list only the edition (if available), the publication year, and the medium of publication you used. If an article is initialed, check the index of authors (in the opening section of each volume) for the author's full name.

> "Technical Education." *Encyclopedia Americana.* 2001 ed. Print.

> Lum, P. Andrea. "Computed Tomography." *World Book.* 2000 ed. Print.

When citing a single definition of several listed, add the abbreviation *Def.* and the particular number or letter for that definition.

> "Macaroni." Def. 2b. *The American Heritage College Dictionary.* 4th ed. 2002. Print.

■ An Article in an Unfamiliar Reference Book

For citations of lesser-known reference works, give full publication information, as for any other sort of book.

> "S Corporation." *The Portable MBA Desk Reference.* Ed. Paul A. Argenti. New York:
> Wiley, 1994. Print.

■ A Government Publication

State the name of the government (country, state, and so on) followed by the name of the agency. Most U.S. federal publications are published by the Government Printing Office (GPO).

> United States. Dept. of Labor. Bureau of Labor Statistics. *Occupational Outlook*
> *Handbook 2006-2007.* Indianapolis: Jist Works, 2006. Print.

When citing the *Congressional Record*, the date, page numbers, and medium you used are all that is required for that source.

> *Cong. Rec.* 5 Feb. 2002: S311–15. Print.

■ A Book in a Series

Give the series name and number (if any), neither italicized nor in quotation marks, followed by a period, at the end of the listing, after the medium of publication.

> Cudworth, Erika. *Environment and Society.* London; New York: Routledge, 2003.
> Print. Routledge Introductions to Environment Ser.

■ A Book with a Title Within Its Title

If the title contains a title normally in quotation marks, keep the quotation marks and italicize the entire title.

> Stuckey-French, Elizabeth. *"The First Paper Girl in Red Oak, Iowa"*
> *and Other Stories.* New York: Doubleday, 2000. Print.

Note: If the title contains a title that is normally italicized, do not italicize that title in your entry:

> Beckwith, Charles E. *Twentieth Century Interpretations of* A Tale of Two Cities: *A*
> *Collection of Critical Essays.* Upper Saddle River: Prentice, 1972. Print.

■ A Sacred Text

The Bible and other such sacred texts are treated as anonymous books. Documentation should read exactly as it is printed on the title page.

> *The Jerusalem Bible.* Garden City: Doubleday, 1966. Print.

■ The Published Proceedings of a Conference

The published proceedings of a conference should be treated as a book. However, if the title of the publication does not identify the conference by title, date, and location, add the appropriate information immediately after the title.

> McIlwaine, Ia C., ed. *Advances in Knowledge Organization.* Vol. 9.
> Proc. of Eighth Intl. ISKO Conf., 13–16 July 2004, London. Wurzburg, Ger.:
> Ergon-Verlag, 2004. Print.

To cite a particular presentation from the published proceedings of a conference, treat it as a work in an anthology.

> Vizine-Goetz, Diane, and Julianne Bea. "Using Literary Warrant to Define a Version
> of the DDC for Automated Classification Services." *Advances in Knowledge*
> *Organization.* Ed. Ia C. McIlwaine. Vol. 9. Proc. of Eighth Intl. ISKO Conf., 13–16
> July 2004, London. Wurzburg, Ger.: Ergon-Verlag, 2004. Print.

■ A Published Dissertation

An entry for a published dissertation contains the same information as a book entry, with a few added details. Add the abbreviation *Diss.* and the degree-granting institution before the publication facts and medium.

> Jansen, James Richard. *Images of Dostoevsky in German Literary*
> *Expressionism.* Diss. U of Utah, 2003. Ann Arbor: UMI, 2003. Print.

■ An Unpublished Dissertation

The entry for an unpublished dissertation lists author, title in quotation marks, degree-granting institution, year of acceptance, and medium. (For a master's thesis, use *MA thesis* or *MS thesis* rather than *Diss.*)

> Vaidhyanathan, Siva. "Unoriginal Sins: Copyright and American Culture." Diss. U
> Texas, 1999. Print.

■ A Pamphlet, Manual, or Other Workplace Document

Treat any such publication as you would a book.

> Grayson, George W. *The North American Free Trade Agreement.* New York: Foreign
> Policy Assn., 1993. Print.

If publication information is missing, list the country of publication in brackets if known. Use n.p. (no place) if the country or the publisher is unknown and n.d. if the date is unknown, just as you would for a book.

> *Pedestrian Safety.* [United States]: n.p., n.d. Print.

■ Works-Cited Entries: Print Periodical Articles

■ Possible Components, in Order

1. Author's name, last name first
2. Title of article, in quotation marks and headline style capitalization
3. Name of periodical, italicized
4. Series number or name, if relevant (not preceded by period or comma)
5. Volume number (for a scholarly journal)
6. Issue number, separated from volume with a period but no space
7. Date of publication (abbreviate all months but May, June, July)
8. Page numbers, preceded by a colon, without "p." or "pp." (For articles continued nonconsecutively, add a plus sign after the first page number.)
9. Medium of publication (Print)
10. Supplementary information as needed

Note: Any components that do not apply are not listed.

■ An Article in a Weekly or Biweekly Magazine

List the author (if identified), article title (in quotation marks), publication title (italicized), full date of publication, and page numbers for the article. Do not include volume and issue numbers.

> Green, Andy. "U2, Neil Young Films Rock Sundance." *Rolling Stone* 7 Feb. 2008: 20.
>   Print.

■ An Article in a Monthly or Bimonthly Magazine

As for a weekly or biweekly magazine, list the author (if identified), article title (in quotation marks), and publication title (italicized). Then identify the month(s) and year of the issue, followed by page numbers for the article. Do not give volume and issue numbers.

> Mead, Walter Russell. "Born Again." *Atlantic Monthly* March 2008: 21–24. Print.

■ An Article in a Scholarly Journal Paginated by Issue

List the volume number immediately after the journal title, followed by a period and the issue number, and then the year of publication (in parentheses). End with the page numbers of the article followed by the medium of publication (Print.).

> Sanchez, Melissa E. "Seduction and Service in *The Tempest*." *Studies in*
>   *Philology* 105.1 (Winter 2008): 50–82. Print.

■ An Article in a Scholarly Journal with Continuous Pagination

An article in a scholarly journal with continuous pagination uses the same citation format, with volume, issue, month or season, and inclusive page numbers.

> Frosch, Thomas R. "The Missing Child in *A Midsummer Night's Dream.*" *American Imago* 64.2 (Winter 2007): 485–511. Print.

■ An Unsigned Article in a Periodical

If no author is identified for an article, list the entry alphabetically by title among your works cited (ignoring any initial *A*, *An*, or *The*).

> "Feeding the Hungry." *Economist.* 371.8374 (2004): 74. Print.

■ A Printed Interview

Begin with the name of the person interviewed if that's who you are quoting.

> Cantwell, Maria. "The New Technocrat." By Erika Rasmusson. *Working Woman* Apr. 2001: 20–21. Print.

Note: If the interview is untitled, the word *Interview* (no italics) and a period follow the interviewee's name.

■ A Newspaper Article

> Segal, Jeff, and Lauren Silva. "Case of Art Imitating Life?" *Wall Street Journal* 3 March 2008, Eastern ed.: C9. Print.

Note: Cite the edition of a major daily newspaper (if given) after the date (1 May 1995, Midwest ed.: 1). If a local paper's name does not include the city of publication, add it in brackets (not italicized) after the name.

To cite an article in a lettered section of the newspaper, list the section and the page number. (For example, A4 would refer to page 4 in section A of the newspaper.) If the sections are numbered, however, use a comma after the year (or the edition); then indicate the section and follow it with a colon, the page number (sec. 1: 20), and the medium of publication you used.

An unsigned newspaper article follows the same format:

> "Bombs—Real and Threatened—Keep Northern Ireland Edgy." *Chicago Tribune* 6 Dec. 2001, sec. 1: 20. Print.

■ A Newspaper Editorial or Letter to the Editor

If an article is an unsigned editorial, put *Editorial* (no italics) and a period after the title.

> "Hospital Power." Editorial. *Bangor Daily News* 14 Sept. 2004: A6. Print.

To identify a letter to the editor, put *Letter* (no italics) and a period after the author's name.

> Sory, Forrest. Letter. *Discover* July 2001: 10. Print.

■ A Review

Begin with the author (if identified) and title of the review. Use the notation *Rev. of* between the title of the review and that of the original work. Identify the author of the original work with the word *by*. Then follow with publication data for the review.

> Dillon, Brian. "Onion Pilfering." Rev. of *Divisadero* by Michael Ondaatje. *London Review of Books* 13 Dec. 2007: 19-20. Print.

Note: If you cite the review of a work by an editor, translator, or director, use *ed., trans.,* or *dir.,* instead of *by*.

■ An Abstract

An abstract is a summary of a work. To cite an abstract, first give the publication information for the original work (if any); then list the publication information for the abstract itself. Add the term *Abstract* and a period between these if the journal title does not include that word. If the journal identifies abstracts by item number, include the word *item* followed by the number. (Add the section identifier [A, B, or C] for those volumes of *Dissertation Abstracts* [DA] and *Dissertation Abstracts International* [DAI] that have one.) If no item number exists, list the page number(s).

> Faber, A. J. "Examining Remarried Couples Through a Bowenian Family System Lens." *Journal of Divorce and Remarriage* 40.4 (2004): 121–33. *Social Work Abstracts* 40 (2004): item 1298. Print.

■ An Article with a Title or Quotation Within Its Title

> Morgenstern, Joe. "Sleeper of the Year: *In the Bedroom* Is Rich Tale of Tragic Love." *Wall Street Journal* 23 Nov. 2001: W1. Print.

Note: Use single quotation marks around the shorter title if it is a title normally punctuated with quotation marks.

■ An Article Reprinted in a Loose-Leaf Collection

The entry begins with original publication information, including the medium of publication, and ends with the name of the loose-leaf volume (*Youth*), editor, volume number, publication information including name of the information service (SIRS), and the article number. In the example below, the plus sign indicates continuing but nonconsecutive pages.

> O'Connell, Loraine. "Busy Teens Feel the Beep." *Orlando Sentinel* 7 Jan. 1993: E1+. Print. *Youth.* Ed. Eleanor Goldstein. Vol. 4. Boca Raton: SIRS, 1993. Art. 41.

■ Works-Cited Entries: Online Sources

■ Components

Citations for online sources generally follow the strategies used for print sources, including the medium of publication (Web). After the author's name and title of the work (either italicized or in quotes, depending on the type of work), include the title of the overall website in italics, and additional information as described below. Because URLs can change, the URL should be provided only if the reader probably cannot locate the source without it, or if your instructor requires it.

1. Author's name
2. Title of the article or work, italicized or in quotation marks
3. Title of the overall website, italicized (if different from item 2)
4. Version or edition used
5. Publisher or sponsor of the site; if not available, use *N.p.*
6. Date of publication, with day, month, and year if available; if nothing is available, use *n.d.*
7. Medium of publication (*Web*)
8. Date of access (day, month, and year)

■ A Site with a URL

If you must include a URL to provide guidance to a site (or because your instructor requires URLs), give it after the date of access, a period, and a space. Enclose it in angle brackets and follow it with a period.

> MacLeod, Donald. "Shake-Up for Academic Publishing." *Guardian Unlimited*.
> Guardian News and Media Ltd., 10 Nov. 2008. Web. 6 Jan. 2011. <http://
> www.guardian.co.uk/Archive/>.

If the URL must be divided between two lines, break it only after a single or double slash. Do not add a hyphen. If possible, include the complete address, including *http://* for the work you are citing.

> "Fort Frederica." *National Parks Service*. U.S. Department of the Interior, n.d. Web.
> 27 Feb. 2011. <http://home.nps.gov/fofr/forteachers/
> curriculummaterials.htm>.

■ A Nonperiodical Publication

Most items online are not posted on a regular schedule; they are nonperiodical. Business pages, blog entries, PDF documents, online books, audio or video posts, and a host of other postings are nonperiodical publications. This includes most websites sponsored by magazines and newspapers. Such items can be identified following the guidelines on the previous page. (For additional guidelines regarding scholarly journals or periodical publications in an online database, see page 515.)

■ Items Existing Only Online

Many publications exist only in online form. Because such publications can move unexpectedly, it is important to include enough information for your reader to locate them again regardless of their new location.

A Typical Online Item

> Booth, Philip. "Robert Frost's Prime Directive." *Poets.org*. Academy of American
> Poets, n.d. Web. 1 Oct. 2011.

An Online Item, No Author Identified

Begin with the title of the work, in quotation marks or italics, as appropriate. Alphabetize this entry by the first significant word of the title ("NetDay" in this case).

> "NetDay AmeriCorps Bridge Program 2001-2003." *NetDay*. Project Tomorrow, n.d.
> Web. 25 Nov. 2011.

A Home Page

If a nonperiodical publication has no title, identify it with a descriptor such as *Home page, Introduction,* or *Online posting* (using no italics or quotation marks). You may add the name of the publication's creator or editor after the overall site title, if appropriate.

> Wheaton, Wil. Home page. *Wil Wheaton dot Net*. N.p., 31 May 2006. Web. 19 Mar.
> 2011.

An Online Item with a Compiler, an Editor, or a Translator

When alphabetizing an entry by its compiler, editor, or translator, treat that person's name as usual, followed by an abbreviation for her or his role. If an author is identified, however, the compiler, editor, or translator follows the item title, with the abbreviation for the role preceding the compiler, editor, or translator's name.

> Webster, Michael, comp. "Books and Articles Cited in 'Notes on the Writings of E.
> E. Cummings.'" *Spring*. E. E. Cummings Society, n.d. 4 Oct. 2011.

> Lao-tzu. *Tao Te Ching*. Trans. J. Legge. *Internet Sacred Text Archive*. John Bruno
> Hare, n.d. Web. 14 Apr. 2011.

■ An Entry in an Online Reference Work

Unless the author of the entry is identified, begin with the entry name in quotation marks. Follow with the usual online publication information.

> "Eakins, Thomas." *Britannica Online Encyclopedia*. Encyclopedia Britannica, 2008.
> Web. 26 Sept. 2008.

■ An Online Poem

List the poet's name, the title of the poem, and any print publication information before the electronic publication details.

> Nemerov, Howard. "Found Poem." *War Stories*. U. of Chicago Press: 1987. Poets.org.
> Web. 5 Oct. 2007.

■ An Online Transcript of a Broadcast

Give the original publication information for the broadcast. Following the medium of publication, add *Transcript,* followed by a period.

> Lehrer, Jim. "Character Above All." *Online NewsHour*. Natl Public Radio, 29 May
> 1996. PBS.org. Web. Transcript. 23 Apr. 2007.

■ An Online Government Publication

As with a governmental publication in print, begin with the name of the government (country, state, and so on) followed by the name of the agency. After the publication title, add the electronic publication information.

> United States. Dept. of Labor. Office of Disability Employment Policy. *Emergency*
> *Preparedness for People with Disabilities*. Apr. 2004. *Disability Employment*
> *Agency*. Web. 12 Sept. 2008.

■ Items Including Print Publication Information

In general, follow the format for printed books. Include publication information for the original print version if available. Follow the date of publication with the electronic information, including the title of the site or database, sponsor, date of electronic posting (or *n.d.* if not available), medium of publication (*Web.*), and your date of access.

> Simon Julian L. *The Ultimate Resource II: People, Materials, and Environment*. College
> Park: U of Maryland, 1996. U of Maryland Libraries. Web. 9 Apr. 2009.

When citing part of an online book (such as the foreword) follow the example on page 505, but end with the online source, the term *Web,* and the date of access.

> Taylor, Bayard. Preface. *Faust*. Trans. Bayard Taylor. Boston: Houghton Mifflin, 1883.
> iii-xvii. Google Book Search. Web. 7 March 2009.

■ Items Including Nonprint Publication Information

For online postings of photographs, videos, sound recordings, works of art, and so on, follow the examples on pages 516–518. In place of the original medium of publication, however, include the title of the database or website (italicized), followed by the medium (*Web.*) and the date of access, as for other online entries.

An Artwork

> Goya, Francisco de. *Saturn Devouring His Children*. 1819-1823. Museo Nacional del
>   Prado, Madrid. *Museodelprado.es*. Web. 13 Dec. 2008.

A Photograph

> Brumfield, William Craft. *Church of Saint Nicholas Mokryi*. 1996. Prints and
>   Photographs Div., Lib. of Cong. *Brumfield Photograph Collection*. Web. 9 May
>   2009.

An Audio Recording

> "Gildy Arrives in Summerfield." *The Great Gildersleeve*. NBC. 31 Aug. 1941.
>   *EThomsen.com*. Web. 13 Apr. 2009.

A Video

> *Sita Sings the Blues*. Prod. Nina Paley. 2008. *Internet Archive*. Web. 5 June 2008.

An Unpublished Manuscript

> "The Work for All Plan." 1933. Mildred Hicks Papers. Manuscript, Archives, and
>   Rare Book Lib., *Emory U. Online Manuscript Resources in Southern Women's
>   History*. Web. 31 Jan. 2009.

■ A Scholarly Journal

Many scholarly journals are published only on the web, with no print version. For such publications, follow the basic guidelines given for print periodicals, though conclude with *Web* instead of *Print,* followed by your date of access. Also, if no page numbers are given, or if each item in the journal is numbered separately, replace the normal page notation with *n. pag.*

> "Wired Style: Principles of English Usage in the Digital Age. Wired." Wired Digital
>   Inc., 1994. Web. 5 Nov. 2008.

■ A Periodical Publication in an Online Database

Articles from different sources may be incorporated into an online database. To cite an article from a database, begin your citation with the usual information for citing print periodicals, but drop the medium of original publication (*Print*). Instead, include the title of the database (italicized), the medium of publication (*Web*), and the date of access.

> Davis, Jerome. "Massacre in Kiev." *Washington Post* 29 Nov. 1999, final ed.: C12.
>   *ProQuest*. Web. 30 Nov. 2008.

■ Works-Cited Entries: Other Sources (Primary, Personal, and Multimedia)

The following examples of works-cited entries illustrate how to cite sources such as television or radio programs, films, live performances, works of art, and other miscellaneous nonprint sources.

■ A Periodically Published Database on CD-ROM or DVD-ROM

Citations for materials published on CD-ROM or DVD-ROM are similar to those for print sources, with these added considerations: (1) The contents of a work may vary from one medium to another; therefore, the citation should always identify the medium. (2) The publisher and vendor of the publication may be different, in which case both must be identified. (3) Because of periodic updates, multiple versions of the same database may exist, which calls for citation if possible of both the date of the document cited and the date of the database itself.

> Ackley, Patricia. "Jobs of the Twenty-First Century." *New Rochelle Informer* 15 (Apr. 1994): A4. New Rochelle Informer Ondisc. Oct. 1994. CD-ROM.

> Baker, Anthony. *The New Earth Science*. Cincinnati: Freeman's P, 1991. New Media Inc., 2004. DVD-ROM.

■ Reference Work on CD-ROM

If you use an encyclopedia or other reference book recorded on CD-ROM, use the form below. If available, include publication information for the printed source.

> *The American Heritage Dictionary of the English Language*. 3rd ed. Boston: Houghton-Mifflin, 1992. Cambridge, MA: Softkey Intl., 1994. CD-ROM.

■ A Television or Radio Program

Include the medium (*Television* or *Radio*) at the end of the citation, followed by a period.

> "U.S. Health Care Gets Boost from Charity." *60 Minutes*. CBS. WBBM, Chicago. 28 Feb. 2008. Television.

■ A Film

The director, distributor, and year of release follow the title. Other information may be included if pertinent. End with the medium, in this case *Film*, followed by a period.

> *Atonement*. Dir. Joe Wright. Perf. James McAvoy, Keira Knightley. Universal Pictures, 2007. Film.

■ A Video Recording or an Audio Recording

Cite a filmstrip, slide program, videocassette, or DVD as you do a film; include the medium of publication last, followed by a period.

> *Monet: Shadow & Light.* Devine Productions, 1999. Videocassette.

If you are citing a specific song on a musical recording, place its title in quotation marks before the title of the recording.

> Bernstein, Leonard. "Maria." *West Side Story.* Columbia, 1995. CD.

■ A Performance

Treat this similarly to a film, adding the location and date of the performance.

> *Chanticleer: An Orchestra of Voices.* Young Auditorium, Whitewater, Wisc. 23 Feb. 2003. Performance.

■ An Artwork on Display

> Titian. *The Entombment.* N.d. Painting. Louvre, Paris.

■ A Letter or Memo Received by the Author (You)

For an unpublished letter or memo, include the form of the material after the date: *TS* for a typescript or printout, and *MS* for a work written by hand.

> Thomas, Bob. Letter to the author. 10 Jan. 2008. TS.

■ An Interview by the Author (You)

> Brooks, Sarah. Personal interview. 15 Oct. 2008.

■ A Cartoon or Comic Strip (in Print)

> Luckovich, Mike. "The Drawing Board." Cartoon. *Time* 17 Sept. 2001: 18. Print.

■ An Advertisement (in Print)

List the subject of the advertisement (product, company, organization, or such), followed by *Advertisement* and a period. Then give the usual publication information.

> Vaio Professional Notebooks. Advertisement. *Campus Technology* Oct. 2004: 45. Print.

■ A Lecture, a Speech, an Address, or a Reading

Provide the speaker's name, the title of the presentation (if known) in quotation marks, the meeting and the sponsoring organization, the location, and the date. End with an appropriate descriptive label such as *Address, Lecture,* or *Reading.*

> Annan, Kofi. "Acceptance of Nobel Peace Prize." Oslo City Hall, Oslo, Norw. 10 Dec. 2001. Speech.

■ A Legal or Historical Document

If your paper requires a number of legal citations, the MLA advises consulting the most recent edition of *The Bluebook: A Uniform System of Citation* (Cambridge: Harvard Law Rev. Assn.: Print). If you are providing only a few such citations, the MLA provides that the titles of laws, acts, and similar documents should appear in regular type (not italicized or enclosed in quotation marks), both within the text and in the list of works cited. The titles are abbreviated, and works are cited by sections, with years included if relevant. End your citation with the medium of publication followed by a period.

> 7 USC. Sec. 308a. 1928. Print.
>
> Do-Not-Call Implementation Act. Pub. L. 108-10. Stat. 117-557. 11 Mar. 2003. Print.

Abbreviate the names of law cases (spelling out the first important word of each party's name). Do not italicize the name in your works-cited list (although it should be italicized within the body of your paper). Follow with the case number or volume, inclusive page or reference numbers, the name of the court, the date (or year) of the decision, the medium consulted, and the date of access for a website.

> Missouri v. Seibert. 02-1371. Supreme Court of the U.S. 28 June 2004. FindLaw.com.
>   Web. 4 June 2009.

■ A Map or Chart

Follow the format for an anonymous book, adding *Map* or *Chart* (without italics), followed by a period, the city and publisher, date, and the medium of publication.

> *Wisconsin Territory*. Map. Madison: Wisconsin Trails, 1988. Print.

■ Sample MLA Paper

Stevie Jeung wrote the following research paper for an American Studies course focusing on crime and punishment in America. The paper examines cultural perceptions of a condemned prisoner's last meal. Because this paper focuses on a humanities topic, Stevie used MLA style for format and documentation. Strictly speaking, MLA format does not require or even recommend a title page or an outline. To see samples of these, go to **www.thecollegewriter.com/4e.** (For more on outlines, you can also see pages 48–53.) You can use Stevie's paper in three ways:

1. To study how a well-written, major research paper develops careful thinking, builds a discussion, and orders supporting points and evidence.

2. To examine how source summaries, paraphrases, and quotations are carefully integrated into the writer's discussion to advance her thinking— a full-length example of the strategies addressed on pages 484–487.

3. To see in detail the format and documentation practices of MLA style, practices that allow the writer to share a professional-looking paper that fairly respects sources used.

Sample Paper: Format, In-Text Citation, and Works-Cited List ■ ˙ ■

Note that MLA format requires that the paper be double-spaced throughout. That formatting is shown in the full version of the paper, which you can find at the website **www.thecollegewriter.com/4e.**

Jeung 1

> The heading supplies identifying details.

Stevie Jeung

Professor Sasha Abramsky

American Studies 101D

17 February 2008

> The title (centered) indicates the paper's topic and theme.

"I Did *Not* Get My Spaghetti-O's":

Death Row Consumption in the Popular Media

> The writer opens with a chronological catalog of executed people and last suppers.

Jesus Christ: Roast lamb, matzo, wine; around AD 30. Perry Smith and Richard Hickock: Identical meals of shrimp, French fries, garlic bread, ice cream and strawberries with whipped cream; 1965. Timothy McVeigh: Two pints of Ben & Jerry's mint chocolate chip ice cream: 2001. Tony Soprano: Holsten's onion rings; 2007. Karl Chamberloin: final meal yet to be consumed; 15 days from now.

1

> The intro zeros in on the topic, focuses on what is odd or difficult to explain, and announces a search for explanations.

While executions historically demand a certain degree of morbid curiosity, the last meals of the condemned seem to stimulate heightened interest. Indeed, a prisoner's final feast has almost become an event in its own right, not only for the prisoner, but for the prison staff and the public. Websites, novels, movies, television shows, newspapers, and even cookbooks report, dissect, criticize, and speculate regarding last meals real and imagined. When confronted with the ultimate consumption of dying people in so many areas of our popular media, the truth becomes alarmingly clear: This is odd behavior. There must be some reason that we institutionally allow our most hated and feared prisoners to choose and enjoy their final meal before we execute them, and there must be some reason that we like to watch and reproduce the event in popular culture.

2

> The analysis focuses on specific examples in film and television.

> Because the film title is identified in the sentence, an in-text citation isn't needed.

The last meal appears in almost every major arena of public entertainment. In *The Green Mile,* a motion picture based on Stephen King's novel of the same

3

name, protagonist John Coffey is wrongfully executed in a heartbreaking, dramatic scene, but not before careful thought about his last meal: "Meatloaf be nice. Mashed taters with gravy. Okra, maybe. I's not picky." Prisoners are also served their last meals on the small screen. Take, for example, FOX's network TV show, *Prison Break,* in which Lincoln Burrows is served his last blueberry pancakes ("Sleight of Hand"). In fact, on an episode of *The Simpsons,* a staple of American television, Homer eats Hans Moleman's last meal of lobster tail and raspberry tort just before Hans is executed, protesting, "But he ate my last meal!" ("Springfield Connection"). Clearly, this animated man did not think it right to be executed without enjoying his final choice of cuisine. Of course, his expression of outrage is followed by, "Are you really allowed to execute people in local jail?" reminding us that *The Simpsons,* however rich with American icons, is not real. Regardless of actual death row ceremony, the Americans who produce and consume these works of fiction expect that a special meal accompanies execution.

Compulsory inclusion of a last meal in fictional executions is one thing, but our fascination does not stop there. Where convicts are executed, the state documents and even publishes details of the last meal and last words before they administer capital punishment. Until recently, Texas, the number one execution state, posted prisoners' last meals on their Justice Department's website ("Death Row"). They discontinued this practice for unclear reasons, but the archived lists from 2003 and earlier are still readily available, and the department continues to publish names, execution dates, case records, and even pictures of the dead and soon-to-be-dead (like Karl Chamberlain, mentioned above). Oklahoma, ranked third among execution states, takes a more voyeuristic approach: "the local newspaper [prints] a blow-by-blow account. Time of injection. Facial expressions. Final meal requests" ("Artist"). While this might seems like a gruesome practice on the state's part, the public does not shy away. In fact, commercial reproduction of this information proves that it's not just reporting; it's entertainment.

[Margin note:] A direct quotation is placed within quotation marks.

[Margin note:] The analysis turns to real executions and state practices.

[Margin note:] An in-text citation uses a shortened title and no page number for a government webpage.

[Margin note:] 4

Jeung 3

The writer explorers the presence of "last supper" interest on the web, using concrete details and examples.

It is evident not only that people read this stuff, but that they actually use available execution and last-meal information to create and market their own masterpieces of morbid exposition. It becomes at once blatantly, amusingly, and disgustingly clear when you stumble across websites like *Last Suppers: Famous Final Meals from Death Row, Meals to Die For,* and *Dead Man Eating,* which faithfully posts the last meal (along with "the skinny" on the day's events and case details) of every person executed in the United States since 2002. The most shocking part is that the *Dead Man Eating* website also sells t-shirts, coffee mugs, and even thong underwear, all of which read "Dead Man Eating: looking for a killer meal?" and feature a crude drawing of a dead man hanging with an ice cream cone in his hand. A more tasteful, if just as morbid, strategy is to publish a "last meal" cookbook or coffee table book. A quick search for "last meal" on Amazon.com yields at least four such books (along with Snoop Dogg's album entitled *Tha Last Meal*). According to its description, one of the books, *Last Suppers: Famous Final Meals from Death Row,* both lists the gritty details of last meals and uses the public's "appetite" for this last-minute courtesy to comment on the death penalty. The book *Meals to Die* For comes from Brian D. Price, a former inmate who personally cooked eleven years' worth of final meals for Texas death row inmates. It reveals recipes, pictures, and even hand-written last-meal requests he received during his incarceration. The last things that our allegedly deadliest murderers eat, then, are not only published for the public, but published *again* with extra details for *sale* to the public. This doubly-consuming public just eats this stuff up.

Free-web resources (fitting the cultural focus of the essay) function as primary sources showing society's fascination with last meals. The sources are all clearly identified.

The analysis draws conclusions from the examples discussed.

With a question, the writer explores possible origins of the phenomenon, and offers a chronological survey.

The more closely we look at it, the more bizarre this cycle of consumption and death appears: a man kills, he eats, we kill him, and then we eat it up. Where does it really begin, though? The "last meal" has a symbolic and ritualistic significance since, well, Jesus and the Last Supper (Peck). At some point, between Jesus and today's American mega-prisons, we began to recognize the last meal as a ritual of institutionalized execution.

Jeung 4

Since the early nineteenth century, Americans have been fascinated with   7
not just execution, but the ritual of a condemned criminal's last day. A large
crowd would turn up to hear the death warrant, sermon, and last words before a
hood was slipped over the offender's head and he or she was hanged by the neck.
Still more people read the details of the execution as it was published, and "if the
offender could not or would not utter any memorable last words, the publisher
had no compunction against compositing them" (Atwell 8). The 1840s brought
the American death penalty's first decline in a trend of fluctuating popularity
that would continue to the present day, but wherever there was a spectacle, there
was an audience. As the death penalty remained popular in the South, so did
reporting the last days of convicts in gross detail.

Each of the states that employ capital punishment uses its own set of   8
rules and procedures. Some states enforce a price limit, while Texas limits a
last meal to the things accessible by the regular prison kitchen staff. In 1995,
the Federal Government administered its first execution since 1969. Timothy
McVeigh's execution prompted development of a 56-page "Execution Protocol,"
"meant to ensure that all executions are carried out 'in an efficient and humane
manner.'" This document clearly outlines a last meal choice as a scheduled
step in the execution process: "At least seven days prior to the execution, the
warden or designee will contact the condemned individual to arrange for his/
her last meal," and "The condemned individual will be served a final meal
at a time determined by the warden" between twelve and three hours prior
to the execution (qtd. in Fritsch). In Texas, the meal would be ready at 3:45
p.m. and delivered at 4 p.m., two hours before lethal injection. This last tray of
food, which would become very public following the execution, was covered
in paper "for privacy" (Price). Although an inmate could request anything, he
or she often received something different: "The local newspaper would always
say they got 24 tacos and 12 enchiladas, but they would actually get four tacos
and two enchiladas" ("Confessions"). After all of this procedure, the report
sensationalizes the last meal, much as early publications sensationalized the last
words.

As the analysis deepens, Stevie refers to scholarly sources, using direct quotation when appropriate and in-text citations noting author and page number.

The analysis compares and contrasts the capital-punishment practices of different government bodies (federal, states).

The citation indicates that the source was quoted in another source.

Jeung 5

9

So why does the state even allow a last meal? Bob Greene argues that "inviting" prisoners to choose a last meal is "hypocritical and insulting to the memory of the victims" because, he poignantly argues, murderers take that foresight and choice from their victims. Perhaps, Tony Karon of *TIME* suggests, the prisoners accept a last bit of freedom and humanity to make up for the "grim act of violence of the state" that is about to occur. Especially considering that prisoners don't always get what they ask for, this seems unlikely. Daniel LaChance notices that although execution practices have historically moved toward anonymity and bureaucracy, the last meal and final speech have incongruently been sustained. His recent paper, "Last Words, Last Meals, and Last Stands: Agency and Individuality in the Modern Execution Process," argues that in giving the prisoners choice in their final meals and words, the state portrays them as autonomous agents who have chosen their deeds and accepted their fates. In other words, the prison system denies a prisoner individuality until his or her last day of life in order to feel righteousness in executing him or her (LaChance). As Sasha Abramsky points out, in the midst of a vengeful prison system this makes perfect sense. It is much more satisfying to exact revenge on a person than on a number. In fact, despite the moves toward more humane and less painful execution, the state can treat mentally ill patients with antipsychotics so that they're "sane enough to be executed" ("Confessions"). Clearly, the "ideal candidate" is an irredeemable individual, sane enough both to feel and participate in the death. In other words, if candidates can choose the last thing they eat, they must have chosen to murder, in which case they deserve to die. Furthermore, resemblance to the biblical Last Supper might justify vengeful treatment in the name of religion, especially for prison staff like Oscar Dees, who believed that God intended him to punish criminals. This powerful, righteous moral logic is published and extended to the public, creating a sense of justice that maintains support for the death penalty. As in *Cool Hand Luke*, this public spectacle of punishment and revenge is a self-serving institution of the prison system itself.

A "why" question pushes forward the analysis; to answer the question, Stevie fluently uses a variety of different sources.

Disagreeing with one source's explanation, the writer turns to another source.

The writer analyzes the moral psychology of the execution rituals, including the last meal.

Jeung 6

The public, however, has its own incentives for gobbling it all up, so to   *10*
speak. Revenge is probably one of them, as is pure, unabashed voyeurism.
American people tend to take the idea of the last meal to heart, though, and
somehow make it their own. Many visitors to the *Dead Man Eating* website and
message boards all over the internet do this by submitting their own "last meal
requests," as if they were going to die tomorrow. Apparently, then, this fixation
on the last meal is not limited to intrusive consumption of execution records;
it extends to the public and their own final food choices. In fact, the subject
of hypothetical last meals has given this icon of criminality and death a fresh,
not-so-morbid vantage point. James L. Dickerson's book, *Last Suppers: If the
world ended tomorrow, what would be your last meal?* asks popular celebrities and
political figures to divulge their last meal of choice. Bill Clinton, for instance,
would like to enjoy chicken enchiladas before his hypothetical death (117), and
professional football coach Mike Ditka (22) fancies pigs in a blanket. *My Last
Supper,* by Melanie Dunea, asks the same of chefs.

Still others forego the macabre enjoyment and the distant speculation   *11*
and use the vivid image of eating for the last time to protest the death penalty
through art. Photographer Jacquelyn C. Black organizes pictures of inmates and
their meals in a book entitled *Last Meal,* in which she also includes statistics.
According to the publisher's description, for example, 10 of the 12 states without
the death penalty have homicide rates below the national average. University of
Oklahoma professor Julie Green paints a series of dinner plates, each depicting
what was on the last plate of a particular inmate. Reading about the executions
in the newspaper "humanized death row" for her and struck her as an invasion
of privacy ("Artist"). Whether they seek revenge or redemption, Americans see
the last meal as a symbol in the life-or-death of justice, on death row and in their
living rooms.

The final episode of *The Sopranos* illustrates the place of "The Last Supper,"   *12*
generally speaking, in the American psyche. Mob leader Tony Soprano sits down
at Holsten's diner in New Jersey and tension builds around him as the other

Exploring an example from television, the writer pulls together the strands of her analysis.

characters bustle about in their respective scenes. The viewer gets the distinct feeling that they are preparing to kill Tony, who looks nervous, as though he knows that his criminal career is about to end in execution. Tony's family arrives at the diner and as he offers a basket of onion rings around the table, and before we find out whether or not he dies, the scene cuts to black ("Made in America"). The end. No more Tony, no more *Sopranos.* This could just be another cliffhanger, but many fans see it as Tony's "Last Supper," and "If Holsten's onion rings—round, crunchy, and, according to one influential diner, the best in the state—didn't symbolize communion wafers, as some viewers of the final scene of *The Sopranos* have theorized, they do now" (Hyman). The point is that the subsequent pilgrimage to Holsten's taken by many fans of the show proves one of two things. Either a) the mega-hit show *did* intend to showcase a symbolic "last meal" for its main character, or b) all of these people are making it up. Either case gives powerful support to the idea that this last ritual of consumption is popularly recognized as the appropriate ending to a life, whether fictional, criminal, or biblical.

The interplay between the public, the media, and the criminal justice system gives the last meal a unique importance to each. The criminal system perpetuates the tradition in its own interest and uses the media to lend righteousness to its questionable and somewhat manipulative actions, but the media and the public interact to derive much greater religious, social, emotional, and political meaning, thus creating a pervasive and lasting icon which permeates popular culture and popular perception. Thomas J. Grasso, executed by lethal injection in Oklahoma (1995), seemed to appreciate the significance of a last meal in the public eye when he gave his last speech: "I did not get my Spaghetti-O's, I got spaghetti. I want the press to know this" ("Last Words").

In her conclusion, the writer answers her original questions and offers a final quotation that drives home her point and harkens back to her title.

13

Jeung 8

Works Cited

Abramsky, Sasha. *American Furies: Crime, Punishment, and Vengeance in the*
Age of Mass Imprisonment. Boston: Beacon Press, 2007. Print.

"Artist serves 'Last Supper' on plates." *Lawrence Journal.* 29 Oct 2006. Web. 5
Feb 2008.

Atwell, Mary Welek. *Evolving Standards of Decency: Popular Culture and*
Capital Punishment. New York: Peter Lang, 2004. Print.

"Confessions of a Death Row Chef." *The Observer.* 14 March 2004. Web. 5 Feb
2008.

"Death Row Information." *Texas Department of Criminal Justice.* 7 Nov 2007.
Web. 5 Feb 2008.

Dickerson, James L. Last Suppers: *If the world ended tomorrow, what would be*
your last meal? USA: Citadel, 2004. Print.

Fritsch, Jane. "Word for Word/Execution Protocol; Please Order Your Last
Meal Seven Days in Advance." *The New York Times.* 22 April 2001. Web.
5 Feb 2008.

The Green Mile. Dir. Frank Darabont. Perf. Tom Hanks, Michael Clarke
Duncan, David Morse, and Bonnie Hunt. Castle Rock, 1999. Film.

Greene, Bob. "They didn't get to choose their last meals." *Jewish World Review.*
12 June 2001. Web. 5 Feb 2008.

Hyman, Vicki. "Chewing Over Tony's Last Meal." *The Star Ledger.* 23 June
2007. Web. 5 Feb 2008.

Karon, Tony. "Why We're Fascinated by Death Row Cuisine." *TIME.* 10
August 2000. Web. 5 Feb 2008.

The list of works cited begins on a separate page and includes the title, header, and page number.

The paper's bibliography lists a range of scholarly books, trade books, scholarly articles, popular articles, and websites on the topic.

Sources are listed in alphabetical order by author (or by title if no author is given) and identified by medium.

LaChance, Daniel. "Last Words, Last Meals, and Last Stands: Agency and
 Individuality in the Modern Execution Process." *Law & Social Inquiry*
 32 (2007): 701-724. JSTOR. Web. 5 Feb 2008.

"Last Words on Death Row." *CNN: The Best of Court TV.* 31 Dec 2007. Web. 5
 Feb 2008.

"Made in America." *The Sopranos.* Dir. David Chase. HBO. 10 June 2007.
 Television.

Peck, John. "Last Meals." *Tuscon Weekly.* 5 Jan 2006. Print. 5 Feb 2008.

Price, Brian D. *Meals to Die For.* USA: Dyna-Paige Corporation, 2001. Print.

"Sleight of Hand." *Prison Break.* Dir. Dwight Little. Fox Network. 7 Nov. 2005.
 Television.

"The Springfield Connection." *The Simpsons.* Dir. Mark Kirkland, Fox
 Network. 7 May. 1995. Television.

Quotation marks and italics are properly used with titles, as are punctuation and abbreviations.

Items are double-spaced throughout. Second and subsequent lines are indented (hanging indent).

Each entry provides complete identifying information, properly formatted.

Reading for Better Writing

1. What are your thoughts about capital punishment, and more broadly about crime and punishment? How did reading Jeung's paper on last meals contribute to your understanding?

2. Did you find her paper engaging? Why or why not?

3. What types of evidence does Jeung use in her paper? Where has she gotten her evidence? Are her resources reliable?

4. How does Jeung distinguish her own thinking from source material? Why are these strategies necessary?

Critical-Thinking and Writing Activities

As directed by your instructor, complete the following critical-thinking and writing activities by yourself or with classmates.

1. The MLA style involves many rules about format and documentation. To make some sense of these rules, answer this question by yourself or with classmates: What is the essential logic of the MLA system?

2. Create MLA works-cited entries for the following publications:

   - An article in the May 27, 2002, issue (vol. 145, no. 11) of *Fortune* magazine by Joseph Nocera: "Return of the Raider" (pages 97–114)

   - Ernest Hemingway's novel *A Farewell to Arms,* published in 1986 by Collier Books, located in New York City

   - The webpage "Aruba," part of *The 2008 World Factbook,* sponsored by the Central Intelligence Agency. No author or publication date is listed. The site was last accessed March 8, 2011, at http://www.cia.gov/library/publications/the-world-factbook/ index.html.

Learning-Outcomes Checklist

As you format your paper and document your research according to MLA guidelines, use the checklist below to review your work.

_____ All borrowed material is acknowledged with an appropriate attributive phrase and/or in-text citation indicating author and page number, as appropriate.

_____ The works-cited list includes entries for all works referred to in the body of the paper: No sources are missing from the list; no extra sources are listed that have no reference within the paper.

_____ The entire works-cited list is properly alphabetized by authors' last names (or by the first main word in the title for anonymous works).

_____ Each works-cited entry contains the maximum amount of identifying and publication information, in the proper order, using all of the accepted abbreviations.

_____ The entire paper is properly formatted, from the first page heading and title to the final works-cited page entry.

_____ Placement, spacing, and margins are correct for the paper's header, the heading, the title, and "Works Cited."

_____ Pagination is correct and consistent.

_____ First lines of paragraphs and inset quotations are properly indented; works-cited entries are properly formatted with a hanging indent.

_____ The paper is cleanly printed single-sided on quality paper.

_____ The paper is properly bound with a paper clip in the upper-left corner.

APA
32 Documentation Format

Those who write papers in the social sciences—psychology, sociology, political science, and education, for example—usually follow the research-writing guidelines of the American Psychological Association (APA). This chapter summarizes these guidelines and helps you use APA format and documentation.

APA format is similar to MLA format in two ways: Both require (1) parenthetical citations within the text and (2) a final listing of all references cited in the paper. But in the social sciences, the date of publication is often much more crucial than it is in the humanities, so the date is highlighted in in-text citations. APA format also requires a cover page and an abstract.

Learning Outcomes

Audio

▶ Understand APA documentation style.

▶ Understand APA in-text citations.

▶ Review in-text citations.

▶ Understand APA references.

▶ Review a sample APA paper.

Visually Speaking ▶ How does the image above connote research in the sciences?

■ APA Research Paper Guidelines

Questions and Answers

Is a separate title page required?	**Yes.** Include your paper's title, your name, and the name of your school on three separate lines, double-spaced, centered, and beginning approximately one-third of the way down from the top of the page. Place a shortened title and page number 1 in the upper-right corner. (See "What about paging?" on the next page.)
What is an abstract and where does it go?	An abstract is required in APA format. An abstract is a 100- to 150-word paragraph summarizing your research paper. (See page 547.) Place your abstract on a new page and label it "Abstract" (centered); type your short title and page number 2 flush right one-half inch from the top.
Are references placed in the text?	**Yes.** Include the author and year, separated by a comma; for quotations, add the page number after a comma and "p."
Do you need a bibliography of sources used in the paper?	**Yes.** Full citations for all sources used (books, periodicals, and so on) are placed in an alphabetized list labeled "References" at the end of the paper.
How are the reference lists to be indented?	Confusion sometimes arises over how the reference lists of APA manuscripts should be indented. Normal paragraph indentation has been called for by APA in the past. However, hanging indentation as shown in this chapter is currently the preferred manuscript form for APA documents, including student papers. As always, ask your instructor if you are in doubt.
Do you need an appendix?	**Maybe.** Ask your instructor. In student papers, charts, tables, and graphs may sometimes be incorporated at appropriate points in the text, making appendices unnecessary.

What about longer quotations?	Type quotations of 40 or more words in block style (all lines flush left) five spaces in from the left margin. Indent the first lines of any additional paragraphs in the long quotation five spaces in from the margin set for the quotation.
What about margins?	Leave a margin of at least one inch on all four sides (if you are binding your paper, leave one and one-half inches at the left margin).
What about paging?	Page numbers appear at the top-right margin, above the first line of text. The title appears in all capital letters at the top-left margin, as a running head. The words "Running head:" precede this title on the title page only.
What about headings?	Headings, like an outline, show the organization of your paper and the importance of each topic. All topics of equal importance should have headings of the same level, or style. Below are the various levels of headings used in APA papers. (In most research papers, only levels 1, 3, and 4 are used.)

Level 1:   **Centered, Bold, Uppercase and Lowercase Heading**

 Flush Left, Bold, Italicized, Uppercase and Lowercase Heading

Level 3:   **Indented, bold, lowercase paragraph heading ending with a period.**

Level 4:   **_Indented, bold, italicized, lowercase paragraph heading ending with a period._**

Any other special instructions?	Always ask whether your school or department has special requirements that may take precedence over these guidelines.

Web Link

Guidelines for In-Text Citations

The Form of an Entry

The APA documentation style is sometimes called the "author–date" system because both the author and the date of the publication must be mentioned in the text when citing a source. Both might appear in the flow of the sentence, like this:

> Children in India are being trafficked for adoption, organ transplants, and labor
> such as prostitution, according to a 2007 article by Nilanjana Ray.

If either name or date does not appear in the text, it must be mentioned within parentheses at the most convenient place, like this:

> According to an article by Nilanjana Ray (2007), children in India . . .
> According to a recent article (Ray, 2007), children in India . . .

Points to Remember

1. When paraphrasing rather than quoting, make it clear where your borrowing begins and ends. Use stylistic cues to distinguish the source's thoughts ("Kalmbach points out . . . ," "Some critics argue . . .") from your own ("I believe . . . ," "It seems obvious, however . . .").

2. When using a shortened title of a work, begin with the word by which the work is alphabetized in your references list (for example, for "Measurement of Stress in Fasting Man," use "Measurement of Stress," not "Fasting Man").

3. When including a parenthetical citation at the end of a sentence, place it before the end punctuation: (Sacks, 1964).

Sample In-Text Citations

■ One Author: A Complete Work

The correct form for a parenthetical reference to a single source by a single author is parenthesis, last name, comma, space, year of publication, parenthesis. Also note that final punctuation should be placed outside the parentheses.

> . . . in this way, the public began to connect certain childhood vaccinations with
> an autism epidemic (Baker, 2008).

■ One Author: Part of a Work

When you cite a specific part of a source, give the page number, chapter, or section, using the appropriate abbreviations (*p.* or *pp.*, *chap.*, or *sec.* For others, see page 536). Always give the page number for a direct quotation.

> . . . while a variety of political and scientific forces were at work in the developing
> crisis, it was parents who pressed the case "that autism had become epidemic and
> that vaccines were its cause" (Baker, 2008, p. 251).

■ One Author: Several Publications in the Same Year

If the same author has published two or more articles in the same year, avoid confusion by placing a small letter *a* after the first work listed in the references list, *b* after the next one, and so on. Determine the order alphabetically by title.

> **Parenthetical Citation:**
>
> Reefs harbor life forms heretofore unknown (Milius, 2001a, 2001b).
>
> **References:**
>
> Milius, D. (2001a). Another world hides inside coral reefs. *Science News, 160*(16), 244.
>
> Milius, D. (2001b). Unknown squids—with elbows—tease science. *Science News, 160*(24), 390.

■ Works by Authors with the Same Last Name

When citing different sources by authors with the same last name, add the authors' initials to avoid confusion, even if the publication dates are different.

> While J. D. Wallace (2009) argued that privatizing social security would benefit only the wealthiest citizens, others such as E. S. Wallace (2011) supported greater control for individuals.

■ Two to Five Authors

In APA style, all authors—up to as many as five must be mentioned in the first text citation, like this:

> Love changes not just who we are, but who we can become, as well (Lewis, Amini, & Lannon, 2000).

Note: The last two authors' names are always separated by a comma and an ampersand (&) when enclosed in parentheses.

For works with **two authors,** list both in every citation. For works with **three to five authors,** list all only the first time; after that, use only the name of the first author followed by "et al.," like this:

> These discoveries lead to the hypothesis that love actually alters the brain's structure (Lewis et al., 2000).

■ Six or More Authors

If your source has six or more authors, refer to the work by the first author's name followed by "et al.," both for the first reference in the text and all references after that. However, be sure to list all the authors (up to six) in your references list.

> According to a recent study, post-traumatic stress disorder (PTSD) continues to dominate the lives of Vietnam veterans, though in modified forms (Trembley et al., 2010).

◾ A Work Authored by an Agency, a Committee, or Other Organization

Treat the name of the group as if it were the last name of the author. If the name is long and easily abbreviated, provide the abbreviation in square brackets. Use the abbreviation without brackets in subsequent references, as follows:

First Text Citation:

A problem for many veterans continues to be heightened sensitivity to noise (National Institute of Mental Health [NIMH], 2005).

Subsequent Citations:

In addition, veterans suffering from PTSD continue to have difficulty discussing their experiences (NIMH, 2005).

◾ A Work with No Author Indicated

If your source lists no author, treat the first few words of the title (capitalized normally) as you would an author's last name. A title of an article or a chapter belongs in quotation marks; the titles of books or reports should be italicized:

. . . including a guide to low-stress postures ("How to Do It," 2001).

◾ A Work Referred to in Another Work

If you need to cite a source that you have found referred to in another source (a "secondary" source), mention the original source in your text. Then, in your parenthetical citation, cite the secondary source, using the words "as cited in."

. . . theorem given by Ullman (as cited in Hoffman, 1998).

Note: In your references list at the end of the paper, you would write out a full citation for Hoffman (not Ullman).

◾ A Work in an Anthology

When citing an article or a chapter in an anthology or a collection, use the authors' names for the specific article, not the names of the anthology's editors. (Similarly, the article should be listed by its authors' names in the references section. See page 537.)

Phonological changes can be understood from a variationist perspective (Guy, 2005).

◾ An Electronic or Other Internet Source

As with print sources, cite an electronic source by the author (or by shortened title if the author is unknown) and the publication date (not the date you accessed the source). If citing a specific part of the source, use an appropriate abbreviation: *p.* for page, ¶ (paragraph symbol) or *para.* for paragraph, and *chap.* for chapter.

One study compared and contrasted the use of web and touch screen transaction log files in a hospital setting (Nicholas, Huntington, & Williams, 2001).

■ A Website

Whenever possible, cite a website by its author and posting date. In addition, refer to a specific page or document rather than to a home page or a menu page. If you are referring to a specific part of a webpage that does not have page numbers, direct your reader, if possible, with a section heading and a paragraph number.

> According to the National Multiple Sclerosis Society (2003, "Complexities" section, para. 2), understanding of MS could not begin until scientists began to research nerve transmission in the 1920s.

■ Two or More Works in a Parenthetical Reference

Sometimes it is necessary to lump several citations into one parenthetical reference. In that case, cite the sources as you usually would, separating the citations with semicolons. Place the citations in alphabetical order, just as they would be ordered in the references list.

> Others report near-death experiences (Rommer, 2000; Sabom, 1998).

■ A Sacred Text or Famous Literary Work

Sacred texts and famous literary works are published in many different editions. For that reason, the original date of publication may be unavailable or not pertinent. In these cases, use your edition's year of translation (for example, *trans. 2003*) or indicate your edition's year of publication (*2003 version*). When you are referring to specific sections of the work, it is best to identify parts, chapters, or other divisions instead of your version's page numbers.

> An interesting literary case of such dysfunctional family behavior can be found in Franz Kafka's *The Metamorphosis*, where it becomes the commandment of family duty for Gregor's parents and sister to swallow their disgust and endure him (trans. 1972, part 3).

Books of the Bible and other well-known literary works may be abbreviated, if no confusion is possible.

> "Generations come and generations go, but the earth remains forever" (*The New International Version Study Bible*, 1985 version, Eccles. 1.4).

■ Personal Communications

If you do the kind of personal research recommended elsewhere in *The College Writer*, you may have to cite personal communications that have provided you with some of your knowledge. Personal communications may include personal letters, phone calls, memos, and so forth. Because they are not published in a permanent form, APA style does not place them among the citations in your references list. Instead, cite them only in the text of your paper in parentheses, like this:

> . . . according to M. T. Cann (personal communication, April 1, 2011).

> . . . by today (M. T. Cann, personal communication, April 1, 2011).

Quick Guide
■ APA References

The references section lists all the sources you have cited in your text (with the exception of personal communications such as phone calls and e-mails). Begin your references list on a new page after the last page of your paper. Number each references page, continuing the numbering from the text. Then format your references list by following the guidelines below.

1. Type the running head in the upper-left corner and the page number in the upper-right corner, approximately one-half inch from the top of the page.

2. Center the title, *References,* approximately one inch from the top; then double-space before the first entry.

3. Begin each entry flush with the left margin. If the entry runs more than one line, indent additional lines approximately one-half inch (five to seven spaces) using a hanging indent.

4. Adhere to the following conventions about spacing, capitalization, and italics:
   - Double-space between all lines on the references page.
   - Use one space following each word and punctuation mark.
   - With book and article titles, capitalize only the first letter of the title (and subtitle) and proper nouns. (Note that this practice differs from the presentation of titles in the body of the essay.)
     Example: The impact of the cold war on Asia.
   - Use italics for titles of books and periodicals, not underlining.

5. List each entry alphabetically by the last name of the author, or, if no author is given, by the title (disregarding A, An, or The). For works with multiple authors, use the first author listed in the publication.

6. Follow these conventions with respect to abbreviations:
   - With authors' names, generally shorten first and middle names to initials, leaving a space after the period. For a work with more than one author, use an ampersand (&) before the last author's name.
   - For publisher locations, use the full city name plus the two-letter U.S. Postal Service abbreviation for the state. For international publishers, include a province and country name.
   - Spell out "Press" in full, but for other publishing information, use the abbreviations below.

Comp. .... compiler, compiled, compiled by	Pt. .... Part
Ed. .... editor(s)	Sec. (sect.) section(s)
N.d. .... no date given	2nd ed. .... Second edition
N.p. .... no place of publication,	Suppl. .... Supplement
no publisher given	Tech. Rep. .... Technical Report
p., pp. .... page(s) (if necessary for clarity)	Trans. (tr.) .... translator, translation

Reference Entries: Books and Other Documents

The general form for a book or brochure entry is this:

> Author, A. (year). *Title.* Location: Publisher.

The entries that follow illustrate the information needed to cite books, sections of a book, brochures, and government publications.

A Book by One Author

> Kuriansky, J. (2007). *Beyond bullets and bombs: Grassroots peacebuilding between Israelis and Palestinians.* Westport, CT: Praeger Press.

A Book by Two or More Authors

List up to seven authors by last name and first initial, separating them by commas, with an ampersand (&) before the last.

> Hooyman, N., & Kramer, B. (2006). *Living through loss: Interventions across the life span.* New York, NY: Columbia University Press.

For eight or more authors, list the first six followed by an ellipsis, and then the last.

An Anonymous Book

If an author is listed as "Anonymous," treat it as the author's name. Otherwise, follow this format:

> *Publication manual of the American Psychological Association* (6th ed.). (2010). Washington, DC: American Psychological Association.

A Chapter from a Book

List the chapter title after the date of publication, followed by a period or appropriate end punctuation. Use *In* before the book title, and follow the book title with the inclusive page numbers of the chapter.

> Tattersall, I. (2002). How did we achieve humanity? In *The monkey in the mirror* (pp. 138–168). New York, NY: Harcourt.

A Single Work from an Anthology

Start with information about the individual work, followed by details about the collection in which it appears, including the page span. For editors' names in the middle of an entry, follow the usual order: initial first, surname last. Note the placement of *Eds.* in parentheses.

> Guy, G. R. (2005). Variationist approaches to phonological change. In B. D. Joseph & R. D. Janda (Eds.), *The handbook of historical linguistics* (pp. 369–400). Malden, MA: Blackwell.

■ One Volume of a Multivolume Edited Work

Indicate the volume in parentheses after the work's title.

> Salzman, J., Smith, D. L., & West, C. (Eds.). (1996). *Encyclopedia of African-American culture and history* (Vol. 4). New York, NY: Simon & Schuster Macmillan.

■ A Separately Titled Volume in a Multivolume Work

> The Associated Press. (1995). *Twentieth-century America: Vol. 8. The crisis of national confidence: 1974–1980.* Danbury, CT: Grolier Educational Corp.

Note: When a work is part of a larger series or collection, as with this example, make a two-part title with the series and the particular volume you are citing.

■ An Edited Work, One in a Series

Start the entry with the work's author, publication date, and title. Then follow with publication details about the series.

> Marshall, P. G. (2002). The impact of the cold war on Asia. In T. O'Neill (Ed.), *World history by era: Vol. 9. The nuclear age* (pp. 162–166). San Diego, CA: Greenhaven Press.

■ A Group Author as Publisher

When the author is also the publisher, simply put *Author* in the spot where you would list the publisher's name.

> Amnesty International. (2007). *Maze of injustice: The failure to protect indigenous women from sexual violence in the USA.* London: Author.

Note: If the publication is a brochure, identify it as such in brackets after the title.

■ An Edition Other Than the First

> Trimmer, J. (2001). *Writing with a purpose* (13th ed.). Boston, MA: Houghton Mifflin.

■ Two or More Books by the Same Author

When you are listing multiple works by the same author, arrange them by the year of publication, earliest first.

> Sacks, O. (1995). *An Anthropologist on Mars: Seven paradoxical tales.* New York, NY: Alfred A. Knopf.

> Sacks, O. (2007). *Musicophilia: Tales of music and the brain.* New York, NY: Alfred A. Knopf.

■ An English Translation

> Setha, R. (1998). *Unarmed* (R. Narasimhan, Trans.). Chennai, India: Macmillan.
> (Original work published 1995)

Note: If you use the original work, cite the original version; the non-English title is followed by its English translation, not italicized, in square brackets.

■ An Article in a Reference Book

Start the entry with the author of the article, if identified. If no author is listed, begin the entry with the title of the article.

> Lewer, N. (1999). Non-lethal weapons. In *World encyclopedia of peace* (pp. 279–
> 280). Oxford, UK: Pergamon Press.

■ A Reprint, Different Form

> Albanov, V. (2000). *In the land of white death: An epic story of survival in the Siberian
> Arctic.* New York, NY: Modern Library. (Original work published 1917)

Note: This work was originally published in Russia in 1917; the 2000 reprint is the first English version. If you are citing a reprint from another source, the parentheses would contain "Reprinted from *Title*, pp. xx–xx, by A. Author, year, Location: Publisher."

■ A Technical or Research Report

> Taylor, B. G., Fitzgerald, N., Hunt, D., Reardon, J. A., & Brownstein, H. H. (2001).
> *ADAM preliminary 2000 findings on drug use and drug markets: Adult male
> arrestees.* Washington, DC: National Institute of Justice.

■ A Government Publication

Generally, refer to the government agency as the author. When possible, provide an identification number for the document after the title in parentheses.

> National Institute on Drug Abuse. (2000). *Inhalant abuse* (NIH Publication No.
> 00–3818). Rockville, MD: National Clearinghouse
> on Alcohol and Drug Information.

For reports obtained from the U.S. Government Printing Office, list location and publisher as "Washington, D.C.: Government Printing Office."

■ Reference Entries: Print Periodical Articles

The general form for a periodical entry is this:

> Author, A. (year). Article title. *Periodical Title, volume number* (issue number), page numbers.

If the periodical does not use volume and issue numbers, include some other designation with the year, such as a date, a month, or a season. The entries that follow illustrate the information and arrangement needed to cite most types of print periodicals.

Note: Issue number is required only for journals that paginate each issue separately.

■ An Article in a Scholarly Journal

> Benson, P., Karlof, K. L., & Siperstein, G. N. (2008). Maternal involvement in the education of young children with autism spectrum disorders. *Autism: The International Journal of Research & Practice, 12*(1), 47–63.

Note: Pay attention to the features of this basic reference to a scholarly journal:

1. Provide the authors' last names and initials, as for a book reference.
2. Place the year of publication in parentheses, followed by a period.
3. Format the article's title in lowercase, except for the first word of the main title and of a subtitle and except for proper nouns, acronyms, or initialisms; do not italicize the article title or place it in quotation marks.
4. Capitalize the first and all main words in the journal title; italicize it.
5. Italicize the volume number but not the issue number; place the issue in parentheses, without a space after the volume number. No issue number is needed if the journal is paginated consecutively throughout a volume.
6. Provide inclusive page numbers, without "pp." or "pages."

■ An Abstract of a Scholarly Article (from a Secondary Source)

When referencing an abstract published separately from an article, provide publication details of the article followed by information about where the abstract was published.

> Shlipak, M. G., Simon, J. A., Grady, O., Lin, F., Wenger, N. K., & Furberg, C. D. (2001, September). Renal insufficiency and cardiovascular events in postmenopausal women with coronary heart disease. *Journal of the American College of Cardiology, 38,* 705–711. Abstract obtained from *Geriatrics, 2001, 56*(12), Abstract No. 5645351.

■ A Journal Article, More Than Seven Authors

> Yamada, A., Suzuki, M., Kato, M., Suzuki, M., Tanaka, S., Shindo, T., Taketani, K., et
> al. (2007). Emotional distress and its correlates among parents of children
> with persuasive developmental disorders. *Psychiatry & Clinical Neurosciences,*
> *61*(6), 651–657.

Note: In the text, abbreviate the parenthetical citation: (Yamada et al., 2007).

■ A Review

To reference a book review or a review of another medium (film, exhibit, and so on), indicate the review and the medium in brackets, along with the title of the work being reviewed by the author listed.

> Hutcheon, L., & Hutcheon, M. (2008). Turning into the mind. [Review of the book
> *Musicophilia: Tales of music and the brain,* by O. Sacks]. *Canadian Medical*
> *Association Journal, 178*(4), 441.

■ A Magazine Article

> Weintraub, B. (2007, October). Unusual suspects. *Psychology Today, 40*(5), 80–87.

Note: If the article is unsigned, begin the entry with the title of the article.

> Tomatoes target toughest cancer. (2002, February). *Prevention, 54*(2), 53.

■ A Newspaper Article

For newspaper articles, include the full publication date, year first followed by a comma, the month (spelled out) and the day. Identify the article's location in the newspaper using page numbers and section letters, as appropriate. If the article is a letter to the editor, identify it as such in brackets following the title. For newspapers, use *p.* or *pp.* before the page numbers; if the article is not on continuous pages, give all the page numbers, separated by commas.

> Schmitt, E., & Shanker, T. (2008, March 18). U.S. adapts cold-war idea to fight
> terrorists. *The New York Times,* pp. 1A, 14A–15A.

> Benderoff, E. (2008, March 14). Facebook sites face scrutiny for March Madness
> pools. *Chicago Tribune,* pp. 2C–3C.

■ A Newsletter Article

Newsletter article entries are similar to newspaper article entries; only a volume number is added.

> Teaching mainstreamed special education students. (2002, February). *The Council*
> *Chronicle,* pp. 11, 6–8.

Reference Entries: Online Sources

When it comes to references for online sources, follow these guidelines:

1. Whenever possible, use the final version of an electronic resource. Typically, this is called the archival copy or the version of record, as opposed to a prepublished version. Right now, that final version is likely the same as the printed version of an article, though there is some movement toward the online publication being the final version (complete with additional data, graphics, and so on).

2. In the reference entry for an electronic source, start with the same elements in the same order for print or other fixed-media resources (author, title, and so on). Then add the most reliable electronic retrieval information that will (a) clarify what version of the source you used and (b) help your reader find the source him- or herself. Determine what you need to include based on these guidelines:

   - Whenever possible, use the electronic document's Digital Object Identifier (DOI). More and more, electronic publishers are using this registration code for the content of journal articles and other documents so that the document can be located on the Internet, even if the URL changes. The DOI will usually be published at the beginning of the article or be available in the article's citation.

     > Author, A. A. (year). Title of article. *Title of Periodical, volume number*(issue number), pages. doi: code

   - If a DOI is not available for the electronic document, give the URL (without a period at the end). Generally, a database name is no longer needed, except for hard-to-find documents and those accessed through subscription-only databases. Use the home- or menu-page URL for subscription-only databases and online reference works.

     > Author, A. A. (year). Title of article. *Title of Periodical, volume number*(issue number), pages. Retrieved from URL

   - If the content of the document is stable (e.g., archival copy or copy of record with DOI), do not include a retrieval date in your reference entry. However, if the content is likely to change or be updated, as is the case with a lot of the material on the free web, then offer a retrieval date. This would be the case with open-web material with no fixed publication date, edition, or version, or material that is prepublished (in preparation, in press).

     > Author, A. A. (year). *Title of document.* Retrieved date from website: URL

■ A Journal Article with DOI

> Oberg, A., Blades, D., & Thom, J. S. (2007). Untying a dreamcatcher: Coming to
> understand possibilities for teaching students of aboriginal inheritance.
> *Educational Studies, 42*(2), 111–139. doi: 10.1080/00131940701513185

Note: Because the DOI references the final version of the article, the retrieval date, URL, and database name are not needed. If the online article is a preprint version, add "Advance online publication" and your retrieval date before the DOI.

■ A Journal Article Without DOI

> Bell, J. B., & Nye, E. C. (2007). Specific symptoms predict suicidal ideation in
> Vietnam combat veterans with Post-Traumatic Stress Disorder. *Military*
> *Medicine, 172*(11), 1144–1147. Retrieved from http://www.ebscohost.com

Note: Because this article has no DOI, the URL is provided for the subscription database search service. If you retrieved the article from the open web, you would supply the exact URL. If the version of the article you access is in press and you have retrieved it from the author's personal or institutional website, place "in press" in parentheses after the author's name and add a retrieval date before the URL.

■ A Newspaper Article

> Sengupta, S. (2008, March 18). Dalai Lama says he'll resign if violence escalates.
> *The New York Times.* Retrieved from http://www.nytimes.com

■ An Article in an Online Magazine (Ezine) not Published in Print

> Pike, D. L. (2008, February). A boy and his dog: On Will Smith, apocalypse, and
> *I Am Legend* [Online exclusive]. *Bright Lights Film Journal.* Retrieved April 17,
> 2008, from http://www.brightlightsfilm.com/59/59legend.html

■ A Book Review

> Shapiro, K. (2007). Mystic chords. [Review of the book *Musicophilia: Tales of music*
> *and the brain,* by O. Sacks]]. *Commentary, 124*(5), 73–77. Retrieved from http:
> //web.ebscohost.com

■ An Electronic Book

> Kafka, F. (2002). *Metamorphosis.* D. Wylie (Trans.). Available from http:
> //www.gutenberg.org/etext/5200

Note: If the URL goes directly to the ebook, use "Retrieved from."

■ Material from an Online Reference Work

> Agonism. (2008). In *Encyclopaedia Britannica*. Retrieved from http://search.eb.com

Note: See pages 466–467 for advice on using Wikipedia.

■ Online Course Material

> Roderiguez, N. *Unit 3, Lecture 3: Sociological Theories of Deviance*. Retrieved from
> University of Houston Website: http://www.uh.edu/~nestor/lecturenotes
> /unit3lecture3.html

■ A Workplace Document or Other "Gray Literature."

"Gray Literature" refers to informative documents (e.g., brochures, fact sheets, white papers) produced by government agencies, corporations, and nonprofit groups. If possible, give a document number or identify the type of document in brackets.

> Foehr, U. G. (2006). *Media multitasking among American youth: Prevelance,*
> *predictors and pairings* (Publication No. 7592). Retrieved from the Kaiser Family
> Foundation: http://www.kff.org/entmedia/upload/7592.pdf

■ Undated Content on Website

> National Institute of Allergy and Infectious Diseases. (n.d.). *Antimicrobial (Drug)*
> *Resistance*. Retrieved June 19, 2008, from http://www3
> .niaid.nih.gov/topics/AntimicrobialResistance/default.htm

■ A Podcast

> Byrd, D., & Block, J. (Producers). (2008, February 5). Antonio Rangel: This is your
> brain on wine. *Earth & Sky: A Clear Voice for Science* [Audio podcast]. Retrieved
> from http://www.earthsky.org/clear-voices/52199

■ Message on a Newsgroup, an Online Forum, or a Discussion Group

> Avnish, J. (2008, March 18). Sex education especially vital to teens nowadays.
> [Online Forum post]. Retrieved from http://groups.google.ca/group/AIDS
> -Beyond-Borders/topics?hl=en

■ A Blog Post

> Koyzis, D. (2007, June 27). Conservative environmentalists. [Web log post].
> Retrieved from http://byzantinecalvinist.blogspot.com/2007_06_01_archive
> .html

Note about URLs: When necessary, break a URL before a slash or other punctuation mark. Do not underline or italicize the URL, place it in angle brackets, or end it with a period.

Reference Entries: Other Sources (Primary, Personal, and Multimedia)

Cite audiovisual media sources and electronic sources as follows.

Specialized Computer Software with Limited Distribution

Standard nonspecialized computer software does not require a reference entry. Treat software as an unauthored work unless an individual has property rights to it.

> Carreau, S. (2001). Champfoot (Version 3.3) [Computer software]. Saint Mandé, France: Author.

Show the software version in parentheses after the title and the medium in brackets.

A Television or Radio Broadcast

Indicate the episode by writers, if possible. Then follow with the airing date, the episode title, and the type of series in brackets. Add the producer(s) as you would the editors(s) of a print medium, and complete the entry with details about the series itself.

> Berger, C. (Writer). (2001, December 19). Feederwatch [Radio series program]. In D. Byrd & J. Block (Producers), Earth & Sky. Austin, TX: The Production Block.

An Audio Recording

Begin the entry with the speaker's or writer's name, not the producer. Indicate the type of recording in brackets.

> Kim, E. (Author, speaker). (2000). *Ten thousand sorrows* [CD]. New York, NY: Random House.

A Music Recording

Give the name and function of the originators or primary contributors. Indicate the recording medium in brackets immediately following the title.

> ARS Femina Ensemble. (Performers). (1998). *Musica de la puebla de Los Angeles: Music by women of baroque Mexico, Cuba, & Europe* [CD]. Louisville, KY: Nannerl Recordings.

A Motion Picture

Give the name and function of the director, producer, or both.

> Cohn, J., & Cohn, E. (Directors). (2007). *No country for old men* [Motion picture]. United States: Miramax Films.

■ A Published Interview, Titled, No Author

Start the entry with the interview's title, followed by publication details.

> Stephen Harper: The Report interview. (2002, January 7). *The Report* (Alberta, BC),
>   *29*, 10–11.

■ A Published Interview, Titled, Single Author

Start the entry with the interviewee's name, followed by the date and the title. Place the interviewer's name in brackets before other publication details.

> Fussman, C. (2002, January). What I've learned. [Interview by Robert McNamara.]
>   *Esquire, 137*, 85.

■ An Unpublished Paper Presented at a Meeting

Indicate when the paper was presented, at what meeting, in what location.

> Lycan, W. (2002, June). *The plurality of consciousness.* Paper presented at the
>   meeting of the Society for Philosophy and Psychology, New York, NY.

■ An Unpublished Doctoral Dissertation

Place the dissertation's title in italics, even though the work is unpublished. Indicate the school at which the writer completed the dissertation.

> Roberts, W. (2001). *Crime amidst suburban wealth* (Unpublished doctoral
>   dissertation). Bowling Green State University, Bowling Green, OH.

■ Sample APA Paper

Student writer Renee Danielle Singh wrote the following research paper on the mystery of the lost colonists of Roanoke Island. In the paper, written for an anthropology class, she explores a range of historical, genetic, and linguistic evidence to resolve this mystery and to explain its continuing relevance. For more on Roanoke's lost colony and the Lumbee People of North Carolina, go to www.thecollegewriter.com/4e. You can use Renee's paper in three ways:

1. To study how a well-written research paper uses a range of resources to build a discussion or line of reasoning that answers a research question.

2. To examine how sources are used and integrated into social-sciences research writing—a full-length discussion of the strategies addressed on pages 484–487.

3. To see in detail the format and documentation practices of APA style.

Note: Often, a social-sciences research paper takes the form of an experiment report. For an example of such a report, go to **www.thecollegewriter.com/4e.**

Note that APA format requires that the paper be double-spaced throughout, with a one-inch margin on all sides. That formatting is shown on the book's website **www.thecollegewriter. com/4e.**

Sample Title Page

Put five spaces between the header and number.	Running head: OUR ROOTS GO BACK TO ROANOKE 1
Type running head (abbreviated title in uppercase letters) flush left.	
Full title, author(s), and school name are centered on the page, typed in uppercase and lowercase.	Our Roots Go Back to Roanoke: Investigating the Link between the Lost Colony and the Lumbee People of North Carolina Renee Danielle Singh University of California Davis

Sample Abstract

OUR ROOTS GO BACK TO ROANOKE   2

Abstract

The abstract summarizes the paper's central issue, its main conclusion, the key reasoning and evidence presented, and the study's significance.

While remaining something of a mystery, the disappearance in the late sixteenth century of a group of colonists from Roanoke Island off North Carolina is likely related to the mystery of the ancestry of the North Carolina's Native American Lumbee tribe. Using evidence from the parallel example of the Catawba Indians, as well as evidence related to baldcypress tree rings, historical analysis, immunology, genetic studies, and linguistic patterns, one can tentatively conclude that the lost colonists were perhaps captured by, intermarried with, and were absorbed by the sixteenth-century ancestors of the Lumbee. This conclusion points to the need for further study, as the Lumbee People's status as Native American is currently contested and needs to be resolved for them to be recognized by the federal government.

APA Research Paper: The Body ■ ▪ ▪

As you review the body of this paper, read the side notes and examine how the writer uses and documents her sources.

> **A running head and page number top each page.**

Our Roots Go Back to Roanoke:
Investigating the Link between the Lost Colony
and the Lumbee People of North Carolina

> **The title is centered one inch from the top, and the paper is double-spaced.**

Introduction: Something Is Terribly Wrong

Consider the following narrative, which features historical information from Kupperman (1984, 1985), Miller (2002), Oberg (1994), and Quinn (1985):

1

> **After referencing multiple sources, the writer provides a narrative to put the main point in context.**

Imagine yourself sailing across the warm waters of the Atlantic. It is a time before airplanes and automobiles, and our nation, which someday will lie just a few miles ahead of you, is still called the "New World." You are on your way to an island off the coast of what will one day be called North Carolina, and you are anxious to see what a small group of colonists has accomplished since their arrival there three years ago. Yes, this is the age of colonization. This is the beginning of a nation.

2

As you draw closer to land, however, you get a strange feeling that something is terribly wrong. No fires are burning on the island, no greeters waving. Instead, an eerie silence fills the air. At once, you cast your anchor and row ashore, hoping that perhaps you've reached the wrong island by mistake. Surely, this is not the island destined to be the first true settlement in the New World? Surely, this is not Roanoke?

3

As you step ashore, your worst fears are confirmed. Pots and other artifacts lay unused on the ground and the shelters show signs of neglect. Footprints and other marks are scattered about as well, but their makers are nowhere in sight. The colonists of Roanoke have vanished.

4

> **The introduction focuses on the research question, suggests an answer, and forecasts a method for finding the answer.**

For over four hundred years, the fate of the lost colonists of Roanoke has remained a mystery. While there are many theories to date concerning what became of them, the most prevalent and well-supported theory argues that the colonists were assimilated into the indigenous tribes of North Carolina (Kupperman, 1984, 1985; Miller, 2002; Oberg, 1994; Quinn, 1985). If that is true, then the lost colonists of Roanoke

5

OUR ROOTS GO BACK TO ROANOKE   4

may be "found" in their suspected descendants: the Lumbee People of North Carolina. By examining the historical, genetic, and linguistic evidence concerning the origins of the Lumbee, we might yet shed light on one of history's greatest mysteries.

Who Are the Lumbee People?

A single tribe of over 50,000 individuals constitutes the Lumbee People, who currently live in Robeson County, North Carolina (Blu, 1980; Bryant & LaFromboise, 2005; Tobert, 2001). Historical records indicate that the Lumbee have been living near Robeson County's Lumber River since the early 1700s, taking their tribal name from this body of water (Blu, 1980; Bryant & LaFromboise, 2005; Tobert, 2001).

Many studies of the Lumbee characterize them as an eclectic tribe because their culture and biology have been highly influenced by non-native groups with whom the tribe has admixed (Blu, 1980; Bryant & LaFromboise, 2005; Tobert, 2001). For example, unlike most traditional tribes, the Lumbee are followers of the Southern Baptist faith. They also speak a dialect often referred to as a "variety of English," and many do not know their tribe's native language, which is Siouan in origin (Blu, 1980; Bryant & LaFromboise, 2005, Tobert, 2001). Additionally, many of the Lumbee exhibit physical characteristics such as blond hair and blue eyes (Blu, 1980; Bryant & LaFromboise, 2005).

How could this admixture have happened? Traditionally, most Native American groups have not been known to admix with outside parties. Indeed, the federal government discourages it by denying benefits to those who practice admixture (Blu, 1980; Bryant & LaFromboise, 2005). However, the Lumbee People are not alone in this respect. Other Native American tribes have also mixed with outsiders.

Admixture and Native American Groups:
The Catawba Indian Example

The Catawba Indians were a group of Native Americans living just outside Rock Hill, South Carolina. As Pollitzer et al. explain (1967), in 1962 the Catawba opted to terminate their reservation status, thus relinquishing all forms of federal recognition. Apparently, reservation life no longer met the needs of their newly acquired Mormon lifestyle. Around the same time, the Catawba allowed outside parties to study their blood types. Over 100 Catawba were typed for the ABO blood

---

The first section offers essential background for the mystery.

In-text citations list the multiple sources for the background information. Dates are featured.

The writer introduces a key concept (admixture) and then explores its relevance.

An attributive phrase for a source is followed by the publication year in parentheses. "Et al." indicates several authors.

6

7

8

9

groups. Physical features such as stature, cephalic index, facial index, and nasal index were also measured, and the data were studied in an attempt to better understand their current genetic composition. In other words, Pollitzer et al. conducted a study to see whether modern-day Catawba Indians were biologically more "white" or "Native American."   *10*

Despite centuries of admixing, a modern Catawba Indian was found to be, on average, 50% white and 50% Native American in genetic composition (Pollitzer et al., 1967). The results of the study surprised many who expected the percentage of white genetic attributes to be much higher (Pollitzer et al., 1967). Like the Lumbee, the Catawba were a nontraditional tribe. They practiced a non-native religion (Mormonism),   *7* abandoned their original Siouan dialect, and exhibited physical features that made some of them indistinguishable from Caucasians. Yet genetic data indicated they were still 50% Native American (Pollitzer et al., 1967).

The example of the Catawba Indians highlights the dangers of   *11* rushing to conclusions about a group's origins and biology based solely on their culture or physical features. The origins and biology of the Lumbee People cannot be studied, therefore, by merely observing modern-day members and associating them with whatever group they most closely resemble culturally and physically. To understand who the Lumbee People are today and from whom they came, we must go back to the beginning. We must go back to Roanoke.

A Mystery in History: The Story of the Lost Colony of Roanoke

Toward the end of the sixteenth century, Europeans had begun to   *12* set up the first permanent settlements in the New World (Kupperman, 1984, 1985; Miller, 2002; Oberg, 1994; Quinn, 1985). One participant was none other than Sir Walter Raleigh, the explorer after whom the capital of North Carolina is named. Raleigh had high hopes for the New World and, in June 1578, he was granted a patent by Queen Elizabeth I to explore and colonize North America. The patent would expire ten years after its issuance; thus, Raleigh had to move quickly. For the next nine years, Raleigh sent ships to and from the New World in search of a good spot to found the first settlement (Kupperman, 1984, 1985; Miller, 2002; Oberg, 1994; Quinn, 1985).

As Kupperman (1984, 1985), Miller (2002), Oberg (1994), and   *13* Quinn (1985) go on to explain, one particular expedition, launched

The writer offers conclusions about the genetic evidence, relating her illustration to her specific topic.

With the last sentence and the new heading, the writer makes a transition to the second part of the mystery.

OUR ROOTS GO BACK TO ROANOKE   6

Referencing multiple sources in attributive phrases and parenthetical citations, the writer provides extensive background on the Roanoke mystery.

in 1584, located a small island off the coast of North Carolina by mistake, after its ship struck a shoal in the sea. The island was later called Roanoke Island. As a result of damage to their ship, the crew of about 100 men was forced to remain on the island, and a fort and other structures were erected as shelters. When a relief ship arrived to rescue the crew, 15 men stayed behind to protect Raleigh's claim to the New World.

In 1587, with time running short, it was hastily agreed that the new settlement would be founded at Chesapeake Bay, Virginia (Kupperman, 1984, 1985; Miller, 2002; Oberg, 1994; Quinn, 1985). In July of that same year, a group of 117 men, women, and children embarked for the New World led by the Portuguese navigator Simon Fernandes. In addition to colonizing Chesapeake Bay, the colonists were given instructions to stop by Roanoke Island and retrieve the 15 volunteers from the previous expedition.   *14*

When the party arrived, however, on July 22, 1587, they found that all 15 men had vanished. It was later determined that the volunteer party had sailed back to England after losing six members during an Indian attack. Despite this discouraging news, the colonists persisted with their plan to found the first new settlement. Unfortunately, for reasons still not clearly understood, Fernandes was unable to deliver the colonists to Chesapeake Bay, and word reached England that the first settlement had been founded on Roanoke Island instead (Kupperman, 1984, 1985; Miller, 2002; Oberg, 1994; Quinn, 1985).   *15*

During August 1587, the colony's governor, John White, was forced to return to England to obtain more supplies. As Kupperman, Miller, Oberg, and Quinn explain, the trip was supposed to take no more than three months, but the arrival of the Spanish Armada prevented White from obtaining a ship for the journey back to Roanoke for three more years. In 1590, when White finally did return, he experienced a horrible fright: All 115 of the original colonists had vanished. Roanoke Island held nothing more than several unused pots and a few scattered footprints.   *16*

A series of questions links the two mysteries of the Lumbee and the Roanoke colonists.

Why would the colonists leave Roanoke? Why risk crossing paths with mainland natives, given what happened to the 15 volunteers who had fled before? And most importantly for our purposes, is there any evidence that they made contact with the indigenous groups of North Carolina?   *17*

Why Leave Roanoke?

Using a heading in the form of a question, the writer explores evidence explaining one part of the mystery.

Recently, scientists from the University of Arkansas and the College of William and Mary discovered several individuals currently living in North Carolina whose roots go back to Roanoke (Stahle et al., 1998). According to Stahle et al., these individuals have been living in the region since the colonists first landed in 1587, and therefore might well be the only living "witnesses" to what occurred (1998).   18

Who are these "witnesses"? The ancient baldcypress trees (*Taxodium distichum*) of North Carolina.   19

As Stahle et al. explain, most trees generate a single ring within their trunks each time a year passes. By counting the rings in a cross section of a tree's trunk, one can determine the age of the tree (1998). Doing so, Stahle et al. confirmed that the baldcypresses were present during the time of Roanoke. Yet tree rings can also provide information on environmental conditions. For example, adequate water available throughout the year results in a wider ring, whereas during a drought the annual ring will be significantly narrower (Stahle et al., 1998). Tree ring data collected from the baldcypress trees of North Carolina suggests that the period between 1587 and 1589 was one of the driest in the area in 800 years (Stahle et al., 1998). Such a severe drought probably led to poor health and poor crop quality on Roanoke Island, thus forcing the colonists to move to the mainland in search of food (Stahle et al., 1998). Yet the question remains: Do we have any evidence of early contact between colonists and Native Americans?   20

Crossing Paths: Early Evidence of Contact Between the Lost Colonists of Roanoke and Indigenous Peoples

The writer adds to her overall argument by exploring another form of evidence related to illness and its effects.

As it turns out, historical records indicate that the lost colonists of Roanoke may have been harboring a dangerous virus: influenza. Mainly affecting the lungs, the influenza virus can easily be spread by simply coming in contact with infected individuals (Mires, 1994). Historians and biologists agree that the New World was free of the virus until the arrival of Europeans during the late sixteenth century (Mires, 1994). In fact, recent documents found by archaeologists from the University of Minnesota indicate that an outbreak of influenza occurred on the mainland of North Carolina at about the same time we speculate the   21 colonists left Roanoke Island (Mires, 1994). If the influenza virus was not present in the New World before the arrival of Europeans, and the only Europeans present in the area during the outbreak were those who arrived with the Roanoke expedition, then it is highly probable that the lost colonists of Roanoke made contact with the indigenous groups of North Carolina and served as vectors for influenza (Mires, 1994).

That being said, we must now turn to a different question, one that has remained unanswered for over four hundred years: What happened to those lost colonists?

22

Tracing Tribes:
A Theory of What Happened to the Lost Colonists

As Kupperman (1984, 1985), Miller (2002), Oberg (1994), and Quinn (1985) all relate, centuries ago a group of natives known as the Eno inhabited North Carolina's wilderness. Archaeological evidence indicates that the Eno were a copper-mining people whose culture centered on this metal. For example, numerous copper ornaments have been found at Eno sites dating back to the sixteenth century, ornaments probably used to decorate Eno houses. As a Siouan-speaking tribe, the Eno were allied with the Occaneechi and other less well-defined Siouan groups dispersed throughout North Carolina. Historical records also suggest that the Eno participated in a slave trading market open to their fellow Siouan allies.

23

Yet historians believe the Eno's copper-based lifestyle was threatened after they lost several tribe members to an influenza epidemic in the late sixteenth century (Kupperman, 1984, 1985; Miller, 2002; Oberg, 1994; Quinn, 1985). Copper mining is not easy, requiring strong individuals to extract the metal sheets from rock formations. Kupperman, Oberg, Miller, and Quinn hypothesize that the Eno captured all 115 of the lost colonists, keeping the men to work the copper mines and selling the women and children to other Siouan-speaking groups involved in the slave market. Indeed, these other Siouan tribes would have been eager to obtain the lost women and children from Roanoke because their numbers would also have been reduced by the recent influenza epidemic. Eventually, the Roanoke women and children would have been assimilated into these other Siouan-speaking tribes (Kupperman, 1984, 1985; Miller, 2002; Oberg, 1994; Quinn, 1985).

24

Building on the discussion of illness in the previous section, the writer explores evidence for the impact of European-borne illness on indigenous people.

All of this begs the question as to whether the Lumbee Pople are *25* descendants of the lost colonists of Roanoke. Answering that question requires that we look not only at the historical evidence but also at the genetic and linguistic evidence.

Are the Lumbee People Descendants of the Lost Colonists of Roanoke?

Historical Clues

Unfortunately, seventeenth-century tribal records for the Eno, the *26* Occaneechi, and the other Siouan-speaking groups of North Carolina are scarce, so these groups cannot be traced directly to the Lumbee People (Kupperman, 1984, 1985; Miller, 2002; Oberg, 1994; Quinn, 1985). However, a document dated 1725 does identify four Siouan-speaking groups living near a river called the "Drowning River" in North Carolina (Blu, 1980). Today, the "Drowning River" is known as the "Lumber River," and tribal records for the Lumbee, which begin in the 1700s, show that the four Siouan-speaking groups are, in fact, the earliest documented ancestors of the Lumbee People (Blu, 1980).

Genetic Clues

During the late 1970s, the Lumbee People were typed for the human *27* leukocyte antigen (HLA) system in an attempt by Grier, Ruderman, and Johnson (1979) to create an HLA profile for the tribe. The HLA system is a group of genes that codes for antigens on the surfaces of cells and is part of a complex known as the human major histocompatibility complex (MHC). Scientists use the prefix "HLA" followed by a letter and a number to identify the allele and HLA locus that is being studied (Grier et al., 1979).

Researchers note that most Native American groups have a high *28* frequency of HLA-B40 (Grier et al., 1979). However, Grier et al. (1979) found that the Lumbee People have an unusually low frequency of HLA-B40. This fact, along with other inconsistencies in the Lumbee HLA profile, indicate that admixture, specifically with European groups, has affected the current genetic composition of the Lumbee (Grier et al., 1979).

Linguistic Clues

Although they originated in part from a Siouan-speaking tribe, *29* modern Lumbee People speak a modified form of English (Torbert, 2001). A linguistic study conducted by Benjamin Torbert from Duke

Using a new heading and a series of subheadings, the writer explores multiple forms of evidence to test her hypothesis.

The writer effectively draws on multiple sources for various types of evidence and reasoning.

OUR ROOTS GO BACK TO ROANOKE   10

University included a consonant cluster analysis of Lumbee speech. A
consonant cluster is a group of consonants not separated by a vowel. For
example, in the word "spring," the "spr-" group would be classified as a
consonant cluster (Tobert, 2001).

Torbert compared the Lumbee dialect with that of other Native   30
American groups in the region and found that, unlike most Native
American tribes in North Carolina, the Lumbee speak a dialect that is
saturated with consonant clusters. Thus, ancestors of the Lumbee People
seem to have adopted consonant clusters after mixing with the lost
colonists of Roanoke—whose own language, like that of most Europeans,
included the frequent use of consonant clusters (Torbert, 2001).

Lumbee Origins and the Study of Human Variation: Ethnicity versus Biological Origins

Unfortunately, we may never know for certain what became of the   31
lost colonists of Roanoke. However, we do know that some evidence
suggests that the Lumbee People of North Carolina may be their
modern-day descendants. As a result, the Lumbee People currently face
a dilemma regarding the issue of racial classification (Blu, 1980; Bryant
& LaFromboise, 2005). Unlike most native peoples in the United States,
the Lumbee People have never been placed on a reservation, and thus
have never been federally recognized as a Native American Group (Blu,
1980; Bryant & LaFromboise, 2005). They do not receive the same federal
benefits as other indigenous groups in the country, a fact reflected in
their poor health and living standards (Beltrane & McQueen, 1979;
Bryant et al., 2004; Humphrey & Kupper, 1982). Simply put, they are
a people with a confused identity (Blu, 1980; Bryant & LaFromboise,
2005). The Lumbee believe that they are Native Americans and would
like to be considered as such, but the federal government has denied
their requests for federal recognition (Blu, 1980; Bryant & LaFromboise,
2005). Stating that the Lumbee have "too open an enrollment policy," the
federal government cites centuries of admixture that have significantly
compromised the Lumbee identity as a tribe (Blu, 1980; Bryant &
LaFromboise, 2005).

Is the federal government correct to assert that the Lumbee are no   32
longer "Native Americans"? Recall that the Catawba Indians of South
Carolina were similar to the Lumbee People in that they, too, frequently
admixed throughout their history and did not look or act very Native

In the final section, the writer explores the relevance of the mystery the paper focuses on: the fate of the people involved.

OUR ROOTS GO BACK TO ROANOKE   11

American anymore (Blu, 1980; Bryant & LaFromboise, 2005). Unlike the Lumbee, however, the Catawba Indians were granted federal recognition even before they proved, genetically, that they were still 50% Native American (Pollitzer et al., 1967). Just how "Native American" does one have to be?

Conclusion: Something Is Still Terribly Wrong

In the conclusion, the writer argues for additional research that will resolve the mystery and bring about justice.

Steps should be taken to answer the question concerning the origins   *33* of the Lumbee once and for all. The HLA profile study, conducted during the late 1970s by Grier et al., for example, is the only genetic study of the Lumbee to date. Modern mitochondrial DNA and possibly Y-chromosome DNA studies should be completed to further clarify the biological identity of the Lumbee tribe. At the same time, steps must be taken to protect the Lumbee People's ethnic identity. Recent cultural studies point out the high occurrence of alcoholism and suicide among the Lumbee as a result of their continuing identity crisis (Beltrane & McQueen, 1979; Bryant et al., 2004; Humphrey & Kupper, 1982). Just as John White found upon his belated return to the deserted colony over four hundred years ago, something is terribly wrong. We must ensure that the Lumbee People do not share the fate of the colonists who disappeared from that infamous island off the coast of North Carolina, the island of Roanoke.

Reading for Better Writing

Working by yourself or with a group, answer these questions.

1. Singh's paper focuses on a historical mystery with current relevance. What strategies make her readers care about the mystery?

2. What types of evidence does Singh use in her paper? Where has she gotten her evidence? Are her resources reliable?

3. How does Singh document her research? How does she distinguish her own thinking from source material? Why are these strategies necessary?

4. Follow-up: More information on the Roanoke mystery and the Lumbee People is available at this book's website, **www.thecollegewriter.com/4e**. After reviewing the resources at the site, offer your own response to the mystery: What do you conclude about what happened and how these developments should impact the current situation in North Carolina?

OUR ROOTS GO BACK TO ROANOKE   12

References

All works referred to in the paper appear on the references page, listed alphabetically by author (or title).

Beltrane, T., & McQueen, D. V. (1979). Urban and rural Indian drinking patterns: The special case of the Lumbee. *International Journal of the Addictions, 14*(4), 533-548.

Blu, K. I. (1980). *The Lumbee problem: The making of an American Indian people.* Cambridge, England: Cambridge University Press.

Bryant, A., Goins, R. T., Bell, R., Herrell, R., Manson, S. M., & Buchwald, D. (2004). Health differences among Lumbee Indians using public and private sources of care. *Journal of Rural Health, 20*(3), 231-236.

Bryant, A., & LaFromboise, T. D. (2005). The racial identity and cultural orientation of Lumbee American Indian high school students. *Cultural Diversity & Ethnic Minority Psychology, 11*(1), 82-89.

Each entry follows APA guidelines for listing authors, dates, titles, and publishing information.

Grier, J. O., Ruderman, R. J., & Johnson, A. H. (1979). HLA profile in the Lumbee Indians of North Carolina. *Transplant Proceedings, 11*(4), 1767-1769.

Humphrey, J. A., & Kupper, H. J. (1982). Homicide and suicide among the Cherokee and Lumbee Indians of North Carolina. *International Journal of Social Psychiatry, 28*(2), 121-128. doi: 10.1177/002076408202800210

Kupperman, K. O. (1984). *Roanoke, the abandoned colony.* Totowa, NJ: Rowman & Allanheld.

Kupperman, K. O. (1985). Roanoke lost. *American Heritage, 36*(5), 81-96.

Capitalization, punctuation, and hanging indentation are consistent with APA format.

Miller, L. (2002). *Roanoke: Solving the mystery of the lost colony.* New York, NY: Penguin.

Mires, P. B. (1994). Contact and contagion: The Roanoke colony and influenza. *Historical Archaeology, 28*(3), 30-38.

Molnar, S. (2002). *Human variation: Races, types, and ethnic groups.* Englewood Cliffs, NJ: Prentice Hall.

Oberg, M. L. (1994). Indians and Englishmen at the first Roanoke colony: A note on Pemisapan's conspiracy, 1585-86. *American Indian Culture & Research Journal, 18*(2), 75-89.

Note: For the complete references list, go to **www.thecollegewriter.com/4e.**

Critical-Thinking and Writing Activities

1. To make sense of APA format rules, answer these questions by yourself or with classmates: What is the essential logic of the APA system? How does this logic reflect research practices and values in the Social Sciences?

2. Create references list entries in correct APA style for the following sources:

   - An article in the October 2001 issue (vol. 29, no. 2) of *Learning & Leading with Technology* magazine by Bob Albrecht and Paul Davis titled "The Metric Backpack" (pages 29–31, 55)

   - The book *The Playful World: How Technology Is Transforming Our Imagination,* by Mark Pesce, published in 2000 by Ballantine Books, located in New York City

   - A webpage by Roger Fouts called "Frequently Asked Questions," part of the *Chimpanzee and Human Communication Institute* site, sponsored by Central Washington University; no publication date; site accessed May 8, 2011, at http://www.cwu.edu/~cwuchci/quanda.html.

Learning-Outcomes Checklist

When you are completing a paper in APA format, use the checklist below to ensure that you are following the format correctly.

_____ All borrowed material is acknowledged with an appropriate attributive phrase and/or in-text citation indicating author(s), publication date, and page number, as appropriate.

_____ All in-text citations effectively point readers to resources in the references list or to personal communication not listed.

_____ The references list includes entries for all works referred to in the body of the paper: No sources are missing from the list; no extra sources are listed that have no reference within the paper. Exception: Personal communications are identified with in-text citations but not in the references list.

_____ The entire references list is properly alphabetized by authors' last names (or by the first main word in the title for anonymous works).

_____ Each references entry (whether for an article, a book, an online document, or other source) contains the maximum amount of identifying and publication information, in the proper order, using the accepted abbreviations.

_____ The paper is properly formatted from the title page to any appendix.

IV. Handbook

33 Marking Punctuation

Period

After Sentences

Use a **period** to end a sentence that makes a statement, requests something, or gives a mild command.

Statement: By 2010, women made up 56 percent of undergraduate students and 59 percent of graduate students.

Request: Please read the instructions carefully.

Mild command: If your topic sentence isn't clear, rewrite it.

Indirect question: The professor asked if we had completed the test.

Note: It is not necessary to place a period after a statement that has parentheses around it and is part of another sentence.

Think about joining a club **(the student affairs office has a list of organizations)** for fun and for leadership experience.

After Initials and Abbreviations

Use a period after an initial and some abbreviations.

Mr.	Mrs.	B.C.E.	Ph.D.	Sen. Russ Feingold
Jr.	Sr.	D.D.S.	U.S.	Booker T. Washington
Dr.	M.A.	p.m.	B.A.	A. A. Milne

Some abbreviations (such as *pm*) also can be written without periods. Use no spacing in abbreviations except when providing a person's initials.

When an abbreviation is the last word in a sentence, use only one period at the end of the sentence.

Mikhail eyed each door until he found the name Rosa Lopez, **Ph.D.**

As Decimal Points

Use a period as a decimal point.

The government spends approximately **$15.5** million each year just to process student loan forms.

Audio
561.1

Exercise

561.2

561.3

Web Link

Ellipsis

562.1

To Show Omitted Words

Use an **ellipsis** (three periods) to show that one or more words have been omitted in a quotation. When typing, leave one space before and after each period.

> **(Original)** We the people of the United States, in order to form a more perfect Union, establish justice, insure domestic tranquility, provide for the common defense, promote the general welfare, and secure the blessings of liberty to ourselves and our posterity, do ordain and establish this Constitution for the United States of America.
>
> —Preamble, U.S. Constitution

> **(Quotation)** "We the people . . . in order to form a more perfect Union . . . establish this Constitution for the United States of America."

Note: Omit internal punctuation (a comma, a semicolon, a colon, or a dash) on either side of the ellipsis marks unless it is needed for clarity.

562.2

To Use After Sentences

If words from a quotation are omitted at the end of a sentence, place the ellipsis after the period or other end punctuation.

> **(Quotation)** "Five score years ago, a great American, in whose symbolic shadow we stand, signed the Emancipation Proclamation. . . . But one hundred years later, we must face the tragic fact that the Negro is still not free."
>
> —Martin Luther King, Jr., "I Have a Dream"

The first word of a sentence following a period and an ellipsis may be capitalized, even though it was not capitalized in the original.

> **(Quotation)** "Five score years ago, a great American . . . signed the Emancipation Proclamation. . . . One hundred years later, . . . the Negro is still not free."

Note: If the quoted material forms a complete sentence (even if it was not in the original), use a period, then an ellipsis.

> **(Original)** I am tired; my heart is sick and sad. From where the sun now stands I will fight no more forever.
>
> —Chief Joseph of the Nez Percé

> **(Quotation)** "I am tired. . . . I will fight no more forever."

562.3

To Show Pauses

Use an ellipsis to indicate a pause or to show unfinished thoughts.

> Listen . . . did you hear that?

> I can't figure out . . . this number doesn't . . . just how do I apply the equation in this case?

Exercise
563.1

Question Mark

After Direct Questions

Use a **question mark** at the end of a direct question.

> What can I know**?** What ought I to do**?** What may I hope**?**
>
> —Immanuel Kant

> Since when do you have to agree with people to defend them from injustice**?**
>
> —Lillian Hellman

563.2

Not After Indirect Questions

No question mark is used after an indirect question.

> After listening to Edgar sing, Mr. Noteworthy asked him if he had ever had formal voice training.

Note: When a single-word question like *how, when,* or *why* is woven into the flow of a sentence, capitalization and special punctuation are not usually required.

> The questions we need to address at our next board meeting are not *why* or *whether,* but *how* and *when.*

563.3

After Quotations That Are Questions

When a question ends with a quotation that is also a question, use only one question mark, and place it within the quotation marks. (Also see 577.4.)

> Do you often ask yourself, "What should I be**?**"

563.4

To Show Uncertainty

Use a question mark within parentheses to show uncertainty about a word or phrase within a sentence.

> This July will be the 34th **(?)** anniversary of the first moon walk.

Note: Do *not* use a question mark in this manner for formal writing.

563.5

For Questions in Parentheses or Dashes

A question within parentheses—or a question set off by dashes—is punctuated with a question mark unless the sentence ends with a question mark.

> You must consult your handbook **(what choice do you have?)** when you need to know a punctuation rule.

> Should I use your charge card (you have one, don't you), or should I pay cash?

> Maybe somewhere in the pasts of these humbled people, there were cases of bad mothering or absent fathering or emotional neglect—**what family surviving the '50s was exempt?**—but I couldn't believe these human errors brought the physical changes in Frank.
>
> —Mary Kay Blakely, *Wake Me When It's Over*

Punctuation Exercises:
Periods, Ellipses, Question Marks

A. End Punctuation

On your own paper, indicate the correct form of end punctuation for each sentence—a period or a question mark.

1. Have you heard of the Ring of Fire
2. It is a volcanically active area
3. The Ring of Fire circles the Pacific
4. How many people has it killed
5. Over 300,000 died from one tsunami
6. Where did the tsunami take place
7. The tsunami ravaged India
8. An earthquake rocked Chile
9. The Ring of Fire is restless
10. How can we predict its catastrophes

B. Ellipses

Copy each sentence, shortening it by removing the bold words and inserting an ellipsis.

1. "Now we are engaged in a great civil war, testing whether that nation, **or any nation so conceived and so dedicated,** can long endure."
2. "We have come to dedicate a portion of that field, as a final resting place for those who here gave their lives **that that nation might live.**"
3. "But, in a larger sense, we can not dedicate—**we can not consecrate—we can not hallow**—this ground."
4. "The brave men, **living and dead,** who struggled here, have consecrated it**, far above our poor power to add or detract.**"
5. "The world will little note, **nor long remember** what we say here, but it can never forget what they did here."

C. Punctuation Practice

Indicate where periods and question marks are needed in the following paragraph by writing the word and the mark after it, and by writing any initials or abbreviations correctly.

Music is the universal language At least that's what people say But have you ever noticed how hard it is to get people to agree on music Play a song by BB King, and some people will be in heaven and others in dread Why would that be Dr Jim Fredericks indicates that the reason may be music's power to reach to our very hearts "Music is intensely personal, and the type of music that makes one person excited and happy may make another person very uncomfortable" Jill Davis, PhD, disagrees She says music is primarily cultural What does music do except make us feel "at home" or feel like a stranger When music alienates us, we dislike it, but when it makes us feel welcome, we like it So, what music makes you feel at home

Exercise

565.1

Comma

Between Independent Clauses

Use a **comma** between independent clauses that are joined by a coordinating conjunction (*and, but, or, nor, for, yet, so*). (See 653.2.)

> Heath Ledger completed his brilliant portrayal as the Joker in *The Dark Knight,* **but** he died before the film was released.

> **Note:** Do not confuse a compound verb with a compound sentence.

> Ledger's Joker became instantly iconic and won him the Oscar for best supporting actor. (compound verb)

> His death resulted from the abuse of prescription drugs, but it was ruled an accident. (compound sentence)

Between Items in a Series

565.2

Use commas to separate individual words, phrases, or clauses in a series. (A series contains at least three items.)

> Many college students must balance studying with **taking care of a family, working a job, getting exercise, and finding time to relax.**

> **Note:** Do *not* use commas when all the items in a series are connected with *or, nor,* or *and.*

> Hmm , , , should I study **or** do laundry **or** go out?

To Separate Adjectives

565.3

Use commas to separate adjectives that *equally* modify the same noun. Notice in the examples below that no comma separates the last adjective from the noun.

> You should exercise regularly and follow a **sensible, healthful** diet.

> A good diet is one that includes lots of **high-protein, low-fat** foods.

Video

To Determine Equal Modifiers

To determine whether the adjectives in a sentence modify a noun *equally*, use these two tests.

1. Reverse the order of the adjectives; if the sentence is clear, the adjectives modify equally. (In the example below, *hot* and *crowded* can be reversed, and the sentence is still clear; *short* and *coffee* cannot.)

   > Matt was tired of working in the **hot, crowded** lab and decided to take a **short coffee** break.

2. Insert *and* between the adjectives; if the sentence reads well, use a comma when *and* is omitted. (The word *and* can be inserted between *hot* and *crowded*, but *and* does not make sense between *short* and *coffee*.)

566.1 ## To Set Off Nonrestrictive Appositives

A specific kind of explanatory word or phrase called an **appositive** identifies or renames a preceding noun or pronoun.

> Albert Einstein, **the famous mathematician and physicist,** developed the theory of relativity.

> **Note:** Do *not* use commas with *restrictive appositives.* A restrictive appositive is essential to the basic meaning of the sentence.

> The famous mathematician and physicist **Albert Einstein** developed the theory of relativity.

566.2 ## To Set Off Adverb Dependent Clauses

Use a comma after most introductory dependent clauses functioning as adverbs.

> **Although Charlemagne was a great patron of learning,** he never learned to write properly. (adverb dependent clause)

You may use a comma if the adverb dependent clause following the independent clause is not essential. Adverb clauses beginning with *even though, although, while,* or another conjunction expressing a contrast are usually not needed to complete the meaning of a sentence.

> Charlemagne never learned to write properly**, even though he continued to practice.**

> **Note:** A comma is *not* used if the dependent clause following the independent clause is needed to complete the meaning of the sentence.

> Maybe Charlemagne didn't learn **because he had an empire to run.**

566.3 ## After Introductory Phrases

Use a comma after introductory phrases.

> **In spite of his practicing,** Charlemagne's handwriting remained poor.

> **Note:** A comma is usually omitted if the phrase follows an independent clause.

> Charlemagne's handwriting remained poor **in spite of his practicing.**

> **Also Note:** You may omit the comma after a short (four or fewer words) introductory phrase unless it is needed to ensure clarity.

> **At 6:00 a.m.** he would rise and practice his penmanship.

566.4 ## To Set Off Transitional Expressions

Use a comma to set off conjunctive adverbs and transitional phrases. (See 571.2–571.3.)

> Handwriting is not**, as a matter of fact,** easy to improve upon later in life; **however,** it can be done if you are determined enough.

> **Note:** If a transitional expression blends smoothly with the rest of the sentence, it does not need to be set off. *Example:* If you are in fact coming, I'll see you there.

Video

A Closer Look
Nonrestrictive and Restrictive Clauses and Phrases

Use Commas with Nonrestrictive Clauses and Phrases

567.1

Exercise

Use commas to enclose **nonrestrictive** (unnecessary) phrases or dependent (adjective) clauses. A nonrestrictive phrase or dependent clause adds information that is not necessary to the basic meaning of the sentence. For example, if the clause or phrase (in **boldface**) were left out of the two examples below, the meaning of the sentences would remain clear. Therefore, commas are used to set off the nonrestrictive information.

> The locker rooms in Swain Hall**, which were painted and updated last summer,** give professors a place to shower. (nonrestrictive clause)

> Work-study programs**, offered on many campuses,** give students the opportunity to earn tuition money. (nonrestrictive phrase)

Don't Use Commas with Restrictive Clauses and Phrases

567.2

Do *not* use commas to set off **restrictive** (necessary) adjective clauses and phrases. A restrictive clause or phrase adds information that the reader needs to understand the sentence. For example, if the adjective clause and phrase (in **boldface**) were dropped from the examples below, the meaning would be unclear.

> Only the professors **who run at noon** use the locker rooms in Swain Hall to shower. (restrictive clause)

> Using tuition money **earned through work-study programs** is the only way some students can afford to go to college. (restrictive phrase)

Using "That" or "Which"

567.3

Video

Use *that* to introduce restrictive (necessary) adjective clauses; use *which* to introduce nonrestrictive (unnecessary) adjective clauses. When the two words are used in this way, the reader can quickly distinguish the necessary information from the unnecessary.

> Campus jobs **that are funded by the university** are awarded to students only. (restrictive)

> The cafeteria**, which is run by an independent contractor,** can hire nonstudents. (nonrestrictive)

Note: Clauses beginning with who can be either restrictive or nonrestrictive.

> Students **who pay for their own education** are highly motivated. (restrictive)

> The admissions counselor**, who has studied student records,** said that many returning students earn high GPAs in spite of demanding family obligations. (nonrestrictive)

568.1   To Set Off Items in Addresses and Dates

Use commas to set off items in an address and the year in a date.

> Send your letter to **1600 Pennsylvania Avenue, Washington, DC 20006, before January 1, 2009,** or send an e-mail to president@whitehouse.gov.

Note: No comma is placed between the state and ZIP code. Also, no comma separates the items if only the month and year are given: January 2009.

568.2   To Set Off Dialogue

Use commas to set off the words of the speaker from the rest of the sentence.

> **"Never be afraid to ask for help,"** advised Ms. Kane.

> **"With the evidence that we now have,"** Professor Thom said**, "many scientists believe there is life on Mars."**

568.3   To Separate Nouns of Direct Address

Use a comma to separate a noun of direct address from the rest of the sentence.

> **Jamie,** would you please stop whistling while I'm trying to work?

568.4   To Separate Interjections

Use a comma to separate a mild interjection from the rest of the sentence.

> **Okay,** so now what do I do?

Note: Exclamation points are used after strong interjections: Wow! You're kidding!

568.5   To Set Off Interruptions

Use commas to set off a word, phrase, or clause that interrupts the movement of a sentence. Such expressions usually can be identified through the following tests: (1) They may be omitted without changing the meaning of a sentence; and (2) they may be placed nearly anywhere in the sentence without changing its meaning.

> For me, **well,** it was just a good job gone!   —Langston Hughes, "A Good Job Gone"

> Lela**, as a general rule,** always comes to class ready for a pop quiz.

568.6   To Separate Numbers

Use commas to separate a series of numbers to distinguish hundreds, thousands, millions, and so on.

> Do you know how to write the amount **$2,025** on a check?

> **25,000   973,240   18,620,197**

To Enclose Explanatory Words

569.1

Use commas to enclose an explanatory word or phrase.

> Time management, **according to many professionals,** is such an important skill that it should be taught in college.

To Separate Contrasted Elements

569.2

Use commas to separate contrasted elements within a sentence.

> We work to become, **not to acquire.**
> —Eugene Delacroix

> Where all think alike, **no one thinks very much.**
> —Walter Lippmann

Before Tags

569.3

Use a comma before tags, which are short statements or questions at the ends of sentences.

> You studied for the test, **right?**

To Enclose Titles or Initials

569.4

Use commas to enclose a title or initials and given names that follow a surname.

> Until Martin, **Sr.,** was 15, he never had more than three months of schooling in any one year.
> —Ed Clayton, *Martin Luther King: The Peaceful Warrior*

> The genealogical files included the names Sanders, **L. H.,** and Sanders, **Lucy Hale.**

Note: Some style manuals no longer require commas around titles.

For Clarity or Emphasis

569.5

Use a comma for clarity or for emphasis. There will be times when none of the traditional rules call for a comma, but one will be needed to prevent misreading or to emphasize an important idea.

> What she does, does matter to us. (clarity)

> It may be those who do most, dream most. (emphasis)
> —Stephen Leacock

Avoid Overusing Commas

The commas (in **red**) below are used incorrectly. Do *not* use a comma between the subject and its verb or the verb and its object.

> Current periodicals on the subject of psychology, are available at nearly all bookstores.

> I think she should read, *Psychology Today.*

Do *not* use a comma before an indirect quotation.

> My roommate said, that she doesn't understand the notes I took.

Punctuation Exercises:

Commas

A. Basic Comma Use

On your own paper, indicate correct comma placement in each sentence by writing down the word preceding each comma. Some sentences have multiple commas.

1. To succeed in college you need focus dedication and hard work.
2. A compatible amiable roommate helps and you will want access to a computer.
3. To keep your sanity a balanced workable schedule is also a must.
4. You should consult with family friends and counselors about course schedules.
5. Between classes jobs and the social scene many students are stretched.
6. College prepares people for life and one way is by teaching them to juggle priorities.
7. Students also must afford books supplies and food.
8. A manageable realistic budget keeps money matters in order.
9. Students should work hard think deeply and enjoy their time in college.
10. With goals such as these students can get the most out of college.

B. Restrictive and Nonrestrictive Clauses and Phrases

For each sentence, indicate correct comma placement by writing down the word preceding each comma. If a sentence needs no commas, write "correct."

1. Author Lauren Beukes who lives in South Africa wrote *Moxyland*.
2. *Moxyland* a dystopian thriller focuses on a world overrun by governmental and corporate domination of technology.
3. Gareth L. Powell who is an author in his own right said the book "gives us a dystopia to rival 1984."
4. Another reviewer said *Moxyland* is a book that changed science fiction.
5. Lauren Beukes an avid user of social media released a *Moxyland* soundtrack and a plush doll which gave two-thirds of its proceeds to a women's charity.

C. Advanced Comma Use

For each sentence, indicate correct comma placement by writing down the word preceding each comma.

1. I live at 3415 West Kane Drive Chicago Illinois.
2. Jamar where do you live?
3. All right who turned out the lights?
4. If you think I turned them out well you're mistaken.
5. I sure would like to receive a check for $5000.

Semicolon

Exercise
571.1

To Join Two Independent Clauses

Use a **semicolon** to join two or more closely related independent clauses that are not connected with a coordinating conjunction. In other words, each of the clauses could stand alone as a separate sentence.

> I was thrown out of college for cheating on the metaphysics exam; I looked into the soul of the boy next to me.
>
> —Woody Allen

Before Conjunctive Adverbs

571.2

Use a semicolon before a conjunctive adverb when the word clarifies the relationship between two independent clauses in a compound sentence. A comma often follows the conjunctive adverb. Common conjunctive adverbs include *also, besides, however, instead, meanwhile, then,* and *therefore.*

> Many college freshmen are on their own for the first time; **however,** others are already independent and even have families.

Before Transitional Phrases

571.3

Use a semicolon before a transitional phrase when the phrase clarifies the relationship between two independent clauses in a compound sentence. A comma usually follows the transitional phrase.

> Pablo was born in the Andes; **as a result,** he loves mountains.

Transitional Phrases

after all	at the same time	in addition	in the first place
as a matter of fact	even so	in conclusion	on the contrary
as a result	for example	in fact	on the other hand
at any rate	for instance	in other words	

To Separate Independent Clauses Containing Commas

571.4

Use a semicolon to separate independent clauses that contain internal commas, even when the independent clauses are connected by a coordinating conjunction.

> Your MP3 player, computer, bike, and other valuables are expensive to replace; so include these items in your homeowner's insurance policy and remember to use the locks on your door, bike, and storage area.

To Separate Items in a Series That Contains Commas

571.5

Use a semicolon to separate items in a series that already contain commas.

> My favorite foods are pizza with pepperoni, onions, and olives; peanut butter and banana sandwiches; and liver with bacon, peppers, and onions.

Exercise

Colon

572.1

After Salutations

Use a **colon** after the salutation of a business letter.

Dear Mr. Spielberg**:**   Dear Professor Higgins**:**   Dear Members**:**

572.2

Between Numbers Indicating Time or Ratios

Use a colon between the hours, minutes, and seconds of a number indicating time.

8**:**30 p.m.   9**:**45 a.m.   10**:**24**:**55

Use a colon between two numbers in a ratio.

The ratio of computers to students is 1**:**20. (one to twenty)

572.3

For Emphasis

Use a colon to emphasize a word, a phrase, a clause, or a sentence that explains or adds impact to the main clause.

I have one goal for myself: to become the first person in my family to graduate from college.

572.4

To Distinguish Parts of Publications

Use a colon between a title and a subtitle, volume and page, and chapter and verse.

*Ron Brown***:** *An Uncommon Life*   *Britannica* 4**:** 211   Psalm 23**:**1–6

572.5

To Introduce Quotations

Use a colon to introduce a quotation following a complete sentence.

John Locke is credited with this prescription for a good life: "A sound mind in a sound body."

Lou Gottlieb, however, offered this version: "A sound mind or a sound body—take your pick."

572.6

To Introduce a List

Use a colon to introduce a list following a complete sentence.

A college student needs a number of things to succeed: basic skills, creativity, and determination.

Avoid Colon Errors

Do *not* use a colon between a verb and its object or complement.

Dave likes**:** comfortable space and time to think. **(Incorrect)**

Dave likes two things**:** comfortable space and time to think. **(Correct)**

**Exercise
573.1**

Video

Hyphen

In Compound Words

Use a **hyphen** to make some compound words.

great-great-grandfather (noun)	starry-eyed (adjective)
mother-in-law (noun)	three-year-old (adjective)

Writers sometimes combine words in new and unexpected ways. Such combinations are usually hyphenated.

> And they pried pieces of **baked-too-fast** sunshine cake from the roofs of their mouths and looked once more into the boy's eyes.
>
> —Toni Morrison, *Song of Solomon*

Note: Consult a dictionary to find how it lists a particular compound word. Some compound words (*living room*) do not use a hyphen and are written separately. Some are written solid (*bedroom*). Some do not use a hyphen when the word is a noun (*ice cream*) but do use a hyphen when it is a verb or an adjective (*ice-cream sundae*).

To Join Letters and Words

573.2

Use a hyphen to join a capital letter or a lowercase letter to a noun or a participle.

T-shirt   U-turn   V-shaped   x-ray

To Join Words in Compound Numbers

573.3

Use a hyphen to join the words in compound numbers from twenty-one to ninety-nine when it is necessary to write them out. (See 592.1.)

Forty-two people found seats in the cramped classroom.

Between Numbers in Fractions

573.4

Use a hyphen between the numerator and the denominator of a fraction, but not when one or both of these elements are already hyphenated.

four-tenths   five-sixteenths   seven thirty-seconds (7/32)

In a Special Series

573.5

Use a hyphen when two or more words have a common element that is omitted in all but the last term.

We have cedar posts in **four-**, **six-**, and **eight**-inch widths.

To Create New Words

573.6

Use a hyphen to form new words beginning with the prefixes *self, ex, all,* and *half.* Also use a hyphen to join any prefix to a proper noun, a proper adjective, or the official name of an office.

post-Depression   mid-May   ex-mayor

574.1 ## To Prevent Confusion

Use a hyphen with prefixes or suffixes to avoid confusion or awkward spelling.

re-cover (not *recover*) the sofa   **shell-like** (not *shelllike*) shape

574.2 ## To Join Numbers

Use a hyphen to join numbers indicating a range, a score, or a vote.

Students study **30-40** hours a week.   The final score was **84-82**.

574.3 ## To Divide Words

Use a hyphen to divide a word between syllables at the end of a line of print.

Guidelines for Word Division

1. Leave enough of the word at the end of the line to identify the word.
2. Never divide a one-syllable word: **rained, skills, through.**
3. Avoid dividing a word of five or fewer letters: **paper, study, July.**
4. Never divide a one-letter syllable from the rest of the word: **omit-ted,** not **o-mitted.**
5. Always divide a compound word between its basic units: **sister-in-law,** not **sis-ter-in-law.**
6. Never divide abbreviations or contractions: **shouldn't,** not **should-n't.**
7. When a vowel is a syllable by itself, divide the word after the vowel: **epi-sode,** not **ep-isode.**
8. Avoid dividing a numeral: **1,000,000,** not **1,000,-000.**
9. Avoid dividing the last word in a paragraph.
10. Never divide the last word in more than two lines in a row.
11. Check a dictionary for acceptable word divisions.

574.4 ## To Form Adjectives

Use a hyphen to join two or more words that serve as a single-thought adjective before a noun.

In real life I am a large, **big-boned** woman with rough, **man-working** hands.

—Alice Walker, "Everyday Use"

Most single-thought adjectives are not hyphenated when they come after the noun. (Check the dictionary to be sure.)

In real life, I am large and **big boned.**

Note: When the first of these words is an adverb ending in *ly,* do not use a hyphen. Also, do not use a hyphen when a number or a letter is the final element in a single-thought adjective.

fresh**ly** painted barn   grade **A** milk (letter is the final element)

Exercise
575.1

Dash

To Set Off Nonessential Elements

Use a **dash** to set off nonessential elements—explanations, examples, or definitions—when you want to emphasize them.

> Near the semester's end—**and this is not always due to poor planning**—some students may find themselves in academic trouble.

> The term *caveat emptor*—**let the buyer beware**—is especially appropriate to Internet shopping.

> **Note:** A dash is indicated by two hyphens--with no spacing before or after--in typewriter-generated material. Don't use a single hyphen when a dash (two hyphens) is required.

To Set Off an Introductory Series

575.2

Use a dash to set off an introductory series from the clause that explains the series.

> **Cereal, coffee, and Facebook**—without these I can't get going in the morning.

To Show Missing Text

575.3

Use a dash to show that words or letters are missing.

> **Mr. —** won't let us marry.
>
> —Alice Walker, *The Color Purple*

To Show Interrupted Speech

575.4

Use a dash (or an ellipsis) to show interrupted or faltering speech in dialogue. (Also see 562.3.)

> Well, **I—ah—had** this terrible case of the flu, **and—then—ah—the** library closed because of that flash flood, **and—well—the** high humidity jammed my printer.
>
> —Excuse No. 101

> "If you *think* you can—"
> "Oh, I *know*—"
> "Don't interrupt!"

For Emphasis

575.5

Use a dash in place of a colon to introduce or to emphasize a word, a series, a phrase, or a clause.

> **Jogging**—that's what he lives for.

> **Life is like a grindstone**—whether it grinds you down or polishes you up depends on what you're made of.

> **This is how the world moves**—not like an arrow, but a boomerang.
>
> —Ralph Ellison

Punctuation Exercises:

Semicolons, Colons, Hyphens, and Dashes

A. Semicolons and Colons

On your own paper, indicate correct placement of semicolons or colons in each sentence by writing down the word preceding each mark.

1. Aaron Copland revolutionized music Leonard Bernstein called him "Moses."
2. Copland wrote ballets such as *Appalachian Spring, Billy the Kid,* and *Rodeo* music for films such as *Our Town* and *The Red Pony* and symphonies such as the *Organ Symphony,* the *Short Symphony,* and his *Third Symphony.*
3. Copland also founded ASCAP the American Society of Composers, Authors, and Publishers.
4. ASCAP made it possible to be a composer it set up royalty standards.
5. Copland was trained in Paris despite that fact, he was all-American.
6. Copland is well known for one piece "Fanfare for the Common Man."
7. Unlike Bernstein, Copland wrote slowly he composed at the piano.
8. At first, Copland composed atonal music he changed his style during the Great Depression.
9. In the '50s, Copland and Bernstein ran up against an antagonist McCarthy.
10. Copland showed the way for young composers he was a kind of "Moses."

B. Hyphens

For each item, write the word or words, inserting hyphens correctly. If an item needs no hyphen, write "correct."

1. forty five
2. midMarch
3. nine thirty seconds
4. father in law
5. recreate (meaning "to create again")
6. a 36 38 score
7. hard working people
8. grade A meat
9. U shaped valley
10. two year old

C. Dashes

For each sentence, indicate correct dash placement by writing the words on either side of the dash.

1. The expression *carpe diem* seize the day was written on the classroom wall.
2. "Faith, hope, and love these three, but the greatest of these is love."
3. He stuttered, "I um well wanted to ask you on a date."
4. Performing before a live audience that's what I love.
5. I will caution you this is what I tell everyone don't give up your dreams.

Quotation Marks

To Punctuate Titles

Exercise
577.1

Use **quotation marks** to punctuate some titles. (Also see 579.2.)

> "Two Friends" (short story)
> "New Car Designs" (newspaper article)
> "Sparks" (song)
> "Multiculturalism and the Language Battle" (lecture title)
> "The New Admissions Game" (magazine article)
> "Reflections on Advertising" (chapter in a book)
> "Blink" (television episode from *Doctor Who*)
> "Annabel Lee" (short poem)

Exercise

Video

For Special Words

577.2

Use quotation marks (1) to show that a word is being discussed as a word, (2) to indicate that a word or phrase is directly quoted, (3) to indicate that a word is slang, or (4) to point out that a word is being used in a humorous or ironic way.

1. A commentary on the times is that the word **"honesty"** is now preceded by **"old-fashioned."**

2. She said she was **"incensed."**

3. I drank a Dixie and ate bar peanuts and asked the bartender where I could hear **"chanky-chank,"** as Cajuns call their music. —William Least Heat-Moon, *Blue Highways*

4. In an attempt to be popular, he works very hard at being **"cute."**

Note: A word used as a word can also be set off with italics.

Placement of Periods or Commas

577.3

Video

Always place periods and commas inside quotation marks.

> "Dr. Slaughter wants you to have liquids, Will," Mama said anxiously. "He said not to give you any solid food tonight." —Olive Ann Burns, *Cold Sassy Tree*

Placement of Exclamation Points or Question Marks

577.4

Video

Place an exclamation point or a question mark inside quotation marks when it punctuates both the main sentence and the quotation *or* just the quotation; place it outside when it punctuates the main sentence.

> Do you often ask yourself, "What should I be?"

> I almost croaked when he asked, "That won't be a problem, will it?"

> Did he really say, "Finish this by tomorrow"?

Placement of Semicolons or Colons

577.5

Always place semicolons or colons outside quotation marks.

> I just read "Computers and Creativity"; I now have some different ideas about the role of computers in the arts.

A Closer Look
Marking Quoted Material

578.1

For Direct Quotations

Use quotation marks before and after a direct quotation—a person's exact words.

> Sitting in my one-room apartment, I remember Mom saying, **"Don't go to the party with him."**

Note: Do *not* use quotation marks for *indirect* quotations.

> I remember Mom saying **that I should not date him.** (These are not the speaker's exact words.)

578.2

For Quoted Passages

Use quotation marks before and after a quoted passage. Any word that is not part of the original quotation must be placed inside brackets.

> **(Original)** First of all, it must accept responsibility for providing shelter for the homeless.

> **(Quotation)** "First of all, it **[the federal government]** must accept responsibility for providing shelter for the homeless."

Note: If you quote only part of the original passage, be sure to construct a sentence that is both accurate and grammatically correct.

> The report goes on to say that the federal government **"must accept responsibility for providing shelter for the homeless."**

578.3

For Long Quotations

If more than one paragraph is quoted, quotation marks are placed before each paragraph and at the end of the last paragraph **(Example A).** Quotations that are five or more lines (MLA style) or forty words or more (APA style) are usually set off from the text by indenting ten spaces from the left margin (a style called "block form"). Do not use quotation marks before or after a block-form quotation **(Example B),** except in cases where quotation marks appear in the original passage **(Example C).**

Example A   **Example B**   **Example C**

578.4

For Quoting Quotations

Use single quotation marks to punctuate quoted material within a quotation.

> **"I was lucky,"** said Jane. **"The proctor announced, 'Put your pencils down,'** just as I was filling in the last answer."

Italics (Underlining)

In Handwritten and Printed Material

Italics is a printer's term for a style of type that is slightly slanted. In this sentence, the word *happiness* is printed in italics. In material that is handwritten or typed on a machine that cannot print in italics, underline each word or letter that should be in italics.

> In <u>The Road to Memphis</u>, racism is a contagious disease.
> (typed or handwritten)

> Mildred Taylor's *The Road to Memphis* exposes racism. (printed)

In Titles

Video

Use italics to indicate the titles of magazines, newspapers, books, pamphlets, full-length plays, films, videos, radio and television programs, book-length poems, ballets, operas, lengthy musical compositions, CDs, paintings and sculptures, legal cases, websites, and the names of ships and aircraft. (Also see 577.1)

> *The Week* (magazine)   *New York Times* (newspaper)
> *The Lost Symbol* (book)   *Yankee Tavern* (play)
> *Enola Gay* (airplane)   *The Fame* (album)
> *ACLU v. State of Ohio* (legal case)   *Billy the Kid* (ballet)
> *Avatar* (film)   *The Thinker* (sculpture)
> *CSI* (television program)   *GeoCities* (website)
> *College Loans* (pamphlet)

When one title appears within another title, punctuate as follows:

> **I read an article entitled "The Making of *Up*."** (title of movie in an article title)

> **He wants to watch *Inside the* New York Times on PBS tonight.**
> (title of newspaper in title of TV program)

For Key Terms

Exercise

Italics are often used for a key term in a discussion or for a technical term, especially when it is accompanied by its definition. Italicize the term the first time it is used. Thereafter, put the term in roman type.

> This flower has a **zygomorphic** (bilateral symmetry) structure.

For Foreign Words and Scientific Names

Use italics for foreign words that have not been adopted into the English language; italics are also used to denote scientific names.

> Say **arrivederci** to your fears and try new activities. (foreign word)

> The voyageurs discovered the shy **Castor canadensis,** or North American beaver. (scientific name)

Exercise
580.1

Video

Parentheses

To Enclose Explanatory or Supplementary Material

Use **parentheses** to enclose explanatory or supplementary material that interrupts the normal sentence structure.

> The RA **(resident assistant)** became my best friend.

580.2

To Set Off Numbers in a List

Use parentheses to set off numbers used with a series of words or phrases.

> Dr. Beck told us **(1)** plan ahead, **(2)** stay flexible, and **(3)** follow through.

580.3

For Parenthetical Sentences

When using a full "sentence" within another sentence, do not capitalize it or use a period inside the parentheses.

> Your friend doesn't have the assignment **(he was just thinking about calling you)**, so you'll have to make a few more calls.

When the parenthetical sentence comes after the main sentence, capitalize and punctuate it the same way you would any other complete sentence.

> But Mom doesn't say boo to Dad; she's always sweet to him. **(Actually she's sort of sweet to everybody.)**
>
> —Norma Fox Mazer, *Up on Fong Mountain*

580.4

To Set Off References

Use parentheses to set off references to authors, titles, pages, and years.

> The statistics are alarming **(see page 9)** and demand action.

> **Note:** For unavoidable parentheses within parentheses (. . . [. . .] . . .), use brackets. Avoid overuse of parentheses by using commas instead.

Diagonal

580.5

To Form Fractions or Show Choices

Use a **diagonal** (also called a *slash*) to form a fraction. Also place a diagonal between two words to indicate that either is acceptable.

> My **walking/running** shoe size is **5 1/2**; my dress shoes are **6 1/2**.

580.6

When Quoting Poetry

When quoting poetry, use a diagonal (with one space before and after) to show where each line ends in the actual poem.

> A dryness is upon the house / My father loved and tended. / Beyond his firm and sculptured door / His light and lease have ended.
>
> —Gwendolyn Brooks, "In Honor of David Anderson Brooks, My Father"

Exercise
581.1

Video

Brackets

With Words That Clarify

Use **brackets** before and after words that are added to clarify what another person has said or written.

> "They'd [**the sweat bees**] get into your mouth, ears, eyes, nose. You'd feel them all over you."
> —Marilyn Johnson and Sasha Nyary, "Roosevelts in the Amazon"

Note: The brackets indicate that the words *the sweat bees* are not part of the original quotation but were added for clarification. (See 578.2.)

Around Comments by Someone Other Than the Author

581.2

Place brackets around comments that have been added by someone other than the author or speaker.

> "In conclusion, *docendo discimus*. Let the school year begin!" [**Huh?**]

Around Editorial Corrections

581.3

Place brackets around an editorial correction or addition.

> "Brooklyn alone has 8 percent of lead poisoning [**victims**] nationwide," said Marjorie Moore.
> —Donna Actie, student writer

Around the Word *Sic*

581.4

Brackets should be placed around the word *sic* (Latin for "so" or "thus") in quoted material; the word indicates that an error appearing in the quoted material was made by the original speaker or writer.

> "There is a higher principal *[sic]* at stake here: Is the school administration aware of the situation?"

Exclamation Point

To Express Strong Feeling

581.5

Use an **exclamation point** to express strong feeling. It may be placed at the end of a sentence (or an elliptical expression that stands for a sentence). Use exclamation points sparingly.

> "That's not the point," said Wangero. "These are all pieces of dresses Grandma used to wear. She did all this stitching by hand. **Imagine!**"
> —Alice Walker, "Everyday Use"

> Su-su-something's crawling up the back of my neck!
> —Mark Twain, Roughing It

> She was on tiptoe, stretching for an orange, when they heard, "**HEY YOU!**"
> —Beverley Naidoo, *Journey to Jo'burg*

Exercise

Exercise

582.1

Apostrophe

In Contractions

Use an **apostrophe** to show that one or more letters have been left out of two words joined to form a contraction.

    don't → **o** is left out   **she'd** → **woul** is left out   **it's** → **i** is left out

    Note: An apostrophe is also used to show that one or more numerals or letters have been left out of numbers or words.

        class of **'02** → **20** is left out   good **mornin'** → **g** is left out

582.2

To Form Plurals

Use an apostrophe and an *s* to form the plural of a letter, a number, a sign, or a word discussed as a word.

    A → **A's**   8 → **8's**   + → **+'s**
    You use too many *and*'s in your writing.

    Note: If two apostrophes are called for in the same word, omit the second one.

    Follow closely the do's and **don'ts** (not **don't's**) on the checklist.

582.3

To Form Singular Possessives

The possessive form of singular nouns is usually made by adding an apostrophe and an s.

    Spock's ears   my **computer's** memory

Video

    Note: When a singular noun of more than one syllable ends with an *s* or a *z* sound, the possessive may be formed by adding just an apostrophe—or an apostrophe and an *s*.

When the singular noun is a one-syllable word, however, the possessive is usually formed by adding both an apostrophe and an *s*.

    Dallas' sports teams *or* **Dallas's** sports teams (two-syllable word)

    Kiss's last concert   my **boss's** generosity (one-syllable words)

582.4

To Form Plural Possessives

The possessive form of plural nouns ending in *s* is made by adding just an apostrophe.

    the **Joneses'** great-grandfather   **bosses'** offices

    Note: For plural nouns not ending in *s*, add an apostrophe and s.
    women's health issues   **children's** program

To Determine Ownership

You will punctuate possessives correctly if you remember that the word that comes immediately before the apostrophe is the owner.

    girl's guitar (*girl* is the owner)   **girls'** guitar (*girls* are the owners)
    boss's office (*boss* is the owner)   **bosses'** office (*bosses* are the owners)

To Show Shared Possession

583.1

When possession is shared by more than one noun, use the possessive form for the last noun in the series.

> Jason, Kamil, and **Elana's** sound system
> (All three own the same system.)

> **Jason's, Kamil's, and Elana's** sound systems
> (Each owns a separate system.)

In Compound Nouns

583.2

The possessive of a compound noun is formed by placing the possessive ending after the last word.

> his **mother-in-law's** name (singular)
> the **secretary of state's** career (singular)

> their **mothers-in-law's** names (plural)
> the **secretaries of state's** careers (plural)

With Indefinite Pronouns

583.3

The possessive form of an indefinite pronoun is made by adding an apostrophe and an *s* to the pronoun. (See 628.4.)

> **everybody's** grades   **no one's** mistake   **one's** choice

In expressions using *else*, add the apostrophe and *s* after the last word.

> **anyone else's**   **somebody else's**

To Show Time or Amount

583.4

Use an apostrophe and an *s* with an adjective that is part of an expression indicating time or amount.

> **yesterday's** news   a **day's** wage   a **month's** pay

---

Punctuation Marks

583.5

´ (é)	**Accent, acute**	:	**Colon**	¶	**Paragraph**
` (è)	**Accent, grave**	,	**Comma**	( )	**Parentheses**
< >	**Angle brackets**	†	**Dagger**	.	**Period**
'	**Apostrophe**	—	**Dash**	?	**Question mark**
*	**Asterisk**	/	**Diagonal/slash**	" "	**Quotation marks**
{ }	**Braces**	(ä)	**Dieresis**	§	**Section**
[ ]	**Brackets**	...	**Ellipsis**	;	**Semicolon**
^	**Caret**	!	**Exclamation point**	˜ (ñ)	**Tilde**
ç	**Cedilla**	-	**Hyphen**	____	**Underscore**
^ (â)	**Circumflex**	.....	**Leaders**		

Punctuation Exercises:

Quotation Marks, Apostrophes, and Other Marks

A. Quotation Marks and Italics (Underlining)

On your own paper, write the titles, opening and closing words of dialogue, and other special words in each sentence. Use quotation marks or italics (underlining) correctly.

1. I read the article Five Cures for Writer's Block in the magazine Writer's Digest.
2. When I used the word interesting, I really meant the word bizarre.
3. The receptionist said, The doctor will be available shortly. While you wait, why don't you read the article New Vaccine in Time magazine?
4. Did the judge just say, Apolo Ohno is disqualified?
5. The music on the album Solar Plexus is what people call jazz fusion.
6. Where is Bill? asked Jacob. Didn't he say he'd be right back?
7. The short story Coffee appeared in the anthology Wake Up.
8. I played The Llama Song; my roommate objected.
9. My roommate said that he had heard that song enough.
10. Doesn't the law state, Any male 18 or over needs to sign up for the draft?

B. Parentheses, Brackets, Diagonals, Exclamation Points

For each sentence, indicate the correct use of these marks by writing the words either enclosed by them or on either side of the mark.

1. The TA teaching assistant in my psychology class is great.
2. "I think that I shall never see A poem lovely as a tree." Joyce Kilmer
3. He signed the letter "Your fiend *sic* Fred."
4. This is not an either or proposition.
5. I want to 1 finish the paper, 2 revise the paper, and 3 be done with the paper.

C. Apostrophes

For each item, write the word or words, inserting apostrophes correctly.

1. didnt
2. dos and donts
3. Daves MP3
4. Jane and Jills room
5. anyones folder
6. mother-in-laws hat
7. Lynnes job
8. wouldve
9. two *ands* and three *ors*
10. mens magazine

34 Checking Mechanics

Capitalization

Audio

Proper Nouns and Adjectives

Exercise

Capitalize all proper nouns and all proper adjectives (adjectives derived from proper nouns). The chart below provides a quick overview of capitalization rules. The pages following explain specific or special uses of capitalization.

Capitalization at a Glance

Days of the week	Sunday, Monday, Tuesday
Months	June, July, August
Holidays, holy days	Thanksgiving, Easter, Hanukkah
Periods, events in history	Middle Ages, World War I
Special events	Tate Memorial Dedication Ceremony
Political parties	Republican Party, Socialist Party
Official documents	the Declaration of Independence
Trade names	Oscar Mayer hot dogs, Pontiac Firebird
Formal epithets	Alexander the Great
Official titles	Mayor John Spitzer, Senator Feinstein
Official state nicknames	the Badger State, the Aloha State
Geographical names	
Planets, heavenly bodies	Earth, Jupiter, the Milky Way
Continents	Australia, South America
Countries	Ireland, Grenada, Sri Lanka
States, provinces	Ohio, Utah, Nova Scotia
Cities, towns, villages	El Paso, Burlington, Wonewoc
Streets, roads, highways	Park Avenue, Route 66, Interstate 90
Sections of the United States and the world	the Southwest, the Far East
Landforms	the Rocky Mountains, the Kalahari Desert
Bodies of water	the Nile River, Lake Superior, Bee Creek
Public areas	Central Park, Yellowstone National Park

586.1   First Words

Capitalize the first word in every sentence and the first word in a full-sentence direct quotation. (Also see 578.1.)

> **Attending** the orientation for new students is a good idea.

> Max suggested, "**Let's** take the guided tour of the campus first."

586.2   Sentences in Parentheses

Capitalize the first word in a sentence that is enclosed in parentheses if that sentence is not contained within another complete sentence.

> The bookstore has the software. (**Now** all I need is the computer.)

> **Note:** Do *not* capitalize a sentence that is enclosed in parentheses and is located in the middle of another sentence. (Also see 580.3.)

> Your college will probably offer everything (**this** includes general access to a computer) that you'll need for a successful year.

586.3   Sentences Following Colons

Capitalize a complete sentence that follows a colon when that sentence is a formal statement, a quotation, or a sentence that you want to emphasize. (Also see 572.5.)

> Sydney Harris had this to say about computers: "**The** real danger is not that computers will begin to think like people, but that people will begin to think like computers."

586.4   Salutation and Complimentary Closing

In a letter, capitalize the first and all major words of the salutation. Capitalize only the first word of the complimentary closing.

> **Dear Personnel Director:**   **Sincerely** yours,

586.5   Sections of the Country

Words that indicate sections of the country are proper nouns and should be capitalized; words that simply indicate direction are not proper nouns.

> Many businesses move to the **South.** (section of the country)

> They move **south** to cut fuel costs and other expenses. (direction)

586.6   Languages, Ethnic Groups, Nationalities, and Religions

Capitalize languages, ethnic groups, nationalities, and religions.

> **African American**   **Latino**   **Navajo**   **French**   **Islam**

Nouns that refer to the Supreme Being and holy books are capitalized.

> **God**   **Allah**   **Jehovah**   **the Koran**   **Exodus**   **the Bible**

Titles

587.1

Capitalize the first word of a title, the last word, and every word in between except articles (*a, an, the*), short prepositions, *to* in an infinitive, and coordinating conjunctions. Follow this rule for titles of books, newspapers, magazines, poems, plays, songs, articles, films, works of art, and stories.

Going to Meet the Man	*Chicago Tribune*
"Nothing Gold Can Stay"	"Jobs in the Cyber Arena"
A Midsummer Night's Dream	*The War of the Roses*

Note: When citing titles in a bibliography, check the style manual you've been asked to follow. For example, in APA style, only the first word of a title is capitalized.

Organizations

587.2

Capitalize the name of an organization or a team and its members.

American Indian Movement	**Democratic Party**
Tampa Bay Buccaneers	**Tucson Drama Club**

Abbreviations

587.3

Capitalize abbreviations of titles and organizations. (Some other abbreviations are also capitalized. See pages 595–596.) (Also see 561.2.)

M.D.   Ph.D.   NAACP   C.E.   B.C.E.   GPA

Letters

587.4

Capitalize letters used to indicate a form or shape.

U-turn   **I**-beam   **S**-curve   **V**-shaped   **T**-shirt

Words Used as Names

587.5

Capitalize words like *father, mother, uncle, senator,* and *professor* when they are parts of titles that include a personal name or when they are substituted for proper nouns (especially in direct address). (Also see 568.3.)

Hello, **Senator** Feingold. (*Senator* is part of the name.)
Our **senator** is an environmentalist.

Who was your chemistry **professor** last quarter?
I had **Professor** Williams for Chemistry 101.

Note: To test whether a word is being substituted for a proper noun, simply read the sentence with a proper noun in place of the word. If the proper noun fits in the sentence, the word being tested should be capitalized. Usually the word is not capitalized if it follows a possessive—*my, his, our, your,* and so on.

Did **Dad (Brad)** pack the stereo in the trailer? (*Brad* works in this sentence.)

Did your **dad (Brad)** pack the stereo in the trailer? (*Brad* does not work in this sentence; the word *dad* follows the possessive *your.*)

588.1   ## Titles of Courses

Words such as *technology, history,* and *science* are proper nouns when they are included in the titles of specific courses; they are common nouns when they name a field of study.

> Who teaches **Art History 202?** (title of a specific course)
>
> Professor Bunker loves teaching **history.** (a field of study)

> **Note:** The words *freshman, sophomore, junior,* and *senior* are not capitalized unless they are part of an official title.
>
> The **seniors** who maintained high GPAs were honored at the **Mount Mary Senior Honors Banquet.**

588.2   ## Internet and E-Mail

The words *Internet* and *World Wide Web* are always capitalized because they are considered proper nouns. When your writing includes a web address (URL), capitalize any letters that the site's owner does (on printed materials or on the site itself). Not only is it respectful to reprint a web address exactly as it appears elsewhere, but, in fact, some web addresses are case-sensitive and must be entered into a browser's address bar exactly as presented.

> When doing research on the **Internet,** be sure to record each site's **web** address **(URL)** and each contact's **e-mail** address.

> **Note:** Some people include capital letters in their e-mail addresses to make certain features evident. Although e-mail addresses are not case-sensitive, repeat each letter in print just as its owner uses it.

Avoid Capitalization Errors

Do not capitalize any of the following:

- A prefix attached to a proper noun
- Seasons of the year
- Words used to indicate direction or position
- Common nouns and titles that appear near, but are not part of, a proper noun

Capitalize	Do Not Capitalize
American	un-American
January, February	winter, spring
The South is quite conservative.	Turn south at the stop sign.
Duluth City College	a Duluth college
Chancellor John Bohm	John Bohm, our chancellor
President Bush	the president of the United States
Earth (the planet)	earthmover
Internet	e-mail

Mechanics Exercises:

Capitalization

A. Capitalization Practice

For each sentence, write the correct form of any incorrectly capitalized or lowercased words. Use your own paper.

1. Vice president Joe Biden will speak in topeka, Kansas, on thursday.

2. What Jarrod meant to say is this: the dallas cowboys have enough talent to win the Super bowl.

3. The beautiful double rainbow in Yellowstone national park seemed like an act of god.

4. Does starbucks have a wireless internet connection?

5. The vehicle in question was driving North along interstate 55 before making a u-turn.

6. are you taking introduction to mass communication 101 with professor Williams next semester?

7. I'm going to the south to visit my brother in the peach state.

8. A story in the *San Francisco chronicle* quoted the Secretary of Agriculture saying, "we are concerned with the development of our farmland."

9. Shoot me an e-mail if you want to go with me to the civil war reenactment.

10. The french restaurant serves an amazing aged Cheese platter.

B. Using Capitalization

For each line of the following e-mail message, write the correct form of any incorrectly capitalized or lowercased words.

> dear Dr. Cruz,   *1*
>
> Thank You for letting me shadow you for a day at St. Vincent Hospital. I very   *2*
> much enjoyed observing the arthroscopic surgery and was impressed with the   *3*
> expertise of the hospital's Staff! I hope we can meet up soon to discuss questions *4*
> about my Human functional anatomy 410 course.   *5*
>
> Best Wishes,   *6*
>
> Kimbra Jenson   *7*

C. Capitalization Errors

Write the correct form of any incorrectly capitalized or lowercased words.

summer	prime minister	David Cameron	m.d.
Vice President	the bible	spanish	

Plurals

590.1

Nouns Ending in a Consonant

Some nouns remain unchanged when used as plurals (*species, moose, halibut,* and so on), but the plurals of most nouns are formed by adding an *s* to the singular form.

> dorm—**dorms**   credit—**credits**   midterm—**midterms**

The plurals of nouns ending in *sh, ch, x, s,* and *z* are made by adding *es* to the singular form.

> lunch—**lunches**   wish—**wishes**   class—**classes**

590.2

Nouns Ending in *y*

The plurals of common nouns that end in *y* (preceded by a consonant) are formed by changing the *y* to *i* and adding *es.*

> dormitory—**dormitories**   sorority—**sororities**   duty—**duties**

The plurals of common nouns that end in *y* (preceded by a vowel) are formed by adding only an s.

> attorney—**attorneys**   monkey—**monkeys**   toy—**toys**

The plurals of all proper nouns ending in *y* (whether preceded by a consonant or a vowel) are formed by adding an *s.*

> the three **Kathys**   the five **Faheys**

590.3

Nouns Ending in *o*

The plurals of words ending in *o* (preceded by a vowel) are formed by adding an *s.*

> radio—**radios**   cameo—**cameos**   studio—**studios**

The plurals of most nouns ending in *o* (preceded by a consonant) are formed by adding *es.*

> echo—**echoes**   hero—**heroes**   tomato—**tomatoes**

Musical terms always form plurals by adding an *s;* check a dictionary for other words of this type.

> alto—**altos**   banjo—**banjos**   solo—**solos**   piano—**pianos**

590.4

Nouns Ending in *f* or *fe*

The plurals of nouns that end in *f* or *fe* are formed in one of two ways: If the final *f* sound is still heard in the plural form of the word, simply add *s;* if the final sound is a *v* sound, change the *f* to *ve* and add an *s.*

> **Plural ends with *f* sound:**   roof—**roofs**   chief—**chiefs**
> **Plural ends with *v* sound:**   wife—**wives**   loaf—**loaves**

> **Note:** The plurals of some nouns that end in *f* or *fe* can be formed by either adding *s* or changing the *f* to *ve* and adding an *s.*
> **Plural ends with either sound:**   hoof—**hoofs, hooves**

Irregular Spelling

Many foreign words (as well as some of English origin) form a plural by taking on an irregular spelling; others are now acceptable with the commonly used *s* or *es* ending. Take time to check a dictionary.

child—**children**	alumnus—**alumni**	syllabus—**syllabi, syllabuses**
goose—**geese**	datum—**data**	radius—**radii, radiuses**

Words Discussed as Words

The plurals of symbols, letters, figures, and words discussed as words are formed by adding an apostrophe and an *s*.

Many colleges have now added **A/B's** and **B/C's** as standard grades.

Note: You can choose to omit the apostrophe when the omission does not cause confusion.

YMCA's or **YMCAs**   **CD's** or **CDs**

Nouns Ending in *ful*

The plurals of nouns that end with *ful* are formed by adding an *s* at the end of the word.

three **teaspoonfuls**   two **tankfuls**   four **bagfuls**

Compound Nouns

The plurals of compound nouns are usually formed by adding an *s* or an *es* to the important word in the compound. (Also see 573.1.)

brothers-in-law   **maids** of honor   **secretaries** of state

Collective Nouns

Collective nouns do not change in form when they are used as plurals.

class (a unit—singular form)

class (individual members—plural form)

Because the spelling of the collective noun does not change, it is often the pronoun used in place of the collective noun that indicates whether the noun is singular or plural. Use a singular pronoun (**its**) to show that the collective noun is singular. Use a plural pronoun (**their**) to show that the collective noun is plural.

The class needs to change **its** motto.

(The writer is thinking of the group as a unit.)

The class brainstormed with **their** professor.

(The writer is thinking of the group as individuals.)

esl Note: To determine whether a plural requires the article *the,* you must first determine whether it is definite or indefinite. Definite plurals use *the,* whereas indefinite plurals do not require any article. (See 672.3–673.1.)

Exercise
592.1

Numbers

Numerals or Words

Numbers from one to one hundred are usually written as words; numbers 101 and greater are usually written as numerals. (APA style uses numerals for numbers 10 and higher.) Hyphenate numbers written as two words if less than one hundred.

two   seven   ten   twenty-five   106   1,079

The same rule applies to the use of ordinal numbers.

second   tenth   twenty-fifth   ninety-eighth   106th   333rd

If numbers greater than 101 are used infrequently in a piece of writing, you may spell out those that can be written in one or two words.

two hundred   fifty thousand   six billion

You may use a combination of numerals and words for very large numbers.

1.5 million   3 billion to 3.2 billion   6 trillion

Numbers being compared or contrasted should be kept in the same style.

8 to **11** years old *or* **eight** to **eleven** years old

Particular decades may be spelled out or written as numerals.

the **'80s** and **'90s** *or* the **eighties** and **nineties**

592.2

Numerals Only

Use numerals for the following forms: decimals, percentages, pages, chapters (and other parts of a book), addresses, dates, telephone numbers, identification numbers, and statistics.

26.2	**8** percent	chapter **7**
pages **287–289**	Highway **36**	**(212) 555–1234**
398-55-0000	a vote of **23** to **4**	May **8, 2007**

Note: Abbreviations and symbols are often used in charts, graphs, footnotes, and so forth, but typically they are not used in texts.

He is **five feet one inch** tall and **ten years old.**

She walked **three and one-half miles** to work through **twelve inches** of snow.

However, abbreviations and symbols may be used in scientific, mathematical, statistical, and technical texts (APA style).

Between **20%** and **23%** of the cultures yielded positive results.

Your **245B** model requires **220V.**

Always use numerals with abbreviations and symbols.

5'4"   8%   10 in.   **3** tbsp.   **6** lb. **8** oz.   **90°F**

Use numerals after the name of local branches of labor unions.

The Office and Professional Employees International Union, Local **8**

Hyphenated Numbers

Hyphens are used to form compound modifiers indicating measurement. They are also used for inclusive numbers and written-out fractions.

a **three-mile** trip   the **2001–2005** presidential term

a **2,500-mile** road trip   **one-sixth** of the pie

a **thirteen-foot** clearance   **three-eighths** of the book

Time and Money

If time is expressed with an abbreviation, use numerals; if it is expressed in words, spell out the number.

4:00 a.m. *or* **four** o'clock (not 4 o'clock)

the **5:15** p.m. train

a **seven o'clock** wake-up call

If money is expressed with a symbol, use numerals; if the currency is expressed in words, spell out the number.

$20 or **twenty** dollars (not 20 dollars)

Abbreviations of time and of money may be used in text.

The concert begins at **7:00** p.m., and tickets cost **$30**.

Words Only

Use words to express numbers that begin a sentence.

Fourteen students "forgot" their assignments.

Three hundred contest entries were received.

> **Note:** Change the sentence structure if this rule creates a clumsy construction.
>
> **Six hundred thirty-nine** students are new to the campus this fall. (Clumsy)
>
> This fall, **639** students are new to the campus. (Better)

Use words for numbers that precede a compound modifier that includes a numeral. (If the compound modifier uses a spelled-out number, use numerals in front of it.)

She sold **twenty 35-millimeter** cameras in one day.

The chef prepared **24 eight-ounce** filets.

Use words for the names of numbered streets of one hundred or less.

Ninth Avenue

123 Forty-fourth Street

Use words for the names of buildings if that name is also its address.

One Thousand State Street   **Two Fifty Park Avenue**

Use words for references to particular centuries.

the twenty-first century   **the fourth century B.C.E.**

Mechanics Exercises:

Plurals and Numbers

A. Plurals

For each of the following words, write the correct plural form on your own paper.

1. team
2. party
3. ratio
4. shelf
5. child

6. sister-in-law
7. video
8. bucketful
9. choir
10. serf

B. Numbers

For each sentence below, write the correct form of any incorrectly used numbers.

1. 4 tiny ducklings crossed a driveway near Six Hundred and Nine Lewis Street.
2. Out of all my friends, Alex woke up 1st around 6 o'clock.
3. The 6 cheeseburgers cost 12 dollars.
4. I read only fifty % of chapter three.
5. At half past 2 the temperature was still seventy degrees Fahrenheit.
6. The recipe calls for two tsp. salt and three oz. butter.

C. Mechanics Practice

In the following paragraph, correct any number errors by writing the line number and the correct form. Also write the plural of each underlined word.

Let me tell you how to grill some wonderful steak. First, consider buying   1
your meat from a butcher rather than from local grocery. The ideal steak cut   2
is between one and a half to 2 inches thick. Next, you will need to prepare the 3
steaks for grilling. Start by trimming excess fat to about one-quarter of an   4
inch thick and seasoning the meat with two tsp. of salt and cracked pepper.   5
Then, when the grill has preheated, grill the steaks for 16 to twenty minutes.   6
If you so choose, rotate the steaks forty-five degrees on both sides for nice   7
diamond grill mark. When the steaks are done, turn off the grill and enjoy.   8
And remember, steak goes great with potato and fresh mushroom.   9

Abbreviations

An **abbreviation** is the shortened form of a word or a phrase. These abbreviations are always acceptable in both formal and informal writing:

   Mr.   Mrs.   Ms.   Dr.   Jr.   a.m. (A.M.)   p.m. (P.M.)

Note: In formal writing, do not abbreviate the names of states, countries, months, days, units of measure, or courses of study. Do not abbreviate the words *Street, Road, Avenue, Company,* and similar words when they are part of a proper name. Also, do not use signs or symbols (%, &, #, @) in place of words. (The dollar sign, however, is appropriate when numerals are used to express an amount of money. See 593.2.)

Also Note: When abbreviations are called for (in charts, lists, bibliographies, notes, and indexes, for example), standard abbreviations are preferred. Reserve the postal abbreviations for ZIP code addresses.

Correspondence Abbreviations

States/Territories

	Standard	Postal
Alabama	Ala.	AL
Alaska	Alaska	AK
Arizona	Ariz.	AZ
Arkansas	Ark.	AR
California	Cal.	CA
Colorado	Colo.	CO
Connecticut	Conn.	CT
Delaware	Del.	DE
District of Columbia	D.C.	DC
Florida	Fla.	FL
Georgia	Ga.	GA
Guam	Guam	GU
Hawaii	Hawaii	HI
Idaho	Idaho	ID
Illinois	Ill.	IL
Indiana	Ind.	IN
Iowa	Ia.	IA
Kansas	Kans.	KS
Kentucky	Ky.	KY
Louisiana	La.	LA
Maine	Me.	ME
Maryland	Md.	MD
Massachusetts	Mass.	MA
Michigan	Mich.	MI
Minnesota	Minn.	MN
Mississippi	Miss.	MS
Missouri	Mo.	MO
Montana	Mont.	MT
Nebraska	Neb.	NE
Nevada	Nev.	NV
New Hampshire	N.H.	NH
New Jersey	N.J.	NJ
New Mexico	N. Mex.	NM
New York	N.Y.	NY
North Carolina	N.C.	NC
North Dakota	N. Dak.	ND
Ohio	Ohio	OH

	Standard	Postal
Oklahoma	Okla.	OK
Oregon	Ore.	OR
Pennsylvania	Pa.	PA
Puerto Rico	P.R.	PR
Rhode Island	R.I.	RI
South Carolina	S.C.	SC
South Dakota	S. Dak.	SD
Tennessee	Tenn.	TN
Texas	Tex.	TX
Utah	Utah	UT
Vermont	Vt.	VT
Virginia	Va.	VA
Virgin Islands	V.I.	VI
Washington	Wash.	WA
West Virginia	W. Va.	WV
Wisconsin	Wis.	WI
Wyoming	Wyo.	WY

Canadian Provinces

	Standard	Postal
Alberta	Alta.	AB
British Columbia	B.C.	BC
Manitoba	Man.	MB
New Brunswick	N.B.	NB
Newfoundland and Labrador	N.F. Lab.	NL
Northwest Territories	N.W.T.	NT
Nova Scotia	N.S.	NS
Nunavut		NU
Ontario	Ont.	ON
Prince Edward Island	P.E.I.	PE
Quebec	Que.	QC
Saskatchewan	Sask.	SK
Yukon Territory	Y.T.	YT

Address Abbreviations

	Standard	Postal
Apartment	Apt.	APT
Avenue	Ave.	AVE
Boulevard	Blvd.	BLVD
Circle	Cir.	CIR
Court	Ct.	CT
Drive	Dr.	DR
East	E.	E
Expressway	Expy.	EXPY
Freeway	Frwy.	FWY
Heights	Hts.	HTS
Highway	Hwy.	HWY
Hospital	Hosp.	HOSP
Junction	Junc.	JCT
Lake	L.	LK
Lakes	Ls.	LKS
Lane	Ln.	LN
Meadows	Mdws.	MDWS
North	N.	N
Palms	Palms	PLMS
Park	Pk.	PK
Parkway	Pky.	PKY
Place	Pl.	PL
Plaza	Plaza	PLZ
Post Office Box	P.O. Box	PO BOX
Ridge	Rdg.	RDG
River	R.	RV
Road	Rd.	RD
Room	Rm.	RM
Rural	R.	R
Rural Route	R.R.	RR
Shore	Sh.	SH
South	S.	S
Square	Sq.	SQ
Station	Sta.	STA
Street	St.	ST
Suite	Ste.	STE
Terrace	Ter.	TER
Turnpike	Tpke.	TPKE
Union	Un.	UN
View	View	VW
Village	Vil.	VLG
West	W.	W

Common Abbreviations

abr. abridged, abridgment
AC, ac alternating current, air-conditioning
ack. acknowledgment
AM amplitude modulation
A.M., a.m. before noon (Latin *ante meridiem*)
AP advanced placement
ASAP as soon as possible
avg., av. average
B.A. bachelor of arts degree
BBB Better Business Bureau
B.C.E. before common era
bibliog. bibliography
biog. biographer, biographical, biography
B.S. bachelor of science degree
C 1. Celsius **2.** centigrade **3.** coulomb
c. 1. circa (about) **2.** cup(s)
cc 1. cubic centimeter **2.** carbon copy **3.** community college
CDT, C.D.T. central daylight time
C.E. common era
CEEB College Entrance Examination Board
chap. chapter(s)
cm centimeter(s)
c/o care of
COD, c.o.d. 1. cash on delivery **2.** collect on delivery
co-op cooperative
CST, C.S.T. central standard time
cu 1. cubic **2.** cumulative
D.A. district attorney
d.b.a., d/b/a doing business as
DC, dc direct current
dec. deceased
dept. department
disc. discount
DST, D.S.T. daylight saving time
dup. duplicate
ed. edition, editor
e.g. for example (Latin *exempli gratia*)
EST, E.S.T. eastern standard time
etc. and so forth (Latin *et cetera*)
F Fahrenheit, French, Friday
FM frequency modulation
F.O.B., f.o.b. free on board
FYI for your information
g 1. gravity **2.** gram(s)
gal. gallon(s)
gds. goods
gloss. glossary
GNP gross national product
GPA grade point average
hdqrs. headquarters

HIV human immunodeficiency virus
hp horsepower
Hz hertz
ibid. in the same place (Latin *ibidem*)
id. the same (Latin *idem*)
i.e. that is (Latin *id est*)
illus. illustration
inc. incorporated
IQ, I.Q. intelligence quotient
IRS Internal Revenue Service
ISBN International Standard Book Number
JP, J.P. justice of the peace
K 1. kelvin (temperature unit) **2.** Kelvin (temperature scale)
kc kilocycle(s)
kg kilogram(s)
km kilometer(s)
kn knot(s)
kw kilowatt(s)
L liter(s), lake
lat. latitude
l.c. lowercase
lit. literary; literature
log logarithm, logic
long. longitude
Ltd., ltd. limited
m meter(s)
M.A. master of arts degree
man. manual
Mc, mc megacycle(s)
MC master of ceremonies
M.D. doctor of medicine (Latin *medicinae doctor*)
mdse. merchandise
MDT, M.D. T. mountain daylight time
mfg. manufacture, manufacturing
mg milligram(s)
mi. 1. mile(s) **2.** mill(s) (monetary unit)
misc. miscellaneous
mL milliliter(s)
mm millimeter(s)
mpg, m.p.g. miles per gallon
mph, m.p.h. miles per hour
MS 1. manuscript **2.** multiple sclerosis
Ms. title of courtesy for a woman
M.S. master of science degree
MST, M.S.T. mountain standard time
NE northeast
neg. negative
N.S.F., n.s.f. not sufficient funds
NW northwest
oz, oz. ounce(s)

PA public-address system
pct. percent
pd. paid
PDT, P.D.T. Pacific daylight time
PFC, Pfc. private first class
pg., p. page
Ph.D. doctor of philosophy
P.M., p.m. after noon (Latin *post meridiem*)
POW, P.O.W. prisoner of war
pp. pages
ppd. 1. postpaid **2.** prepaid
PR, P.R. public relations
PSAT Preliminary Scholastic Aptitude Test
psi, p.s.i. pounds per square inch
PST, P.S.T. Pacific standard time
PTA, P.T.A. Parent-Teacher Association
R.A. residence assistant
RF radio frequency
R.P.M., rpm revolutions per minute
R.S.V.P., r.s.v.p. please reply (French *répondez s'il vous plaît*)
SAT Scholastic Aptitude Test
SE southeast
SOS 1. international distress signal 2. any call for help
Sr. 1. senior (after surname) **2.** sister (religious)
SRO, S.R.O. standing room only
std. standard
SW southwest
syn. synonymous, synonym
tbs., tbsp. tablespoon(s)
TM trademark
UHF, uhf ultrahigh frequency
v 1. physics: velocity **2.** volume
V electricity: volt
VA Veterans Administration
VHF, vhf very high frequency
VIP informal: very important person
vol. 1. volume **2.** volunteer
vs. versus, verse
W 1. electricity: watt(s) **2.** physics: (also **w**) work **3.** west
whse., whs. warehouse
whsle. wholesale
wkly. weekly
w/o without
wt. weight
www World Wide Web

Acronyms and Initialisms

Acronyms

An **acronym** is a word formed from the first (or first few) letters of words in a set phrase. Even though acronyms are abbreviations, they require no periods.

radar	radio detecting and ranging
CARE	Cooperative for Assistance and Relief Everywhere
NASA	National Aeronautics and Space Administration
VISTA	Volunteers in Service to America
FICA	Federal Insurance Contributions Act

Initialisms

An **initialism** is similar to an acronym except that the initials used to form this abbreviation are pronounced individually.

CIA	Central Intelligence Agency
FBI	Federal Bureau of Investigation
FHA	Federal Housing Administration

Common Acronyms and Initialisms

AIDS	acquired immune deficiency syndrome	OSHA	Occupational Safety and Health Administration
APR	annual percentage rate	PAC	political action committee
CAD	computer-aided design	PIN	personal identification number
CAM	computer-aided manufacturing	POP	point of purchase
CETA	Comprehensive Employment and Training Act	PSA	public service announcement
FAA	Federal Aviation Administration	REA	Rural Electrification Administration
FCC	Federal Communications Commission	RICO	Racketeer Influenced and Corrupt Organizations (Act)
FDA	Food and Drug Administration	ROTC	Reserve Officers' Training Corps
FDIC	Federal Deposit Insurance Corporation	SADD	Students Against Destructive Decisions
FEMA	Federal Emergency Management Agency	SASE	self-addressed stamped envelope
FHA	Federal Housing Administration	SPOT	satellite positioning and tracking
FTC	Federal Trade Commission	SSA	Social Security Administration
IRS	Internal Revenue Service	SUV	sport-utility vehicle
MADD	Mothers Against Drunk Driving	SWAT	Special Weapons and Tactics
NAFTA	North American Free Trade Agreement	TDD	telecommunications device for the deaf
NATO	North Atlantic Treaty Organization	TMJ	temporomandibular joint
OEO	Office of Economic Opportunity	TVA	Tennessee Valley Authority
ORV	off-road vehicle	VA	Veterans Administration
		WHO	World Health Organization

Mechanics Exercises:

Abbreviations, Acronyms, and Initialisms

A. Abbreviations

On your own paper, indicate whether the following abbreviations would be acceptable in a formal piece of writing. Write "yes" for appropriate and "no" for inappropriate.

1. MN

2. Sask.

3. Dr.

4. R.A.

5. P.M.

6. Jr.

7. Ave.

8. Misc.

9. Mrs.

10. $5.25

B. Acronyms

Indicate whether each term is an acronym or an initialism.

1. PSA

2. FDA

3. MADD

4. NATO

5. NASA

6. TMJ

7. VA

8. SWAT

9. IRS

10. FAA

C. Initialisms

For each sentence, write the correct abbreviation, acronym, or initialism of the underlined word or words.

1. <u>Mister</u> Anderson of the <u>Federal Deposit Insurance Corporation</u> called today regarding the bank's membership status.

2. We cruised south on Falcon <u>Drive</u> in our new <u>sport-utility vehicle</u>.

3. The student's low <u>grade point average</u> negated a high score on the <u>Scholastic Aptitude Test</u>.

4. Do you know the <u>latitude</u> and <u>longitude</u> of Key West, <u>Florida</u>?

5. You can add two <u>teaspoons</u> salt and one <u>tablespoon</u> basil for extra flavor.

Basic Spelling Rules

Write i Before e

Write *i* before *e* except after *c*, or when sounded like *a* as in *neighbor* and *weigh*.

believe   **relief**   **receive**   **eight**

> **Note:** This sentence contains eight exceptions:
>
> **Neither sheik dared leisurely seize either weird species of financiers.**

Words with Consonant Endings

When a one-syllable word (*bat*) ends in a consonant (*t*) preceded by one vowel (*a*), double the final consonant before adding a suffix that begins with a vowel (*batting*).

sum—**summary**   god—**goddess**

> **Note:** When a multisyllable word (*control*) ends in a consonant (*l*) preceded by one vowel (*o*), the accent is on the last syllable (*con trol´*), and the suffix begins with a vowel (*ing*)— the same rule holds true: Double the final consonant (*controlling*).

prefer—**preferred**   begin—**beginning**
forget—**forgettable**   admit—**admittance**

Words with a Final Silent e

If a word ends with a silent *e*, drop the *e* before adding a suffix that begins with a vowel. Do *not* drop the *e* when the suffix begins with a consonant.

state—**stating**—**statement**   like—**liking**—**likeness**
use—**using**—**useful**   nine—**ninety**—**nineteen**

> **Note:** Exceptions are **judgment, truly, argument, ninth.**

Words Ending in y

When *y* is the last letter in a word and the *y* is preceded by a consonant, change the *y* to *i* before adding any suffix except those beginning with *i*.

fry—**fries, frying**   hurry—**hurried, hurrying**
lady—**ladies**   ply—**pliable**
happy—**happiness**   beauty—**beautiful**

> **Note:** When forming the plural of a word that ends with a *y* that is preceded by a vowel, add *s*.

toy—**toys**   play—**plays**   monkey—**monkeys**

TIP: Never trust your spelling to even the best spell checker. Carefully proofread and use a dictionary for words you know your spell checker does not cover.

Commonly Misspelled Words

The commonly misspelled words that follow are hyphenated to show where they would logically be broken at the end of a line.

A
ab-bre-vi-ate
abrupt
ab-scess
ab-sence
ab-so-lute (-ly)
ab-sorb-ent
ab-surd
abun-dance
ac-a-dem-ic
ac-cede
ac-cel-er-ate
ac-cept (-ance)
ac-ces-si-ble
ac-ces-so-ry
ac-ci-den-tal-ly
ac-com-mo-date
ac-com-pa-ny
ac-com-plice
ac-com-plish
ac-cor-dance
ac-cord-ing
ac-count
ac-crued
ac-cu-mu-late
ac-cu-rate
ac-cus-tom (-ed)
ache
achieve (-ment)
ac-knowl-edge
ac-quaint-ance
ac-qui-esce
ac-quired
ac-tu-al
adapt
ad-di-tion (-al)
ad-dress
ad-e-quate
ad-journed
ad-just-ment
ad-mi-ra-ble
ad-mis-si-ble
ad-mit-tance
ad-van-ta-geous
ad-ver-tise-ment
ad-ver-tis-ing

ad-vice (n.)
ad-vis-able
ad-vise (v.)
ad-vis-er
ae-ri-al
af-fect
af-fi-da-vit
a-gainst
ag-gra-vate
ag-gres-sion
a-gree-able
a-gree-ment
aisle
al-co-hol
a-lign-ment
al-ley
al-lot-ted
al-low-ance
all right
al-most
al-ready
al-though
al-to-geth-er
a-lu-mi-num
al-um-nus
al-ways
am-a-teur
a-mend-ment
a-mong
a-mount
a-nal-y-sis
an-a-lyze
an-cient
an-ec-dote
an-es-thet-ic
an-gle
an-ni-hi-late
an-ni-ver-sa-ry
an-nounce
an-noy-ance
an-nu-al
a-noint
a-non-y-mous
an-swer
ant-arc-tic
an-tic-i-pate

anx-i-ety
anx-ious
a-part-ment
a-pol-o-gize
ap-pa-ra-tus
ap-par-ent (-ly)
ap-peal
ap-pear-ance
ap-pe-tite
ap-pli-ance
ap-pli-ca-ble
ap-pli-ca-tion
ap-point-ment
ap-prais-al
ap-pre-ci-ate
ap-proach
ap-pro-pri-ate
ap-prov-al
ap-prox-i-mate-ly
ap-ti-tude
ar-chi-tect
arc-tic
ar-gu-ment
a-rith-me-tic
a-rouse
ar-range-ment
ar-riv-al
ar-ti-cle
ar-ti-fi-cial
as-cend
as-cer-tain
as-i-nine
as-sas-sin
as-sess (-ment)
as-sign-ment
as-sist-ance
as-so-ci-ate
as-so-ci-a-tion
as-sume
as-sur-ance
as-ter-isk
ath-lete
ath-let-ic
at-tach
at-tack (-ed)
at-tempt

at-tend-ance
at-ten-tion
at-ti-tude
at-tor-ney
at-trac-tive
au-di-ble
au-di-ence
au-dit
au-thor-i-ty
au-to-mo-bile
au-tumn
aux-il-ia-ry
a-vail-a-ble
av-er-age
aw-ful
aw-ful-ly
awk-ward

B
bac-ca-lau-re-ate
bach-e-lor
bag-gage
bal-ance
bal-loon
bal-lot
ba-nan-a
ban-dage
bank-rupt
bar-gain
bar-rel
base-ment
ba-sis
bat-tery
beau-ti-ful
beau-ty
be-com-ing
beg-gar
be-gin-ning
be-hav-ior
be-ing
be-lief
be-lieve
ben-e-fi-cial
ben-e-fit (-ed)
be-tween
bi-cy-cle

bis-cuit
bliz-zard
book-keep-er
bought
bouil-lon
bound-a-ry
break-fast
breath (n.)
breathe (v.)
brief
bril-liant
Brit-ain
bro-chure
brought
bruise
bud-get
bul-le-tin
buoy-ant
bu-reau
bur-glar
bury
busi-ness
busy

C
caf-e-te-ria
caf-feine
cal-en-dar
cam-paign
can-celed
can-di-date
can-is-ter
ca-noe
ca-pac-i-ty
cap-i-tal
cap-i-tol
cap-tain
car-bu-ret-or
ca-reer
car-i-ca-ture
car-riage
cash-ier
cas-se-role
cas-u-al-ty
cat-a-log
ca-tas-tro-phe

caught
cav-al-ry
cel-e-bra-tion
cem-e-ter-y
cen-sus
cen-tu-ry
cer-tain
cer-tif-i-cate
ces-sa-tion
chal-lenge
chan-cel-lor
change-a-ble
char-ac-ter (-is-tic)
chauf-feur
chief
chim-ney
choc-o-late
choice
choose
Chris-tian
cir-cuit
cir-cu-lar
cir-cum-stance
civ-i-li-za-tion
cli-en-tele
cli-mate
climb
clothes
coach
co-coa
co-er-cion
col-lar
col-lat-er-al
col-lege
col-le-giate
col-lo-qui-al
colo-nel
col-or
co-los-sal
col-umn
com-e-dy
com-ing
com-mence
com-mer-cial
com-mis-sion
com-mit
com-mit-ment
com-mit-ted
com-mit-tee
com-mu-ni-cate
com-mu-ni-ty
com-par-a-tive

com-par-i-son
com-pel
com-pe-tent
com-pe-ti-tion
com-pet-i-tive-ly
com-plain
com-ple-ment
com-plete-ly
com-plex-ion
com-pli-ment
com-pro-mise
con-cede
con-ceive
con-cern-ing
con-cert
con-ces-sion
con-clude
con-crete
con-curred
con-cur-rence
con-cur-rence
con-demn
con-de-scend
con-di-tion
con-fer-ence
con-ferred
con-fi-dence
con-fi-den-tial
con-grat-u-late
con-science
con-sci-en-tious
con-scious
con-sen-sus
con-se-quence
con-ser-va-tive
con-sid-er-ably
con-sign-ment
con-sis-tent
con-sti-tu-tion
con-tempt-ible
con-tin-u-al-ly
con-tin-ue
con-tin-u-ous
con-trol
con-tro-ver-sy
con-ven-ience
con-vince
cool-ly
co-op-er-ate
cor-dial
cor-po-ra-tion
cor-re-late
cor-re-spond

cor-re-spond-
  ence
cor-rob-o-rate
cough
coun-cil
coun-sel
coun-ter-feit
coun-try
cour-age
cou-ra-geous
cour-te-ous
cour-te-sy
cous-in
cov-er-age
cred-i-tor
cri-sis
crit-i-cism
crit-i-cize
cru-el
cu-ri-os-i-ty
cu-ri-ous
cur-rent
cur-ric-u-lum
cus-tom
cus-tom-ary
cus-tom-er
cyl-in-der

D

dai-ly
dair-y
dealt
debt-or
de-ceased
de-ceit-ful
de-ceive
de-cid-ed
de-ci-sion
dec-la-ra-tion
dec-o-rate
de-duct-i-ble
de-fend-ant
de-fense
de-ferred
def-i-cit
def-i-nite (-ly)
def-i-ni-tion
del-e-gate
de-li-cious
de-pend-ent
de-pos-i-tor
de-pot

de-scend
de-scribe
de-scrip-tion
de-sert
de-serve
de-sign
de-sir-able
de-sir-ous
de-spair
des-per-ate
de-spise
des-sert
de-te-ri-o-rate
de-ter-mine
de-vel-op
de-vel-op-ment
de-vice
de-vise
di-a-mond
di-a-phragm
di-ar-rhe-a
dic-tio-nary
dif-fer-ence
dif-fer-ent
dif-fi-cul-ty
di-lap-i-dat-ed
di-lem-ma
din-ing
di-plo-ma
di-rec-tor
dis-agree-able
dis-ap-pear
dis-ap-point
dis-ap-prove
dis-as-trous
dis-ci-pline
dis-cov-er
dis-crep-an-cy
dis-cuss
dis-cus-sion
dis-ease
dis-sat-is-fied
dis-si-pate
dis-tin-guish
dis-trib-ute
di-vide
di-vis-i-ble
di-vi-sion
doc-tor
doesn't
dom-i-nant
dor-mi-to-ry

doubt
drudg-ery
du-pli-cate
dye-ing
dy-ing

E

ea-ger-ly
ear-nest
eco-nom-i-cal
econ-o-my
ec-sta-sy
e-di-tion
ef-fer-ves-cent
ef-fi-ca-cy
ef-fi-cien-cy
eighth
ei-ther
e-lab-o-rate
e-lec-tric-i-ty
el-e-phant
el-i-gi-ble
e-lim-i-nate
el-lipse
em-bar-rass
e-mer-gen-cy
em-i-nent
em-pha-size
em-ploy-ee
em-ploy-ment
e-mul-sion
en-close
en-cour-age
en-deav-or
en-dorse-ment
en-gi-neer
En-glish
e-nor-mous
e-nough
en-ter-prise
en-ter-tain
en-thu-si-as-tic
en-tire-ly
en-trance
en-vel-op (v.)
en-ve-lope (n.)
en-vi-ron-ment
equip-ment
equipped
e-quiv-a-lent
es-pe-cial-ly
es-sen-tial

es-tab-lish
es-teemed
et-i-quette
ev-i-dence
ex-ag-ger-ate
ex-ceed
ex-cel-lent
ex-cept
ex-cep-tion-al-ly
ex-ces-sive
ex-cite
ex-ec-u-tive
ex-er-cise
ex-haust (-ed)
ex-hi-bi-tion
ex-hil-a-ra-tion
ex-is-tence
ex-or-bi-tant
ex-pect
ex-pe-di-tion
ex-pend-i-ture
ex-pen-sive
ex-pe-ri-ence
ex-plain
ex-pla-na-tion
ex-pres-sion
ex-qui-site
ex-ten-sion
ex-tinct
ex-traor-di-nar-y
ex-treme-ly

F

fa-cil-i-ties
fal-la-cy
fa-mil-iar
fa-mous
fas-ci-nate
fash-ion
fa-tigue (-d)
fau-cet
fa-vor-ite
fea-si-ble
fea-ture
Feb-ru-ar-y
fed-er-al
fem-i-nine
fer-tile
fic-ti-tious
field
fierce
fi-ery

fi-nal-ly
fi-nan-cial-ly
fo-li-age
for-ci-ble
for-eign
for-feit
for-go
for-mal-ly
for-mer-ly
for-tu-nate
for-ty
for-ward
foun-tain
fourth
frag-ile
fran-ti-cal-ly
freight
friend
ful-fill
fun-da-men-tal
fur-ther-more
fu-tile

G

gad-get
gan-grene
ga-rage
gas-o-line
gauge
ge-ne-al-o-gy
gen-er-al-ly
gen-er-ous
ge-nius
gen-u-ine
ge-og-ra-phy
ghet-to
ghost
glo-ri-ous
gnaw
go-ril-la
gov-ern-ment
gov-er-nor
gra-cious
grad-u-a-tion
gram-mar
grate-ful
grat-i-tude
grease
grief
griev-ous
gro-cery
grudge

grue-some
guar-an-tee
guard
guard-i-an
guer-ril-la
guess
guid-ance
guide
guilty
gym-na-si-um
gyp-sy
gy-ro-scope

H

hab-i-tat
ham-mer
hand-ker-chief
han-dle (-d)
hand-some
hap-haz-ard
hap-pen
hap-pi-ness
ha-rass
har-bor
hast-i-ly
hav-ing
haz-ard-ous
height
hem-or-rhage
hes-i-tate
hin-drance
his-to-ry
hoarse
hol-i-day
hon-or
hop-ing
hop-ping
horde
hor-ri-ble
hos-pi-tal
hu-mor-ous
hur-ried-ly
hy-drau-lic
hy-giene

I

i-am-bic
i-ci-cle
i-den-ti-cal
id-io-syn-cra-sy
il-leg-i-ble
il-lit-er-ate

il-lus-trate
im-ag-i-nary
im-ag-i-na-tive
im-ag-ine
im-i-ta-tion
im-me-di-ate-ly
im-mense
im-mi-grant
im-mor-tal
im-pa-tient
im-per-a-tive
im-por-tance
im-pos-si-ble
im-promp-tu
im-prove-ment
in-al-ien-able
in-ci-den-tal-ly
in-con-ve-nience
in-cred-i-ble
in-curred
in-def-i-nite-ly
in-del-ible
in-de-pend-ence
in-de-pend-ent
in-dict-ment
in-dis-pens-able
in-di-vid-u-al
in-duce-ment
in-dus-tri-al
in-dus-tri-ous
in-ev-i-ta-ble
in-fe-ri-or
in-ferred
in-fi-nite
in-flam-ma-ble
in-flu-en-tial
in-ge-nious
in-gen-u-ous
in-im-i-ta-ble
in-i-tial
ini-ti-a-tion
in-no-cence
in-no-cent
in-oc-u-la-tion
in-quir-y
in-stal-la-tion
in-stance
in-stead
in-sti-tute
in-struc-tor
in-sur-ance
in-tel-lec-tu-al

in-tel-li-gence
in-ten-tion
in-ter-cede
in-ter-est-ing
in-ter-fere
in-ter-mit-tent
in-ter-pret (-ed)
in-ter-rupt
in-ter-view
in-ti-mate
in-va-lid
in-ves-ti-gate
in-ves-tor
in-vi-ta-tion
ir-i-des-cent
ir-rel-e-vant
ir-re-sis-ti-ble
ir-rev-er-ent
ir-ri-gate
is-land
is-sue
i-tem-ized
i-tin-er-ar-y

J

jan-i-tor
jeal-ous (-y)
jeop-ar-dize
jew-el-ry
jour-nal
jour-ney
judg-ment
jus-tice
jus-ti-fi-able

K

kitch-en
knowl-edge
knuck-le

L

la-bel
lab-o-ra-to-ry
lac-quer
lan-guage
laugh
laun-dry
law-yer
league
lec-ture
le-gal
leg-i-ble

leg-is-la-ture
le-git-i-mate
lei-sure
length
let-ter-head
li-a-bil-i-ty
li-a-ble
li-ai-son
lib-er-al
li-brar-y
li-cense
lieu-ten-ant
light-ning
lik-able
like-ly
lin-eage
liq-ue-fy
liq-uid
lis-ten
lit-er-ary
lit-er-a-ture
live-li-hood
log-a-rithm
lone-li-ness
loose
lose
los-ing
lov-able
love-ly
lun-cheon
lux-u-ry

M

ma-chine
mag-a-zine
mag-nif-i-cent
main-tain
main-te-nance
ma-jor-i-ty
mak-ing
man-age-ment
ma-neu-ver
man-u-al
man-u-fac-ture
man-u-script
mar-riage
mar-shal
ma-te-ri-al
math-e-mat-ics
max-i-mum
may-or
mean-ness

meant
mea-sure
med-i-cine
me-di-eval
me-di-o-cre
me-di-um
mem-o-ran-dum
men-us
mer-chan-dise
mer-it
mes-sage
mile-age
mil-lion-aire
min-i-a-ture
min-i-mum
min-ute
mir-ror
mis-cel-la-neous
mis-chief
mis-chie-vous
mis-er-a-ble
mis-ery
mis-sile
mis-sion-ary
mis-spell
mois-ture
mol-e-cule
mo-men-tous
mo-not-o-nous
mon-u-ment
mort-gage
mu-nic-i-pal
mus-cle
mu-si-cian
mus-tache
mys-te-ri-ous

N

na-ive
nat-u-ral-ly
nec-es-sary
ne-ces-si-ty
neg-li-gi-ble
ne-go-ti-ate
neigh-bor-hood
nev-er-the-less
nick-el
niece
nine-teenth
nine-ty
no-tice-able
no-to-ri-ety

nu-cle-ar
nui-sance

O

o-be-di-ence
o-bey
o-blige
ob-sta-cle
oc-ca-sion
oc-ca-sion-al-ly
oc-cu-pant
oc-cur
oc-curred
oc-cur-rence
of-fense
of-fi-cial
of-ten
o-mis-sion
o-mit-ted
op-er-ate
o-pin-ion
op-po-nent
op-por-tu-ni-ty
op-po-site
op-ti-mism
or-di-nance
or-di-nar-i-ly
orig-i-nal
out-ra-geous

P

pag-eant
pam-phlet
par-a-dise
para-graph
par-al-lel
par-a-lyze
pa-ren-the-ses
pa-ren-the-sis
par-lia-ment
par-tial
par-tic-i-pant
par-tic-i-pate
par-tic-u-lar-ly
pas-time
pa-tience
pa-tron-age
pe-cu-liar
per-ceive
per-haps
per-il
per-ma-nent

per-mis-si-ble
per-pen-dic-u-lar
per-se-ver-ance
per-sis-tent
per-son-al (-ly)
per-son-nel
per-spi-ra-tion
per-suade
phase
phe-nom-e-non
phi-los-o-phy
phy-si-cian
piece
planned
pla-teau
plau-si-ble
play-wright
pleas-ant
plea-sure
pneu-mo-nia
pol-i-ti-cian
pos-sess
pos-ses-sion
pos-si-ble
prac-ti-cal-ly
prai-rie
pre-cede
pre-ce-dence
pre-ced-ing
pre-cious
pre-cise-ly
pre-ci-sion
pre-de-ces-sor
pref-er-a-ble
pref-er-ence
pre-ferred
prej-u-dice
pre-lim-i-nar-y
pre-mi-um
prep-a-ra-tion
pres-ence
prev-a-lent
pre-vi-ous
prim-i-tive
prin-ci-pal
prin-ci-ple
pri-or-i-ty
pris-on-er
priv-i-lege
prob-a-bly
pro-ce-dure
pro-ceed

pro-fes-sor
prom-i-nent
pro-nounce
pro-nun-ci-a-tion
pro-pa-gan-da
pros-e-cute
pro-tein
psy-chol-o-gy
pub-lic-ly
pump-kin
pur-chase
pur-sue
pur-su-ing
pur-suit

Q

qual-i-fied
qual-i-ty
quan-ti-ty
quar-ter
ques-tion-naire
quite
quo-tient

R

raise
rap-port
re-al-ize
re-al-ly
re-cede
re-ceipt
re-ceive
re-ceived
rec-i-pe
re-cip-i-ent
rec-og-ni-tion
rec-og-nize
rec-om-mend
re-cur-rence
ref-er-ence
re-ferred
reg-is-tra-tion
re-hearse
reign
re-im-burse
rel-e-vant
re-lieve
re-li-gious
re-mem-ber
re-mem-brance
rem-i-nisce
ren-dez-vous

re-new-al
rep-e-ti-tion
rep-re-sen-ta-tive
req-ui-si-tion
res-er-voir
re-sis-tance
re-spect-a-bly
re-spect-ful-ly
re-spec-tive-ly
re-spon-si-bil-i-ty
res-tau-rant
rheu-ma-tism
rhyme
rhythm
ri-dic-u-lous
route

S

sac-ri-le-gious
safe-ty
sal-a-ry
sand-wich
sat-is-fac-to-ry
Sat-ur-day
scarce-ly
scene
scen-er-y
sched-ule
schol-ar-ship
sci-ence
scis-sors
sec-re-tary
seize
sen-si-ble
sen-tence
sen-ti-nel
sep-a-rate
ser-geant
sev-er-al
se-vere-ly
shep-herd
sher-iff
shin-ing
siege
sig-nif-i-cance
sim-i-lar

si-mul-ta-ne-ous
since
sin-cere-ly
ski-ing
sol-dier
sol-emn
so-phis-ti-cat-ed
soph-o-more
so-ror-i-ty
source
sou-ve-nir
spa-ghet-ti
spe-cif-ic
spec-i-men
speech
sphere
spon-sor
spon-ta-ne-ous
sta-tion-ary
sta-tion-ery
sta-tis-tic
stat-ue
stat-ure
stat-ute
stom-ach
stopped
straight
strat-e-gy
strength
stretched
study-ing
sub-si-dize
sub-stan-tial
sub-sti-tute
sub-tle
suc-ceed
suc-cess
suf-fi-cient
sum-ma-rize
su-per-fi-cial
su-per-in-tend-
   ent
su-pe-ri-or-i-ty
su-per-sede
sup-ple-ment
sup-pose

sure-ly
sur-prise
sur-veil-lance
sur-vey
sus-cep-ti-ble
sus-pi-cious
sus-te-nance
syl-la-ble
sym-met-ri-cal
sym-pa-thy
sym-pho-ny
symp-tom
syn-chro-nous

T

tar-iff
tech-nique
tele-gram
tem-per-a-ment
tem-per-a-ture
tem-po-rary
ten-den-cy
ten-ta-tive
ter-res-tri-al
ter-ri-ble
ter-ri-to-ry
the-ater
their
there-fore
thief
thor-ough (-ly)
though
through-out
tired
to-bac-co
to-geth-er
to-mor-row
tongue
to-night
touch
tour-na-ment
tour-ni-quet
to-ward
trag-e-dy
trai-tor
tran-quil-iz-er

trans-ferred
trea-sur-er
tru-ly
Tues-day
tu-i-tion
typ-i-cal
typ-ing

U

unan-i-mous
un-con-scious
un-doubt-ed-ly
un-for-tu-nate-ly
unique
u-ni-son
uni-ver-si-ty
un-nec-es-sary
un-prec-e-
dent-ed
un-til
up-per
ur-gent
us-able
use-ful
using
usu-al-ly
u-ten-sil
u-til-ize

V

va-can-cies
va-ca-tion
vac-u-um
vague
valu-able
va-ri-ety
var-i-ous
veg-e-ta-ble
ve-hi-cle
veil
ve-loc-i-ty
ven-geance
vi-cin-i-ty
view
vig-i-lance
vil-lain

vi-o-lence
vis-i-bil-i-ty
vis-i-ble
vis-i-tor
voice
vol-ume
vol-un-tary
vol-un-teer

W

wan-der
war-rant
weath-er
Wednes-day
weird
wel-come
wel-fare
where
wheth-er
which
whole
whol-ly
whose
width
wom-en
worth-while
wor-thy
wreck-age
wres-tler
writ-ing
writ-ten
wrought

Y

yel-low
yes-ter-day
yield

Steps to Becoming a Better Speller

1. **Be patient.** Becoming a good speller takes time.

2. **Check the correct pronunciation of each word you are attempting to spell.**

   Knowing the correct pronunciation of each word can help you to remember its spelling.

3. **Note the meaning and history of each word as you are checking the dictionary for the pronunciation.**

   Knowing the meaning and history of a word provides you with a better notion of how the word is properly used, and it can help you remember the word's spelling.

4. **Before you close the dictionary, practice spelling the word.**

   You can do so by looking away from the page and trying to "see" the word in your "mind's eye." Write the word on a piece of paper. Check the spelling in the dictionary and repeat the process until you are able to spell the word correctly.

5. **Learn some spelling rules.**

   The four rules in this handbook (page 599) are four of the most useful—although there are others.

6. **Make a list of the words that you misspell.**

   Select the first ten words and practice spelling them.

   First: Read each word carefully; then write it on a piece of paper. Look at the written word to see that it's spelled correctly. Repeat the process for those words that you misspelled.

   Then: Ask someone to read the words to you so you can write them again. Then check for misspellings. Repeat both steps with your next ten words.

7. **Write often.**

   As noted educator Frank Smith said,

   "There is little point in learning to spell
   if you have little intention of writing."

Mechanics Exercises:

Spelling

On your own paper, correct any spelling errors in the following letter by writing the line number and the correct spelling of the word(s).

Dear Dr. Hanson: *1*

I wanted to pass along an updat regarding my project for the Undergraduate   *2*

Recearch Conference. I'm makin great progress, but I have a few questions.   *3*

I'll start with my progress: *4*

- As of Febuary 21, my primary and secondary research is in excelent   *5*
  order.   *6*
- I've completed writng, revising, and editing my literature review.   *7*
- I beleive I will finish a first draft by the end of the week.   *8*

Here are my questions for you: *9*

- Should I make a PowerPoint version for my presentation?   *10*
- Who is in charge of advertiseing for the event?   *11*
- How soon from now will room asignments be announced?   *12*

I've really enjoyed researching the relatinship between stress and eating   *13*

habits among college students. You'll find the introduction to my   *14*

presentation in the enclosed pamflet.   *15*

Thanks for takin the time to read over these materials.   *16*

Sinserely,   *17*

Jim White   *18*

Audio

Video

35 Using the Right Word

a, an Use *a* as the article before words that begin with consonant sounds and before words that begin with the long vowel sound *u* (yü). Use *an* before words that begin with other vowel sounds.

> **An** older student showed Kris **an** easier way to get to class.
> **A** uniform is required attire for **a** cafeteria worker.

607.1

a lot, alot, allot *Alot* is not a word; *a lot* (two words) is a vague descriptive phrase that should be used sparingly, especially in formal writing. *Allot* means to give someone a share.

> Prof Dubi **allots** each of us five spelling errors per semester, and he thinks that's **a lot**.

607.2

accept, except The verb *accept* means "to receive or believe"; the preposition *except* means "other than."

> The instructor **accepted** the student's story about being late, but she wondered why no one **except** him had forgotten about the change to daylight saving time.

607.3

adapt, adopt, adept *Adapt* means "to adjust or change to fit"; *adopt* means "to choose and treat as your own" (a child, an idea). *Adept* is an adjective meaning "proficient or well trained."

> After much thought and deliberation, we agreed to **adopt** the black Lab from the shelter. Now we have to agree on how to **adapt** our lifestyle to fit our new roommate.

607.4

adverse, averse *Adverse* means "hostile, unfavorable, or harmful." *Averse* means "to have a definite feeling of distaste—disinclined."

> Groans and other **adverse** reactions were noted as the new students, **averse** to strenuous exercise, were ushered past the X-5000 pump-and-crunch machine.

607.5

advice, advise *Advice* is a noun meaning "information or recommendation"; *advise* is a verb meaning "to recommend."

> Successful people will often give you sound **advice**, so I **advise** you to listen.

607.6

affect, effect *Affect* means "to influence"; the noun *effect* means "the result."

> The employment growth in a field will **affect** your chances of getting a job. The **effect** may be a new career choice.

607.7

608.1   **aid, aide** As a verb, *aid* means "to help"; as a noun, *aid* means "the help given." An *aide* is a person who acts as an assistant.

608.2   **all, of** Of is seldom needed after all.

> **All** the reports had an error in them.
> **All** the speakers spoke English.
> **All of** us voted to reschedule the meeting.
> (Here *of* is needed for the sentence to make sense.)

608.3   **all right, alright** *Alright* is the incorrect form of *all right*. (**Note:** The following are spelled correctly: *always, altogether, already, almost.*)

608.4   **allude, elude** *Allude* means "to indirectly refer to or hint at something"; *elude* means "to escape attention or understanding altogether."

> Ravi often **alluded** to wanting a supper invitation by mentioning the "awfully good" smells from the kitchen. These hints never **eluded** Ma's good heart.

608.5   **allusion, illusion** *Allusion* is an indirect reference to something or someone, especially in literature; *illusion* is a false picture or idea.

> Did you recognize the **allusion** to David in the reading assignment? Until I read that part, I was under the **illusion** that the young boy would run away from the bully.

608.6   **already, all ready** *Already* is an adverb meaning "before this time" or "by this time." *All ready* is an adjective form meaning "fully prepared." (**Note:** Use *all ready* if you can substitute *ready* alone in the sentence.)

> By the time I was a junior in high school, I had **already** taken my SATs. That way, I was **all ready** to apply early to college.

608.7   **altogether, all together** *Altogether* means "entirely." *All together* means "in a group" or "all at once." (**Note:** Use *all together* if you can substitute *together* alone in the sentence.)

> **All together** there are 35,000 job titles to choose from. That's **altogether** too many to even think about.

608.8   **among, between** *Among* is used when emphasizing distribution throughout a body or a group of three or more; *between* is used when emphasizing distribution to two individuals.

> There was discontent **among** the relatives after learning that their aunt had divided her entire fortune **between** a canary and a favorite waitress at the local cafe.

608.9   **amoral, immoral** *Amoral* means "neither moral (right) nor immoral (wrong)"; *immoral* means "wrong, or in conflict with traditional values."

> Carnivores are **amoral** in their hunt; poachers are **immoral** in theirs.

608.10   **amount, number** *Amount* is used for bulk measurement. *Number* is used to count separate units. (See also **fewer.**)

> The **number** of new instructors hired next year will depend on the **amount** of revenue raised by the new sales tax.

and etc. Don't use *and* before etc. since *et cetera* means "and the rest." 609.1

> Did you remember your textbook, notebook, handout, **etc.**?

annual, biannual, semiannual, biennial, perennial An *annual* event happens once every 609.2
year. A *biannual* event happens twice a year (*semiannual* is the same as *biannual*). A *biennial*
event happens every two years. A *perennial* event happens throughout the year, every year.

anxious, eager Both words mean "looking forward to," but *anxious* also connotes fear or 609.3
concern.

> The professor is **eager** to move into the new building, but she's a little **anxious** that
> students won't be able to find her new office.

anymore, any more *Anymore* (an adverb) means "any longer"; *any more* means "any 609.4
additional."

> We won't use that textbook **anymore**; call if you have **any mor**e questions.

any one (of), anyone *Any one* means "any one of a number of people, places, or things"; 609.5
anyone is a pronoun meaning "any person."

> Choose **any one** of the proposed weekend schedules. **Anyone** wishing to work on
> Saturday instead of Sunday may do so.

appraise, apprise *Appraise* means "to determine value." *Apprise* means "to inform." 609.6

> Because of the tax assessor's recent **appraisal** of our home, we were **apprised** of an
> increase in our property tax.

as Don't use *as* in place of *whether* or *if*. 609.7

> I don't know **as** I'll accept the offer. (Incorrect)
> I don't know **whether** I'll accept the offer. (Correct)

Don't use *as* when it is unclear whether it means *because* or *when*.

> We rowed toward shore **as** it started raining. (Unclear)
> We rowed toward shore **because** it started raining. (Correct)

assure, ensure, insure (See insure.)

bad, badly *Bad* is an adjective, used both before nouns and as a predicate adjective after 609.8
linking verbs. *Badly* is an adverb.

> Christina felt **bad** about serving us **bad** food.
> Larisa played **badly** today.

beside, besides *Beside* means "by the side of." *Besides* means "in addition to." 609.9

> **Besides** the two suitcases you've already loaded into the trunk, remember the smaller
> one **beside** the van.

between, among (See among.)

bring, take *Bring* suggests the action is directed toward the speaker; *take* suggests the action 609.10
is directed away from the speaker.

> If you're not going to **bring** the video to class, **take** it back to the resource center.

Using the Right Word Exercises:

Using the Right Word I

A. Selecting the Right Word

On your own paper, write the correct word from those in parentheses for each sentence.

1. Hunter was (*accepted, excepted*) into a summer internship program at an accounting firm.
2. The celebrity was unable to (*allude, elude*) the paparazzi outside of the night club.
3. Juan is quite (*adapt, adopt, adept*) at playing the electric guitar.
4. Does (*anyone, any one*) know of a scenic location for a Sunday picnic?
5. I feel (*anxious, eager*) around people who are loud and outgoing.
6. Today was a good day because it did not go as (*bad, badly*) as yesterday.
7. (*Altogether, All together*) thirty-five people waited outside of the movie theater for the premiere of the new movie.
8. Are you under the (*allusion, illusion*) that the young businesswoman will abandon her friends?
9. The new round of layoffs may (*affect, effect*) my position with the company.
10. What (*amount, number*) of money will it take to purchase a plane ticket to France?

B. Replacing Incorrect Words

For each sentence below, write the misused words, cross them out, and write the correct words beside them.

1. Phil appraised his buddy about the affects of pushing a car more than 3,000 miles without a oil change.

2. Do you mean to elude that I'm in need of some fashion advise?

3. A strong friendship among Cary and Nyssa helped get them through an averse situation.

can, may In formal contexts, *can* is used to mean "being able to do"; *may* is used to mean "having permission to do."

> **May** I borrow your bicycle to get to the library? Then I **can** start working on our group project.

611.1

capital, capitol The noun *capital* refers to a city or to money. The adjective *capital* means "major or important" or "seat of government." *Capitol* refers to a building.

> The **capitol** is in the **capital** city for a **capital** reason. The city government contributed **capital** for the building expense.

611.2

cent, sent, scent *Cent* is a coin; *sent* is the past tense of the verb "send"; *scent* is an odor or a smell.

> For forty-one **cents**, I **sent** my friend a love poem in a perfumed envelope. She adored the **scent** but hated the poem.

611.3

chord, cord *Chord* may mean "an emotion or a feeling," but it also may mean "the combination of three or more tones sounded at the same time," as with a guitar *chord*. A *cord* is a string or a rope.

> The guitar player strummed the opening **chord**, which struck a responsive **chord** with the audience.

611.4

chose, choose *Chose* (chōz) is the past tense of the verb *choose* (chüz). (See 637.)

> For generations, people **chose** their careers based on their parents' careers; now people **choose** their careers based on the job market.

611.5

climactic, climatic *Climactic* refers to the climax, or high point, of an event; *climatic* refers to the climate, or weather conditions.

> Because we are using the open-air amphitheater, **climatic** conditions will just about guarantee the wind gusts we need for the **climactic** third act.

611.6

☑
Exercise

coarse, course *Coarse* means "of inferior quality, rough, or crude"; *course* means "a direction or a path taken." *Course* also means "a class or a series of studies."

> A basic writing **course** is required of all students.
>
> Due to years of woodworking, the instructor's hands are rather **coarse**.

611.7

compare with, compare to Things in the same category are *compared with* each other; things in different categories are *compared to* each other.

> **Compare** Christopher Marlowe's plays **with** William Shakespeare's plays.
>
> My brother **compared** reading *The Tempest* **to** visiting another country.

611.8

complement, compliment *Complement* means "to complete or go well with." *Compliment* means "to offer an expression of admiration or praise."

> We wanted to **compliment** Zach on his decorating efforts; the bright yellow walls **complement** the purple carpet.

611.9

comprehensible, comprehensive *Comprehensible* means "capable of being understood"; *comprehensive* means "covering a broad range, or inclusive."

> The theory is **comprehensible** only to those who have a **comprehensive** knowledge of physics.

611.10

612.1 **comprise, compose** *Comprise* means "to contain or consist of"; *compose* means "to create or form by bringing parts together."

> Fruitcake **comprises** a variety of nuts, candied fruit, and spice.
>
> Fruitcake is **composed of** (not *comprised of*) a variety of ingredients.

612.2 **conscience, conscious** A *conscience* gives one the capacity to know right from wrong. *Conscious* means "awake or alert, not sleeping or comatose."

> Your **conscience** will guide you, but you have to be **conscious** to hear what it's "saying."

612.3 **continual, continuous** *Continual* often implies that something is happening often, recurring; *continuous* usually implies that something keeps happening, uninterrupted.

> The **continuous** loud music during the night gave the building manager not only a headache but also **continual** phone calls.

612.4 **counsel, council, consul** When used as a noun, *counsel* means "advice"; when used as a verb, *counsel* means "to advise." *Council* refers to a group that advises. A *consul* is a government official appointed to reside in a foreign country.

> The city **council** was asked to **counsel** our student **council** on running an efficient meeting. Their **counsel** was very helpful.

612.5 **decent, descent, dissent** *Decent* means "good." *Descent* is the process of going or stepping downward. *Dissent* means "disagreement."

> The food was **decent**.
>
> The elevator's fast **descent** clogged my ears.
>
> Their **dissent** over the decisions was obvious in their sullen expressions.

612.6 **desert, dessert** *Desert* is barren wilderness. *Dessert* is food served at the end of a meal. The verb *desert* means "to abandon."

612.7 **different from, different than** Use *different* from in formal writing; use either form in informal or colloquial settings.

> Rafael's interpretation was **different from** Andrea's.

612.8 **discreet, discrete** *Discreet* means "showing good judgment, unobtrusive, modest"; *discrete* means "distinct, separate."

> The essay question had three **discrete** parts.
>
> Her roommate had apparently never heard of quiet, **discreet** conversation.

612.9 **disinterested, uninterested** Both words mean "not interested." However, *disinterested* is also used to mean "unbiased or impartial."

> A person chosen as an arbitrator must be a **disinterested** party.
>
> Professor Eldridge was **uninterested** in our complaints about the assignment.

effect, affect (See affect.)

612.10 **elicit, illicit** *Elicit* is a verb meaning "to bring out." *Illicit* is an adjective meaning "unlawful."

> It took a hand signal to **elicit** the **illicit** exchange of cash for drugs.

eminent, imminent *Eminent* means "prominent, conspicuous, or famous"; *imminent* means "ready or threatening to happen."

613.1

With the island's government about to collapse, assassination attempts on several **eminent** officials seemed **imminent**.

ensure, insure, assure (See **insure**.)

except, accept (See **accept**.)

explicit, implicit *Explicit* means "expressed directly or clearly defined"; *implicit* means "implied or unstated."

613.2

The professor **explicitly** asked that the experiment be wrapped up on Monday, **implicitly** demanding that her lab assistants work on the weekend.

farther, further *Farther* refers to a physical distance; *further* refers to additional time, quantity, or degree.

613.3

Further research showed that walking **farther** rather than faster would improve his health.

fewer, less *Fewer* refers to the number of separate units; *less* refers to bulk quantity.

613.4

Because of spell checkers, students can produce papers containing **fewer** errors in **less** time.

figuratively, literally *Figuratively* means "in a metaphorical or analogous way—describing something by comparing it to something else"; *literally* means "actually."

613.5

The lab was **literally** filled with sulfurous gases—**figuratively** speaking, dragon's breath.

first, firstly Both words are adverbs meaning "before another in time" or "in the first place." However, do not use *firstly*, which is stiff and unnatural sounding.

613.6

Firstly I want to see the manager. (Incorrect)

First I want to see the manager. (Correct)

Exercise

Note: When enumerating, use the forms *first, second, third, next, last*—without the *ly*.

fiscal, physical *Fiscal* means "related to financial matters"; *physical* means "related to material things."

613.7

The school's **fiscal** work is handled by its accounting staff.

The **physical** work is handled by its maintenance staff.

for, fore, four *For* is a conjunction meaning "because" or is a preposition used to indicate the object or recipient of something; *fore* means "earlier" or "the front"; *four* is the word for the number 4.

613.8

The crew brought treats **for** the barge's **four** dogs, who always enjoy the breeze at the **fore** of the vessel.

former, latter When two things are being discussed, *former* refers to the first thing, and *latter* to the second.

613.9

Our choices are going to a movie or eating at the Pizza Palace: The **former** is too expensive, and the **latter** too fattening.

Using the Right Word Exercises:

Using the Right Word II

A. Selecting the Right Word

On your own paper, write the correct word from those in parentheses for each sentence.

1. The (*capital, capitol*) building looked radiant with the fall sunshine beaming on its white dome.

2. That jacket would (*complement, compliment*) the colors of your dress.

3. The museum had three (*discreet, discrete*) levels, each with a different theme.

4. Darren took (*counsel, council, consul*) from his internship coordinator regarding his career path.

5. Would you (*comprise, compose*) an updated report on our position in the New York power and electric industry?

6. Our destination along Interstate 43 was (*farther, further*) than we expected.

7. The (*climactic, climatic*) point of the baseball game occurred when Vicki caught a foul ball.

8. The (*decent, descent, dissent*) down Pike's Peak Mountain was a scary experience.

9. I was so sleepy that I felt barely (*conscience, conscious*).

10. The (*cent, sent, scent*) coming from the garbage left us all gagging for fresh air.

B. Replacing Incorrect Words

For each sentence below, write the misused words, cross them out, and write the correct words beside them.

1. Our second coarse was descent, but the desert was the real winner.

2. The farther we delay restructuring our finances, the worse our physical situation will be.

3. My aunt is firstly a good judge of character and second an imminent authority on all things Milwaukee.

good, well *Good* is an adjective; *well* is nearly always an adverb. (When used to indicate state of health, *well* is an adjective.)

615.1

> A **good** job offers opportunities for advancement, especially for those who do their jobs **well**.

heal, heel *Heal* (a verb) means "to mend or restore to health"; a *heel* (noun) is the back part of a human foot.

615.2

healthful, healthy *Healthful* means "causing or improving health"; *healthy* means "possessing health."

615.3

> **Healthful** foods and regular exercise build **healthy** bodies.

I, me *I* is a subject pronoun; *me* is used as an object of a preposition, a direct object, or an indirect object. (See 630.1.) (A good way to know if *I* or *me* should be used in a compound subject is to eliminate the other subject; the sentence should make sense with the pronoun—*I* or *me*—alone.)

615.4

Video

> My roommate and **me** went to the library last night. (Incorrect)
>
> My roommate and **I** went to the library last night. (Correct: Eliminate "my roommate and"; the sentence still makes sense.)
>
> Rasheed gave the concert tickets to Erick and **I**. (Incorrect)
>
> Rasheed gave the concert tickets to Erick and **me**. (Correct: Eliminate "Erick and"; the sentence still makes sense.)

illusion, allusion (See allusion.)

immigrate (to), emigrate (from) *Immigrate* means "to come into a new country or environment." *Emigrate* means "to go out of one country to live in another."

615.5

> **Immigrating** to a new country is a challenging experience.
>
> People **emigrating** from their homelands face unknown challenges.

imminent, eminent (See eminent.)

imply, infer *Imply* means "to suggest without saying outright"; *infer* means "to draw a conclusion from facts." (A writer or a speaker *implies*; a reader or a listener *infers*.)

615.6

> Dr. Rufus **implied** I should study more; I **inferred** he meant my grades had to improve, or I'd be repeating the class.

ingenious, ingenuous *Ingenious* means "intelligent, discerning, clever"; *ingenuous* means "unassuming, natural, showing childlike innocence and candidness."

615.7

> Gretchen devised an **ingenious** plan to work and receive college credit for it.
>
> Ramón displays an **ingenuous** quality that attracts others.

insure, ensure, assure *Insure* means "to secure from financial harm or loss," *ensure* means "to make certain of something," and *assure* means "to put someone's mind at rest."

615.8

> Plenty of studying generally **ensures** academic success.
>
> Nicole **assured** her father that she had **insured** her new car.

interstate, intrastate *Interstate* means "existing between two or more states"; *intrastate* means "existing within a state."

615.9

616.1   **irregardless, regardless** *Irregardless* is a nonstandard synonym for *regardless*.

> **Irregardless** of his circumstance, José is cheerful. (Incorrect)
> **Regardless** of his circumstance, José is cheerful. (Correct)

616.2   **it's, its** *It's* is the contraction of "it is." *Its* is the possessive form of "it."

> **It's** not hard to see why my husband feeds that alley cat; **its** pitiful limp and mournful mewing would melt any heart.

616.3   **later, latter** *Later* means "after a period of time." *Latter* refers to the second of two things mentioned.

> The **latter** of the two restaurants you mentioned sounds good.
> Let's meet there **later**.

616.4   **lay, lie** *Lay* means "to place." *Lay* is a transitive verb. (See 632.2.) Its principal parts are *lay, laid, laid.* (See 637.)

> If you **lay** another book on my table, I won't have room for anything else.
> Yesterday, you **laid** two books on the table.
> Over the last few days, you must have **laid** at least 20 books there.

Lie means "to recline." *Lie* is an intransitive verb. (See 632.2.) Its principal parts are *lie, lay, lain.*

> The cat **lies** down anywhere it pleases.
> It **lay** down yesterday on my tax forms.
> It has **lain** down many times on the kitchen table.

616.5   **learn, teach** *Learn* means "to acquire information"; *teach* means "to give information."

> Sometimes it's easier to **teach** someone else a lesson than it is to **learn** one yourself.

616.6   **leave, let** *Leave* means "to allow something to remain behind." *Let* means "to permit."

> Please **let** me help you carry that chair; otherwise, **leave** it for the movers to pick up.

616.7   **lend, borrow** *Lend* means "to give for temporary use"; *borrow* means "to receive for temporary use."

> I asked Haddad to **lend** me $15 for a CD, but he said I'd have to find someone else to **borrow** the money from.

less, fewer (See **fewer**.)

616.8   **liable, libel** *Liable* is an adjective meaning "responsible according to the law" or "exposed to an adverse action"; the noun *libel* is a written defamatory statement about someone, and the verb *libel* means "to publish or make such a statement."

> Supermarket tabloids, **liable** for ruining many a reputation, make a practice of **libeling** the rich and the famous.

616.9   **liable, likely** *Liable* means "responsible according to the law" or "exposed to an adverse action"; *likely* means "in all probability."

> Rain seems **likely** today, but if we cancel the game, we are still **liable** for paying the referees.

like, as *Like* should not be used in place of *as*. *Like* is a preposition, which is followed by its object (a noun, a pronoun, or a noun phrase). *As* is a subordinating conjunction, which introduces a clause. Do not use *like* as a subordinating conjunction. Use *as* instead.

> You don't know her **like** I do. (Incorrect)
>
> You don't know her **as** I do. (Correct)
>
> **Like** the others in my study group, I do my work as any serious student would— carefully and thoroughly. (Correct)

617.1

literally, figuratively (See figuratively.)

loose, lose, loss The adjective *loose* (lüs) means "free, untied, unrestricted"; the verb *lose* (lüz) means "to misplace or fail to find or control"; the noun *loss* (lòs) means "something that is misplaced and cannot be found."

> Her sadness at the **loss** of her longtime companion caused her to **lose** weight, and her clothes felt uncomfortably **loose**.

617.2

may, can (See can.)

maybe, may be Use *maybe* as an adverb meaning "perhaps;" use *may be* as a verb phrase.

> She **may be** the computer technician we've been looking for. **Maybe** she will upgrade the software and memory.

617.3

miner, minor A *miner* digs in the ground for ore. A *minor* is a person who is not legally an adult. The adjective *minor* means "of no great importance."

> The use of **minors** as coal **miners** is no **minor** problem.

617.4

number, amount (See amount.)

OK, okay This expression, spelled either way, is appropriate in informal writing; however, avoid using it in papers, reports, or formal correspondence of any kind.

> Your proposal is satisfactory [not okay] on most levels.

617.5

oral, verbal *Oral* means "uttered with the mouth"; *verbal* means "relating to or consisting of words and the comprehension of words."

> The actor's **oral** abilities were outstanding, her pronunciation and intonation impeccable, but I doubted the playwright's **verbal** skills after trying to decipher the play's meaning.

617.6

passed, past *Passed* is a verb. *Past* can be used as a noun, an adjective, or a preposition.

> That little pickup truck **passed** my 'Vette! (verb)
>
> My stepchildren hold on dearly to the **past**. (noun)
>
> I'm sorry, but my **past** life is not your business. (adjective)
>
> The officer drove **past** us, not noticing our flat tire. (preposition)

617.7

peace, piece *Peace* means "tranquility or freedom from war." A *piece* is a part or fragment.

> Someone once observed that **peace** is not a condition, but a process—a process of building goodwill one **piece** at a time.

617.8

Using the Right Word Exercises:

Using the Right Word III

A. Selecting the Right Word

On your own paper, write the correct word from those in parentheses for each sentence.

1. Raphael injured his (*heal, heel*) when he took out the trash shoeless.

2. (*Irregardless, Regardless*) of how you feel about the assignment, you have to get it done by Friday.

3. Could you (*borrow, lend*) me three quarters for laundry?

4. My car suffered (*miner, minor*) damages from last night's hailstorm.

5. You (*maybe, may be*) upset with me, but I hope you will soon forgive me.

6. Before you look to the future, you should recognize lessons from the (*passed, past*).

7. Can you (*insure, ensure, assure*) me that I will receive an annual review?

8. Andrew (*immigrated, emigrated*) from Australia.

9. The offender was found (*liable, libel*) for all medical expenses.

10. The Taj Mahal was incredible; I was most impressed by (*it's, its*) majesty.

B. Replacing Incorrect Words

For each sentence below, write the misused words, cross them out, and write the correct words beside them.

1. Despite feeling under the weather, Andre was good enough to give a verbal presentation at a company meeting.

2. Teresa inferred I should look for a new job, while I implied she meant I had no chance for a promotion.

3. Before you lie down another box, make sure the shelf is sturdy enough; otherwise it is liable to collapse.

people, person Use *people* to refer to human populations, races, or groups; use *person* to refer to an individual or the physical body.

619.1

> What the American **people** need is a good insect repellent.
>
> The forest ranger recommends that we check our **persons** for wood ticks when we leave the woods.

percent, percentage *Percent* means "per hundred"; for example, 60 percent of 100 jelly beans would be 60 jelly beans. *Percentage* refers to a portion of the whole. Generally, use the word *percent* when it is preceded by a number. Use *percentage* when no number is used.

619.2

> Each person's **percentage** of the reward amounted to $125—25 **percent** of the $500 offered by Crime Stoppers.

personal, personnel *Personal* (an adjective) means "private." *Personnel* (a noun) are people working at a particular job.

619.3

> Although choosing a major is a **personal** decision, it can be helpful to consult with guidance **personnel**.

perspective, prospective *Perspective* (a noun) is a point of view or the capacity to view things realistically; *prospective* is an adjective meaning "expected in or related to the future."

619.4

> From my immigrant neighbor's **perspective**, any job is a good job.
>
> **Prospective** students wandered the campus on visitors' day.

pore, pour, poor The noun *pore* is an opening in the skin; the verb *pore* means "to gaze intently." *Pour* means "to move with a continuous flow." *Poor* means "needy or pitiable."

619.5

> **Pour** hot water into a bowl, put your face over it, and let the steam open your **pores**. Your **poor** skin will thank you.

precede, proceed To *precede* means "to go or come before"; *proceed* means "to move on after having stopped" or "go ahead."

619.6

> Our biology instructor often **preceded** his lecture with these words:
>
> "OK, sponges, **proceed** to soak up more fascinating facts!"

principal, principle As an adjective, *principal* means "primary." As a noun, it can mean "a school administrator" or "a sum of money." A *principle* (noun) is an idea or a doctrine.

619.7

> His **principal** gripe is lack of freedom. (adjective)
>
> My son's **principal** expressed his concerns to the teachers. (noun)
>
> After 20 years, the amount of interest was higher than the **principal**. (noun)
>
> The **principle** of *caveat emptor* guides most consumer groups. (noun)

quiet, quit, quite *Quiet* is the opposite of noisy. *Quit* means "to stop or give up." *Quite* (an adverb) means "completely" or "to a considerable extent."

619.8

> The meeting remained **quite quiet** when the boss told us he'd **quit**.

quote, quotation *Quote* is a verb; *quotation* is a noun.

619.9

> The **quotation** I used was from Woody Allen. You may **quote** me on that.

real, very, really Do not use the adjective *real* in place of the adverbs *very* or *really*.

619.10

> My friend's cake is usually **very** [not *real*] fresh, but this cake is **really** stale.

620.1   **right, write, wright, rite**   *Right* means "correct or proper"; it also refers to that which a person has a legal claim to, as in *copyright*. Write means "to inscribe or record." A *wright* is a person who makes or builds something. *Rite* is a ritual or ceremonial act.

> Did you **write** that it is the **right** of the **shipwright** to perform the **rite** of christening—breaking a bottle of champagne on the bow of the ship?

620.2   **scene, seen**   *Scene* refers to the setting or location where something happens; it also may mean "sight or spectacle." *Seen* is the past participle of the verb "see."

> An exhibitionist likes to be **seen** making a **scene**.

620.3   **set, sit**   *Set* means "to place." *Sit* means "to put the body in a seated position." *Set* is a transitive verb; *sit* is an intransitive verb (See 632.2.).

> How can you just **sit** there and watch as I **set** the table?

620.4   **sight, cite, site**   *Sight* means "the act of seeing" (a verb) or "something that is seen" (a noun). *Cite* (a verb) means "to quote" or "to summon to court." *Site* means "a place or location" (noun) or "to place on a site" (verb).

> After **sighting** the faulty wiring, the inspector **cited** the building contractor for breaking two city codes at a downtown work **site**.

620.5   **some, sum**   *Some* refers to an unknown thing, an unspecified number, or a part of something. *Sum* is a certain amount of money or the result of adding numbers together.

> **Some** of the students answered too quickly and came up with the wrong **sum**.

620.6   **stationary, stationery**   *Stationary* means "not movable"; *stationery* refers to the paper and envelopes used to write letters.

> Odina uses **stationery** that she can feed through her portable printer. Then she drops the mail into a **stationary** mail receptacle at the mall.

take, bring   (See bring.)

teach, learn   (See learn.)

620.7   **than, then**   *Than* is used in a comparison; *then* is an adverb that tells when.

> Study more **than** you think you need to. **Then** you will probably be satisfied with your grades.

620.8   **their, there, they're**   *Their* is a possessive personal pronoun. *There* is an adverb used as a filler word or to point out location. *They're* is the contraction for "they are."

> Look over **there**. **There** is a comfortable place for students to study for **their** exams, so **they're** more likely to do a good job.

620.9   **threw, through**   *Threw* is the past tense of "throw." *Through* (a preposition) means "from one side of something to the other."

> In a fit of frustration, Sachiko **threw** his cell phone right **through** the window.

620.10   **to, too, two**   *To* is a preposition that can mean "in the direction of." *To* is also used to form an infinitive. *Too* (an adverb) means "also" or "very." *Two* is the number 2.

> **Two** causes of eye problems among students are lights that fail **to** illuminate properly and computer screens with **too** much glare.

vain, vane, vein *Vain* means "valueless or fruitless"; it may also mean "holding a high regard for oneself." *Vane* is a flat piece of material set up to show which way the wind blows. *Vein* refers to a blood vessel or a mineral deposit.

> The weather **vane** indicates the direction of the wind; the blood **vein** determines the direction of flowing blood; and the **vain** mind moves in no particular direction, content to think only about itself.

621.1

vary, very The verb *vary* means "to change"; the adverb *very* means "to a high degree."

> To ensure the **very** best employee relations, the workloads should not **vary** greatly from worker to worker.

621.2

verbal, oral (See oral.)

waist, waste The noun *waist* refers to the part of the body just above the hips. The verb *waste* means "to squander" or "to wear away, decay"; the noun *waste* refers to material that is unused or useless.

> His **waist** is small because he **wastes** no opportunity to exercise.

621.3

wait, weight *Wait* means "to stay somewhere expecting something." *Weight* refers to a degree or unit of heaviness.

> The **weight** of sadness eventually lessens; one must simply **wait** for the pain to dissipate.

621.4

ware, wear, where The noun *ware* refers to a product that is sold; the verb *wear* means "to have on or to carry on one's body"; the adverb *where* asks the question "In what place?" or "In what situation?"

> The designer boasted, "**Where** can one **wear** my **wares**? Anywhere."

621.5

weather, whether *Weather* refers to the condition of the atmosphere. *Whether* refers to a possibility.

> **Weather** conditions affect all of us, **whether** we are farmers or plumbers.

621.6

well, good (See good.)

which, that (See 567.3.)

who, which, that *Who* refers to people. *Which* refers to nonliving objects or to animals. (*Which* should never refer to people.) *That* may refer to animals, people, or nonliving objects. (See also 567.3.)

621.7

who, whom *Who* is used as the subject of a verb; *whom* is used as the object of a preposition or as a direct object.

> Captain Mather, to **whom** the survivors owe their lives, is the man **who** is being honored today.

621.8

who's, whose *Who's* is the contraction for "who is." *Whose* is a possessive pronoun.

> **Whose** car are we using, and **who's** going to pay for the gas?

621.9

your, you're *Your* is a possessive pronoun. *You're* is the contraction for "you are."

> If **you're** like most Americans, you will have held eight jobs by **your** fortieth birthday.

621.10

Using the Right Word Exercises:

Using the Right Word IV

A. Selecting the Right Word

On your own paper, write the correct word from those in parentheses for each sentence.

1. The (*principal, principle*) of relativity applies to any scientific investigation.

2. Vince gave an interesting (*perspective, prospective*) on the importance of workplace writing proficiency.

3. The large piece of rock that fell from the cliff face remained (*stationary, stationery*) near the entrance to the hiking trail.

4. Have you decided (*weather, whether*) to take your boyfriend to your Thanksgiving dinner?

5. If (*your, you're*) planning to begin work on Monday, we'll have the training materials ready for you.

6. Latoya tried in (*vain, vane, vein*) to find her missing car keys.

7. I think Christopher Nolan's *Inception* is even better (*than, then*) *The Dark Knight*.

8. The professor reminded her students to (*sight, cite, site*) any sources they use in their papers.

9. Mack and Gordon discussed (*who's, whose*) car they should take to the mall.

10. Although not recommended, pulling an all-night study session is considered a (*right, write, wright, rite*) of passage among college students.

B. Replacing Incorrect Words

For each sentence below, write the misused words, cross them out, and write the correct words beside them.

1. The company began making personal changes by interviewing perspective suitors.

2. Students whom wish to proceed with the medical mission trip will need to bring there applications to the volunteer office.

3. Hopefully the some of my two checks will not go to waist at the casino.

36 Understanding Grammar

Audio

Grammar is the study of the structure and features of the language, consisting of rules and standards that are to be followed to produce acceptable writing and speaking. **Parts of speech** refers to the eight different categories that indicate how words are used in the English language—as *nouns, pronouns, verbs, adjectives, adverbs, prepositions, conjunctions,* or *interjections.*

Noun

623.1

A **noun** is a word that names something: a person, a place, a thing, or an idea.

Toni Morrison/author	*Lone Star*/film	Renaissance/era
UC-Davis/university	*A Congress of Wonders*/book	

Exercise

esl Note: See 671.1–672.2 for information on count and noncount nouns.

Classes of Nouns

All nouns are either proper nouns or common nouns. Nouns may also be classified as *individual* or *collective,* or *concrete* or *abstract.*

Proper Nouns

623.2

A **proper noun,** which is always capitalized, names a specific person, place, thing, or idea.

Rembrandt, Bertrand Russell (people)

Stratford-upon-Avon, Tower of London (places)

The Night Watch, **Rosetta stone** (things)

New Deal, Christianity (ideas)

Common Nouns

623.3

A **common noun** is a general name for a person, a place, a thing, or an idea. Common nouns are not capitalized.

optimist, instructor (people)	**cafeteria, park** (places)
computer, chair (things)	**freedom, love** (ideas)

624.1   ### Collective Nouns

A **collective noun** names a group or a unit.

     family   audience   crowd   committee   team   class

624.2   ### Concrete Nouns

A **concrete noun** names a thing that is tangible (can be seen, touched, heard, smelled, or tasted).

     child   The White Stripes   gym   village   microwave oven   pizza

624.3   ### Abstract Nouns

An **abstract noun** names an idea, a condition, or a feeling—in other words, something that cannot be seen, touched, heard, smelled, or tasted.

     beauty   Jungian psychology   anxiety   agoraphobia   trust

Forms of Nouns

Nouns are grouped according to their *number*, *gender*, and *case*.

624.4   ### Number of Nouns

Number indicates whether a noun is singular or plural.

A singular noun refers to one person, place, thing, or idea.

     student   laboratory   lecture   note   grade   result

A plural noun refers to more than one person, place, thing, or idea.

     students   laboratories   lectures   notes   grades   results

624.5   ### Gender of Nouns

Gender indicates whether a noun is masculine, feminine, neuter, or indefinite.

     Masculine:
         father   king   brother   men   colt   rooster
     Feminine:
         mother   queen   sister   women   filly   hen
     Neuter (without sex):
         notebook   monitor   car   printer
     Indefinite or common (masculine or feminine):
         professor   customer   children   doctor   people

Case of Nouns

The **case** of a noun tells what role the noun plays in a sentence. There are three cases: *nominative, possessive,* and *objective.*

A noun in the **nominative case** is used as a subject. The subject of a sentence tells who or what the sentence is about.

> **Dean Henning** manages the College of Arts and Communication.

Note: A noun is also in the nominative case when it is used as a predicate noun (or predicate nominative). A predicate noun follows a linking verb, usually a form of the *be* verb (such as *am, is, are, was, were, be, being, been*), and repeats or renames the subject.

> Ms. Yokum is the **person** to talk to about the college's impact in our community.

A noun in the **possessive case** shows possession or ownership. In this form, it acts as an adjective.

> Our **president's** willingness to discuss concerns with students has boosted campus morale.

A noun in the **objective case** serves as an object of the preposition, a direct object, an indirect object, or an object complement.

> To survive, institutions of higher **learning** sometimes cut **budgets** in spite of **protests** from **students** and **instructors**. (*Learning* is the object of the preposition *of, protests* is the object of the preposition *in spite of, budgets* is the direct object of the verb *cut,* and *students* and *instructors* are the objects of the preposition *from.*)

A Closer Look
at Direct and Indirect Objects

A **direct object** is a noun (or pronoun) that identifies what or who receives the action of the verb.

> Budget cutbacks reduced class **choices**. (*Choices* is the direct object of the active verb *reduced.*)

An **indirect object** is a noun (or pronoun) that identifies the person *to whom* or *for whom* something is done, or the thing *to which or for which* something is done. An indirect object is always accompanied by a direct object.

> Recent budget cuts have given **students** fewer class choices. (*Choices* is the direct object of *have given; students* is the indirect object.)

esl Note: Not every transitive verb is followed by *both* a direct object and an indirect object. Both can, however, follow *give, send, show, tell, teach, find, sell, ask, offer, pay, pass,* and *hand.*

Grammar Exercises:

Nouns

A. Classes of Nouns

On your own paper, identify the class or classes that correctly describe the underlined noun in each sentence.

1. Jenna used a <u>pencil</u> to sketch a design for the new recreational center.
   - a. proper noun
   - b. common noun
   - c. concrete noun

2. My <u>team</u> won a regional debate championship.
   - a. collective noun
   - b. common noun
   - c. abstract noun

3. The end of the movie left me with deep <u>disappointment</u>.
   - a. common noun
   - b. concrete noun
   - c. abstract noun

4. Tomorrow night I'm going to the <u>Arizona Diamondbacks</u> game.
   - a. proper noun
   - b. abstract noun
   - c. common noun

5. Can someone buy me a <u>soda</u> at the store?
   - a. collective noun
   - b. concrete noun
   - c. abstract noun

6. I'm trying to work up the <u>motivation</u> to go to the gym.
   - a. proper noun
   - b. common noun
   - c. abstract noun

B. Case of Nouns

For each sentence identify the case of the underlined noun.

1. Social media websites have changed the way we receive <u>news</u>.
   - a. nominative case
   - b. possessive case
   - c. objective case

2. <u>Kings of Leon</u> play rock music.
   - a. nominative case
   - b. possessive case
   - c. objective case

3. <u>Justin's</u> favorite restaurant is on LaGrange Avenue.
   - a. nominative case
   - b. possessive case
   - c. objective case

C. Gender of Nouns

Write down the feminine nouns from the list below.

desk   writer   princess   child   pilot   tree   waitress

Pronoun

627.1

A **pronoun** is a word that is used in place of a noun.

> Roger was the most interesting 10-year-old **I** ever taught. **He** was a good thinker and thus a good writer. **I** remember **his** paragraph about the cowboy hat **he** received from **his** grandparents. **It** was "too new looking." The brim was not rolled properly. But the hat's imperfections were not the main idea in Roger's writing. No, the main idea was how **he** was fixing the hat **himself** by wearing it when **he** showered.

Antecedents

627.2

An **antecedent** is the noun or pronoun that the pronoun refers to or replaces. Most pronouns have antecedents, but not all do. (See 628.4.)

> As the wellness **counselor** checked *her* chart, several **students** *who* were waiting *their* turns shifted uncomfortably. (*Counselor* is the antecedent of *her*; *students* is the antecedent of *who* and *their*.)

> **Note:** Each pronoun must agree with its antecedent in number, person, and gender. (See pages 629–630 and 659.)

627.3

Classes of Pronouns

Personal

I, me, my, mine / we, us, our, ours / you, your, yours
they, them, their, theirs / he, him, his, she, her, hers, it, its

Reflexive and Intensive

myself, yourself, himself, herself, itself, ourselves, yourselves, themselves

Relative

who, whose, whom, which, that

Indefinite

all	anything	everybody	most	no one	some
another	both	everyone	much	nothing	somebody
any	each	everything	neither	one	someone
anybody	each one	few	nobody	other	something
anyone	either	many	none	several	such

Interrogative

who, whose, whom, which, what

Demonstrative

this, that, these, those

Reciprocal

each other, one another

Classes of Pronouns

There are several classes of pronouns: *personal, reflexive and intensive, relative, indefinite, interrogative,* and *demonstrative.*

628.1   Personal Pronouns

A **personal pronoun** refers to a specific person or thing.

> *Marge* started **her** car; **she** drove the antique *convertible* to Monterey, where **she** hoped to sell **it** at an auction.

628.2   Reflexive and Intensive Pronouns

A **reflexive pronoun** is formed by adding *-self* or *-selves* to a personal pronoun. A reflexive pronoun can act as a direct object or an indirect object of a verb, an object of a preposition, or a predicate nominative.

> Charles loves **himself**. (direct object of *loves*)
> Charles gives **himself** A's for fashion sense. (indirect object of *gives*)
> Charles smiles at **himself** in store windows. (object of preposition *at*)
> Charles can be **himself** anywhere. (predicate nominative)

An **intensive pronoun** intensifies, or emphasizes, the noun or pronoun it refers to.

> Leo **himself** taught his children to invest their lives in others.
> The lesson was sometimes painful—but they learned it **themselves**.

628.3   Relative Pronouns

A **relative pronoun** relates an adjective dependent (relative) clause to the noun or pronoun it modifies. (The noun is italicized in each example below; the relative pronoun is in bold.)

> *Freshmen* **who** believe they have a lot to learn are absolutely right.
> Just navigating this *campus,* **which** is huge, can be challenging.

Make sure you know when to use the relative pronouns *who* or *whom* and *that* or *which*. (See 567.3, 621.7, 621.8, and 651.3.)

628.4   Indefinite Pronouns

An **indefinite pronoun** refers to unnamed or unknown people, places, or things.

> **Everyone** seemed amused when I was searching for my classroom in the student center. (The antecedent of *everyone* is unnamed.)
> **Nothing** is more unnerving than rushing at the last minute into the wrong room for the wrong class. (The antecedent of *nothing* is unknown.)

Most indefinite pronouns are singular, so when they are used as subjects, they should have singular verbs. (See pages 655–658.)

Interrogative Pronouns

629.1

An **interrogative pronoun** asks a question.

> So **which** will it be—highlighting and attaching a campus map to the inside of your backpack, or being lost and late for the first two weeks?

Note: When an interrogative pronoun modifies a noun, it functions as an adjective.

Demonstrative Pronouns

629.2

A **demonstrative pronoun** points out people, places, or things.

> We advise **this:** Bring along as many maps and schedules as you need.
> **Those** are useful tools. **That** is the solution.

Note: When a demonstrative pronoun modifies a noun, it functions as an adjective.

Forms of Personal Pronouns

The **form** of a personal pronoun indicates its *number* (singular or plural), its *person* (first, second, or third), its *case* (nominative, possessive, or objective), and its *gender* (masculine, feminine, neuter, or indefinite).

Number of Pronouns

629.3

A **personal pronoun** is either singular (*I, you, he, she, it*) or plural (*we, you, they*).

> **He** should have a budget and stick to it. (singular)
> **We** can help new students learn about budgeting. (plural)

Person of Pronouns

629.4

The **person** of a pronoun indicates whether the person is speaking (first person), is spoken to (second person), or is spoken about (third person).

First person is used to name the speaker(s).

> I know **I** need to handle **my** stress in a healthful way, especially during exam week; **my** usual chips-and-doughnuts binge isn't helping. (singular)
> **We** all decided to bike to the tennis court. (plural)

Second person is used to name the person(s) spoken to.

> Maria, **you** grab the rackets, okay? (singular)
> John and Tanya, can **you** find the water bottles? (plural)

Third person is used to name the person(s) or thing(s) spoken about.

> Today's students are interested in wellness issues. **They** are concerned about **their** health, fitness, and nutrition. (plural)
> Maria practices yoga and feels **she** is calmer for **her** choice. (singular)
> One of the advantages of regular exercise is that **it** raises one's energy level. (singular)

630.1

Case of Pronouns

The **case** of each pronoun tells what role it plays in a sentence. There are three cases: *nominative, possessive,* and *objective.*

A pronoun in the **nominative case** is used as a subject. The following are nominative forms: *I, you, he, she, it, we, they.*

> **He** found an old map in the trunk.

> My friend and **I** went biking. (not *me*)

A pronoun is also in the nominative case when it is used as a predicate nominative, following a linking verb (*am, is, are, was, were, seems*) and renaming the subject.

> It was **he** who discovered electricity. (not *him*)

A pronoun in the **possessive case** shows possession or ownership: *my, mine, our, ours, his, her, hers, their, theirs, its, your, yours.* A possessive pronoun before a noun acts as an adjective: *your* coat.

> That coat is **hers.**   This coat is **mine.**   **Your** coat is lost.

A pronoun in the **objective case** can be used as the direct object, indirect object, object of a preposition, or object complement: *me, you, him, her, it, us, them.*

> Professor Adler hired **her**. (*Her* is the direct object of the verb *hired*.)

> He showed Mary and **me** the language lab. (*Me* is the indirect object of the verb *showed*.)

> He introduced the three of **us**—Mary, Shavonn, and **me**—to the faculty.
> (*Us* is the object of the preposition *of*; *me* is part of the appositive renaming *us*.)

630.2

Gender of Pronouns

The **gender** of a pronoun indicates whether the pronoun is masculine, feminine, neuter, or indefinite. (See page 106.)

| **Masculine:** | **Neuter** (without sex): |
| he, him, his | it, its |

| **Feminine:** | **Indefinite** (masculine or feminine): |
| she, her, hers | they, them, their |

630.3

Number, Person, and Case of Personal Pronouns

	Nominative Case	Possessive Case	Objective Case
First Person Singular	I	my, mine	me
Second Person Singular	you	your, yours	you
Third Person Singular	he, she, it	his, her, hers, its	him, her, it
First Person Plural	we	our, ours	us
Second Person Plural	you	your, yours	you
Third Person Plural	they	their, theirs	them

Grammar Exercises:

Pronouns

A. Classes of Pronouns

On your own paper, identify the class of the underlined pronoun in each sentence.

1. Krunal asked <u>himself</u> if he should reprioritize his responsibilities.

    a. personal   b. reflexive   c. relative

2. <u>Who</u> is coming to the pep rally?

    a. demonstrative   b. relative   c. interrogative

3. <u>That</u> is quite possibly the most worthless product I've ever used.

    a. demonstrative   b. reflexive   c. interrogative

4. Victoria washed <u>her</u> car on the way home from work.

    a. personal   b. intensive   c. indefinite

5. <u>Some</u> of the hamburgers were undercooked.

    a. personal   b. intensive   c. indefinite

6. The new fitness center, <u>which</u> is awesome, is open until 10:00 p.m.

    a. personal   b. relative   c. reflexive

B. Person of Pronouns

For each sentence, indicate whether the underlined pronoun is written in the first, second, or third person.

1. Russell is excited for <u>his</u> new opportunity at the sailing club.

    a. first person   b. second person   c. third person

2. Hey Britney, can <u>you</u> pass me the salt and pepper?

    a. first person   b. second person   c. third person

3. I was hoping I could make the start of the play, but <u>my</u> class schedule interfered with my plans.

    a. first person   b. second person   c. third person

C. Case of Pronouns

Write down the objective-case pronouns from the list below.

his   me   your   us   he   they   them   him

632.1

Exercise

Verb

A **verb** shows action *(pondered, grins)*, links words *(is, seemed)*, or accompanies another action verb as an auxiliary or helping verb *(can, does)*.

>Harry **honked** the horn. (shows action)
>Harry **is** impatient. (links words)
>Harry **was** honking the truck's horn. (accompanies the verb *honking*)

Classes of Verbs

Verbs are classified as action, auxiliary (helping), or linking (state of being).

632.2

Action Verbs: Transitive and Intransitive

As its name implies, an **action verb** shows action. Some action verbs are *transitive*; others are *intransitive*. (The term *action* does not always refer to a physical activity.)

>Rain **splashed** the windshield. (transitive verb)
>Josie **drove** off the road. (intransitive verb)

Transitive verbs have direct objects that receive the action (625.2, 647.5).

>The health care industry **employs** more than 7 million **workers** in the United States. (*Workers* is the direct object of the action verb *employs*.)

Intransitive verbs communicate action that is complete in itself. They do not need an object to receive the action.

>My new college roommate **smiles** and **laughs** a lot.

>**Note:** Some verbs can be either transitive or intransitive.
>Ms. Hull **teaches** physiology and microbiology. (transitive)
>She **teaches** well. (intransitive)

632.3

Auxiliary (Helping) Verbs

Auxiliary verbs (helping verbs) help to form some of the *tenses* (634.1), the *mood* (635.2), and the *voice* (635.1) of the main verb. In the following example, the auxiliary verbs are in **bold**, and the main verbs are in *italics*.

>I *believe*, I **have** always *believed*, and I **will** always *believe* in private enterprise as the backbone of economic well-being in America. —Franklin D. Roosevelt

Common Auxiliary Verbs

am	been	could	does	have	might	should	will
are	being	did	had	is	must	was	would
be	can	do	has	may	shall	were	

>**esl Note:** "Be" auxiliary verbs are always followed by either a verb ending in *ing* or a past participle. Also see "Common Modal Auxiliary Verbs" (677.2).

Linking (State of Being) Verbs

A **linking verb** is a special form of intransitive verb that links the subject of a sentence to a noun, a pronoun, or an adjective in the predicate. (See the chart below.)

The streets **are** flooded. (adjective)   The streets **are** rivers! (noun)

Common Linking Verbs

am   are   be   become   been   being   is   was   were

Additional Linking Verbs

appear   feel   look   seem   sound   grow   remain   smell   taste

Note: The verbs listed as "additional linking verbs" above function as linking verbs when they do not show actual action. An adjective usually follows these linking verbs.

The thunder **sounded** ominous. (adjective)

My little brother **grew** frightened. (adjective)

Note: When these same words are used as action verbs, an adverb or a direct object may follow them.

I **looked** carefully at him. (adverb)

My little brother **grew** corn for a science project. (direct object)

Forms of Verbs

A verb's *form* differs depending on its *number* (singular, plural), *person* (first, second, third), *tense* (present, past, future, present perfect, past perfect, future perfect), *voice* (active, passive), and *mood* (indicative, imperative, subjunctive).

Number of a Verb

Number indicates whether a verb is singular or plural. The verb and its subject both must be singular, or they both must be plural. (See "Subject–Verb Agreement," pages 655–658.)

My college **enrolls** high schoolers in summer programs. (singular)

Many colleges **enroll** high schoolers in summer courses. (plural)

Person of a Verb

Person indicates whether the subject of the verb is *first, second,* or *third person*. The verb and its subject must be in the same person. Verbs usually have a different form only in **third person singular of the present tense**.

	First Person	**Second Person**	**Third Person**
Singular	I think	you think	he/she/it thinks
Plural	we think	you think	they think

634.1 Tense of a Verb

Tense indicates the time of an action or state of being. There are three basic tenses (*past, present, and future*) and three verbal aspects (*progressive, perfect, and perfect progressive*).

634.2 Present Tense

Present tense expresses action happening at the present time or regularly.

> In the United States, more than 75 percent of workers **hold** service jobs.

Present progressive tense also expresses action that is happening continually, in an ongoing fashion at the present time, but it is formed by combining *am, are,* or *is* and the present participle (ending in *ing*) of the main verb.

> More women than ever before **are working** outside the home.

Present perfect tense expresses action that began in the past and has recently been completed or that continues up to the present time.

> My sister **has taken** four years of swimming lessons.

Present perfect progressive tense also expresses an action that began in the past but stresses the continuing nature of the action. Like the present progressive tense, it is formed by combining auxiliary verbs (*have been* or *has been*) and present participles.

> She **has been taking** them since she was six years old.

634.3 Past Tense

Past tense expresses action that was completed at a particular time in the past.

> A hundred years ago, more than 75 percent of laborers **worked** in agriculture.

Past progressive tense expresses past action that continued over an interval of time. It is formed by combining *was* or *were* with the present participle of the main verb.

> A century ago, my great-grandparents **were farming**.

Past perfect tense expresses an action in the past that was completed at a specific time before another past action occurred.

> By the time we sat down for dinner, my cousins **had eaten** all the olives.

Past perfect progressive tense expresses a past action but stresses the continuing nature of the action. It is formed by using *had been* along with the present participle.

> They **had been eating** the olives all afternoon.

634.4 Future Tense

Future tense expresses action that will take place in the future.

> Next summer I **will work** as a lifeguard.

Future progressive tense expresses an action that will be continuous in the future.

> I **will be working** for the park district at North Beach.

Future perfect tense expresses future action that will be completed by a specific time.

> By 10:00 p.m., I **will have completed** my research project.

Future perfect progressive tense also expresses future action that will be completed by a specific time but (as with other perfect progressive tenses) stresses the action's continuous nature. It is formed using *will have been* along with the present participle.

> I **will have been researching** the project for three weeks by the time it's due.

Voice of a Verb

Voice indicates whether the subject is acting or being acted upon.

Active voice indicates that the subject of the verb is performing the action.

> People **update** their resumés on a regular basis. (The subject, *People*, is acting; *resumés* is the direct object.)

Passive voice indicates that the subject of the verb is being acted upon or is receiving the action. A passive verb is formed by combining a *be* verb with a past participle.

> Your resumé **should be updated** on a regular basis. (The subject, *resumé*, is receiving the action.)

Using Active Voice

Generally, use active voice rather than passive voice for more direct, energetic writing. To change your passive sentences to active ones, do the following: First, find the noun that is doing the action and make it the subject. Then find the word that had been the subject and use it as the direct object.

> **Passive:** The winning goal **was scored** by Eva. (The subject, *goal*, is not acting.)
> **Active:** Eva **scored** the winning goal. (The subject, *Eva*, is acting.)

Note: When you want to emphasize the receiver more than the doer—or when the doer is unknown—use the passive voice. (Much technical and scientific writing regularly uses the passive voice.)

Mood of a Verb

The mood of a verb indicates the tone or attitude with which a statement is made.

Indicative mood, the most common, is used to state a fact or to ask a question.

> **Can** any theme **capture** the essence of the complex 1960s culture? President John F. Kennedy's directive [stated below] **represents** one ideal popular during that decade.

Imperative mood is used to give a command. (The subject of an imperative sentence is *you*, which is usually understood and not stated in the sentence.)

> **Ask** not what your country can do for you—**ask** what you can do for your country.
> —John F. Kennedy

Subjunctive mood is used to express a wish, an impossibility or unlikely condition, or a necessity. The subjunctive mood is often used with *if* or *that*. The verb forms below create an atypical subject–verb agreement, forming the subjunctive mood.

> If I **were** rich, I would travel for the rest of my life. (a wish)
>
> If each of your brain cells **were** one person, there would be enough people to populate 25 planets. (an impossibility)
>
> The English Department requires that every student **pass** a proficiency test. (a necessity)

636.1 Verbals

A **verbal** is a word that is made from a verb, but it functions as a noun, an adjective, or an adverb. There are three types of verbals: *gerunds, infinitives,* and *participles.*

636.2 Gerunds

A **gerund** ends in *ing* and is used as a noun.

> **Waking** each morning is the first challenge. (subject)
>
> I start **moving** at about seven o'clock. (direct object)
>
> I work at **jump-starting** my weary system. (object of the preposition)
>
> As Woody Allen once said, "Eighty percent of life is **showing up**." (predicate nominative)

636.3 Infinitives

An infinitive is *to* and the base form of the verb. The infinitive may be used as a noun, an adjective, or an adverb.

> **To succeed** is not easy. (noun)
>
> That is the most important thing **to remember**. (adjective)
>
> Students are wise **to work** hard. (adverb)

> **esl Note:** It can be difficult to know whether a gerund or an infinitive should follow a verb. It's helpful to become familiar with lists of specific verbs that can be followed by one but not the other. (See 676.2–677.1.)

636.4 Participles

A **present participle** ends in *ing* and functions as an adjective. A **past participle** ends in *ed* (or another past tense form) and also functions as an adjective.

> The **studying** students were annoyed by the **partying** ones.
>
> The students **playing** loud music were **annoying**.
>
> (These participles function as adjectives: *studying* students and *partying* students. Notice, however, that *playing* has a direct object: *music.* All three types of verbals may have direct objects. See 649.3.)

Using Verbals

Make sure that you use verbals correctly; look carefully at the examples below.

Verbal: **Diving** is a popular Olympic sport.
(*Diving* is a gerund used as a subject.)

Diving gracefully, the Olympian hoped to get high marks.
(*Diving* is a participle modifying *Olympian.*)

Verb: The next competitor was **diving** in the practice pool.
(Here, *diving* is a verb, not a verbal.)

Irregular Verbs

Irregular verbs can often be confusing. That's because the past tense and past participle of irregular verbs are formed by changing the word itself, not merely by adding *d* or *ed*. The following list contains the most troublesome irregular verbs.

Common Irregular Verbs and Their Principal Parts

Present Tense	Past Tense	Past Participle	Present Tense	Past Tense	Past Participle	Present Tense	Past Tense	Past Participle
am, be	was, were	been	fly	flew	flown	see	saw	seen
arise	arose	arisen	forget	forgot	forgotten,	set	set	set
awake	awoke,	awoken,			forgot	shake	shook	shaken
	awaked	awaked	freeze	froze	frozen	shine (light)	shone	shone
beat	beat	beaten	get	got	gotten	shine (polish)	shined	shined
become	became	become	give	gave	given	show	showed	shown
begin	began	begun	go	went	gone	shrink	shrank	shrunk
bite	bit	bitten, bit	grow	grew	grown	sing	sang	sung
blow	blew	blown	hang (execute)	hanged	hanged	sink	sank	sunk
break	broke	broken	hang (suspend)	hung	hung	sit	sat	sat
bring	brought	brought	have	had	had	sleep	slept	slept
build	built	built	hear	heard	heard	speak	spoke	spoken
burn	burnt,	burnt,	hide	hid	hidden	spend	spent	spent
	burned	burned	hit	hit	hit	spring	sprang	sprung
burst	burst	burst	keep	kept	kept	stand	stood	stood
buy	bought	bought	know	knew	known	steal	stole	stolen
catch	caught	caught	lay	laid	laid	strike	struck	struck,
choose	chose	chosen	lead	led	led			stricken
come	came	come	leave	left	left	strive	strove	striven
cost	cost	cost	lend	lent	lent	swear	swore	sworn
cut	cut	cut	let	let	let	swim	swam	swum
dig	dug	dug	lie (deceive)	lied	lied	swing	swung	swung
dive	dived, dove	dived	lie (recline)	lay	lain	take	took	taken
do	did	done	make	made	made	teach	taught	taught
draw	drew	drawn	mean	meant	meant	tear	tore	torn
dream	dreamed,	dreamed,	meet	met	met	tell	told	told
	dreamt	dreamt	pay	paid	paid	think	thought	thought
drink	drank	drunk	prove	proved	proved,	throw	threw	thrown
drive	drove	driven			proven	wake	woke,	woken,
eat	ate	eaten	put	put	put		waked	waked
fall	fell	fallen	read	read	read	wear	wore	worn
feel	felt	felt	ride	rode	ridden	weave	wove	woven
fight	fought	fought	ring	rang	rung	wind	wound	wound
find	found	found	rise	rose	risen	wring	wrung	wrung
flee	fled	fled	run	ran	run	write	wrote	written

Grammar Exercises:

Verbs

A. Classes of Verbs

On your own paper, identify the class of the underlined verb in each sentence.

1. Shawn <u>sprinted</u> back to his apartment to retrieve his homework.

    a. action verb   b. auxiliary verb   c. linking verb

2. The streets <u>were</u> teeming with partygoers.

    a. action verb   b. auxiliary verb   c. linking verb

3. Niki's gaze <u>remained</u> fixed on the ice-cream cone.

    a. action verb   b. auxiliary verb   c. linking verb

4. I think I <u>should</u> take time to study the new material.

    a. action verb   b. auxiliary verb   c. linking verb

B. Forms of Verbs

For each sentence, identify the tense of the underlined verb.

1. Before we even got to the concert, the band <u>had played</u> my favorite song.

    a. past tense   b. past progressive tense   c. past perfect tense

2. On Sunday I <u>will finish</u> my manuscript.

    a. future tense   b. future progressive tense   c. future perfect tense

3. The mechanics <u>have been working</u> for ten straight hours.

    a. present progressive tense   b. present perfect tense
    c. past progressive tense

4. Yesterday at this time I <u>was relaxing</u> on the beach.

    a. past tense   b. past progressive tense   c. past perfect tense

C. Irregular Verbs

Write the past tense of the following irregular verbs.

1. buy   **6.** lay

2. prove   **7.** wear

3. swim   **8.** fly

4. lead   **9.** give

5. pay   **10.** sleep

Adjective

639.1

An **adjective** describes or modifies a noun or pronoun. The articles *a*, *an*, and *the* are adjectives.

> Advertising is **a big** and **powerful** industry. (*A*, *big*, and *powerful* modify the noun *industry*.)

Numbers are also adjectives.

> **Fifty-three** relatives came to my party.

639.2

Note: Many demonstrative, indefinite, and interrogative forms may be used as either adjectives or pronouns (*that*, *these*, *many*, *some*, *whose*, and so on). These words are adjectives if they come before a noun and modify it; they are pronouns if they stand alone.

> **Some** advertisements are less than truthful. (*Some* modifies *advertisements* and is an adjective.)

> **Many** cause us to chuckle at their outrageous claims. (*Many* stands alone; it is a pronoun and replaces the noun *advertisements*.)

Proper Adjectives

639.3

Proper adjectives are created from proper nouns and are capitalized.

> **English** has been influenced by advertising slogans. (proper noun)

> The **English** language is constantly changing. (proper adjective)

Predicate Adjectives

639.4

A **predicate adjective** follows a form of the *be* verb (or other linking verb) and describes the subject. (See 633.1.)

> At its best, advertising is **useful**; at its worst, **deceptive**. (*Useful* and *deceptive* modify the noun *advertising*.)

Forms of Adjectives

639.5

Adjectives have three forms: *positive*, *comparative*, and *superlative*.

The **positive form** is the adjective in its regular form. It describes a noun or a pronoun without comparing it to anyone or anything else.

> Joysport walking shoes are **strong** and **comfortable**.

The **comparative form** (*-er*, *more*, or *less*) compares two things. (*More* and *less* are used generally with adjectives of two or more syllables.)

> Air soles make Mile Eaters **stronger** and **more comfortable** than Joysports.

The **superlative form** (*-est*, *most*, or *least*) compares three or more things. (*Most* and *least* are used most often with adjectives of two or more syllables.)

> My old Canvas Wonders are the **strongest**, **most comfortable** shoes of all!

esl Note: Two or more adjectives before a noun should have a certain order when they do not modify the noun equally. (See 565.3.)

640.1

Exercise

Adverb

An **adverb** describes or modifies a verb, an adjective, another adverb, or a whole sentence. An adverb answers questions such as *how, when, where, why, how often,* or *how much.*

> The temperature fell **sharply**. (*Sharply* modifies the verb *fell.*)
>
> The temperature was **quite** low. (*Quite* modifies the adjective *low.*)
>
> The temperature dropped **very quickly**. (*Very* modifies the adverb *quickly,* which modifies the verb *dropped.*)
>
> **Unfortunately**, the temperature stayed cool. (*Unfortunately* modifies the whole sentence.)

640.2

Types of Adverbs

Adverbs can be grouped in four ways: *time, place, manner,* and *degree.*

Time (These adverbs tell *when, how often,* and *how long.*)

> **today, yesterday   daily, weekly   briefly, eternally**

Place (These adverbs tell *where, to where,* and *from where.*)

> **here, there   nearby, beyond   backward, forward**

Manner (These adverbs often end in *ly* and tell *how* something is done.)

> **precisely   regularly   regally   smoothly   well**

Degree (These adverbs tell *how much* or *how little.*)

> **substantially   greatly   entirely   partly   too**

640.3

Forms of Adverbs

Adverbs have three forms: *positive, comparative,* and *superlative.*

The **positive form** is the adverb in its regular form. It describes a verb, an adjective, or another adverb without comparing it to anyone or anything else.

> With Joysport shoes, you'll walk **fast**. They support your feet **well**.

The **comparative form** (*-er, more,* or *less*) compares two things. (*More* and *less* are used generally with adverbs of two or more syllables.)

> Wear Jockos instead of Joysports, and you'll walk **faster**. Jockos' special soles support your feet **better** than the Joysports do.

The **superlative form** (*-est, most,* or *least*) compares three or more things. (*Most* and *least* are used most often with adverbs of two or more syllables.)

> Really, I walk **fastest** wearing my old Canvas Wonders. They seem to support my feet, my knees, and my pocketbook **best** of all.

Regular Adverbs			**Irregular Adverbs**		
positive	**comparative**	**superlative**	**positive**	**comparative**	**superlative**
fast	faster	fastest	well	better	best
effectively	more effectively	most effectively	badly	worse	worst

Preposition

641.1

A **preposition** is a word (or group of words) that shows the relationship between its object (a noun or pronoun following the preposition) and another word in the sentence.

> **Regarding** your reasons **for** going **to** college, do they all hinge **on** getting a good job **after** graduation? (In this sentence, *reasons, going, college, getting,* and *graduation* are objects of their preceding prepositions *regarding, for, to, on,* and *after.*)

Prepositional Phrases

641.2

A **prepositional phrase** includes the preposition, the object of the preposition, and the modifiers of the object. A prepositional phrase may function as an adverb or an adjective.

> A broader knowledge **of the world** is one benefit **of higher education**.
> (The two phrases function as adjectives modifying the nouns *knowledge* and *benefit* respectively.)

> He placed the flower **in the window**. (The phrase functions as an adverb modifying the verb *placed*.)

Prepositions

641.3

aboard	back of	excepting	notwithstanding	save
about	because of	for	of	since
above	before	from	off	subsequent to
according to	behind	from among	on	through
across	below	trom between	on account ot	throughout
across from	beneath	from under	on behalf of	'til
after	beside	in	onto	to
against	besides	in addition to	on top of	together with
along	between	in behalf of	opposite	toward
alongside	beyond	in front of	out	under
alongside of	by	in place of	out of	underneath
along with	by means of	in regard to	outside	until
amid	concerning	inside	outside of	unto
among	considering	inside of	over	up
apart from	despite	in spite of	over to	upon
around	down	instead of	owing to	up to
as far as	down from	into	past	with
aside from	during	like	prior to	within
at	except	near	regarding	without
away from	except for	near to	round	

esl Note: Prepositions often pair up with a verb and become part of an idiom, a slang expression, or a two-word verb. (See pages 678 and 693–696.)

Conjunction

642.1

Exercise

A **conjunction** connects individual words or groups of words.

When we came back to Paris, it was clear **and** cold **and** lovely.

—Ernest Hemingway

642.2

Coordinating Conjunctions

Coordinating conjunctions usually connect a word to a word, a phrase to a phrase, or a clause to a clause. The words, phrases, or clauses joined by a coordinating conjunction are equal in importance or are of the same type.

Civilization is a race between education **and** catastrophe.

—H. G. Wells

642.3

Correlative Conjunctions

Correlative conjunctions are a type of coordinating conjunction used in pairs.

There are two inadvisable ways to think: **either** believe everything **or** doubt everything.

642.4

Subordinating Conjunctions

Subordinating conjunctions connect two clauses that are not equally important. A subordinating conjunction connects a dependent clause to an independent clause. The conjunction is part of the dependent clause.

Experience is the worst teacher; it gives the test **before** it presents the lesson. (The clause *before it presents the lesson* is dependent. It connects to the independent clause *it gives the test*.)

642.5

Conjunctions	
Coordinating:	and, but, or, nor, for, so, yet
Correlative:	either, or; neither, nor; not only, but (but also); both, and; whether, or
Subordinating:	after, although, as, as if, as long as, because, before, even though, if, in order that, provided that, since, so that, though, unless, until, when, whenever, where, while

Note: Relative pronouns (628.3) can also connect clauses.

Interjection

642.6

An **interjection** communicates strong emotion or surprise (*oh, ouch, hey,* and so on). Punctuation (often a comma or an exclamation point) is used to set off an interjection.

Hey! Wait! Well, so much for catching the bus.

Grammar Exercises:

Adjectives, Adverbs, Prepositions, Conjunctions, and Injections

A. Forms of Adjectives

On your own paper, write the correct form (positive, comparative, or superlative) of the adjective shown in parentheses for each sentence.

1. I ate the _____ chicken wings I had ever tasted in my life. (*spicy*)
2. The Internet connection at the coffeehouse is _____ than the connection at the library. (*fast*)
3. Arizona is known for its _____ and dry climate. (*hot*)
4. Online shopping is _____ than mall shopping. (*efficient*)

B. Types of Adverbs

Indicate whether the adverb reveals time, place, manner, or degree.

1. completely
2. smartly
3. easily
4. briefly
5. everywhere
6. tomorrow

C. Conjunctions

On your own paper, create a three-column table and label the columns "Coordinating," "Subordinating," and "Correlative." Then sort out the conjunctions below into their appropriate columns.

after	even though	so that
although	for	that
and	if	though
as	in order that	unless
as if	neither/nor	until
as long as	nor	when
because	not only/but also	whenever
before	or	where
both/and	provided that	while
but	since	yet
either/or	so	

A Closer Look
at the Parts of Speech

Noun

A **noun** is a word that names something: a person, a place, a thing, or an idea.

Toni Morrison/author	*Lone Star*/film
UC–Davis/university	Renaissance/era
A Congress of Wonders/book	

Pronoun

A **pronoun** is a word used in place of a noun.

I	my	that	themselves	which
it	ours	they	everybody	you

Verb

A **verb** is a word that expresses action, links words, or acts as an auxiliary verb to the main verb.

are	break	drag	fly	run	sit	was
bite	catch	eat	is	see	tear	were

Adjective

An **adjective** describes or modifies a noun or pronoun. (The articles *a*, *an*, and *the* are adjectives.)

The carbonated drink went down easy on **that hot, dry** day.
(*The* and *carbonated* modify *drink; that, hot,* and *dry* modify *day.*)

Adverb

An **adverb** describes or modifies a verb, an adjective, another adverb, or a whole sentence. An adverb generally answers questions such as *how, when, where, how often,* or *how much.*

greatly	precisely	regularly	there
here	today	partly	quickly
slowly	yesterday	nearly	loudly

Preposition

A **preposition** is a word (or group of words) that shows the relationship between its object (a noun or pronoun that follows the preposition) and another word in the sentence. Prepositions introduce prepositional phrases, which are modifiers.

across for with out to of

Conjunction

A **conjunction** connects individual words or groups of words.

and because but for or since so yet

Interjection

An **interjection** is a word that communicates strong emotion or surprise. Punctuation (often a comma or an exclamation point) is used to set off an interjection from the rest of the sentence.

Stop! No! What, am I invisible?

Audio

Exercise

37 Constructing Sentences

645.1

A **sentence** is made up of at least a subject (sometimes understood) and a verb and expresses a complete thought. Sentences can make statements, ask questions, give commands, or express feelings.

The web delivers the universe in a box.

Using Subjects and Predicates

645.2

Sentences have two main parts: a **subject** and a **predicate**.

Technology frustrates many people.

Exercise

> **Note:** In the sentence above, *technology* is the subject—the sentence talks about technology. *Frustrates many people* is the complete predicate—it tells what the subject is doing.

The Subject

645.3

The **subject** names the person or thing either performing the action, receiving the action, or being described or renamed. The subject is most often a noun or a pronoun.

Technology is an integral part of almost every business.
Manufacturers need technology to compete in the world market.
They could not go far without it.

A verbal phrase or a noun dependent clause may also function as a subject.

To survive without technology is difficult. (infinitive phrase)
Downloading information from the web is easy. (gerund phrase)
That the information age would arrive was inevitable. (noun dependent clause)

> **Note:** To determine the subject of a sentence, ask yourself *who* or *what* performs or receives the action or is described. In most sentences, the subject comes before the verb; however, in many questions and some other instances, that order is reversed. (See 652.2, 652.3, 656.1, and 686.)

> **esl Note:** Some languages permit the omission of a subject in a sentence; English does not. A subject must be included in every sentence. (The only exception is an "understood subject," which is discussed at 646.4.)

646.1

Simple Subject

A **simple subject** is the subject without the words that describe or modify it.

> Thirty years ago, reasonably well-trained **mechanics** could fix any car on the road.

646.2

Complete Subject

A **complete subject** is the simple subject *and* the words that describe or modify it.

> Thirty years ago, **reasonably well-trained mechanics** could fix any car on the road.

646.3

Compound Subject

A **compound subject** is composed of two or more simple subjects joined by a conjunction and sharing the same predicate(s).

> Today, **mechanics** and **technicians** would need to master a half million manual pages to fix every car on the road.

> **Dealerships** and their service **departments** must sometimes explain that situation to the customers.

646.4

Understood Subject

Sometimes a subject is **understood**. This means it is not stated in the sentence, but a reader clearly understands what the subject is. An understood subject occurs in a command (imperative sentence). (See 652.3.)

> **(You)** Park on this side of the street. (The subject *you* is understood.)

> Put the CD player in the trunk.

646.5

Delayed Subject

In sentences that begin with *There is*, *There was*, or *Here is*, the subject follows the verb.

> There are 70,000 **fans** in the stadium. (The subject is *fans*; *are* is the verb. *There* is an expletive, an empty word.)

> Here is a **problem** for stadium security. (*Problem* is the subject. *Here* is an adverb.)

The subject is also delayed in questions.

> Where was the **event**? (*Event* is the subject.)

> Was **Dave Matthews** playing? (*Dave Matthews* is the subject.)

The Predicate (Verb)

647.1

The **predicate**, which contains the verb, is the part of the sentence that either tells what the subject is doing, tells what is being done to the subject, or describes or renames the subject.

Students **need technical skills as well as basic academic skills**.

Simple Predicate

647.2

A **simple predicate** is the complete verb without the words that describe or modify it. (The complete verb can consist of more that one word.)

Today's workplace **requires** employees to have a range of skills.

Complete Predicate

647.3

A **complete predicate** is the verb, all the words that modify or explain it, and any objects or complements.

Today's workplace **requires employees to have a range of skills**.

Compound Predicate

647.4

A **compound predicate** is composed of two or more verbs, all the words that modify or explain them, and any objects or complements.

Engineers **analyze problems** and **calculate solutions**.

Direct Object

647.5

A **direct object** is the part of the predicate that receives the action of an active transitive verb. A direct object makes the meaning of the verb complete.

Marcos visited several **campuses**. (The direct object *campuses* receives the action of the verb *visited* by answering the question "Marcos visited what?")

Exercise

Note: A direct object may be compound.

A counselor explained the academic **programs** and the application **process**.

Indirect Object

647.6

An **indirect object** is the word(s) that tells *to whom/to what* or *for whom/for what* something is done. A sentence must have a direct object before it can have an indirect object.

I showed our **children** my new school.

Use these questions to find an indirect object:
- What is the verb?   *showed*
- *Showed* what?   *school* (direct object)
- Showed *school* to whom?   *children* (indirect object)

I wrote **them** a note.

Note: An indirect object may be compound.

I gave the **instructor** and a few **classmates** my e-mail address.

Constructing Sentences Exercises:

Subjects and Predicates

A. Subjects

1. On your own paper, write the complete subject of each numbered sentence in the following paragraph. Then underline the simple subjects. (You will find one compound subject.)

> (1) Every modern war seems to have its own terrible illness for soldiers. (2) In World War I, blistered skin and ravaged lungs resulted from exposure to mustard gas. (3) World War II saw the problem of "shell shock." (4) Agent Orange was blamed for causing cancer in Vietnam War veterans. (5) The Gulf War saw the rise of "post-traumatic stress disorder." (6) And many veterans of combat in Iraq and Iran return with "mild traumatic brain injury" due to improvised explosive devices.

2. Create your own sentence with an understood subject.

3. Create your own sentence with a delayed subject.

B. Predicates

1. Write the complete predicate of each numbered sentence in the following paragraph. Then underline the simple predicates. (You will find one compound predicate.)

> (1) Women today have more than one choice for professional assistance with childbirth. (2) The obstetrician of your parents' era is trained to diagnose abnormalities and is prepared to deal with emergencies. (3) Today's midwife practitioner, on the other hand, is focused upon normal deliveries. (4) This makes the two occupations quite complementary.

2. List the direct objects in the numbered sentences of the following paragraph. If a sentence also includes an indirect object, list that in parentheses after the direct object.

> (1) Different situations bring you happiness. (2) Various pursuits deliver satisfaction. (3) And many agree that parents pass along their values and goals to their children. (4) So your own offspring will also receive this intangible inheritance.

Using Phrases

649.1

Exercise

A **phrase** is a group of related words that functions as a single part of speech. A phrase lacks a subject, a predicate, or both. There are three phrases in the following sentence:

> **Examples of technology can be found in ancient civilizations.**
>
> **of technology**
> (prepositional phrase that functions as an adjective; no subject or predicate)
>
> **can be found**
> (verb phrase—all of the words of the verb; no subject)
>
> **in ancient civilizations**
> (prepositional phrase that functions as an adverb; no subject or predicate)

Types of Phrases

There are several types of phrases: *verb, verbal, prepositional, appositive,* and *absolute.*

Verb Phrase

649.2

A **verb phrase** consists of a main verb and its helping verbs.

> Students, worried about exams, **have camped** at the library all week.

Verbal Phrase

649.3

Exercise

A **verbal phrase** is a phrase that expands on one of the three types of verbals: *gerund, infinitive,* or *participle.* (See 636.)

A **gerund phrase** consists of a gerund and its modifiers and objects. The whole phrase functions as a noun. (See 636.2.)

> **Becoming a marine biologist** is Rashanda's dream. (The gerund phrase is used as the subject of the sentence.)
>
> She has acquainted herself with the various methods for **collecting sea-life samples.** (The gerund phrase is the object of the preposition *for.*)

An **infinitive phrase** consists of an infinitive and its modifiers and objects. The whole phrase functions as a noun, an adjective, or an adverb. (See 636.3.)

> **To dream** is the first step in any endeavor. (The infinitive phrase functions as a noun used as the subject.)
>
> Remember **to make a plan to realize your dream.** (The infinitive phrase *to make a plan* functions as a noun used as a direct object; *to realize your dream* functions as an adjective modifying *plan.*)
>
> Finally, apply all of your talents and skills **to achieve your goals.** (The infinitive phrase functions as an adverb modifying *apply.*)

A **participial phrase** consists of a present or past participle (a verb form ending in *ing* or *ed*) and its modifiers. The phrase functions as an adjective. (See 636.4.)

> **Doing poorly in biology,** Theo signed up for a tutor. (The participial phrase modifies the noun *Theo.*)
>
> Some students **frustrated by difficult course work** don't seek help. (The participial phrase modifies the noun *students.*)

650.1

Functions of Verbal Phrases			
	Noun	Adjective	Adverb
Gerund	■		
Infinitive	■	■	■
Participial		■	

650.2

Prepositional Phrase

A **prepositional phrase** is a group of words beginning with a preposition and ending with its object, a noun or a pronoun. Prepositional phrases are used mainly as adjectives and adverbs. See 641.3 for a list of prepositions.

> Denying the existence **of exam week** hasn't worked **for anyone** yet.
> (The prepositional phrase *of exam week* is used as an adjective modifying the noun *existence; for anyone* is used as an adverb modifying the verb *has worked*.)

> Test days still dawn and GPAs still plummet **for the unprepared student.**
> (The prepositional phrase *for the unprepared student* is used as an adverb modifying the verbs *dawn* and *plummet*.)

> **esl Note:** Do not mistake the following adverbs for nouns and incorrectly use them as objects of prepositions: *here, there, everywhere.*

650.3

Appositive Phrase

An **appositive phrase**, which follows a noun or a pronoun and renames it, consists of a noun and its modifiers. An appositive adds new information about the noun or pronoun it follows.

> The Olympic-size pool, **a prized addition to the physical education building,** gets plenty of use. (The appositive phrase renames *pool*.)

650.4

Absolute Phrase

An **absolute phrase** consists of a noun and a participle (plus the participle's object, if there is one, and any modifiers). It usually modifies the entire sentence.

> **Their enthusiasm sometimes waning,** the students who cannot swim are required to take lessons. (The noun *enthusiasm* is modified by the present participle *waning;* the entire phrase modifies *students*.)

 Phrases can add valuable information to sentences, but some phrases add nothing but "fat" to your writing. For a list of phrases to avoid, see page 103.

Using Clauses

A **clause** is a group of related words that has both a subject and a verb.

Independent/Dependent Clauses

An **independent clause** contains at least one subject and one verb, presents a complete thought, and can stand alone as a sentence; a **dependent clause** (also called a subordinate clause) does not present a complete thought and cannot stand alone (make sense) as a sentence.

> Though airplanes are twentieth-century inventions (dependent clause), people have always dreamed of flying (independent clause).

Exercise

651.1

Types of Clauses

There are three basic types of dependent, or subordinate, clauses: *adverb, adjective,* and *noun.* These dependent clauses are combined with independent clauses to form complex and compound-complex sentences.

Exercise

Adverb Clause

651.2

An **adverb clause** is used like an adverb to modify a verb, an adjective, or an adverb. All adverb clauses begin with subordinating conjunctions. (See 642.4.)

> **Because Orville won a coin toss**, he got to fly the power-driven air machine first. (The adverb clause modifies the verb *got.*)

Adjective Clause

651.3

An **adjective clause** is used like an adjective to modify a noun or a pronoun. Adjective clauses begin with relative pronouns *(which, that, who).* (See 628.3.)

> The men **who invented the first airplane** were brothers, Orville and Wilbur Wright. (The adjective clause modifies the noun *men. Who* is the subject of the adjective clause.)
> The first flight, **which took place December 17, 1903,** was made by Orville. (The adjective clause modifies the noun *flight. Which* is the subject of the adjective clause.)

Noun Clause

651.4

A **noun clause** is used in place of a noun. Noun clauses can appear as subjects, as direct or indirect objects, as predicate nominatives, or as objects of prepositions. Noun clauses can also play a role in the independent clause. They are introduced by subordinating words such as *what, that, when, why, how, whatever, who, whom, whoever,* and *whomever.*

> He wants to know **what made modern aviation possible.** (The noun clause functions as the object of the infinitive.)
> **Whoever invents an airplane with vertical takeoff ability** will be a hero. (The noun clause functions as the subject.)

Note: If you can replace a whole clause with the pronoun *something* or *someone,* it is a noun clause.

Using Sentence Variety

A sentence can be classified according to the kind of statement it makes and according to the way it is constructed.

Kinds of Sentences

Sentences can make five basic kinds of statements: *declarative, interrogative, imperative, exclamatory,* or *conditional.*

652.1   ### Declarative Sentence

Declarative sentences make statements. They tell us something about a person, a place, a thing, or an idea.

> In 1955, Rosa Parks refused to follow segregation rules on a bus in Montgomery, Alabama.

652.2   ### Interrogative Sentence

Interrogative sentences ask questions.

> Do you think Ms. Parks knew she was making history?
>
> Would you have had the courage to do what she did?

652.3   ### Imperative Sentence

Imperative sentences give commands. They often contain an understood subject (*you*). (See 646.4.)

> Read chapters 6 through 10 for tomorrow.

esl Note: Imperative sentences with an understood subject are the only sentences in which it is acceptable to have no subjects stated.

652.4   ### Exclamatory Sentence

Exclamatory sentences communicate strong emotion or surprise. They are punctuated with exclamation points.

> I simply can't keep up with these long reading assignments!
>
> Oh my gosh, you scared me!

652.5   ### Conditional Sentence

Conditional sentences express two circumstances. One of the circumstances depends on the other circumstance. The words *if, when,* or *unless* are often used in the dependent clause in conditional sentences.

> **If** you practice a few study-reading techniques, college reading loads will be manageable.
>
> **When** I manage my time, it seems I have more of it.
>
> Don't ask me to help you **unless** you are willing to do the reading first.

Structure of Sentences

A sentence may be *simple, compound, complex,* or *compound-complex,* depending on how the independent and dependent clauses are combined.

Simple Sentence

653.1

A **simple sentence** contains one independent clause. The independent clause may have compound subjects and verbs, and it may also contain phrases.

> My **back aches.**
> (single subject: *back;* single verb: *aches*)
>
> My **teeth** and my **eyes hurt.**
> (compound subject: *teeth* and *eyes;* single verb: *hurt*)
>
> My **memory** and my **logic come** and **go.**
> (compound subject: *memory* and *logic;* compound verb: *come* and *go*)
>
> **I must need a vacation.**
> (single subject: *I;* single verb: *must need;* direct object: *vacation*)

Compound Sentence

653.2

A **compound sentence** consists of two independent clauses. The clauses must be joined by a semicolon, by a comma and a coordinating conjunction *(and, but, or, nor, so, for, yet),* or by a semicolon followed by a conjunctive adverb *(besides, however, instead, meanwhile, then, therefore)* and a comma.

> I had eight hours of sleep**, so** why am I so exhausted?
>
> I take good care of myself; I get enough sleep.
>
> I still feel fatigued**; therefore,** I must need more exercise.

Complex Sentence

653.3

A **complex sentence** contains one independent clause (in bold) and one or more dependent clauses (underlined).

> <u>When I can</u>, **I get eight hours of sleep.** (<u>dependent clause</u>; independent clause)
>
> <u>When I get up on time</u>, and <u>if someone hasn't used up all the milk,</u>
> **I eat breakfast.** (<u>two dependent clauses</u>; independent clause)

When the dependent clause comes before the independent clause, use a comma.

Compound-Complex Sentence

653.4

A **compound-complex sentence** contains two or more independent clauses (in bold type) and one or more dependent clauses (underlined).

> <u>If I'm not in a hurry</u>, **I take leisurely walks,** and **I try to spot some wildlife.**
> (<u>dependent clause</u>; two independent clauses)
>
> **I saw a hawk** <u>when I was walking</u>, and **other smaller birds were chasing it.**
> (dependent clause, <u>independent</u> clause; independent clause)

Exercise

Constructing Sentences Exercises:

Phrases, Clauses, and Sentence Variety

A. Phrases and Clauses

On your own paper, identify the numbered phrases (gerund, infinitive, participial, prepositional, appositive, or absolute), and clauses (adverb, adjective, or noun). Note that not every type is represented.

> The marionette, (1) a type of puppet manipulated by strings or rods, has been around for millennia. Stringed puppets have been found in Egyptian tombs from around 2000 B.C. Greek philosophers such as Xenophon wrote about these articulated puppets as early as 422 B.C. (2) To control their marionettes, the ancient Romans used rods from above, and Italy retains a strong tradition of articulated puppetry from these Roman roots. (3) Employed in religious performances during ancient times, marionettes found similar use in morality plays during the Renaissance. Most likely, the term "marionette" originated as a diminutive form (4) of the Virgin Mary's name in these plays. Starting in the eighteenth century, entire operas were performed by marionettes in theaters such as the Salzburg Marionette Theatre in Austria, (5) which continues performances to this day. Of course, marionettes have also starred in television and film, and (6) since puppetry is still a valued storytelling art, chances are you've seen them perform at your local grade school.

B. Sentence Variety

Identify each sentence in the following paragraph by kind (declarative, interrogative, imperative, exclamatory, or conditional).

> (1) Do you realize how far personal computers have come since their early days? (2) Understand that the first examples were marketed to scientists and researchers. (3) After that came kits for hobbyists to build and program their own machines. (4) The introduction of the microprocessor chip allowed PCs to proliferate after 1975. (5) If blinkenlights.com is correct, the HP 9830, originally sold in 1972, qualifies as the very first personal computer, being a fully built desktop machine with a keyboard and display. (6) Other people argue that the Commodore PET in 1977 better suited that designation because it was commercially available to everyone. (7) In any case, the popular Apple II and the IBM-PC then solidified the personal computer's role in business and at home.

Audio

38 Avoiding Sentence Errors

Subject–Verb Agreement

655.1

The subject and verb of any clause must agree in both *person* and *number*. Person indicates whether the subject of the verb is *first, second,* or *third person*. *Number* indicates whether the subject and verb are *singular* or *plural*. (See 633.2 and 633.3.)

	Singular	**Plural**
First Person	I think	we think
Second Person	you think	you think
Third Person	he/she/it thinks	they think

Exercise

Agreement in Number

655.2

A verb must agree in number (singular or plural) with its subject.

> The **student was** rewarded for her hard work. (Both the subject *student* and the verb *was* are singular; they agree in number.)

Note: Do not be confused by phrases that come between the subject and the verb. Such phrases may begin with words like *in addition to, as well as,* or *together with*.

> The **instructor**, as well as the students, is expected to attend the orientation. (*Instructor,* not *students,* is the subject.)

Compound Subjects

655.3

Compound subjects connected with *and* usually require a plural verb.

> **Dedication and creativity are** trademarks of successful students.

Note: If a compound subject joined by *and* is thought of as a unit, use a singular verb.

> **Macaroni and cheese is** always available in the cafeteria.

(Also see 656.3 and 656.4.)

656.1   Delayed Subjects

Delayed subjects occur when the verb comes *before* the subject in a sentence. In these inverted sentences, the true (delayed) subject must still agree with the verb.

> There **are** many nontraditional **students** on our campus.
> Here **is** the **syllabus** you need.
> (*Students* and *syllabus* are the subjects of these sentences, not the adverbs *there* and *here*.)

Note: Using an inverted sentence, on occasion, will lend variety to your writing style. Simply remember to make the delayed subjects agree with the verbs.

> However, included among the list's topmost items **was "revise research paper."**
> (Because the true subject here is singular—one item—the singular verb *was* is correct.)

656.2   Titles as Subjects

When the subject of a sentence is the title of a work of art, literature, or music, the verb should be singular. This is also true of a word (or phrase) being used as a word (or phrase).

> *Lyrical Ballads* **was** published in 1798 by two of England's greatest poets, Wordsworth and Coleridge. (Even though the title of the book, *Lyrical Ballads,* is plural in form, it is still a single title being used as the subject, correctly taking the singular verb *was.*)

> **"Over-the-counter drugs" is** a phrase that means nonprescription medications. (Even though the phrase is plural in form, it is still a single phrase being used as the subject, correctly taking the singular verb *is.*)

656.3   Singular Subjects with *Or* or *Nor*

Singular subjects joined by *or* or *nor* take a singular verb.

> Neither a **textbook** nor a **notebook is required** for this class.

Note: When the subject nearer a present-tense verb is the singular pronoun *I* or *you,* the correct singular verb does not end in *s.* (See the chart on page 666.1.)

> Neither **Marcus** nor **I feel** (not *feels*) right about this.

> Either **Rosa** or **you have** (not *has*) to take notes for me.

> Either **you** or **Rosa has** to take notes for me.

656.4   Singular/Plural Subjects

When one of the subjects joined by *or* or *nor* is singular and one is plural, the verb must agree with the subject nearer the verb.

> Neither the **professor** nor her **students were** in the lab. (The plural subject *students* is nearer the verb; therefore, the plural verb *were* agrees with *students.*)

> Neither the **students** nor the **professor was** in the lab. (The singular subject *professor* is nearer the verb; therefore, the singular verb *was* is used to agree with *professor.*)

Collective Nouns

657.1

Generally, **collective nouns** (*faculty, pair, crew, assembly, congress, species, crowd, army, team, committee,* and so on) take a singular verb. However, if you want to emphasize differences among individuals in the group or are referring to the group as individuals, you can use a plural verb.

> My lab **team takes** its work very seriously. (*Team* refers to the group as a unit; it requires a singular verb, *takes*.)
>
> The **team assume** separate responsibilities for each study they undertake. (In this example, *team* refers to individuals within the group; it requires a plural verb, *assume*.)

> **Note:** Collective nouns such as (the) *police, poor, elderly,* and *young* use plural verbs.
>
> The police direct traffic here between 7:00 and 9:00 a.m.

Plural Nouns with Singular Meaning

657.2

Some nouns that are plural in form but singular in meaning take a singular verb: *mumps, measles, news, mathematics, economics, robotics,* and so on.

> **Economics is** sometimes called "the dismal science."
>
> The economic **news is** not very good.

> **Note:** The most common exceptions are *scissors, trousers, tidings,* and *pliers.*
>
> The **scissors are** missing again.
>
> **Are** these **trousers** prewashed?

With Linking Verbs

657.3

When a sentence contains a linking verb (usually a form of *be*)—and a noun or pronoun comes before and after that verb—the verb must agree with the subject, not the predicate nominative (the noun or pronoun coming after the verb).

> The cause of his problem **was** poor study habits. (*Cause* requires a singular verb, even though the predicate nominative, *habits*, is plural.)
>
> His poor study habits **were** the cause of his problem. (*Habits* requires a plural verb, even though the predicate nominative, *cause*, is singular.)

Nouns Showing Measurement, Time, and Money

657.4

Mathematical phrases and phrases that name a period of time, a unit of measurement, or an amount of money take a singular verb.

> Three and three **is** six.
>
> Eight pages **is** a long paper on this topic.
>
> In my opinion, two dollars **is** a high price for a cup of coffee.

658.1   Relative Pronouns

When a **relative pronoun** *(who, which, that)* is used as the subject of a dependent clause, the number of the verb is determined by that pronoun's antecedent. (The *antecedent* is the word to which the pronoun refers.)

> This is one of the **books that are** required for English class.
> (The relative pronoun *that* requires the plural verb *are* because its antecedent is *books*, not the word *one*. To test this type of sentence for agreement, read the *of* phrase first: *Of the books that are . . .*)

> **Note:** Generally, the antecedent is the nearest noun or pronoun to the relative pronoun and is often the object of a preposition. Sometimes, however, the antecedent is not the nearest noun or pronoun, especially in sentences with the phrase "the only one of."

> Dr. Graciosa wondered why Claire was the only **one** of her students **who was** not attending lectures regularly. (In this case, the addition of the modifiers *the only* changes the meaning of the sentence. The antecedent of *who* is *one*, not *students*. Only one student was not attending.)

658.2   Indefinite Pronoun with Singular Verb

Many indefinite pronouns *(someone, somebody, something; anyone, anybody, anything; no one, nobody, nothing; everyone, everybody, everything; each, either, neither, one, this)* serving as subjects require a singular verb.

> **Everybody is** welcome to attend the chancellor's reception.

> **No one was** sent an invitation.

> **Note:** Although it may seem to indicate more than one, *each* is a singular pronoun and requires a singular verb. Do not be confused by words or phrases that come between the indefinite pronoun and the verb.

> **Each** of the new students **is** (not *are*) **encouraged** to attend the reception.

658.3   Indefinite Pronoun with Plural Verb

Some indefinite pronouns *(both, few, many, most,* and *several)* are plural; they require a plural verb.

> **Few are** offered the opportunity to study abroad.

> **Most take** advantage of opportunities closer to home.

658.4   Indefinite Pronoun or Quantity Word with Singular/Plural Verb

Some indefinite pronouns or quantity words *(all, any, most, part, half, none,* and *some)* may be either singular or plural, depending on the nouns they refer to. Look inside the prepositional phrase to see what the antecedent is.

> **Some** of the students **were** missing. (*Students,* the noun that *some* refers to, is plural; therefore, the pronoun *some* is considered plural, and the plural verb *were* is used to agree with it.)

> **Most** of the lecture **was** over by the time we arrived. (Because *lecture* is singular, *most* is also singular, requiring the singular verb *was*.)

Pronoun–Antecedent Agreement

A pronoun must agree in number, person, and gender (sex) with its *antecedent*. The antecedent is the word to which the pronoun refers.

> **Yoshi** brought **his** laptop computer and e-book to school. (The pronoun *his* refers to the antecedent *Yoshi*. Both the pronoun and its antecedent are singular, third person, and masculine; therefore, the pronoun is said to agree with its antecedent.)

Singular Pronoun

Use a singular pronoun to refer to such antecedents as *each, either, neither, one, anyone, anybody, everyone, everybody, somebody, another, nobody,* and *a person.*

> **Each** of the maintenance vehicles has **their** doors locked at night. (Incorrect)
>
> **Each** of the maintenance vehicles has **its** doors locked at night. (Correct: Both *Each* and *its* are singular.)
>
> **Somebody** left **his or her** (not *their*) vehicle unlocked. (Correct)

Plural Pronoun

When a plural pronoun *(they, their)* is mistakenly used with a singular indefinite pronoun (such as *everyone* or *everybody*), you may correct the sentence by replacing *their* or *they* with optional pronouns *(her or his* or *he or she),* or make the antecedent plural.

> **Everyone** must learn to wait **their** turn. (Incorrect)
>
> **Everyone** must learn to wait **her or his** turn. (Correct: Optional pronouns *her* or *his* are used.)
>
> **People** must learn to wait **their** turns. (Correct: The singular antecedent, *Everyone,* is changed to the plural antecedent, *People.*)

Two or More Antecedents

When two or more antecedents are joined by *and,* they are considered plural.

> **Tomas** and **Jamal** are finishing **their** assignments.

When two or more singular antecedents are joined by *or* or *nor,* they are considered singular.

> **Connie** or **Shavonn** left **her** headset in the library.

> **Note:** If one of the antecedents is masculine and one feminine, the pronouns should likewise be masculine and feminine.
>
> Is **Ahmad** or **Phyllis** bringing **his or her** laptop computer?

> **Note:** If one of the antecedents joined by *or* or *nor* is singular and one is plural, the pronoun is made to agree with the nearer antecedent.
>
> Neither **Ravi** nor **his friends** want to spend **their** time studying.
>
> Neither **his friends** nor **Ravi** wants to spend **his** time studying.

Avoiding Sentence Errors Exercises:

Agreement

A. Subject-Verb Agreement

On you own paper, correct the agreement errors in the following paragraph by writing down the line number and any incorrect verb, crossed out, with the correct form beside it.

> There is in beautiful Barcelona, Spain, many surprises to be found. 1
> Barcelona, Spain's second-largest city, and Madrid, the country's capital, 2
> has a traditional rivalry. At one time, the population of Barcelona were 3
> forbidden to speak the city's native tongue, Catalan, by a royal decree from 4
> Madrid. Today, however, neither Spanish nor Catalan are discriminated 5
> against in the region. One of the sites that belongs on every tour, the 6
> outlandish cathedral La Sagrada Familia ("The Sacred Family"), was 7
> designed by Antoni Gaudi. Everyone using the word "gaudy" actually has 8
> Gaudi's name on his or her tongue. A series of thirteenth- to fifteenth- 9
> century palaces now house the Museo Picasso, which display a history 10
> of Picasso's work and his many years living in Barcelona. *Les Demoiselles* 11
> *d'Avignon,* or *The Young Ladies of Avignon,* are one example of a painting 12
> inspired by his time in Barcelona. Whether you prefer cobblestone streets 13
> with centuries-old buildings or asphalt streets with modern shops and 14
> taverns, each are found in Barcelona. At night, every one of the streets 15
> seem to have a festive air, reflecting the vivacity of Spanish culture. 16

B. Pronoun-Antecedent and Subject-Verb Agreement

Provide the correct pronoun or verb for each blank in the following sentences. Use the directions or choices in parentheses.

1. Some people _____ math with an abacus. (*do/does*)

2. This counting device has been used for thousands of years, and _____ is still very popular in Eastern nations. (pronoun for "device")

3. The earliest examples _____ employed between 2700 and 2300 B.C. in Sumeria. (*was/were*)

4. As recently as the 1990s, school children in the Soviet Union were taught to use _____ . (pronoun for "examples" in the previous sentence)

5. Pocket-sized abacuses _____ still popular in Japan, despite the availability of portable calculators. (*is/are*)

6. Expert abacus users _____ able to add, subtract, multiply, divide, and even calculate square roots and cube roots very quickly. (*is/are*)

Shifts in Sentence Construction

A shift is an improper change in structure midway through a sentence. The following examples will help you identify and fix several different kinds of shifts.

Exercise

Shift in Person

661.1

Shift in person is mixing first, second, or third person within a sentence. (See 629.4 and 633.3.)

Exercise

> *Shift:* **One** may get spring fever unless **you** live in California or Florida. (The sentence shifts from third person, *one*, to second person, *you*.)
>
> Corrected: **You** may get spring fever unless **you** live in California or Florida. (Stays in second person)
>
> Corrected: **People** may get spring fever unless **they** live in California or Florida. (*People*, a third person plural noun, requires a third person plural pronoun, *they*.)

Shift in Tense

661.2

Shift in tense is using more than one tense in a sentence when only one is needed.

Exercise

> *Shift:* Sheila **looked** at nine apartments in one weekend before she **had chosen** one. (Tense shifts from past to past perfect for no reason.)
>
> Corrected: Sheila **looked** at nine apartments in one weekend before she **chose** one. (Tense stays in past.)

Shift in Voice

661.3

Shift in voice is mixing active with passive voice. Usually, a sentence beginning in active voice should remain so to the end.

> *Shift:* As you look (active voice) for just the right place, many interesting apartments **will probably be seen.** (passive voice)
>
> Corrected: As you look (active voice) for just the right place, **you will probably see** (active voice) many interesting apartments.

Unparallel Construction

661.4

Unparallel construction occurs when the kind of words or phrases being used shifts or changes in the middle of a sentence.

Exercise

Exercise

> *Shift:* In my hometown, people pass the time shooting pool, pitching horseshoes, and at softball games. (Sentence shifts from a series of general phrases, *shooting pool* and *pitching horseshoes*, to the prepositional phrase *at softball games.*)
>
> Parallel: In my hometown, people pass the time **shooting pool, pitching horseshoes, and playing softball**. (Now all three activities are gerund phrases—they are consistent, or parallel.)

Quick Guide

■ Avoiding Sentence Problems

Does every subject agree with its verb? (See pages 655–658.)

- ■ In person and number?
- ■ When a word or phrase comes between the subject and the verb?
- ■ When the subject is delayed?
- ■ When the subject is a title?
- ■ When a compound subject is connected with o*r*?
- ■ When the subject is a collective noun (*faculty, team,* or *crowd*)?
- ■ When the subject is a relative pronoun *(who, which, that)*?
- ■ When the subject is an indefinite pronoun (*everyone, anybody,* or *many*)?

Does every pronoun agree with its antecedent? (See page 659.)

- ■ When the pronoun is a singular indefinite pronoun such as *each, either,* or *another*?
- ■ When two antecedents are joined with *and*?
- ■ When two antecedents are joined with *or*?

Did you unintentionally create inappropriate shifts? (See page 661.)

- ■ In person?
- ■ In tense?
- ■ From active voice to passive voice?
- ■ In another unparallel construction?

Are all your sentences complete? (See pages 662–664.)

- ■ Have you used sentence fragments?
- ■ Are some sentences "spliced" or run together?

Did you use any misplaced modifiers or ambiguous wording? (See pages 665–667.)

- ■ Have you used misplaced or dangling modifiers?
- ■ Have you used incomplete comparisons or indefinite references?

Did you use any nonstandard language? (See pages 668–669.)

- ■ Have you used slang or colloquial language?
- ■ Have you used double negatives or double prepositions?

Preposition

A **preposition** combines with a noun to form a prepositional phrase, which acts as a modifier—an adverb or an adjective. See pages 641 and 644 for a list of common prepositions and for more information about prepositions.

684.1

Using *in, on, at,* and *by*

In, on, at, and *by* are four common prepositions that refer to time and place. Here are some examples of how these prepositions are used in each case.

To show time

> **on** a specific day or date: **on** June 7, **on** Wednesday
>
> **in** part of a day: **in** the afternoon
>
> **in** a year or month: **in** 2008, **in** April
>
> **in** a period of time: completed **in** an hour
>
> **by** a specific time or date: **by** noon, **by** the fifth of May
>
> **at** a specific time of day or night: **at** 3:30 this afternoon

To show place

> **at** a meeting place or location: **at** school, **at** the park
>
> **at** the edge of something: standing **at** the bar
>
> **at** the corner of something: turning **at** the intersection
>
> **at** a target: throwing a dart **at** the target
>
> **on** a surface: left **on** the floor
>
> **on** an electronic medium: **on** the Internet, **on** television
>
> **in** an enclosed space: **in** the box, **in** the room
>
> **in** a geographic location: **in** New York City, **in** Germany
>
> **in** a print medium: **in** a journal
>
> **by** a landmark: **by** the fountain

TIP: Do not insert a preposition between a transitive verb and its direct object. Intransitive verbs, however, are often followed by a prepositional phrase (a phrase that begins with a preposition).

> I **cooked** hot dogs on the grill. (transitive verb)
>
> I **ate** in the park. (intransitive verb)

684.2

Phrasal Prepositions

Some prepositional phrases begin with more than one preposition. These **phrasal prepositions** are commonly used in both written and spoken communication. A list of common phrasal prepositions follows:

according to	because of	in case of	on the side of
across from	by way of	in spite of	up to
along with	except for	instead of	with respect to

Shifts in Sentence Construction

A shift is an improper change in structure midway through a sentence. The following examples will help you identify and fix several different kinds of shifts.

Shift in Person

661.1

Shift in person is mixing first, second, or third person within a sentence. (See 629.4 and 633.3.)

> *Shift:* **One** may get spring fever unless **you** live in California or Florida.
> (The sentence shifts from third person, *one*, to second person, *you*.)
>
> *Corrected:* **You** may get spring fever unless **you** live in California or Florida.
> (Stays in second person)
>
> *Corrected:* **People** may get spring fever unless **they** live in California or Florida.
> (*People*, a third person plural noun, requires a third person plural pronoun, *they*.)

Shift in Tense

661.2

Shift in tense is using more than one tense in a sentence when only one is needed.

> *Shift:* Sheila **looked** at nine apartments in one weekend before she **had chosen** one. (Tense shifts from past to past perfect for no reason.)
>
> *Corrected:* Sheila **looked** at nine apartments in one weekend before she **chose** one. (Tense stays in past.)

Shift in Voice

661.3

Shift in voice is mixing active with passive voice. Usually, a sentence beginning in active voice should remain so to the end.

> *Shift:* As you look (active voice) for just the right place, many interesting apartments **will probably be seen.** (passive voice)
>
> *Corrected:* As you look (active voice) for just the right place, **you will probably see** (active voice) many interesting apartments.

Unparallel Construction

661.4

Unparallel construction occurs when the kind of words or phrases being used shifts or changes in the middle of a sentence.

> *Shift:* In my hometown, people pass the time shooting pool, pitching horseshoes, and at softball games. (Sentence shifts from a series of general phrases, *shooting pool* and *pitching horseshoes*, to the prepositional phrase *at softball games*.)
>
> *Parallel:* In my hometown, people pass the time **shooting pool, pitching horseshoes, and playing softball**. (Now all three activities are gerund phrases—they are consistent, or parallel.)

Fragments, Comma Splices, and Run-Ons

Except in a few special situations, you should use complete sentences when you write. By definition, a complete sentence expresses a complete thought. However, a sentence may actually contain several ideas, not just one. The trick is getting those ideas to work together to form a clear, interesting sentence that expresses your exact meaning. Among the most common sentence errors that writers make are fragments, comma splices, and run-ons.

662.1

Exercise

Fragments

A **fragment** is a phrase or dependent clause used as a sentence. It is not a sentence, however, because a phrase lacks a subject, a verb, or some other essential part, and a dependent clause must be connected to an independent clause to complete its meaning.

> *Fragment:* Pete gunned the engine. Forgetting that the boat was hooked to the truck. (This is a sentence followed by a fragment. This error can be corrected by combining the fragment with the sentence.)

> **Corrected:** Pete gunned the engine, forgetting that the boat was hooked to the truck.

> *Fragment:* Even though my best friend had a little boy last year. (This clause does not convey a complete thought. We need to know what is happening despite the birth of the little boy.)

> **Corrected:** Even though my best friend had a little boy last year, **I do not comprehend the full meaning of "motherhood."**

662.2

Video

Exercise

Comma Splices

A **comma splice** is a mistake made when two independent clauses are connected ("spliced") with only a comma. The comma is not enough: A period, semicolon, or conjunction is needed.

> *Splice:* People say that being a stay-at-home mom or dad is an important job, their actions tell a different story.

> **Corrected:** People say that being a stay-at-home mom or dad is an important job, **but** their actions tell a different story. (The coordinating conjunction *but*, added after the comma, corrects the splice.)

> **Corrected:** People say that being a stay-at-home mom or dad is an important job; their actions tell a different story. (A semicolon—rather than just a comma—makes the sentence correct.)

> **Corrected:** People say that being a stay-at-home mom or dad is an important job. **Their** actions tell a different story. (A period creates two sentences and corrects the splice.)

Run-Ons

A run-on sentence is actually two sentences (two independent clauses) joined without adequate punctuation or a connecting word.

> *Run-on:* The Alamo holds a special place in American history it was the site of an important battle between the United States and Mexico.

> **Corrected:** **The Alamo holds a special place in American history because it was the site of an important battle between the United States and Mexico.** (A subordinating conjunction is added to fix the run-on by making the second clause dependent.)

> *Run-on:* Antonio de Santa Anna, the president of Mexico who once held a funeral for his amputated leg, is the same Santa Anna who stormed the Alamo he led his troops to victory over the Texan rebels defending that fort. Two famous American frontiersmen died they were James Bowie and Davy Crockett. Santa Anna enjoyed fame, power, and respect among his followers. He died in 1876 he was poor, blind, and ignored.

> **Corrected:** Antonio de Santa Anna, the president of Mexico who once held a funeral for his amputated leg, is the same Santa Anna who stormed the Alamo. He led his troops to victory over the Texan rebels defending that fort. Two famous American frontiersmen were killed in the battle; they were James Bowie and Davy Crockett. Santa Anna enjoyed fame, power, and respect among his followers. When he died in 1876, he was poor, blind, and ignored.

The writer corrected the run-on sentences in the paragraph above by adding punctuation and making one sentence a dependent clause. While doing so, the writer also made a few changes to improve the ideas. The writer makes further improvements in the paragraph below by revising one sentence and by combining two sets of short sentences into one stronger sentence.

> **Improved:** Antonio de Santa Anna, the president of Mexico who once held a funeral for his amputated leg, is the same Santa Anna who stormed the Alamo. He led his troops to victory over Texan rebels defending that fort. Two famous American frontiersmen, **James Bowie and Davy Crockett, were killed in the battle**. Santa Anna enjoyed fame, power, and respect among his followers; **but when** he died in 1876, he was poor, blind, and ignored.

fyi Once you make a correction, you may see an opportunity to add, cut, or improve something else. Correcting and editing sentences can be frustrating at times, but with practice, these processes can become some of the more enjoyable parts of the writing process.

Avoiding Sentence Errors Exercises:
Shifts in Construction, Fragments, Comma Splices, and Run-Ons

A. Identifying Errors

On your own paper, identify the type of sentence error illustrated by each example below. If the error is a shift in construction, tell which type. (See page 661.)

1. Much music in the Western world is based upon a "diatonic scale" of seven notes, five half steps separate all but two notes in a complete diatonic scale.
2. A quick look at the piano keyboard to understand this scale.
3. From C to B, for example, you can count seven white keys and five black keys, and one can see that each black key is a half step between the white keys on either side.
4. There is no black key between E and F, nor between B and C, so these notes were understood to be only a half step apart.
5. One advantage of this arrangement of black and white keys is that pianists can easily tell the difference between notes as they touch the keyboard imagine if there were nothing but white keys all a half step apart!

B. Correcting Errors

In the following paragraph, locate each sentence error (fragment, comma splice, run-on, and unparallel construction). Identify each with the sentence number and name of the error. Then write the sentence correctly.

(1) When you're listening to jazz, you're hearing a uniquely American style of music. (2) From the American South, a fusion of African and European traditions. (3) As Art Blakely, an originator of bebop drumming, is quoted saying, "No America, no jazz." (4) The earliest jazz bands emerged in New Orleans around the turn of the twentieth century here black gospel music and Latin American brass met, and Dixieland was spawned in the 1910s. (5) During the 1920s, many popular and influential jazz musicians found their way to Chicago clubs, recordings in the Windy City began to spread the sound to other parts of the country. (6) New York City also played an important role in jazz history by adding piano, incorporating jazz into swing music, and through sales of jazz records. (7) During the late 1920s and the 1930s, local jazz bands formed all around the country, establishing the style firmly in American culture.

Misplaced and Dangling Modifiers

Writing is thinking. Before you can write clearly, you must think clearly. Nothing is more frustrating for the reader than having to reread writing just to understand its basic meaning. Look carefully at the common errors that follow. Then use this section as a checklist when you revise. Always avoid leaving misplaced or dangling modifiers in your finished work.

Exercise

Misplaced Modifiers

665.1

Misplaced modifiers are descriptive words or phrases so separated from what they are describing that the reader is confused.

Video

> *Misplaced:* The neighbor's dog has nearly been barking nonstop for two hours. (*Nearly* been barking?)
>
> *Corrected:* The neighbor's dog has been barking nonstop **for nearly two hours**. (Watch your placement of *only, just, nearly, barely,* and so on.)
>
> *Misplaced:* The commercial advertised an assortment of combs for active people with unbreakable teeth. (*People* with unbreakable teeth?)
>
> *Corrected:* The commercial advertised an assortment of combs **with unbreakable teeth for active people**. (*Combs* with unbreakable teeth)
>
> *Misplaced:* The pool staff gave large beach towels to the students marked with chlorine-resistant ID numbers. (*Students* marked with chlorine-resistant ID numbers?)
>
> *Corrected:* The pool staff gave large beach towels **marked with chlorine-resistant ID numbers to the students**. (*Towels* marked with chlorine-resistant ID numbers)

Dangling Modifiers

665.2

Dangling modifiers are descriptive phrases that tell about a subject that isn't stated in the sentence. These often occur as participial phrases containing *ing* or *ed* words.

> *Dangling:* After standing in line all afternoon, the manager informed us that all the tickets had been sold. (It sounds as if the manager has been *standing in line all afternoon.*)
>
> *Corrected:* **After we had stood in line all afternoon,** the manager informed us that all the tickets had been sold.
>
> *Dangling:* After living in the house for one month, the electrician recommended we update all the wiring. (It sounds as if the electrician has been *living in the house.*)
>
> *Corrected:* After living in the house for one month, **we hired an electrician, who recommended we update all the wiring.**

Ambiguous Wording

Sloppy sentences confuse readers. No one should have to wonder, "What does this writer mean?" When you revise and edit, check for indefinite pronoun references, incomplete comparisons, and unclear wording.

666.1 Indefinite Pronoun References

An **indefinite reference** is a problem caused by careless use of pronouns. There must always be a word or phrase nearby (its antecedent) that a pronoun clearly replaces.

Indefinite: When Tonya attempted to put her dictionary on the shelf, it fell to the floor. (The pronoun *it* could refer to either the dictionary or the shelf since both are singular nouns.)

Corrected: When Tonya attempted to put her dictionary on the shelf, **the shelf** fell to the floor.

Indefinite: Juanita reminded Kerri that she needed to photocopy her resumé before going to her interview. (Who *needed to photocopy her resumé*—Juanita or Kerri?)

Corrected: Juanita reminded Kerri **to photocopy her resumé before going to her interview.**

666.2 Incomplete Comparisons

Incomplete comparisons—leaving out words that show exactly what is being compared to what—can confuse readers.

Incomplete: After completing our lab experiment, we concluded that helium is lighter. (*Lighter* than what?)

Corrected: After completing our lab experiment, we concluded that helium is lighter **than oxygen.**

666.3 Unclear Wording

One type of ambiguous writing is wording that has two or more possible meanings due to an unclear reference to something elsewhere in the sentence. (See 666.1.)

Unclear: I couldn't believe that my sister bought a cat with all those allergy problems. (Who has the *allergy problems*—the cat or the sister?)

Corrected: I couldn't believe that my sister, **who is very allergic, bought a cat**.

Unclear: Dao intended to wash the car when he finished his homework, but he never did. (It is unclear which he *never did*—wash the car or finish his homework.)

Corrected: Dao intended to wash the car when he finished his homework, **but he never did manage to wash the car**.

Avoiding Sentence Errors Exercises:

Misplaced and Dangling Modifiers and Ambiguous Wording

A. Correcting Sentences

On your own paper, rewrite the following sentences to correct misplaced and dangling modifiers and ambiguous wording.

1. When it touched down on the moon in 1969, the onboard guidance computer of the *Apollo 11's Eagle* lander contained less than 80 kilobytes of memory.
2. The cheapest mp3 player today at least has 1 gigabyte.
3. That's equivalent to 14,000 *Apollo 11* computers roughly in one device.
4. Even a typical smartphone or handheld computer could theoretically control about 5,000 lunar landers at once, properly programmed!
5. Imagine using your phone or pocket game to land 5,000 *Apollo* craft in your car or bedroom.
6. Of course, you couldn't see all the lunar-lander controls at once because of their tiny screens.
7. After spending almost a day on the moon's surface, NASA had the crew launch back into orbit and return to Earth.
8. The *Eagle's* journey to the moon had made it a sensation around the world.
9. The crew were all heroes, but they certainly liked the Earth better.
10. Today the Science Museum in London displays a lunar-lander replica for visitors in full size.

B. Correcting Errors in Context

Locate a misplaced modifier and several indefinite-pronoun-reference errors in the following paragraph. For each error, write the sentence number, identify the error type, and rewrite the sentences correctly.,

> (1) One famous Russian joke lampoons the *nouveau-riche* Russians, known as "New Russians," by comparing cars. (2) In this joke, unexpectedly, a New Russian and an old man wake up in an emergency room. (3) The New Russian asks the old man how he ended up there. (4) The old man replies, "I put my war-trophy Messerschmitt jet engine on my old Zaporozhets car to make it go faster. (5) But after a couple of miles I lost control and crashed into a tree. (6) How about you?" (7) He answers that when an old Zaporozhets passed his new Ferrari on the highway, he thought it had stalled. (8) So he opened the door and stepped out.

☑️
Exercise

Nonstandard Language

Nonstandard language is language that does not conform to the standards set by schools, media, and public institutions. It is often acceptable in everyday conversation and in fictional writing but seldom is used in formal speech or other forms of writing.

668.1   Colloquial Language

Colloquial language is wording used in informal conversation that is unacceptable in formal writing.

> *Colloquial:* Hey, wait up! Cal wants to go with.
>
> *Standard:* **Hey, wait!** Cal wants to go with us.

668.2   Double Preposition

The use of certain **double prepositions**—*off of, off to, from off*—is unacceptable.

> *Double Preposition:* Pick up the dirty clothes from off the floor.
>
> *Standard:* Pick up the dirty clothes **from the floor.**

668.3   Substitution

Avoid substituting *and* for *to.*

> *Substitution:* Try and get to class on time.
>
> *Standard:* **Try to** get to class on time.

Avoid substituting *of* for *have* when combining with *could, would, should,* or *might.*

> *Substitution:* I should of studied for that exam.
>
> *Standard:* **I should have** studied for that exam.

668.4   Double Negative

A **double negative** is a sentence that contains two negative words used to express a single negative idea. Double negatives are unacceptable in academic writing.

> *Double Negative:* After paying for essentials, I haven't got no money left.
>
> *Standard:* **I haven't got** any money left. / **I have no** money left.

668.5   Slang

Avoid the use of **slang** or any "in" words in formal writing.

> *Slang:* The way the stadium roof opened was way cool.
>
> *Standard:* The way the stadium roof opened **was remarkable.**

Avoiding Sentence Errors Exercises:
Nonstandard Language

A. Correcting Sentences

On your own paper, identify the type of error exhibited in each sentence below (colloquialism, double preposition, substitution, double negative, or slang). Then correct it.

1. Would you of guessed that soccer is the world's most popular sport?
2. The word "soccer" is Oxford slang for "association," 'cause officially the game is "Association Football."
3. In most countries the sport's called "football," or some variation like *fútbol* or *fußball*.
4. The World Cup is a wicked awesome competition played every four years.
5. Soccer rules were set up in England in 1863, and they haven't hardly changed since then.
6. The point of the game is to try and kick the ball into the other team's goal area.
7. Normally play continues until someone commits a foul or kicks a ball off of the field.
8. Most players aren't not allowed to touch the ball with their hands.
9. If you've ever watched soccer, though, you might of seen the goalie engage the ball that way.
10. The other players don't have no official titles.
11. Most times, though, there are forwards, defenders, and midfielders.
12. According to the rules, games needn't never go into overtime; they can end in a tie.
13. But some games can just keep agoin' in overtime till somebody scores.
14. The U.S. team did pretty good for itself in the 2010 games.
15. Some folks say that Europeans feel closer to us since our team rocked big time and stayed in the competition so long.
16. I wonder what they would of thought if the U.S. had won!
17. Personally, though, I was rooting for Spain from the get go.
18. If you're interested, it doesn't hardly take much equipment to play soccer.
19. All's you really need's a ball and maybe some markers for the goals.
20. Well, you also gotta have two teams with eleven players each.

B. Correcting Your Own Writing

Spend 5 minutes writing freely about a sport you find interesting. Imagine describing that sport to someone unfamiliar with it, or simply explain your own interest in it. When you have finished, review your writing for nonstandard language and make any necessary corrections.

Quick Guide

■ Avoiding Sentence Problems

Does every subject agree with its verb? (See pages 655–658.)

- In person and number?
- When a word or phrase comes between the subject and the verb?
- When the subject is delayed?
- When the subject is a title?
- When a compound subject is connected with o*r*?
- When the subject is a collective noun (*faculty, team,* or *crowd*)?
- When the subject is a relative pronoun (*who, which, that*)?
- When the subject is an indefinite pronoun (*everyone, anybody,* or *many*)?

Does every pronoun agree with its antecedent? (See page 659.)

- When the pronoun is a singular indefinite pronoun such as *each, either,* or *another*?
- When two antecedents are joined with *and*?
- When two antecedents are joined with *or*?

Did you unintentionally create inappropriate shifts? (See page 661.)

- In person?
- In tense?
- From active voice to passive voice?
- In another unparallel construction?

Are all your sentences complete? (See pages 662–664.)

- Have you used sentence fragments?
- Are some sentences "spliced" or run together?

Did you use any misplaced modifiers or ambiguous wording? (See pages 665–667.)

- Have you used misplaced or dangling modifiers?
- Have you used incomplete comparisons or indefinite references?

Did you use any nonstandard language? (See pages 668–669.)

- Have you used slang or colloquial language?
- Have you used double negatives or double prepositions?

Multilingual and ESL Guidelines

39

English may be your second, third, or fifth language. As a multilingual learner, you bring to your writing the culture and knowledge of the languages you use. This broader perspective enables you to draw on many experiences and greater knowledge as you write and speak. Whether you are an international student or someone who has lived in North America a long time and is now learning more about English, this chapter provides you with important information about writing in English.

Five Parts of Speech

Noun

Audio

Count Nouns

671.1

Count nouns refer to things that can be counted. They can have *a*, *an*, *the*, or *one* in front of them. One or more adjectives can come between the articles *a*, *an*, *the*, or *one* and the singular count noun.

> **an apple, one orange, a plum, a purple plum**

Count nouns can be singular, as in the examples above, or plural, as in the examples below.

> **plums, apples, oranges**

> **Note:** When count nouns are plural, they can have the article *the*, a number, or a demonstrative adjective in front of them. (See 673.1 and 673.3.)
>
> I used **the** plums to make a pie.
>
> He placed **five** apples on my desk.
>
> **These** oranges are so juicy!

The *number* of a noun refers to whether it names a single thing (*book*), in which case its number is *singular*, or whether it names more than one thing (*books*), in which case the number of the noun is *plural*.

> **Note:** There are different ways in which the plural form of nouns is created. For more information, see pages 590–591.

Exercise

Web Link

672.1

Noncount Nouns

Noncount nouns refer to things that cannot be counted. Do not use *a*, *an*, or *one* in front of them. They have no plural form, so they always take a singular verb. Some nouns that end in *s* are not plural; they are noncount nouns.

> **fruit, furniture, rain, thunder, advice, mathematics, news**

Abstract nouns name ideas or conditions rather than people, places, or objects. Many abstract nouns are noncount nouns.

> The students had **fun** at the party. Good **health** is a wonderful gift.

Collective nouns name a whole category or group and are often noncount nouns.

> **homework, furniture, money**

> **Note:** The parts or components of a group or category named by a noncount noun are often count nouns. For example, *report* and *assignment* are count nouns that are parts of the collective, noncount noun *homework*.

672.2

Two-Way Nouns

Some nouns can be used as either count or noncount nouns, depending on what they refer to.

> I would like a **glass** of water. (count noun)

> **Glass** is used to make windows. (noncount noun)

Articles and Other Noun Markers

672.3

Specific Articles

Use articles and other noun markers or modifiers to give more information about nouns. The **specific** (or **definite**) **article** *the* is used to refer to a specific noun.

> I found **the** book I misplaced yesterday.

672.4

Indefinite Articles and Indefinite Adjectives

Exercise

Use the **indefinite article** *a* or *an* to refer to a nonspecific noun. Use *an* before singular nouns beginning with the vowels *a*, *e*, *i*, *o*, and *u*. Use *a* before nouns beginning with all other letters of the alphabet, the consonants. Exceptions do occur: *a* unit; *a* university.

> I always take **an** apple to work.

> It is good to have **a** book with you when you travel.

Indefinite adjectives can also mark nonspecific nouns—*all, any, each, either, every, few, many, more, most, neither, several, some* (for singular and plural count nouns); *all, any, more, most, much, some* (for noncount nouns).

> **Every** student is encouraged to register early.

> **Most** classes fill quickly.

Determining Whether to Use Articles 673.1

Listed below are a number of guidelines to help you determine whether to use an article and which one to use.

Use *a* or *an* with singular count nouns that do not refer to one specific item.

A zebra has black and white stripes. **An apple** is good for you.

Do not use *a* or *an* with plural count nouns.

Zebras have black and white stripes. **Apples** are good for you.

Do not use *a* or *an* with noncount nouns.

Homework needs to be done promptly.

Use *the* with singular count nouns that refer to one specific item.

The apple you gave me was delicious.

Use *the* with plural count nouns.

The zebras at Brookfield Zoo were healthy.

Use *the* with noncount nouns.

The money from my uncle is a gift.

Do not use *the* with most singular proper nouns.

Mother Theresa loved the poor and downcast.

Note: There are many exceptions: *the* Sahara Desert, *the* University of Minnesota, *the* Fourth of July

Use *the* with plural nouns.

the Joneses (both Mr. and Mrs. Jones), **the Rocky Mountains, the United States**

Possessive Adjectives 673.2

The possessive case of nouns and pronouns can be used as adjectives to mark nouns.

possessive nouns: *Tanya's, father's, store's*

The car is **Tanya's,** not her **father's.**

possessive pronouns: *my, your, his, her, its, our*

My hat is purple.

Demonstrative Adjectives 673.3

Demonstrative pronouns can be used as adjectives to mark nouns.

Demonstrative adjectives: *this, that, these, those* (for singular and plural count nouns); *this, that* (for noncount nouns)

Those chairs are lovely. Where did you buy **that** furniture?

Multilingual/ESL Exercises:
Nouns, Articles, and Other Noun Markers

A. Count and Noncount Nouns

On your own paper, make a list of count nouns from the following paragraph. Next make a list of noncount nouns.

> We live in a time of confusing economics. On the one hand, it is 1
> necessary to spend money to keep the economy stimulated. Manufacturers 2
> use every psychological trick they can identify to coax consumers to buy 3
> more products. As a matter of fact, advertisers work to make the public want 4
> things it doesn't actually need. On the other hand, citizens are expected to 5
> invest and save for emergencies and for their retirement. Shame is used as a 6
> motivator to accomplish this. Unfortunately, in a world where citizens have 7
> been relabeled as consumers, the psychology of sales too often outweighs the 8
> shadow of shame. 9

B. Articles and Other Noun Markers

For each numbered blank, write an appropriate article or noun marker as needed. (If none is needed, write "none needed.") Then identify each added article or adjective by type (specific article, indefinite article, indefinite adjective, possessive adjective, demonstrative adjective, or quantifier).

> Does (1)_____ family own a dog? If so, what made you choose (2)_____ breed instead of a different one? In (3)_____ house, we have (4) _____ dogs. (5)_____ dog is a Chihuahua and (6)_____ other is (7)_____ Bichon Frise. The Chihuahua barks at (8)_____ people but not at others. Well, to be truthful, he always barks at (9)_____ strangers, but seldom at a family member or (10)_____ friend. (11)_____ Bichon Frise is too friendly and excited to bark. He jumps on each and (12)_____ person who visits us. Scientists say that (13)_____ dogs originally descended from (14)_____ wolf. From my observation of (15)_____ Chihuaha and Bichon Frise, it is obvious that different dogs descended differently.

Quantifiers

675.1

Expressions of quantity and measure are often used with nouns. Below are some of these expressions and guidelines for using them.

The following expressions of quantity can be used with count nouns: *each, every, both, a couple of, a few, several, many, a number of.*

> We enjoyed **both** concerts we attended. **A couple of** songs performed were familiar to us.

Use a number to indicate a specific quantity of a continuum.

> I saw **fifteen** cardinals in the park.

To indicate a specific quantity of a noncount noun, use *a* + quantity (such as *bag, bottle, bowl, carton, glass,* or *piece*) + *of* + noun.

> I bought **a carton of milk, a head of lettuce, a piece of cheese,** and **a bag of flour** at the grocery store.

The following expressions can be used with noncount nouns: *a little, much, a great deal of.*

> We had **much** wind and **a little** rain as the storm passed through yesterday.

The following expressions of quantity can be used with both count and noncount nouns: *no/ not any, some, a lot of, lots of, plenty of, most, all, this, that.*

> I would like **some** apples *(count noun)* and **some** rice *(noncount noun),* please.

Verb

As the main part of the predicate, a verb conveys much of a sentence's meaning. Using verb tenses and forms correctly ensures that your readers will understand your sentences as you intend them to. For a more thorough review of verbs, see pages 632–638.

Exercise

Progressive (Continuous) Tenses

675.2

Progressive or continuous tense verbs express action in progress (see page 634).

To form the **present progressive** tense, use the helping verb *am, is,* or *are* with the *ing* form of the main verb.

> He **is washing** the car right now.
> Kent and Chen **are studying** for a test.

To form the **past progressive** tense, use the helping verb *was* or *were* with the *ing* form of the main verb.

> Yesterday he **was working** in the garden all day.
> Julia and Juan **were watching** a movie.

To form the future progressive tense, use *will* or a phrase that indicates the future, the helping verb *be,* and the *ing* form of the main verb.

> Next week he **will be painting** the house.
> He **plans to be painting** the house soon.

676.1

Exercise

Note that some verbs are generally not used in the progressive tenses, such as the following groups of frequently used verbs:

- Verbs that express thoughts, attitudes, and desires: *know, understand, want, prefer*
- Verbs that describe appearances: *seem, resemble*
- Verbs that indicate possession: *belong, have, own, possess*
- Verbs that signify inclusion: *contain, hold*

    Kala **knows** how to ride a motorcycle.

    NOT THIS: Kala is **knowing** how to ride a motorcycle.

676.2

Objects and Complements of Verbs

Active transitive verbs take objects. These can be direct objects, indirect objects, or object complements. Linking verbs take subject complements—predicate nominatives or predicate adjectives—that rename or describe the subject.

676.3

Infinitives as Objects

Infinitives can follow many verbs, including these: *agree, appear, attempt, consent, decide, demand, deserve, endeavor, fail, hesitate, hope, intend, need, offer, plan, prepare, promise, refuse, seem, tend, volunteer, wish.* (See 636.3 for more on infinitives.)

    He **promised to bring** some samples.

The following verbs are among those that can be followed by a noun or pronoun plus the infinitive: *ask, beg, choose, expect, intend, need, prepare, promise, want.*

    I **expect you to be** there on time.

Note: Except in the passive voice, the following verbs must have a noun or pronoun before the infinitive: *advise, allow, appoint, authorize, cause, challenge, command, convince, encourage, forbid, force, hire, instruct, invite, order, permit, remind, require, select, teach, tell, tempt, trust.*

    I will **authorize Emily to use** my credit card.

Unmarked infinitives (no *to*) can follow these verbs: *have, help, let, make.*

    These glasses **help me see** the board.

676.4

Gerunds as Objects

Gerunds can follow these verbs: *admit, avoid, consider, deny, discuss, dislike, enjoy, finish, imagine, miss, postpone, quit, recall, recommend, regret.* (Also see 636.2.)

    I **recommended hiring** Ian for the job.

Here *hiring* is the direct object of the active verb *recommended*, and *Ian* is the object of the gerund.

Infinitives or Gerunds as Objects

677.1

Either **gerunds** or **infinitives** can follow these verbs: *begin, continue, hate, like, love, prefer, remember, start, stop, try.*

> I **hate having** cold feet. I **hate to have** cold feet. (In either form, the verbal phrase is the direct object of the verb hate.)

> **Note:** Sometimes the meaning of a sentence will change depending on whether you use a gerund or an infinitive.

> I stopped to smoke. (I *stopped* weeding the garden *to smoke* a cigarette.)

> I stopped smoking. (I no longer smoke.)

Common Modal Auxiliary Verbs

677.2

Modal auxiliary verbs are a kind of auxiliary verb. (See 632.3.) They help the main verb express meaning. Modals are sometimes grouped with other helping or auxiliary verbs.

Modal verbs must be followed by the base form of a verb without *to* (not by a gerund or an infinitive). Also, modal verbs do not change form; they are always used as they appear in the following chart.

Modal	Expresses	Sample Sentence
can	ability	I *can* program a VCR.
could	ability	I *could* babysit Tuesday.
	possibility	He *could* be sick.
might	possibility	I *might* be early.
may, might	possibility	I *may* sleep late Saturday.
	request	*May* I be excused?
must	strong need	I *must* study more.
have to	strong need	I *have to* (have got to) exercise.
ought to	feeling of duty	I *ought to* (should) help Dad.
should	advisabillity	She *should* retire.
	expectation	I *should* have caught that train.
shall	intent	*Shall* I stay longer?
will	intent	I *will* visit my grandma soon.
would	intent	I *would* live to regret my offer.
	repeated action	He *would* walk in the meadow.
would + you	polite request	*Would you* help me?
could + you	polite request	*Could you* type this letter?
will + you	polite request	*Will you* give me a ride?
can + you	polite request	*Can you* make supper tonight?

Common Two-Word Verbs

This chart lists some common verbs in which two words—a verb and a preposition—work together to express a specific action. A noun or pronoun is often inserted between the parts of the two-word verb when it is used in a sentence: *break it down, call it off.*

break down	to take apart or fall apart
call off	cancel
call up	make a phone call
clear out	leave a place quickly
cross out	draw a line through
do over	repeat
figure out	find a solution
fill in/out	complete a form or an application
fill up	fill a container or tank
* **find out**	discover
* **get in**	enter a vehicle or building
* **get out of**	leave a car, a house, or a situation
* **get over**	recover from a sickness or a problem
give back	return something
give in/up	surrender or quit
hand in	give homework to a teacher
hand out	give someone something
hang up	put down a phone receiver
leave out	omit or don't use
let in/out	allow someone or something to enter or go out
look up	find information
mix up	confuse
pay back	return money or a favor
pick out	choose
point out	call attention to
put away	return something to its proper place
put down	place something on a table, the floor, and so on.
put off	delay doing something
shut off	turn off a machine or light
* **take part**	participate
talk over	discuss
think over	consider carefully
try on	put on clothing to see if it fits
turn down	lower the volume
turn up	raise the volume
write down	write on a piece of paper

* These two-word verbs should not have a noun or pronoun inserted between their parts.

Spelling Guidelines for Verb Forms

The same spelling rules that apply when adding a suffix to other words apply to verbs as well. Most verbs need a suffix to indicate tense or form. The third-person singular form of a verb, for example, usually ends in *s*, but it can also end in *es*. Formation of *ing* and *ed* forms of verbs and verbals needs careful attention, too. Consult the rules below to determine which spelling is correct for each verb. (For general spelling guidelines, see page 599.)

There may be exceptions to these rules when forming the past tense of irregular verbs because the verbs are formed by changing the word itself, not merely by adding *d* or *ed*. (See the chart of irregular verbs on page 637.)

Past Tense: Adding *ed*

679.1

Add *ed* . . .

- When a verb ends with two consonants:
  touch—**touched**   ask—**asked**   pass—**passed**

- When a verb ends with a consonant preceded by two vowels:
  heal—**healed**   gain—**gained**

- When a verb ends in *y* preceded by a vowel:
  annoy—**annoyed**   flay—**flayed**

- When a multisyllable verb's last syllable is not stressed (even when the last syllable ends with a consonant preceded by a vowel):
  budget—**budgeted**   enter—**entered**   interpret—**interpreted**

Change *y* to *i* and add *ed* when a verb ends in a consonant followed by *y:*
  liquefy—**liquefied**   worry—**worried**

Double the final consonant and add *ed* . . .

- When a verb has one syllable and ends with a consonant preceded by a vowel:
  wrap—**wrapped**   drop—**dropped**

- When a multisyllable verb's last syllable (ending in a consonant preceded by a vowel) is stressed:
  admit—**admitted**   confer—**conferred**   abut—**abutted**

Past Tense: Adding *d*

679.2

Add *d* . . .

- When a verb ends with *e:*
  chime—**chimed**   tape—**taped**

- When a verb ends with *ie:*
  tie—**tied**   die—**died**   lie—**lied**

680.1

Present Tense: Adding *s* or *es*

Add *es* . . .

- When a verb ends in *ch, sh, s, x,* or *z*:
  watch—**watches**   fix—**fixes**

- To *do* and *go:*
  do—**does**   go—**goes**

Change *y* to *i* and add *es* when the verb ends in a consonant followed by *y*:
liquefy—**liquefies**   quantify—**quantifies**

Add *s* to most other verbs, including those already ending in *e* and those that end in a vowel followed by *y:*
write—**writes**   buy—**buys**

680.2

Present Tense: Adding *ing*

Drop the *e* and add *ing* when the verb ends in *e:*
drive—**driving**   rise—**rising**

Double the final consonant and add *ing* . . .

- When a verb has one syllable and ends with a consonant preceded by a single vowel:
  wrap—**wrapping**   sit—**sitting**

- When a multisyllable verb's last syllable (ending in a consonant preceded by a single vowel) is stressed:
  forget—**forgetting**   begin—**beginning**   abut—**abutting**

Change *ie* to *y* and add *ing* when a verb ends with *ie:*
tie—**tying**   die—**dying**   lie—**lying**

Add *ing* . . .

- When a verb ends with two consonants:
  touch—**touching**   ask—**asking**   pass—**passing**

- When a verb ends with a consonant preceded by two vowels:
  heal—**healing**   gain—**gaining**

- When a verb ends in *y:*
  buy—**buying**   study—**studying**   cry—**crying**

- When a multisyllable verb's last syllable is not stressed (even when the last syllable ends with a consonant preceded by a vowel):
  budget—**budgeting**   enter—**entering**   interpret—**interpreting**

> **Note:** Never trust your spelling to even the best computer spell checker. Carefully proofread. Use a dictionary for questionable words your spell checker may miss.

Multilingual/ESL Exercises:

Verbs, Objects, and Complements

A. Errors in Context

On your own paper, correct any verb, object, and complement errors in the sentences below. Write down the error, crossed out, with the correction beside it.

> (1) Evolutionary psychologist Robert Dunbar suggest that brain size directly affects behavior in terms of how many individuals a mammal can to care about. (2) A chimpanzee is possessing an emotional connection with about 50 other chimpanzees. (3) If a tribe's size grow beyond that, the group tends fighting. (4) Studies of human brain size predict that humans are having the ability to care for roughly 150 other people, and Dunbar says research bears that out. (5) Fortunately, humans decide building hierarchies to support larger societies. (6) Also, people can conceiving of a universal family of humanity. (7) Can you to think that way?

B. Forming Tenses

Write the correct past tense for each of the verbs listed below. (Note that some of these verbs have irregular past-tense forms.)

1. say _____

2. go _____

3. derive _____

4. maintain _____

5. parrot _____

6. make _____

7. lift _____

8. offer _____

Write the correct present tense form (adding *s* or *es*) for each of these verbs.

1. will _____

2. come _____

3. wonder _____

4. verify _____

5. speak _____

6. display _____

7. propagate _____

8. go _____

Write the correct present tense form (adding *ing*) for each of these verbs.

1. activate _____

2. portray _____

3. begin _____

4. start _____

5. manage _____

6. travel _____

7. monopolize _____

8. fly _____

Adjective

682.1 Placing Adjectives

Exercise

You probably know that an adjective often comes before the noun it modifies. When several adjectives are used in a row to modify a single noun, it is important to arrange the adjectives in the well-established sequence used in English writing and speaking. The following list shows the usual order of adjectives. (Also see 565.3.)

First, place . . .

1. articles . . . . **a, an, the**
   demonstrative adjectives . . . . **that, those**
   possessives . . . . **my, her, Misha's**

Then place words that . . .

2. indicate time . . . .**first, next, final**
3. tell how many . . . .**one, few, some**
4. evaluate . . . . **beautiful, dignified, graceful**
5. tell what size . . . . **big, small, short, tall**
6. tell what shape. . . . . **round, square**
7. describe a condition . . . . **messy, clean, dark**
8. tell what age. . . . . **old, young, new, antique**
9. tell what color . . . . **blue, red, yellow**
10. tell what nationality . . . . **English, Chinese, Mexican**
11. tell what religion . . . . **Buddhist, Jewish, Protestant**
12. tell what material . . . . **satin, velvet, wooden**

Finally, place nouns . . .

13. used as adjectives . . . . **computer [monitor], spice [rack]**

    my second try (1 + 2 + noun)
    gorgeous young white swans (4 + 8 + 9 + noun)

682.2 Present and Past Participles as Adjectives

Both the **present participle** and the **past participle** can be used as adjectives. (Also see 636.4.) Exercise care in choosing whether to use the present participle or the past participle. A participle can come either before a noun or after a linking verb.

A **present participle** used as an adjective should describe a person or thing that is causing a feeling or situation.

> His **annoying** comments made me angry.

A **past participle** should describe a person or thing that experiences a feeling or situation.

> He was **annoyed** because he had to wait so long.

> **Note:** Within each of the following pairs, the present (*ing* form) and past (*ed* form) participles have different meanings.
>
> | | | |
> |---|---|---|
> | annoying/annoyed | depressing/depressed | fascinating/fascinated |
> | boring/bored | exciting/excited | surprising/surprised |
> | confusing/confused | exhausting/exhausted | |

Nouns as Adjectives

Exercise

Nouns sometimes function as adjectives by modifying another noun. When a noun is used as an adjective, it is always singular.

> Many European cities have **rose** gardens.
>
> Marta recently joined a **book** club.

TIP: Try to avoid using more than two nouns as adjectives for another noun. These "noun compounds" can get confusing. Prepositional phrases may get the meaning across better than long noun strings.

> *Correct:* Omar is a **crew** member in the **restaurant** kitchen during **second** shift.
>
> *Not correct:* Omar is a **second-shift restaurant kitchen crew** member.

Adverb

Placing Adverbs

Consider the following guidelines for placing adverbs correctly. See page 640 for more information about adverbs.

Place adverbs that tell how often (*frequently, seldom, never, always, sometimes*) after a helping (auxiliary) verb and before the main verb. In a sentence without a helping verb, adverbs that tell *how often* are placed before an action verb but after a linking verb.

> The salesclerk will **usually** help me.

Place adverbs that tell when (*yesterday, now, at five o'clock*) at the end of a sentence.

> Auntie El came home **yesterday.**

Adverbs that tell where (*upside-down, around, downstairs*) usually follow the verb they modify. Many prepositional phrases (*at the beach, under the stairs, below the water*) function as adverbs that tell where.

> We waited **on the porch.**

Adverbs that tell how (*quickly, slowly, loudly*) can be placed either at the beginning, in the middle, or at the end of a sentence—but not between a verb and its direct object.

> **Softly** he called my name. He **softly** called my name. He called my name **softly.**

Place adverbs that modify adjectives directly before the adjective.

> That is a **most** unusual dress.

Adverbs that modify clauses are most often placed in front of the clause, but they can also go inside or at the end of the clause.

> **Fortunately,** we were not involved in the accident.
> We were not involved, **fortunately,** in the accident.
> We were not involved in the accident, **fortunately.**

Note: Adverbs that are used with verbs that have direct objects must *not* be placed between the verb and its object.

> *Correct:* Luis **usually** catches the most fish.   **Usually,** Luis catches the most fish.
>
> *Not correct:* Luis catches **usually** the most fish.

Preposition

A **preposition** combines with a noun to form a prepositional phrase, which acts as a modifier—an adverb or an adjective. See pages 641 and 644 for a list of common prepositions and for more information about prepositions.

684.1

Using *in, on, at,* and *by*

In, on, at, and *by* are four common prepositions that refer to time and place. Here are some examples of how these prepositions are used in each case.

To show time

    on a specific day or date: *on* June 7, *on* Wednesday

    in part of a day: *in* the afternoon

    in a year or month: *in* 2008, *in* April

    in a period of time: completed *in* an hour

    by a specific time or date: *by* noon, *by* the fifth of May

    at a specific time of day or night: *at* 3:30 this afternoon

To show place

    at a meeting place or location: *at* school, *at* the park

    at the edge of something: standing *at* the bar

    at the corner of something: turning *at* the intersection

    at a target: throwing a dart *at* the target

    on a surface: left *on* the floor

    on an electronic medium: *on* the Internet, *on* television

    in an enclosed space: *in* the box, *in* the room

    in a geographic location: *in* New York City, *in* Germany

    in a print medium: *in* a journal

    by a landmark: *by* the fountain

TIP: Do not insert a preposition between a transitive verb and its direct object. Intransitive verbs, however, are often followed by a prepositional phrase (a phrase that begins with a preposition).

    I **cooked** hot dogs on the grill. (transitive verb)

    I **ate** in the park. (intransitive verb)

684.2

Phrasal Prepositions

Some prepositional phrases begin with more than one preposition. These **phrasal prepositions** are commonly used in both written and spoken communication. A list of common phrasal prepositions follows:

according to	because of	in case of	on the side of
across from	by way of	in spite of	up to
along with	except for	instead of	with respect to

Multilingual/ESL Exercises:
Adjectives, Adverbs, Prepositions

A. Adjective Order

On your own paper, rewrite the following phrases to place the adjectives in the proper order.

1. sandstone first square several red gigantic the blocks

2. a sticky brown few last delicious figs

3. rough-barked old some round huge trees

B. Present and Past Participles

Choose the correct adjective form (present or past participle) in each case below.

1. Deborah was <u>annoying/annoyed</u> that her wedding dress was not finished.

2. The <u>exciting/excited</u> day was quickly approaching, but the preparation was making her <u>exhausting/exhausted</u>.

3. Then <u>surprising/surprised</u> news arrived: An old high school friend was coming to help!

4. Her fiancé Trevor was confusing/confused at first that her old friend, Michael, was willing to be a "bridesmaid."

5. Trevor figured that Michael must be a <u>fascinating/fascinated</u> fellow.

C. *At, By, In,* or *On*

Write the best preposition—*at, by, in,* or *on*—for each blank in the sentences below.

1. _____ what time do you get up most mornings?

2. Do you come to school _____ car, _____ bike, _____ bus, or do you walk?

3. After school, I have to work _____ a pizza parlor most evenings.

4. The pizza restaurant is _____ the downtown area, _____ the public library.

5. I like pizza with mushrooms _____ it.

6. The place I work posts free coupons _____ its website.

7. The current coupon expires _____ June 8.

8. We have tables, so you can eat _____ the store if you like.

9. Our pizzas are cooked _____ a wood-burning oven.

10. Once, I cooked a pizza _____ my grill at home, over charcoal.

Exercise

Understanding Sentence Basics

Simple sentences in the English language follow the five basic patterns shown below. (See pages 645–654 for more information.)

Subject + Verb

┌─S─┐┌─V─┐
Naomie winked.

Some verbs like *winked* are intransitive. Intransitive verbs do not need a direct object to express a complete thought. (See 632.2.)

Subject + Verb + Direct Object

┌─S─┐ ┌─V─┐┌─DO─┐
Harris grinds his teeth.

Some verbs like *grinds* are transitive. Transitive verbs *do* need a direct object to express a complete thought. (See 632.2.)

Subject + Verb + Indirect Object + Direct Object

┌─S─┐┌─V─┐ ┌─IO──┐ ┌─DO──┐
Elena offered her friend an anchovy.

The direct object names who or what receives the action; the indirect object names to whom or for whom the action was done.

Subject + Verb + Direct Object + Object Complement

┌──── S ────┐┌─V─┐ DO ┌────── OC ──────┐
The chancellor named Ravi the outstanding student of 2010.

The object complement renames or describes the direct object.

Subject + Linking Verb + Predicate Nominative (or Predicate Adjective)

┌─S─┐LV ┌────PN────┐   ┌─S─┐LV┌───PA───┐
Paula is a computer programmer.   **Paula is very intelligent.**

A linking verb connects the subject to the predicate noun or predicate adjective. The predicate noun renames the subject; the predicate adjective describes the subject.

Inverted Order

In the sentence patterns above, the subject comes before the verb. In a few types of sentences, such as those below, the subject comes *after* the verb.

LV┌─S─┐ ┌─PN─┐   LV ┌──S──┐
Is Larisa a poet?   **There was a meeting.**

(A question)   (A sentence beginning with "there")

Exercise

Sentence Problems

This section looks at potential trouble spots and sentence problems. For more information about English sentences, their parts, and how to construct them, see pages 645 through 654 in the handbook. Pages 655 through 670 cover the types of problems and errors found in English writing. The guide to avoiding sentence problems found on page 670 is an excellent editing tool.

Double Negatives

687.1

When making a sentence negative, use *not* or another negative adverb (*never, rarely, hardly, seldom,* and so on), but not both. Using both results in a double negative (see 668.4).

Subject–Verb Agreement

687.2

Be sure the subject and verb in every clause agree in person and number. (See pages 655–658.)

The **student was** rewarded for her hard work.

The **students were** rewarded for their hard work.

The **instructor,** as well as the students, **is** expected to attend the orientation.

The **students,** as well as the instructor, **are** expected to attend the orientation.

Omitted Words

687.3

Do not omit subjects or the expletives *there* or *here*. In all English clauses and sentences (except imperatives in which the subject *you* is understood), there must be a subject.

Correct: Your mother was very quiet; **she** seemed to be upset.
Not correct: Your mother was very quiet; seemed to be upset.

Correct: **There** is not much time left.
Not correct: Not much time left.

Repeated Words

687.4

Do not repeat the subject of a clause or sentence.

Correct: The doctor prescribed an antibiotic.
Not correct: The doctor, **she** prescribed an antibiotic.

Do not repeat an object in an adjective dependent clause.

Correct: I forgot the flowers that I intended to give to my hosts.
Not correct: I forgot the flowers that I intended to give **them** to my hosts.

Note: Sometimes the relative pronoun that begins the adjective dependent clause is omitted but understood.

I forgot the flowers I intended to give to my hosts.
(The relative pronoun *that* is omitted.)

688.1

Exercise

Conditional Sentences

Conditional sentences express a situation requiring that a condition be met in order to be true. Selecting the correct verb tense for use in the two clauses of a conditional sentence can be problematic. Below you will find an explanation of the three types of conditional sentences and the verb tenses that are needed to form them.

1. **Factual conditionals:** The conditional clause begins with *if, when, whenever,* or a similar expression. Furthermore, the verbs in the conditional clause and the main clause should be in the same tense.

    Whenever we **had** time, we **took** a break and **went** for a swim.

2. **Predictive conditionals** express future conditions and possible results. The conditional clause begins with *if* or *unless* and has a present tense verb. The main clause uses a modal (*will, can, should, may, might*) plus the base form of the verb.

    Unless we **find** a better deal, we **will buy** this sound system.

3. **Hypothetical past conditionals** describe a situation that is unlikely to happen or that is contrary to fact. To describe situations in the past, the verb in the conditional clause is in the past perfect tense, and the verb in the main clause is formed from *would have, could have,* or *might have* plus the past participle.

    If we **had started out** earlier, we **would have arrived** on time.

Note: If the hypothetical situation is a present or future one, the verb in the conditional clause is in the past tense, and the verb in the main clause is formed from *would, could,* or *might* plus the base form of the verb.

    If we **bought** groceries once a week, we **would** not **have** to go to the store so often.

688.2

Quoted and Reported Speech

Quoted speech is the use of exact words from another source in your own writing; you must enclose these words in quotation marks. It is also possible to report nearly exact words without quotation marks. This is called **reported speech,** or indirect quotation. (See pages 577–578 for a review of the use of quotation marks.)

Direct quotation: Felicia said, "Don't worry about tomorrow."

Indirect quotation: Felicia said that you don't have to worry about tomorrow.

In the case of a question, when a direct quotation is changed to an indirect quotation, the question mark is not needed.

Direct quotation: Ahmad asked, "Which of you will give me a hand?"

Indirect quotation: Ahmad asked which of us would give him a hand.

Notice how pronouns are often changed in indirect quotations.

Direct quotation: My friends said, "**You**'re crazy."

Indirect quotation: My friends said that **I** was crazy.

Note: In academic writing, the use of another source's spoken or written words in one's own writing without proper acknowledgment is called *plagiarism*. Plagiarism is severely penalized in academic situations. (See pages 474–477.)

Multilingual/ESL Exercises:
Sentence Problems

A. Errors in Context

On your own paper, correct the error(s) in each sentence below. Write down the error, crossed out, with the correction beside it.

> (1) Flying by commercial jet can be a great way to travel if you have a long way to go and needs to get there quickly. (2) You can't never ignore, however, that the convenience comes with a price. (3) Security checks is becoming more intrusive every year. (4) Also, airlines they are reducing flights, crowding planes, and charging for services like meals. (5) If you wanted a leisurely vacation, you do better to choose different transportation. (6) An ocean voyage it takes longer but doesn't cause no jet lag. (7) People makes the same mistake with their road trips. (8) They gets in a car and rushes down the highway to a destination. (9) If they took a train instead, they relax and watch the countryside. (10) A jeep or a motorcycle are another great way to make a road trip. (11) Because these vehicles are open to the air, can feel in touch with the terrain. (12) If you were to travel back roads, you enjoy the journey as much as the arrival.

B. Quoted and Reported Speech

Rewrite direct quotations as indirect quotations and vice versa.

1. Kimi told Hal, "I pay my bills with income from my online writing."
2. "How did you get started?" he asked.
3. She answered that their friend Toi had introduced her to a site for essayists.
4. She told him, "I had to fill out an application and submit a sample of work."
5. She said they made her revise her biography several times before accepting it.

C. Defining Problems

In your own words, define each of the following sentence problems or types.

1. Double negatives
2. Omitted words
3. Repeated words
4. Conditional sentences
5. Quoted speech
6. Reported speech

Exercise

Numbers, Word Parts, and Idioms

Numbers

As a multilingual/ESL learner, you may be accustomed to a way of writing numbers that is different than the way it is done in North America. Become familiar with the North American conventions for writing numbers. Pages 592–593 show you how numbers are written and punctuated in both word and numeral form.

690.1

Using Punctuation with Numerals

Note that the **period** is used to express percentages (5.5%, 75.9%) and the **comma** is used to organize large numbers into units (7,000; 23,100; 231,990,000). Commas are not used, however, in writing the year (2011). (Also see 568.1 and 568.6.)

690.2

Cardinal Numbers

Cardinal numbers are used when counting a number of parts or objects. Cardinal numbers can be used as nouns (she counted to **ten**), pronouns (I invited many guests, but only **three** came), or adjectives (there are **ten** boys here).

Write out in words the numbers one through one hundred. Numbers 101 and greater are often written as numerals. (See 592.1.)

690.3

Ordinal Numbers

Ordinal numbers show place or succession in a series: the fourth row, the twenty-first century, the tenth time, and so on. Ordinal numbers are used to talk about the parts into which a whole can be divided, such as a fourth or a tenth, and as the denominator in fractions, such as one-fourth or three-fifths. Written fractions can also be used as nouns (I gave him **four-fifths**) or as adjectives (a **four-fifths** majority).

> **Note:** See the list below for names and symbols of the first twenty-five ordinal numbers. Consult a college dictionary for a complete list of cardinal and ordinal numbers.

First	1st	Tenth	10th	Nineteenth	19th
Second	2nd	Eleventh	11th	Twentieth	20th
Third	3rd	Twelfth	12th	Twenty-first	21st
Fourth	4th	Thirteenth	13th	Twenty-second	22nd
Fifth	5th	Fourteenth	14th	Twenty-third	23rd
Sixth	6th	Fifteenth	15th	Twenty-fourth	24th
Seventh	7th	Sixteenth	16th	Twenty-fifth	25th
Eighth	8th	Seventeenth	17th		
Ninth	9th	Eighteenth	18th		

Exercise

Prefixes, Suffixes, and Roots

Following is a list of many common word parts and their meanings. Learning them can help you determine the meaning of unfamiliar words as you come across them in your reading. For instance, if you know that *hemi* means "half," you can conclude that *hemisphere* means "half of a sphere."

Prefixes	Meaning	Suffixes	Meaning
a, an	not, without	able, ible	able, can do
anti, ant	against	age	act of, state of
co, con, com	together, with	al	relating to
di	two, twice	ate	cause, make
dis, dif	apart, away	en	made of
ex, e, ec, ef	out	ence, ency	action, quality
hemi, semi	half	esis, osis	action, process
il, ir, in, im	not	ice	condition, quality
inter	between	ile	relating to
intra	within	ish	resembling
multi	many	ment	act of, state of
non	not	ology	study, theory
ob, of, op, oc	toward, against	ous	full of, having
per	throughout	sion, tion	act of, state of
post	after	some	like, tending to
super, supr	above, more	tude	state of
trans, tra	across, beyond	ward	in the direction of
tri	three		
uni	one		

Roots	Meaning	Roots	Meaning
acu	sharp	ject	throw
am, amor	love, liking	log, ology	word, study, speech
anthrop	man	man	hand
aster, astr	star	micro	small
auto	self	mit, miss	send
biblio	book	nom	law, order
bio	life	onym	name
capit, capt	head	path, pathy	feeling, suffering
chron	time	rupt	break
cit	to call, start	scrib, script	write
cred	believe	spec, spect, spic	look
dem	people	tele	far
dict	say, speak	tempo	time
erg	work	tox	poison
fid, feder	faith, trust	vac	empty
fract, frag	break	ver, veri	true
graph, gram	write, written	zo	animal

Multilingual/ESL Exercises:

Numbers and Word Parts

A. Punctuating Numerals

On your own paper, write the following numbers. Add or correct punctuation as necessary to suit North American style. (Some of the numbers are already correct, and two items need to be punctuated correctly as percentages.)

A. 3000

B. 44

C. 9.400.207,33

D. 200,000,01

E. 600000009

F. 23,7%

G. Dec. 21 2012

H. 100

I. 1.877,14

J. 17,7%

B. Numbers in Text

Write each number below as it should appear in text.

A. 900

B. 4/5

C. 99

D. 24

E. 101

F. 42

G. 17

H. 1/3

I. 70

J. 1,001

C. Prefixes, Suffixes, and Roots

Break each of the following terms into its component parts (prefix, root, and/or suffix) and define it in your own words.

1. semiserious

2. pseudonym

3. toxicology

4. bibliography

5. verified

6. coauthor

7. westward

8. microfinance

9. antipathy

10. international

11. infantile

12. postponement

13. astrophysics

14. ticklish

15. multihued

16. incredulous